All the programs from Zen of Assembly Language ~~are also~~ available on diskette **for the IBM PC.** You can order this diskette directly from the author, using the order form below.

Order Form
Shipping information—please print

Name _____

Street _____

City _____ State _____ Zip _____

Date _____

Please send me

_____ diskettes to accompany **Zen of Assembly Language**

at $10.00 each; $15.00 each outside U.S. and Canada.

Check method of payment

☐ check ☐ money order ☐ cash
(Credit cards and C.O.D. payments are not accepted.)

Amount enclosed $ _____

Mail to: **Michael Abrash**
7 Adirondack Street
South Burlington, VT 05403

Price includes postage and handling and applicable sales tax. Price and availability subject to change without notice.

Zen of Assembly Language

Volume I, Knowledge

Scott, Foresman
Assembly Language Programming Series

Jeff Duntemann, Editor

Zen of Assembly Language

Volume I, Knowledge

Michael Abrash

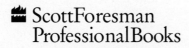

ScottForesman
ProfessionalBooks

An Imprint of ScottForesman

Cover photo: Courtesy of International Business Machines Corporation

Library of Congress Cataloging-in-Publication Data

Abrash, Michael.
    Zen of assembly language / Michael Abrash.
       p. cm.
     ISBN 0-673-38602-3 (v. 1)
      1. Assembler language (Computer program language)   I. Title.
  QA76.73.A8A27   1990
  005.265—dc20   89-24258
                                               CIP

2 3 4 5 6 MVN 94 93 92 91

ISBN 0-673-38602-3

Notice of Liability

The information in this book is distributed on an "As is" basis, without warranty. Neither the author nor Scott, Foresman and Company shall have any liability to customer or any other person or entity with respect to any liability, loss, or damage caused or alleged to be caused directly or indirectly by the programs contained herein. This includes, but is not limited to, interruption of service, loss of data, loss of business or anticipatory profits, or consequential damages from the use of the programs.

For Shay and Emily

Trademarks

◆◆◆

Foreword to the Scott, Foresman Assembly Language Programming Series

◆◆

There is really only one kind of book on 8086/8088 assembly language today; one that contains a chapter on the central processing unit (CPU) registers, perhaps a chapter on memory addressing modes, which is then followed by a long tour of the instruction set with (at most) a few two- or three-line examples of how the instructions are put together. Few of these books mention the PC at all, and those that do generally stop after demonstrating a few BIOS calls that are too slow to be useful anyway.

This is no way to teach assembly language.

Assembly language is, after all, the language of the machine. This means that it is the language of a specific, particular machine; the use of assembly language on that machine is inextricably tied to the architecture and peculiarities of that machine. Teaching assembly language on the PC requires teaching the PC as well or what is taught won't be especially useful.

This realization led to one of the two design goals of this series: to teach assembly language in the context of the PC standard so that those learning assembler will be able to apply it immediately without also having to bury themselves in books about the PC. At an advanced level (as Michael Abrash brilliantly demonstrates in *Zen of Assembly Language*) the border between machine code and the machine itself begins to blur. Hidden performance thieves (Michael calls them "the cycle eaters") like DMA refresh and video memory wait states lurk behind every instruction. Arcana such as the difference between 8-bit and 16-bit I/O ports can mean the difference between slow software and fast software or in extreme cases, between software that works and software that crashes and burns. Without understanding the PC's hardware, the assembly language programmer is at the mercy of such villains—the more sophisticated the program becomes, the more it is exposed to such dangers.

The second design goal addresses both the nature of the subject and the nature of the audience: no single book can turn a green programmer into a Zen-level expert. The subject is large and complex; what's worse, the details of assembly language are an interconnected web that make serial discussion of any assembly language topic without "forward references" to more advanced topics almost impossible. This means that the same broad set of topics must be taught in each book, but that the level of detail be gradually increased in moving from beginner to expert.

The goal, then, was to define a series of books that gradually moves from absolute beginner level to world-class programmer, covering the same old CPU and assembly language each time, but covering it in a fashion appropriate to the gradually escalating skills that the reader is building. This is what we have done.

Assembly Language from Square One takes the bold step of treating assembly language as a programmer's *first* language. In doing so, it must explain not only what assembly language is, but what *programming* is, and it does so without apology. As the ground-level book on the topic, *Assembly Language from Square One* lays the groundwork for assembly language programming on the PC, which includes considerable discussion of the PC itself. The idea is to get the newcomer to become familiar with the jargon and the concepts behind the language, both of which bewilder the newcomer far more often than assembly language itself.

The journeyman's course in assembly language lies in *Assembly Language Magic,* which assumes that the programmer has the jargon and context for assembly language and needs to work at the considerable spread of the instruction set itself. *Assembly Language Magic* provides a great many short but complete demonstration programs that exercise the full range of the instruction set of the 8086/8088 microprocessors. Most books fail to adequately address how instructions work together and tend to treat instructions in isolation. Programs do not consist of one instruction, and any intermediate-level assembly language book that does not provide numerous complete and working programs simply will not do the student any lasting good.

Finally, there is the difference between assembly language programs that work and assembly language programs that work *well.* Writing in assembler is difficult compared with writing in C or Pascal, and if the resulting assembly language programs are no smaller or no faster than an equivalent program in C or Pascal, there's very little point to the extra effort. I have yet to see any assembly language book make this point, much less dwell on it. *Zen of Assembly Language* carries the theme that assembly language, which offers a higher level of control than any other language, must be written with a knowledge of the machine, the individual instructions, and the relationships among instructions that transcend all three. Without this second-level understanding, the programmer might as well return to C or Pascal, because the payback will not be enough to justify the effort.

Zen of Assembly Language assumes that the programmer understands the general principles of assembly language and shows how to melt the program into the machine in a way calculated to get the very most out of both. Wait states, DMA, the prefetch queue, planning for and measuring performance—these are the topics that await the Zen programmer in assembly language. Master *Zen of Assembly Language* and you will have mastered assembly language.

Until, like Michael Abrash, you discover some new unturned stone in the garden.

With these books, and other books to come, we hope to put the subject of assembly language for the PC at your fingertips. The subject deserves better than it has gotten at the hands of the computer book industry, and with the Scott, Foresman Assembly Series we hope to put that situation aright.

Jeff Duntemann

The Books in the Scott, Foresman Assembly Language Programming Series

Assembly Language from Square One
by Jeff Duntemann
ISBN 0-673-38590-6

Assembly Language Magic
by William H. Murray, III and Chris H. Pappas
ISBN 0-673-38766-6

Zen of Assembly Language Volume I, Knowledge
by Michael Abrash
ISBN 0-673-38602-3

Introduction: Pushing the Envelope

◆◆

This is the book I wished for with all my heart seven years ago, when I started programming the IBM PC: the book that unlocks the secrets of writing superb assembly language code. There was no such book then, so I had to learn the hard way, through experimentation and through trial and error. Over the years, I waited in vain for that book to appear; I looked everywhere without success for a book about advanced assembly language programming, a book written specifically for assembly language programmers who want to get better rather than for would-be assembly language programmers. I'm sure many of you have waited for such a book as well. Well, wait no longer: this is that book.

Zen of Assembly Language assumes that you're already familiar with assembly language. Not an expert, but at least acquainted with the registers and instructions of the 8088 and with the use of one of the popular PC assemblers. Your familiarity with assembly language will allow us to skip over the droning tutorials about the use of the assembler and the endless explanations of binary arithmetic that take up hundreds of pages in introductory books. We're going to jump into high performance programming right from the start, and when we come up for air 16 chapters from now, your view of assembly language will be forever altered for the better. Then we'll leap right into Volume II, applying our newfound knowledge of assembly language to ever more sophisticated programming tasks.

In short, *Zen of Assembly Language* is about nothing less than how to become the best assembly language programmer you can be.

Why Assembly Language?

For years, people have been predicting—hoping for—the demise of assembly language, claiming that the world is ready to move on to less primitive approaches to programming . . . and for years, the best programs around have been written in assembly language. Why is this? Simply because assembly language is hard to work with, but—when properly used—produces programs of unparalleled performance. Mediocre programmers have a terrible time working with assembly language; on the other hand, assembly language is, without fail, the language that PC gurus use when they need the best possible code.

Which brings us to you.

Do you want to be a guru? I'd imagine so, if you're reading this book. You've set yourself an ambitious and difficult goal, and your success is far from guaranteed. There's no sure-fire recipe for becoming a guru, any more than there's a recipe for becoming a chess grand master. There is, however, one way you can greatly improve your chances: become an expert assembly language programmer. Assembly language by itself won't make you a guru, but without it you'll never reach your full potential as a programmer.

Why is assembly language so important in this age of optimizing compilers and program generators? Assembly language is fundamentally different from all other languages, as we'll see throughout *Zen of Assembly Language*. Assembly language lets you use every last resource of the PC to push the performance envelope; only in assembly language can you press right up against the inherent limits of the PC.

If you aren't pushing the envelope, there's generally no reason to program in assembler. High level languages are certainly easier to use, and nowadays most high level languages let you get at the guts of the PC—display memory, DOS functions, interrupt vectors, and so on—without having to resort to assembler. If, on the other hand, you're striving for the sort of performance that will give your programs snappy interfaces and crackling response times, you'll find assembly language to be almost magical, for no other language even approaches assembler for sheer speed.

Of course, no one tests the limits of the PC with his or her first assembler program; that takes time and practice. While many PC programmers know something about assembler, few are experts. If you are a typical programmer, you have typed in the assembler code from an article or two, read a book about assembler programming, and perhaps written a few assembler programs of your own, but you don't yet feel you've mastered the language. If you fall into this category, you've surely sensed the remarkable potential of assembler, but you're also keenly aware of how hard it is to write good assembler code and how much you have yet to learn. In all likelihood, you're not sure how to sharpen your assembler skills and take that last giant step toward mastery of your PC.

This book is for you.

Welcome to the most exciting and esoteric aspect of the IBM PC. *Zen of Assembly Language* will teach you how to create blindingly fast code for the IBM PC. More important still, it will teach you how to continue to develop your assembler programming skills on your own. *Zen of Assembly Language* will show you a way to learn what you need to know as the need arises, and it is that way of learning that will serve you well for years to come. There are facts and code aplenty in this book and in the companion volume, but it is a way of thinking and learning that lies at the heart of *Zen of Assembly Language*.

Don't take the title to mean that this is a mystical book in any way. In the context of assembly language programming, Zen is a technique that brings intuition and nonobvious approaches to bear on difficult problems and puzzles. If you would rather think of high performance assembler programming as something more mundane, such as right-brained thinking or plain old craftsmanship, go right ahead; good assembler programming is a highly individualized process.

Zen of Assembly Language is specifically about assembly language for the IBM PC (and, by definition, compatible computers). In particular, the bulk of this volume will focus on the capabilities of the 8088 processor that lies at the heart of the PC. However, many of the findings and almost all of the techniques I'll discuss can also be applied to assembly language programming for the other members of Intel's 808X processor family, including the 80286 and 80386 processors, as we'll see toward the end of this volume. *Zen of Assembly Language* doesn't much apply to computers built around other processors, such as the 68XXX family, the Z80, the 8080, or the 6502, because a great deal of the Zen of assembly language in the case of the IBM PC derives from the highly unusual architecture of the 808X family. (In fact, the processors in the 808X family lend themselves beautifully to assembly language, much more so than other currently popular processors.)

While I will spend a chapter looking specifically at the 80286 found in the AT and PS/2 models 50 and 60 and at the 80386 found in the PS/2 model 80, I'll concentrate primarily on the 8088 processor found in the IBM PC and XT, for a number of reasons. First, there are at least 15 million 8088-based computers around, ensuring that good 8088 code isn't going to go out of style any time soon. Second, the 8088 is far and away the slowest of the processors used in IBM-compatible computers, so no matter how carefully code is tailored to the subtleties of the 8088, it's still going to run much faster on an 80286 or 80386. Third, many of the concepts I'll present regarding the 8088 apply to the 80286 and 80386 as well, but to different degrees. Given that there are simply too many processors around to cover in detail (and the 80486 on the way), I'd rather pay close attention to the 8088, the processor for which top-quality code is most critical, and provide you with techniques that will allow you to learn on your own how best to program other processors.

We'll return to this topic in Chapter 15, when we will, in fact, discuss other 808X-family processors, but for now, take my word for it: when it comes to optimization, the 8088 is the processor of choice.

What You'll Need

The tools you'll need to follow this book are simple: a text editor to create ASCII program files, the Microsoft Macro Assembler version 5.0 or a compatible assembler (Turbo Assembler is fine) to assemble programs, and the Microsoft Linker or a compatible linker to link programs into an executable form.

There are several types of reference material you should have available as you pursue assembler mastery. You will certainly want a general reference on 8088 assembler. *The 8086 Book,* written by Rector and Alexy and published by Osborne/McGraw-Hill, is a good reference, although you should beware of the unusually high number of typographic errors. Also useful is the spiral-bound reference manual that comes with MASM, which contains an excellent summary of the instruction sets of the 8088, 8086, 80186, 80286, and 80386. IBM's hardware, BIOS, and DOS technical reference manuals are also useful references, containing as they do detailed information about the resources available to assembler programmers.

If you're the type who digs down to the hardware of the PC in the pursuit of knowledge, you'll find Intel's handbooks and reference manuals invaluable (albeit none too easy to read), since Intel manufactures the 8088 and many of the support chips used in the PC. There's simply no way to understand what a hardware component is capable of doing in the context of the PC without a comprehensive description of everything that part can do, and that's exactly what Intel's literature provides.

Finally, keep an eye open for articles on assembly language programming. Articles provide a steady stream of code from diverse sources and are your best sources of new approaches to assembler programming.

By the way, the terms *assembler* and *assembly language* are generally interchangeable. While assembly language is perhaps technically more accurate (since Assembler is also the name of the software that assembles assembly language code), assembler is a widely used shorthand that I'll use throughout this book.

Acknowledgments

Special thanks to Jeff Duntemann, who made it all happen, to Noah Oremland, who proofed every word, encouraged me, and even laughed at my jokes, and to Amy Davis of Scott, Foresman and Co., who made this book possible. Thanks also to Tom Blakeslee, John T. Cockerham, Dan Gochnauer, Dan Illowsky, Bob Jervis, Darrel Johanssen, Dave Miller, Ted Mirecki, Phil Mummah, Kent Porter, and Tom Wilson for information, feedback and encouragement. Finally, thanks to Orion Instruments for the use of an OmniLab.

Odds and Ends

I'd like to identify the manufacturers of the products I'll refer to in this volume. Microsoft makes the Microsoft Macro Assembler (MASM), the Microsoft Linker (LINK), CodeView (CV), and Symdeb (SYMDEB). Borland International makes Turbo assembler (TASM), Turbo C (TC), Turbo Link (TLINK), and Turbo Debugger (TD). SLR Systems makes OPTASM, an assembler. Finally, Orion Instruments makes OmniLab, which integrates high performance oscilloscope, logic analyzer, stimulus generator, and disassembler instrumentation in a single PC-based package.

In addition, I'd like to point out that while I've made every effort to ensure that the code in this volume works as it should, no one's perfect. Please let me know if you find bugs. Also, please let me know what works for you and what doesn't in this book; teaching is not a one-way street.

The Path to the Zen of Assembly Language

Zen of Assembly Language consists of four major parts, contained in two volumes. Parts One and Two are in this volume, Volume I, while Parts Three and Four are in Volume II, *Zen of Assembly Language: The Flexible Mind.* While the book you're reading stands on its own as a tutorial in high performance assembler code, the two volumes together cover the whole of superior assembler programming, from hardware to implementation. I strongly recommend that you read both.

The four parts of *Zen of Assembly Language* are organized as follows:

Part One introduces the concept of the Zen of assembler and presents the tools we'll use to delve into assembler code performance.

Part Two covers various and sundry pieces of knowledge about assembler programming, examines the resources available for programming the PC, and probes fundamental hardware aspects that affect code performance.

Part Three (in Volume II) examines the process of creating superior code, combining the detailed knowledge of Part Two with varied and often unorthodox coding approaches.

Part Four (also in Volume II) illustrates the Zen of assembler in the form of a working animation program.

In general, Parts One and Two discuss the raw stuff of performance, while Parts Three and Four show how to integrate that raw performance with algorithms and applications, although there is considerable overlap. The four parts together teach all aspects of the Zen of assembler: concept, knowledge, the flexible mind, and implementation. Together, we will follow that path down the road to mastery of the IBM PC.

Shall we begin?

Michael Abrash

Contents

◆◆◆

Part One   **The Zen of Assembly Language**   *1*

1   Zen?   *3*

1.1 The Zen of Assembly Language in a Nutshell   *4*

1.2 Assembler Is Fundamentally Different from Other
    Languages   *5*

1.3 Knowledge   *8*

1.4 The Flexible Mind   *9*

1.5 Where to Begin?   *11*

2   Assume Nothing   *12*

2.1 The Zen Timer   *14*

2.2 The Zen Timer Is a Means, Not an End   *22*

2.3 Starting the Zen Timer   *23*

2.4 Time and the PC   *23*

2.5 Stopping the Zen Timer   *27*

2.6 Reporting Timing Results   *28*

2.7 Notes on the Zen Timer   *29*

2.8 A Sample Use of the Zen Timer   *30*

2.9 The Long-Period Zen Timer   *34*

2.10 Stopping the Clock   *36*

2.11 A Sample Use of the Long-period Zen Timer   *48*

2.12 Further Reading   *52*

2.13 Armed with the Zen Timer, Onward and Upward   *53*

Part Two   **Knowledge**   *55*

3   Context   *57*

3.1 From the Bottom Up   *58*

3.2 The Traditional Model   *59*

3.3 Cycle Eaters   *61*

3.4 Code Is Data   *65*

3.5 Inside the 8088   *65*

3.6 Stepchild of the 8086   *69*

3.7 Which Model to Use   *73*

4 Things Mother Never Told You: Under the Programming Interface   *74*

4.1 Cycle Eaters Revisited   *75*

4.2 The 8-Bit Bus Cycle Eater   *76*

4.3 The Prefetch Queue Cycle Eater   *83*

4.4 Dynamic RAM Refresh: The Invisible Hand   *94*

4.5 Wait States   *100*

4.6 Cycle Eaters: A Summary   *110*

4.7 What Does It All Mean?   *110*

5 Night of the Cycle Eaters   *112*

5.1 No, We're Not In Kansas Anymore   *114*

5.2 There's Still No Such Beast as a "True" Execution Time   *116*

5.3 The True Nature of Instruction Execution   *124*

5.4 Back to the Programming Interface   *130*

6 The 8088   *132*

6.1 An Overview   *134*

6.2 Resources   *135*

6.3 Registers   *135*

6.4 The 8088's Register Set   *136*

6.5 The General-Purpose Registers   *138*

6.6 The Segment Registers   *141*

6.7 The Instruction Pointer   *144*

6.8 The Flags Register   *144*

6.9 There's More to Life Than Registers   *149*

7 Memory Addressing 151

7.1 Definitions *153*
7.2 The Memory Architecture of the 8088 *154*
7.3 Segments and Offsets *155*
7.4 Segment Handling *168*
7.5 Offset Handling *198*
7.6 *mod-reg-rm* Addressing *199*
7.7 Non-*mod-reg-rm* Memory Addressing *224*
7.8 Initializing Memory *258*
7.9 A Brief Note on I/O Addressing *261*

8 Strange Fruit of the 8080 265

8.1 The 8080 Legacy *266*
8.2 Accumulator-Specific Instructions *270*
8.3 Pushing and Popping the 8080 Flags *289*
8.4 A Brief Digression on Optimization *292*

9 Around and about the Instruction Set 296

9.1 Shortcuts for Handling Zero and Constants *297*
9.2 inc and dec *304*
9.3 Carrying Results along in a Flag *310*
9.4 Byte-to-Word and Word-to-Doubleword Conversion *312*
9.5 xchg is Handy When Registers Are Tight *316*
9.6 Destination: Register *319*
9.7 neg and not *321*
9.8 Rotates & Shifts *324*
9.9 ASCII and Decimal Adjust *333*
9.10 Mnemonics That Cover Multiple Instructions *342*

10 String Instructions: The Magic Elixir 345

10.1 A Quick Tour of the String Instructions *347*
10.2 Hither and Yon with the String Instructions *359*

11   String Instruction Applications   *403*

11.1 String Handling with lods and stos   *404*

11.2 Block Handling with movs   *413*

11.3 Searching with scas   *430*

11.4 Comparing Memory with Memory Using cmps   *457*

11.5 A Note about Returning Values   *487*

11.6 Putting String Instructions to Work in Unlikely Places   *489*

11.7 A Note on Handling Blocks Larger Than 64 K Bytes   *505*

12   Don't Jump!   *507*

12.1 How Slow Is It?   *509*

12.2 Branching and Calculation of the Target Address   *510*

12.3 Branching and the Prefetch Queue   *517*

12.4 Branching and the *Second* Byte of the Instruction Branched To   *525*

13   Not-Branching   *532*

13.1 Think Functionally   *533*

13.2 rep: Looping without Branching   *537*

13.3 Look-up Tables: Calculating without Branching   *538*

13.4 Take the Branch Less Travelled By   *539*

13.5 Yes, Virginia, There *Is* a Faster 32-Bit Negate!   *544*

13.6 Arrange Your Code to Eliminate Branches   *555*

13.7 loop May Not Be Bad, but Lord Knows It's Not Good: In-Line Code   *589*

13.8 A Note on Self-Modifying Code   *615*

14   If You Must Branch . . .   *618*

14.1 Don't Go Far   *619*

14.2 Replacing call and ret with jmp   *627*

14.3 Use int Only When You Must   *636*

14.4 Forward References Can Waste Time and Space   *643*

14.5 Saving Space with Branches   *646*

14.6 Double-Duty Tests   *653*

14.7 The Looping Instructions   *657*

14.8 Only jcxz Can Test *and* Branch in a Single Bound   *668*

14.9 Jump and Call Tables   *670*

14.10 Forward References Rear Their Collective Ugly Head Once
More   *692*

15   Other Processors   695

15.1 Why Optimize for the 8088?   *696*

15.2 Which Processors Matter?   *698*

15.3 Things Mother Never Told You, Part II   *701*

15.4 New Instructions and Features   *714*

15.5 Optimization Rules: The More Things Change . . .   *717*

15.6 popf and the 80286   *721*

15.7 Coprocessors and Peripherals   *728*

16   Onward to the Flexible Mind   732

16.1 A Taste of What You've Learned   *734*

16.2 Zenning   *735*

16.3 Knowledge and Beyond   *741*

Appendices

A 8086/8088 Instruction Set Reference   *743*

B The Extended ASCII Code and Symbol Set   *825*

Zen of
Assembly Language
Volume I, Knowledge

Part One

The Zen of Assembly Language

> If I am asked, then, what Zen teaches, I would answer, Zen teaches nothing. Whatever teachings there are in Zen, they come out of one's own mind. We teach ourselves; Zen merely points the way.
>
> —D. T. Suzuki, *An Introduction to Zen Buddhism*

Chapter 1

◆◆◆

Zen?

1.1	The Zen of Assembly Language in a Nutshell
1.2	Assembler Is Fundamentally Different from Other Languages
1.3	Knowledge
1.4	The Flexible Mind
1.5	Where to Begin?

What is the Zen of assembly language? Many things: a set of programming skills that lets you write incredibly fast programs, a technique for turning ideas into code, a process of looking at problems in new ways and finding fresh solutions, and more. Perhaps a brief story would be the best way to introduce the Zen of assembly language.

1.1 ◆ The Zen of Assembly Language in a Nutshell

Some time ago, I was asked to work over a critical assembler subroutine in order to make it run as fast as possible. The task of the subroutine was to construct a nybble out of 4 bits read from different bytes, rotating and combining the bits so that they ultimately ended up neatly aligned in bits 3 to 0 of a single byte. (In case you're curious, the object was to construct a 16-color pixel from bits scattered over 4 bytes.) I examined the subroutine line by line, saving a cycle here and a cycle there, until the code truly seemed to be optimized. When I was done, the key part of the code looked something like this:

```
LoopTop:
      lodsb              ;get the next byte to extract a bit from
      and   al,ah        ;isolate the bit we want
      rol   al,cl        ;rotate the bit into the desired position
      or    bl,al        ;insert the bit into the final nibble
      dec   cx           ;the next bit goes 1 place to the right
      dec   dx           ;count down the number of bits
      jnz   LoopTop      ;process the next bit, if any
```

Now, it's hard to write code that's much faster than seven assembler instructions, only one of which accesses memory, and most programmers would have called it a day at this point; still, something bothered me, so I spent a little time going over the code again. Suddenly, the answer struck me—the code was rotating each bit into place separately, so that a multi-bit rotation was being performed every time the loop was executed, for a total of four separate time-consuming multi-bit rotations! *Although the instructions were optimized individually, the overall approach did not make the best possible use of the instructions.*

I changed the code to the following:

```
LoopTop:
    lodsb                ;get the next byte to extract a bit from
    and    al,ah         ;isolate the bit we want
    or     bl,al         ;insert the bit into the final nibble
    rol    bl,1          ;make room for the next bit
    dec    dx            ;count down the number of bits
    jnz    LoopTop       ;process the next bit, if any
    rol    bl,cl         ;rotate all four bits into their final
                         ; positions at the same time
```

This moved the costly multi-bit rotation out of the loop, so that it was performed just once, rather than four times. Although the new code may not look much different from the original and, in fact, still contains exactly the same number of instructions, the performance of the entire subroutine was improved by about 10 percent with just this one change. (Incidentally, that wasn't the end of the optimization; I eliminated the **dec** and **jnz** instructions by expanding the four iterations of the loop into in-line code, but that's a tale for another chapter.)

The point is this: to write truly superior assembler programs, you need to know what the various instructions do, which instructions execute fastest, and more. You also must learn to look at your programming problems from a variety of perspectives, so that you can put those fast instructions to work in the most effective ways. And that, in a nutshell, is the Zen of assembly language.

1.2 ◆ Assembler Is Fundamentally Different from Other Languages

Is it really so hard as all that to write good assembler code for the IBM PC? Yes! Thanks to the decidedly quirky nature of the 8088 processor, assembly language differs fundamentally from other languages and is undeniably harder to work with. On the other hand, the potential of assembler code is much greater than that of other languages. The Zen of assembly language is the way to tap that potential.

To understand why this is so, consider how a program is written. A programmer examines the requirements of an application, designs a solution at some level of abstraction, and then makes that design come alive in a code implementation. If not handled properly, the transformation that takes place between conception and implementation can reduce performance tremendously; for example, a programmer who implements a routine to search a list of 100,000 sorted items with a linear rather than a binary search will end up with a disappointingly slow program.

No matter how well an implementation is derived from the corresponding design, however, high level languages such as C and Pascal inevitably introduce additional transformation inefficiencies, as shown in Figure 1.1. High level languages provide artificial environments that lend themselves relatively well to human programming skills, in order to ease the transition from design to implementation. The price for this ease of implementation is a considerable loss of efficiency in transforming source code into machine language. This is particularly true given that the 8088, with its specialized memory-addressing instructions and segmented memory architecture, does not lend itself particularly well to compiler design.

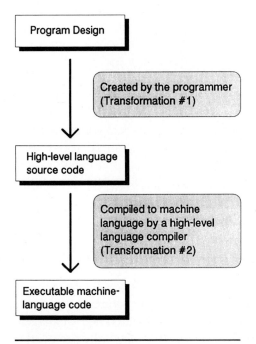

FIGURE 1.1   The process of turning a design into executable code by way of a high level language involves two transformations: one performed by the programmer to generate source code, and another performed by the compiler to turn source code into machine language instructions. Consequently, the machine language code generated by compilers is usually less than optimal given the requirements of the original design.

Assembler, on the other hand, is simply a human-oriented representation of machine language. As a result, assembler provides a difficult programming environment—the bare hardware and systems software of the computer—*but properly constructed assembler programs suffer no transformation loss* (Fig. 1.2). The key, of course, is the programmer, because in assembler the programmer must essentially perform the transformation from the application specification to machine language entirely on his or her own. (The assembler merely handles the direct translation from assembler to machine language.)

The first part of the Zen of assembly language, then, is self-reliance. An assembler is nothing more than a tool that lets you design machine

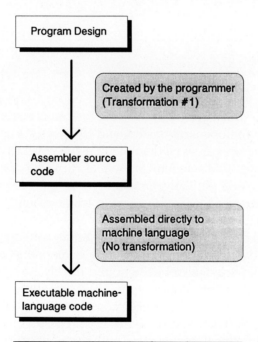

FIGURE 1.2   Only one transformation is required when creating an assembler program, and that single transformation is completely under the programmer's control. Assemblers perform no transformation from source code to machine language; instead, they merely map assembler instructions to machine language instructions on a one-to-one basis. As a result, the programmer is able to produce machine language code that's precisely tailored to the needs of each task a given application requires.

language programs without having to think in hexadecimal codes, so assembly language programmers, unlike all other programmers, must take full responsibility for the quality of their code. Because assemblers provide little help at any level higher than the generation of machine language, the assembler programmer must be capable both of coding any programming construct directly and of controlling the PC at the lowest practical level—the operating system, the BIOS, and the hardware where necessary. High level languages handle most of this transparently to the programmer, but in assembler everything is fair (and necessary) game, which brings us to another aspect of the Zen of assembly language.

Knowledge.

1.3 ◆ Knowledge

In the IBM PC world, you can never have enough knowledge, and every item you add to your store will make your programs better. Thorough familiarity with both the operating system and BIOS interfaces is important; because those interfaces are well-documented and reasonably straightforward, my advice is to get IBM's documentation and a good book or two and bring yourself up to speed. Similarly, familiarity with the hardware of the IBM PC is required. Although that topic covers a lot of ground—display adapters, keyboards, serial ports, printer ports, timer and DMA channels, memory organization, and more—most of the hardware is well-documented, and articles about programming major hardware components appear frequently, so this sort of knowledge can be acquired readily enough.

The single most critical part of the hardware, and the one about which it is hardest to learn, is the 8088 processor. The 8088 has a complex, irregular instruction set, and, unlike most processors, the 8088 is neither straightforward nor well-documented with regard to true code performance. What's more, assembler is so difficult to learn that most articles and books that present assembler code settle for code that works rather than code that pushes the 8088 to its limits. In fact, because most articles and books are written for inexperienced assembler programmers, very little information of any sort is available about how to generate high-quality assembler code for the 8088. As a result, knowledge about programming the 8088 effectively is by far the hardest knowledge to gather. A good portion of this book is devoted to seeking out such knowledge. Be forewarned, though: no matter how much you learn about programming the IBM PC in assembler, there's always more to discover.

1.4 ◆ The Flexible Mind

Is the never-ending collection of information all there is to the Zen of assembly language, then? Hardly. Knowledge is simply a necessary base on which to build. Let's take a moment to examine the objectives of good assembler programming, and the remainder of the Zen of assembly language will fall into place.

Basically, there are only two possible objectives to high-performance assembler programming: depending on the requirements of the application, keep to a minimum either the number of processor cycles the program takes to run or the number of bytes in the program (or some combination of the two). We'll look at ways to achieve these objectives, but we'll be concerned with saving cycles more often than with saving bytes, because the PC offers relatively more memory than it does processing horsepower. In fact, we'll find that we can often improve performance two to three times *over tight assembler code* if we're willing to expend additional bytes in order to save cycles. It's not always desirable to use such techniques to speed up code, owing to the heavy memory requirements, but it is almost always possible.

You will notice that my short list of objectives for high-performance assembler programming does not include traditional objectives such as easy maintenance and speed of development. Those are indeed important considerations—to persons and companies that develop and distribute software. People who *buy* software, on the other hand, care only about how well it performs, not how it was developed. Nowadays, developers spend so much time focusing on such admittedly important issues as code maintainability and reusability, source code control, choice of development environment, and the like that they forget rule 1: from the user's perspective, performance is fundamental. Comment your code, design it carefully, and write non–time-critical portions in a high level language, if you wish, but when you write the portions that interact with the user or affect response time, performance must be your paramount objective. Assembler is the path to that goal.

Knowledge of the sort described earlier is absolutely essential to fulfilling either of the objectives of assembler programming. What that knowledge doesn't do by itself is meet the need to write code that both performs to the requirements of the application at hand and operates in the PC environment as efficiently as possible. Knowledge makes that possible, but your programming instincts make it happen. And it is that intuitive, on-the-fly integration of a program specification and a sea of facts about the PC that is the heart of the Zen of assembly language.

As with Zen of any sort, mastering the Zen of assembly language is more a matter of learning than of being taught. You will have to find your own path of learning, although I will start you on your way with this book. The subtle facts and examples I provide will help you gain the necessary experience, but you must continue the journey on your own. Each program you create will expand your programming horizons and increase the options available to you for meeting the next challenge. The ability of your mind to find surprising new and better ways to craft superior code from a concept—the flexible mind, if you will—is the linchpin of good assembler code, and you will develop this skill only by doing.

Never underestimate the importance of the flexible mind. Good assembler code is better than good compiled code. Many people would have you believe otherwise, but they're wrong. That doesn't mean high level languages are useless; far from it. High level languages are the best choice for the majority of programmers and for the bulk of the code of most applications. When the *best* code—the fastest or smallest code possible—is needed, though, assembler is the only way to go.

Simple logic dictates that no compiler can know as much about what a piece of code needs to do or can adapt to those needs as well as the person who wrote the code. Given that superior information and adaptability, an assembly language programmer can generate better code than a compiler, all the more so because compilers are constrained by the limitations of high level languages and by the process of transformation from high level language to machine language. Consequently, carefully optimized assembler is not just the language of choice but the *only* choice for the 1 percent to 10 percent of all code, usually small, well-defined subroutines, that determines overall program performance, and it is the only choice for code that must be as compact as possible. In the run-of-the-mill, non-time-critical portions of your programs, it makes no sense to waste time and effort writing optimized assembler code. Concentrate your efforts on loops and the like instead—but in areas where you need the finest code quality, accept no substitutes.

Note, I said that an assembler programmer *can* generate better code than a compiler, not *will* generate better code. Although it is true that good assembler code is better than good compiled code, it is also true that bad assembler code is often much worse than bad compiled code. Because the assembler programmer has so much control over the program, he or she has unlimited opportunities to waste cycles and bytes. The sword cuts both ways, and good assembler code requires more, not less, forethought and planning than good code written in a high level language.

The gist of all this is simply that good assembler programming is done in the context of a solid overall framework unique to each program, and the flexible mind is the key to creating that framework and holding it together.

1.5 ◆ Where to Begin?

To summarize, the Zen of assembly language is a combination of knowledge, perspective, and way of thinking that makes possible the genesis of first-rate assembler programs. Given that, where should we begin our explorations of the Zen of assembly language? Development of the flexible mind is an obvious step. Still, the flexible mind is no better than the knowledge at its disposal. We have much knowledge to acquire before we can begin to discuss the flexible mind, and, in truth, we don't even know yet how to acquire knowledge about 8088 assembler, let alone what that knowledge might be. The first step in the journey toward the Zen of assembly language, then, would seem to be learning how to learn.

Chapter 2

Assume Nothing

2.1	The Zen Timer
2.2	The Zen Timer Is a Means, Not an End
2.3	Starting the Zen Timer
2.4	Time and the PC
2.5	Stopping the Zen Timer
2.6	Reporting Timing Results
2.7	Notes on the Zen Timer
2.8	A Sample Use of the Zen Timer
2.9	The Long-Period Zen Timer
2.10	Stopping the Clock
2.11	A Sample Use of the Long-Period Zen Timer
2.12	Further Reading
2.13	Armed with the Zen Timer, Onward and Upward

When you're pushing the envelope in assembler, you're likely to become more than a little compulsive about finding approaches that let you wring more speed from your computer. In the process, you're bound to make mistakes, which is fine, so long as you watch for those mistakes and learn from them.

A case in point: a few years back, I came across an article about 8088 assembly language called "Optimizing for Speed." Now, *optimize* is not a word to be used lightly; *Webster's Ninth New Collegiate Dictionary* defines *optimize* as "to make as perfect, effective, or functional as possible," which certainly leaves little room for error. The author had, however, chosen to refine a small, well-defined 8088 assembly language routine consisting of about 30 instructions that did nothing more than expand 8 bits to 16 bits by duplicating each bit. (We'll discuss this code and various optimizations to it at length in Chapter 7.)

The author of "Optimizing . . ." had clearly fine tuned the code with care, examining alternative instruction sequences and adding up cycles until he arrived at an implementation he calculated to be nearly 50 percent faster than the original routine. In short, he had used all the information at his disposal to improve his code, and had, as a result, saved cycles by the bushel. There was, in fact, only one slight problem with the optimized version of the routine.

It ran slower than the original version!

As diligent as the author had been, he had nonetheless committed a cardinal sin of 8088 assembly language programming: he had assumed that the information available to him was both correct and complete. While the execution times provided by Intel for its processors are indeed correct, they are incomplete; the other—and often more important—part of code performance is instruction *fetch* time, a topic to which I will return in later chapters.

Had the author taken the time to measure the true performance of his code, he wouldn't have put his reputation on the line with relatively low-performance code. What's more, had he measured the performance of his code and found it to be unexpectedly slow, curiosity might well have led him to experiment further and thereby add to his store of reliable information about the 8088. And there you have an important part of the Zen of assembler: after crafting the best code possible, you should check it in action to see if it's really doing what you think it is. If it's not behaving as expected, that's all to the good, since solving mysteries is the path to knowledge. You'll learn more in this way, I assure you, than from any manual or book on assembly language.

Assume nothing. I cannot emphasize this strongly enough: When you care about performance, do your best to improve the code and then *measure* the improvement. If you don't measure performance, you're just guessing, and if you're guessing, you're not very likely to write top-notch code.

Ignorance about true performance can be costly. When I wrote video games for a living, I spent days at a time trying to wring more performance from my graphics drivers. I rewrote whole sections of code just to save a few cycles, juggled registers, and relied heavily on blurry fast register-to-register shifts and adds. As I was writing my last game, I discovered that the program ran perceptibly faster if I used look-up tables instead of shifts and adds for my calculations. It *shouldn't* have run faster, according to my cycle counting, but it did. In truth, instruction fetching was rearing its head again, as it often does in programming the 8088, and the fetching of the shifts and adds was taking as much as four times the nominal execution time of those instructions.

Ignorance can also produce considerable wasted effort. I recall a debate in the letters column of one computer magazine about exactly how quickly text can be drawn on a Color/Graphics Adapter (CGA) screen without causing snow. The letter writers counted every cycle in their timing loops, just as the author had in the anecdote that started this chapter. Like that author, the letter writers had failed to take the prefetch queue into account. In fact, they had neglected the effects of video wait states as well, so the code they discussed was actually *much* slower than their estimates. The proper test would, of course, have been to run the code to see whether snow resulted, since the only true measure of code performance is observing it in action.

2.1 ◆ The Zen Timer

One key to mastering the Zen of assembler is having a tool with which to measure code performance. The most accurate way to measure performance is with expensive hardware, but reasonable measurements can be made at no cost with the PC's 8253 timer chip, which counts at a rate of slightly over 1 million times per second. The 8253 can be started at the beginning of a block of code of interest and stopped at the end of that code, with the resulting count indicating, with an accuracy of about 1 microsecond, how long the code took to execute. (A microsecond is one millionth of a second and is abbreviated μsec). To be precise, the 8253 counts once every 838.1 nanoseconds. (A nanosecond is one billionth of a second and is abbreviated nsec).

Listing 2-1 shows 8253-based timer software, consisting of three subroutines: **ZTimerOn**, **ZTimerOff**, and **ZTimerReport**. For the remainder of this book, I'll refer to these routines collectively as the *Zen timer*.

```
1   ;
2   ; *** Listing 2-1 ***
3   ;
4   ; The precision Zen timer (PZTIMER.ASM)
5   ;
6   ; Uses the 8253 timer to time the performance of code that takes
7   ; less than about 54 milliseconds to execute, with a resolution
8   ; of better than 10 microseconds.
9   ;
10  ; By Michael Abrash 4/26/89
11  ;
12  ; Externally callable routines:
13  ;
14  ;   ZTimerOn: Starts the Zen timer, with interrupts disabled.
15  ;
16  ;   ZTimerOff: Stops the Zen timer, saves the timer count,
17  ;        times the overhead code, and restores interrupts to the
18  ;        state they were in when ZTimerOn was called.
19  ;
20  ;   ZTimerReport: Prints the net time that passed between starting
21  ;        and stopping the timer.
22  ;
23  ; Note: If longer than about 54 ms passes between ZTimerOn and
24  ;        ZTimerOff calls, the timer turns over and the count is
25  ;        inaccurate. When this happens, an error message is displayed
26  ;        instead of a count. The long-period Zen timer should be used
27  ;        in such cases.
28  ;
29  ; Note: Interrupts *MUST* be left off between calls to ZTimerOn
30  ;        and ZTimerOff for accurate timing and for detection of
31  ;        timer overflow.
32  ;
33  ; Note: These routines can introduce slight inaccuracies into the
34  ;        system clock count for each code section timed even if
35  ;        timer 0 doesn't overflow. If timer 0 does overflow, the
36  ;        system clock can become slow by virtually any amount of
37  ;        time, since the system clock can't advance while the
38  ;        precison timer is timing. Consequently, it's a good idea
39  ;        to reboot at the end of each timing session. (The
40  ;        battery-backed clock, if any, is not affected by the Zen
41  ;        timer.)
42  ;
43  ; All registers, and all flags except the interrupt flag, are
44  ; preserved by all routines. Interrupts are enabled and then disabled
45  ; by ZTimerOn, and are restored by ZTimerOff to the state they were
46  ; in when ZTimerOn was called.
47  ;
48
```

```
49    Code    segment word public 'CODE'
50            assume  cs:Code, ds:nothing
51            public  ZTimerOn, ZTimerOff, ZTimerReport
52
53    ;
54    ; Base address of the 8253 timer chip.
55    ;
56    BASE_8253               equ     40h
57    ;
58    ; The address of the timer 0 count registers in the 8253.
59    ;
60    TIMER_0_8253            equ     BASE_8253 + 0
61    ;
62    ; The address of the mode register in the 8253.
63    ;
64    MODE_8253               equ     BASE_8253 + 3
65    ;
66    ; The address of Operation Command Word 3 in the 8259 Programmable
67    ; Interrupt Controller (PIC) (write only, and writable only when
68    ; bit 4 of the byte written to this address is 0 and bit 3 is 1).
69    ;
70    OCW3                    equ     20h
71    ;
72    ; The address of the Interrupt Request register in the 8259 PIC
73    ; (read only, and readable only when bit 1 of OCW3 = 1 and bit 0
74    ; of OCW3 = 0).
75    ;
76    IRR                     equ     20h
77    ;
78    ; Macro to emulate a POPF instruction in order to fix the bug in some
79    ; 80286 chips which allows interrupts to occur during a POPF even when
80    ; interrupts remain disabled.
81    ;
82    MPOPF macro
83            local   p1, p2
84            jmp short p2
85    p1:     iret                    ;jump to pushed address & pop flags
86    p2:     push    cs              ;construct far return address to
87            call    p1              ; the next instruction
88            endm
89
90    ;
91    ; Macro to delay briefly to ensure that enough time has elapsed
92    ; between successive I/O accesses so that the device being accessed
93    ; can respond to both accesses even on a very fast PC.
94    ;
95    DELAY   macro
96            jmp     $+2
97            jmp     $+2
98            jmp     $+2
99            endm
100
101   OriginalFlags           db      ?       ;storage for upper byte of
102                                            ; FLAGS register when
103                                            ; ZTimerOn called
104   TimedCount              dw      ?       ;timer 0 count when the timer
105                                            ; is stopped
106   ReferenceCount          dw      ?       ;number of counts required to
107                                            ; execute timer overhead code
```

```
108    OverflowFlag              db       ?              ;used to indicate whether the
109                                                      ; timer overflowed during the
110                                                      ; timing interval
111    ;
112    ; String printed to report results.
113    ;
114    OutputStr        label    byte
115                     db       0dh, 0ah, 'Timed count: ', 5 dup (?)
116    ASCIICountEnd    label    byte
117                     db       ' microseconds', 0dh, 0ah
118                     db       '$'
119    ;
120    ; String printed to report timer overflow.
121    ;
122    OverflowStr      label    byte
123              db     0dh, 0ah
124              db     '****************************************************'
125              db     0dh, 0ah
126              db     '* The timer overflowed, so the interval timed was  *'
127              db     0dh, 0ah
128              db     '* too long for the precision timer to measure.      *'
129              db     0dh, 0ah
130              db     '* Please perform the timing test again with the     *'
131              db     0dh, 0ah
132              db     '* long-period timer.                                *'
133              db     0dh, 0ah
134              db     '****************************************************'
135              db     0dh, 0ah
136              db     '$'
137
138    ;****************************************************************************
139    ;* Routine called to start timing.                                          *
140    ;****************************************************************************
141
142    ZTimerOn         proc     near
143
144    ;
145    ; Save the context of the program being timed.
146    ;
147              push   ax
148              pushf
149              pop    ax              ;get flags so we can keep
150                                     ; interrupts off when leaving
151                                     ; this routine
152              mov    cs:[OriginalFlags],ah   ;remember the state of the
153                                     ; Interrupt flag
154              and    ah,0fdh         ;set pushed interrupt flag
155                                     ; to 0
156              push   ax
157    ;
158    ; Turn on interrupts, so the timer interrupt can occur if it's
159    ; pending.
160    ;
161              sti
162    ;
163    ; Set timer 0 of the 8253 to mode 2 (divide-by-N), to cause
164    ; linear counting rather than count-by-two counting. Also
165    ; leaves the 8253 waiting for the initial timer 0 count to
166    ; be loaded.
```

```
167    ;
168            mov     al,00110100b                ;mode 2
169            out     MODE_8253,al
170    ;
171    ; Set the timer count to 0, so we know we won't get another
172    ; timer interrupt right away.
173    ; Note: this introduces an inaccuracy of up to 54 ms in the system
174    ; clock count each time it is executed.
175    ;
176            DELAY
177            sub     al,al
178            out     TIMER_0_8253,al             ;lsb
179            DELAY
180            out     TIMER_0_8253,al             ;msb
181    ;
182    ; Wait before clearing interrupts to allow the interrupt generated
183    ; when switching from mode 3 to mode 2 to be recognized. The delay
184    ; must be at least 210 ns long to allow time for that interrupt to
185    ; occur. Here, 10 jumps are used for the delay to ensure that the
186    ; delay time will be more than long enough even on a very fast PC.
187    ;
188            rept 10
189            jmp     $+2
190            endm
191    ;
192    ; Disable interrupts to get an accurate count.
193    ;
194            cli
195    ;
196    ; Set the timer count to 0 again to start the timing interval.
197    ;
198            mov     al,00110100b                ;set up to load initial
199            out     MODE_8253,al                ; timer count
200            DELAY
201            sub     al,al
202            out     TIMER_0_8253,al             ;load count lsb
203            DELAY
204            out     TIMER_0_8253,al             ;load count msb
205    ;
206    ; Restore the context and return.
207    ;
208            MPOPF                               ;keeps interrupts off
209            pop     ax
210            ret
211
212    ZTimerOn        endp
213
214    ;****************************************************************
215    ;* Routine called to stop timing and get count.               *
216    ;****************************************************************
217
218    ZTimerOff proc  near
219
220    ;
221    ; Save the context of the program being timed.
222    ;
223            push    ax
224            push    cx
225            pushf
```

```
226     ;
227     ; Latch the count.
228     ;
229             mov     al,00000000b            ;latch timer 0
230             out     MODE_8253,al
231     ;
232     ; See if the timer has overflowed by checking the 8259 for a pending
233     ; timer interrupt.
234     ;
235             mov     al,00001010b            ;OCW3, set up to read
236             out     OCW3,al                 ; Interrupt Request register
237             DELAY
238             in      al,IRR                  ;read Interrupt Request
239                                             ; register
240             and     al,1                    ;set AL to 1 if IRQ0 (the
241                                             ; timer interrupt) is pending
242             mov     cs:[OverflowFlag],al    ;store the timer overflow
243                                             ; status
244     ;
245     ; Allow interrupts to happen again.
246     ;
247             sti
248     ;
249     ; Read out the count we latched earlier.
250     ;
251             in      al,TIMER_0_8253         ;least significant byte
252             DELAY
253             mov     ah,al
254             in      al,TIMER_0_8253         ;most significant byte
255             xchg    ah,al
256             neg     ax                      ;convert from countdown
257                                             ; remaining to elapsed
258                                             ; count
259             mov     cs:[TimedCount],ax
260     ; Time a zero-length code fragment, to get a reference for how
261     ; much overhead this routine has. Time it 16 times and average it,
262     ; for accuracy, rounding the result.
263     ;
264             mov     cs:[ReferenceCount],0
265             mov     cx,16
266             cli                             ;interrupts off to allow a
267                                             ; precise reference count
268     RefLoop:
269             call    ReferenceZTimerOn
270             call    ReferenceZTimerOff
271             loop    RefLoop
272             sti
273             add     cs:[ReferenceCount],8   ;total + (0.5 * 16)
274             mov     cl,4
275             shr     cs:[ReferenceCount],cl  ;(total) / 16 + 0.5
276     ;
277     ; Restore original interrupt state.
278     ;
279             pop     ax                      ;retrieve flags when called
280             mov     ch,cs:[OriginalFlags]   ;get back the original upper
281                                             ; byte of the FLAGS register
282             and     ch,not 0fdh             ;only care about original
283                                             ; interrupt flag...
284             and     ah,0fdh                 ;...keep all other flags in
```

```
285                                               ; their current condition
286             or      ah,ch                     ;make flags word with original
287                                               ; interrupt flag
288             push    ax                        ;prepare flags to be popped
289     ;
290     ; Restore the context of the program being timed and return to it.
291     ;
292             MPOPF                             ;restore the flags with the
293                                               ; original interrupt state
294             pop     cx
295             pop     ax
296             ret
297
298     ZTimerOff endp
299
300     ;
301     ; Called by ZTimerOff to start timer for overhead measurements.
302     ;
303
304     ReferenceZTimerOn       proc    near
305     ;
306     ; Save the context of the program being timed.
307     ;
308             push    ax
309             pushf                   ;interrupts are already off
310     ;
311     ; Set timer 0 of the 8253 to mode 2 (divide-by-N), to cause
312     ; linear counting rather than count-by-two counting.
313     ;
314             mov     al,00110100b    ;set up to load
315             out     MODE_8253,al    ; initial timer count
316             DELAY
317     ;
318     ; Set the timer count to 0.
319     ;
320             sub     al,al
321             out     TIMER_0_8253,al ;load count lsb
322             DELAY
323             out     TIMER_0_8253,al ;load count msb
324     ;
325     ; Restore the context of the program being timed and return to it.
326     ;
327             MPOPF
328             pop     ax
329             ret
330
331     ReferenceZTimerOn       endp
332
333     ;
334     ; Called by ZTimerOff to stop timer and add result to ReferenceCount
335     ; for overhead measurements.
336     ;
337
338     ReferenceZTimerOff proc near
339     ;
340     ; Save the context of the program being timed.
341     ;
342             push    ax
343             push    cx
```

```
344              pushf
345       ;
346       ; Latch the count and read it.
347       ;
348              mov      al,00000000b            ;latch timer 0
349              out      MODE_8253,al
350              DELAY
351              in       al,TIMER_0_8253         ;lsb
352              DELAY
353              mov      ah,al
354              in       al,TIMER_0_8253         ;msb
355              xchg     ah,al
356              neg      ax                      ;convert from countdown
357                                               ; remaining to amount
358                                               ; counted down
359              add      cs:[ReferenceCount],ax
360       ;
361       ; Restore the context of the program being timed and return to it.
362       ;
363              MPOPF
364              pop      cx
365              pop      ax
366              ret
367
368       ReferenceZTimerOff endp
369
370       ;*****************************************************************
371       ;* Routine called to report timing results.                    *
372       ;*****************************************************************
373
374       ZTimerReport      proc      near
375
376              pushf
377              push     ax
378              push     bx
379              push     cx
380              push     dx
381              push     si
382              push     ds
383       ;
384              push     cs       ;DOS functions require that DS point
385              pop      ds       ; to text to be displayed on the screen
386              assume   ds:Code
387       ;
388       ; Check for timer 0 overflow.
389       ;
390              cmp      [OverflowFlag],0
391              jz       PrintGoodCount
392              mov      dx,offset OverflowStr
393              mov      ah,9
394              int      21h
395              jmp      short EndZTimerReport
396       ;
397       ; Convert net count to decimal ASCII in microseconds.
398       ;
399       PrintGoodCount:
400              mov      ax,[TimedCount]
401              sub      ax,[ReferenceCount]
402              mov      si,offset ASCIICountEnd - 1
```

```
403      ;
404      ; Convert count to microseconds by multiplying by .8381.
405      ;
406              mov     dx,8381
407              mul     dx
408              mov     bx,10000
409              div     bx               ;* .8381 = * 8381 / 10000
410      ;
411      ; Convert time in microseconds to 5 decimal ASCII digits.
412      ;
413              mov     bx,10
414              mov     cx,5
415      CTSLoop:
416              sub     dx,dx
417              div     bx
418              add     dl,'0'
419              mov     [si],dl
420              dec     si
421              loop    CTSLoop
422      ;
423      ; Print the results.
424      ;
425              mov     ah,9
426              mov     dx,offset OutputStr
427              int     21h
428      ;
429      EndZTimerReport:
430              pop     ds
431              pop     si
432              pop     dx
433              pop     cx
434              pop     bx
435              pop     ax
436              MPOPF
437              ret
438
439      ZTimerReport    endp
440
441      Code    ends
442              end
```

2.2 ◆ The Zen Timer Is a Means, Not an End

We're going to spend the rest of this chapter seeing what the Zen timer can do, examining how it works, and learning how to use it. The Zen timer will be our principal tool for the remainder of *Zen of Assembly Language*, so it's essential that you learn what the Zen timer can do and how to use it. On the other hand, it is by no means essential that you understand exactly how the Zen timer works. (Interesting? Yes. Essential? No.)

In other words, the Zen timer isn't really part of the knowledge we seek; rather, it's one tool with which we'll acquire that knowledge. Consequently, you shouldn't worry if you don't fully grasp the inner workings of the Zen timer. Instead, focus on learning how to use the timer, since we will use it frequently throughout *The Zen of Assembly Language.*

2.3 ◆ Starting the Zen Timer

ZTimerOn is called at the start of a segment of code to be timed. **ZTimerOn** saves the context of the calling code, disables interrupts, sets timer 0 of the 8253 to mode 2 (divide-by-N mode), sets the initial timer count to 0, restores the context of the calling code, and returns. (I'd like to note that while Intel's documentation for the 8253 seems to indicate that a timer won't reset to 0 until it finishes counting down, in actual practice timers seems to reset to 0 as soon as they're loaded.)

Two aspects of **ZTimerOn** are worth discussing further. One point of interest is that **ZTimerOn** disables interrupts. (**ZTimerOff** later restores interrupts to the state they were in when **ZTimerOn** was called.) Were interrupts not disabled by **ZTimerOn**, keyboard, mouse, timer, and other interrupts could occur during the timing interval, and the time required to service those interrupts would incorrectly and erratically appear to be part of the execution time of the code being measured. As a result, code timed with the Zen timer should not require any hardware interrupts during the interval between any call to **ZTimerOn** and the corresponding call to **ZTimerOff**, and should not enable interrupts during that time.

2.4 ◆ Time and the PC

A second interesting point about **ZTimerOn** is that it may introduce some small inaccuracy into the system clock time whenever it is called. To understand why this is so, we need to examine the way in which both the 8253 and the PC's system clock (which keeps the current time) work.

The 8253 actually contains three timers (Fig. 2.1), all three driven by the system board's 14.31818-megahertz crystal. Divided by 12, this yields a 1.19318-MHz clock to the timers, so the timers count once every 838.1 nsec. Each timer counts down in a programmable way, generating a signal on its output pin when it counts down to 0. Each timer can be halted at any time via a 0 level on its gate input; when a timer's gate input is 1, that timer counts constantly. All in all, the 8253's timers are inherently very flexible

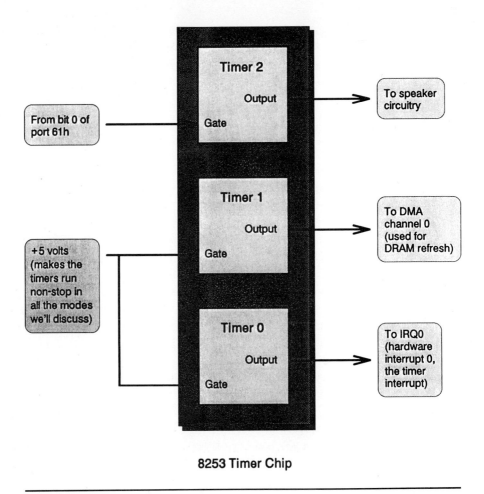

8253 Timer Chip

FIGURE 2.1   The configuration of the 8253 timer chip in the PC. Of the
                     8253's three timers, only timer 2 is wired so that its gate
                     input is under program control; the gate inputs of timers
                     0 and 1 are always enabled, so there is no documented
                     way to get either timer 0 or timer 1 to stop counting. Only
                     timer 0 is connected so that it is capable of generating an
                     interrupt.

devices; unfortunately, much of the flexibility depends on how the timers
are connected to external circuitry, and in the PC the timers are connected
with specific purposes in mind.

Timer 2 drives the speaker, although it can be used for other timing purposes when the speaker is not in use. As shown in Figure 2.1, timer 2 is the only timer with a programmable gate input in the PC; that is, timer 2 is the only timer that can be started and stopped under program control in the manner specified by Intel. On the other hand, the *output* of timer 2 is connected only to the speaker. In particular, timer 2 cannot generate an interrupt to get the 8088's attention.

Timer 1 is dedicated to providing dynamic RAM refresh and should not be tampered with, lest system crashes result.

Finally, timer 0 is used to drive the system clock. As programmed by the BIOS at power-up, every 65,536 (64 K) counts, or 54.925 milliseconds, timer 0 generates a rising edge on its output line. (A millisecond is one-thousandth of a second, and is abbreviated msec). This line is connected to the hardware interrupt 0 (IRQ0) line on the system board, so every 54.925 msec, timer 0 causes hardware interrupt 0 to occur.

The interrupt vector for IRQ0 is set by the BIOS at power-up time to point to a BIOS routine, **TIMER_INT**, that maintains a time-of-day count. **TIMER_INT** keeps a 16-bit count of IRQ0 interrupts in the BIOS data area at address 0000:046C (all addresses are given in segment:offset hexadecimal pairs); this count turns over once an hour (less a few microseconds), and when it does, **TIMER_INT** updates a 16-bit hour count at address 0000:046E in the BIOS data area. This routine is the basis for the current time and date that DOS supports via functions 2Ah (2A hexadecimal) through 2Dh and by way of the Date and Time commands.

Each timer channel of the 8253 can operate in any of six modes. Timer 0 normally operates in mode 3, square wave mode. In square wave mode, the initial count is counted down 2 at a time; when the count reaches 0, the output state is changed. The initial count is again counted down 2 at a time, and the output state is toggled back when the count reaches 0. The result is a square wave that changes state more slowly than the input clock by a factor of the initial count. In its normal mode of operation, timer 0 generates an output pulse that is low for about 27.5 msec and high for about 27.5 msec; this pulse is sent to the 8259 interrupt controller, and its rising edge generates a timer interrupt once every 54.925 msec.

Square wave mode is not very useful for precision timing, because it counts down by 2 twice per timer interrupt, thereby rendering exact timings impossible. Fortunately, the 8253 offers another timer mode, mode 2 (divide-by-N mode), which is both a good substitute for square wave mode and a perfect mode for precision timing.

Divide-by-N mode counts down by 1 from the initial count. When the count reaches 0, the timer turns over and starts counting down again without stopping, and a pulse is generated for a single clock period. While the pulse is not held for nearly as long as in square wave mode, it doesn't matter, since the 8259 interrupt controller is configured in the PC to be edge-triggered and, so, registers only the existence of a pulse from timer 0, not the duration of the pulse. As a result, timer 0 continues to generate timer interrupts in divide-by-N mode, and the system clock continues to maintain good time.

Why not use timer 2 instead of timer 0 for precision timing? After all, timer 2 has a programmable gate input and isn't used for anything but sound generation. The problem with timer 2 is that its output can't generate an interrupt; in fact, timer 2 can't do anything but drive the speaker. We need the interrupt generated by the output of timer 0 to tell us when the count has overflowed, and we will see shortly that the timer interrupt also makes it possible to time much longer periods than the Zen timer shown in Listing 2-1 supports.

In fact, the Zen timer shown in Listing 2-1 can time intervals of only up to about 54 msec, since that is the period that can be measured by timer 0 before its count turns over and repeats. Fifty-four msec may not seem like a very long time, but an 8088 can perform more than 1000 divides in 54 msec, and division is the instruction the 8088 performs most slowly. If a measured period turns out to be longer than 54 msec (that is, if timer 0 has counted down and turned over), the Zen timer will display a message to that effect. A long-period Zen timer for use in such cases will be presented later in this chapter.

The Zen timer determines whether timer 0 has turned over by checking to see whether an IRQ0 interrupt is pending. (Remember, interrupts are off while the Zen timer runs, so the timer interrupt cannot be recognized until the Zen timer stops and enables interrupts.) If an IRQ0 interrupt is pending, then timer 0 has turned over and generated a timer interrupt. Recall that **ZTimerOn** initially sets timer 0 to 0, in order to allow for the longest possible period (about 54 msec) before timer 0 reaches 0 and generates the timer interrupt.

Now we're ready to look at the ways in which the Zen timer can introduce inaccuracy into the system clock. Since timer 0 is initially set to 0 by the Zen timer, and since the system clock ticks only when timer 0 counts off 54.925 msec and reaches 0 again, an average inaccuracy of one half of 54.925 msec, or about 27.5 msec, is incurred each time the Zen timer is started. In addition, a timer interrupt is generated when timer 0 is switched from mode 3 to mode 2, advancing the system clock by up to 54.925 msec, although this happens only the first time the Zen timer is run after a warm or cold boot. Finally, up to 54.925 msec can again be lost when **ZTimerOff** is called, since that routine again sets the timer count to 0. Net result: the system clock runs up to 110 msec (about 1/9 sec) slow each time the Zen timer is used.

Potentially far greater inaccuracy can be generated by timing code that takes longer than about 110 msec to execute. Recall that all interrupts, including the timer interrupt, are disabled while timing code with the Zen timer. The 8259 interrupt controller is capable of remembering, at most, one pending timer interrupt, so all timer interrupts after the first during any given Zen timing interval are ignored. Consequently, if a timing interval exceeds 54.9 msec, the system clock effectively stops 54.9 msec after the timing interval starts and doesn't restart until the timing interval ends, losing time all the while.

The effects on the system time of the Zen timer aren't a matter for great concern, as they are temporary, lasting only until the next warm or cold boot. Systems that have battery-backed clocks, such as ATs, automatically reset the correct time whenever the computer is booted, and systems without battery-backed clocks prompt for the correct date and time when booted. Also, even repeated use of the Zen timer usually makes the system clock slow by no more than a total of a few seconds, unless code that takes much longer than 54 msec to run is timed (in which case the Zen timer will notify you that the code is too long to time).

Nonetheless, it's a good idea to reboot your computer at the end of each session with the Zen timer, to make sure that the system clock is correct.

2.5 ◆ Stopping the Zen Timer

At some point after **ZTimerOn** is called, **ZTimerOff** must always be called to mark the end of the timing interval. **ZTimerOff** saves the context of the calling program, latches and reads the timer 0 count, converts that count from the countdown value that the timer maintains to the number of counts elapsed since **ZTimerOn** was called, and stores the result. Immediately after latching the timer 0 count—and before enabling interrupts—**ZTimerOff** checks the 8259 interrupt controller to see if a timer interrupt is pending, setting a flag to mark that the timer overflowed if indeed a timer interrupt is pending. After that, **ZTimerOff** executes just the overhead code of **ZTimerOn** and **ZTimerOff** sixteen times and averages and saves the results in order to determine how many of the counts in the timing result just obtained were incurred by the overhead of the Zen timer rather than by the code being timed. Finally, **ZTimerOff** restores the context of the calling program, including the state of the interrupt flag that was in effect when **ZTimerOn** was called to start timing, and returns.

One interesting aspect of **ZTimerOff** is the manner in which timer 0 is stopped in order to read the timer count. We don't actually have to stop the timer to read the count; the 8253 provides a special latched read feature for the specific purpose of reading the count while a time is running. (That's a good thing, too. We've no documented way to stop timer 0 if we wanted to, since its gate input isn't connected, though later in this chapter, we'll see that it can be stopped after all.) We simply tell the 8253 to latch the current count and it does so without breaking stride.

2.6 ◆ Reporting Timing Results

ZTimerReport may be called to display timing results at any time after both **ZTimerOn** and **ZTimerOff** have been called. **ZTimerReport** first checks to see whether the timer overflowed (counted down to 0 and turned over) before **ZTimerOff** was called; if it did overflow, **ZTimerOff** prints a message to that effect and returns. Otherwise, **ZTimerReport** subtracts the reference count (representing the overhead of the Zen timer) from the count measured between the calls to **ZTimerOn** and **ZTimerOff**, converts the result from timer counts to microseconds, and prints the resulting time in microseconds to the standard output.

Note that **ZTimerReport** need not be called immediately after **ZTimerOff**. In fact, after a given call to **ZTimerOff**, **ZTimerReport** can be called at any time up until the next call to **ZTimerOn**.

You may want to use the Zen timer to measure several portions of a program while it executes normally, in which case it may not be desirable to have the text printed by **ZTimerReport** interfere with the program's normal display. There are many ways to deal with this. One approach is to remove the invocations of the DOS print string function (INT 21h with AH equal to 9) from **ZTimerReport**, instead running the program under a debugger that supports screen flipping (such as Symdeb or Codeview), placing a breakpoint at the start of **ZTimerReport**, and directly observing the count in microseconds as **ZTimerReport** calculates it.

A second approach is modification of **ZTimerReport** to place the result at some safe location in memory, such as an unused portion of the BIOS data area. A third approach is alteration of **ZTimerReport** to print the result over a serial port to a terminal or to another PC serving as a terminal. Similarly, Symdeb (and undoubtedly other debuggers as well) can be run from a remote terminal by running Mode to set up the serial port, then starting Symdeb and executing the command =**com1** or =**com2**.

Yet another approach is to modify **ZTimerReport** to send the result to the printer via either DOS function 5 or BIOS interrupt 17h.

A final approach is to modify **ZTimerReport** to print the result to the auxiliary output via DOS function 4 and to then write and load a special device driver named **AUX**, to which DOS function 4 output would automatically be directed. This device driver could send the result anywhere you desire. The result might go to the secondary display adapter, over a serial port, or to the printer, or it could simply be stored in a buffer within the driver, to be dumped at a later time. (Credit for this final approach goes to Michael Geary, and thanks go to David Miller for passing the idea on to me.)

You may well want to devise still other approaches better suited to your needs than those I've presented. Go to it! I've just thrown out a few possibilities to get you started.

2.7 ◆ Notes on the Zen Timer

The Zen timer subroutines are designed to be near called from assembly language code running in the public segment **Code**. The Zen timer subroutines can, however, be called from any assembler or high level language code that generates OBJ files that are compatible with the Microsoft Linker simply by modifying the segment that the timer code runs in to match the segment used by the code being timed, or by changing the Zen timer routines to far procedures and making far calls to the Zen timer code from the code being timed. All three subroutines preserve all registers and all flags except the interrupt flag, so calls to these routines are transparent to the calling code.

If you do change the Zen timer routines to far procedures in order to call them from code running in another segment, be sure to make *all* the Zen timer routines far, including **ReferenceZTimerOn** and **ReferenceZTimerOff**. (You'll have to put **far ptr** overrides on the calls from **ZTimerOff** to the latter two routines if you do make them far.) If the reference routines aren't the same type (near or far) as the other routines, they won't reflect the true overhead incurred by starting and stopping the Zen timer.

Please be aware that the inaccuracy that the Zen timer can introduce into the system clock time does not affect the accuracy of the performance measurements reported by the timer itself. The 8253 counts once every 838 nsec, giving a count resolution of about 1 μsec, although factors such as the prefetch queue (see below), dynamic RAM refresh, and internal timing variations in the 8253 make it perhaps more accurate to describe the Zen timer as measuring code performance with an accuracy of better than 10 μsec. In fact, we'll see in Chapter 5 why the Zen timer is actually most accurate in assessing code performance when timing intervals that are longer than about 100 μsec. At any rate, we're most interested in using the Zen timer to assess the relative performance of various code sequences—that is, using it to compare and tweak code—and the timer is more than accurate enough for that purpose.

The Zen timer works on all PC-compatible computers I've tested it on, including XTs, ATs, PS/2 computers, and 80386-based AT-compatible machines. Of course, I haven't been able to test it on *all* PC compatibles, but I don't expect any problems; computers on which the Zen timer doesn't run can't truly be called "IBM PC-compatible."

On the other hand, there is certainly no guarantee that code performance as measured by the Zen timer will be the same on compatible computers as on genuine IBM machines, or that absolute or relative code performance will be similar even on different IBM models; in fact, quite the opposite is true. For example, every PS/2 computer, even the relatively slow Model 30, executes code much faster than does a PC or XT. As another example, I set out to do the timings for this book on an XT-compatible computer, only to find that the computer wasn't quite IBM-compatible with regard to code performance. The differences were minor, but my experience illustrates the risk of assuming without actually checking that a specific make of computer will perform in a certain way.

Not that this variation between computers makes the Zen timer one whit less useful; quite the contrary. The Zen timer is an excellent tool for evaluating code performance over the entire spectrum of PC-compatible computers.

2.8 ◆ A Sample Use of the Zen Timer

Listing 2-2 shows a test bed program for measuring code performance with the Zen timer. This program sets DS equal to CS (for reasons we'll discuss shortly), includes the code to be measured from the file TESTCODE, and calls **ZTimerReport** to display the timing results. Consequently, the code being measured should be in the file TESTCODE and should contain calls to **ZTimerOn** and **ZTimerOff.**

```
1    ;
2    ; *** Listing 2-2 ***
3    ;
4    ; Program to measure performance of code that takes less than
5    ; 54 ms to execute. (PZTEST.ASM)
6    ;
7    ; Link with PZTIMER.ASM (Listing 2-1). PZTEST.BAT (Listing 2-4)
8    ; can be used to assemble and link both files. Code to be
9    ; measured must be in the file TESTCODE; Listing 2-3 shows
10   ; a sample TESTCODE file.
11   ;
12   ; By Michael Abrash 4/26/89
13   ;
14   mystack segment para stack 'STACK'
15           db      512 dup(?)
16   mystack ends
17   ;
18   Code    segment para public 'CODE'
19           assume  cs:Code, ds:Code
20           extrn   ZTimerOn:near, ZTimerOff:near, ZTimerReport:near
21   Start   proc    near
22           push    cs
23           pop     ds      ;set DS to point to the code segment,
24                           ; so data as well as code can easily
25                           ; be included in TESTCODE
26   ;
27           include TESTCODE ;code to be measured, including
28                           ; calls to ZTimerOn and ZTimerOff
29   ;
30   ; Display the results.
31   ;
32           call    ZTimerReport
33   ;
34   ; Terminate the program.
35   ;
36           mov     ah,4ch
37           int     21h
38   Start   endp
39   Code    ends
40           end     Start
```

Listing 2-3 shows some sample code to be timed. This listing measures the time required to execute 1000 loads of AL from the memory variable **MemVar**. Note that Listing 2-3 calls **ZTimerOn** to start timing, performs 1000 **mov** instructions in a row, and calls **ZTimerOff** to end timing. When Listing 2-3 is named TESTCODE and included by Listing 2-2, Listing 2-2 calls **ZTimerReport** to display the execution time after the code in Listing 2-3 has been run.

It's worth noting that Listing 2-3 begins by jumping around the memory variable **MemVar**. This approach lets us avoid reproducing Listing 2-2 in its entirety for each code fragment we want to measure. The key is that by defining any needed data right in the code segment and jumping around that data, each listing becomes self-contained and can be plugged directly into Listing 2-2 as TESTCODE. Listing 2-2 sets DS equal to CS before doing

```
1    ;
2    ; *** Listing 2-3 ***
3    ;
4    ; Measures the performance of 1000 loads of AL from
5    ; memory. (Use by renaming to TESTCODE, which is
6    ; included by PZTEST.ASM (Listing 2-2). PZTIME.BAT
7    ; (Listing 2-4) does this, along with all assembly
8    ; and linking.)
9    ;
10           jmp     Skip      ;jump around defined data
11   ;
12   MemVar  db      ?
13   ;
14   Skip:
15   ;
16   ; Start timing.
17   ;
18           call    ZTimerOn
19   ;
20           rept    1000
21           mov     al,[MemVar]
22           endm
23   ;
24   ; Stop timing.
25   ;
26           call    ZTimerOff
```

anything else, precisely so that data can be embedded in code fragments
being timed. Note that only after the initial jump is performed in Listing 2-3
is the Zen timer started, since we don't want to include the execution time
of start-up code in the timing interval. That's why the calls to **ZTimerOn**
and **ZTimerOff** are in TESTCODE, not in PZTEST.ASM; this way, we have
full control over which portion of TESTCODE is timed, and we can keep
setup code and the like out of the timing interval.

Listing 2-3 is used by naming it TESTCODE, assembling Listing 2-2
(which includes TESTCODE) and Listing 2-1 with MASM, and linking the
two resulting OBJ files together by way of the Microsoft Linker. Listing
2-4 shows a batch file, PZTIME.BAT, which does all that; when run, this
batch file generates and runs the executable file PZTEST.EXE. PZTIME.BAT
(Listing 2-4) assumes that the file PZTIMER.ASM contains Listing 2-1 and
that the file PZTEST.ASM contains Listing 2-2. The command line parameter
to PZTIME.BAT is the name of the file to be copied to TESTCODE and
included into PZTEST.ASM. (Note that Turbo Assembler can be substituted
for MASM by replacing "masm" with "tasm" and "link" with "tlink" in Listing
2-4. The same will be true of Listing 2-7.)

```
1    echo off
2    rem
3    rem *** Listing 2-4 ***
```

```
4    rem
5    rem **********************************************************************
6    rem * Batch file PZTIME.BAT, which builds and runs the precision  *
7    rem * Zen timer program PZTEST.EXE to time the code named as the  *
8    rem * command-line parameter. Listing 2-1 must be named           *
9    rem * PZTIMER.ASM, and Listing 2-2 must be named PZTEST.ASM. To    *
10   rem * time the code in LST2-3, you'd type the DOS command:         *
11   rem *                                                              *
12   rem * pztime lst2-3                                                *
13   rem *                                                              *
14   rem * Note that MASM and LINK must be in the current directory or *
15   rem * on the current path in order for this batch file to work.   *
16   rem *                                                              *
17   rem * This batch file can be speeded up by assembling PZTIMER.ASM *
18   rem * once, then removing the lines:                               *
19   rem *                                                              *
20   rem * masm pztimer;                                                *
21   rem * if errorlevel 1 goto errorend                                *
22   rem *                                                              *
23   rem * from this file.                                              *
24   rem *                                                              *
25   rem * By Michael Abrash 4/26/89                                    *
26   rem **********************************************************************
27   rem
28   rem Make sure a file to test was specified.
29   rem
30   if not x%1==x goto ckexist
31   echo **********************************************************************
32   echo * Please specify a file to test.                              *
33   echo **********************************************************************
34   goto end
35   rem
36   rem Make sure the file exists.
37   rem
38   :ckexist
39   if exist %1 goto docopy
40   echo **********************************************************************
41   echo * The specified file, "%1," doesn't exist.
42   echo **********************************************************************
43   goto end
44   rem
45   rem copy the file to measure to TESTCODE.
46   rem
47   :docopy
48   copy %1 testcode
49   masm pztest;
50   if errorlevel 1 goto errorend
51   masm pztimer;
52   if errorlevel 1 goto errorend
53   link pztest+pztimer;
54   if errorlevel 1 goto errorend
55   pztest
56   goto end
57   :errorend
58   echo **********************************************************************
59   echo * An error occurred while building the precision Zen timer.   *
60   echo **********************************************************************
61   :end
```

Assuming that Listing 2-3 is named LST2-3 and Listing 2-4 is named PZTIME.BAT, the code in Listing 2-3 would be timed with the command:

pztime LST2-3

which performs all assembly and linking and reports the execution time of the code in Listing 2-3.

When the above command is executed on a PC, the time reported by the Zen timer is 3619 μsec, or about 3.62 μsec per load of AL from memory. (While the exact number is 3.619 μsec per load of AL, I'm going to round off that last digit from now on. No matter how many repetitions of a given instruction are timed, there's just too much noise in the timing process, between dynamic RAM refresh, the prefetch queue, and the internal state of the 8088 at the start of timing, for that last digit to have any significance.) Given the PC's 4.77-MHz clock, this works out to about 17 cycles per **mov**, which is actually a good bit longer than Intel's specified 10-cycle execution time for this instruction. (See Appendix A for official execution times.) Fear not, the Zen timer is right: **mov al,[MemVar]** really does take 17 cycles as used in Listing 2-3. Exactly why that is so is just what this book, and particularly the next three chapters, are all about.

In order to perform any of the timing tests in this book, enter Listing 2-1 and name it PZTIMER.ASM, enter Listing 2-2 and name it PZTEST.ASM, and enter Listing 2-4 and name it PZTIME.BAT. Then simply enter the listing you wish to run into the file *filename* and enter the command:

pztime filename

In fact, that's exactly how I timed each of the listings in this book. Code fragments you write yourself can be timed in just the same way. If you wish to time code directly in place in your programs, rather than in the test bed program of Listing 2-2, simply insert calls to **ZTimerOn**, **ZTimerOff**, and **ZTimerReport** in the appropriate places and link PZTIMER to your program.

2.9 ◆ The Long-Period Zen Timer

With a few exceptions, the Zen timer presented above will serve us well for the remainder of this book, since we'll be focusing on relatively short code sequences that generally take much less than 54 msec to execute.

Occasionally, however, we will need to time longer intervals. What's more, it is very likely that you will want to time code sequences longer than 54 msec at some point in your programming career. Accordingly, I've also developed a Zen timer for such periods. The long-period Zen timer (so named to contrast with the precision Zen timer just presented) shown in Listing 2-5 can measure periods of up to 1 hour.

The key difference between the long-period Zen timer and the precision Zen timer is that the long-period timer leaves interrupts enabled during the timing period. As a result, timer interrupts are recognized by the PC, allowing the BIOS to maintain an accurate system clock time over the timing period. Theoretically, this enables measurement of indefinitely long periods. Practically speaking, however, there is no need for a timer that can measure more than a few minutes, since the DOS time of day and date functions (or, indeed, the Date and Time commands in a batch file) serve perfectly well for longer intervals. Since very long timing intervals aren't needed, the long-period Zen timer uses a simplified means of calculating elapsed time that is limited to measuring intervals of an hour or less. If a period longer than an hour is timed, the long-period Zen timer prints a message to the effect that it is unable to time an interval of that length.

For implementation reasons, the long-period Zen timer is also incapable of timing code that starts before midnight and ends after midnight; if that eventuality occurs, the long-period Zen timer reports that it was unable to time the code because midnight was crossed. If this happens to you, just time the code again, secure in the knowledge that at least you won't run into the problem for another 23-some hours.

You should not use the long-period Zen timer to time code that requires interrupts to be disabled for more than 54 msec at a stretch during the timing interval, since when interrupts are disabled the long-period Zen timer is subject to the same 54-msec maximum measurement time as the precision Zen timer.

While allowing the timer interrupt to occur permits long intervals to be timed, that same interrupt makes the long-period Zen timer less accurate than the precision Zen timer, since the time the BIOS spends handling timer interrupts during the timing interval is included in the time measured by the long-period timer. Likewise, any other interrupts that occur during the timing interval, most notably keyboard and mouse interrupts, will increase the measured time.

The long-period Zen timer has some of the same effects on the system time as the precision Zen timer, so it's a good idea to reboot the system after a session with the long-period Zen timer. The long-period Zen timer does not, however, have the same potential for introducing major inaccuracy into the system clock time during a single timing run, since it leaves interrupts enabled and therefore allows the system clock to update normally.

2.10 ◆ Stopping the Clock

There's a potential problem with the long-period Zen timer: in order to measure times longer than 54 msec, we must maintain not one but two timing components, the timer 0 count and the BIOS time-of-day count. The time-of-day count measures the passage of 54.9-msec intervals, whereas the timer 0 count measures time within those intervals. We need to read the two time components simultaneously to get a clean reading. Otherwise, we may read the timer count just before it turns over and generates an interrupt, then read the BIOS time-of-day count just after the interrupt has occurred and caused the time-of-day count to turn over. The result would be a 54-msec measurement error. (The opposite sequence—reading the time-of-day count and then the timer count—can result in a 54-msec inaccuracy in the other direction.)

The only way to avoid this problem is to stop timer 0, read both the timer and time-of-day counts while the timer is stopped, and then restart the timer. Alas, the gate input to timer 0 isn't program controllable in the PC, so there's no documented way to stop the timer. (The latched read feature we used in the Listing 2-1 doesn't stop the timer; it latches a count, but the timer keeps running.) What to do?

As it turns out, an undocumented feature of the 8253 makes it possible to stop the timer dead in its tracks. Setting the timer to a new mode, waiting for an initial count to be loaded, causes the timer to stop until the count is loaded. Surprisingly, the timer count remains readable and correct while the timer is awaiting the initial load.

In my experience, this approach works beautifully with fully 8253-compatible chips; however, there's no guarantee that it will always work, since it programs the 8253 in an undocumented way. What's more, IBM chose not to implement compatibility with this particular 8253 feature in the custom chips used in PS/2 computers. On PS/2 computers, we have no choice but to latch the timer 0 count and then stop the BIOS count (by disabling interrupts) as quickly as possible. We'll just have to accept the fact that on PS/2 computers we may occasionally get a reading that's off by 54 msec, and leave it at that.

I've set up Listing 2-5 so that it can assemble to either use or not use the undocumented timer-stopping feature. The **PS2** equate selects between the two modes of operation. If **PS2** is 1 (as it is in Listing 2-5), then the latch-and-read method is used; if **PS2** is 0, then the undocumented timer stop approach is used. The latch-and-read method will work on all PC-compatible computers, but it may occasionally produce results that are incorrect by 54 msec. The timer stop approach avoids synchronization problems, but doesn't work on all computers.

Moreover, because it uses an undocumented feature, the timer stop approach could conceivably cause erratic 8253 operation, which could in turn seriously affect your computer's operation until the next reboot. In non–8253-compatible systems, I've observed not only wildly incorrect timing results, but also failure of a floppy drive to operate properly after the long-period Zen timer has run with **PS2** set to 0, so be alert for signs of trouble if you do set **PS2** to 0.

Rebooting should clear up any timer-related problems of the sort described above. (This gives us another reason to reboot at the end of each code-timing session.) You should *immediately* reboot and set the **PS2** equate to 1 if you get erratic or obviously incorrect results with the long-period Zen timer when **PS2** is set to 0. If you want to set **PS2** to 0, it would be a good idea to time a few of the listings in this book with **PS2** set first to 1 and then to 0, to make sure that your results match the results described herein. If they're consistently different, you should set **PS2** to 1.

While the non–PS/2 version is more dangerous than the PS/2 version, it also produces more accurate results when it does work. If you have a non–PS/2 PC-compatible computer, the choice between the two timing approaches is yours.

If you do leave the **PS2** equate at 1 in Listing 2-5, you should repeat each code-timing run several times before relying on the results to be accurate to more than 54 msec, since variations may result from the possible lack of synchronization between the timer 0 count and the BIOS time-of-day count. In fact, it's a good idea to time code more than once no matter which version of the long-period Zen timer you're using, since interrupts, which must be enabled in order for the long-period timer to work properly, may occur at any time and can alter execution time substantially.

Finally, please note that the *precision* Zen timer works perfectly well on both PS/2 and non-PS/2 computers. The PS/2 and 8253 considerations we've just discussed apply only to the long-period Zen timer.

```
1   ;
2   ; *** Listing 2-5 ***
3   ;
4   ; The long-period Zen timer. (LZTIMER.ASM)
5   ; Uses the 8253 timer and the BIOS time-of-day count to time the
6   ; performance of code that takes less than an hour to execute.
```

```
 7   ; Because interrupts are left on (in order to allow the timer
 8   ; interrupt to be recognized), this is less accurate than the
 9   ; precision Zen timer, so it is best used only to time code that takes
10   ; more than about 54 milliseconds to execute (code that the precision
11   ; Zen timer reports overflow on). Resolution is limited by the
12   ; occurrence of timer interrupts.
13   ;
14   ; By Michael Abrash 4/26/89
15   ;
16   ; Externally callable routines:
17   ;
18   ;   ZTimerOn: Saves the BIOS time of day count and starts the
19   ;       long-period Zen timer.
20   ;
21   ;   ZTimerOff: Stops the long-period Zen timer and saves the timer
22   ;       count and the BIOS time-of-day count.
23   ;
24   ;   ZTimerReport: Prints the time that passed between starting and
25   ;       stopping the timer.
26   ;
27   ; Note: If either more than an hour passes or midnight falls between
28   ;       calls to ZTimerOn and ZTimerOff, an error is reported. For
29   ;       timing code that takes more than a few minutes to execute,
30   ;       either the DOS TIME command in a batch file before and after
31   ;       execution of the code to time or the use of the DOS
32   ;       time-of-day function in place of the long-period Zen timer is
33   ;       more than adequate.
34   ;
35   ; Note: The PS/2 version is assembled by setting the symbol PS2 to 1.
36   ;       PS2 must be set to 1 on PS/2 computers because the PS/2's
37   ;       timers are not compatible with an undocumented timer-stopping
38   ;       feature of the 8253; the alternative timing approach that
39   ;       must be used on PS/2 computers leaves a short window
40   ;       during which the timer 0 count and the BIOS timer count may
41   ;       not be synchronized. You should also set the PS2 symbol to
42   ;       1 if you're getting erratic or obviously incorrect results.
43   ;
44   ; Note: When PS2 is 0, the code relies on an undocumented 8253
45   ;       feature to get more reliable readings. It is possible that
46   ;       the 8253 (or whatever chip is emulating the 8253) may be put
47   ;       into an undefined or incorrect state when this feature is
48   ;       used.
49   ;
50   ;   ****************************************************************
51   ;   * If your computer displays any hint of erratic behavior      *
52   ;   * after the long-period Zen timer is used, such as the floppy *
53   ;   * drive failing to operate properly, reboot the system, set   *
54   ;   * PS2 to 1 and leave it that way!                             *
55   ;   ****************************************************************
56   ;
57   ; Note: Each block of code being timed should ideally be run several
58   ;       times, with at least two similar readings required to
59   ;       establish a true measurement, in order to eliminate any
60   ;       variability caused by interrupts.
61   ;
62   ; Note: Interrupts must not be disabled for more than 54 ms at a
63   ;       stretch during the timing interval. Because interrupts
64   ;       are enabled, keys, mice, and other devices that generate
65   ;       interrupts should not be used during the timing interval.
```

```
66    ;
67    ; Note: Any extra code running off the timer interrupt (such as
68    ;         some memory-resident utilities) will increase the time
69    ;         measured by the Zen timer.
70    ;
71    ; Note: These routines can introduce inaccuracies of up to a few
72    ;         tenths of a second into the system clock count for each
73    ;         code section timed. Consequently, it's a good idea to
74    ;         reboot at the conclusion of timing sessions. (The
75    ;         battery-backed clock, if any, is not affected by the Zen
76    ;         timer.)
77    ;
78    ; All registers and all flags are preserved by all routines.
79    ;
80
81    Code    segment word public 'CODE'
82            assume  cs:Code, ds:nothing
83            public  ZTimerOn, ZTimerOff, ZTimerReport
84
85    ;
86    ; Set PS2 to 0 to assemble for use on a fully 8253-compatible
87    ; system; when PS2 is 0, the readings are more reliable if the
88    ; computer supports the undocumented timer-stopping feature,
89    ; but may be badly off if that feature is not supported. In
90    ; fact, timer-stopping may interfere with your computer's
91    ; overall operation by putting the 8253 into an undefined or
92    ; incorrect state.  Use with caution!!!
93    ;
94    ; Set PS2 to 1 to assemble for use on non-8253-compatible
95    ; systems, including PS/2 computers; when PS2 is 1, readings
96    ; may occasionally be off by 54 ms, but the code will work
97    ; properly on all systems.
98    ;
99    ; A setting of 1 is safer and will work on more systems,
100   ; while a setting of 0 produces more reliable results in systems
101   ; which support the undocumented timer-stopping feature of the
102   ; 8253. The choice is yours.
103   ;
104   PS2     equ     1
105   ;
106   ; Base address of the 8253 timer chip.
107   ;
108   BASE_8253            equ     40h
109   ;
110   ; The address of the timer 0 count registers in the 8253.
111   ;
112   TIMER_0_8253         equ     BASE_8253 + 0
113   ;
114   ; The address of the mode register in the 8253.
115   ;
116   MODE_8253            equ     BASE_8253 + 3
117   ;
118   ; The address of the BIOS timer count variable in the BIOS
119   ; data segment.
120   ;
121   TIMER_COUNT          equ     46ch
122   ;
123   ; Macro to emulate a POPF instruction in order to fix the bug in some
124   ; 80286 chips which allows interrupts to occur during a POPF even when
```

```
125     ; interrupts remain disabled.
126     ;
127     MPOPF macro
128             local   p1, p2
129             jmp short p2
130     p1:     iret                            ;jump to pushed address & pop flags
131     p2:     push    cs                      ;construct far return address to
132             call    p1                      ; the next instruction
133             endm
134
135     ;
136     ; Macro to delay briefly to ensure that enough time has elapsed
137     ; between successive I/O accesses so that the device being accessed
138     ; can respond to both accesses even on a very fast PC.
139     ;
140     DELAY   macro
141             jmp     $+2
142             jmp     $+2
143             jmp     $+2
144             endm
145
146     StartBIOSCountLow       dw      ?       ;BIOS count low word at the
147                                             ; start of the timing period
148     StartBIOSCountHigh      dw      ?       ;BIOS count high word at the
149                                             ; start of the timing period
150     EndBIOSCountLow         dw      ?       ;BIOS count low word at the
151                                             ; end of the timing period
152     EndBIOSCountHigh        dw      ?       ;BIOS count high word at the
153                                             ; end of the timing period
154     EndTimedCount           dw      ?       ;timer 0 count at the end of
155                                             ; the timing period
156     ReferenceCount          dw      ?       ;number of counts required to
157                                             ; execute timer overhead code
158     ;
159     ; String printed to report results.
160     ;
161     OutputStr       label   byte
162                     db      0dh, 0ah, 'Timed count: '
163     TimedCountStr   db      10 dup (?)
164                     db      ' microseconds', 0dh, 0ah
165                     db      '$'
166     ;
167     ; Temporary storage for timed count as it's divided down by powers
168     ; of ten when converting from doubleword binary to ASCII.
169     ;
170     CurrentCountLow         dw      ?
171     CurrentCountHigh        dw      ?
172     ;
173     ; Powers of ten table used to perform division by 10 when doing
174     ; doubleword conversion from binary to ASCII.
175     ;
176     PowersOfTen     label   word
177             dd      1
178             dd      10
179             dd      100
180             dd      1000
181             dd      10000
182             dd      100000
183             dd      1000000
```

```
184              dd        10000000
185              dd        100000000
186              dd        1000000000
187    PowersOfTenEnd  label    word
188    ;
189    ; String printed to report that the high word of the BIOS count
190    ; changed while timing (an hour elapsed or midnight was crossed),
191    ; and so the count is invalid and the test needs to be rerun.
192    ;
193    TurnOverStr      label    byte
194              db        0dh, 0ah
195              db        '**************************************************'
196              db        0dh, 0ah
197              db        '* Either midnight passed or an hour or more passed *'
198              db        0dh, 0ah
199              db        '* while timing was in progress. If the former was  *'
200              db        0dh, 0ah
201              db        '* the case, please rerun the test; if the latter   *'
202              db        0dh, 0ah
203              db        '* was the case, the test code takes too long to    *'
204              db        0dh, 0ah
205              db        '* run to be timed by the long-period Zen timer.    *'
206              db        0dh, 0ah
207              db        '* Suggestions: use the DOS TIME command, the DOS   *'
208              db        0dh, 0ah
209              db        '* time function, or a watch.                       *'
210              db        0dh, 0ah
211              db        '**************************************************'
212              db        0dh, 0ah
213              db        '$'
214
215    ;********************************************************************
216    ;* Routine called to start timing.                                 *
217    ;********************************************************************
218
219    ZTimerOn         proc     near
220
221    ;
222    ; Save the context of the program being timed.
223    ;
224              push      ax
225              pushf
226    ;
227    ; Set timer 0 of the 8253 to mode 2 (divide-by-N), to cause
228    ; linear counting rather than count-by-two counting. Also stops
229    ; timer 0 until the timer count is loaded, except on PS/2
230    ; computers.
231    ;
232              mov       al,00110100b      ;mode 2
233              out       MODE_8253,al
234    ;
235    ; Set the timer count to 0, so we know we won't get another
236    ; timer interrupt right away.
237    ; Note: this introduces an inaccuracy of up to 54 ms in the system
238    ; clock count each time it is executed.
239    ;
240              DELAY
241              sub       al,al
242              out       TIMER_0_8253,al          ;lsb
```

```
243              DELAY
244              out       TIMER_0_8253,al          ;msb
245      ;
246      ; In case interrupts are disabled, enable interrupts briefly to allow
247      ; the interrupt generated when switching from mode 3 to mode 2 to be
248      ; recognized. Interrupts must be enabled for at least 210 ns to allow
249      ; time for that interrupt to occur. Here, 10 jumps are used for the
250      ; delay to ensure that the delay time will be more than long enough
251      ; even on a very fast PC.
252      ;
253              pushf
254              sti
255              rept 10
256              jmp       $+2
257              endm
258              MPOPF
259      ;
260      ; Store the timing start BIOS count.
261      ; (Since the timer count was just set to 0, the BIOS count will
262      ; stay the same for the next 54 ms, so we don't need to disable
263      ; interrupts in order to avoid getting a half-changed count.)
264      ;
265              push      ds
266              sub       ax,ax
267              mov       ds,ax
268              mov       ax,ds:[TIMER_COUNT+2]
269              mov       cs:[StartBIOSCountHigh],ax
270              mov       ax,ds:[TIMER_COUNT]
271              mov       cs:[StartBIOSCountLow],ax
272              pop       ds
273      ;
274      ; Set the timer count to 0 again to start the timing interval.
275      ;
276              mov       al,00110100b             ;set up to load initial
277              out       MODE_8253,al             ; timer count
278              DELAY
279              sub       al,al
280              out       TIMER_0_8253,al          ;load count lsb
281              DELAY
282              out       TIMER_0_8253,al          ;load count msb
283      ;
284      ; Restore the context of the program being timed and return to it.
285      ;
286              MPOPF
287              pop       ax
288              ret
289
290      ZTimerOn        endp
291
292      ;*******************************************************************
293      ;* Routine called to stop timing and get count.                   *
294      ;*******************************************************************
295
296      ZTimerOff proc  near
297
298      ;
299      ; Save the context of the program being timed.
300      ;
```

```
301          pushf
302          push    ax
303          push    cx
304   ;
305   ; In case interrupts are disabled, enable interrupts briefly to allow
306   ; any pending timer interrupt to be handled. Interrupts must be
307   ; enabled for at least 210 ns to allow time for that interrupt to
308   ; occur. Here, 10 jumps are used for the delay to ensure that the
309   ; delay time will be more than long enough even on a very fast PC.
310   ;
311          sti
312          rept    10
313          jmp     $+2
314          endm
315
316   ;
317   ; Latch the timer count.
318   ;
319
320   if PS2
321
322          mov     al,00000000b
323          out     MODE_8253,al            ;latch timer 0 count
324   ;
325   ; This is where a one-instruction-long window exists on the PS/2.
326   ; The timer count and the BIOS count can lose synchronization;
327   ; since the timer keeps counting after it's latched, it can turn
328   ; over right after it's latched and cause the BIOS count to turn
329   ; over before interrupts are disabled, leaving us with the timer
330   ; count from before the timer turned over coupled with the BIOS
331   ; count from after the timer turned over. The result is a count
332   ; that's 54 ms too long.
333   ;
334
335   else
336
337   ;
338   ; Set timer 0 to mode 2 (divide-by-N), waiting for a 2-byte count
339   ; load, which stops timer 0 until the count is loaded. (Only works
340   ; on fully 8253-compatible chips.)
341   ;
342          mov     al,00110100b            ;mode 2
343          out     MODE_8253,al
344          DELAY
345          mov     al,00000000b            ;latch timer 0 count
346          out     MODE_8253,al
347
348   endif
349
350          cli                             ;stop the BIOS count
351   ;
352   ; Read the BIOS count. (Since interrupts are disabled, the BIOS
353   ; count won't change.)
354   ;
355          push    ds
356          sub     ax,ax
357          mov     ds,ax
358          mov     ax,ds:[TIMER_COUNT+2]
```

```
359            mov      cs:[EndBIOSCountHigh],ax
360            mov      ax,ds:[TIMER_COUNT]
361            mov      cs:[EndBIOSCountLow],ax
362            pop      ds
363      ;
364      ; Read the timer count and save it.
365      ;
366            in       al,TIMER_0_8253              ;lsb
367            DELAY
368            mov      ah,al
369            in       al,TIMER_0_8253              ;msb
370            xchg     ah,al
371            neg      ax                           ;convert from countdown
372                                                  ; remaining to elapsed
373                                                  ; count
374            mov      cs:[EndTimedCount],ax
375      ;
376      ; Restart timer 0, which is still waiting for an initial count
377      ; to be loaded.
378      ;
379
380      ife PS2
381
382            DELAY
383            mov      al,00110100b                 ;mode 2, waiting to load a
384                                                  ; 2-byte count
385            out      MODE_8253,al
386            DELAY
387            sub      al,al
388            out      TIMER_0_8253,al              ;lsb
389            DELAY
390            mov      al,ah
391            out      TIMER_0_8253,al              ;msb
392            DELAY
393
394      endif
395
396            sti                      ;let the BIOS count continue
397      ;
398      ; Time a zero-length code fragment, to get a reference for how
399      ; much overhead this routine has. Time it 16 times and average it,
400      ; for accuracy, rounding the result.
401      ;
402            mov      cs:[ReferenceCount],0
403            mov      cx,16
404            cli                                   ;interrupts off to allow a
405                                                  ; precise reference count
406      RefLoop:
407            call     ReferenceZTimerOn
408            call     ReferenceZTimerOff
409            loop     RefLoop
410            sti
411            add      cs:[ReferenceCount],8    ;total + (0.5 * 16)
412            mov      cl,4
413            shr      cs:[ReferenceCount],cl   ;(total) / 16 + 0.5
414      ;
415      ; Restore the context of the program being timed and return to it.
416      ;
417            pop      cx
```

```
418             pop     ax
419             MPOPF
420             ret
421
422     ZTimerOff endp
423
424     ;
425     ; Called by ZTimerOff to start the timer for overhead measurements.
426     ;
427
428     ReferenceZTimerOn       proc    near
429     ;
430     ; Save the context of the program being timed.
431     ;
432             push    ax
433             pushf
434     ;
435     ; Set timer 0 of the 8253 to mode 2 (divide-by-N), to cause
436     ; linear counting rather than count-by-two counting.
437     ;
438             mov     al,00110100b    ;mode 2
439             out     MODE_8253,al
440     ;
441     ; Set the timer count to 0.
442     ;
443             DELAY
444             sub     al,al
445             out     TIMER_0_8253,al         ;lsb
446             DELAY
447             out     TIMER_0_8253,al         ;msb
448     ;
449     ; Restore the context of the program being timed and return to it.
450     ;
451             MPOPF
452             pop     ax
453             ret
454
455     ReferenceZTimerOn       endp
456
457     ;
458     ; Called by ZTimerOff to stop the timer and add the result to
459     ; ReferenceCount for overhead measurements. Doesn't need to look
460     ; at the BIOS count because timing a zero-length code fragment
461     ; isn't going to take anywhere near 54 ms.
462     ;
463
464     ReferenceZTimerOff proc near
465     ;
466     ; Save the context of the program being timed.
467     ;
468             pushf
469             push    ax
470             push    cx
471
472     ;
473     ; Match the interrupt-window delay in ZTimerOff.
474     ;
475             sti
476             rept    10
```

```
477               jmp     $+2
478               endm
479
480               mov     al,00000000b
481               out     MODE_8253,al              ;latch timer
482       ;
483       ; Read the count and save it.
484       ;
485               DELAY
486               in      al,TIMER_0_8253           ;lsb
487               DELAY
488               mov     ah,al
489               in      al,TIMER_0_8253           ;msb
490               xchg    ah,al
491               neg     ax                        ;convert from countdown
492                                                 ; remaining to elapsed
493                                                 ; count
494               add     cs:[ReferenceCount],ax
495       ;
496       ; Restore the context and return.
497       ;
498               pop     cx
499               pop     ax
500               MPOPF
501               ret
502
503       ReferenceZTimerOff endp
504
505       ;********************************************************************
506       ;* Routine called to report timing results.                       *
507       ;********************************************************************
508
509       ZTimerReport    proc    near
510
511               pushf
512               push    ax
513               push    bx
514               push    cx
515               push    dx
516               push    si
517               push    di
518               push    ds
519       ;
520               push    cs        ;DOS functions require that DS point
521               pop     ds        ; to text to be displayed on the screen
522               assume  ds:Code
523       ;
524       ; See if midnight or more than an hour passed during timing. If so,
525       ; notify the user.
526       ;
527               mov     ax,[StartBIOSCountHigh]
528               cmp     ax,[EndBIOSCountHigh]
529               jz      CalcBIOSTime              ;hour count didn't change,
530                                                 ; so everything's fine
531               inc     ax
532               cmp     ax,[EndBIOSCountHigh]
533               jnz     TestTooLong               ;midnight or two hour
534                                                 ; boundaries passed, so the
535                                                 ; results are no good
```

```
536              mov       ax,[EndBIOSCountLow]
537              cmp       ax,[StartBIOSCountLow]
538              jb        CalcBIOSTime             ;a single hour boundary
539                                                ; passed-that's OK, so long as
540                                                ; the total time wasn't more
541                                                ; than an hour
542
543     ;
544     ; Over an hour elapsed or midnight passed during timing, which
545     ; renders the results invalid. Notify the user. This misses the
546     ; case where a multiple of 24 hours has passed, but we'll rely
547     ; on the perspicacity of the user to detect that case.
548     ;
549     TestTooLong:
550              mov       ah,9
551              mov       dx,offset TurnOverStr
552              int       21h
553              jmp       short ZTimerReportDone
554     ;
555     ; Convert the BIOS time to microseconds.
556     ;
557     CalcBIOSTime:
558              mov       ax,[EndBIOSCountLow]
559              sub       ax,[StartBIOSCountLow]
560              mov       dx,54925                 ;number of microseconds each
561                                                ; BIOS count represents
562              mul       dx
563              mov       bx,ax                    ;set aside BIOS count in
564              mov       cx,dx                    ; microseconds
565     ;
566     ; Convert timer count to microseconds.
567     ;
568              mov       ax,[EndTimedCount]
569              mov       si,8381
570              mul       si
571              mov       si,10000
572              div       si              ;* .8381 = * 8381 / 10000
573     ;
574     ; Add timer and BIOS counts together to get an overall time in
575     ; microseconds.
576     ;
577              add       bx,ax
578              adc       cx,0
579     ;
580     ; Subtract the timer overhead and save the result.
581     ;
582              mov       ax,[ReferenceCount]
583              mov       si,8381          ;convert the reference count
584              mul       si               ; to microseconds
585              mov       si,10000
586              div       si              ;* .8381 = * 8381 / 10000
587              sub       bx,ax
588              sbb       cx,0
589              mov       [CurrentCountLow],bx
590              mov       [CurrentCountHigh],cx
591     ;
592     ; Convert the result to an ASCII string by trial subtractions of
593     ; powers of 10.
594     ;
```

```
595          mov       di,offset PowersOfTenEnd - offset PowersOfTen - 4
596          mov       si,offset TimedCountStr
597   CTSNextDigit:
598          mov       bl,'0'
599   CTSLoop:
600          mov       ax,[CurrentCountLow]
601          mov       dx,[CurrentCountHigh]
602          sub       ax,PowersOfTen[di]
603          sbb       dx,PowersOfTen[di+2]
604          jc        CTSNextPowerDown
605          inc       bl
606          mov       [CurrentCountLow],ax
607          mov       [CurrentCountHigh],dx
608          jmp       CTSLoop
609   CTSNextPowerDown:
610          mov       [si],bl
611          inc       si
612          sub       di,4
613          jns       CTSNextDigit
614   ;
615   ;
616   ; Print the results.
617   ;
618          mov       ah,9
619          mov       dx,offset OutputStr
620          int       21h
621   ;
622   ZTimerReportDone:
623          pop       ds
624          pop       di
625          pop       si
626          pop       dx
627          pop       cx
628          pop       bx
629          pop       ax
630          MPOPF
631          ret
632
633   ZTimerReport       endp
634
635   Code       ends
636          end
```

2.11 ◆ A Sample Use of the Long-Period Zen Timer

The long-period Zen timer has exactly the same calling interface as the precision Zen timer and can be used in place of it simply by being linked to the code to be timed in place of the precision timer code. Whenever the precision Zen timer informs you that the code being timed takes too long for the precision timer to handle, all you have to do is link in the long-period timer instead.

Listing 2-6 shows a test bed program for the long-period Zen timer. While this program is similar to Listing 2-2, it's worth noting that the former waits a few seconds before calling **ZTimerOn,** allowing any pending keyboard interrupts to be processed. Since interrupts must be left on in order to time periods longer than 54 msec, the interrupts generated by keystrokes (including the upstroke of the **Enter** key press that starts the program), or any interrupts, for that matter, could incorrectly inflate the time recorded by the long-period Zen timer. In light of this, you should resist the temptation to type ahead, move the mouse, or the like while the long-period Zen timer is timing.

```
1     ;
2     ; *** Listing 2-6 ***
3     ;
4     ; Program to measure performance of code that takes longer than
5     ; 54 ms to execute. (LZTEST.ASM)
6     ;
7     ; Link with LZTIMER.ASM (Listing 2-5). LZTEST.BAT (Listing 2-7)
8     ; can be used to assemble and link both files. Code to be
9     ; measured must be in the file TESTCODE; Listing 2-8 shows
10    ; a sample TESTCODE file.
11    ;
12    ; By Michael Abrash 4/26/89
13    ;
14    mystack segment para stack 'STACK'
15            db     512 dup(?)
16    mystack ends
17    ;
18    Code    segment para public 'CODE'
19            assume cs:Code, ds:Code
20            extrn  ZTimerOn:near, ZTimerOff:near, ZTimerReport:near
21    Start   proc   near
22            push   cs
23            pop    ds      ;point DS to the code segment,
24                           ; so data as well as code can easily
25                           ; be included in TESTCODE
26    ;
27    ; Delay for 6-7 seconds, to let the Enter keystroke that started the
28    ; program come back up.
29    ;
30            mov    ah,2ch
31            int    21h             ;get the current time
32            mov    bh,dh           ;set the current time aside
33    DelayLoop:
34            mov    ah,2ch
35            push   bx              ;preserve start time
36            int    21h             ;get time
37            pop    bx              ;retrieve start time
38            cmp    dh,bh           ;is the new seconds count less than
39                                   ; the start seconds count?
40            jnb    CheckDelayTime  ;no
41            add    dh,60           ;yes, a minute must have turned over,
42                                   ; so add one minute
```

```
43    CheckDelayTime:
44              sub     dh,bh          ;get time that's passed
45              cmp     dh,7           ;has it been more than 6 seconds yet?
46              jb      DelayLoop      ;not yet
47    ;
48              include TESTCODE       ;code to be measured, including calls
49                                     ; to ZTimerOn and ZTimerOff
50    ;
51    ; Display the results.
52    ;
53              call    ZTimerReport
54    ;
55    ; Terminate the program.
56    ;
57              mov     ah,4ch
58              int     21h
59    Start     endp
60    Code      ends
61              end     Start
```

As with the precision Zen timer, the program in Listing 2-6 is used
by naming the file containing the code to be timed TESTCODE, then
assembling both Listing 2-6 and Listing 2-5 with MASM and linking the
two files together by way of the Microsoft Linker. Listing 2-7 shows a
batch file, named LZTIME.BAT, which does all of the above, generating
and running the executable file LZTEST.EXE. LZTIME.BAT assumes that the
file LZTIMER.ASM contains Listing 2-5 and that the file LZTEST.ASM contains
Listing 2-6.

```
1     echo off
2     rem
3     rem *** Listing 2-7 ***
4     rem
5     rem ******************************************************************
6     rem * Batch file LZTIME.BAT, which builds and runs the              *
7     rem * long-period Zen timer program LZTEST.EXE to time the code     *
8     rem * named as the command-line parameter. Listing 2-5 must be      *
9     rem * named LZTIMER.ASM, and Listing 2-6 must be named              *
10    rem * LZTEST.ASM. To time the code in LST2-8, you'd type the        *
11    rem * DOS command:                                                  *
12    rem *                                                               *
13    rem * lztime lst2-8                                                 *
14    rem *                                                               *
15    rem * Note that MASM and LINK must be in the current directory or   *
16    rem * on the current path in order for this batch file to work.     *
17    rem *                                                               *
18    rem * This batch file can be speeded up by assembling LZTIMER.ASM   *
19    rem * once, then removing the lines:                                *
20    rem *                                                               *
21    rem * masm lztimer;                                                 *
22    rem * if errorlevel 1 goto errorend                                 *
23    rem *                                                               *
24    rem * from this file.                                               *
25    rem *                                                               *
```

```
26    rem * By Michael Abrash 4/26/89                                    *
27    rem ***********************************************************
28    rem
29    rem Make sure a file to test was specified.
30    rem
31    if not x%1==x goto ckexist
32    echo ***********************************************************
33    echo * Please specify a file to test.                           *
34    echo ***********************************************************
35    goto end
36    rem
37    rem Make sure the file exists.
38    rem
39    :ckexist
40    if exist %1 goto docopy
41    echo ***********************************************************
42    echo * The specified file, "%1," doesn't exist.
43    echo ***********************************************************
44    goto end
45    rem
46    rem copy the file to measure to TESTCODE.
47    :docopy
48    copy %1 testcode
49    masm lztest;
50    if errorlevel 1 goto errorend
51    masm lztimer;
52    if errorlevel 1 goto errorend
53    link lztest+lztimer;
54    if errorlevel 1 goto errorend
55    lztest
56    goto end
57    :errorend
58    echo ***********************************************************
59    echo * An error occurred while building the long-period Zen timer. *
60    echo ***********************************************************
61    :end
```

Listing 2-8 shows sample code that can be timed with the test bed program of Listing 2-6. Listing 2-8 measures the time required to execute 20,000 loads of AL from memory, a period too long for the precision Zen timer to handle.

When LZTIME.BAT is run on a PC with the following command line (assuming the code in Listing 2-8 is the file LST2-8):

lztime lst2-8

the result is 72,544 μsec, or about 3.63 μsec per load of AL from memory. This is just slightly longer than the time per load of AL measured by the precision Zen timer, as we would expect given that interrupts are left enabled by the long-period Zen timer. The extra fraction of a microsecond measured per multiply reflects the time required to execute the BIOS code that handles the 18.2 timer interrupts that occur each second.

```
 1   ;
 2   ; *** Listing 2-8 ***
 3   ;
 4   ; Measures the performance of 20000 loads of AL from
 5   ; memory. (Use by renaming to TESTCODE, which is
 6   ; included by LZTEST.ASM (Listing 2-6). LZTIME.BAT
 7   ; (Listing 2-7) does this, along with all assembly
 8   ; and linking.)
 9   ;
10   ; Note: takes about 10 minutes to assemble on a PC with
11   ;       MASM 5.0.
12   ;
13           jmp      Skip      ; jump around defined data
14   ;
15   MemVar  db       ?
16   ;
17   Skip:
18   ;
19   ; Start timing.
20   ;
21           call     ZTimerOn
22   ;
23           rept     20000
24           mov      al,[MemVar]
25           endm
26   ;
27   ; Stop timing.
28   ;
29           call     ZTimerOff
```

Note that the above command takes about 10 minutes to finish on a PC, with most of that time spent assembling Listing 2-8. Why? Because MASM is notoriously slow at assembling **rept** blocks, and the block in Listing 2-8 is repeated 20,000 times.

2.12 ◆ Further Reading

For those of you who wish to pursue the mechanics of code measurement further, one good article about measuring code performance with the 8253 timer is "Programming Insight: High-Performance Software Analysis on the IBM PC," by Byron Sheppard, which appeared in the January, 1987 issue of *Byte*. For complete if somewhat cryptic information on the 8253 timer itself, I refer you to Intel's *Microsystem Components Handbook,* which is also a useful reference for a number of other PC components, including the 8259 Programmable Interrupt Controller and the 8237 DMA Controller. For details about the way the 8253 is used in the PC, as well as a great deal of additional information about the PC's hardware and BIOS resources, I suggest you consult IBM's series of technical reference manuals for the PC, XT, AT, Model 30, Models 50 and 60, and Model 80.

For our purposes, however, it's not critical that you understand exactly how the Zen timer works. All you really need to know is what it can do and how to use it, and we've accomplished that in this chapter.

2.13 ◆ Armed with the Zen Timer, Onward and Upward

The Zen timer is not perfect. For one thing, the finest resolution to which it can measure an interval is at best about 1 μsec, a period in which a 25-MHz 80386 computer can execute as many as twelve instructions (although a PC would be hard pressed to manage two instructions in a microsecond). Another problem is that the timing code itself interferes with the state of the prefetch queue at the start of the code being timed, because the timing code is not necessarily fetched and does not necessarily access memory in exactly the same time sequence as the code immediately preceding the code under measurement normally does. This prefetch effect can introduce as much as 3 to 4 μsec of inaccuracy. (The nature of this problem will become more apparent when we discuss the prefetch queue.) Similarly, the state of the prefetch queue at the end of the code being timed affects how long the code that stops the timer takes to execute. Consequently, the Zen timer tends to be more accurate for longer code sequences, since the relative magnitude of the inaccuracy introduced by the Zen timer becomes less over longer periods.

Imperfections notwithstanding, the Zen timer is a good tool for exploring 8088 assembly language, and it's a tool we'll use well for the remainder of this book. With the timer in hand, let's begin our trek toward the Zen of assembler, dispelling old assumptions and acquiring new knowledge along the way.

Part Two

Knowledge

> There are more things in heaven and earth, Horatio, than are dreamt of in your philosophy.
>
> —Shakespeare, *Hamlet*

Chapter 3

Context

3.1	From the Bottom Up
3.2	The Traditional Model
3.3	Cycle Eaters
3.4	Code Is Data
3.5	Inside the 8088
3.6	Stepchild of the 8086
3.7	Which Model to Use

One of my favorite stories—and I am not making this up—concerns a C programmer who wrote a function to clear the screen. His function consisted of just two statements, a call to another function that printed a space character and a **for** statement that repeated that function call 2000 times. While this fellow's function cleared the screen perfectly well, it didn't do it particularly quickly or attractively; in fact, the whole process was perfectly visible to the naked eye, with the cursor racing from the top to the bottom of the screen. Nonetheless, the programmer was incensed when someone commented that the function seemed rather slow. How could it possibly be any faster, he wondered, when it was already the irreducible minimum of two statements long?

Of course, the function wasn't two statements long in any meaningful sense; its true length would have to be measured in terms of all the machine language instructions generated by those two C statements plus all the instructions executed by the function that printed the space character. By comparison with a single **rep stosw** instruction, which is the preferred way to clear the screen, this fellow's screen clear function was undoubtedly very long indeed.

The programmer's mistake was one of context. While his solution seemed optimal by the standards of the C environment he was programming in, it was considerably less ideal when applied to the PC, the environment in which the code actually had to run. While human-oriented abstractions such as high level languages and system software have their virtues, most notably the ability to mask the complexities of processors and hardware, speed is not necessarily among those virtues.

We certainly don't want to make the same mistake, so we'll begin our search for knowledge by establishing a context for assembler programming, a usable framework within which to work for the remainder of this book. This is more challenging than it might at first glance seem, for the PC looks quite different to an assembler programmer—especially an assembler programmer interested in performance—than it does to a high level language programmer. The difference is that a good assembler programmer sees the PC as it really is—hardware, software, warts, and all—a perspective all too few programmers ever have the opportunity to enjoy.

3.1 ◆ From the Bottom Up

In this volume, we're going to explore the knowledge needed for top-notch assembler programming. We'll start at the bottom, with the hardware of the PC, and we'll work our way up through the 8088's registers, memory addressing capabilities, and instruction set. In Volume II of *Zen of Assembly Language,* we'll put that knowledge to work in the context of higher-level optimization, algorithm implementation, program design, and the like. We're not going to spend time on topics suchas BIOS and DOS calls that are well documented elsewhere, for we've a great deal of new ground to cover.

The next three chapters, which discuss the ways in which the hardware of the PC affects performance, are the foundation for everything that follows, and they also cover the most difficult material in *Zen of Assembly Language.* Don't worry if you don't understand everything you read in the upcoming chapters; the same topics will come up again and again, from a variety of perspectives, throughout *Zen of Assembly Language.* Read through Chapters 3 through 5 once now, absorbing as much as you can. After you've finished Volume I, come back to these chapters and read them again.

You'll be amazed at how much sense they make—and at how much you've learned.

Let's begin our explorations.

3.2 ◆ The Traditional Model

Figure 3.1 shows the traditional assembler programming model of the PC. In this model, the assembler program is separated from the hardware by layers of system software, such as DOS, the BIOS, and device drivers. Although this model recognizes that it is possible for assembler programs to make end runs around the layers to access any level of system software or the hardware directly, programs are supposed to request services from the highest level that can fulfill a given request (preferably DOS), thereby gaining hardware independence, which brings with it portability to other systems with different hardware but the same system software.

This model has many admirable qualities and should be followed whenever possible. For example, because the DOS file system masks incompatibilities between the dozens of disk and disk controller models on the market, there's generally nothing to be gained and much to be lost by programming a disk controller directly. Similarly, the BIOS sometimes hides differences between makes of keyboards, so keystrokes should not be taken directly from the hardware unless that's absolutely necessary. Every assembler programmer should be thoroughly aware of the services provided by

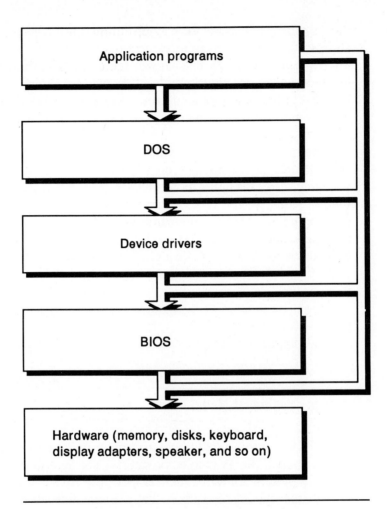

FIGURE 3.1   The traditional view of the PC's resources, in which application programs rest on layers of system software and hardware. In this scheme, application programs are supposed to communicate only with the highest possible layer (preferably DOS), although they can, if necessary, make end runs around the layers directly to any needed level. While this arrangement has advantages as regards portability and compatibility with future computers and operating systems, it is less than ideal for performance.

DOS and the BIOS and should use them whenever they're good enough for a given purpose.

A moment's thought will show, however, that it's not always desirable to follow the model of Figure 3.1. Disk-backup software programs the disk controller directly and sells handsomely, while keyboard macro programs and many pop-up programs read the keyboard directly. Part of your job as a programmer is knowing when to break the rules embodied by Figure 3.1, and breaking the rules is tempting because this model has major failings when it comes to performance.

One shortcoming of the model of Figure 3.1 is that DOS and the BIOS provide inadequate services in some areas and no services at all in others. For instance, the half-hearted support DOS and the BIOS provide for serial communications is an insult to the potential of the PC's communications hardware. Likewise, the graphics primitives offered by the BIOS are so slow and limited as to be virtually useless. While device drivers can extend DOS's capabilities in some areas, many of the drivers are themselves embarrassingly slow and limited. As an example, the ANSI.SYS driver, which provides extended screen control in text mode, is so sluggish that a single screen update can take a second and more, quite a contrast with the instant screen updates most text editors and word processors offer.

When you use a system service, you're accepting someone else's solution to a problem; while it may be a good solution, you don't know that unless you check. After all, you may well be a better programmer than the author of the system software, and you're bound to be better attuned to your particular needs than he was. In short, you should know the system services well and use them fully, but you should also learn when it pays to replace them with your own code.

3.3 ◆ Cycle Eaters

The second shortcoming of the model shown in Figure 3.1 is that it makes the hardware seem to be just another system resource, and a rather remote and uninteresting resource at that. Nothing could be further from the truth! After all, in order to be useful programs must ultimately perform input from and output to the real world, and all input and output requires interaction with the hardware. True, DOS and the BIOS may handle much of your I/O, but DOS and the BIOS themselves are nothing more than assembly-language programs.

Also, programs access memory almost continuously, and memory is of course part of the PC's hardware. It's hard to write a code sequence of more than a few dozen instructions in which memory isn't accessed at least once as either a stack operand or as a direct instruction operand. I/O ports are also accessed heavily in some applications. Every single memory and I/O access of any kind must interact with the hardware via the PC's data bus.

It's easy to think of the PC's hardware and bus as being transparent to programs; hardware appears to be available on demand, while the bus seems to be nothing more than a path for data to take on the way to and from the hardware. Not so. While the PC bus is in fact generally transparent to programs, the many demands on the bus and the relatively low rate at which the bus, the 8088, and the PC's memory together can support data transfers can have a significant effect on performance, as we'll see shortly. Moreover, there are a number of memory and I/O devices for the PC that can't access data fast enough to keep up with the PC bus; to compensate, they make the 8088 wait, sometimes for several cycles, while they catch up. Inevitably, program performance suffers from these characteristics of the hardware and bus.

For the remainder of this book, I'm going to refer to PC bus- and hardware-resident gremlins that affect code performance as *cycle eaters*. There are cycle eaters of many sorts, of which the prefetch queue and display adapter cycle eaters are perhaps the best known; 8-bit cards in ATs and dynamic RAM refresh are other examples. Cycle eaters are undeniably difficult to pin down. Once you've identified and understood them, though, you'll be among the elite few who can deal with the most powerful—and least understood—aspect of assembler programming.

Just how important are cycle eaters? Well, thanks to the display adapter cycle eater, the code in Listing 3-1, which accesses memory on an Enhanced

```
1    ;
2    ; *** Listing 3-1 ***
3    ;
4    ; Times speed of memory access to Enhanced Graphics
5    ; Adapter graphics mode display memory at A000:0000.
6    ;
7            mov     ax,0010h
8            int     10h                  ;select hi-res EGA graphics
9                                         ; mode 10 hex (AH=0 selects
10                                        ; BIOS set mode function,
11                                        ; with AL=mode to select)
12   ;
13           mov     ax,0a000h
14           mov     ds,ax
15           mov     es,ax                ;move to & from same segment
16           sub     si,si                ;move to & from same offset
17           mov     di,si
18           mov     cx,800h              ;move 2K words
```

```
19            cld
20            call    ZTimerOn
21            rep     movsw           ;simply read each of the first
22                                    ; 2K words of the destination segment,
23                                    ; writing each byte immediately back
24                                    ; to the same address. No memory
25                                    ; locations are actually altered; this
26                                    ; is just to measure memory access
27                                    ; times
28            call    ZTimerOff
29
30            mov     ax,0003h
31            int     10h             ;return to text mode
```

Graphics Adapter (EGA), runs in 26.06 msec. That's more than twice as long as the 11.24 msec of the Listing 3-2, which is identical to Listing 3-1 except that it accesses normal system memory rather than display memory. That's a difference in performance as great as that between an 8-MHz AT and a 16-MHz 80386 machine! Clearly, cycle eaters cannot be ignored, and in the chapters to come we'll spend considerable time tracking them down and devising ways to work around them.

Given cycle eaters and our understanding of layered system software as simply another sort of code, the programming model shown in Figure 3.2 is more appropriate than that in Figure 3.1. All system and application software, whether it is generated from high level or from assembler source code, ultimately becomes a series of machine language instructions for the 8088. The 8088 executes each of those instructions in turn, accessing memory and devices as needed by way of the PC bus. In this three-level structure, the 8088 provides software with a programming interface, and in

```
1     ;
2     ; *** Listing 3-2 ***
3     ;
4     ; Times speed of memory access to normal system
5     ; memory.
6     ;
7             mov     ax,ds
8             mov     es,ax           ;move to & from same segment
9             sub     si,si           ;move to & from same offset
10            mov     di,si
11            mov     cx,800h         ;move 2K words
12            cld
13            call    ZTimerOn
14            rep     movsw           ;simply read each of the first
15                                    ; 2K words of the destination segment,
16                                    ; writing each byte immediately back
17                                    ; to the same address. No memory
18                                    ; locations are actually altered; this
19                                    ; is just to measure memory access
20                                    ; times
21            call    ZTimerOff
```

turn rests on the PC's hardware. Thanks to cycle eaters, the PC's hardware and bus emerge as important factors in performance.

The primary virtue of Figure 3.2 is that it moves us away from the comfortable, human-oriented perspective of Figure 3.1 and forces us to view program execution at a level that more clearly reveals the true nature

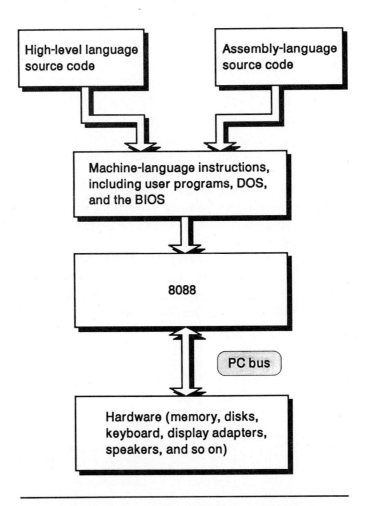

FIGURE 3.2   For high-performance assembler programming, this view of the PC's resources is more useful than that of layered system software. Here, the emphasis is on the interaction between machine language instructions, the 8088, and the hardware, with cycle eaters potentially present in the PC's hardware and bus.

of the beast—as nothing more than the performance of a sequence of instructions that command the 8088 to perform actions which in some cases involve accessing memory and/or devices over the PC bus. From the software side, we can now see that, in the end, all code consists of machine language instructions, so the distinction between high level languages, system software, and assembler vanishes. From the hardware side, we can see that the 8088 is not the lowest level, and we can begin to appreciate the many ways in which hardware can directly affect code performance.

We need to see still more of the beast, however, and the place to start is with the equivalence of code and data.

3.4 ◆ Code Is Data

Code is nothing more than data that the 8088 interprets as instructions. The most obvious case of this is self-modifying code, where the 8088 treats its code as data in order to modify it, then executes those same bytes as instructions. There are many other examples, though. After all, what is a compiler but a program that transforms source code data into machine language data? Both code and data consist of byte values stored in system memory; the only thing that differentiates code from any other sort of data is that the bytes that code is made of have a special meaning to the 8088, in that when fetched as instructions they instruct the 8088 to perform a series of (presumably related) actions. In other words, the meaning of byte values as code rather than data is strictly a matter of context.

Why is this important? It's important because the 8088 is really two processors in one, and therein lies a tale.

3.5 ◆ Inside the 8088

Internally, the 8088 consists of two complementary processors: the bus interface unit (BIU) and the execution unit (EU) (Fig. 3.3). The EU is what we normally think of as being a processor; it contains the flags, the general-purpose registers, and the arithmetic logic unit (ALU) and executes instructions. In fact, the EU performs just about every function you could want from a processor except one: it does not access memory or perform I/O. That's the BIU's job, so whenever the EU needs a memory or I/O

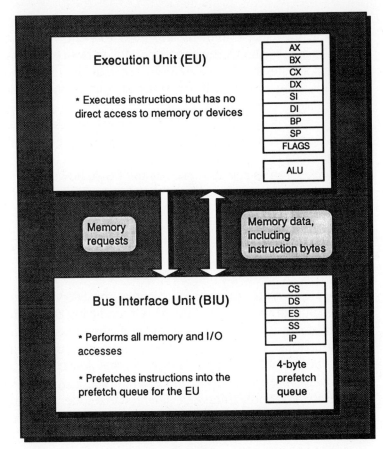

The 8088

FIGURE 3.3   Internally, the 8088 consists of two separate processing
sections operating in parallel. The execution unit (EU)
contains the general-purpose registers, the flags, and the
ALU, and executes instructions, while the bus interface
unit (BIU) contains the instruction pointer and the segment registers, and performs all memory accesses for the
EU. The BIU not only performs all reads and writes of
memory operands, but also prefetches the next few instruction bytes from memory during idle times, storing the
bytes in a 4-byte internal instruction prefetch queue until
the EU requests them. If a branch is performed, all instruction bytes in the prefetch queue are discarded.

access performed, it sends a request to the BIU, which carries out the access, transferring the data according to the EU's specifications. The two units are capable of operating in parallel whenever they've got independent tasks to perform; put another way, the BIU can access memory or I/O at the same time that the EU is processing an instruction, so long as neither task is dependent on the other.

Each BIU memory access transfers 1 byte, since the 8088 has an 8-bit external data bus. The 8088 is designed so that each byte access takes a minimum of 4 cycles. Given the PC's 4.77-MHz processor clock, which results in a 209.5-nsec cycle time, the 8088 supports a maximum data transfer rate of 1 byte/838 nsec, or about 1.2 bytes/μsec. That's an important number, and we'll come back to it shortly.

The EU is capable of working with both 8- and 16-bit memory operands. Because the 8088 can access memory only 1 byte at a time, however, the BIU splits each of the EU's 16-bit memory requests into a pair of 8-bit accesses. Since each 8-bit access requires a minimum of 4 cycles to execute, each 16-bit memory request takes at least 8 cycles, or 1.676 μsec. The instruction timings shown in Appendix A reflect the additional overhead of word memory accesses by adding 4 additional cycles per memory access to instruction execution times when word rather than byte memory operands are used.

The BIU contains all the memory-related logic of the 8088, including the segment registers and the instruction pointer, which points to the next instruction to be executed. Since code is just another sort of data, it makes sense that the instruction pointer resides in the BIU; after all, code bytes are read from memory just as data bytes are. In fact, the BIU takes on a bit of autonomy when it comes to fetching instructions. Whenever the EU isn't making any memory or I/O requests, the BIU uses the otherwise idle time to fetch the bytes at the addresses immediately following the current instruction, on the reasonable theory that those addresses are likely to contain the next instructions that the EU will want. The BIU of the 8088 can store up to 4 potential instruction bytes in an internal prefetch queue, and other 8086-family processors can store more bytes still.

Instruction prefetching isn't always advantageous. In particular, if the instruction the 8088 is currently executing results in a branch of any sort, the bytes in the instruction queue are of no value, since they are the bytes the 8088 would have executed had the branch *not* been performed. As a result, all the 8088 can do when a branch occurs is discard all the bytes in the prefetch queue and start fetching instructions all over again.

Nonetheless, the prefetching scheme often allows the BIU to have the next instruction byte waiting when the EU comes calling for it. Bear in mind that the EU and BIU can operate at the same time; it's only when the EU is waiting for the BIU to finish a memory or I/O operation for it that the EU is held up. The virtue of the 8088's internal architecture, then, is that the EU can increase its effective processing time because the BIU often coprocesses with it. Since instruction fetches occur in a constant stream (usually much more frequently than memory operand accesses) instruction prefetching is the most important sort of coprocessing the BIU performs.

It's worth noting at this point that the execution time specified by Intel for any given instruction running on the 8088 (as shown in Appendix A) assumes that the BIU has already prefetched that instruction and has it ready and waiting for the EU. *If the next instruction is not waiting for the EU when the EU completes the current instruction, at least some of the time required to fetch the next instruction must be added to its specified execution time in order to arrive at the actual execution time.*

The degree to which the EU and BIU can coprocess during instruction fetching is not uniform for all types of code; in fact, it varies considerably depending on the mix of instructions being executed. Multiplication and division instructions are ideal for coprocessing, since the BIU can prefetch until the queue is full while these very long instructions execute. Among other instructions, oddly enough, it is code that performs many memory accesses that allows the EU and BIU to coprocess most effectively, because the 8088 is relatively slow at executing instructions that access memory (as we'll see in Chapter 7). While a single memory-accessing instruction is being executed, the BIU can often prefetch 1 to 4 instruction bytes (depending on the instruction being performed) and still leave time for the memory access to occur. Execution of a memory-accessing instruction and prefetching of the next instruction can generally proceed simultaneously, so such instructions often run at close to full speed.

Ironically, code that primarily performs register-only operations and rarely accesses memory affords little opportunity for prefetching, because register-only instructions execute so rapidly that the BIU can't fetch instruction bytes nearly as rapidly as the EU can execute them. To see why this is so, recall that the 8088 can fetch 1 byte every 4 cycles (or 0.838 μsec). The **shr** instruction is 2 bytes long, so it takes 1.676 μsec to fetch each **shr** instruction. However, the EU can *execute* a **shr** in just 2 cycles, or 0.419 μsec, four times as rapidly as the BIU can fetch the same instruction.

The instruction queue can be depleted quickly by register-only instructions. *Given enough such instructions in a row, the overall time required to complete a series of register-only instructions is determined almost entirely by the time required to fetch the instructions from memory.* This is precisely the respect in which Figure 3.2 fails us; because of the prefetch queue, the instructions the 8088 executes must be viewed as data, stored along with other program data and accessed through the same PC bus and BIU, as shown in Figure 3.4. Seen in this light, it becomes apparent that instruction fetches are subject to the same cycle eaters as are memory operand accesses. What's more, the BIU emerges as potentially the greatest cycle eater of all, as code and data bytes struggle to get through the BIU fast enough to keep the EU busy, a phenomenon I'll refer to from now on as the prefetch queue cycle eater. As we will see, designing code to work around the prefetch queue cycle eater and keep the EU busy is a difficult but rewarding task.

3.6 ◆ Stepchild of the 8086

You might justifiably wonder why Intel would design a processor with an EU that can execute instructions faster than the BIU can possibly fetch them. The answer is that they didn't; they designed the 8086, then created the 8088 as a poor man's 8086.

The 8086 is completely software compatible with the 8088, and in fact differs from it in only one important respect, the width of the external data bus (the bus that goes off-chip to memory and peripherals); where the 8088 has an 8-bit wide external data bus, the 8086 has a 16-bit wide bus. (The 8086 also has a 6- rather than 4-byte prefetch queue, which gives it an advantage in keeping the EU busy.) Both the 8086 and the 8088 have 16-bit EUs and 16-bit internal data buses, but while the 8086's BIU can fulfill most 16-bit memory requests with a single memory access, the 8088's BIU must convert 16-bit memory requests into 8-bit memory accesses. Figure 3.5, which charts internal and external data bus sizes for processors from the 8080 through the 80386, shows that the 8088 is something of an aberration in that it is the only widely used processor in the 8086 family with mismatched internal and external data bus sizes. (The 80386SX, which may well become a successful inexpensive substitute for the 80386, also has mismatched internal and external bus sizes, and as a result suffers from many of the same performance constraints as the 8088.)

There is a significant price to be paid for the 8088's mismatched bus sizes. Why? Well, the 8086 was designed to support efficient and balanced memory access, with the external data bus generally in use as much as possible without becoming a bottleneck. In other words, the 16-bit external data bus of the 8086 was designed to provide a memory access rate roughly equal to the processing rate of the 16-bit EU. While the 8088 offers the same

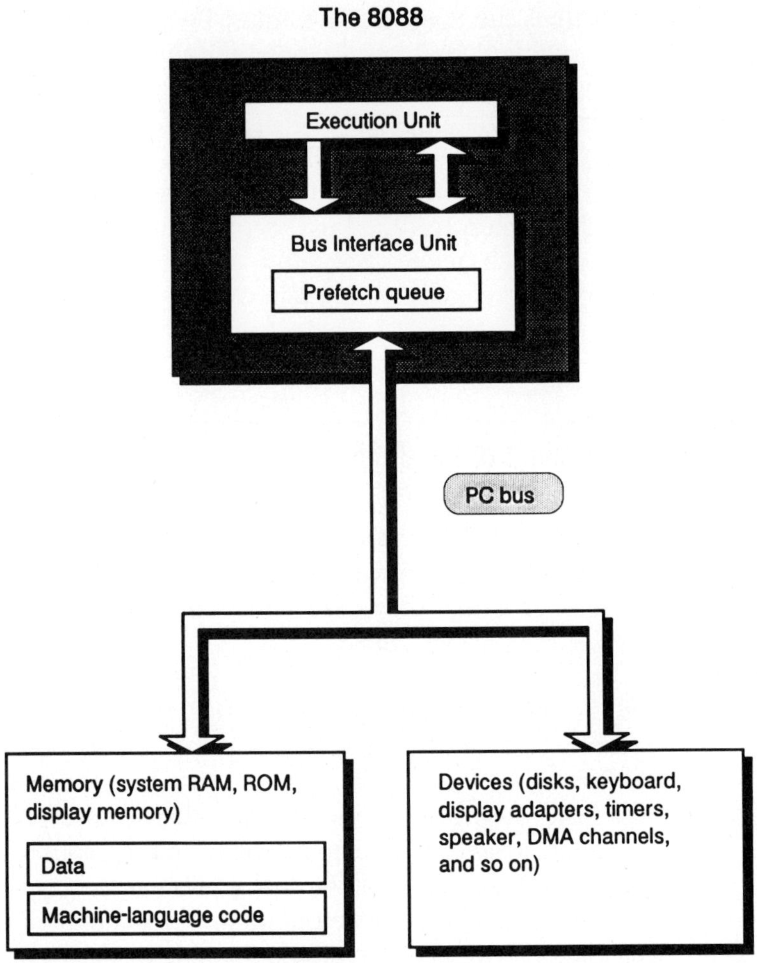

The 8088

FIGURE 3.4   This view of the PC's resources reflects the true nature of code as data stored in system memory. Code is stored in memory, so it must be fetched by the bus interface unit (BIU) just as data must; consequently, any cycle eaters present between system memory and the BIU affect the 8088's code-fetching speed as well as its data-fetching speed. In addition, all memory accesses must pass through the BIU a byte at a time at a rate no faster than 1.2 bytes/microsecond (1 byte per 4 cycles), and serious bottlenecks can develop since code and data fetching can demand data transfer rates as high as 1 byte/209 nsec (1 byte per cycle).

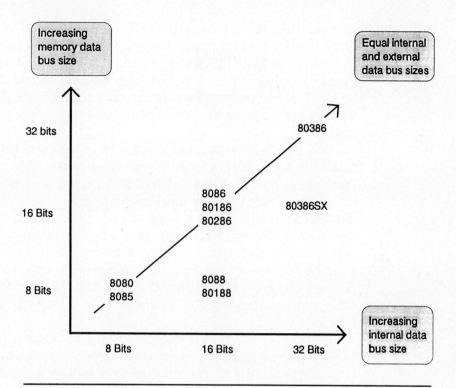

FIGURE 3.5   Most of the processors in the 8086's extended family have
identical internal and external data bus sizes. The 8088
is unusual in that it has a 16-bit internal data bus but an
8-bit external data bus, a mismatch that makes the 8088
a significantly slower processor than the 8086, especially
when running high-performance assembler code. Under
certain circumstances, code can run as much as four times
more slowly on an 8088 than on an 8086.

internal 16-bit architecture as the 8086, the 8-bit external data bus of the
8088 can provide only half the maximum memory access rate of the 8086,
so the balance of the 8086 is lost.

The obvious effect of the 8088's mismatched bus sizes is that accesses
to word-sized memory operands take 4 cycles longer on an 8088 than
on an 8086, but that's actually not the most significant fallout of the 8-bit
external data bus. More significant is the prefetch queue cycle eater, which
is the result of the inability of the 8088's BIU to fetch instructions and

operands over the 8-bit external data bus as fast as the 16-bit EU can process them, thereby limiting the performance of the 8088's fastest instructions. In contrast, the 8086, for which the EU was originally designed, has little trouble keeping the EU supplied with instructions and data; the 8086's BIU fetches 2 instruction bytes in the same time it takes the 8088 to fetch a single byte, making the 8086 instruction fetching rate twice that of the 8088.

How significant is the performance impact of the 8088's 8-bit external data bus? While normal code is estimated to run only about one third faster on an 8086 than on an 8088, high-performance 8086 code can, as we've already seen, run as much as four times slower on an 8088 once the prefetch queue empties, because code performance is limited by the rate at which the BIU can transfer data a byte at a time. In the case where both the 8088 and 8086 prefetch queues are emptied, the 8086 runs fast assembler code only twice as fast as the 8088, but the 8086 has a bigger prefetch queue than the 8088 and fetches instructions twice as fast, so the 8086 queue empties much more slowly. In any case, twice as fast is nothing to sniff at.

In short, the 8086 is just like the 8088—except that it's somewhere between 0 percent and 300 percent faster, depending on what code happens to be executing. The typical performance advantage is somewhere between 33 percent and 100 percent for high-performance assembler code.

Why, then, does the 8088 exist, and why has it become so popular? An 8-bit–bus version of the 8086 (that is, the 8088) was desirable in the late 1970s because at that time it was significantly more expensive to build a computer with a 16-bit data bus than with an 8-bit data bus. The 8088 allowed the construction of low-cost, low-performance computers that would run 8086 software, albeit more slowly. As it turned out, the cost advantage of an 8-bit memory data bus quickly became relatively insignificant, and the 8088 might have vanished into obscurity had IBM not selected it for the PC; then we might never have had the pleasure of wrestling with the prefetch queue cycle eater. IBM *did* select the 8088 for the PC, however, and the rest is history.

Incidentally, an imbalance between processing speed and memory access speed remains a factor today with the 80286-based IBM AT and with many 80386-based computers. The memory in those computers often does not run at the speeds the processors are capable of, and assembler code encounters the same sorts of performance losses when running on those computers as it does on the 8088. We'll return to that topic in Chapter 15.

3.7 ◆ Which Model to Use

Each of the three programming models I've presented offers a useful perspective on assembler programming for the PC. However, it is the model shown in Figure 3.4 that best reflects the true nature of the 8088, so that model is the most useful of the three for tapping the unique potential of assembler. While we'll use elements of all three models in *Zen of Assembly Language,* we'll concentrate on the perspective of Figure 3.4 as we explore high-performance assembler programming.

Keep the following concepts in mind as you read on:

◆ *All code is machine language in the end.* Don't assume that anyone else's code, even system software, is best suited for your needs.

◆ *1.2 bytes/μsec.* At its best, the 8088's BIU can transfer data no faster than this.

◆ *The 8088 is not the lowest level.* Know how the PC's hardware and bus affect memory access speed.

◆ *Code is data.* When the BIU and the PC's hardware and bus affect memory access speed, they affect code fetching as well as data access, since code is just another sort of data in system memory.

Short and simple as the above list may seem, in it you will find every one of the concepts that form the foundation of the Zen of assembly language—and with them the key to high-performance code.

Chapter 4

Things Mother Never Told You: Under the Programming Interface

4.1	Cycle Eaters Revisited
4.2	The 8-Bit Bus Cycle Eater
4.3	The Prefetch Queue Cycle Eater
4.4	Dynamic RAM Refresh: The Invisible Hand
4.5	Wait States
4.6	Cycle Eaters: A Summary
4.7	What Does It All Mean?

Over the last few chapters we've seen that programming has many levels, ranging from the familiar (high level languages, DOS calls, and the like) to the esoteric (cycle eaters). In this chapter we're going to jump right in at the lowest level by examining the cycle eaters that live beneath the programming interface.

Why start at the lowest level? Simply because cycle eaters affect the performance of all assembler code and yet are almost unknown to most programmers. A full understanding of virtually everything else we'll discuss in *Zen of Assembly Language* requires an understanding of cycle eaters and their implications. That's no simple task, and in fact it is in precisely that area that most books and articles about assembler programming fall short.

Nearly all literature on assembler programming discusses only the programming interface: the instruction set, the registers, the flags, and the BIOS and DOS calls. Those topics cover the functionality of assembler programs most thoroughly—but it's performance above all else that we're after. No one ever tells you about the raw stuff of performance, which lies *beneath* the programming interface, in the dimly seen realm, populated by instruction prefetching, dynamic RAM refresh, and wait states, where software meets hardware. This area is the domain of hardware engineers, and its effect on code performance is almost never discussed. And yet it is only by understanding the mechanisms operating at this level that we can fully understand and most effectively improve the performance of our code.

Which brings us to cycle eaters.

4.1 ◆ Cycle Eaters Revisited

You'll recall that cycle eaters are gremlins that live on the bus or in peripherals, slowing the performance of 8088 code so that it doesn't execute at full speed. Because cycle eaters live outside the execution unit of the 8088, they can affect the 8088 *only* when it performs a bus access (a memory or I/O read or write). Internally, the 8088 is a 16-bit processor, capable of running at full speed at all times, unless external data is required. External data must traverse the 8088's external data bus and the PC's data bus 1 byte at a time to and from peripherals, with cycle eaters lurking at every step along the way. What's more, external data includes not only memory operands *but also instruction bytes,* so even instructions with no memory operands can suffer from cycle eaters. Since some of the 8088's fastest instructions are register-only instructions, that's important indeed.

The major cycle eaters are:

◆ The 8088's 8-bit external data bus
◆ The prefetch queue
◆ Dynamic RAM refresh
◆ Wait states, notably display memory wait states and, in the AT and 80386 computers, system memory wait states.

The locations of these cycle eaters in the PC are shown in Figure 4.1. We'll cover each of the cycle eaters in turn in this chapter. The material won't be easy, since cycle eaters are among the most subtle aspects of assembler programming. By the same token, however, this will be one of the most important and rewarding chapters in the book. Don't worry if you don't grasp everything in this chapter, but do read it all, even if the going gets a bit rough. Cycle eaters play a key role in later chapters, so some familiarity with them is highly desirable. Then, too, those later chapters illustrate cycle eaters in action, which should help clear up any aspects of cycle eaters about which you're uncertain.

4.2 ◆ The 8-Bit Bus Cycle Eater

Look! Down on the motherboard! It's a 16-bit processor! It's an 8-bit processor! It's . . .

  . . . an 8088!

Fans of the 8088 call it a 16-bit processor. Fans of other 16-bit processors call the 8088 an 8-bit processor. Unbiased as we are, we know that the truth of the matter is that the 8088 is a 16-bit processor that often *performs* like an 8-bit processor.

As we saw in Chapter 3, the 8088 is internally a full 16-bit processor, equivalent to an 8086. In terms of the instruction set, the 8088 is clearly a 16-bit processor, capable of performing any given 16-bit operation—addition, subtraction, even multiplication or division—with a single instruction. Externally, however, the 8088 is unequivocally an 8-bit processor, since the external data bus is only 8 bits wide. In other words, the programming interface is 16 bits wide, but the hardware interface is only 8 bits wide, as shown in Figure 4.2. The result of this mismatch is sim-

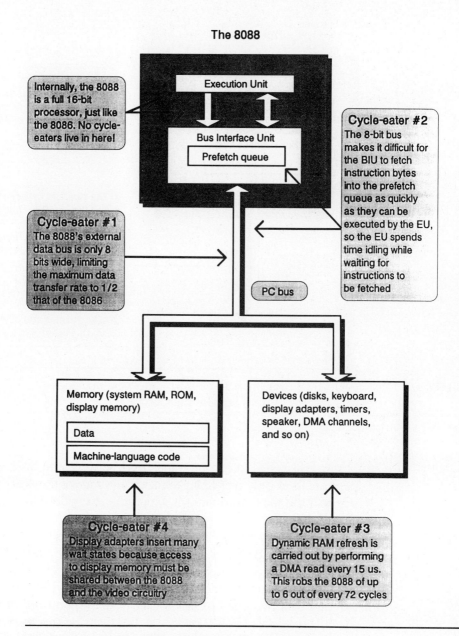

The 8088

Execution Unit

Internally, the 8088 is a full 16-bit processor, just like the 8086. No cycle-eaters live in here!

Bus Interface Unit

Prefetch queue

Cycle-eater #2
The 8-bit bus makes it difficult for the BIU to fetch instruction bytes into the prefetch queue as quickly as they can be executed by the EU, so the EU spends time idling while waiting for instructions to be fetched

Cycle-eater #1
The 8088's external data bus is only 8 bits wide, limiting the maximum data transfer rate to 1/2 that of the 8086

PC bus

Memory (system RAM, ROM, display memory)

Data

Machine-language code

Devices (disks, keyboard, display adapters, timers, speaker, DMA channels, and so on)

Cycle-eater #4
Display adapters insert many wait states because access to display memory must be shared between the 8088 and the video circuitry

Cycle-eater #3
Dynamic RAM refresh is carried out by performing a DMA read every 15 us. This robs the 8088 of up to 6 out of every 72 cycles

FIGURE 4.1   The locations of the major cycle eaters in the IBM PC. Note that all the cycle eaters are external to the execution unit of the 8088.

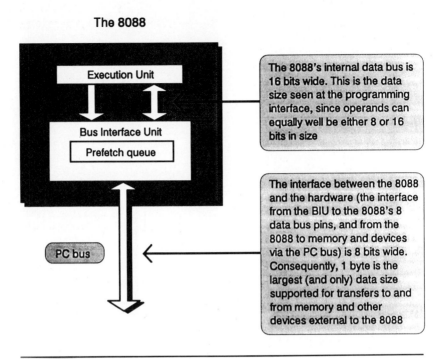

The 8088

Execution Unit

Bus Interface Unit

Prefetch queue

PC bus

The 8088's internal data bus is 16 bits wide. This is the data size seen at the programming interface, since operands can equally well be either 8 or 16 bits in size

The interface between the 8088 and the hardware (the interface from the BIU to the 8088's 8 data bus pins, and from the 8088 to memory and devices via the PC bus) is 8 bits wide. Consequently, 1 byte is the largest (and only) data size supported for transfers to and from memory and other devices external to the 8088

FIGURE 4.2   Internally the 8088 is a 16-bit microprocessor, but externally the 8088 is only an 8-bit microprocessor.

ple: word-sized data can be transferred between the 8088 and memory or peripherals at only one half the maximum rate of the 8086, which is to say one half the maximum rate for which the execution unit (EU) of the 8088 was designed.

As shown in Figure 4.1, the 8-bit bus cycle eater lies squarely on the 8088's external data bus. Technically, it might be more accurate to place this cycle eater in the bus interface unit (BIU), which breaks 16-bit memory accesses into paired 8-bit accesses, but it is really the limited width of the external data bus that constricts data flow into and out of the 8088. True, the PC's bus is also only 8 bits wide, but that's just to match the 8088's 8-bit bus; even if the PC's bus were 16 bits wide, data could still pass into and out of the 8088 only 1 byte at a time.

Each bus access by the 8088 takes 4 clock cycles, or 0.838 μsec in the PC, and transfers 1 byte. That means that the maximum rate at which data can be transferred into and out of the 8088 is 1 byte every 0.838 μsec. While 8086 bus accesses also take 4 clock cycles, each 8086 bus access can transfer either 1 byte or 1 word, for a maximum transfer rate of 1 *word* every 0.838 μsec. Consequently, for word-sized memory accesses the 8086 has an effective transfer rate of 1 byte every 0.419 μsec. By contrast, every word-sized access on the 8088 requires two 4-cycle bus accesses, one for the high byte of the word and one for the low byte. As a result, the 8088 has an effective transfer rate for word-sized memory accesses of just 1 word every 1.676 μsec—and that, in a nutshell, is the 8-bit bus cycle eater.

The Impact of the 8-Bit Bus Cycle Eater

One obvious effect of the 8-bit bus cycle eater is that word-sized accesses to memory operands on the 8088 take 4 cycles longer than byte-sized accesses. That's why the instruction timings in Appendix A add 4 cycles for every word-sized access to a memory operand. For instance,

```
mov     ax,word ptr [MemVar]
```

takes 4 cycles longer to read the word at address **MemVar** than

```
mov     al,byte ptr [MemVar]
```

takes to read the byte at address **MemVar**. (Actually, the difference between the two isn't very likely to be exactly 4 cycles, for reasons that will become clear when we discuss the prefetch queue and dynamic RAM refresh cycle eaters later in this chapter.)

What's more, in some cases one instruction can perform multiple word-sized accesses, incurring that 4-cycle penalty on each access. For example, adding a value to a word-sized memory variable requires two word-sized accesses—one to read the destination operand from memory prior to adding to it, and one to write the result of the addition back to the destination operand—and thus incurs not one but two 4-cycle penalties. As a result,

```
add     word ptr [MemVar],ax
```

takes about eight cycles longer to execute than

```
add     byte ptr [MemVar],al
```

String instructions can suffer more than other instructions from the 8-bit bus cycle eater. Believe it or not, a single **rep movsw** instruction can lose as much as

$$524{,}280 \text{ cycles} = 131{,}070 \text{ word-sized memory accesses} \times 4 \text{ cycles}$$

to the 8-bit bus cycle eater! In other words, one 8088 instruction (admittedly, an instruction that does a great deal) can take over 1/10 second longer on an 8088 than on an 8086, simply because of the 8-bit bus. *One tenth of a second!* That's a phenomenally long time in computer terms; in one tenth of a second, the 8088 can perform more than 50,000 additions and subtractions.

The upshot of all this is simply that the 8088 can transfer word-sized data to and from memory at only half the speed of the 8086, which inevitably causes performance problems when coupled with an EU that can process word-sized data every bit as fast as an 8086. These problems show up with any code that uses word-sized memory operands. More ominously, as we will see shortly, the 8-bit bus cycle eater can cause performance problems with other sorts of code as well.

What to Do about the 8-Bit Bus Cycle Eater

The obvious implication of the 8-bit bus cycle eater is that byte-sized memory variables should be used whenever possible. After all, the 8088 performs *byte-sized* memory accesses just as quickly as the 8086. For instance, Listing 4-1, which uses a byte-sized memory variable as a loop counter, runs in 10.03 μsec per loop. That's 20 percent faster than the 12.05 μsec per loop execution time of Listing 4-2, which uses a word-sized counter. Why the difference in execution times? Simply because each word-sized **dec** performs four byte-sized memory accesses (two to read the word-sized operand and two to write the result back to memory), whereas each byte-sized **dec** performs only two byte-sized memory accesses in all.

```
 1    ;
 2    ; *** Listing 4-1 ***
 3    ;
 4    ; Measures the performance of a loop which uses a
 5    ; byte-sized memory variable as the loop counter.
 6    ;
 7             jmp      Skip
 8    ;
 9    Counter db       100
10    ;
11    Skip:
12             call     ZTimerOn
13    LoopTop:
14             dec      [Counter]
15             jnz      LoopTop
16             call     ZTimerOff
```

```
 1   ;
 2   ; *** Listing 4-2 ***
 3   ;
 4   ; Measures the performance of a loop which uses a
 5   ; word-sized memory variable as the loop counter.
 6   ;
 7           jmp     Skip
 8   ;
 9   Counter dw      100
10   ;
11   Skip:
12           call    ZTimerOn
13   LoopTop:
14           dec     [Counter]
15           jnz     LoopTop
16           call    ZTimerOff
```

I'd like to make a brief aside concerning code optimization in the listings in this book. Throughout the book I've modelled the sample code after working code so that the timing results are applicable to real-world programming. In Listings 4-1 and 4-2, for instance, I could have shown a still greater advantage for byte-sized operands simply by performing 1000 **dec** instructions in a row, with no branching at all. However, **dec** instructions don't exist in a vacuum, so in the listings I used code that both decremented the counter and tested the result. The difference is the difference between decrementing a memory location (simply an instruction) and using a loop counter (a functional instruction sequence). If you come across code in *Zen of Assembly Language* that seems less than optimal, my desire to provide code that's relevant to real programming problems may be the reason. On the other hand, optimal code is an elusive thing indeed; by no means should you assume that the code in this book is ideal! Examine it, question it, and improve upon it, for an inquisitive, skeptical mind is an important part of the Zen of assembly language.

Back to the 8-bit bus cycle eater. As I've said, you should strive to use byte-sized memory variables whenever possible. That does *not* mean that you should use two byte-sized memory accesses to manipulate a word-sized memory variable in preference to one word-sized memory access, as, for instance, with:

```
mov     dl,byte ptr [MemVar]
mov     dh,byte ptr [MemVar+1]
```

versus

```
mov     dx,word ptr [MemVar]
```

Recall that every access to a memory byte takes at least 4 cycles; that limitation is built right in to the 8088. The 8088 is also built so that the second byte-sized memory access to a 16-bit memory variable takes just those 4 cycles and no more. There's no way you can manipulate the second byte of a word-sized memory variable faster with a second separate byte-sized instruction in less than 4 cycles. As a matter of fact, you're bound to access that second byte much more slowly with a separate instruction, thanks to the overhead of instruction fetching and execution, address calculation, and the like.

For example, consider Listing 4-3, which performs 1000 word-sized reads from memory. This code runs in 3.77 μsec per word read. That's 45 percent faster than the 5.49 μsec per word read of Listing 4-4, which reads the same 1000 words as Listing 4-3 but does so with 2000 byte-sized reads. Both listings perform exactly the same number of memory accesses—2000 accesses, each byte-sized, as all 8088 memory accesses must be. (Remember

```
1    ;
2    ; *** Listing 4-3 ***
3    ;
4    ; Measures the performance of reading 1000 words
5    ; from memory with 1000 word-sized accesses.
6    ;
7            sub     si,si
8            mov     cx,1000
9            call    ZTimerOn
10      rep lodsw
11           call    ZTimerOff
```

that the BIU must perform two byte-sized memory accesses in order to handle a word-sized memory operand.) However, Listing 4-3 is considerably faster, because it expends only 4 additional cycles to read the second byte of each word, whereas Listing 4-4 performs a second **lodsb**, requiring 13 cycles, to read the second byte of each word.

In short, if you must perform a 16-bit memory access, let the 8088 break

```
1    ;
2    ; *** Listing 4-4 ***
3    ;
4    ; Measures the performance of reading 1000 words
5    ; from memory with 2000 byte-sized accesses.
6    ;
7            sub     si,si
8            mov     cx,2000
9            call    ZTimerOn
10      rep lodsb
11           call    ZTimerOff
```

the access into two byte-sized accesses for you. The 8088 is more efficient at that task than your code can possibly be.

Chapter 9 has more examples of ways in which you can take advantage of the 8088's relative speed at handling the second byte of a word-sized memory operand to improve your code. However, that advantage is only relative to the time taken to access two byte-sized memory operands; you're still better off using single byte-sized memory accesses rather than word-sized accesses whenever possible. Word-sized variables should be stored in registers to the greatest extent feasible, since registers are inside the 8088, where 16-bit operations are just as fast as 8-bit operations because the 8-bit cycle eater can't get at them. In fact, it's a good idea to keep as many variables of all sorts in registers as you can. Instructions with register-only operands execute very rapidly, partially because they avoid both the time-consuming memory accesses and the lengthy address calculations associated with memory operands.

There is yet another reason why register operands are preferable to memory operands, and it's an unexpected effect of the 8-bit bus cycle eater. Instructions with only register operands tend to be shorter (in terms of bytes) than instructions with memory operands, and when it comes to performance, shorter is usually better. To explain why that is true and how it relates to the 8-bit bus cycle eater, I must digress for a moment.

For the last few pages, you may well have been thinking that the 8-bit bus cycle eater, while a nuisance, doesn't seem particularly subtle or difficult to quantify. After all, Appendix A tells us exactly how many cycles each instruction loses to the 8-bit bus cycle eater, doesn't it?

Yes and no. It's true that in general we know approximately how much longer a given instruction will take to execute with a word-sized memory operand than with a byte-sized operand, although the dynamic RAM refresh and wait state cycle eaters can raise the cost of the 8-bit bus cycle eater considerably, as we'll see later in this chapter. However, *all* word-sized memory accesses lose 4 cycles to the 8-bit bus cycle eater, and there's one sort of word-sized memory access we haven't discussed yet: instruction fetching. The ugliest manifestation of the 8-bit bus cycle eater is in fact the prefetch queue cycle eater.

4.3 ◆ The Prefetch Queue Cycle Eater

Simply put, here's the prefetch queue cycle eater: the 8088's 8-bit external data bus keeps the BIU from fetching instruction bytes as fast as the 16-bit

EU can execute them, so the EU often lies idle while waiting for the next instruction byte to be fetched.

Why does this happen? Recall that the 8088 is an 8086 internally, but accesses word-sized memory data at only one half the maximum rate of the 8086, owing to the 8088's 8-bit external data bus. Unfortunately, instructions are among the word-sized data the 8086 fetches, meaning that the 8088 can fetch instructions at only one half the speed of the 8086. On the other hand, the 8086-equivalent EU of the 8088 can *execute* instructions every bit as fast as the 8086. The net result is that the EU burns up instruction bytes much faster than the BIU can fetch them, and ends up idling while waiting for instruction bytes to arrive.

The BIU can fetch instruction bytes at a maximum rate of 1 byte every 4 cycles—*and that 4-cycle-per-instruction byte rate is the ultimate limit on overall instruction execution time, regardless of EU speed.* While the EU may execute a given instruction that's already in the prefetch queue in less than 4 cycles per byte, over time the EU can't execute instructions any faster than they can arrive—and they can't arrive faster than 1 byte every 4 cycles.

Clearly, then, the prefetch queue cycle eater is nothing more than one aspect of the 8-bit bus cycle eater. Often, 8088 code runs at less than the EU's maximum speed because the 8-bit data bus can't keep up with the demand for instruction bytes. That's straightforward enough. So why all the fuss about the prefetch queue cycle eater?

What makes the prefetch queue cycle eater tricky is that it's undocumented and unpredictable. That is, with a word-sized memory access, such as

```
mov     [bx],ax
```

it's well documented that an extra 4 cycles will always be required to write the upper byte to AX to memory. Not so with the prefetch queue. For instance, the instruction

```
shr     ax,1
shr     ax,1
shr     ax,1
shr     ax,1
shr     ax,1
```

should execute in 10 cycles, according to the specifications in Appendix A, since each **shr** takes 2 cycles to execute. Those specifications contain Intel's official instruction execution times, but in this case—and in many others—the specifications are drastically inaccurate. Why? Because they describe execution time *once an instruction reaches the prefetch queue.* They say nothing about whether a given instruction will be in the prefetch queue when it's time for that instruction to run, or how long it will take that instruction to reach the prefetch queue if it's not there already. Thanks to the poor performance of the 8088's external data bus, that's a glaring omission—but, alas, an unavoidable one. Let's look at why the official execution times are wrong and why that can't be helped.

Official Execution Times Are Only Part of the Story

The sequence of five **shr** instructions in the last example is 10 bytes long. That means that it can never execute in less than 24 cycles, even if the 4-byte prefetch queue is full when it starts, since 6 instruction bytes would still remain to be fetched, at 4 cycles per fetch. If the prefetch queue is empty at the start, the sequence *could* take 40 cycles. In short, thanks to instruction fetching, the code won't run at its documented speed and could take up to four times as long as it is supposed to.

Why does Intel document EU execution time rather than overall in-struction execution time, which includes both instruction fetch time and EU execution time? As described in Chapter 3, instruction fetching isn't per-formed as part of instruction execution by the EU, but is instead carried on in parallel by the BIU whenever the external data bus isn't in use or whenever the EU runs out of instruction bytes to execute. Sometimes the BIU can use spare bus cycles to prefetch instruction bytes before the EU needs them, so instruction fetching takes no time at all, practically speak-ing. At other times the EU executes instructions faster than the BIU can fetch them and instruction fetching becomes a significant part of overall execution time. As a result, *the effective fetch time for a given instruction varies greatly, depending on the code mix preceding that instruction.* Simi-larly, the state in which a given instruction leaves the prefetch queue affects the overall execution time of subsequent instructions.

In other words, while the execution time for a given instruction is constant, the fetch time for that instruction depends on the context in which the instruction is executing (the amount of prefetching the preceding instructions allowed) and can vary from a full 4 cycles per instruction byte to no time at all. As we'll see later, other cycle eaters, such as DRAM refresh and display memory wait states, can cause prefetching variations even during different executions of the *same* code sequence. Given that, it's meaningless to talk about the prefetch time of a given instruction, except in the context of a specific code sequence.

So now you know why the official instruction execution times are often wrong, and why Intel can't provide better specifications. You also know why you must time your code if you want to know how fast it really is.

There Is No Such Beast as a "True" Instruction Execution Time

The effect of the code preceding an instruction on the execution time of that instruction makes the Zen timer trickier to use than you might expect and complicates the interpretation of results reported by the Zen timer. For one thing, the Zen timer is best used to time code sequences that are more than a few instructions long; below 10 μsec or so, prefetch queue effects and the limited resolution of the clock driving the timer can cause problems.

Some slight prefetch queue–induced inaccuracy usually exists even when the Zen timer is used to time longer code sequences, since the calls to the Zen timer usually alter the code's prefetch queue from its normal state. (As we'll see in Chapter 12, branches—jumps, calls, returns, and the like—empty the prefetch queue.) Ideally, the Zen timer is used to measure the performance of an entire subroutine, so the prefetch queue effects of the branches at the start and end of the subroutine are similar to the effects of the calls to the Zen timer when you're measuring the subroutine's performance.

Another way in which the prefetch queue cycle eater complicates the use of the Zen timer involves the practice of timing the performance of a few instructions over and over. I'll often repeat one or two instructions 100 or 1000 times in a row in listings in this book in order to get timing intervals that are long enough to provide reliable measurements. However, as we just learned, the actual performance of any 8088 instruction depends on the code mix preceding any given use of that instruction, which in turn affects the state of the prefetch queue when the instruction starts executing. Alas, the execution time of an instruction preceded by dozens of identical instructions reflects just one of many possible prefetch states (and not a very realistic state, at that), and some of the other prefetch states may well produce distinctly different results.

For example, consider the code in Listings 4-5 and 4-6. Listing 4-5 shows our familiar **shr** case. Here, because the prefetch queue is always empty, execution time should work out to about 4 cycles per byte, or 8 cycles per **shr**, as shown in Figure 4.3. (Figure 4.3 illustrates the relationship between instruction fetching and execution in a simplified way, and is not intended to show the exact timing of 8088 operations.) That's quite a contrast to the

```
1    ;
2    ; *** Listing 4-5 ***
3    ;
4    ; Measures the performance of 1000 SHR instructions
5    ; in a row. Since SHR executes in 2 cycles but is
6    ; 2 bytes long, the prefetch queue is always empty,
7    ; and prefetching time determines the overall
8    ; performance of the code.
9    ;
10            call    ZTimerOn
11           rept    1000
12           shr     ax,1
13           endm
14           call    ZTimerOff
```

```
1    ;
2    ; *** Listing 4-6 ***
3    ;
4    ; Measures the performance of 1000 MUL/SHR instruction
5    ; pairs in a row. The lengthy execution time of MUL
6    ; should keep the prefetch queue from ever emptying.
7    ;
8            mov     cx,1000
9            sub     ax,ax
10           call    ZTimerOn
11           rept    1000
12           mul     ax
13           shr     ax,1
14           endm
15           call    ZTimerOff
```

official 2-cycle execution time of **shr**. In fact, the Zen timer reports that
Listing 4-5 executes in 1.81 μsec per byte, or slightly *more* than 4 cycles
per byte. (The extra time is the result of the dynamic RAM refresh cycle
eater, which we'll discuss shortly.) Going strictly by Listing 4-5, we would
conclude that the "true" execution time of **shr** is 8.64 cycles.

Now let's examine Listing 4-6. Here each **shr** follows a **mul** instruction.
Since **mul** instructions take so long to execute that the prefetch queue is
always full when they finish, each **shr** should be ready and waiting in the
prefetch queue when the preceding **mul** ends. As a result, we'd expect that
each **shr** would execute in 2 cycles; together with the 118-cycle execution
time of multiplying 0 times 0, the total execution time should come to 120
cycles per **shr/mul** pair, as shown in Figure 4.4. And, by God, when we
run Listing 4-6 we get an execution time of 25.14 μsec per **shr/mul** pair,
or *exactly* 120 cycles! According to these results, the "true" execution time
of **shr** would seem to be 2 cycles, quite a change from the conclusion we
drew from Listing 4-5.

The key point is this: we've seen one code sequence in which **shr** took
8-plus cycles to execute, and another in which it took only 2 cycles. Are we

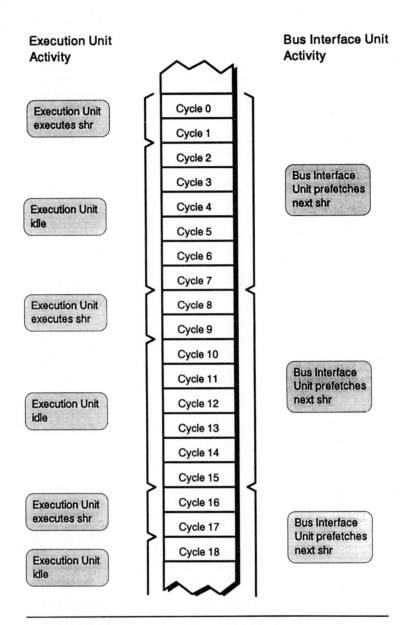

Execution Unit Activity

- Execution Unit executes shr
- Execution Unit idle
- Execution Unit executes shr
- Execution Unit idle
- Execution Unit executes shr
- Execution Unit idle

Cycle 0
Cycle 1
Cycle 2
Cycle 3
Cycle 4
Cycle 5
Cycle 6
Cycle 7
Cycle 8
Cycle 9
Cycle 10
Cycle 11
Cycle 12
Cycle 13
Cycle 14
Cycle 15
Cycle 16
Cycle 17
Cycle 18

Bus Interface Unit Activity

- Bus Interface Unit prefetches next shr
- Bus Interface Unit prefetches next shr
- Bus Interface Unit prefetches next shr

FIGURE 4.3   Instruction prefetching determines the overall execution time of a sequence of fast register-only instructions, such as **shr ax,1**, because such a sequence drains instruction bytes from the prefetch queue. In this example, overall execution time is four times longer than execution unit execution time, thanks to the prefetch queue cycle eater. This figure is for illustrative purposes only, and is not intended to show the exact timings of 8088 operations.

Execution Unit Activity

Bus Interface Unit Activity

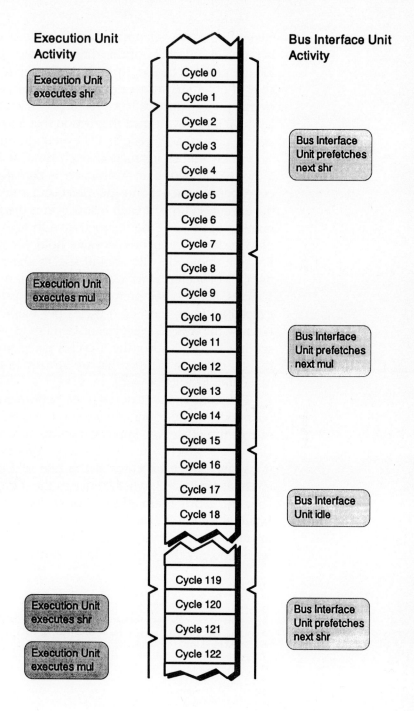

FIGURE 4.4

Execution unit execution time determines the overall execution time of a sequence of slow instructions, such as **mul**, because such a sequence allows the prefetch queue to stay well stocked with instruction bytes. In this example, overall execution time exactly matches execution unit execution time, and the prefetch queue cycle eater has no effect. This figure is for illustrative purposes only, and is not intended to show the exact timings of 8088 operations.

Execution Unit executes shr

Execution Unit executes mul

Bus Interface Unit prefetches next shr

Bus Interface Unit prefetches next mul

Bus Interface Unit idle

Cycle 0
Cycle 1
Cycle 2
Cycle 3
Cycle 4
Cycle 5
Cycle 6
Cycle 7
Cycle 8
Cycle 9
Cycle 10
Cycle 11
Cycle 12
Cycle 13
Cycle 14
Cycle 15
Cycle 16
Cycle 17
Cycle 18

Cycle 119
Cycle 120
Cycle 121
Cycle 122

Execution Unit executes shr

Execution Unit executes mul

Bus Interface Unit prefetches next shr

talking about two different forms of **shr** here? Of course not—the difference is purely a reflection of the differing states in which the preceding code left the prefetch queue. In Listing 4-5, each **shr** after the first few follows a slew of other **shr** instructions that have sucked the prefetch queue dry, so overall performance reflects instruction fetch time. By contrast, each **shr** in Listing 4-6 follows a **mul** instruction that leaves the prefetch queue full, so overall performance reflects EU execution time.

Clearly, either instruction fetch time *or* EU execution time—or even a mix of the two, if an instruction is partially prefetched—can determine code performance. Some people use a rule of thumb that assumes that the execution time of each instruction is the produce of 4 cycles times the number of bytes in the instruction. Although that's often true for register-only code, it frequently doesn't hold for code that accesses memory. For one thing, the rule should specify the product of 4 cycles times the number of *memory accesses*, not instruction bytes, since all accesses take 4 cycles. For another, memory-accessing instructions often have slower EU execution times than the 4 cycles per memory access rule would dictate, because the 8088 doesn't calculate memory addresses very rapidly, as we'll see in Chapter 7. Also, the 4 cycles per instruction byte rule isn't true for register-only instructions that are already in the prefetch queue when the preceding instruction ends.

The truth is that it never hurts performance to reduce either the cycle count or the byte count of a given bit of code, but there's no guarantee that one or the other will improve performance either. For example, consider Listing 4-7, which consists of a series of 4-cycle, 2-byte **mov al,0** instructions, and which executes at the rate of 1.81 μsec per instruction. Now consider Listing 4-8, which replaces the 4-cycle **mov al,0** with the 3-cycle (but still 2-byte) **sub al,al**. Despite its 1-cycle-per-instruction advantage, Listing 4-8 runs at exactly the same speed as Listing 4-7. The reason: both instructions are 2 bytes long, and in both cases it is the 8-cycle instruction fetch time, not the 3- or 4-cycle EU execution time, that limits performance.

```
1    ;
2    ; *** Listing 4-7 ***
3    ;
4    ; Measures the performance of repeated MOV AL,0 instructions,
5    ; which take 4 cycles each according to Intel's official
6    ; specifications.
7    ;
8            sub     ax,ax
9            call    ZTimerOn
10           rept    1000
11           mov     al,0
12           endm
13           call    ZTimerOff
```

```
1   ;
2   ; *** Listing 4-8 ***
3   ;
4   ; Measures the performance of repeated SUB AL,AL instructions,
5   ; which take 3 cycles each according to Intel's official
6   ; specifications.
7   ;
8           sub     ax,ax
9           call    ZTimerOn
10          rept    1000
11          sub     al,al
12          endm
13          call    ZTimerOff
```

As you can see, it's easy to be drawn into thinking you're saving cycles when you're not. You can only improve the performance of a specific bit of code by reducing the factor—instruction fetch time or execution time, or sometimes a mix of the two—that's limiting the performance of that code.

In case you missed it in all the excitement, the variability of prefetching means that our method of testing performance by executing 1000 instructions in a row by no means produces "true" instruction execution times, any more than the official execution times in Appendix A are "true" times. The fact of the matter is that a given instruction takes at least as long to execute as the time given for it in Appendix A, but may take as much as 4 cycles per byte longer, depending on the state of the prefetch queue when the preceding instruction ends. The only true execution time for an instruction is a time measured in a certain context, and that time is meaningful *only* in that context.

Look at it this way. We've firmly established that there's no number you can attach to a given instruction that's always that instruction's true execution time. In fact, as we'll see in the rest of this chapter and in the next, there are other cycle eaters that can work with the prefetch queue cycle eater to cause the execution time of an instruction to vary to an even greater extent than we've seen so far. That's okay, though, because the execution time of a single instruction is not what we're really after.

What we *really* want is to know how long useful working code takes to run, not how long a single instruction takes, and the Zen timer gives us the tool we need to gather that information. Granted, it would be easier if we could just add up neatly documented instruction execution times—but that's not going to happen. Without actually measuring the performance of a given code sequence, you simply don't know how fast it is. For crying out loud, even the people who *designed* the 8088 at Intel couldn't tell you exactly how quickly a given 8088 code sequence executes on the PC just by looking at it! Get used to the idea that execution times are only meaningful in context, learn the rules of thumb in this book, and use the Zen timer to measure your code.

Approximating Overall Execution Times

Don't think that because overall instruction execution time is determined by both instruction fetch time and EU execution time, the two times should be added together when estimating performance. For example, practically speaking, each **shr** in Listing 4-5 does not take 8 cycles of instruction fetch time plus 2 cycles of EU execution time to execute. Figure 4.3 shows that while a given **shr** is executing, the fetch of the next **shr** is starting, and since the two operations are overlapped for 2 cycles, there's no sense in charging the time to both instructions. You could think of the extra instruction fetch time for **shr** in Listing 4-5 as being 6 cycles, which yields an overall execution time of 8 cycles when added to the 2 cycles of EU execution time.

Alternatively, you could think of each **shr** in Listing 4-5 as taking 8 cycles to fetch and then executing in effectively 0 cycles while the next **shr** is being fetched. Whichever perspective you prefer is fine. The important point is that the time during which the execution of one instruction and the fetching of the next instruction overlap should be counted only toward the overall execution time of one of the instructions. For all intents and purposes, one of the two instructions runs at no performance cost whatsoever while the overlap exists.

As a working definition, we'll consider the execution time of a given instruction in a particular context to start when the first byte of the instruction is sent to the EU and to end when the first byte of the next instruction is sent to the EU. We'll discuss this further in Chapter 5.

What to Do about the Prefetch Queue Cycle Eater

Reducing the impact of the prefetch queue cycle eater is one of the overriding objectives in creating high-performance assembler code. How can you do this? One effective technique is to minimize access to memory operands, since such accesses compete with instruction fetching for precious memory accesses. You can also greatly reduce instruction fetch time simply by your choice of instructions: *keep your instructions short.* Less time is required to fetch instructions that are 1 or 2 bytes long than instructions that are 5 or 6 bytes long. Reduced instruction fetching lowers minimum execution time (minimum execution time is the product of 4 cycles times the number of instruction bytes) and often leads to faster overall execution.

While short instructions minimize overall prefetch time, they ironically actually often suffer relatively more from the prefetch queue bottleneck than do long instructions. Short instructions generally have such fast execution times that they drain the prefetch queue despite their small size. For example, consider the **shr** of Listing 4-5, which runs at only 25 percent of its EU execution time even though it's only 2 bytes long, thanks to the prefetch queue bottleneck. Short instructions are nonetheless generally faster than long instructions, thanks to the combination of fewer instruction bytes and faster EU execution times, and should be used as much as possible—just don't expect them to run at their documented speeds.

More than anything, the above rules boil down to using the registers as much as possible, both because register-only instructions are short and because they don't perform memory accesses to read or write operands. (Using the registers is a topic we'll return to repeatedly in *Zen of Assembly Language.*) However, using the registers is a rule of thumb, not a commandment. In some circumstances, it may actually be *faster* to access memory. (The look-up table technique, which we'll encounter in Chapter 7, is one such case.) What's more, the performance of the prefetch queue (and hence the performance of each instruction) differs from one code sequence to the next, and can even differ during different executions of the same code sequence.

All in all, writing good assembler code is as much an art as a science. As a result, you should follow the rules of thumb described in *Zen of Assembly Language*—and then time your code to see how fast it really is. You should experiment freely, but always remember that actual, measured performances is the bottom line.

The prefetch queue cycle eater looms over the performance of all 8088 code. We'll encounter it again and again in this book, and in every case it will make our code slower than it would otherwise be. An understanding of the prefetch queue cycle eater provides deep insight into what makes some 8088 code much faster than other, seemingly similar 8088 code, and is a key to good assembler programming. You'll never conquer this cycle eater, but with experience and the Zen timer you can surely gain the advantage.

Holding up the 8088

Over the last two chapters I've taken you further and further into the depths of the PC, telling you again and again that you must understand the computer at the lowest possible level in order to write good code. At this point, you may well wonder, "Have we gotten low enough?"

Not quite yet. The 8-bit bus and prefetch queue cycle eaters are low level indeed, but we've one level yet to go. Dynamic RAM refresh and wait states (our next topics) together form the lowest level at which the hardware of the PC affects code performance. Below this level, the PC is of interest only to hardware engineers.

Before we begin our discussion of dynamic RAM refresh, let's step back for a moment to take an overall look at this lowest level of cycle eaters. In truth, the distinctions between wait states and dynamic RAM refresh don't much matter to a programmer. What is important is that you understand this: *under certain circumstances, devices on the PC bus can stop the 8088 for 1 or more cycles, making your code run more slowly than it seemingly should.*

Unlike the other cycle eaters we've encountered, wait states and dynamic RAM refresh are strictly external to the 8088, as shown in Figure 4.1. Adapters on the PC's bus, such as video and memory cards, can insert wait states on any 8088 bus access, the idea being that they won't be able to complete the access properly unless the access is stretched out. Likewise, the channel of the DMA controller dedicated to dynamic RAM refresh can request control of the bus at any time, although the 8088 must relinquish the bus before the DMA controller can take over. This means that your code can't directly control wait states or dynamic RAM refresh. However, code *can* sometimes be designed to minimize the effects of these cycle eaters, and even when the cycle eaters slow your code and there isn't a thing in the world you can do about it, you're still better off understanding that you're losing performance and knowing why your code doesn't run as fast as it's supposed to than you are programming in ignorance.

Let's start with dynamic RAM (DRAM) refresh, which affects the performance of every program that runs on the PC.

4.4 ♦ Dynamic RAM Refresh: The Invisible Hand

DRAM refresh is sort of an act of God. By that I mean that DRAM refresh invisibly and inexorably steals up to 8.33 percent of all available memory access time from your programs. Although you *could* stop DRAM refresh, you wouldn't want to, since that would be a sure prescription for crashing your computer. In the end, thanks to DRAM refresh, almost all code runs a bit slower on the PC than it otherwise would, and that's that.

A bit of background: a static RAM (SRAM) chip is a memory chip that retains its contents indefinitely, so long as power is maintained. In contrast, each of several blocks of bits in a dynamic RAM (DRAM) chip retains its contents for only a short time after it's accessed for a read or write. In order to get a DRAM chip to store data for an extended period, each of the blocks of bits in that chip must be accessed regularly, so that the chip's stored data stays refreshed and valid. So long as this is done often enough, a DRAM chip will retain its contents indefinitely.

All of the PC's system memory consists of DRAM chips. (Some PC-compatible computers are built with SRAM chips, but IBM PCs, XTs, and ATs use only DRAM chips for system memory.) Each DRAM chip in the PC must be completely refreshed once every 4 msec (give or take a little) in order to ensure the integrity of the data it stores. Obviously, it's highly desirable that the memory in the PC retain the correct data indefinitely, so each DRAM chip in the PC *must* always be fully refreshed within 4 msec of the last refresh. Since there's no guarantee that a given program will access each and every block of bits in every DRAM once every 4 msec, the PC contains special circuitry and programming for providing DRAM refresh.

How DRAM Refresh Works in the PC

Timer 1 of the 8253 timer chip is programmed at power-up to generate a signal once every 72 cycles, or once every 15.08 μsec. That signal goes to channel 0 of the 8237 DMA controller, which requests the bus from the 8088 upon receiving the signal. (DMA stands for *direct memory access,* the ability of a device other than the 8088 to control the bus and access memory directly, without any help from the 8088.) As soon as the 8088 is between memory accesses, it gives control of the bus to the 8237, which in conjunction with special circuitry on the PC's motherboard then performs a single 4-cycle read access to 1 of 256 possible addresses, advancing to the next address on each successive access. (The read access is only for the purpose of refreshing the DRAM; the data read isn't used.)

The 256 addresses accessed by the refresh DMA accesses are arranged so that taken together they properly refresh all the memory in the PC. By accessing one of the 256 addresses every 15.08 μsec, all of the PC's DRAM is refreshed in

3.86 msec = 256 $\times$ 15.08 μsec

just about the desired 4 msec time I mentioned earlier. (Only the first 640 Kb of memory is refreshed; video adapters and other adapters above 640 Kb containing memory that requires refreshing must provide their own DRAM refresh.)

Don't sweat the details here. The important point is this: for at least 4 out of every 72 cycles, the PC's bus is given over to DRAM refresh and is not available to the 8088, as shown in Figure 4.5. That means that as much as 5.56 percent of the PC's already inadequate bus capacity is lost. However,

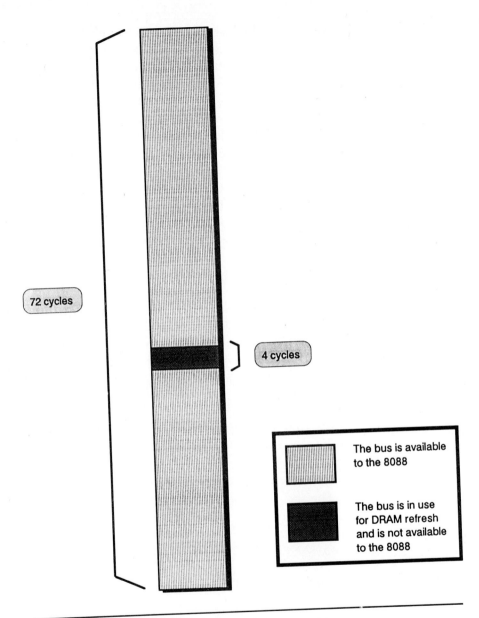

72 cycles

4 cycles

The bus is available
to the 8088

The bus is in use
for DRAM refresh
and is not available
to the 8088

FIGURE 4.5   The PC's bus is given over to providing dynamic RAM
(DRAM) refresh for at least 4 cycles out of every 72 cycles.

DRAM refresh doesn't necessarily stop the 8088 for 4 cycles. The EU of the 8088 can keep processing while DRAM refresh is occuring, unless the EU needs to access memory. Consequently, DRAM refresh can slow code performance anywhere from 0 percent to 5.56 percent (and actually a bit more, as we'll see shortly), depending on the extend to which DRAM refresh occupies cycles during which the 8088 would otherwise be accessing memory.

The Impact of DRAM Refresh

Let's look at examples from opposite ends of the spectrum in terms of the impact of DRAM refresh on code performance. First, consider the series of **mul** instructions in Listing 4-9. Since a 16-bit **mul** executes in between 118 and 133 cycles and is only 2 bytes long, there should be plenty of time for the prefetch queue to fill after each instruction, even after DRAM refresh has taken its slice of memory access time. Consequently, the prefetch queue should be able to keep the EU well supplied with instruction bytes at all times. Since the listing uses no memory operands, the EU should never have to wait for data from memory, and DRAM refresh should have no impact on performance. (Remember that the EU can operate normally during DRAM refreshes so long as it doesn't need to request a memory access from the BIU.)

Running Listing 4-9, we find that each **mul** executes in 24.72 μsec, or exactly 118 cycles. Since that's the shortest time in which **mul** can execute, we can see that no performance is lost to DRAM refresh. Listing 4-9 clearly illustrates that DRAM refresh affects code performance only when a DRAM refresh forces the EU of the 8088 to wait for a memory access.

```
1    ;
2    ; *** Listing 4-9 ***
3    ;
4    ; Measures the performance of repeated MUL instructions,
5    ; which allow the prefetch queue to be full at all times,
6    ; to demonstrate a case in which DRAM refresh has no impact
7    ; on code performance.
8    ;
9            sub     ax,ax
10           call    ZTimerOn
11           rept    1000
12           mul     ax
13           endm
14           call    ZTimerOff
```

Now let's look at the series of **shr** instructions shown in Listing 4-10. Since **shr** executes in 2 cycles but is 2 bytes long, the prefetch queue should

```
1    ;
2    ; *** Listing 4-10 ***
3    ;
4    ; Measures the performance of repeated SHR instructions,
5    ; which empty the prefetch queue, to demonstrate the
6    ; worst-case impact of DRAM refresh on code performance.
7    ;
8            call    ZTimerOn
9            rept    1000
10           shr     ax,1
11           endm
12           call    ZTimerOff
```

be empty while the listing executes, with the 8088 prefetching instruction bytes nonstop. As a result, the time per instruction of Listing 4-10 should precisely reflect the time required to fetch the instruction bytes.

Since 4 cycles are required to read each instruction byte, we'd expect each **shr** to execute in 8 cycles, or 1.676 μsec, if there were no DRAM refresh. In fact, each **shr** in Listing 4-10 executes in 1.81 μsec, indicating that DRAM refresh is taking 7.4 percent of the program's execution time. That's nearly 2 percent more than our worst-case estimate of the loss to DRAM refresh overhead! In fact, the result indicates that DRAM refresh is stealing not 4 but 5.33 cycles out of every 72 cycles. How can this be?

The answer is that a given DRAM refresh can actually hold up CPU memory accesses for as many as 6 cycles, depending on the timing of the DRAM refresh's DMA request relative to the 8088's internal instruction execution state. When the code in Listing 4-10 runs, each DRAM refresh holds up the CPU for either 5 or 6 cycles, depending on where the 8088 is in executing the current **shr** instruction when the refresh request occurs. Now we see that things can get even worse than we thought: *DRAM refresh can steal as much as 8.33 percent of available memory access time (6 out of every 72 cycles) from the 8088.*

Which of the two cases we've examined reflects reality? Although either *can* happen, the latter—significant performance reduction, ranging as high as 8.33 percent—is far more likely to occur. This is especially true for high-performance assembler code, which uses fast instructions that tend to cause nonstop instruction fetching.

What to Do about the DRAM Refresh Cycle Eater

Hmmm. When we discovered the prefetch queue cycle eater, we learned to use short instructions. When we discovered the 8-bit bus cycle eater, we learned to use byte-sized memory operands whenever possible and to keep word-sized variables in registers. What can we do to work around the DRAM refresh cycle eater?

Nothing.

As I've said before, DRAM refresh is an act of God. DRAM refresh is a fundamental, unchanging part of the PC's operation, and there's nothing you or I can do about it. If refresh were any less frequent, the reliability of the PC would be compromised, so tinkering with either timer 1 or DMA channel 0 to reduce DRAM refresh overhead is out. Nor is there any way to structure code to minimize the impact of DRAM refresh. Sure, some instructions are affected less by DRAM refresh than others, but how many multiplies and divides in a row can you really use? I suppose that code *could* conceivably be structured to leave a free memory access every 72 cycles, so DRAM refresh wouldn't have any effect. In the old days when code size was measured in bytes, not K bytes, and processors were less powerful (and less complex) programmers did in fact use similar tricks to eke every last bit of performance from their code. When programming the PC, however, the prefetch queue cycle eater would make such careful code synchronization a difficult task indeed, and any modest performance improvement that did result could never justify the increase in programming complexity and the limits on creative programming that such an approach would impose. There's no way around it: useful code accesses memory frequently and at irregular intervals, and over the long haul DRAM refresh always exacts its price.

If you're still harboring thoughts of reducing the overhead of DRAM refresh, consider this. Instructions that tend not to suffer very much from DRAM refresh are those that have a high ratio of execution time to instruction fetch time, and those aren't the fastest instructions of the PC. It certainly wouldn't make sense to use slower instructions just to reduce DRAM refresh overhead, for it's *total* execution time—DRAM refresh, instruction fetching, and all—that matters.

The important thing to understand about DRAM refresh is that it generally slows your code down; the extent of that performance reduction can vary considerably and unpredictably, depending on how the DRAM refreshes interact with your code's pattern of memory accesses. When you use the Zen timer and get a fractional cycle count for the execution time of an instruction, that's often DRAM refresh at work. (The display adapter cycle eater is another possible culprit.) Whenever you get two timing results that differ less or more than they seemingly should, that's usually DRAM refresh too. Thanks to DRAM refresh, variations of up to 8.33 percent in PC code performance are par for the course.

4.5 ◆ Wait States

Wait states are cycles during which a bus access by the 8088 to a device on the PC's bus is temporarily halted by that device while it gets ready to complete the read or write. Wait states are well and truly the lowest level of code performance. Everything we have discussed (and will discuss), even DMA accesses, can be affected by wait states.

Wait states exist because the 8088 must be able to coexist with any adapter, no matter how slow (within reason). The 8088 expects to be able to complete each bus access (a memory or I/O read or write) in 4 cycles, but adapters can't always respond that quickly, for a number of reasons. For example, display adapters must split access to display memory between the 8088 and the circuitry that generates the video signal based on the contents of display memory, so they often can't immediately fulfill a request by the 8088 for a display memory read or write. To resolve this conflict, display adapters can tell the 8088 to wait during bus accesses by inserting one or more wait states, as shown in Figure 4.6. The 8088 simply sits and idles as long as wait states are inserted, then completes the access as soon as the display adapter indicates its readiness by no longer inserting wait states. The same would be true of any adapter that couldn't keep up with the 8088.

Mind you, this is all transparent to the code running on the 8088. An instruction that encounters wait states runs exactly as if there were no wait states, but slower. Wait states are nothing more or less than wasted time as far as the 8088 and your programs are concerned.

By understanding the circumstances in which wait states can occur, you can avoid them when possible. Even when it's not possible to work around wait states, it's still to your advantage to understand how they can cause your code to run more slowly.

First, let's learn a bit more about wait states by contrast with DRAM refresh. Unlike DRAM refresh, wait states do not occur on any regularly scheduled basis and are of no particular duration. Wait states can occur only when an instruction performs a memory or I/O read or write. Both the presence of wait states and the number of wait states inserted on any given bus access are controlled entirely by the device being accessed. When it comes to wait states, the 8088 is passive, merely accepting whatever wait states the accessed device chooses to insert during the course of the access. All this makes perfect sense given that the whole point of the wait state mechanism is to allow a device to stretch out any access to itself for however much time it needs to perform the access.

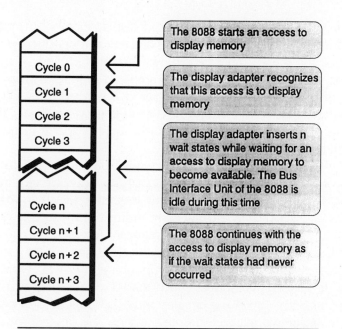

Cycle 0	The 8088 starts an access to display memory
Cycle 1	The display adapter recognizes that this access is to display memory
Cycle 2	
Cycle 3	The display adapter inserts n wait states while waiting for an access to display memory to become available. The Bus Interface Unit of the 8088 is idle during this time
Cycle n	
Cycle n + 1	The 8088 continues with the access to display memory as if the wait states had never occurred
Cycle n + 2	
Cycle n + 3	

FIGURE 4.6   Both the video circuitry and the 8088 often try to access display memory at the same time. Display adapters resolve such conflicts by holding up 8088 accesses with wait states until the video circuitry no longer needs to access display memory. This figure is for illustrative purposes only, and is not intended to show the exact timings of 8088 operations.

Like DRAM refresh, wait states don't stop the 8088 completely. The EU can continue processing while wait states are inserted, so long as it doesn't need to perform a bus access. However, in the PC wait states most often occur when an instruction accesses a memory operand, so in fact the EU usually is stopped by wait states. (Instruction fetches rarely wait in a PC because system memory is zero wait state. AT memory routinely inserts one wait state, however, as we'll see in Chapter 15.)

As it turns out, wait states pose a serious problem in just one area in the PC. Although any adapter *can* insert wait states, in the PC only display adapters do so to an extent that seriously affects performance.

The Display Adapter Cycle Eater

Display adapters must serve two masters, and that creates a fundamental performance problem. Master 1 is the circuitry that drives the display screen.

This circuitry must constantly read display memory in order to obtain the information used to draw the characters or dots displayed on the screen. Since the screen must be redrawn between 50 and 70 times per second, and since each redraw of the screen can require as many as 36,000 reads of display memory (more in Super-VGA modes), master 1 is a demanding master indeed. No matter how demanding master 1 gets, though, its needs must *always* be met—otherwise the quality of the picture on the screen will suffer.

Master 2 is the 8088, which reads from and writes to display memory in order to manipulate the bytes that the video circuitry reads to form the picture on the screen. Master 2 is less important than master 1, since the 8088 affects display quality only indirectly. In other words, if the video circuitry has to wait for display memory accesses, the picture will develop holes, snow, and the like, but if the 8088 has to wait for display memory accesses, the program will just run a bit slower—no big deal.

It matters a great deal which master is more important, for while both the 8088 and the video circuitry must gain access to display memory, only one of the two masters can read or write display memory at any one time. Potential conflicts are resolved by flat-out guaranteeing the video circuitry however many accesses to display memory it needs; the 8088 waits for whatever display memory accesses are left over.

It turns out that the 8088 has to do a lot of waiting, for three reasons. First, the video circuitry can take as much as about 90 percent of the available display memory access time, as shown in Figure 4.7, leaving as little as about 10 percent of all display memory accesses for the 8088. (These percentages vary considerably among the many EGA and VGA clones.)

Second, because dots (or *pixels,* short for "picture elements") must be drawn on the screen at a constant speed, display adapters can provide memory accesses only at fixed intervals. As a result, time can be lost while the 8088 synchronizes with the start of the next display adapter memory access, even if the video circuitry isn't accessing display memory at that time, as shown in Figure 4.8.

Finally, the time it takes a display adapter to complete a memory access is related to the speed of the clock that generates pixels on the screen rather than to the memory access speed of the 8088. Consequently, the time taken for display memory to complete an 8088 read or write access is often longer than the time taken for system memory to complete an access, even if the 8088 lucks into hitting a free display memory access just as it becomes available, again as shown in Figure 4.8. Any or all of the three factors I've described can result in wait states, slowing the 8088 and creating the display adapter cycle eater.

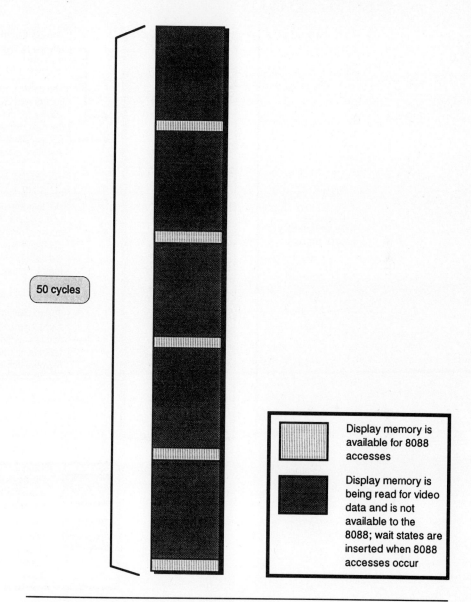

50 cycles

Display memory is available for 8088 accesses

Display memory is being read for video data and is not available to the 8088; wait states are inserted when 8088 accesses occur

FIGURE 4.7 The video circuitry, which scans display memory for pixel data, can take as much as about 90 percent of available display memory access time, leaving as little as about 10 percent of all display memory accesses free for the use of the 8088.

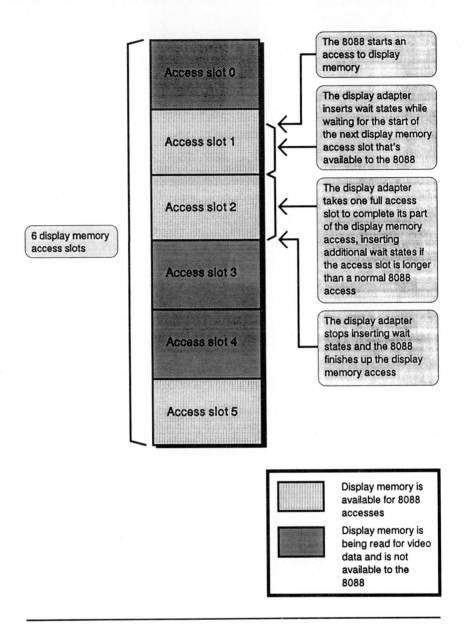

The 8088 starts an access to display memory

The display adapter inserts wait states while waiting for the start of the next display memory access slot that's available to the 8088

The display adapter takes one full access slot to complete its part of the display memory access, inserting additional wait states if the access slot is longer than a normal 8088 access

The display adapter stops inserting wait states and the 8088 finishes up the display memory access

6 display memory access slots

Access slot 0

Access slot 1

Access slot 2

Access slot 3

Access slot 4

Access slot 5

Display memory is available for 8088 accesses

Display memory is being read for video data and is not available to the 8088

FIGURE 4.8   Accesses to display memory are available only at fixed intervals and are of fixed lengths. Both the intervals and the lengths are controlled by the display adapter, and are the same regardless of the speed of the computer in which the display adapter is installed. This figure is for illustrative purposes only, and is not intended to show the exact timings of 8088 operations.

If some of this is Greek to you, don't worry. The important point is that display memory is not very fast compared to normal system memory. How slow is it? *Incredibly* slow. Remember how slow the PC*jr* was? In case you've forgotten, I'll refresh your memory: the PC*jr* was at best only half as fast as the PC. The PC*jr* had an 8088 running at 4.77 MHz, just like the PC—why do you suppose it was so much slower? I'll tell you why: *all the memory in the PC*jr *was display memory.*

Enough said.

All the memory in the PC is *not* display memory, however, and unless you're thickheaded enough to put code in display memory, the PC isn't going to run as slowly as a PC*jr*. (Putting code or other nonvideo data in unused areas of display memory sounds like a neat idea—until you consider the effect on instruction prefetching of cutting the 8088's already poor memory access performance in half. Running your code from display memory is sort of like running on the hypothetical 8084—an 8086 with a *4-bit* bus. Not recommended!) Given that your code and data reside in normal system memory below the 640-K mark, how great an impact does the display adapter cycle eater have on performance?

The answer varies considerably depending on what display adapter and what display mode we're talking about. The display adapter cycle eater is worst with the Enhanced Graphics Adapter (EGA) and the Video Graphics Array (VGA). While the Color/Graphics Adapter (CGA), Monochrome Display Adapter (MDA), and Hercules Graphics Card (HGC) all suffer from the display adapter cycle eater as well, they suffer to lesser degrees. Since the EGA and the VGA represent the standards for PC graphics now and for the foreseeable future, and since those are the hardest graphics adapters to wring performance from, for the remainder of this chapter we'll restrict our discussion to the EGA and VGA.

The Impact of the Display Adapter Cycle Eater

Even on the EGA and VGA, the effect of the display adapter cycle eater depends on the display mode selected. In text mode, the display adapter cycle eater is rarely a major factor. It's not that the cycle eater isn't present; however, a mere 4000 bytes control the entire text mode display, and even with the display adapter cycle eater it just doesn't take that long to manipulate 4000 bytes. Even if the display adapter cycle eater were to cause the 8088 to take as much as 5 μsec per display memory access—more than 5 times normal—it would still take only

$$40 \text{ msec} = 4000 \times 2 \times 5 \text{ } \mu\text{sec}$$

to read *and* write every byte of display memory. That's a lot of time as measured in 8088 cycles, but it's less than the blink of an eye in human time, and video performance matters only in human time. After all, the whole point of drawing graphics is to convey visual information, and if that information can be presented faster than the eye can see, that is, by definition, fast enough.

That's not to say that the display adapter cycle eater *can't* matter in text mode. In Chapter 2, I recounted the story of a debate among readers of a magazine about exactly how quickly characters could be written to display memory without causing snow. The writers carefully added up Intel's instruction cycle times to see how many writes to display memory they could squeeze into a single horizontal retrace interval. (On a CGA, it's only during the short horizontal retrace interval and the longer vertical retrace interval that display memory can be accessed in 80-column text mode without causing snow.) Of course, we now know that their cardinal sin was to ignore the prefetch queue; even if there were no wait states, their calculations would have been overly optimistic. There *are* display memory wait states as well, however, so the calculations were not just optimistic but wildly optimistic.

Text mode situations such as the above notwithstanding, where the display adapter cycle eater really kicks in is in graphics mode, and most especially in the high-resolution graphics modes of the EGA and VGA. The problem here is not that there are necessarily more wait states per access in high-resolution graphics modes (that varies from adapter to adapter and mode to mode). Rather, the problem is simply that there are many more bytes of display memory per screen in these modes than in lower-resolution graphics modes and in text modes, so many more display memory accesses, each with its share of display memory wait states, are required in order to draw an image of a given size. When accessing the many thousands of bytes used in the high-resolution graphics modes, the cumulative effects of display memory wait states can seriously affect code performance, even as measured in human time.

For example, if we assume the same 5 μsec per display memory access for the EGA's high-res graphics mode (mode 10h) that we assumed for text mode, it would take

$$260 \text{ msec} = 26,000 \times 2 \times 5 \text{ } \mu\text{sec}$$

to scroll the screen once in the EGA's high-res graphics mode. That's more than 1/4 second—noticeable by human standards, an eternity by computer standards.

That sounds pretty serious, but we did make an unfounded assumption about memory access speed. Let's get some hard numbers. Listing 4-11 accesses display memory at the 8088's maximum speed, by way of a **rep movsw** with display memory as both source and destination. The code in Listing 4-11 executes in 3.18 μsec per access to display memory—not as long as we had assumed, but a long time nonetheless.

```
1    ;
2    ; *** Listing 4-11 ***
3    ;
4    ; Times speed of memory access to Enhanced Graphics
5    ; Adapter graphics mode display memory at A000:0000.
6    ;
7            mov     ax,0010h
8            int     10h                 ;select hi-res EGA graphics
9                                        ; mode 10 hex (AH=0 selects
10                                       ; BIOS set mode function,
11                                       ; with AL=mode to select)
12   ;
13           mov     ax,0a000h
14           mov     ds,ax
15           mov     es,ax               ;move to & from same segment
16           sub     si,si               ;move to & from same offset
17           mov     di,si
18           mov     cx,800h             ;move 2K words
19           cld
20           call    ZTimerOn
21           rep     movsw               ;simply read each of the first
22                                       ; 2K words of the destination segment,
23                                       ; writing each byte immediately back
24                                       ; to the same address. No memory
25                                       ; locations are actually altered; this
26                                       ; is just to measure memory access
27                                       ; times
28           call    ZTimerOff
29   ;
30           mov     ax,0003h
31           int     10h                 ;return to text mode
```

For comparison, let's see how long the same code takes when accessing normal system RAM instead of display memory. The code in Listing 4-12, which performs a **rep movsw** from the code segment to the code segment, executes in 1.39 μsec per display memory access. That means that, on average, 1.79 μsec (more than 8 cycles!) are lost to the display adapter cycle eater on each access. In other words, the display adapter cycle eater can *more than double* the execution time of 8088 code!

Bear in mind that we're talking about a worst case here; the impact of the display adapter cycle eater is proportional to the percentage of time a given code sequence spends accessing display memory. A line-drawing subroutine, which executes perhaps a dozen instructions for each display

```
1    ;
2    ; *** Listing 4-12 ***
3    ;
4    ; Times speed of memory access to normal system
5    ; memory.
6    ;
7            mov     ax,ds
8            mov     es,ax           ;move to & from same segment
9            sub     si,si           ;move to & from same offset
10           mov     di,si
11           mov     cx,800h         ;move 2K words
12           cld
13           call    ZTimerOn
14   rep     movsw                   ;simply read each of the first
15                                   ; 2K words of the destination segment,
16                                   ; writing each byte immediately back
17                                   ; to the same address. No memory
18                                   ; locations are actually altered; this
19                                   ; is just to measure memory access
20                                   ; times
21           call    ZTimerOff
```

memory access, generally loses less performance to the display adapter cycle eater than does a block copy or scrolling subroutine that uses **rep movs** instructions. Scaled and three-dimensional graphics, which spend a great deal of time performing calculations (often using *very* slow floating-point arithmetic), tend to suffer still less.

In addition, code that accesses display memory infrequently tends to suffer only about half of the maximum display memory wait states, because, on average, such code accesses display memory halfway between one available display memory access slot and the next. As a result, code that accesses display memory less intensively than the code in Listing 4-11 will on average lose 4 or 5, rather than 8-plus, cycles to the display adapter cycle eater on each memory access.

Nonetheless, the display adapter cycle eater always takes its toll on graphics code. Interestingly, that toll becomes relatively much higher on ATs and 80386 machines, because while those computers can execute many more instructions per microsecond than can the PC, it takes just as long to access display memory on those computers as on the PC. Remember, the limited speed of access to a graphics adapter is an inherent characteristic of the adapter, so the fastest computer around can't access display memory one iota faster than the adapter will allow. We'll discuss this further in Chapter 15.

What to Do about the Display Adapter Cycle Eater

What can we do about the display adapter cycle eater? Well, we can minimize display memory accesses whenever possible. In particular, we can try to avoid read/modify/write display memory operations of the sort used to mask individual pixels and clip images. Why? Because read/modify/write operations require two display memory accesses (one read and one write) each time display memory is manipulated. Instead, we should try to use writes of the sort that set all the pixels in a given byte of display memory at once, since such writes don't require accompanying read accesses. The key here is that only half as many display memory accesses are required to write a byte to display memory as to read a byte from display memory, mask part of it off and alter the rest, and write the byte back to display memory. Half as many display memory accesses means half as many display memory wait states.

Along the same line, the display adapter cycle eater makes the popular exclusive-or animation technique, which requires paired reads and writes of display memory, less-than-ideal for the PC. Exclusive-or animation should be avoided in favor of simply writing images to display memory whenever possible, as we'll see in Chapter 11.

Another principle for display adapter programming is to perform multiple accesses to display memory very rapidly, in order to make use of as many of the scarce accesses to display memory as possible. This is especially important when many large images need to be drawn quickly, since only by using virtually every available display memory access can many bytes be written to display memory in a short period of time. Repeated string instructions are ideal for making maximum use of display memory accesses; of course, repeated string instructions can be used only on whole bytes, so this is another point in favor of modifying display memory a byte at a time.

These concepts certainly need examples and clarification, along with some working code; that coming up in Volume II of *Zen of Assembly Language.* Why not now? Well, in Volume II we'll be able to devote a whole chapter to display adapter programming, and by that point we'll have the benefit of an understanding of the flexible mind, which is certainly a plus for this complex topic.

For now, all you really need to know about the display adapter cycle eater is that you can lose more than 8 cycles of execution time on each access to display memory. For intensive access to display memory, the loss really can be as high as 8-plus cycles, while for average graphics code the loss is closer to 4 cycles; in either case, the impact on performance is significant. There is only one way to discover just how significant the impact of the display adapter cycle eater is for any particular graphics code, and that is, of course, to measure the performance of that code.

If you're interested in the detailed operation of the display adapter cycle eater, I suggest you read my article, "The Display Adapter Bottleneck," in the January 1987 issue of *PC Tech Journal.*

4.6 ◆ Cycle Eaters: A Summary

We've covered a great deal of sophisticated material in this chapter, so don't feel bad if you haven't understood everything you've read; it will all become clear as you read on. What's really important is that you come away from this chapter understanding that:

◆ The 8-bit bus cycle eater causes each access to a word-sized operand to be 4 cycles longer than an equivalent access to a byte-sized operand.

◆ The prefetch queue cycle eater can cause instruction execution times to be as much as four times longer than the times specified in Appendix A.

◆ The DRAM refresh cycle eater slows most PC code, with performance reductions as great as 8.33 percent.

◆ The display adapter cycle eater typically doubles, and can more than triple, the length of the standard 4-cycle access to display memory, with intensive display memory access suffering most.

This basic knowledge about cycle eaters puts you in a good position to understand the results reported by the Zen timer, and that means that you're well on your way to writing high-performance assembler code. We will put this knowledge to work throughout the remainder of *Zen of Assembly Language.*

4.7 ◆ What Does It All Mean?

There you have it: life under the programming interface. It's not a particularly pretty picture, for the inhabitants of that strange realm where hardware and software meet are little-known cycle eaters that sap the speed from your unsuspecting code. Still, some of those cycle eaters can be minimized by keeping instructions short, using the registers, using byte-sized memory operands, and accessing display memory as little as possible. None of the cycle eaters can be eliminated, and DRAM refresh can scarcely be addressed at all; still, aren't you better off knowing how fast your code *really* runs—and why—than you were reading the "official" execution times and guessing?

So far we've only examined cycle eaters singly. Unfortunately, cycle eaters don't work alone, and together they're still more complex and unpredictable than they are taken one at a time. The intricate relationship between the cycle eaters is our next topic.

Chapter 5

Night of the Cycle Eaters

5.1	No, We're Not in Kansas Anymore
5.2	There's Still No Such Beast as a "True" Execution Time
5.3	The True Nature of Instruction Execution
5.4	Back to the Programming Interface

When sorrows come, they come not single spies,
But in battalions.

Shakespeare, *Hamlet*

Thus far we've explored what might be called the science of assembler programming. We've dissected in considerable detail the many factors that affect code performance, greatly increasing our understanding of the PC in the process. We've approached the whole business in a logical fashion, measuring 8 cycles here, accounting for 6 cycles there, always coming up with reasonable explanations for the phenomena we observe. In short, we've acted as if assembler programming for the PC can be reduced to a well-understood, cut-and-dried cookbook discipline once we know enough.

I'm here to tell you, it ain't so.

Assembler programming for the PC can't be reduced to a science, and cycle eaters are the reason why. The 8-bit bus and prefetch queue cycle eaters give every code sequence on the PC unique and hard-to-predict performance characteristics. Throw in the DRAM refresh and display adapter cycle eaters and you've got virtually infinite possibilities not only for the performance of different code sequences but also for the performance of the *same* code sequence at different times! There is simply *no way* to know in advance exactly how fast a specific instance of an instruction will execute, and there's no way to be sure what code is the fastest for a particular purpose. Instead, what we must do is use the Zen timer to gain experience and develop rules of thumb, write code by feel as much as by prescription, and measure the actual performance of what we write.

In other words, we must become Zen programmers.

As you read this, you may understand but not believe. Surely, you think, there must be a way to know what the best code is for a given task. How can it not be possible to come up with a purely rational solution to a problem that involves that most rational of man's creations, the computer?

The answer lies in the nature of the computer in question. While it's true that it's not impossible to understand the exact performance of a given piece of code on the IBM PC, because of the 8-bit bus and prefetch queue cycle eaters it *is* extremely complex and requires expensive hardware. And then, when you fully understand the performance of that piece of code, what have you got? Only an understanding of one out of millions of possible code sequences, each of which is a unique problem requiring just as much analysis as the first code sequence.

That's bad enough, but the two remaining cycle eaters make the problem of understanding code performance more complex still. The DRAM refresh and display adapter cycle eaters don't affect the execution of each instruction equally; they occur periodically and have varying impacts on performance when they do occur, thereby causing instruction performance to vary as a function not only of the sequence of instructions but also of time. In other words, the understanding you gain of a particular code sequence *may not even be valid the next time that code runs,* thanks to the varying effects of the DRAM refresh and display adapter cycle eaters.

In short, it is true that the exact performance of assembler code is indeed a solvable problem in the classic sense, since everything about the performance of a given execution of a given chunk of code is knowable given enough time, effort, and expensive hardware. It is equally true, however, that the exact performance of assembler code over time is such a complex problem that it might as well be unsolvable, since that hard won knowledge would be so specific as to be of no use. We are going to spend the rest of this chapter proving that premise. First we'll look at some of the interactions between the cycle eaters; those interactions make the prediction of code performance still more complex than we've seen so far. After that we'll look at every detail of 170 cycles in the life of the PC. What we'll find is that if we set out to understand the exact performance of an entire assembler program, we could well spend the rest of our lives at that task—and would be no better off than we were before.

The object of this chapter is to convince you that when it comes to writing assembler code there's no complete solution, no way to understand every detail or get precise, unvarying answers about performance. We *can* come close, though, by understanding the basic operation of the PC, developing our intuition, following rules of thumb such as keeping instructions short, and always measuring code performance. Those approaches are precisely what this book is about, and are the foundation of the Zen of assembler.

5.1   ◆ No, We're Not in Kansas Anymore

You may be feeling a bit lost at this point. That's certainly understandable, for the last two chapters have covered what is surely the most esoteric aspect of assembler programming. I must tell you that this chapter will be more of the same.

Follow along as best you can, but don't be concerned if some of the material is outside your range right now. Both the following chapters and experience will give you a better feel for what this chapter is about. It's important that you be exposed to these concepts now, though, so you can recognize them when you run into them later. The key concept to bring away from this chapter is that the cycle eaters working together make for such enormous variability of code performance that there's no point in worrying about exactly what's happening in the execution of a given instruction or sequence of instructions. Instead, we must use rules of thumb and a programming "feel" developed with experience, and we must focus on overall performance as measured with the Zen timer.

Cycle Eaters by the Battalion

Taken individually the cycle eaters are formidable, as we saw in the last chapter. Cycle eaters don't line up neatly and occur one at a time, though. Like the proverbial 900-pound gorilla, they appear whenever they want. Frequently one cycle eater will occur during the course of another cycle eater, with compound (and complex) effects.

For example, it's perfectly legal to put code in display memory and execute that code; however, as the instruction bytes of that code are fetched they'll be subjected to the display adapter cycle eater, which means that each instruction byte could easily take twice as long as usual to fetch. Naturally, this will intensify the already serious effects of the prefetch queue cycle eater. (Remember that the prefetch queue cycle eater is simply the result of the inability of the 8088 to fetch instruction bytes quickly enough.) In this case, the display adapter and prefetch queue cycle eaters together could make overall execution times five to ten times longer than the times listed in Appendix A!

As another example, the DRAM refresh and 8-bit bus cycle eaters can work together to increase the variability of code performance. When DRAM refresh occurs during an instruction that accesses a word-sized memory operand, the instruction's memory accesses are held up until the DRAM refresh is completed. However, the exact amount by which the instruction's accesses are delayed (and which access is delayed, as well) depends on exactly where in the course of execution the instruction was when the DRAM refresh came along. If the DRAM refresh happens just as the 8088 was about to begin a bus access, the 8088 can be held up for a long time. If, however, the DRAM refresh happens while the 8088 is performing internal operations, such as address calculations or instruction decoding, the impact on performance will be less.

The point is not, Lord knows, that you should understand how every cycle eater affects every other cycle eater and how together and separately they affect each instruction in your code. Quite the opposite, in fact. *I* certainly don't understand all the interactions between cycle eaters and code performance, and frankly I don't ever expect (or want) to. Rather, what I'm telling you (again) is that a complete understanding of the performance of a given code sequence is so complex and varies so greatly with context that there's no point in worrying about it. As a result, high-performance assembler code is produced by programming according to intuition and experience and then measuring performance, not from looking up execution times and following rigid rules. In a way that's all to the good: experienced, intuitive assembler programmers are worth a great deal, because no compiler can rival a good assembler programmer's ability to deal with cycle eaters and the complexity of code execution on the 8088.

One fallout of the nearly infinite variability of code performance is that the exact performance of a given instruction is, for all intents and purposes, undefined. So many factors affect performance, and those factors can vary so easily with time and context, that there's just no use to trying to tag a given instruction with a single execution time. In other words . . .

5.2 ◆ There's Still No Such Beast as a "True" Execution Time

Thanks to the combined efforts of the cycle eaters, it's more true than ever that there's no such thing as a single "true" execution time for a given instruction. As you'll recall, I said that in the last chapter. Why do I keep bringing it up? Because I don't want you to look at the times reported by our tests of 1000 repetitions of the same instruction and think that those times are the true execution times of that instruction. They aren't—any more than the official cycle times in Appendix A are the true times. *There is no such thing as a true execution time on the 8088.* There are only execution times in context.

Do you remember the varying performances of **shr** in different contexts in Chapter 4? Well, that was just for repeated instances of one or two instructions. Imagine how much variation cycle eaters could induce in the performance of a sequence of 10 or 20 different instructions, especially if some of the instructions accessed word-sized display memory operands. You should always bear in mind that a time reported by the Zen timer is accurate only for the particular code sequence you've timed, not for all instances of a given instruction in all code sequences.

There's just no way around it: *you must measure the performance of your code to know how fast it is.* Yes, I know, it would be awfully nice just to be able to look up instruction execution times and be done with it. That's not the way the 8088 works, though—and the odd architecture of the 8088 is what the Zen of assembler is all about.

170 Cycles in the Life of a PC

Next, we're going to examine every detail of instruction execution on the PC over a period of 170 cycles. One reason for doing this is to convince anyone who may still harbor the notion that there must be some way to come up with hard and fast execution times that it's a fool's quest. Another reason is to illustrate many of the concepts we've developed in the last two chapters.

A third reason is simple curiosity. We'll spend most of this book measuring instruction execution times and inferring how cycle eaters and instruction execution are interacting. Why not take a look at the real thing? It won't answer any fundamental questions, but it will give us a feel for what's going on under the programming interface.

The Test Setup

The code we'll observe is shown in Listing 5-1. This code is an endless loop in which the value stored in the variable **i** is copied to the variable **j** over and over by way of AH. The **DS:** override prefixes on the variables, while not required, make it clear that both variables are accessed by way of DS.

The detailed performance of the code in Listing 5-1 was monitored with the logic analyzer capability of the OmniLab multipurpose electronic test instrument manufactured by Orion Instruments. (Not coincidentally, I was part of the team that developed the OmniLab software.) OmniLab's probes were hooked up to a PC's 8088 and bus, Listing 5-1 was started, and a snapshot of code execution was captured and studied.

By the way, OmniLab, a high-performance but relatively low-priced instrument, costs (circa 1989) about $9,000. Money is one reason why you probably won't want to analyze code performance in great detail yourself!

The following lines of the 8088 were monitored with OmniLab: the 16 lines that carry addresses, 8 of which also carry data, the READY line (used to hold the 8088 up during DRAM refresh), and the QS1 and QS0 lines (which signal transfers of instruction bytes from the prefetch queue to the execution unit [EU]). The /MEMR and /MEMW lines on the PC bus were monitored to observe memory accesses. The 8088 itself provides additional information about bus cycle timing and type, but the lines described above will show us program execution in plenty of detail for our purposes.

```
1    ;
2    ; *** Listing 5-1 ***
3    ;
4    ; Copies a byte via AH endlessly, for the purpose of
5    ; illustrating the complexity of a complete understanding
6    ; of even the simplest instruction sequence on the PC.
7    ;
8    ; Note: This program is an endless loop, and never exits!
9    ;
10   ; Compile and link as a standalone program; not intended
11   ; for use with the Zen timer.
12   ;
13   mystack segment para stack 'STACK'
14           db        512 dup(?)
15   mystack ends
16   ;
17   Code    segment word public 'CODE'
18           assume  cs:Code, ds:Code
19   Start   proc    near
20           push    cs
21           pop     ds
22           jmp     Skip
23   ;
24   i       db      1
25   j       db      0
26   ;
27   Skip:
28           rept    1000
29           mov     ah,ds:[i]
30           mov     ds:[j],ah
31           endm
32           jmp     Skip
33   Start   endp
34   Code    ends
35           end     Start
```

Odds are that you, the reader, are not a hardware engineer. After all, this *is* a book about software, however far it may seem to stray at times. Consequently, I'm not going to show the execution of Listing 5-1 in the form of the timing diagrams of which hardware engineers are so fond. Timing diagrams are fine for observing the state of a single line but are hard to follow at an overall level, which is precisely what we want to see. Instead, I've condensed the information I collected with OmniLab into an event timeline, shown in Figure 5.1.

The Results

Figure 5.1 shows 170 consecutive 8088 cycles. To the left of the cycle timeline, Figure 5.1 shows the timing of instruction byte transfers from the prefetch queue to the EU. This information was provided by the QS1 and QS0 pins of the 8088. To the right of the cycle timeline Figure 5.1 shows

Execution Unit Activity

Bus Interface Unit Activity

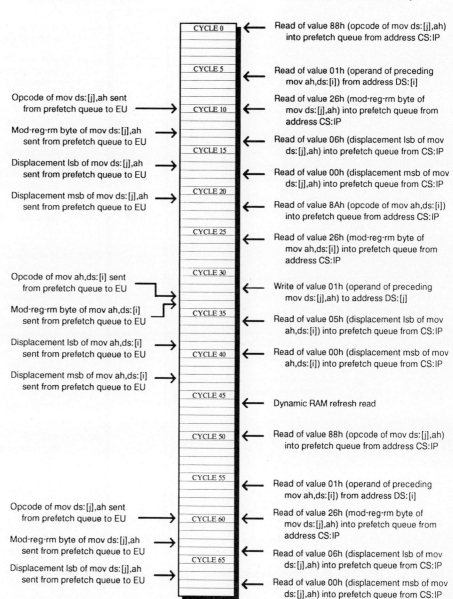

FIGURE 5.1

A timeline showing 170 cycles during the execution of the code in Listing 5-1. This figure illustrates the interleaving of instruction fetches, transfers of instruction bytes to the execution unit, and accesses to memory operands that routinely occurs during the execution of 8088 code. Various cycle eaters cause each of the two instructions (**mov ah,ds:[i]** and **mov ds:[j],ah**) to execute at different speeds at different times. Note that the sequence of events repeats at cycle 144.

Opcode of mov ds:[j],ah sent from prefetch queue to EU

Mod-reg-rm byte of mov ds:[j],ah sent from prefetch queue to EU

Displacement lsb of mov ds:[j],ah sent from prefetch queue to EU

Displacement msb of mov ds:[j],ah sent from prefetch queue to EU

Opcode of mov ah,ds:[i] sent from prefetch queue to EU

Mod-reg-rm byte of mov ah,ds:[i] sent from prefetch queue to EU

Displacement lsb of mov ah,ds:[i] sent from prefetch queue to EU

Displacement msb of mov ah,ds:[i] sent from prefetch queue to EU

Opcode of mov ds:[j],ah sent from prefetch queue to EU

Mod-reg-rm byte of mov ds:[j],ah sent from prefetch queue to EU

Displacement lsb of mov ds:[j],ah sent from prefetch queue to EU

CYCLE 0
CYCLE 5
CYCLE 10
CYCLE 15
CYCLE 20
CYCLE 25
CYCLE 30
CYCLE 35
CYCLE 40
CYCLE 45
CYCLE 50
CYCLE 55
CYCLE 60
CYCLE 65

Read of value 88h (opcode of mov ds:[j],ah) into prefetch queue from address CS:IP

Read of value 01h (operand of preceding mov ah,ds:[i]) from address DS:[i]

Read of value 26h (mod-reg-rm byte of mov ds:[j],ah) into prefetch queue from address CS:IP

Read of value 06h (displacement lsb of mov ds:[j],ah) into prefetch queue from address CS:IP

Read of value 00h (displacement msb of mov ds:[j],ah) into prefetch queue from address CS:IP

Read of value 8Ah (opcode of mov ah,ds:[i]) into prefetch queue from address CS:IP

Read of value 26h (mod-reg-rm byte of mov ah,ds:[i]) into prefetch queue from address CS:IP

Write of value 01h (operand of preceding mov ds:[j],ah) to address DS:[j]

Read of value 05h (displacement lsb of mov ah,ds:[i]) into prefetch queue from CS:IP

Read of value 00h (displacement msb of mov ah,ds:[i]) into prefetch queue from CS:IP

Dynamic RAM refresh read

Read of value 88h (opcode of mov ds:[j],ah) into prefetch queue from address CS:IP

Read of value 01h (operand of preceding mov ah,ds:[i]) from address DS:[i]

Read of value 26h (mod-reg-rm byte of mov ds:[j],ah) into prefetch queue from address CS:IP

Read of value 06h (displacement lsb of mov ds:[j],ah) into prefetch queue from CS:IP

Read of value 00h (displacement msb of mov ds:[j],ah) into prefetch queue from CS:IP

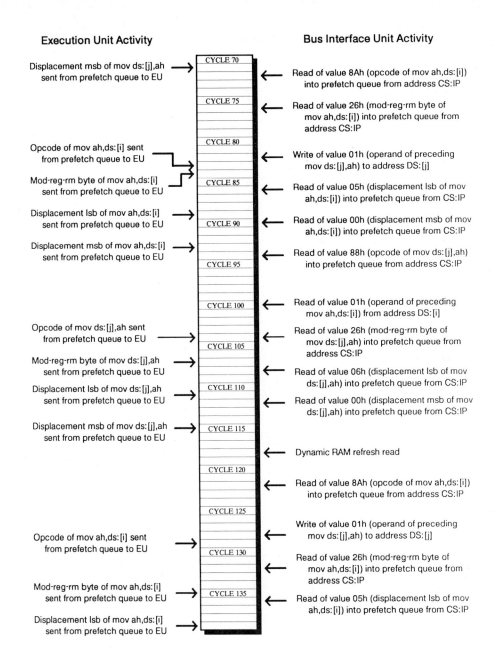

FIGURE 5.1   (*Continued*)

Execution Unit Activity

Bus Interface Unit Activity

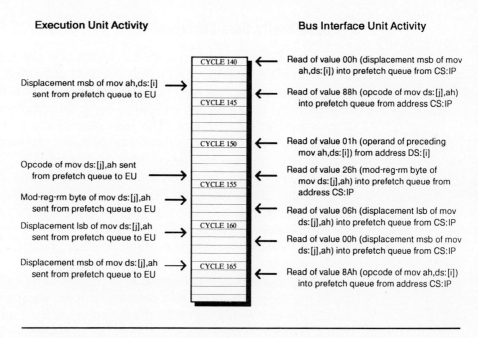

Displacement msb of mov ah,ds:[i]
sent from prefetch queue to EU →

Read of value 00h (displacement msb of mov
ah,ds:[i]) into prefetch queue from CS:IP

← Read of value 88h (opcode of mov ds:[j],ah)
into prefetch queue from address CS:IP

← Read of value 01h (operand of preceding
mov ah,ds:[i] from address DS:[i]

Opcode of mov ds:[j],ah sent
from prefetch queue to EU →

← Read of value 26h (mod-reg-rm byte of
mov ds:[j],ah) into prefetch queue from
address CS:IP

Mod-reg-rm byte of mov ds:[j],ah
sent from prefetch queue to EU →

← Read of value 06h (displacement lsb of mov
ds:[j],ah) into prefetch queue from CS:IP

Displacement lsb of mov ds:[j],ah
sent from prefetch queue to EU →

← Read of value 00h (displacement msb of mov
ds:[j],ah) into prefetch queue from CS:IP

Displacement msb of mov ds:[j],ah →
sent from prefetch queue to EU

← Read of value 8Ah (opcode of mov ah,ds:[i])
into prefetch queue from address CS:IP

CYCLE 140
CYCLE 145
CYCLE 150
CYCLE 155
CYCLE 160
CYCLE 165

FIGURE 5.1   (*Continued*)

the timing of bus read and write accesses. The timing of these accesses was provided by the /MEMR and /MEMW lines of the PC bus, and the data and addresses were provided by the address/data lines of the 8088. One note for the technically oriented: since bus accesses take 4 cycles from start to finish, I considered the read and write accesses to complete on the last cycle during which /MEMR or /MEMW was active.

Take a minute to look over Figure 5.1 before we begin our discussion. Bear in mind that Figure 5.1 is actually a simplified, condensed version of the information that actually appeared on the 8088's pins. In other words, if you choose to analyze cycle-by-cycle performance yourself, the data will be considerably *harder* to interpret than Figure 5.1!

Code Execution Isn't All That Exciting

The first thing that surely strikes you about Figure 5.1 is that it's awfully tedious, even by assembler standards. During the entire course of the figure only seven instructions are executed—not much to show for all the events listed. The monotony of picking apart code execution is one reason why such a detailed level of understanding of code performance isn't desirable.

The 8088 Really Does Coprocess

The next notable aspect of Figure 5.1 is that you can truly see the two parts of the 8088—the EU and the bus interface unit (BIU)—coprocessing. The left side of the timeline shows the times at which the EU receives instruction bytes to execute, indicating the commencement and continuation of instruction execution. The right side of the timeline shows the times at which the BIU reads or writes bytes from or to memory, indicating instruction fetches and accesses to memory operands.

The two sides of the timeline overlap considerably. For example, at cycle 10 the EU receives the opcode byte of **mov ds:[j],ah** from the prefetch queue at the same time that the BIU prefetches the *mod-reg-rm* byte for the same instruction. (We'll discuss *mod-reg-rm* bytes in detail in Chapter 7.) Clearly, the two parts of the 8088 are processing independently during cycle 10.

The EU and BIU aren't always able to process independently, however. The EU spends a considerable amount of time waiting for the BIU to provide the next instruction byte, thanks to the prefetch queue cycle eater. This is apparent during cycles 129 through 135, where the EU must wait 6 cycles for the *mod-reg-rm* byte of **mov ah,ds:[i]** to arrive. Back at cycle 84, the EU only had to wait 1 cycle for the same byte to arrive. Why the difference?

The difference is the result of the DRAM refresh that occurred at cycle 118, preempting the bus and delaying prefetching so that the *mod-reg-rm* byte of **mov ah,ds:[i]** wasn't available until cycle 135. What's particularly interesting is that this variation occurs even though the sequence of instructions is exactly the same at cycle 83 as at cycle 129. In this case, it's the DRAM refresh cycle eater that causes identical instructions in identical code sequences to execute at different speeds. Another time, it might be the display adapter cycle eater that causes the variation, or the prefetch queue cycle eater, or a combination of the three. This is an important lesson in the true nature of code execution: *the same instruction sequence may execute at different speeds at different times.*

When Does an Instruction Execute?

One somewhat startling aspect of Figure 5.1 is that it makes it clear that there is no such thing as the time interval during which a given instruction—and only that instruction—executes. There is the time at which a given byte of an instruction is prefetched, there is a time at which a given byte of an instruction is sent to the EU, and there is a time at which each memory operand byte of an instruction is accessed. None of those times really marks the start or end of an instruction, though, and the instruction fetches and memory accesses of one instruction usually overlap with those of other instructions. Figure 5.2 illustrates the full range of action of each of the instructions in Figure 5.1. (In Figure 5.2, and in Figure 5.3 as well, the two sides of the timeline are equivalent; there is no specific meaning to text on, say, the left side as there is in Figure 5.1. I simply alternate sides in order to keep one instruction from running into the next.)

For example, at cycle 143 the last instruction byte of **mov ah,ds:[i]** is sent to the EU. At cycle 144 the opcode of the next instruction, **mov ds:[j],ah**, is prefetched. Not until cycle 150 is the operand of **mov ah,ds:[i]** read, and not until cycle 154 is the opcode byte of **mov ds:[j],ah** sent to the EU. Which instruction is executing between cycles 143 and 154?

It's easiest to consider execution to start when the opcode byte of an instruction is sent to the EU and to end when the opcode byte of the next instruction is sent, as shown in Figure 5.3. Under this approach, the current instruction is charged with any instruction fetch time for the opcode byte of the next instruction that isn't overlapped with EU execution of the current instruction. This is consistent with our conclusion in Chapter 4 that execution time is, practically speaking, EU execution time plus any instruction fetch time that's not overlapped with the EU execution time of another instruction. Therefore, **mov ah,ds:[i]** executes during cycles 129 through 153.

In truth, though, the first hint of **mov ah,ds:[i]** occurs at cycle 122, when the opcode byte is fetched. In fact, since read accesses to memory take 4 cycles, the 8088 must have begun fetching the opcode byte earlier still. Figure 5.2 assumes that the 8088 starts bus accesses 2 cycles before the cycle during which /MEMR or /MEMW becomes inactive. That assumption may be off by a cycle, but none of our conclusions would be altered if that were the case. Consequently, the instruction **mov ah,ds:[i]** occupies the attention of at least some part of the 8088 from around cycle 120 up through cycle 153, or 34 cycles, as shown in Figure 5.2.

Figure 5.3 shows that **mov ah,ds:[i]** doesn't take 34 cycles to execute, however. The instruction fetching that occurs during cycles 120 through 128 is overlapped with the execution of the preceding instruction, so those cycles aren't counted against the execution time of **mov ah,ds:[i]**. The instruction does take 25 cycles to execute, though, illustrating the power of the cycle eaters: according to Appendix A, **mov ah,ds:[i]** should execute in 14 cycles, so just two of the cycle eaters, the prefetch queue and DRAM refresh, have nearly doubled the actual execution time of the instruction in this context.

FIGURE 5.2

An illustration of the overlap of instruction execution in the 8088. This figure summarizes the information in Figure 5.1 to show the period of time during which each instruction occupies the attention of at least some part of the 8088 by involvement in instruction fetching, execution, or access to a memory operand. It's inappropriate to count the full time shown for an instruction as that instruction's execution time; times during which instructions overlap should be charged to only one instruction, because the 8088 increases overall performance at those times by coprocessing. Note that bus accesses are assumed to start 2 cycles before the cycle after which the /MEMR or /MEMW line becomes inactive, since bus cycles take 4 cycles in all. As a result, the bus access start times shown may be off by a cycle, but the implications of this figure remain the same regardless.

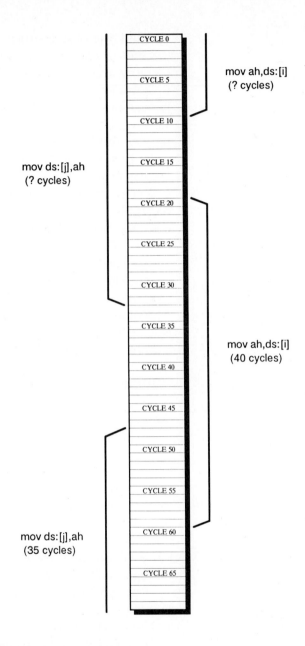

mov ah,ds:[i]
(? cycles)

mov ds:[j],ah
(? cycles)

mov ah,ds:[i]
(40 cycles)

mov ds:[j],ah
(35 cycles)

5.3 ◆ The True Nature of Instruction Execution

Figure 5.1 makes it perfectly clear that at the lowest level code execution is really nothing more than two parallel chains of execution, one taking place in the EU and one taking place in the BIU. What's more, the BIU

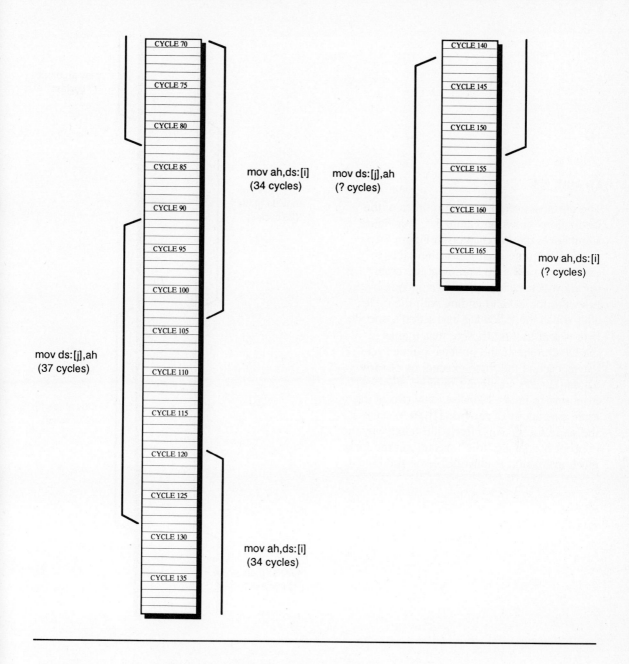

CYCLE 70
CYCLE 75
CYCLE 80
CYCLE 85
CYCLE 90
CYCLE 95
CYCLE 100
CYCLE 105
CYCLE 110
CYCLE 115
CYCLE 120
CYCLE 125
CYCLE 130
CYCLE 135

CYCLE 140
CYCLE 145
CYCLE 150
CYCLE 155
CYCLE 160
CYCLE 165

mov ah,ds:[i]
(34 cycles)

mov ds:[j],ah
(? cycles)

mov ah,ds:[i]
(? cycles)

mov ds:[j],ah
(37 cycles)

mov ah,ds:[i]
(34 cycles)

interleaves instruction fetches for one instruction with memory operand accesses for another instruction. Thus, instruction execution really consists of three interleaved streams of events.

Unfortunately, assembler itself tests the limits of human comprehension of processor actions. Thinking in terms of the interleaved streams of

FIGURE 5.3

The effective overall execution times of the instructions shown in Figure 5.1. This figure summarizes the information in Figure 5.1 to show the time each instruction takes to execute, as measured starting at the cycle during which each instruction's opcode byte is sent to the EU and ending with the cycle after which the following instruction's opcode byte is sent to the EU. Note that, thanks to the DRAM refresh and prefetch queue cycle eaters, each of the three executions of **mov ah,ds:[i]** takes a different number of cycles from start to finish. Likewise, only two of the three executions of **mov ds:[j],ah** execute at the same speed. This clearly illustrates why the concept of a single "true" execution time for a given instruction is unworkable on the PC.

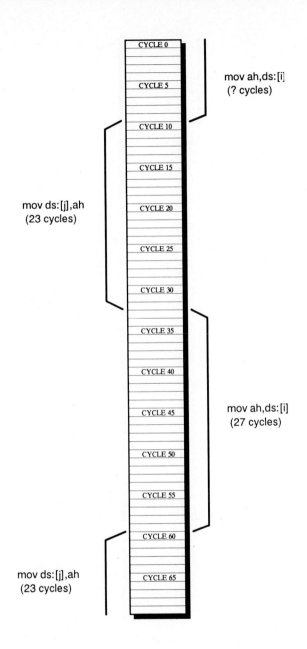

events shown in Figure 5.1 is too much for any mere mortal. It's ridiculous to expect that an assembler programmer could visualize interleaved instruction fetches, EU execution, and memory operand fetches as he writes code, and in fact no one even tries to do so.

And that is yet another reason why an understanding of code performance at the level shown in Figure 5.1 isn't desirable.

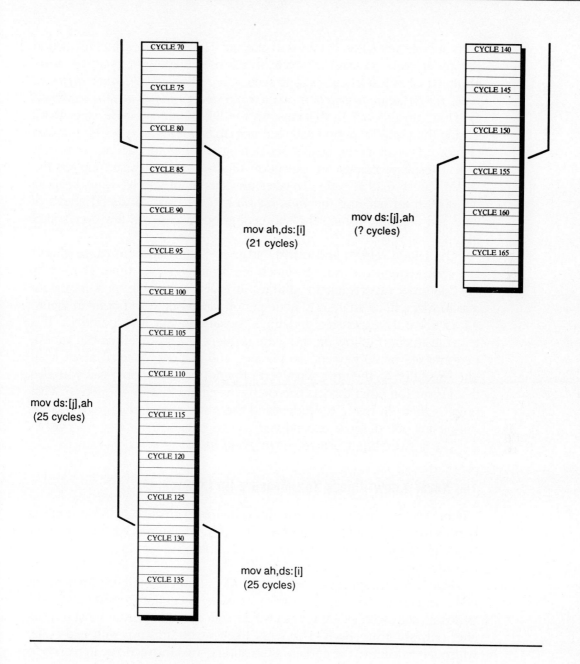

Variability

This brings us to an excellent illustration of the variability of performance, even for the same instruction in the same code sequence executing at different times. As we just discovered, the **mov ah,ds:[i]** instruction that starts at cycle 129 takes 25 cycles to execute. However, the same instruction starting at cycle 33 takes 27 cycle to execute. Starting at cycle 83, **mov ah,ds:[i]** takes just 21 cycles to execute. *That's three significantly different times for the same instruction executing in the same instruction sequence!*

How can this be? In this case it's the DRAM refresh cycle eater that's stirring things up by periodically holding up 8088 bus accesses for 4 cycles or more. This alters the 8088's prefetching and memory access sequence, with a resultant change in execution time. As we discussed earlier, the DRAM refresh read at cycle 118 takes up valuable bus access time, keeping the 8088 from fetching the *mod-reg-rm* byte of **mov ah,ds:[i]** ahead of time and thereby pushing the succeeding bus accesses a few cycles later in time.

The DRAM refresh and display adapter cycle eaters can cause almost any code sequence to vary in much the same way over time. That's why the Zen timer reports fractional times. It is also the single most important reason why a microanalysis of code performance of the sort done in Figure 5.1 is not only expensive and time consuming but also pointless. If a given instruction following the same sequence of instructions can vary in performance by 20 percent, 50 percent, 100 percent, or even more from one execution to the next, what sort of performance number can you give that instruction other than as part of the overall instruction sequence? What point is there in trying to understand the instruction's exact performance during any one of those executions?

The answer, briefly stated, is: *no point at all.*

You Never Know Unless You Measure (in Context!)

I hope I've convinced you that the actual performance of 8088 code is best viewed as the interaction of many highly variable forces, the net result of which is measurable but hardly predictable. But just in case I haven't, consider this...

Figure 5.1 illustrates the execution of one of the simplest imaginable code sequences. The exact pattern of code execution repeats after 144 cycles, so even with DRAM refresh we have an execution pattern that repeats after only six instructions. That's not likely to be the case with real code, which rarely features the endless alternation of two instructions. In real code the code mix changes endlessly, so DRAM refresh and the prefetch queue cycle eater normally result in a far greater variety of execution sequences than in Figure 5.1.

Also, only two of the four cycle eaters are active in Figure 5.1. Since Listing 5-1 uses no word-sized operands, the 8-bit bus cycle eater has no effect other than to slow instruction prefetching. Likewise, Listing 5-1 doesn't access display memory, so the display adapter cycle eater doesn't affect performance. Imagine if we threw those cycle eaters into Figure 5.1 as well!

Worse still, in the real world interrupts occur often and asynchronously, flushing the prefetch queue and often changing the fetching, execution, and memory operand access patterns of whatever code happens to be running. Most notable among these interrupts is the timer interrupt, which occurs every 54.9 msec. Because the timer interrupt may occur after any instruction and doesn't always take the same amount of time, it can cause execution to settle into new patterns. For example, after I captured the sequence shown in Figure 5.1 I took another snapshot of the execution of Listing 5-1. *The second snapshot did not match the first.* The timer interrupt had kicked execution into a different pattern, in which the same instructions were executed, with the same results—but not at exactly the same speeds.

Other interrupts, such as those from keyboards, mice, and serial ports, can similarly alter program performance. Of course, interrupts and cycle eaters don't change the *effects* of code—**add ax,1** always adds 1 to AX, and so on—but they can drastically change the performance of a given instruction in a given context. That's why we focus on the overall performance of code sequences in context, as measured with the Zen timer, rather than on the execution times of individual instructions.

The Longer, the Better

Now is a good time to point out that the longer the instruction sequence you measure, the less variability you'll normally get from one execution to the next. Over time, the perturbations caused by the DRAM refresh cycle eater tend to average out, since DRAM refresh occurs on a regular basis. Similarly, a lengthy code sequence that accesses display memory multiple times will tend to suffer a fairly consistent loss of performance to the display adapter cycle eater. By contrast, a short code sequence that accesses display memory just once may vary greatly in performance from one run to the next, depending on how many wait states occur on the one access during a given run.

In short, you should time either long code sequences or repeated executions of shorter code sequences. While there's no strict definition of "long" in this context, the effects of the DRAM refresh and display adapter cycle eaters should largely even out in sequences longer than about 100 μsec. While you can certainly use the Zen timer to measure shorter intervals, you should take multiple readings in such cases, to make sure that the variations the cycle eaters can cause from one run to the next aren't skewing your readings.

Odds and Ends

There are a few more interesting observations to be made about Figure 5.1. For one thing, we can clearly see that while bus accesses are sometimes farther apart than 4 cycles, they are never any closer together. This confirms our earlier observation that bus cycles take a minimum of 4 cycles.

On the other hand, instruction bytes can be transferred from the prefetch queue to the EU at a rate of 1 byte per cycle when the EU needs them that quickly. This reinforces the notion that the EU can use up instruction bytes faster than the BIU can fetch them. In fact, we can see the EU waiting for an instruction byte fetch from cycle 130 to cycle 135, as discussed earlier. It's worth noting that after the instruction byte transfer to the EU at cycle 135, the next two instruction byte transfers occur at cycles 139 and 143, each occurring 4 cycles after the previous transfer. That mimics the 4 cycles separating the fetches of those instruction bytes, and that's no coincidence. During these cycles the EU does nothing but wait for the BIU to fetch instruction bytes—the most graphic demonstration yet of the prefetch queue cycle eater.

The prefetch queue cycle eater can be observed in another way in Figure 5.1. A careful reading of Figure 5.1 will make it apparent that the prefetch queue never contains more than 2 bytes at any time. In other words, the prefetch queue not only never fills, it never gets more than 2 bytes ahead of the EU. Moreover, we can see at cycles 33 and 34 that the EU can empty those 2 bytes from the prefetch queue in just 2 cycles. There's no doubt but what the BIU often fights a losing battle in trying to keep the EU supplied with instruction bytes.

5.4 ◆ Back to the Programming Interface

It's not important that you grasp everything in this chapter, so long as you understand that the factors affecting the performance of an instruction in a given context are complex and vary with time. These complex and varied factors make it virtually impossible to know beforehand at what speed code will actually run. They also make it both impractical and pointless to understand exactly—down to the cycle—why a particular instruction or code sequence performs as well or as poorly as it does.

As a result, high-performance assembler programming must be an intuitive art, rather than a cut-and-dried cookbook process. That's why this book is called *Zen of Assembly Language,* not *The Assembly Language Programming Reference Guide.* That's also why you *must* time your code if you want to know how fast it is.

Cycle eaters underlie the programming interface, the topic we'll tackle next. Together, cycle eaters and the programming interface constitute the knowledge aspect of the Zen of assembly language. Ultimately, the concept of the flexible mind rests on knowledge, and algorithms and implementation rest on the flexible mind. In short, cycle eaters are the foundation of the Zen of assembler, and as such they will pop up frequently in the following chapters in a variety of contexts. The constant application of our understanding of the various cycle eaters to working code should clear up any uncertainties you may still have about the cycle eaters.

Next, we'll head up out of the land of the cycle eaters to the programming interface, the far more familiar domain of registers, instructions, memory addressing, DOS calls, and the like. After our journey to the land of the cycle eaters, however, don't be surprised if the programming interface looks a little different. Assembler code never looks quite the same to a programmer who understands the true nature of performance.

Chapter 6

◆◆

The 8088

6.1	An Overview
6.2	Resources
6.3	Registers
6.4	The 8088's Register Set
6.5	The General-Purpose Registers
6.6	The Segment Registers
6.7	The Instruction Pointer
6.8	The Flags Register
6.9	There's More to Life Than Registers

The programming interface consists of many elements, including memory, the programmable portions of the PC's hardware, the BIOS, DOS, and the 8088, as we saw in Chapter 3. Although all of those elements are important, it's the 8088 that sets the tone for the IBM PC.

There's certainly more to a PC than an 8088 and some memory. Just ask any of several companies that came out with 8088-based computers that were *almost* IBM compatible, perhaps differing only in the BIOS or the display adapter, and paid dearly for their nonconformity. Nonetheless, 8088 compatibility is the fundamental requirement for any computer that would call itself PC compatible. Other factors—memory, disk space, display technology, and so on—add specific capabilities to the PC, but the PC can never do more than the 8088 is capable of, no matter how powerful the rest of the computer is. For instance, the PC is flat out incapable of addressing more than 1 Mb of memory at one time, because that limitation is inherent in the 8088.

What's more, while the BIOS, DOS, and the programmable aspects of the PC's hardware are well-documented in a variety of books, data sheets, articles, and the like, the 8088 itself is usually described either in cryptic shorthand, as in Appendix A, or in gentle, vague terms for the uninitiated (baby talk, to be blunt). What's lacking in the PC world is a comprehensive and comprehensible discussion of the 8088 from the perspective of writing compact, high-performance code. Consequently, for the remainder of this volume we will focus our efforts primarily on using the resources of the 8088 to create top-notch code.

The 8088 gives us a lot of ground to cover—registers, memory addressing, instructions, and so on—enough to take up the next nine chapters, in fact. You are undoubtedly already familiar with some of the material we'll cover, but you are almost certainly not familiar with *all* of it, and every bit of knowledge about the 8088 helps in generating good assembler code.

While the next nine chapters cover many aspects of the 8088, they are not intended to be either comprehensive or tutorial in nature. You should already know how to program the 8088 in assembly language; at any rate, I'm not going to teach you how to do so in this book. What I *am* going to do is establish a consistent terminology, so you can be sure of what I mean by "direct addressing" or "the *mod-reg-rm* byte"; then we'll discuss the resources of the 8088 in detail, exploring implications for high-performance assembler code as we go.

We'll start this chapter with a quick overview of the 8088, and then we'll begin our exploration of the resources of the 8088 with the register set.

6.1 ◆ An Overview

In a nutshell, the 8088 is a 16-bit processor with an 8-bit data bus, capable of addressing 1 Mb of memory in total but no more than four 64-Kb blocks at any one time, and that via a remarkably awkward segmented memory scheme. The register space is limited, but the instruction set is powerful and flexible, albeit highly irregular. The 4.77-MHz clock speed of the 8088 as implemented in the IBM PC is slow by today's standards, and both instruction execution and memory access are relatively slow as well. What the whole 8088 package as used in the PC amounts to is a fairly low-performance processor that is hard to program.

Why am I saying such unflattering things about the 8088? Because I want you to understand how hard it is to write good 8088 code. As you may have guessed, there is a saving grace to the 8088; as implemented in the PC the 8088 can support just enough performance and memory to run some splendid software—software carefully crafted to work around the 8088's weaknesses and take maximum advantage of its strengths. Those strengths and weaknesses lie hidden in the 8088's instruction set, and we will spend the rest of this book ferreting them out.

Before we begin, you must understand one thing: the 8088 is a hodge-podge of a processor. Not a *random* hodgepodge, mind you—there are good reasons why the 8088 is what it is—but a hodgepodge nonetheless. Internally, the 8088 is a 16-bit processor, thanks to its derivation from the 8086, as discussed in Chapter 3. Externally, the 8088 is an 8-bit processor, owing to its genesis in the 1970s, when the cost difference between 8- and 16-bit buses was significant. The design of the 8086, including the register set and many instructions, was heavily influenced by the 8-bit 8080 processor, as we'll see in Chapter 8. Finally, the memory architecture of the 8088 is a remnant of an era when both chip space and the number of pins per chip were severely limited and memory was extremely expensive. The 8088 is an excellent representative of the transitional state of the microcomputer industry a decade ago: striving for state-of-the-art while maintaining a link with the past, all in too little silicon. From a programmer's perspective, though, the 8088 is simply a bit of a mess.

That certainly doesn't mean the 8088 isn't worth bothering with nowadays, as attested to by 10 million or so 8088-based computers. It does, however, mean that programming the 8088 properly in assembler is not simple, since code that takes maximum advantage of the unique nature of the 8088 is generally much faster than code that uses the processor in a straightforward manner. We must take time to understand the strengths and weaknesses of the 8088 intimately, then learn how to best structure our code in light of that knowledge.

6.2 ◆ Resources

Over the next nine chapters, we'll look at the capabilities and resources of the 8088. We'll learn a great deal about high-performance assembler programming, and we'll also lay the groundwork for the higher level assembler programming techniques of Volume II.

We'll spend the remainder of this chapter looking at the registers and flags of the 8088. In Chapter 7 we'll cover the 8088's memory-addressing capabilities, and in Chapter 8 we'll start to cover the 8088's large and varied instruction set. The resources of the 8088 are both fascinating and essential, for in their infinite permutations and combinations they are your set of tools for creating the best possible code for the IBM PC.

6.3 ◆ Registers

The register set of a processor is a key to understanding the processor's personality, since registers are typically where most of the action in a processor takes place. The 8088's register set is something of a mixed bag. Since the 8088 is a 16-bit processor internally, register-only instructions (instructions without memory operands) tend to be fast and compact, so the registers of the 8088 are one key to fast code. On the other hand, the 8088's registers are no more regular than anything else about the processor. Each register offers unique, specialized (and hard to remember) functions; together, these oddball register functions make up what my friend and editor Jeff Duntemann calls "the register hidden agenda," the not obvious but powerful register capabilities that considerably increase both the difficulty and the potential power of 8088 assembler programming.

Let me give you an example. Many years ago, a friend who had just made the transition from programming the Apple II to programming the IBM PC had a program that crashed every so often for no apparent reason. We spent a good deal of time examining his program before we could isolate the cause of his problems. As it turned out, he was using SP as a working register for short stretches, storing values in it, performing arithmetic with it, and all-in-all using SP as if it were just another general-purpose register.

While SP can theoretically be used as a general-purpose register, in fact it is almost always dedicated to maintaining the stack. My friend's problem was that keyboard and timer interrupts, which use the stack, were occurring while he had SP loaded with values that didn't point to a valid stack, so interrupts were pushing return addresses and flags into random areas of memory. When I asked him how he could possibly have made such an obvious mistake, he explained that his approach would have worked perfectly well on the Apple II, where there are no interrupts.

There are two important points here. One is that by not understanding SP's portion of the register hidden agenda—the role of SP as a stack pointer in an interrupt-driven system—my friend had wasted considerable development time. The second point is that, had he understood the register hidden agenda better, he could have extended his odd approach to generate some genuinely innovative code.

How? Well, SP really *is* a general-purpose register when it's not being used to maintain a stack. My friend's mistake had been his assumption that the stack is inactive when no calls, returns, pushes, or pops are occurring; this assumption is incorrect because interrupts may take place at any time. Suppose, though, that he had simply disabled interrupts for those brief periods when he needed an eighth general-purpose register for speed. Why, then his use of SP would have been not only acceptable but nearly brilliant!

Alas, disabling interrupts and using SP would not have been truly brilliant, for nonmaskable interrupts, used to signal parity errors and used by some display adapters as well, can occur and use the stack even when interrupts are disabled. In general, I recommend that you not use SP as a general-purpose register, even with interrupts disabled. Although the chances of a nonmaskable interrupt occurring are slim, they are nonetheless real.

All of which simply serves to reinforce the notion that the more we know about the 8088, the better our code will be. That's why we'll take the time to review the 8088's registers, even though you may be familiar with much of the material already, and that's why we'll cover the 8088's other resources for most of the rest of this volume. The more thorough your understanding of the 8088, the greater the potential of your assembler code.

6.4 ◆ The 8088's Register Set

Figure 6.1 shows the 8088's register set to be a mix of general- and special-purpose registers. The 8088 offers only seven truly general-purpose

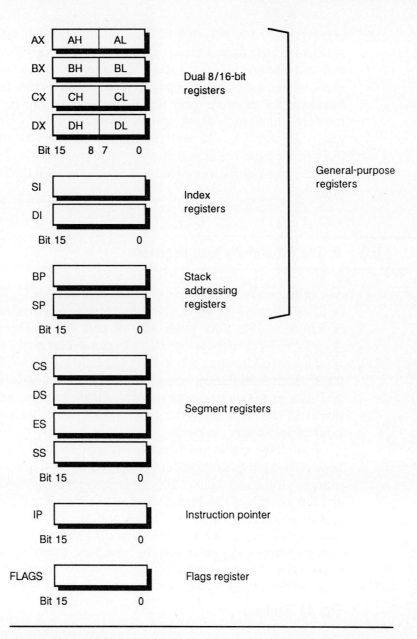

FIGURE 6.1   The 8088's register set

registers—AX, BX, CX, DX, SI, DI, and BP—a small set that seems even smaller because four of these registers double as memory-addressing registers and because the slow speed of memory access dictates use of registers whenever possible. Only certain registers can be used for many functions; for example, only BX, BP, SI, and DI can be used to generate memory-addressing offsets, and then only in certain combinations. Likewise, only AX, BX, CX, and DX can be accessed as either single 16-bit registers or paired 8-bit registers.

Let's take a quick tour of the registers, looking at the unique capabilities of each.

6.5 ◆ The General-Purpose Registers

Any of the eight general-purpose registers—AX, BX, CX, DX, SI, DI, BP, or SP—may serve as an operand to virtually any instruction that accepts operands, such as **add**, **push**, **shl**, or **call**. Put another way, any general-purpose register may be used as an operand by any instruction that uses *mod-reg-rm* addressing, the most commonly-used addressing mode of the 8088, which we'll discuss in the next chapter. Most of the logical, arithmetic, and data movement operations of the 8088 can use any of the general-purpose registers, and it is the general-purpose registers that are most often used as instruction operands.

Four of the eight general-purpose registers—AX, BX, CX, and DX—can be accessed either as paired 8-bit registers or as single 16-bit registers. For example, the upper byte of BX can be accessed as BH for 8-bit operations, and the lower byte can be accessed as BL. The eight 8-bit general-purpose registers—AH, AL, BH, BL, CH, CL, DH, and DL—can be used as 8-bit operands with any instructions that use *mod-reg-rm* addressing, just as the eight 16-bit general-purpose registers can be used as 16-bit operands with those instructions.

The AX Register

The AX register is the 16-bit accumulator. The lower byte of AX can be accessed as the AL register, which is the 8-bit accumulator; the upper byte of AX can be accessed as the AH register, which is not an accumulator of any sort. The accumulator is always both one of the source operands and the destination for multiply and divide instructions. The accumulator must also be the source for **out** instructions and the destination for **in** instructions, and is the source or destination register for the string instructions **lods**, **stos**, and **scas**, as we'll see in Chapter 10. There are special instructions for sign-extending the accumulator to larger data types: **cbw** for converting a signed byte in AL to a signed word in AX, and **cwd** for converting a signed word in AX to a signed doubleword in DX:AX. Finally, there are a number of accumulator-specific instructions that are particularly efficient; we'll discuss those instructions in Chapters 8 and 9.

There are several instructions that use part or all of the AX register in odd ways. In Chapter 7 we'll discuss **xlat**, the only instruction that can use AL for memory addressing. In Chapter 8 we'll discuss **lahf** and **sahf**, which transfer the lower byte of the flags register to and from AH. In Chapter 8 we'll also discuss a special form of **xchg** that requires that AX be one operand. Finally, the decimal- and ASCII-adjust instructions—**aaa**, **aad**, **aam**, **aas**, **daa**, and **das**—alter AL or AX in specific ways to compensate for the effects of ASCII or BCD arithmetic. These instructions are so different from the other members of the 8088 instruction set that we'll defer further discussion of them until Chapter 9.

The BX Register

The BX register is the only register among the dual 8/16-bit registers that can be used for memory addressing (with the sole exception of AL in the case of **xlat**). The lower byte of BX is accessible as BL and the upper byte is accessible as BH; neither BH nor BL alone can be used for memory addressing.

Like the other general-purpose registers, BX (or BH or BL) may serve as an operand to any instruction that uses *mod-reg-rm* addressing. In addition, BX (but not BH or BL) can be used as a base register for memory addressing. That is, the contents of BX can be used to generate the address of a memory operand, as discussed in the next chapter, by any instruction that uses *mod-reg-rm* addressing, and by **xlat** as well.

The CX Register

The CX register is designed for specialized counting purposes. The lower byte of CX is accessible as CL and the upper byte as CH; CL can be used for certain specialized 8-bit counting purposes, but CH cannot. CX is used as a counter by the **loop**, **loopz**, **loopnz**, and **jcxz** instructions, which we'll look at in Chapter 14, and is also used as a counter by the string instructions when they're used with the **rep** prefix, as we'll see in Chapter 10. CL can be used to specify a rotation or shift count for any of the rotate or shift instructions, such as **ror**, **shl**, and **rcl**, as described in Chapter 9.

The DX Register

The DX register is the least specialized of the general-purpose registers; the only unique functions of DX are serving as the upper word of the destination on 16-bit by 16-bit multiplies, serving as the upper word of the source and the destination for the remainder on 32-bit by 16-bit divides, addressing I/O ports when used with **in** and **out**, and serving as the upper word of the destination for **cbw**. The lower byte of DX is accessible as DL, and the upper byte is accessible as DH.

The SI Register

The SI register specializes as the source memory-addressing register for the string instructions **lods** and **movs** and as the destination memory-addressing register for the string instruction **cmps**, as we'll see in Chapter 10.

Like the other general-purpose registers, SI may serve as an operand to any instruction that uses *mod-reg-rm* addressing. In addition, SI can be used as an index register for memory addressing by any instruction that uses *mod-reg-rm* addressing, as we'll see in the next chapter, and, of course, by the above-mentioned string instructions as well.

The DI Register

The DI register specializes as the destination memory-addressing register for the string instructions **stos** and **movs**, and as the source memory-addressing register for the string instructions **scas** and **cmps**, as we'll see in Chapter 10.

Like the other general-purpose registers, DI may serve as an operand to any instruction that uses *mod-reg-rm* addressing. In addition, DI can be used as an index register for memory addressing by any instruction that uses *mod-reg-rm* addressing, as we'll see in the next chapter, and by the above-mentioned string instructions as well.

The BP Register

The BP register specializes as the stack frame-addressing register. Like the other general-purpose registers, BP may serve as an operand to any instruction that uses *mod-reg-rm* addressing. Like BX, BP can also be used as a base register for memory addressing by any instruction that uses *mod-reg-rm* addressing, as discussed in the next chapter. However, while

BX normally addresses the data segment, BP normally addresses the stack segment. This makes BP ideal for addressing parameters and temporary variables stored in stack frames, a topic to which we'll return in the next chapter.

The SP Register

The SP register is technically a general-purpose register, but in actual practice it almost always serves as the highly specialized stack pointer, and is rarely used as a general-purpose register. SP points to the offset of the top of the stack in the stack segment, and is automatically incremented and decremented as the stack is accessed via **push**, **pop**, **call**, **ret**, **int**, and **iret** instructions.

Like the other general-purpose registers, SP may serve as an operand to any instruction that uses *mod-reg-rm* addressing. In general, SP is modified through the above-mentioned stack-oriented instructions, but SP also may be subtracted from, added to, or loaded directly in order to allocate or deallocate a temporary storage block on the stack or switch to a new stack.

One note: never push SP directly, as in

```
push sp
```

The reason is that the 80286 doesn't handle the pushing of SP in quite the same way as the 8088 does; the 80286 pushes SP before decrementing it by 2, whereas the 8088 pushes SP *after* decrementing it. As a result, code that uses **push sp** may not work in the same way on all computers. In normal code you'll rarely need to push SP, but if you do, you can simply pass the value through another register, as in

```
mov     ax,sp
push ax
```

The above sequence will work exactly the same way on any 8086-family processor.

6.6 ◆ The Segment Registers

Each of the four segment registers—CS, DS, ES, and SS—points to the start of a 64-Kb block, or segment, within which certain types of memory accesses may be performed. For instance, the stack must always reside in the segment pointed to by SS. Except as noted, segment registers can only be copied to or loaded from a memory operand, the stack, or a general-purpose register. Segment registers cannot be used as operands to instructions such as **add**, **dec**, or **and**, a property that complicates considerably the handling of blocks of memory larger than 64 Kb.

Since a segment register stores a 16-bit value just as a general-purpose register does, it sometimes becomes tempting to use one of the segment registers (almost always ES or DS, although SS could conceivably be used under certain circumstances) for temporary storage. Be aware, however, that because segment registers take on more specialized meanings in the protected modes of the 80286 and 80386 processors, you should avoid using this technique in code that may at some time need to be ported to protected mode. That doesn't mean you shouldn't use segment registers for temporary storage, as we'll see in the next chapter, just that you should be aware of the possible complications.

We'll discuss segments and segment registers at length in the next chapter; what's coming up next is just a quick glance at the segment registers and their uses.

The CS Register

The CS register points to the code segment, the 64-Kb block within which IP points to the offset of the next instruction byte to be executed. The CS:IP pair cannot *ever* point to the wrong place for even one instruction; if it did, an incorrect instruction byte would be fetched and executed next. Consequently, both CS and IP must be set whenever CS is changed, and the setting of both registers must be accomplished by a single instruction. Although CS can be pushed, copied to memory, or copied to a general-purpose register, it can't be loaded directly from any of those sources. The only instructions that can load CS are the far versions of **jmp**, **call**, and **ret**, as well as **int** and **iret**; what all those instructions have in common is that they load both CS and IP at the same time. Both **int** and the far version of **call** push both CS and IP on the stack so that **iret** or **ret** can return to the instruction following the **int** or **call**.

In addition, segment override prefixes can be used to select CS as the segment accessed by many memory operands that normally access DS.

The DS Register

The DS register points to the data segment, the segment within which most memory operands reside by default. (Note, however, that many memory-addressing instructions can access any of the four segments with the help of a segment override prefix.)

DS can be copied to or loaded from a memory operand, the stack, or a general-purpose register. It can also be loaded, along with any general-purpose register, from a doubleword operand with the **lds** instruction.

The ES Register

The ES register points to the extra segment, the segment within which certain string instruction operands must reside. In addition, segment override prefixes can be used to select ES as the segment accessed by many memory operands that normally access DS.

ES can be copied to or loaded from a memory operand, the stack, or a general-purpose register. ES can also be loaded, along with any general-purpose register, from a doubleword operand with the **les** instruction.

The SS Register

The SS register points to the stack segment, the segment within which SP points to the top of the stack. The instruction **push** stores its operand in the stack segment, and **pop** retrieves its operand from the stack segment. In addition, **call**, **ret**, **int**, and **iret** all access the stack. Memory accesses performed with BP as a base register also default to accessing the stack segment. Finally, segment override prefixes can be used to select SS as the segment accessed by many memory operands that normally access DS.

Although SS can be loaded directly, like DS and ES, you must always remember that SS and SP operate as a pair and together must point to a valid stack whenever stack operations might occur. As discussed above, interrupts can occur at any time, so when you load SS, interrupts *must* be off until both SS and SP have been loaded to point to the new stack. Intel thoughtfully provided a feature designed to take care of such problems. Whenever you load a segment register via **mov** or **pop**, interrupts are automatically disabled until the *following* instruction has finished. For example, in the following code

```
mov   ss,dx
mov   sp,ax
```

interrupts are disabled from the start of the first **mov** until the end of the second. After the second **mov**, interrupts are again enabled or disabled as they were before the first **mov**, depending on the state of the interrupt flag.

Unfortunately, there was a bug in early 8088 chips that caused the automatic interrupt disabling described above to malfunction. Consequently, it's safest to explicitly disable interrupts when loading SS:SP, as follows:

```
cli
mov   ss,dx
mov   sp,ax
sti
```

6.7 ◆ The Instruction Pointer

IP, the instruction pointer, is an internal 8088 register that is not directly accessible as an instruction operand. IP contains the offset in the code segment at which the next instruction to be executed resides. After one instruction is started, IP is normally advanced to point to the next instruction; however, branching instructions, such as **jmp** and **call**, load IP with the offset of the instruction being branched to. The instructions **call** and **int** automatically push IP, allowing **ret** or **iret** to continue execution at the instruction following the **call** or **int**.

As we've discussed, in one sense the instruction pointer points to the next instruction to be *fetched* from memory rather than the next instruction to be executed. This distinction arises because the bus interface unit (BIU) of the 8088 can prefetch several instructions ahead of the instruction being carried out by the execution unit (EU). From the programmer's perspective, though, the instruction pointer always simply points to the next instruction byte to be executed; the 8088 handles all the complications of prefetching internally in order to present us with this consistent programming interface.

6.8 ◆ The Flags Register

The flags register contains the nine bit-sized status flags of the 8088, as shown in Figure 6.2. Six of these flags—CF, PF, AF, ZF, SF, and OF, collectively known as the status flags—reflect the status of logical and arithmetic operations; two—IF and DF—control aspects of the 8088's operation; and one—TF—is used only by debugging software.

The flags are generally tested singly (or occasionally in pairs or even three at a time, as when testing signed operands); however, many arithmetic

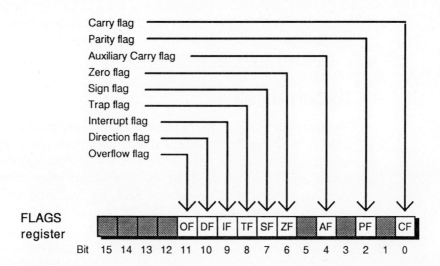

FIGURE 6.2   The 8088's flags

and logical instructions set all six status flags to indicate result statuses, and a few instructions work directly with all or half of the flags register at once. For example, **pushf** pushes the flags register onto the stack, and **popf** pops the word on top of the stack into the flags register. (We'll encounter an interesting complication with **popf** on the 80286 in Chapter 15.) In Chapter 8 we'll discuss **lahf** and **sahf**, which copy the lower byte of the flags register to and from the AH register. Interrupts, both software (via **int**) and hardware (via the INTR pin), push the flags register on the stack, followed by CS and IP; **iret** reverses the action of an interrupt, popping the three words on top of the stack into IP, CS, and the flags register.

One more note: bear in mind that the six status flags are not set by every instruction. On some processors the status flags always reflect the contents of the accumulator, but not so with the 8088, where only specific instructions affect specific flags. For example, **inc** affects all the status flags *except* the carry flag; although that can be a nuisance, it can also be used to good advantage in summing multi-word memory operands, as we'll see in Chapter 9.

Along the same line, some instructions, such as division, leave some or all of the status flags in undefined states; that is, the flags are changed, but there is no guarantee as to what values they are changed to. Because **mov** and most branching instructions don't affect the status flags at all, you can, if you're clever, carry the result of an operation along for several instructions, a technique we'll look at in Chapter 9.

Let's briefly examine each flag.

The Carry Flag (CF)

The carry flag (CF for short) is set to 1 by additions that result in sums too large to fit in the destination and by subtractions that result in differences less than 0, and is set to 0 by arithmetic and logical operations that produce results small enough to fit in the destination when viewed as unsigned integers. (The logical operations **and**, **or**, and **xor** always set CF to 0, since they always produce results that fit in the destination.) Also, when a shift or rotate instruction shifts a bit out of an operand's most significant bit (msb) or least significant bit (lsb), that bit is transferred to CF. As a special case, both the carry and overflow flags are set to 1 by multiplication, except when the result is small enough to fit in the lower half of the destination (considered as a signed number for **imul** and as an unsigned number for **mul**).

The primary purpose of CF is to support addition, subtraction, rotation, and shifting of multi-byte or multi-word operands. In these applications, CF conveys the msb or lsb of one 8- or 16-bit operation to the next operation, as for example in the 32-bit right shift

```
shr   dx,1      ;shift upper 16 bits
rcr   ax,1      ;shift lower 16 bits, including the bit
              ; shifted down from the upper 16 bits
```

Note that this makes CF the only flag that can participate directly in arithmetic operations.

CF can also be tested with the **jc** (which can be thought of as standing for "jump carry") and **jnc** ("jump no carry") conditional jump instructions. The instruction **jc** is also known as both **jb** ("jump below") and **jnae** ("jump not above or equal"). All three instructions assemble to the same machine code. Likewise, **jnc** is also known as both **jae** ("jump above or equal") and **jnb** ("jump not below"). The carry and zero flags together can be tested with **ja** and **jbe**. **ja** is also known as **jnbe** ("jump not below or equal"), and **jbe** is also known as **jna** ("jump not above"). These conditional jumps are often used to determine unsigned greater than/less than/equal relationships between operands.

Alone among the six status flags, CF can be set, reset, and toggled directly, with the **clc** ("clear carry"), **stc** ("set carry"), and **cmc** ("complement carry") instructions. This can be useful for returning a status from a subroutine, or for modifying the action of **adc**, **sbb**, **rcl**, or any other instruction that includes CF in its calculations.

Note that CF is *not* affected by **inc** or **dec**, although it is affected by **add** and **sub**. (We'll see one use for this trait of **inc** and **dec** in Chapter 9.) Also, be aware that since **neg** is logically equivalent to subtracting an operand from 0, CF is always set by **neg**, except when the operand is 0. (Zero minus anything other than zero always causes borrow).

The Parity Flag (PF)

The parity flag (PF for short) is set to 1 whenever the least significant byte of the result of an arithmetic or logical operation contains an even number of bits that are set to 1, and it is set to 0 whenever the least significant byte contains an odd number of bits that are 1.

PF can be tested only with the **jp** ("jump parity") and **jnp** ("jump no parity") conditional jump instructions. The instruction **jp** is also known as **jpe** ("jump parity even"), and **jnp** is also known as **jpo** ("jump parity odd"). Generally, PF is useful for generating and testing parity bits for data storage and transmission. Apart from that, I know of no good uses for PF, although such uses may well exist.

The Auxiliary Carry Flag (AF)

The auxiliary carry flag (AF for short) is set to 1 if an arithmetic or logical operation results in carry out of bit 3 of the destination and is set to 0 otherwise. Alone among the six status flags, AF cannot be tested by any conditional jump instruction. In fact, the only instructions that pay any attention at all to AF are **aaa**, **aas**, **daa**, and **das**, which use AF to help sort out the results of ASCII or BCD arithmetic. Apart from ASCII and BCD arithmetic, which we'll discuss in Chapter 9, I've never found a use for AF.

The Zero Flag (ZF)

The zero flag (ZF for short) is set to 1 if an arithmetic or logical operation produces a 0 result, or to 0 otherwise. ZF is generally used to test for equality of two operands or for zero results via the **jz** ("jump zero") and **jnz** ("jump not zero") conditional jumps, also known as **je** ("jump equal") and **jne** ("jump not equal"), respectively. As discussed above, ZF and CF can be tested together with a variety of conditional jumps. The zero, sign, and overflow flags together can be tested with **jg** ("jump greater"), also known as **jnle** ("jump not less or equal") and with **jle**, also known as **jng** ("jump not greater"). These conditional jumps are often used to determine signed greater than/less than/equal relationships between operands.

The Sign Flag (SF)

The sign flag (SF for short) is set to the state of the most significant bit of the result of an arithmetic or logical operation. For signed arithmetic, the most significant bit is the sign of the operand, so an SF setting of 1 indicates a negative result.

SF is generally used to test for negative results via the **js** ("jump sign") and **jns** ("jump no sign") conditional jumps. As discussed above, the sign, zero, and overflow flags together can be tested with **jg** and **jle**. The sign and overflow flags together can be tested with **jl** ("jump less") and **jge** ("jump greater or equal"). The instruction **jl** is also known as **jnge** ("jump not greater or equal") and **jge** is also known as **jnl** ("jump not less").

The Overflow Flag (OF)

The overflow flag (OF for short) is set to 1 if the carry into the most significant bit of the result of an operation and the carry out of that bit don't match. Overflow indicates that the result, interpreted as a signed result, is too large to fit in the destination and is therefore not a valid signed result of the operation. (It may still be a valid unsigned result, however; CF is used to detect too large and too small unsigned results.) In short, OF is set to 1 if the result has overflowed (grown too large for) the destination in terms of signed arithmetic. I know of no use for OF other than in signed arithmetic. The logical operations **and**, **or**, and **xor** always set OF to 0.

OF can be tested in any of several ways. The **jo** ("jump overflow") and **jno** ("jump no overflow") instructions branch or don't branch depending on the state of OF. As described above, the **jl**, **jnl**, **jle**, **jnle**, **jg**, **jng**, **jge**, and **jnge** instructions branch or don't branch depending on the states of OF, SF, and sometimes ZF. Finally, the **into** instruction executes an **int 4** if and only if OF is set.

The Interrupt Flag (IF)

The interrupt flag (IF for short) enables and disables maskable hardware interrupts. When IF is 1, all hardware interrupts are recognized by the 8088. When IF is 0, maskable interrupts (that is, those interrupts signalled on the INTR pin) are not recognized until such time as IF is set to 1. (Nonmaskable interrupts—interrupts signalled on the NMI pin—are recognized by the 8088 regardless of the setting of IF, as are software interrupts, which are invoked with the **int** instruction.) IF is set to 1 (enabling interrupts) with **sti** and is set to 0 (disabling interrupts) with **cli**. IF is also automatically set to 0 when a hardware interrupt occurs or an **int** instruction is executed. In addition, as described in the discussion of the SS register above, interrupts are automatically disabled until the end of the following instruction whenever a segment register is loaded.

The PC is an interrupt-based computer, so interrupts should in general be disabled as infrequently and for as short a time as possible. System resources such as the keyboard and time-of-day clock are interrupt based and won't function properly if interrupts are off for too long. You really only need to disable interrupts in code that could malfunction if it is interrupted, such as code that services time-sensitive hardware or code that uses multiple prefix bytes per instruction. (The latter, as discussed in Chapter 10, should be avoided whenever possible.)

Leave interrupts enabled at all other times.

The Direction Flag (DF)

The direction flag (DF for short) controls the direction in which the pointer registers used by the string instructions (SI and DI) count. When DF is 1 (as set with **std**), string instruction pointer registers decrement after each memory access; when DF is 0 (as set with **cld**), string instruction pointer registers increment. We'll discuss the direction flag in detail when we cover the string instructions in Chapter 10.

The Trap Flag (TF)

The trap flag (TF for short) instructs the 8088 to execute a software interrupt 1 after the next instruction. This is specifically intended to allow debugging software to single-step through code; it has no other known use.

6.9 ◆ There's More to Life Than Registers

The register set is just one aspect of the 8088, albeit an important aspect indeed. The other key features of the 8088 are memory addressing, which expands the 8088's working data set from the few bytes that can be stored in the registers to the million bytes that can be stored in memory, and the instruction set, which allows manipulation of registers and memory locations and provides program flow control (branching and decision making) as well. We'll look at memory addressing next, then move on to the limitless possibilities of the instruction set.

Chapter 7

◆◆

Memory Addressing

7.1	Definitions
7.2	The Memory Architecture of the 8088
7.3	Segments and Offsets
7.4	Segment Handling
7.5	Offset Handling
7.6	*mod-reg-rm* Addressing
7.7	Non–*mod-reg-rm* Memory Addressing
7.8	Initializing Memory
7.9	A Brief Note on I/O Addressing

The 8088's registers are very powerful, and critically important to writing high-performance code—but there are scarcely a dozen of them, and they certainly can't do the job by themselves. We need more than seven—or 70, or 700, or even 7000—general-purpose storage locations. We need storage that's capable of storing characters, numbers, and instruction bytes in great quantities (remember that instruction bytes are just another sort of data)—and, of course, that's just what we get by way of the 1 megabyte of memory that the 8088 supports.

(The PC has only 640 Kb of system RAM, but nonetheless supports a full megabyte of addressable memory. The memory above the 640-K mark is occupied by display memory and by BIOS code stored in ROM (*read only memory*); this memory can always be read from and can, in some cases—display memory, for example—be written to as well.)

Not only does the 8088 support 1 Mb of memory, but it also provides many powerful and flexible ways to get at that memory. We'll skim through the many memory-addressing modes and instructions quickly, but we're not going to spend a great deal of time on their basic operation.

Why not spend more time describing the memory-addressing modes and instructions? One reason is that I've assumed throughout *Zen of Assembly Language* that you're at least passingly familiar with assembler, thereby avoiding a lot of rehashing and explaining—and memory addressing is fundamental to almost any sort of assembler programming. If you really don't know the basic memory-addressing modes, a refresher on assembler in general might be in order before you continue with *Zen of Assembly Language*.

The other reason for not spending much time on the operation of the memory-addressing modes is that we have another—and sadly neglected—aspect of memory addressing to discuss: performance.

You see, while the 8088 lets you address a great deal of memory, it isn't particularly fast at accessing all that memory. This is especially true when it deals with blocks of memory larger than 64 Kb, but is *always* true to some extent. Memory-accessing instructions are often very long and are always very slow.

Worse, many people don't seem to understand the sharp distinction between memory and registers. Some "experts" would have you view memory locations as extensions of your register set. With this sort of thinking, the instructions

```
mov    dx,ax
```

and

```
mov    dx,MemVar
```

are logically equivalent. Well, the instructions *are* logically equivalent in the sense that they both move data into DX—but they're polar opposites when it comes to performance. The register-only **mov** is half the length in bytes and anywhere from two to seven times faster than the **mov** from memory, and that's fairly typical of the differences between register-only and memory-addressing instructions.

So you see, saying that memory is logically equivalent to registers is something like saying that a bus is logically equivalent to a 747. Sure, you can buy a ticket to get from one place to another with either mode of transportation . . . but which would *you* rather cross the country in?

As we'll see in this chapter, and, indeed, throughout the rest of *Zen of Assembly Language,* one key to optimizing 8088 code is using the registers heavily while avoiding memory whenever you can. Pick your spots for such optimizations carefully, though. Optimize instructions in tight loops and in time-critical code, but let initialization and setup code slide; it's just not worth the time and effort required to optimize code that doesn't much affect overall performance or response time.

Slow and lengthy as memory-accessing instructions are, you're going to end up using them a great deal in your code. (Just try to write a useful program that doesn't access memory!) In light of that, we're going to review the memory-addressing architecture and modes of the 8088 and then look at the performance implications of accessing memory. We'll see why memory accesses are slow, and we'll see that not all memory-addressing modes or memory-addressing instructions are created equal in terms of size and performance. (In truth, the differences between the various memory-addressing modes and instructions are just about as great as those between register-only and memory-accessing instructions.) Along the way, we'll come across a number of useful techniques for writing high-performance code for the PC, most notably look-up tables. By the end of this chapter, we'll be ready to dive into the instruction set in a big way.

We've got a lot of ground to cover, so let's get started.

7.1 ◆ Definitions

I'm going to take a moment to define some terms I'll use in this chapter to describe operands to various instructions; for example, **mov ax,*segreg*** refers to copying the contents of a segment register into AX.

reg refers to any 8- or 16-bit general-purpose register; *reg8* refers to any 8-bit (byte-sized) general-purpose register; and *reg16* refers to any 16-bit (word-sized) general-purpose register.

segreg refers to any segment register.

mem refers to any 8-, 16-, or 32-bit memory operand: *mem8* refers to any byte-sized memory operand; *mem16* refers to any word-sized memory operand; and *mem32* refers to any doubleword–sized memory operand.

reg/mem refers to any 8- or 16-bit register or memory operand. As you'd expect, *reg/mem8* refers to any byte-sized register or memory operand, and *reg/mem16* refers to any word-sized register or memory operand.

immed refers to any immediate (constant) instruction operand. (Immediate addressing is discussed in detail below.) *immed8* refers to any byte-sized immediate operand, and *immed16* refers to any word-sized immediate operand.

Square Brackets Mean Memory Addressing

The use of square brackets is optional when a memory location is being addressed by name. That is, the following two instructions assemble to exactly the same code:

```
mov     dx,MemVar
mov     dx,[MemVar]
```

However, addressing memory without square brackets is an extension of the "memory and registers are logically equivalent" mindset. I strongly recommend that you use square brackets on all memory references in order to keep the distinction between memory and registers clear in your mind. This practice also helps distinguish between immediate and memory operands.

7.2 ◆ The Memory Architecture of the 8088

The ability to address 1 Mb of memory, while unimpressive by today's standards, was quite remarkable when the PC was first introduced, 64 Kb then being standard for "serious" microcomputers. In fact, it could be argued that the 8088's 1-Mb address space is the single factor most responsible for the success of the IBM PC and for the exceptional software that quickly became available for it. Realistically, the letters IBM were probably more important, but all that memory didn't hurt; quantities of memory make new sorts of software possible, and can often compensate for limited processor power in the form of look-up tables, RAM disks, data caching, and in-line code. All in all, the PC's then-large memory capacity made possible a quantum leap in software quality.

On the other hand, the 8088 actually addresses all that memory in what is perhaps the most awkward manner ever conceived—by addressing 64-Kb blocks off each of the four segment registers. This scheme means that programs must perform complex and time-consuming calculations in order to access the full 1 Mb of memory in a general way. One of the ways in which assembler programs can outstrip compiled programs is by cleverly structuring code and data so that sequential memory accesses generally involve only memory within the four segments that are addressable at any one time, thereby avoiding the considerable overhead associated with calculating full addresses and frequently reloading the segment registers.

In short, the 8088's memory architecture is the best of worlds and the worst of worlds: the best because a great deal of memory is addressable (at least by 1981 standards), the worst because it's hard to access all that memory quickly. That said, let's look at the 8088's memory architecture in detail. Most likely you know what we're about to discuss, but bear with me; I want to make sure we're all speaking the same language before I go on to more advanced subjects.

7.3 ◆ Segments and Offsets

Twenty bits are needed to address 1 Mb of memory, and every one of the 1 million-plus memory addresses the 8088 can handle can indeed be expressed as a 20-bit number. However, programs do *not* address memory with 20-bit addresses. There's a good reason for that: 20-bit addresses would be most impractical. For one thing, the 8088's registers contain only 16 bits, so they couldn't be used to point to 20-bit addresses. For another, 3, rather than 2, bytes would be needed to store each address loaded by a program, making for bloated code. In general, the 8088 just wasn't designed to handle straight 20-bit addresses.

(You may well ask why the 8088 wasn't designed better. "Better" is a slippery term, and the 8088 certainly has been successful. Nonetheless, that's a good question, which I'll answer in Chapter 8. A hint: much of the 8088's architecture is derived from the 8080, which could address only 64 Kb in all. The 8088 strongly reflects early microcomputer technology, not least in its limitation to 1 Mb in total.)

Well, if the PC doesn't use straight 20-bit addresses, what does it use? It uses paired segments and offsets, which together form an address denoted as segment:offset. For example, the address 23F0:1512 is the address composed of the segment value 23F0 hex and the offset value 1512 hex. (I'll always show segment:offset pairs in hexadecimal, which is by far the easiest numbering scheme for memory addressing.) Both segments and offsets are 16-bit values.

Wait one minute! We're looking for 20-bit addresses, not 32-bit addresses. Why do we need 16 bits of segment and 16 bits of offset?

Actually, we *don't* need 16 bits of segment. We could manage to address 1 Mb perfectly well with a mere 4 bits of segment, but that's not the way Intel set up the segment:offset addressing scheme. I might add that there's some justification for using segments and offsets. The segment:offset approach is a reasonable compromise between the need to use memory efficiently that predominated in the late 1970s and the need for an architecture that could stretch to accommodate the far more sophisticated memory demands of the 8088's successors. The 80286 uses an extension of the segment:offset approach to address 16 Mb of memory in a fully protected multi-tasking environment, and the 80386 goes far beyond that, as we'll see in Chapter 15.

Anyway, although we need only 4 bits of segment, we get 16 bits, and none of them are ignored by the 8088. Twenty-bit addresses are formed from segment:offset pairs by shifting the segment 4 bits to the left and adding it to the offset, as shown in Figure 7.1.

I'd like to take a moment to note that, for the remainder of this book, I'll use light lines in figures to signify memory addressing and heavy lines to show data movement, as in Figure 7.1. In the future, I'll show segment:offset memory addressing by simply joining the lines from the segment register and any registers and/or displacements (fixed values) used to generate an offset, as in Figure 7.7, avoiding the shift-and-add complications of Figure 7.1A; the 4-bit left shift of the segment and the addition to the offset to generate a 20-bit memory address, which occur whenever a segment:offset address is used, are implied. Also, when the segment isn't germane to the discussion at hand, I may omit it and show only the offset component or components; although unseen, the segment is implied, since one segment register must participate in forming virtually every 20-bit memory address, as we'll see shortly.

Figure 7.1 also illustrates another practice I'll follow in figures that involve memory addressing: the shading of registers and memory locations that change value, making it easy to spot the effects of various operations. In Figure 7.1, only the contents of AL are altered; consequently, only AL is shaded.

I'll generally follow the sequence of Figure 7.1—memory address,

FIGURE 7.1

Twenty-bit memory addresses are constructed by shifting a segment left 4 bits and adding an offset to the shifted value. This figure illustrates memory addressing during the operation of the instruction **mov al,[bx]**: **(A)** The construction of the 20-bit address from DS and BX; **(B)** the addressed data being read from memory; **(C)** the final state of the PC, with the addressed value stored in AL. Note that AL is shaded to indicate that it has changed; this will be standard practice in figures involving memory addressing.

Also note that light lines are used to denote memory addressing and

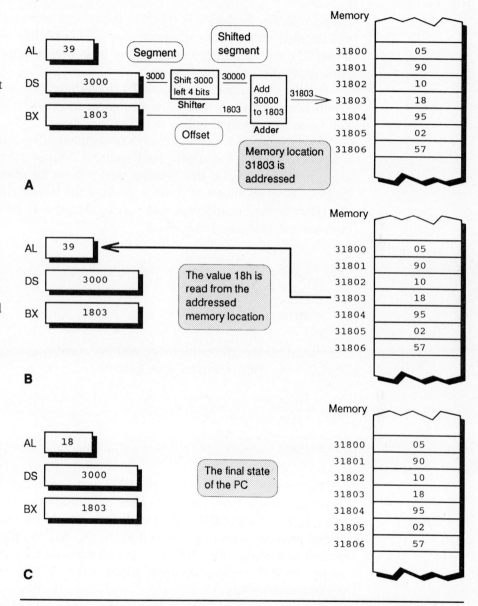

heavy lines are used to denote data movement. For simplicity, I'll omit the shifting and adding steps in showing memory addressing in the future, although they always occur. Instead, I'll simply join the lines from segments and offsets; segment shifting and adding are implied.

Finally, note that all numbers are in hexadecimal, as they will be in all memory-addressing figures unless otherwise noted.

memory access, final state of the PC—in memory-addressing figures. While this detailed, step-by-step approach may seem a bit like overkill right now, it will be most useful for illustrating the 8088's more complex instructions, particularly the string instructions.

Finally, the numbers in Figure 7.1, including both addresses and data, are in hexadecimal. Numbers in all figures involving memory addressing will be in hexadecimal unless noted otherwise.

To continue with our discussion of segment:offset addressing, shifting a segment value left 4 bits is equivalent to shifting it left 1 hexadecimal digit; that's one reason that hexadecimal is a useful notation for memory addresses. Put another way, if the segment is the hexadecimal value *ssss* and the offset is the hexadecimal value *xxxx*, then the 20-bit memory address *mmmmm* is calculated as follows:

$$
\begin{array}{r}
s\ s\ s\ s\ 0 \\
+\quad x\ x\ x\ x \\
\hline
=\ mmmmm
\end{array}
$$

For example, the 20-bit memory address corresponding to 23F0:1512 is 25412 (hex). This is arrived at as follows:

$$
\begin{array}{r}
23F00 \\
+\quad 1512 \\
\hline
=\ 25412
\end{array}
$$

By the way, it happens that the 8088 isn't particularly fast at calculating 20-bit addresses from segment:offset pairs. Although it takes the 8088's bus interface unit (BIU) only 4 cycles to complete a memory access, the fastest memory-accessing instruction the PC has to offer (**xlat**) takes 11 cycles to run. Other memory-accessing instructions take longer, some much longer. We'll delve into the implications of the 8088's poor memory access performance shortly.

Several questions should leap immediately into your mind if you've never encountered segments and offsets before. Where do these odd beasts live? What's to prevent more than one segment:offset pair from pointing to the same 20-bit address? What happens when the sum of the two gets too large to fit in 20 bits?

To answer the first question first, segment values reside in the four segment registers: CS, DS, ES, and SS. One (and only one) of these four registers participates in calculating the address for almost every memory access the PC makes. (Interrupts are exceptions to this rule, since interrupt vectors are read from fixed locations in the first kilobyte of memory.) Segments are, practically speaking, part of every memory access your code will ever make.

CS is always used for code addresses, such as addresses involved in instruction fetching and branching. DS is usually used for accessing memory operands; most instructions can use any segment to access memory operands, but DS is generally the most efficient register for data access. SS is used for maintaining the stack and to access data in stack frames. Finally, ES is used to access data anywhere in the 8088's address space; since it's not dedicated to any other purpose, it's useful for pointing to rarely used segments. ES is particularly useful in conjunction with the string instructions, as we'll see in Chapter 10. In Chapter 6 we discussed exactly what sort of memory accesses operate relative to each segment register by default; we'll continue that discussion later in this chapter, and look at ways to override the default segment selections in some cases.

Offsets are not so simple as segments. The 8088 can calculate offsets in a number of different ways, depending on the addressing mode being used. Both registers and instructions can contain offsets, and registers and/or constant values can be added together on the fly by the 8088 in order to calculate offsets. In various addressing modes, components of offsets may reside in BX, BP, SI, DI, SP, and AL, and offset components can be built in to instructions as well.

We'll discuss the loading and use of the segment registers and the calculation and use of offsets below. First, though, let's answer our two remaining questions.

Segment:Offset Pairs Aren't Unique

The answer to question number two, what's to prevent more than one segment:offset pair from pointing to the same 20-bit address, is: nothing. There's no rule that says two segment:offset pairs can't point to the same address, and in fact many segment:offset pairs do evaluate to any given address—4096 segment:offset pairs for every address, to be precise. For example, the following segment:offset pairs all point to the 20-bit address 00410: 0000:0410, 0001:0400, 0002:03F0, 0003:03E0, and so on up to 0041:0000.

You may have noticed that we've accounted for only 42h segment:offset pairs, not 4096 of them, and that leads in neatly to the answer to our third and final question. When the sum of a segment shifted left 4 bits plus an offset exceeds 20 bits, it wraps back around to address 00000. Basically, any bits that carry out of bit 19 (into what would be bit 20 if the 8088 had 21 addressing bits) are thrown away. The segment:offset pair FFFF:0010 points to the address 00000 as follows:

```
   FFFF0
+  0010
  ───────
  100000
   ↑
  carry
```

with the 1 that carries out of bit 19 discarded to leave 00000.

Now we can see what the other 4,000-odd segment:offset pairs that point to address 00410 are. FFFF:0420 points to 00410, as do FFFE:0430, F042:FFF0, and a host of segment:offset pairs in between. I doubt you'll want to take advantage of that knowledge (in fact, there is a user-selectable trick that can be played on the 80286 and 80386 to disable wrapping at FFFFF, so you shouldn't count on wrapping if you can help it), but if you *do* ever happen to address past the end of memory, that's how it works on the 8088.

Good News and Bad News

Now that we know how segments and offsets work, what are the implications for assembler programs? The obvious implication is that we can address 1 Mb of memory, and that's good news, since we can use memory in myriad ways to improve performance. For example, we'll see how look-up tables can turn extra memory into improved performance later in this chapter. Likewise, in Chapter 13 we'll see how in-line code lets you trade off bytes for performance. Much of top-notch assembler programming involves balancing memory requirements against performance, so the more memory we have available, the merrier.

The bad news is this: although there's a lot of memory, it's available only in 64-Kb chunks. The four segment registers can point to only four 64-Kb segments at any given time, as shown in Figure 7.2. If you want to access a memory location that's not in any of the four segments currently pointed to, there is *no way* to do that with a single instruction. You must first load a segment register to point to a segment containing the desired memory location, a process that takes a minimum of 1, and often 2, instructions. Only then can you access the desired memory location.

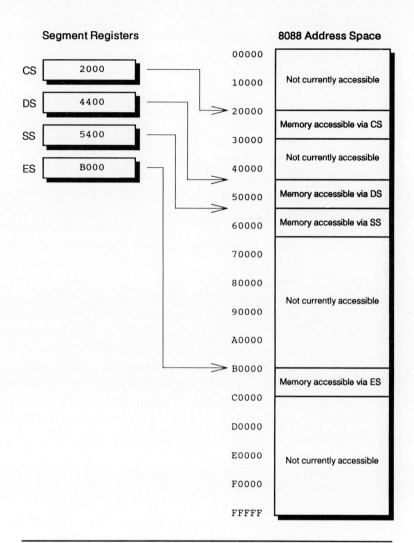

FIGURE 7.2 Out of the one-million-plus bytes that the 8088 can address, only the data in the four 64-Kb blocks pointed to currently by the segment registers can be accessed without reloading a segment register.

Worse, there are problems dealing with blocks of memory larger than 64 Kb, because there's no easy way to perform calculations involving full 20-bit addresses, and because 64 Kb is the largest block of memory that can be addressed by way of a single segment register without reloading the segment register. It's easy enough to access a block up to 64 Kb in size:

point a segment register to the start of the block, and then point wherever you wish. For example, the following bit of code would calculate the 16-bit sum of all the bytes in a 64-Kb array:

```
            mov     bx,seg Test Array
            mov     ds,bx             ;point to segment:offset of start of
            mov     bx,offset TestArray  ;array to sum
            sub     cx,cx             ;count 64 K bytes
            mov     ax,cx             ;set initial sum to 0
            mov     dh,ah             ;set DH to 0 for summing later
SumLoop:
            mov     dl,[bx]           ;get the next array element
            add     ax,dx             ;add the array element to the sum
            inc     bx                ;point to the next array element
            loop    SumLoop
```

Easy enough, eh? Ah, but it all falls apart when a block of memory is larger than 64 Kb or when a block crosses a segment boundary. The problem is that in either of those cases the segment must change as well as the offset, for there's simply no way for an offset to reach more than 64 K bytes away from any given segment register setting. If a register containing an offset reaches the end of a segment (reaches the value 0FFFFh), it simply wraps back to zero when it's incremented. Likewise, the instruction sequence

```
      mov     si,0ffffh
      mov     al,[si+1]
```

merely manages to load AL with the contents of offset 0. Basically, whenever an offset exceeds 16 bits in size, the excess bits are ignored, just as the excess bits are ignored when a segment:offset pair adds up to an address past the 1-Mb overall limit on 8088 memory.

So we need to work with the whole segment:offset pair in order to handle blocks larger than 64 Kb. Is that such a problem? Unfortunately, the answer is yes. The 8088 has no particular aptitude for calculations involving more than 16 bits, and is very bad at handling segments. There's no way to increment a segment:offset pair as a unit, and, in fact, there's no way to modify a segment register other than by copying it to a general-purpose register, modifying that register, and copying the result back to the segment register. All in all, it's as difficult to work with blocks of memory larger than 64 Kb as it is easy to work with blocks no larger than 64 Kb.

For example, here's typical code to calculate the 16-bit sum of a 128-Kb array, of the sort that a high level language might generate. (Actually, the following code is a good deal *better* than most high level languages would generate, but what the heck, let's give them the benefit of the doubt!) The code:

```
        mov  bx,seg TestArray
        mov  ds,bx          ;point to segment:offset of start of
        mov  bx,offset TestArray ;array to sum
        sub  cx,cx          ;count 128 K bytes with SI:CX
        mov  si,2
        mov  ax,cx          ;set initial sum to 0
        mov  dh,ah          ;set DH to 0 for summing later
SumLoop:
        mov  dl,[bx]        ;get the next array element
        add  ax,dx         ;add the array element to the sum
        inc  bx            ;point to the next array element
        and  bx,0fh        ;time to advance the segment?
        jnz  SumLoopEnd    ;not yet
        mov  di,ds         ;advance the segment by 1; since BX has
        inc  di            ; just gone from 15 to 0, we've advanced
        mov  ds,di         ; 1 byte in all
SumLoopEnd:
        loop SumLoop       ;count down 32-bit counter
        dec  si
        jnz  SumLoop
```

More good news.   While the code above is undeniably a mess, things are not quite so grim as they might seem. In fact, the news is pretty good when it comes to handling multiple segments in assembler. For one thing, assembler is *much* better than other languages at handling segments efficiently. Only in assembler do you have complete control over all your segments; that means that you can switch the segments as needed in order to make sure that they are pointing to the data in which you're currently interested. What's more, in assembler you can structure your code and data so that they fall naturally into 64-Kb blocks, allowing most of your accesses at any one time to fall within the currently loaded segments.

In high level languages you almost always suffer both considerable performance loss and significant increase in code size when you start using multiple code or data segments, but in assembler it's possible to maintain nearly peak performance even with many segments. In fact, segment handling is one area in which assembler truly distinguishes itself, and we'll see examples of assembler's fine touch with segments in this chapter, in Chapter 14, and in Volume II of *Zen of Assembly Language*.

There's one more reason that handling multiple code or data segments isn't much of a problem in assembler, and that's that the assembler programmer knows exactly what his code needs to do and can optimize accordingly. For example, suppose that we know that the array **TestArray** in the last example is guaranteed to start at offset 0 in the initial data segment. Given that extra knowledge, we can put together the following version of the above code to sum a 128-Kb array:

```
            mov  bx,seg TestArray
            mov  ds,bx          ;point to segment:offset of start of
            sub  bx,bx          ;array to sum, which we know starts
                                ; at offset 0
            mov  cx,2           ;count two 64 Kb blocks
            sub  ax,ax          ;set initial sum to 0
            mov  dh,ah          ;set DH to 0 for summing later
SumLoop:
            mov  dl,[bx]        ;get the next array element
            add  ax,dx         ;add the array element to the sum
            inc  bx            ;point to the next array element
            jnz  SumLoop       ;until we wrap at the end of a 64 Kb block
            mov  si,ds
            add  si,1000h      ;advance the segment by 64 K bytes
            mov  ds,si
            loop SumLoop       ;count off this 64 Kb block
```

Compare the code within the inner loop above to that in the inner loop of the previous version of this example. The difference is striking. This inner loop is every bit as tight as that of the code for handling blocks of 64 Kb and smaller; in fact, it's slightly *tighter,* as **jnz** is faster than **loop**. Consequently, there shouldn't be much difference in performance between the last example and the 64-Kb and less version. Nonetheless, a basic rule of the Zen of assembly language is that we should check our assumptions, so let's toss the three approaches to summing arrays into the Zen timer and see what comes out.

Listing 7-1 measures the time required to calculate the 16-bit sum of a 64-Kb block without worrying about segments. This code runs in 619 msec, or 9.4 μsec per byte summed. (Note that the Listings 7-1 through 7-3 must be timed with the long-period Zen timer, via LZTIME.BAT, since they take more than 54 msec to run.)

```
1    ;
2    ; *** Listing 7-1 ***
3    ;
4    ; Calculates the 16-bit sum of all bytes in a 64Kb block.
5    ;
6    ; Time with LZTIME.BAT, since this takes more than
7    ; 54 ms to run.
8    ;
9            call    ZTimerOn
10           sub     bx,bx       ;we'll just sum the data ségment
11           sub     cx,cx       ;count 64K bytes
12           mov     ax,cx       ;set initial sum to 0
13           mov     dh,ah       ;set DH to 0 for summing later
14   SumLoop:
15           mov     dl,[bx]     ;get this byte
16           add     ax,dx       ;add the byte to the sum
17           inc     bx          ;point to the next byte
18           loop    SumLoop
19           call    ZTimerOff
```

Listing 7-2 measures the time required to calculate the 16-bit sum of a 128-Kb block. As is always the case with a memory block larger than 64 Kb, segments must be dealt with, and that shows in the performance of Listing 7-2: 2,044 msec, or 15.6 μsec per byte summed. In other words, Listing 7-1, which doesn't concern itself with segments, sums bytes 66 percent faster than Listing 7-2.

```
1    ;
2    ; *** Listing 7-2 ***
3    ;
4    ; Calculates the 16-bit sum of all bytes in a 128Kb block.
5    ;
6    ; Time with LZTIME.BAT, since this takes more than
7    ; 54 ms to run.
8    ;
9            call    ZTimerOn
10           sub     bx,bx       ;we'll just sum the 128Kb starting
11                               ; at DS:0
12           sub     cx,cx       ;count 128K bytes with SI:CX
13           mov     si,2
14           mov     ax,cx       ;set initial sum to 0
15           mov     dh,ah       ;set DH to 0 for summing later
16   SumLoop:
17           mov     dl,[bx]     ;get this byte
18           add     ax,dx       ;add the byte to the sum
19           inc     bx          ;point to the next byte
20           and     bx,0fh      ;time to advance the segment?
21           jnz     SumLoopEnd  ;not yet
22           mov     di,ds       ;advance the segment by 1; since BX
23           inc     di          ; has just gone from 15 to 0, we've
24           mov     ds,di       ; advanced 1 byte in all
25   SumLoopEnd:
26           loop    SumLoop
27           dec     si
28           jnz     SumLoop
29           call    ZTimerOff
```

Finally, Listing 7-3 implements 128-Kb block–handling code that takes advantage of the knowledge that the block of memory being summed starts at offset 0 in the initial data segment. We've speculated that Listing 7-3 should perform on a par with Listing 7-1, because their inner loops are similar . . . and the Zen timer bears that out, reporting that Listing 7-3 runs in 1239 msec, or 9.5 μsec per byte summed.

Assumptions confirmed.

```
1    ;
2    ; *** Listing 7-3 ***
3    ;
4    ; Calculates the 16-bit sum of all bytes in a 128Kb block
5    ; using optimized code that takes advantage of the knowledge
6    ; that the first byte summed is at offset 0 in its segment.
7    ;
8    ; Time with LZTIME.BAT, since this takes more than
9    ; 54 ms to run.
10   ;
11         call    ZTimerOn
12         sub     bx,bx   ;we'll just sum the 128Kb starting
13                         ; at DS:0
14         mov     cx,2    ;count two 64Kb blocks
15         mov     ax,bx   ;set initial sum to 0
16         mov     dh,ah   ;set DH to 0 for summing later
17   SumLoop:
18         mov     dl,[bx] ;get this byte
19         add     ax,dx   ;add the byte to the sum
20         inc     bx      ;point to the next byte
21         jnz     SumLoop ;go until we wrap at the end of a
22                         ; 64Kb block
23         mov     si,ds
24         add     si,1000h ;advance the segment by 64K bytes
25         mov     ds,si
26         loop    SumLoop ;count down 64Kb blocks
27         call    ZTimerOff
```

Notes on Optimization

There are several points to be made about Listings 7-1 through 7-3. First, they graphically illustrate that you should focus your optimization efforts on inner loops. Listing 7-3 is considerably bigger and more complex than Listing 7-1, but by moving the complexity and extra bytes out of the inner loop, we've managed to keep performance high in Listing 7-3.

Now, you may well object that in the process of improving the performance of Listing 7-3, we've altered the code so that it will work only under certain circumstances, and that's my second point. Truly general-purpose code runs slowly, whether it's written in assembler, C, BASIC, or COBOL. Your advantage as a programmer—and your *great* advantage as an assembler programmer—is that you know exactly what your code needs to do

. . . so why write code that wastes cycles and bytes doing extra work? I stipulated that the start offset was at 0 in the initial data segment, and Listing 7-3 is a response to that stipulation. If the conditions to be met had been different, then we would have come up with a different solution.

Do you see what I'm driving at? I hope so, for it's central to the Zen of assembly language. A key to creating good assembler code is to write lean code. Your code should do everything you need done—and nothing more.

I'll finish up by pointing out that Listings 7-1 through 7-3 are excellent examples of both the hazards of using memory blocks larger than 64 Kb and the virtues of using assembler when you must deal with large blocks. It's rare that you'll be able to handle blocks larger than 64 Kb as efficiently as you can blocks that fit within a single segment; Listing 7-3 does take advantage of a very convenient special case. However, it's equally rare that you won't be able to handle large blocks much more efficiently in assembler than you ever could in a high level language.

A Final Word on Segment:Offset Addressing

Let's review what we've learned about segment:offset addressing and assembler. The architecture of the 8088 limits us to addressing at most four segments—64-Kb blocks of memory—at any time, with each segment pointed to by a different segment register. Accessing data in a segment that is not currently pointed to by any segment register is a time-consuming, awkward process, as is handling data that spans multiple blocks. Fortunately, assembler is adept at handling segments, and gives us considerable freedom to structure our programs so that we're usually working within the currently loaded segments at any one time.

On balance, segment:offset addressing is one of the less attractive features of the 8088. For us, however, it's actually an advantage, since it allows assembler, with its superb control over the 8088, to far outstrip high level languages. We won't deal with segments a great deal in the remainder of this volume, as we'll be focusing on detailed optimizations, but the topic will come up from time to time. In Volume II, we'll tackle the subject of segment management in a big way.

The remainder of this chapter will deal only with data addressing—that is, the addressing of instruction operands. Code addressing, in the forms of instruction fetching and branching, is a very real part of PC performance (heck, instruction fetching is perhaps the single most important performance factor of all!), but it's also very different from the sort of memory addressing we'll be discussing. We learned as much as we'll ever need to know (possibly more) about instruction fetching back in Chapters 4 and 5, so we won't pursue that aspect of code addressing any further. However, Chapters 12 through 14 discuss code addressing as it relates to branching in considerable detail.

7.4 ◆ Segment Handling

Now that we know what segments are, let's look at ways to handle the segment registers, in particular how to load them quickly. What we are *not* going to do is discuss the directives that let you create segments and the storage locations within them.

Why not discuss the segment directives? For one thing, there are enough directives, segment and otherwise, to fill a book by themselves. For another, there are already several such books, including the manuals that come with MASM and TASM and the other books in this series. *Zen of Assembly Language* is about writing efficient code, not about using MASM, so I'll assume you already know how to use the **segment**, **ends**, and **assume** directives to define segments and **db**, **dw**, and the like to create and reserve storage. If that's not the case, brush up before you continue reading. We'll use all of the above directives in *Zen of Assembly Language*, and we'll discuss **assume** at some length later in this chapter, but we won't spend time covering the basic functionality of the segment and data directives.

What Can You Do with Segment Registers? Not Much

Segment registers are by no means as flexible as general-purpose registers. What can't you do with segment registers that you can do with general-purpose registers? Let me answer that question with a story.

There's a peculiar sort of puzzle that's standard fare in children's magazines. Such puzzles typically consist of a drawing with a few intentional mistakes (a farmer milking a donkey, for example—a risky proposition at best), captioned "What's wrong with this picture?" Invariably, the answer is printed upside down at the bottom of the page.

I dimly recall from my childhood a takeoff that *MAD* magazine did on those puzzles. *MAD* showed a picture in which everything—and I do mean *everything*—was wrong. Just as with the real McCoy, this picture was accompanied by the caption "What's wrong with this picture?" and by the answer at the bottom of the page.

In *MAD*, the answer was, "Better yet, what's *right* with this picture?"

Segment registers are sort of like *MAD*'s puzzle. What can't you do with segment registers? Better yet, what *can* you do with segment registers? Well, you can use them to address memory—and that's about it.

Any segment register can be copied to a general-purpose register or memory location. Any segment register other than CS can be loaded from a general-purpose register or memory location. Any segment register can be pushed onto the stack, and any segment register except CS can be popped from the stack.

And that's *all*.

Segment registers can't be used for arithmetic. They can't be operands to logical instructions, and they can't take part in comparisons. One segment register can't even be copied directly to another. Basically, segment registers can't do a blessed thing except get loaded and get copied to a register or memory.

Now, there *are* reasons why segments are so hard to work with. For one thing, it's not all that important that segment registers be manipulated quickly. They aren't changed as often as general-purpose registers—at least, they shouldn't be, if you're interested in decent performance. Segment registers rarely need to be manipulated arithmetically or logically, and when the need does arise, they can always be copied to general-purpose registers and manipulated there. Nonetheless, greater flexibility in handling segment registers would be nice; however, a major expansion of the 8088's instruction set—requiring additional circuitry inside the 8088—would have been required in order to allow us to handle segment registers as we do general-purpose registers, and it seems likely that the 8088's designers had other, higher-priority uses for their limited chip space.

There's another reason why segments can only be loaded and copied, and it has to do with the protected mode of the 80286 and 80386 processors. Protected mode, which we'll return to in Chapter 15, is a second mode of the 80286 and 80386, not compatible with either MS-DOS or the 8088, that makes much more memory available for program use than the familiar 1 Mb of MS-DOS/8088–compatible real mode.

In protected mode, the segment registers don't contain memory addresses; instead, they contain segment selectors, which the 80286 and 80386 use to look up the actual segment information (location and attributes such as writability) in a table. Not only would it make no sense to perform arithmetic and the like on segment selectors, as selectors don't correspond directly to memory addresses, but because the segment registers are central to the memory protection scheme of the 80286 and 80386, they simply *cannot* be loaded arbitrarily—the 80286 and 80386 flat out don't allow that to happen by instantly causing a trap whenever an invalid selector is loaded.

What's more, it can take quite a while to load a segment register in protected mode. In real mode, moves to and from segment registers are just as fast as transfers involving general-purpose registers, but that's not the case in protected mode. For example, **mov es,ax** takes 2 cycles in real mode and 17 cycles in protected mode.

Given all of the above, all you'd generally want to do in protected mode is load the segment registers with known good segment selectors provided to you by the operating system. That doesn't affect real mode, which is all we care about, but since real mode and protected mode share most instructions, the segment-register philosophy of protected mode (which Intel no doubt had as a long-range goal even before they designed the 8088) carries over to real mode.

And now you know why the 8088 offers so little in the way of segment register manipulation capability.

Using Segment Registers for Temporary Storage

That brings us to another interesting point: the use of segment registers for temporary storage. The 8088 has only seven available general-purpose registers (remember, we can't use SP for anything but the stack most of the time), and sometimes it would be awfully handy to have somewhere to store a 16-bit value for a little while. Can we use the segment registers for that purpose?

Some people would answer no, because code that uses segments for temporary storage can't easily be ported to protected mode. I don't buy that, for reasons I'll explain when we get to **les**. My answer is, Yes . . . when they're available. Two of the segment registers are never available, one is available occasionally, and one may or may not be readily available, depending on your code.

Some segments are always in use. CS is always busy pointing to the segment of the next instruction to be executed; if you were to load CS with an arbitrary value for even 1 instruction, your program would surely crash. Clearly, it's not a good idea to use CS for temporary storage. (Actually, this isn't even a potential problem, as Intel has thoughtfully not implemented the instructions, **mov** and **pop**, that might load CS directly; MASM will simply generate an error if you try to assemble **pop cs** or **mov cs,[*mem16*]**. CS can be loaded only by far branches: far calls, far returns, far jumps, and interrupts.)

SS isn't in use during every cycle as CS is, but unless interrupts are off, SS *might* be used on any cycle. Even if interrupts are off, nonmaskable interrupts can occur, and of course your code will often use the stack directly. The risks are too great, the rewards too few. Don't use SS for temporary storage.

DS can be used for temporary storage whenever it's free; however, DS is usually used to point to the default data segment. Only rarely will you have a tight loop in which memory isn't accessed (it's not worth bothering with such optimizations except in the tightest, most time-critical code), and memory is usually accessed most efficiently via DS. There certainly are cases in which DS is free—loops that use **scas** to scan the segment pointed to by ES, for example—but such cases are few and far between. Far more common is the case in which DS is saved and then pointed to another segment, as follows:

```
        push  ds                        ;preserve  normal  DS  setting
        mov   bx,seg  TestArray
        mov   ds,bx                     ;point  DS:BX  to  array  in  which
        mov   bx,offset  TestArray      ;  to  flip  all  bits
        mov   cx,TEST_ARRAY_LENGTH      ;#  of  bytes  to  flip
FlipLoop:
        not   byte  ptr  [bx]           ;flip  all  bits  in  current  byte
        inc   bx                        ;point  to  next  byte
        loop  FlipLoop
        pop   ds                        ;restore  normal  DS  setting
```

This approach allows instructions within the loop to access memory without the segment override prefix required when ES is used. (More on segment override prefixes shortly.)

In short, feel free to use DS for temporary storage if it's free, but don't expect that situation to arise too often.

Which brings us to the use of ES for temporary storage. ES is by far the best segment register to use for temporary storage; not being dedicated to any full-time function, it's usually free for any sort of use at all, including temporary storage.

Let's look at an example of code that uses ES for temporary storage to good effect. This sample code sums selected points in a two-dimensional word-sized array. Let's start by tallying up the registers this code will use. (A bit backward, true, but we're focusing on the use of ES for temporary storage at the moment, and this is the best way to go about it.)

In the sample code, the list of subscripts of points to be added in the major dimension will be stored at DI, and the list of subscripts in the minor dimension will be stored at BX. CX will contain the number of points to be summed, and BP will contain the final sum. AX and DX will be used for multiplying, and, as usual, SP will be used to point to the stack. Finally, when the code begins, SI will contain the offset of the start of the array.

Let's see . . . that covers all eight general-purpose registers. Unfortunately, we need yet another storage location, this one to serve as a working pointer into the array. There are many possible solutions to this problem, including using the **xchg** instruction (which we'll cover in the next chapter), storing values in memory (slow), pushing and popping SI (also slow), or disabling interrupts and using SP (can unduly delay interrupts and carries some risk). Instead, here's a solution that uses ES for temporary storage; it's not necessarily the *best* solution, but it does nicely illustrate the use of ES for temporary storage:

```
;
; Sums selected points in a two-dimensional array.
;
; Input:
;     BX = list of minor dimension coordinates to sum
;     CX = number of points to sum
;     DS:SI = start address of array
;     DI  = list of major dimension coordinates to sum
;
; Output:
;     BP = sum of selected points
;
; Registers altered: AX, BX, CX, DX, SI, DI, BP, ES
;
        mov es,si            ;set aside the array start offset
        sub bp,bp            ;initialize sum to 0
TwoDimArraySumLoop:
        mov ax,ARRAY_WIDTH;convert the next major dimension
        mul  word ptr [di]   ;coordinate to an offset in the array
                             ; (wipes out DX)
        add  ax,[bx]         ;add in the minor dimension coordinate
        shl  ax,1            ;make it a word-sized lookup
        mov si,es            ;point to the start of the array
        add  si,ax           ;point to the desired data point
        add  bp,[si]         ;add it to the total
        inc  di              ;point to the next major dimension coordinate
        inc  di
        inc  bx              ;point to the next minor dimension coordinate
        inc  bx
        loop TwoDimArraySumLoop
```

If you find yourself running out of registers in a tight loop and you're not using the segment pointed to by ES, by all means reload one of your registers from ES if that will help.

Setting and Copying Segment Registers

As I've said, loading segment registers is one area in which assembler has a tremendous advantage over high level languages. High level languages tend to use DS to point to a default data segment all the time, loading ES every single time any other segment is accessed. In assembler, we can either load a new segment into DS as needed, or we can load ES and leave it loaded for as long as we need to access a given segment.

We'll see examples of efficient segment use throughout *Zen of Assembly Language,* especially when we discuss strings, so I'm not going to go into more detail here. What I am going to do is discuss the *process* of loading segment registers, because it is by no means obvious what is the most efficient segment-loading mechanism.

For starters, let's divide segment loading into two categories, setting and copying. *Segment setting* refers to loading a segment register to point to a certain segment, whereas *segment copying* refers to loading one segment register with the contents of another. I'm making this distinction because the instruction sequences used for the two sorts of segment loading differ considerably.

Let's tackle segment copying first. Segment copying is useful when you want two segment registers to point to the same segment. For example, you'll want ES to point to the same segment as DS if you're using **rep movs** to copy data within the segment pointed to by DS, because DS and ES are the default source and destination segments, respectively, for **movs**. There are two good ways to load ES to point to the same segment as DS, given that we can't copy one segment register directly to another:

```
push ds
pop  es
```

and

```
mov  ax,ds
mov  es,ax
```

(Any general-purpose register would serve as well as AX.)

Each of the above approaches has its virtues. The **push/pop** approach is extremely compact at just 2 bytes and affects no other registers. Un-fortunately, it takes a less than snappy 27 cycles to run. By contrast, the **mov/mov** approach officially takes just 4 cycles to run; 16 cycles (4 bytes at 4 cycles to fetch each byte) is a more realistic figure, but either way, **mov/mov** is clearly faster than **push/pop**. On the other hand, **mov/mov** takes twice as many bytes as **push/pop**, and destroys the contents of a general-purpose register as well.

There's no clear winner here. Use the **mov/mov** approach to copy segment registers when you're interested in speed and can spare a general-purpose register, and use the **push/pop** approach when bytes and/or registers are at a premium. I'll use both approaches in this book, generally using **push/pop** in non–time-critical code and **mov/mov** when speed really counts. Why waste the bytes when the cycles don't matter?

That brings us to an important point about assembler programming. There is rarely such a beast as the "best code" in assembler; instead, there's code that's good in a given context. In any situation, the choice of fast code, small code, understandable code, portable code, maintainable code, structured code, or whatever other sort of code you can dream up is purely up to you. If you make the right decisions, your code will beat high level language code hands down, because you know more about your code and can think far more flexibly than any high level language possibly can.

Now let's look at ways to set segment registers. Segment registers can't be loaded directly with a segment value, but they can be loaded either through a general-purpose register or from memory. The two approaches aren't always interchangeable: one requires that the segment name be available as an immediate operand, whereas the other requires that a memory variable be set to the desired segment value. Nonetheless, you can generally set things up so that either approach can be used, if you really want to—so which is best?

Well, loading a segment register through a general-purpose register, as in

```
mov   ax,DATA
mov   es,ax
```

officially takes 6 cycles. Since the two instructions together are 5 bytes long, however, this approach could take as much as 20 cycles if the prefetch queue is empty. By contrast, loading from memory, as in

```
mov   es,[DataSeg]
```

officially takes only 18 cycles, is only 4 bytes long, and doesn't destroy a general-purpose register. (Note that the last approach assumes that the memory variable **DataSeg** has previously been set to point to the desired segment.) Loading from memory sounds better, doesn't it?

It isn't.

Remember, it's not just the number of instruction byte fetches that affects performance—*it's the number of memory accesses of all sorts.* When a segment register is loaded from memory, two memory accesses are performed to read the segment value; together with the 4 instruction bytes, that means that, in all, six memory accesses are performed when a segment register is loaded from memory. Consequently, loading a segment register from memory takes anywhere from 18 to 24 (six memory accesses at 4 cycles per access) cycles, which stacks up poorly against the 6 to 20 cycles required to load a segment register through a general-purpose register.

In short, it's clearly faster to load segment registers through general-purpose registers.

That's not to say that there aren't times when you'll want to load a segment register directly from memory. If you're *really* tight on space, you can save a byte every time you load a segment by using the 4-byte load from memory rather than the 5-byte load through a general-purpose register. (This is worthwhile only if there are multiple segment load instructions, since the memory variable containing the segment address takes 2 bytes.) Also, if the segment you want to work with varies as your program runs (for example, if your code can access either display memory or a display buffer in system RAM), then loading the segment register from memory is the way to go. The following code is clearly the best way to load ES to point to a display buffer that may be at any of several segments:

```
mov   es,[DisplayBufferSegment]
```

Here, **DisplayBufferSegment** is set externally to point to the segment in which all screen drawing should be performed at any given time.

Finally, segments are often passed as stack frame parameters from high level languages to assembler subroutines—to point to far data buffers and the like—and in those cases segments can best be loaded directly from stack frames into segment registers. (We'll discuss stack frames later in this chapter.) It's easy to forget that segments can be loaded directly from *any* addressable memory location, as we'll see in Chapter 16. All too many people load segments from stack frames like this:

```
mov    ax,[bp+BufferSegment]
mov    es,ax
```

when the following is shorter, faster, and doesn't use any general-purpose registers:

```
mov    es,[bp+BufferSegment]
```

As it happens, though, lone segment values are rarely passed as stack frame parameters. Instead, segment:offset pairs that provide a full 20-bit pointer to a specific data element are usually passed. These can be loaded as follows:

```
mov    es,[bp+BufferSegment]
mov    di,[bp+BufferOffset]
```

However, the designers of the 8088 anticipated the need for loading 20-bit pointers and gave us two most useful instructions for just that purpose: **lds** and **les**.

Loading 20-Bit Pointers with lds and les

The instruction **lds** loads *both* DS and any one general-purpose register from a doubleword of memory, and **les** similarly loads *both* ES and a general-purpose register, as shown in Figure 7.3.

While both instructions are useful, **les** is by far the more commonly used of the two. Since most programs leave DS pointing to the default data segment whenever possible, it's rare that we'd want to load DS as part of a segment:offset pointer. True, it does happen, but generally only when we want to point temporarily to a block of far memory for faster processing in a tight loop.

ES, on the other hand, is the segment of choice when a segment:offset pointer is needed, because it's not generally reserved for any other purpose. Consequently, **les** is usually used to load segment:offset pointers.

The instructions **lds** and **les** actually don't come in for all that much use in pure assembler programs. The reason is that efficient assembler programs tend to be organized so that segments rarely need to be changed, so such programs tend to work with 16-bit pointers most of the time. After all, while **lds** and **les** are efficient considering all they do, they're still slow, with official execution times of at least 29 cycles. If you need to

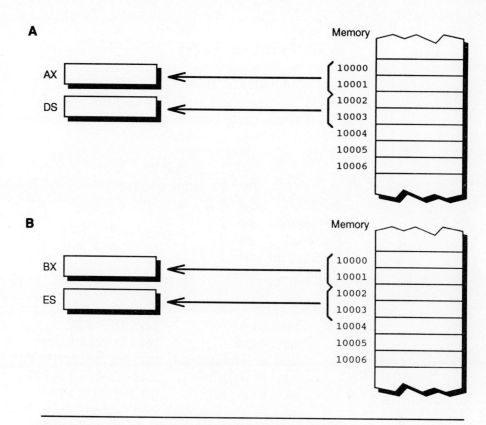

FIGURE 7.3   **(A)** The operation of **lds**, which loads both DS and a
general-purpose register (AX in this case) at once from a
doubleword of memory. **(B)** The operation of **les**, which
loads both ES and a general-purpose register (BX in this
case) at once.

load segment:offset pointers, use **lds** and **les**, but try to load only offsets
whenever you can.

One place where there's no way to avoid loading segments is in
assembler code that's called from a high level language, especially when
the large data model (the model that supports more than 64 Kb of data) is
used. When a high level language passes a far pointer as a parameter to an
assembler subroutine, the full 20-bit pointer must be loaded from memory
before it can be used, and there **lds** and **les** work beautifully.

Suppose that we have a C statement that calls the assembler subroutine
AddTwoFarInts as follows:

```
int Sum;
int far *FarPtr1, far *FarPtr2;
    :
Sum = AddTwoFarInts(FarPtr1, FarPtr2);
```

AddTwoFarInts could be written without **les** as follows:

```
Parms           struc
                dw   ?   ;pushed BP
                dw   ?   ;return address
Ptr1Offset      dw   ?
Ptr1Segment     dw   ?
Ptr2Offset      dw   ?
Ptr2Segment     dw   ?
Parms           ends
;
AddTwoFarInts   proc near
        push bp                  ;save caller's BP
        mov  bp,sp               ;point to stack frame
        mov  es,[Ptr1Segment]    ;load segment part of Ptr1
        mov  bx,[Ptr1Offset]     ;load offset part of Ptr1
        mov  ax,es:[bx]          ;get first int to add
        mov  es,[Ptr2Segment]    ;load segment part of Ptr2
        mov  bx,[Ptr2Offset]     ;load offset part of Ptr2
        add  ax,es:[bx]          ;add the two ints together
        pop  bp                  ;restore caller's BP
        ret
AddTwoFarInts   endp
```

The subroutine is considerably more efficient when **les** is used, however:

```
Parms    struc
    dw   ?    ;pushed BP
    dw   ?    ;return address
Ptr1 dd   ?
Ptr2 dd   ?
Parms    ends
;
AddTwoFarInts   proc near
        push bp             ;save caller's BP
        mov  bp,sp          ;point to stack frame
```

```
        les    bx,[Ptr1]    ;load both segment and offset of Ptr1
        mov    ax,es:[bx]   ;get first int to add
        les    bx,[Ptr2]    ;load both segment and offset of Ptr2
        add    ax,es:[bx]   ;add the two ints together
        pop    bp           ;restore caller's BP
        ret
AddTwoFarInts   endp
```

(We'll talk about **struc**, stack frames, and segment overrides, such as **es:**, later in this chapter.)

High level languages use **les** all the time to point to data that's not in the default data segment, and that hurts performance significantly. Most high level languages aren't very smart about using **les**, either. For example, high level languages tend to load a full 20-bit pointer into ES:BX every time through a loop, even though ES never gets changed from the last pass through the loop. That's one reason why high level languages don't perform very well with more than 64 Kb of data.

You can usually easily avoid **les**-related performance problems in assembler. Consider Listing 7-4, which adds one far array to another far array in the same way that most high level languages would, storing both far pointers in memory variables and loading each pointer with **les** every time it's used. (Actually, that Listing 7-4 is better than your average high level language subroutine because it uses **loop**, whereas most high level languages use less efficient instruction sequences to handle looping.) Listing 7-4 runs in 43.42 msec, or 43 μsec per array element addition.

```
1    ;
2    ; *** Listing 7-4 ***
3    ;
4    ; Adds one far array to another far array as a high-level
5    ; language would, loading each far pointer with LES every
6    ; time it's needed.
7    ;
8            jmp     Skip
9    ;
10   ARRAY_LENGTH      equ     1000
11   Array1  db      ARRAY_LENGTH dup (1)
12   Array2  db      ARRAY_LENGTH dup (2)
13   ;
14   ; Adds one byte-sized array to another byte-sized array.
15   ; C-callable.
16   ;
17   ; Input: parameters on stack as in AddArraysParms
18   ;
19   ; Output: none
20   ;
21   ; Registers altered: AL, BX, CX, ES
```

```
22   ;
23   AddArraysParms  struc
24           dw      ?          ;pushed BP
25           dw      ?          ;return address
26   FarPtr1 dd      ?          ;pointer to array to be added to
27   FarPtr2 dd      ?          ;pointer to array to add to the
28                              ; other array
29   AddArraysLength dw ?       ;# of bytes to add
30   AddArraysParms  ends
31   ;
32   AddArrays       proc    near
33           push    bp                 ;save caller's BP
34           mov     bp,sp              ;point to stack frame
35           mov     cx,[bp+AddArraysLength]
36                              ;get the length to add
37   AddArraysLoop:
38           les     bx,[bp+FarPtr2] ;point to the array to add
39                              ; from
40           inc     word ptr [bp+FarPtr2]
41                              ;point to the next byte
42                              ; of the array to add from
43           mov     al,es:[bx]  ;get the array element to
44                              ; add
45           les     bx,[bp+FarPtr1] ;point to the array to add
46                              ; to
47           inc     word ptr [bp+FarPtr1]
48                              ;point to the next byte
49                              ; of the array to add to
50           add     es:[bx],al  ;add to the array
51           loop    AddArraysLoop
52           pop     bp                 ;restore caller's BP
53           ret
54   AddArrays       endp
55   ;
56   Skip:
57           call    ZTimerOn
58           mov     ax,ARRAY_LENGTH
59           push    ax      ;pass the length to add
60           push    ds      ;pass segment of Array2
61           mov     ax,offset Array2
62           push    ax      ;pass offset of Array2
63           push    ds      ;pass segment of Array1
64           mov     ax,offset Array1
65           push    ax      ;pass offset of Array1
66           call    AddArrays
67           add     sp,10   ;clear the parameters
68           call    ZTimerOff
```

Now look at Listing 7-5, which does exactly the same thing that Listing 7-4 does, except that it loads the far pointers *outside* the loop and keeps them in the registers for the duration of the loop, using the segment-loading techniques that we learned earlier in this chapter. How much difference does it make to keep the far pointers in registers at all times? Listing 7-5 runs in 19.69 msec—*more than twice as fast as Listing 7-4.*

```
1     ;
2     ; *** Listing 7-5 ***
3     ;
4     ; Adds one far array to another far array as only assembler
5     ; can, loading the two far pointers once and keeping them in
6     ; the registers during the entire loop for speed.
7     ;
8              jmp      Skip
9     ;
10    ARRAY_LENGTH       equ      1000
11    Array1  db         ARRAY_LENGTH dup (1)
12    Array2  db         ARRAY_LENGTH dup (2)
13    ;
14    ; Adds one byte-sized array to another byte-sized array.
15    ; C-callable.
16    ;
17    ; Input: parameters on stack as in AddArraysParms
18    ;
19    ; Output: none
20    ;
21    ; Registers altered: AL, BX, CX, DX, ES
22    ;
23    AddArraysParms    struc
24             dw        ?           ;pushed BP
25             dw        ?           ;return address
26    FarPtr1 dd         ?           ;pointer to array to be added to
27    FarPtr2 dd         ?           ;pointer to array to add to the
28                                   ; other array
29    AddArraysLength dw ?           ;# of bytes to add
30    AddArraysParms    ends
31    ;
32    AddArrays          proc     near
33             push      bp              ;save caller's BP
34             mov       bp,sp           ;point to stack frame
35             push      si              ;save registers used by many
36             push      di              ; C compilers for register
37                                       ; variables
38             mov       cx,[bp+AddArraysLength]
39                                       ;get the length to add
40             les       si,[bp+FarPtr2] ;point to the array to add
41                                       ; from
42             mov       dx,es           ;set aside the segment
43             les       bx,[bp+FarPtr1] ;point to the array to add
44                                       ; to
45             mov       di,es           ;set aside the segment
46    AddArraysLoop:
47             mov       es,dx           ;point ES:SI to the next
48                                       ; byte of the array to add
49                                       ; from
50             mov       al,es:[si]      ;get the array element to
51                                       ; add
52             inc       si              ;point to the next byte of
53                                       ; the array to add from
54             mov       es,di           ;point ES:BX to the next
55                                       ; byte of the array to add
56                                       ; to
57             add       es:[bx],al      ;add to the array
58             inc       bx              ;point to the next byte of
59                                       ; the array to add to
```

```
60                loop    AddArraysLoop
61                pop     di              ;restore registers used by
62                pop     si              ; many C compilers for
63                                        ; register variables
64                pop     bp              ;restore caller's BP
65                ret
66     AddArrays          endp
67     ;
68     Skip:
69                call    ZTimerOn
70                mov     ax,ARRAY_LENGTH
71                push    ax      ;pass the length to add
72                push    ds      ;pass segment of Array2
73                mov     ax,offset Array2
74                push    ax      ;pass offset of Array2
75                push    ds      ;pass segment of Array1
76                mov     ax,offset Array1
77                push    ax      ;pass offset of Array1
78                call    AddArrays
79                add     sp,10   ;clear the parameters
80                call    ZTimerOff
```

Now you know why I keep saying that assembler can handle segments much better than high level languages can. Listing 7-5 isn't the ultimate in that regard, however; we can carry that concept a step further still, as shown in Listing 7-6.

Listing 7-6 brings the full power of assembler to bear on the task of adding two arrays. Listing 7-6 sets up the segments so that they never once need to be loaded within the loop. What's more, Listing 7-6 arranges the registers so that the powerful **lodsb** string instruction can be used in place of a **mov** and an **inc**. (We'll discuss the string instructions in Chapter 10. For now, just take my word that the string instructions are good stuff.) In short, Listing 7-6 organizes segment and register use so that as much work as possible is moved out of the loop and so that the most efficient instructions can be used.

The results are stunning.

Listing 7-6 runs in just 13.79 msec, more than three times as fast as Listing 7-4, even though Listing 7-4 uses the efficient **loop** and **les** instructions. This example is a powerful reminder of two important aspects of the Zen of assembly language. First, you must strive to play to the strengths of the 8088 (such as the string instructions) while sidestepping its weaknesses (such as the segments and slow memory access speed). Second, *you must always concentrate on moving cycles out of loops.* The **lds** and **les** instructions outside the loop in Listing 7-6 effectively run 1000 times faster than the **les** instructions inside the loop in Listing 7-4, since the latter are executed 1000 times but the former are executed only once.

```
1    ;
2    ; *** Listing 7-6 ***
3    ;
4    ; Adds one far array to another far array by temporarily
5    ; switching segments in order to allow the use of the most
6    ; efficient possible instructions within the loop.
7    ;
8            jmp     Skip
9    ;
10   ARRAY_LENGTH    equ     1000
11   Array1 db       ARRAY_LENGTH dup (1)
12   Array2 db       ARRAY_LENGTH dup (2)
13   ;
14   ; Adds one byte-sized array to another byte-sized array.
15   ; C-callable.
16   ;
17   ; Input: parameters on stack as in AddArraysParms
18   ;
19   ; Output: none
20   ;
21   ; Registers altered: AL, BX, CX, ES
22   ;
23   ; Direction flag cleared
24   ;
25   AddArraysParms  struc
26           dw      ?          ;pushed BP
27           dw      ?          ;return address
28   FarPtr1 dd      ?          ;pointer to array to be added to
29   FarPtr2 dd      ?          ;pointer to array to add to the
30                              ; other array
31   AddArraysLength dw ?       ;# of bytes to add
32   AddArraysParms  ends
33   ;
34   AddArrays       proc    near
35           push    bp                 ;save caller's BP
36           mov     bp,sp              ;point to stack frame
37           push    si                 ;save register used by many
38                                      ; C compilers for register
39                                      ; variables
40           push    ds                 ;save normal DS, since we're
41                                      ; going to switch data
42                                      ; segments for the duration
43                                      ; of the loop
44           mov     cx,[bp+AddArraysLength]
45                                      ;get the length to add
46           les     bx,[bp+FarPtr1]    ;point to the array to add
47                                      ; to
48           lds     si,[bp+FarPtr2]    ;point to the array to add
49                                      ; from
50           cld                        ;make LODSB increment SI
51   AddArraysLoop:
52           lodsb                      ;get the array element to
53                                      ; add
54           add     es:[bx],al         ;add to the other array
55           inc     bx                 ;point to the next byte of
56                                      ; the array to add to
57           loop    AddArraysLoop
58           pop     ds                 ;restore normal DS
59           pop     si                 ;restore register used by
```

```
60                                      ; many C compilers for
61                                      ; register variables
62              pop      bp             ;restore caller's BP
63              ret
64    AddArrays         endp
65    ;
66    Skip:
67              call     ZTimerOn
68              mov      ax,ARRAY_LENGTH
69              push     ax        ;pass the length to add
70              push     ds        ;pass segment of Array2
71              mov      ax,offset Array2
72              push     ax        ;pass offset of Array2
73              push     ds        ;pass segment of Array1
74              mov      ax,offset Array1
75              push     ax        ;pass offset of Array1
76              call     AddArrays
77              add      sp,10     ;clear the parameters
78              call     ZTimerOff
```

Loading Doublewords with les

While **les** isn't often used to load segment:offset pointers in pure assembler programs, it has another less obvious use: loading doubleword values into the general-purpose registers.

Normally, a doubleword value is loaded into two general-purpose registers with two instructions. Here's the standard way to load DX:AX from the doubleword memory variable **DVar**:

```
mov   ax,word ptr [DVar]
mov   dx,word ptr [DVar+2]
```

There's nothing *wrong* with this approach, but it does take between 4 and 8 bytes and between 34 and 48 cycles. We can cut the time nearly in half, and can usually reduce the size as well, by using **les** in a most unusual way:

```
les   ax,[DVar]
mov   dx,es
```

The only disadvantage of using **les** to load doubleword values is that it wipes out the contents of ES; if that isn't a problem, there's simply no reason to load doubleword values any other way.

Once again, there are people who will tell you that it's a bad idea to load ES with anything but specific segment values because such code won't work if you port it to run in protected mode on the 80286 and

80836. While that's a consideration, it's not an overwhelming one. For one thing, most code will never be ported to protected mode. For another, protected mode programming, which we'll touch on in Chapter 15, differs from normal 8088 assembler programming in a number of ways; using **les** to load doubleword values is unlikely to be the most difficult part of porting code to protected mode, especially if you have to rewrite the code to run under a new operating system. Still, if protected mode concerns you, use a macro such as

```
LOAD_32_BITS  macro  Address
ifdef PROTECTED_MODE
    mov   ax,word ptr [Address]
    mov   dx,word ptr [Address+2]
else
    les   ax,dword ptr [Address]
    mov   dx,es
endif
    endm
        :
    LOAD_32_BITS  DwordVar
```

to load 32-bit values.

The **les** approach to loading doubleword values is not only fast but has a unique virtue: it's indivisible. In other words, there's no way an interrupt can occur after the lower word of a doubleword is read and before the upper word is read. For example, suppose we want to read the timer count the BIOS maintains at 0000:046C. We *could* read the count like this:

```
sub   ax,ax
mov   es,ax
mov   ax,es:[46ch]
mov   dx,es:[46eh]
```

There's a problem with this code, though. Every 54.9 msec, the timer generates an interrupt which starts the BIOS timer tick handler. The BIOS handler then increments the timer count. If an interrupt occurs right after **mov ax,es:[46ch]** in the above code (before **mov dx,es:[46eh]** can execute), we would read half of the value before it's advanced and half of the value after it's advanced. If this happened as an hour or a day turned over, we could conceivably read a count that's seriously wrong, with potentially disastrous implications for any program that relies on precise time synchronization. Over time, such a misread of the timer is bound to happen if we use the above code.

We could solve the problem by disabling interrupts while we read the count:

```
sub    ax,ax
mov    es,ax
cli
mov    ax,es:[46ch]
mov    dx,es:[46eh]
sti
```

but there's a better solution. There's no way **les** can be interrupted as it reads a doubleword value, so we'll just load our doubleword thus:

```
sub  ax,ax
mov  es,ax
les  ax,es:[46ch]
mov  dx,es
```

This last bit of code is shorter, faster, and uninterruptible. In short, it's perfect for our needs. In fact, we could have put **les** to good use reading the BIOS timer count in the long-period Zen timer, way back in Listing 2-5. Why didn't I use it there? The truth is that I didn't know about using **les** to load doublewords when I wrote the timer (which just goes to show that there's always more to learn about the 8088). When I did learn about loading doublewords with **les**, it didn't make any sense to tinker with code that worked perfectly well just to save a few bytes and cycles, particularly because the timer count load isn't time critical.

Remember, it's worth optimizing for speed only when the cycles you save make a significant difference, which usually means inside tight loops.

Segment:Offset and Byte Ordering in Memory

Our discussion of **les** brings up the topic of how multi-byte values are stored in memory on the 8088. That's an interesting topic indeed; on occasion we'll need to load just the segment part of a 20-bit pointer from memory, or we'll want to modify only the upper byte of a word variable. The answer to our question is simple but by no means obvious: *multi-byte values are always stored with the least significant byte at the lowest address.*

For example, when you execute **mov ax,[WordVar]**, AL is loaded from address **WordVar**, and AH is loaded from address **WordVar+1**, as shown in Figure 7.4. Put another way, this:

```
mov   ax,[WordVar]
```

is logically equivalent to this:

```
mov   al,byte ptr [WordVar]
mov   ah,byte ptr [WordVar+1]
```

although the single-instruction version is much faster and smaller. All word-sized values (including address displacements, which we'll get to shortly) follow this least significant byte–first memory ordering.

Similarly, segment:offset pointers are stored with the least significant byte of the offset at the lowest memory address, the most significant byte of the offset next, the least significant byte of the segment after that, and the most significant byte of the segment at the highest memory address, as shown in Figure 7.5. This:

```
les   dx,dword ptr [FarPtr]
```

is logically equivalent to this:

```
mov   dx,word ptr [FarPtr]
mov   es,word ptr [FarPtr+2]
```

which is in turn logically equivalent to this:

```
mov   dl,byte ptr [FarPtr]
mov   dh,byte ptr [FarPtr+1]
mov   al,byte ptr [FarPtr+2]
mov   ah,byte ptr [FarPtr+3]
mov   es,ax
```

This organization applies to all segment:offset values stored in memory, including return addresses placed on the stack by far calls, far pointers used by far indirect calls, and interrupt vectors.

There's nothing magical about having the least significant byte at the lowest address; it's just the approach Intel chose. Other processors store values with most significant byte at the lowest address, and there's a

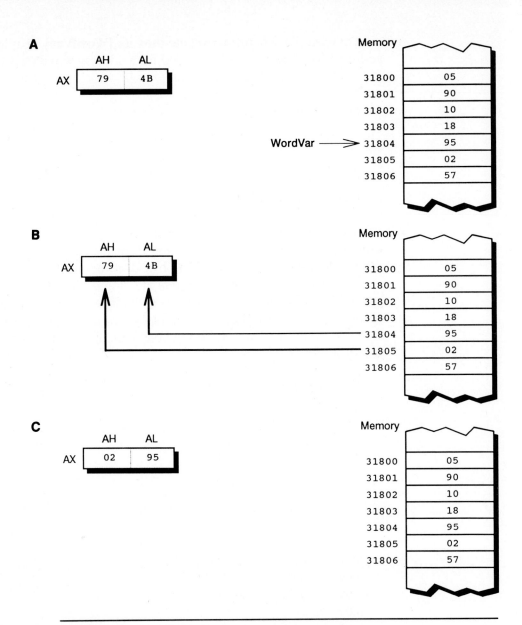

FIGURE 7.4 The 8088 always considers the least significant byte of word-sized memory accesses to be at the lower memory address. **(A)** The state of the PC as **mov ax,[WordVar]** begins. **(B)** Memory being accessed, with the least significant byte at the lower memory address. **(C)** Data from the least significant byte is indeed loaded into AL, and data from the most significant byte is loaded into AH.

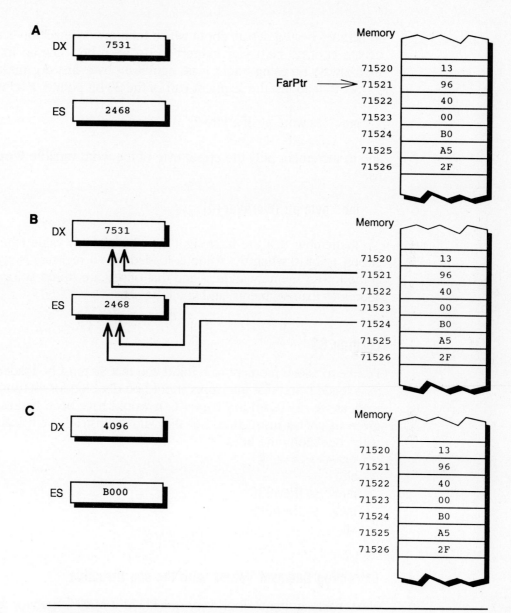

FIGURE 7.5   The 8088 always considers the least significant word of doubleword-sized memory accesses to be at the lower memory address. **(A)** The state of the PC as **les dx,dword ptr [FarPtr]** begins. **(B)** Memory being accessed, with the least significant word at the lower memory address. **(C)** The data from the least significant word is indeed loaded into DX and the data from the most significant word is loaded into ES.

sometimes heated debate about which memory organization is better. That debate is of no particular interest to us; we'll be using an Intel chip, so we'll always be using Intel's least significant byte–first organization.

So, to load just the segment part of the 20-bit pointer **FarPtr**, we'd use

```
mov   es,word ptr [FarPtr+2]
```

and to increment only the upper byte of the word variable **WordPtr**, we'd use

```
inc   byte ptr [WordVar+1]
```

Remember that the least significant byte of any value (the byte that's closest to bit 0 when the value is loaded into a register) is always stored at the lowest memory address and that offsets are stored at lower memory addresses than segments, and you'll be set.

Loading SS

I'd like to take a moment to remind you that SP must be loaded whenever SS is loaded, and that interrupts should be disabled for the duration of the load, as we discussed in Chapter 6. It would have been handy if Intel had given us an **lss** instruction, but they didn't. Instead, we'll load SS and SP with code along the lines of

```
cli
mov   ss,[NewSS]
mov   sp,[NewSP]
sti
```

Extracting Segment Values with the seg Directive

Next, we're going to look very quickly at a MASM operator and a MASM directive. As I've said, this is not a book about MASM, but these features are closely related to the efficient use of segments.

The **seg** operator returns the segment within which the following symbol (label or variable name) resides. In the following code, **seg WordVar** returns the segment **Data**, which is then loaded into ES and used to assume ES to that segment:

```
        Data segment
        WordVar    dw   0
        Data ends
        Code segment
            assume     cs:Code, es:Nothing
                :
            mov   ax,seg WordVar
            mov   es,ax
            assume   es:seg WordVar
                :
        Code ends
```

You may well ask why it's worth bothering with **seg** when we could simply have used the segment name **Data** instead. The answer is that you may not know or may not have direct access to the segment name for variables that are declared in other modules. For example, suppose that **WordVar** were external in our last example:

```
        extrn WordVar:word
    Code segment
        assume     cs:Code, es:Nothing
            :
        mov   ax,seg WordVar
        mov   es,ax
        assume     es:seg WordVar
            :
    Code ends
```

This code still returns the segment of **WordVar** properly, even though we don't necessarily have any idea at all what the name of that segment might be.

In short, **seg** makes it easier to work with multiple segments in multi-module programs.

Joining Segments

Selected assembler modules can share the same code and/or data segments even when multiple code and data segments are used. In other words, in assembler you can choose to share segments between modules or not, in contrast to high level languages, which generally force you to choose between all or no modules sharing segments. (This is not always the case, however, as we'll see in Chapter 14.)

The mechanism for joining or separating segments is the **segment** directive. If each of two modules has a segment of the same name, and if those segments are created as public segments (via the **public** option to the **segment** directive), then the segments will be joined into a single, shared segment. If they are code segments, you can use near calls (faster and smaller than far calls) between the modules. If they are data segments, there's no need for one module to load segment registers in order to access data in the other.

All in all, shared segments allow multiple-module programs to produce code that's as efficient as single-module code, with the segment registers changed as infrequently as possible. In the same program in which multiple modules share a given segment, however, other modules—or even other parts of the same modules—may share segments of different names or may have segments that are private (unique to that module). As a result, assembler programs can strike an effective balance between performance and available memory: efficient offset-only addressing most of the time, along with access to as many segments and as much memory as the PC can handle on an as-needed basis.

There are many ways to join segments, including grouping them and declaring them common, and there are many options to the **segment** directive. We need to get on with our discussion of memory addressing, so we won't cover MASM's segment-related directives further, but I strongly suggest that you read carefully the discussion of those directives in your assembler's manual. In fact, you should make it a point to read your assembler's manual cover to cover—it may not be the most exciting reading around, but I guarantee that there are tricks and tips there that you'll find nowhere else.

Although we won't discuss MASM's segment-related directives again, we will explore the topic of effective segment use again in Chapter 10 (as it relates to the string instructions), Chapter 14 (as it relates to branching), and in Volume II of *Zen of Assembly Language*.

Segment Override Prefixes

As we saw in Chapter 6, all memory accesses default to accessing memory relative to one of the four segment registers. Instructions come from CS, stack accesses and memory accesses that use BP as a pointer occur within SS, string instruction accesses via DI are in ES, and everything else is normally in DS. In some—but by no means all—cases, segments other than the default segments can be accessed by way of segment override prefixes, special bytes that can precede (prefix) instructions in order to cause those instructions to use any one of the four segment registers.

Let's start by listing the types of memory accesses segment override prefixes *can't* affect. Instructions are always fetched from CS; there's no way to alter that. The stack pointer is always used as a pointer into SS, no matter what. ES is always the segment to which string instruction accesses via DI go, regardless of segment override prefixes. Basically, accesses to explicitly named memory operands and string instruction accesses via SI are the ones that are affected by segment override prefixes. (The segment accessed by the unusual **xlat** instruction, which we'll encounter later in this chapter, can also be overridden.)

The default segment for a memory operand is overridden by placing the prefix **CS:**, **DS:**, **ES:**, or **SS:** on that memory operand. For example

```
sub    bx,bx
mov    ax,es:[bx]
```

loads AX with the word at offset 0 in ES, as opposed to:

```
sub    bx,bx
mov    ax,[bx]
```

which loads AX with the word at offset 0 in DS.

Segment override prefixes are handy in a number of situations. They're good for accessing data out of CS when you're not sure where DS is pointing or when DS is pointing temporarily to some segment that doesn't contain the data you want. (CS is the one segment upon whose setting you can absolutely rely at any given time, since you know that if a given instruction is being executed CS *must* be pointing to the segment containing that instruction. Consequently, CS is a good place to put jump tables and temporary variables in multi-segment programs and is a particularly handy segment in which to stash data in interrupt handlers, which start up with only CS among the four segment registers set to a known value.)

In many programs, especially those involving high-level languages, DS and SS normally point to the same segment, since it's convenient to have both stack frame variables and static/global variables in the same segment. When that's the case, **ss:** prefixes can be used to point to data in the default data segment when DS is otherwise occupied. Even when SS doesn't point to the default data segment, segment override prefixes still let you address data on the stack using pointer registers other than BP.

Segment override prefixes are particularly handy when you need to access data in two to four segments at once. Suppose, for example, that we need to add two far word-sized arrays together and store the resulting array in the default data segment. Assuming that SS and DS both point to the default data segment, segment override prefixes let us keep all our pointers and counters in the registers as we add the arrays, as follows:

```
        push ds               ;save normal DS
        les  di,[FarPtr2]     ;point ES:DI to one source array
        mov  bx,[DestPtr]     ;point SS:BX to the destination array
        mov  cx,[AddLength]   ;array length
        lds  si,[FarPtr1]     ;point DS:SI to the other source array
        cld                   ;make LODSW count up
Add3Loop:
        lodsw                 ;get the next entry from one array
        add  ax,es:[di]       ;add it to the other array
        mov  ss:[bx],ax       ;save the sum in a third array
        inc  di               ;point to the next entries
        inc  di
        inc  bx
        inc  bx
        loop Add3Loop
        pop  ds               ;restore normal DS
```

Had we needed to, we could also have stored data in CS by using **cs:**.

Handy as segment override prefixes are, you shouldn't use them too heavily if you can help it. They're fine for one-shot actions such as branching through a jump table in CS or retrieving a byte from the BIOS data area by way of ES, but they're to be avoided whenever possible inside tight loops. The reason: segment override prefixes officially take 2 cycles to execute, and, since they're 1 byte long, they can actually take up to 4 cycles to fetch and execute—and 4 cycles is a significant amount of time inside a tight loop.

Whenever you can, organize your segments outside loops so that segment override prefixes aren't needed inside loops. For example, consider Listing 7-7, which uses a segment override prefix while stripping the high bit of every byte in an array in the segment addressed via ES. Listing 7-7 runs in 2.95 msec.

```
1  ;
2  ; *** Listing 7-7 ***
3  ;
```

```
4     ; Strips the high bit of every byte in a byte-sized array,
5     ; using a segment override prefix.
6     ;
7               jmp     Skip
8     ;
9     ARRAY_LENGTH      equ     1000
10    TestArray         db      ARRAY_LENGTH dup (0ffh)
11    ;
12    ; Strips the high bit of every byte in a byte-sized array.
13    ;
14    ; Input:
15    ;       CX = length of array
16    ;       ES:BX = pointer to start of array
17    ;
18    ; Output: none
19    ;
20    ; Registers altered: AL, BX
21    ;
22    StripHighBits     proc    near
23              mov     al,not 80h        ;bit pattern for stripping
24                                        ; high bits, loaded into a
25                                        ; register outside the loop
26                                        ; so we can use fast
27                                        ; register-to-memory ANDing
28                                        ; inside the loop
29    StripHighBitsLoop:
30              and     es:[bx],al        ;strip this byte's high bit
31              inc     bx                ;point to next byte
32              loop    StripHighBitsLoop
33              ret
34    StripHighBits     endp
35    ;
36    Skip:
37              call    ZTimerOn
38              mov     bx,seg TestArray
39              mov     es,bx
40              mov     bx,offset TestArray   ;point to array
41                                            ; which will have
42                                            ; high bits stripped
43              call    StripHighBits         ;strip the high bits
44              call    ZTimerOff
```

Now consider Listing 7-8, which does the same thing as Listing 7-7, except that DS is set to match ES outside the loop. Because DS is the default segment for the memory accesses we perform inside the loop, there's no longer any need for a segment override prefix . . . and that one change improves performance by nearly 14%, reducing total execution time to 2.59 msec.

```
1     ;
2     ; *** Listing 7-8 ***
3     ;
4     ; Strips the high bit of every byte in a byte-sized array
5     ; without using a segment override prefix.
6     ;
```

```
 7              jmp      Skip
 8    ;
 9    ARRAY_LENGTH    equ      1000
10    TestArray       db       ARRAY_LENGTH dup (0ffh)
11    ;
12    ; Strips the high bit of every byte in a byte-sized array.
13    ;
14    ; Input:
15    ;      CX = length of array
16    ;      ES:BX = pointer to start of array
17    ;
18    ; Output: none
19    ;
20    ; Registers altered: AL, BX
21    ;
22    StripHighBits    proc    near
23              push     ds              ;save normal DS
24              mov      ax,es           ;point DS to the array's
25              mov      ds,ax           ; segment
26              mov      al,not 80h      ;bit pattern for stripping
27                                       ; high bits, loaded into a
28                                       ; register outside the loop
29                                       ; so we can use fast
30                                       ; register-to-memory ANDing
31                                       ; inside the loop
32    StripHighBitsLoop:
33              and      [bx],al         ;strip this byte's high bit
34              inc      bx              ;point to next byte
35              loop     StripHighBitsLoop
36              pop      ds              ;restore normal DS
37              ret
38    StripHighBits    endp
39    ;
40    Skip:
41              call     ZTimerOn
42              mov      bx,seg TestArray
43              mov      es,bx
44              mov      bx,offset TestArray    ;point to array
45                                              ; which will have
46                                              ; high bits stripped
47              call     StripHighBits          ;strip the high bits
48              call     ZTimerOff
```

The lesson is clear: don't use segment override prefixes in tight loops unless you have no choice.

assume and Segment Override Prefixes

Even if you don't put them there, segment override prefixes can find their way into your code courtesy of the assembler and the **assume** directive. The latter, **assume**, tells MASM what segments are currently addressable via the segment registers. Whenever MASM doesn't think the default segment register for a given instruction can reach the desired segment but thinks that another segment register can, *MASM sticks in a segment override prefix without telling you it's doing so.* As a result, your code can get bigger and slower without you knowing about it.

Take a look at this code:

```
Code segment
      assume   cs:code
Start proc       far
      jmp   Skip
ByteVar    db  0
Skip:
      push  cs
      pop   ds   ;set DS to point to the segment Code
      inc   [ByteVar]
          :
Code ends
```

You know and I know that DS can be used to address **ByteVar** in this code, since the first thing the code does is set DS equal to CS, thereby loading DS to point to the segment **Code**. Unfortunately, the assembler does *not* know that. The **assume** directive told the assembler only that CS points to **Code**, and **assume** is all the assembler has to go by. Given this correct but not complete information, the assembler concludes that **ByteVar** must be addressed via CS and inserts a **cs:** segment override prefix, so the **inc** instruction assembles as if **inc cs:[ByteVar]** had been used.

The result is a wasted byte and several wasted cycles. Worse yet, you have no idea that the segment override prefix has been inserted unless you either generate and examine a listing file or view the assembled code as it runs in a debugger. The assembler is just trying to help by taking some of the burden of segment selection away from you, but the outcome is all too often code that's invisibly bloated with segment override prefixes.

The solution is simple. *Keep the assembler's segment assumptions correct at all times by religiously using the **assume** directive every time you load a segment.* The above example would have assembled correctly—without a segment override prefix—if only we had inserted the line

```
assume   ds:Code
```

before attempting to access **ByteVar**.

7.5 ◆ Offset Handling

At long last, we've completed our discussion of segments. Now it's time to move on to the other half of the memory-addressing equation, offsets.

Offsets are handled somewhat differently from segments. Segments are simply loaded into the segment registers, which are then used to address memory as half of a segment:offset address. Offsets can also be loaded into registers and used directly as half of a segment:offset address, but just as often offsets are built into instructions, and they can also be calculated on the fly by summing the contents of one or two registers and/or offsets built into instructions.

At any rate, we'll quickly cover offset loading, and then we'll look at the many ways to generate offsets for memory addressing. The offset portion of memory addressing is one area in which the 8088 is very flexible, and, as we'll see, there's no single best way to address memory.

Loading offsets

Offsets are loaded with the **offset** operator. The **offset** operator is analogous to the **seg** operator we encountered earlier; the difference, of course, is that **offset** extracts the offset of a label or variable name rather than the segment. For example,

```
mov   bx,offset WordVar
```

loads BX with the offset of the variable **WordVar**. If some segment register already points to the segment containing **WordVar**, then BX can be used to address memory, as for example in

```
mov   bx,seg WordVar
mov   es,bx
mov   bx,offset WordVar
mov   ax,es:[bx]
```

We'll discuss the many ways in which offsets can be used to address memory next.

Before we get to using offsets to address memory, there are a couple of points I'd like to make. The first point is that the **lea** instruction can also be used to load offsets into registers; however, an understanding of **lea** requires an understanding of the 8088's addressing modes, so we'll defer the discussion of **lea** until later in this chapter.

The second point is a shortcoming of MASM that you must be aware of when you use **offset** on variables that reside in segment groups. If you are using the **group** directive to make segment groups, you must always specify the group name as well as the variable name when you use the offset operator. For example, if the segment **_DATA** is in the group **DGROUP**, and **WordVar** is in **_DATA**, you *must* load the offset of **WordVar** as follows:

```
mov   di,offset DGROUP:WordVar
```

If you don't specify the group name, as in

```
mov   di,offset WordVar
```

the offset of **WordVar** relative to **_DATA** rather than **DGROUP** is loaded; given that segment groups are organized with all segments in the group addressed in a single combined segment, an offset relative to **_DATA** may not work at all.

I realize that the above discussion won't make much sense if you haven't encountered the **group** directive (lucky you!). I've never found segment groups to be necessary in pure assembler code, but they are often needed when sharing segments between high-level language code and assembler. If you do find yourself using segment groups, all you need to remember is this: *when loading the offset of a variable that resides within a segment group with the* **offset** *operator, always specify the group name along with the variable name.*

7.6 ◆ *mod-reg-rm* Addressing

There are a number of ways in which the offset of an instruction operand can be specified. Collectively, the ways of specifying operand offsets are known as addressing modes. Most of the 8088's addressing modes fall into a category known as *mod-reg-rm* addressing modes. We're going to discuss *mod-reg-rm* addressing modes next; later in the chapter we'll discuss non-*mod-reg-rm* addressing modes.

The *mod-reg-rm* addressing modes are so named because they're specified by a second instruction byte, known as the *mod-reg-rm* byte, that follows instruction opcodes in order to specify the memory and/or register operands for many instructions. The *mod-reg-rm* byte gets its name because the various fields within the byte are used to specify the memory address-

ing *mode*, the *register* used for one operand, and the *register* or *memory*
location used for the other operand, as shown in Figure 7.6. (Figure 7.6
should make it clear that at most only one *mod-reg-rm* operand can be
a memory operand; one or both operands must be register operands, for
there just aren't enough bits in a *mod-reg-rm* byte to specify two memory
operands.)

Simply put, the *mod-reg-rm* byte tells the 8088 where to find an instruction's operand or operands. (It's up to the opcode byte to specify the
data size as well as which operand is the source and which the destination.) When a memory operand is used, the *mod-reg-rm* byte tells the 8088
how to add together the contents of registers (BX or BP and/or SI or DI)
and/or a fixed value built into the instruction (a displacement) in order to
generate the operand's memory offset. The offset is then combined with
the contents of one of the segment registers to make a full 20-bit memory
address, as we saw earlier in this chapter, and that 20-bit address serves as
the instruction operand. Figure 7.7 illustrates the operation of the complex
base+index+displacement addressing mode, in which an offset is generated by adding BX or BP, SI or DI, and a fixed displacement. (Note that
displacements are built right into instructions, coming immediately after
mod-reg-rm bytes, as illustrated by Figure 7.9.)

For example, if the opcode for **mov reg8,[reg/mem8] (8Ah)** is
followed by the *mod-reg-rm* byte 17h, that indicates that the register DL
is to be loaded from the memory location pointed to by BX, as shown
in Figure 7.8. Put the other way around, **mov dl,[bx]** assembles to the
2-byte sequence 8Ah 17h, where the first byte is the opcode for **mov
reg8,[reg/mem8]** and the second byte is the *mod-reg-rm* byte that selects
DL as the destination and the memory location pointed to by BX as the
source.

You may well wonder how the *mod-reg-rm* byte works with one-
operand instructions, such as **neg word ptr ds:[140h]**, or with instructions
that have constant data as one operand, such as **sub [WordVar],1**. The
answer is that in these cases the *reg* field isn't used for source or destination
control; instead, it's used as an extension of the opcode byte. So, for
instance, **neg [reg/mem16]** has an opcode byte of 0F7h and always has
bits 5 to 3 of the *mod-reg-rm* byte set to 011b. Bits 7 to 6 and 2 to 0 of the
mod-reg-rm byte still select the memory addressing mode for the single
operand, but bits 5 to 3, together with the opcode byte, now simply tell
the 8088 that the instruction is **neg [reg/mem16]**, as shown in Figure 7.9.
The **not [reg/mem16]** instruction also has an opcode byte of 0F7h, but it
is distinguished from **neg [reg/mem16]** by bits 5 to 3 of the *mod-reg-rm*
byte, which are 010b for **not** and 011b for **neg**.

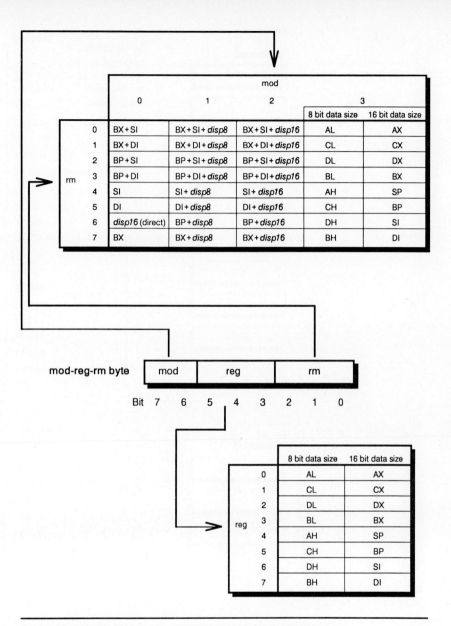

FIGURE 7.6   The interpretation of *mod-reg-rm* byte. The *mod-reg-rm*
byte specifies two operands. One may reside either in
a register or in memory; while the other must reside in
a register. The *mod* and *rm* fields together specify the
register/memory operand, while the *reg* field specifies the
register operand.

Note that it's the opcode byte, not the *mod-reg-rm*
byte, that specifies both the size of the operation and
which of the two operands specified by the *mod-reg-rm*
byte is source and which is destination.

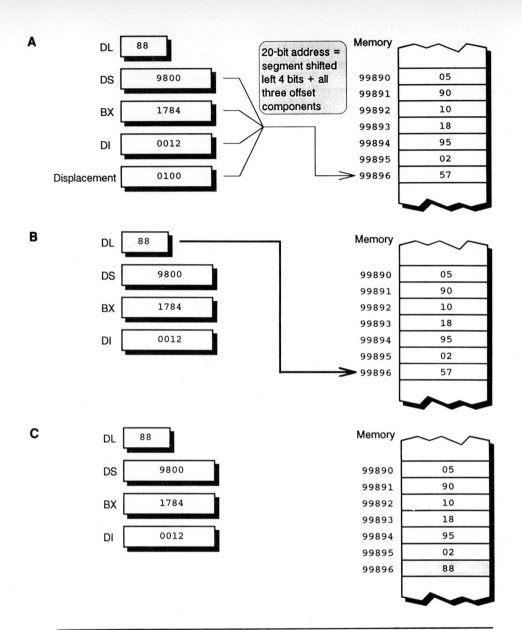

FIGURE 7.7 The operation of the instruction **mov [bx+di+100h],dl**, which uses base+index+displacement addressing. **(A)** The three offset components, BX, DI, and the displacement of 100h, are added together, and the resulting offset is added to DS shifted left 4 bits. The 20-bit result is used to address the byte of memory written to in **B. (C)** The completed operation, with the value in DL written to the addressed byte.

Note that displacements are built in to instructions, coming immediately after *mod-reg-rm* bytes.

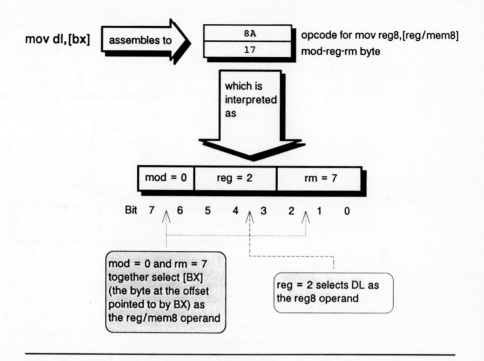

FIGURE 7.8   The interpretation of the bytes assembled for the instruction **mov dl,[bx]**, illustrating the encoding of *mod-reg-rm*
bytes.

At any rate, the mechanics of *mod-reg-rm* addressing aren't what we
need to concern ourselves with; the assembler takes care of such details,
thank goodness. We do, however, need to concern ourselves with the
implications of *mod-reg-rm* addressing, particularly size and performance
issues.

What's *mod-reg-rm* Addressing Good For?

The first thing to ask is, What is *mod-reg-rm* addressing good for? What
mod-reg-rm addressing does best is address memory in a very flexible way.
No other addressing mode approaches *mod-reg-rm* addressing for the sheer
number of ways in which memory offsets can be generated.

Look at Figure 7.6, and try to figure out how many source/destination
combinations are possible with *mod-reg-rm* addressing. The answer
is simple, as there are 8 bits in a *mod-reg-rm* byte; 256 possible

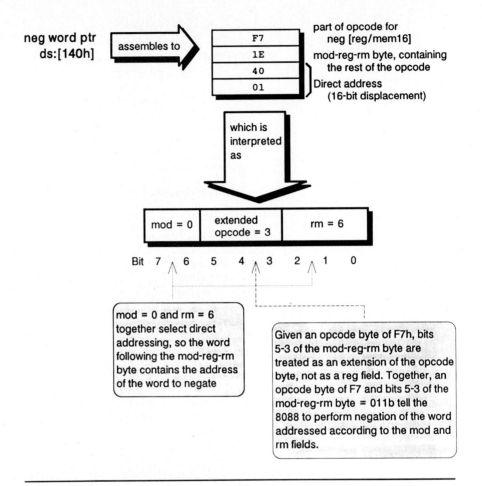

FIGURE 7.9   The interpretation of the bytes assembled for the instruction **neg word ptr ds:[140h]**, illustrating that in
single-operand *mod-reg-rm* instructions, bits 5 to 3 of the
mod-reg-rm byte serve as an extension of the opcode byte
rather than as the *reg* field.

source/destination combinations are supported. Any general-purpose register can be one operand, and any general-purpose register or memory
location can be the other operand.

If we look at memory addressing alone, we see that there are 24 distinct
ways to generate a memory offset. (Eight of the 32 possible selections
that can be made with bits 7 to 6 and 3 to 0 of the *mod-reg-rm* byte
select general-purpose registers.) Some of those 24 selections differ only

in whether 1 or 2 displacement bytes are present, leaving us with the following 16 completely distinct memory-addressing modes:

[*disp* 16]   [bp+*disp*]
[bx]   [bx+*disp*]
[si]   [si+*disp*]
[di]   [di+*disp*]
[bp+si]   [bp+si+*disp*]
[bp+di]   [bp+di+*disp*]
[bx+si]   [bx+si+*disp*]
[bx+di]   [bx+di+*disp*]

For two-operand instructions, each of those memory addressing modes can serve as either source or destination, with either a constant value or one of the eight general-purpose registers as the other operand.

Basically, *mod-reg-rm* addressing lets you select a memory offset in any of 16 ways (or a general-purpose register, if you prefer), and say, Use this as an operand. The other operand can't involve memory, but it can be any general-purpose register or (usually) a constant value. (There's no inherent support in *mod-reg-rm* addressing for constant operands. Special, separate opcodes must be used to specify constant operands for instructions that support such operands, and a few *mod-reg-rm* instructions, such as **mul**, don't accept constant operands at all.)

mod-reg-rm addressing is flexible indeed.

Displacements and Sign-Extension

I've said that displacements can be specified with either 1 or 2 bytes. The obvious question is: what determines which size is used? That's an important question, because displacement bytes directly affect program size, which in turn indirectly affects performance via the prefetch queue cycle eater.

Except in the case of direct addressing, which we'll discuss shortly, displacements in the range −128 to +127 are stored as 1 byte, then automatically sign-extended by the 8088 to a word when the instructions containing them are executed. (Expressed in unsigned hexadecimal, −128 to +127 covers two ranges: 0 to 7Fh and 0FF80h to 0FFFFh.) Sign extension involves copying bit 7 of the byte to bits 15 to 8, so a byte value of 80h sign extends to 0FF80h, and a byte value of 7Fh sign extends to 0007Fh. Basically, sign extension converts signed byte values to signed word values;

since the maximum range of a signed byte is −128 to +127, that's the maximum range of a 1-byte displacement as well.

The implication of this should be obvious: you should try to use displacements in the range −128 to +127 whenever possible, in order to reduce program size and improve performance. One caution, however: displacements must be either numbers or symbols equated to numbers in order for the assembler to be able to assemble them as single bytes. (Numbers and symbols work equally well. In

```
SAMPLE_DISPLACEMENT  equ 1
    :
    mov ax,[bx+SAMPLE_DISPLACEMENT]
    mov ax,[bx+9]
```

both **mov** instructions assemble with 1-byte displacements.)

Displacements must be constant values in order to be stored in sign-extended bytes because when a named memory variable is used, the assembler has no way of knowing where in the segment the variable will end up. Other parts of the segment may appear in other parts of the module or may be linked in from other modules, and the linker may also align the segment to various memory boundaries; any of these can have the effect of moving a given variable in the segment to an offset that doesn't fit in a sign extended byte. As a result, the following **mov** instruction assembles with a 2-byte displacement, even though it appears to be at offset 0 in its segment:

```
Data segment
MemVar   db   10 dup (?)
Data ends
        :
    mov al,[MemVar+bx]
```

Naming the *mod-reg-rm* Addressing Modes

The 16 distinct memory addressing modes supported by the *mod-reg-rm* byte are often given a slew of confusing names, such as "implied addressing," "based relative addressing," and "direct indexed addressing." Generally, there's little need to name addressing modes; you'll find you use them much more than you talk about them. However, we will need to refer to the modes later in this book, so let me explain my preferred addressing mode–naming scheme.

I find it simplest to give a name to each of the three possible components of a memory offset—*base* for BX or BP, *index* for SI or DI, *displacement* for a 1- or 2-byte fixed value—and then just refer to an addressing mode with all the components of that mode. That way, **mov [bx],al** uses base addressing, **add ax,[si+1]** uses index+displacement addressing, and **mov dl,[bp+di+1000h]** uses base+index+displacement addressing. The names may be long at times, but they're never ambiguous or hard to remember.

Direct Addressing

There is one exception to the above naming scheme, and that's direct addressing. Direct addressing is used when a memory address is referenced with just a 16-bit displacement, as in **mov bx,[WordVar]** or **mov es:[410h],al**. You might expect direct addressing to be called displacement addressing, but it's not, for three reasons. First, the address used in direct addressing is not, strictly speaking, a displacement, because it isn't relative to any register. Second, direct addressing is a time-honored term that came into use long before the 8088 was around, so experienced programmers are more likely to speak of direct addressing than of displacement addressing.

Third, direct addressing is a bit of an anomaly in *mod-reg-rm* addressing. It's pretty obvious why we'd *want* to have direct addressing available; surely you'd rather do this:

```
mov   dx,[WordVar]
```

than this:

```
mov   bx,offset WordVar
mov   dx,[bx]
```

It's just plain handy to be able to access a memory location directly by name.

Now look at Figure 7.6 again. Direct addressing really doesn't belong in that figure at all, does it? The *mod-reg-rm* encoding for direct addressing should by rights be taken by base addressing using only BP. However, there *is* no addressing mode that can use only BP; if you assemble the instruction **mov [bp],al**, you'll find that it actually assembles as **mov [bp+0],al**, with a 1-byte displacement.

In other words, the designers of the 8088 rightly considered direct addressing important enough to build it into *mod-reg-rm* addressing in place of a little-used addressing mode. (BP is designed to point to stack frames, as we'll see shortly, and there's rarely any use for BP-only base addressing in stack frames.)

Along the same lines, note that direct addressing always uses a 16-bit displacement. Direct addressing does not use an 8-bit sign-extended displacement even if the address is in the range −128 to +127.

Miscellaneous Information about Memory Addressing

Be aware that all *mod-reg-rm* addressing defaults to accessing the segment pointed to by DS—*except* when BP is used as part of the *mod-reg-rm* address. Any *mod-reg-rm* addressing involving BP accesses the segment pointed to by SS by default. (If DS and SS point to the same segment, as they often do, you can use BP-based addressing modes to point to normal data if necessary, and you can use the other *mod-reg-rm* addressing modes to point to data on the stack.) However, *mod-reg-rm* addressing can always be forced to use any segment register with a segment override prefix.

There are a few other addressing terms that I should mention now. *Indirect addressing* is commonly used to refer to any sort of memory addressing that uses a register (BX, BP, SI, or DI, or any of the valid combinations) to point to memory. We'll also use indirect to refer to branches that branch to destinations specified by memory operands, as in **jmp word ptr [SubroutinePointer]**. We'll discuss indirect branching in detail in Chapter 14.

Immediate addressing is a non-*mod-reg-rm* form of addressing in which the operand is a constant value that's built right into the instruction. We'll cover immediate addressing when we're done with *mod-reg-rm* addressing.

Finally, I'd like to make it clear that a displacement is nothing more than a fixed (constant) value that's added into the memory offset calculated by a *mod-reg-rm* byte. It's called a displacement because it specifies the number of bytes by which the addressed offset should be displaced from the offset specified by the registers used to point to memory. In **mov si,[bx+1]**, the displacement is 1; the address from which SI is loaded is displaced 1 byte from the memory location pointed to by BX. In **mov ax,[si+WordVar]**, the displacement is the offset of **WordVar**. We won't know exactly what that offset is unless we look at the code with a debugger, but it's a constant value nonetheless.

Don't get caught up worrying about the exact meaning of the term displacement, or indeed of any of the memory-addressing terms. In a way, the terms are silly; **mov ax,[bx]** is base addressing and **mov ax,[si]** is index addressing, but both load AX from the address pointed to by a register, both are 2 bytes long, and both take 13 cycles to execute. The difference between the two is purely semantic from a programmer's perspective.

Notwithstanding, we needed to establish a common terminology for the *mod-reg-rm* memory addressing modes, and we've done so. Now that we understand how *mod-reg-rm* addressing works and how wonderfully flexible it is, let's look at its dark side.

mod-reg-rm Addressing: The Dark Side

Gee, if *mod-reg-rm* addressing is so flexible, why don't we use it for all memory accesses? For that matter, why does the 8088 even *have* any other addressing modes?

One reason is that *mod-reg-rm* addressing doesn't work with all instructions. For example, the string instructions can't use *mod-reg-rm* addressing, and neither can **xlat**, which we'll encounter later in this chapter. Nonetheless, most instructions, including **mov**, **add**, **adc**, **sub**, **sbb**, **cmp**, **and**, **or**, **xor**, **neg**, **not**, **mul**, **div**, and more, do support *mod-reg-rm* addressing, so it would seem that there must be some other reason for the existence of other addressing modes.

And indeed there is. In fact, there are two reasons, speed and size. *mod-reg-rm* addressing is more flexible than other addressing modes, and it also produces the largest, slowest code around.

It's easy to understand why *mod-reg-rm* addressing produces larger code than other memory addressing modes. The bits needed to encode *mod-reg-rm* addressing's many possible source, destination, and addressing mode combinations increase the size of *mod-reg-rm* instructions, and displacement bytes can make *mod-reg-rm* instructions larger still. It stands to reason that the string instruction **lods**, which always loads AL from the memory location pointed to by DS:SI, should have fewer instruction bytes than the *mod-reg-rm* instruction **mov al,[si]**, which selects AL from 8 possible destination registers, and which selects the memory location pointed to by SI from among 32 possible source operands.

It's less obvious why *mod-reg-rm* addressing is slower than other memory addressing modes. One major reason falls out from the larger size of *mod-reg-rm* instructions; we've already established that instructions with more instruction bytes tend to run more slowly, simply because it takes time to fetch those extra instruction bytes. That's not the whole story, however. It takes the 8088 a variable but considerable amount of time—5 to

12 cycles—to calculate memory addresses from *mod-reg-rm* bytes. Those lengthy calculations, known as effective address (EA) calculations, are our next topic.

Before we proceed to EA calculations, I'd like to point out that slow and bulky as *mod-reg-rm* addressing is, it's still the workhorse memory addressing mode of the 8088. It's also the addressing mode used by many register-only instructions, such as **add dx,bx** and **mov al,dl**, with the *mod-reg-rm* byte selecting register rather than memory operands. My goodness, some instructions don't even *have* a non–*mod-reg-rm* addressing mode. Without a doubt, you'll be using *mod-reg-rm* addressing often in your code, so we'll take the time to learn how to use it well.

Nonetheless, the less flexible addressing modes are generally shorter and faster than *mod-reg-rm* addressing. As we'll see throughout *Zen of Assembly Language,* one key to writing high-performance code is avoiding *mod-reg-rm* addressing as much as possible.

Why Memory Accesses Are Slow

As I've already said, *mod-reg-rm* memory accesses are slow partly because instructions that use *mod-reg-rm* addressing tend to have many instruction bytes. The *mod-reg-rm* byte itself adds 1 byte beyond the opcode byte, and a displacement, if used, will add 1 or 2 more bytes. Remember, 4 cycles are required to fetch each and every one of those instruction bytes.

Taken a step farther, that line of thinking reveals why *all* instructions that access memory are slow: memory is slow. It takes 4 cycles per byte to access memory in any way. That means that an instruction like **mov bx,[WordVar]**, which is 4 bytes long and reads a word-sized memory variable, must perform 6 memory accesses in all; at 4 cycles a pop, that adds up to a minimum execution time of 24 cycles. Even a 2-byte memory-accessing instruction spends a minimum of 12 cycles just accessing memory. By contrast, most register-only operations are 1 to 2 bytes long and have execution unit (EU) execution times of 2 to 4 cycles, so the *maximum* execution times for register-only instructions tend to be 4 to 8 cycles.

I've said it before, and I'll say it again: *avoid accessing memory whenever you can.* Memory is just plain slow.

In actual use, many memory-accessing instructions turn out to be even slower than memory access times alone would explain. For example, the fastest possible *mod-reg-rm* memory-accessing instruction, **mov *reg8*,[bx]** (BP, SI, or DI would do as well as BX), has an EU execution time of 13 cycles, although only three memory accesses (requiring 12 cycles) are performed. Similarly, string instructions, **xlat**, **push**, and **pop** take more cycles than can be accounted for solely by memory accesses.

The full explanation for the poor performance of the 8088's memory-accessing instructions lies in the microcode of the 8088 (the built-in bit patterns that sequence the 8088 through the execution of each instruction), which is undeniably slower than it might be. (Check out the execution times of the 8088's instructions on the 80286 and 80386, and you'll see that it's possible to execute the 8088's instructions in many fewer cycles than the 8088 requires.) That's not something we can change; about all we can do is choose the fastest available instruction for each task, and we'll spend much of *Zen of Assembly Language* doing just that.

There is one aspect of memory addressing that we *can* change, however, and that's EA calculation time—the amount of time it takes the 8088 to calculate memory addresses.

Some *mod-reg-rm* Memory Accesses Are Slower than Others

A given instruction that uses *mod-reg-rm* addressing doesn't always execute in the same number of cycles. The EU execution time of *mod-reg-rm* instructions comes in two parts: a fixed EU execution time and an effective address (EA) calculation time that varies depending on the *mod-reg-rm* addressing mode used. The two times added together constitute the overall execution time of each *mod-reg-rm* instruction.

Each *mod-reg-rm* instruction has its own fixed EU execution time, which remains the same for all addressing modes. For example, the fixed execution time of **add bl,[*mem*]** is 9 cycles, as shown in Appendix A; this value is constant, no matter what *mod-reg-rm* addressing mode is used.

The EA calculation time, on the other hand, depends not in the least on which instruction is being executed. EA calculation time is determined solely by the *mod-reg-rm* addressing mode used and nothing else, as shown in Figure 7.10. As you can see in Figure 7.10, the time it takes the 8088 to calculate an effective address can vary greatly, ranging from a mere 5 cycles if a single register is used to point to memory all the way up to 11 or 12 cycles if the sum of two registers and a displacement is used to point to memory. (Segment override prefixes require an additional 2 cycles each, as we saw earlier.) When I discuss the performance of an instruction that uses *mod-reg-rm* addressing, I often say that it takes at least a certain number of cycles to execute. What *at least* means is that the instruction will take that many cycles if the fastest *mod-reg-rm* addressing mode—base- or

Addressing mode	Effective address calculation time

Base
    [BP]
    [BX]
	5 cycles

Index
    [SI]
    [DI]
	5 cycles

Direct [MemVar]	6 cycles

Base + Index
    [BP + DI]
    [BX + SI]
	7 cycles

Base + Index
    [BX + DI]
    [BP + SI]
	8 cycles

Base + Displacement
    [BX + disp]
    [BP + disp]
	9 cycles

Index + Displacement
    [SI + disp]
    [DI + disp]
	9 cycles

Base + Index + Displacement
    [BP + DI + disp]
    [BX + SI + disp]
	11 cycles

Base + Index + Displacement
    [BX + DI + disp]
    [BP + SI + disp]
	12 cycles

FIGURE 7.10   Effective address (EA) calculation times.

index-only—is used, and longer if some other *mod-reg-rm* addressing mode is selected.

Only *mod-reg-rm* memory operands require EA calculations. There is no EA calculation time for register operands, or for memory operands accessed with non–*mod-reg-rm* addressing modes.

In short, EA calculation time means that the choice of *mod-reg-rm* addressing mode directly affects performance. Let's take a closer look at the performance implications of EA calculations.

Performance Implications of Effective Address Calculations

There are a number of interesting points to be made about EA calculation time. For starters, it should be clear that EA calculation time is a big reason why instructions that use *mod-reg-rm* addressing are slow. The minimum EA calculation time of 5 cycles, on top of 8 or more cycles of fixed execution time, is no bargain; the maximum EA calculation time of 12 cycles is a grim prospect indeed.

For example, **add bl,[si]** takes 13 cycles to execute (8 cycles of fixed execution time and 5 cycles of EA calculation time), which is certainly not terrific by comparison with the 3-cycle execution time of **add bl,dl**. (Instruction fetching alters the picture somewhat, as we'll see shortly.) At the other end of the EA calculation spectrum, **add bl,[bx+di+100h]** takes 20 cycles to execute, which is horrendous no matter what you compare it to.

The lesson seems clear: use faster *mod-reg-rm* addressing modes whenever you can. While that's true, it's not necessarily obvious which *mod-reg-rm* addressing modes are faster. Base-only addressing and index-only addressing are the *mod-reg-rm* addressing modes of choice, because they add only 5 cycles of EA calculation time and 1 byte, the *mod-reg-rm* byte. For instance, **mov dl,[bp]** is just 2 bytes long and takes a fairly reasonable 13 cycles to execute.

Direct addressing, which has an EA calculation time of 6 cycles, is only slightly slower than base or index addressing so far as official execution time goes. However, direct addressing requires 2 additional instruction bytes (the 16-bit displacement) beyond the *mod-reg-rm* byte, so it's actually a good deal slower than base or index addressing. The instruction **mov dl,[ByteVar]** officially takes 14 cycles to execute, but given that it is 4 bytes long and performs a memory access, 20 cycles is a more accurate execution time.

Base+index addressing (**mov al,[bp+di]** and the like) takes 1 to 2 cycles more for EA calculation time than does direct addressing, but is nonetheless superior to direct addressing in most cases. The key: base+index addressing requires only the 1 *mod-reg-rm* byte. Base+index addressing instructions are 2 bytes shorter than equivalent direct addressing instructions, and that translates into a considerable instruction-fetching/performance advantage.

The rule is: *use displacement-free* mod-reg-rm *addressing modes whenever you can.* Instructions that use displacements are always 1 to 2 bytes longer than those that use displacement-free *mod-reg-rm* addressing modes, and that means that there's generally a prefetching penalty for using displacements. There's also a substantial EA calculation time penalty for base+displacement, index+displacement, or base+index+displacement addressing. If you must use displacements, use 1-byte displacements as much as possible; we'll see an example of this when we get to stack frames later in this chapter.

Now, bear in mind that the choice of *mod-reg-rm* addressing mode really matters only inside loops or in time-critical code. If you're going to load DX from memory just once in a long subroutine, it doesn't much matter if you take a few extra cycles to load it with direct addressing rather than base or index addressing. It certainly isn't worth loading, say, BX to point to memory, as in:

```
mov   bx,offset MemVar
mov   dx,[bx]
```

to use base or index addressing just once. The **mov** instruction used to load BX takes 4 cycles and 3 bytes, more than negating any advantage base addressing has over direct addressing.

Inside loops, however, it's well worth using the most efficient addressing mode available. Listing 7-9, which adds up the elements of a byte-sized array using base+index+displacement addressing every time through the loop, runs in 1.17 msec. Listing 7-10, which changes the addressing mode to base+index by adding the displacement into the base outside the loop, runs in 1.01 msec, nearly 16 percent faster than Listing 7-9. Finally, Listing 7-11, which performs all the addressing calculations outside the loop and uses plain old base-only addressing, runs in just 0.95 msec, 6 percent faster still. (The string instruction **lods** is even faster than **mov al,[bx]**, as we'll see in Chapter 10. Always think of your non–*mod-reg-rm* alternatives.) Clearly, the choice of addressing mode matters considerably inside tight loops.

We've learned two basic rules, then: 1. *Use displacement-free* mod-reg-rm *addressing modes whenever you can.* 2. *Calculate memory addresses outside loops and use base-only or index-only addressing whenever possible.* The **lea** instruction, which we'll get to shortly, is most useful for calculating memory addresses outside loops.

```
1    ;
2    ; *** Listing 7-9 ***
3    ;
4    ; Adds up the elements of a byte-sized array using
5    ; base+index+displacement addressing inside the loop.
6    ;
7            jmp     Skip
8    ;
9    ARRAY_LENGTH    equ     1000
10   TestArray       db      ARRAY_LENGTH dup (1)
11   TEST_START_OFFSET equ   200     ;we'll add elements 200-299
12   TEST_LENGTH     equ     100     ; of TestArray
13   ;
14   Skip:
15           call    ZTimerOn
16           mov     bx,TEST_START_OFFSET
17                                   ;for base+index+displacement
18           sub     si,si           ; addressing
19           sub     ax,ax           ;initialize sum
20           sub     dl,dl           ;store 0 in DL so we can use
21                                   ; it for faster register-
22                                   ; register adds in the loop
23           mov     cx,TEST_LENGTH  ;# of bytes to add
24   SumArrayLoop:
25           add     al,[TestArray+bx+si] ;add in the next byte
26           adc     ah,dl           ; to the 16-bit sum
27           inc     si              ;point to next byte
28           loop    SumArrayLoop
29           call    ZTimerOff
```

```
1    ;
2    ; *** Listing 7-10 ***
3    ;
4    ; Adds up the elements of a byte-sized array using
5    ; base+index addressing inside the loop.
6    ;
7            jmp     Skip
8    ;
9    ARRAY_LENGTH    equ     1000
10   TestArray       db      ARRAY_LENGTH dup (1)
11   TEST_START_OFFSET equ   200     ;we'll add elements 200-299
12   TEST_LENGTH     equ     100     ; of TestArray
13   ;
14   Skip:
15           call    ZTimerOn
16           mov     bx,offset TestArray+TEST_START_OFFSET
17                                   ;build the array start
18                                   ; offset right into the
19                                   ; base so we can use
20                                   ; base+index addressing,
21           sub     si,si           ; with no displacement
22           sub     ax,ax           ;initialize sum
23           sub     dl,dl           ;store 0 in DL so we can use
24                                   ; it for faster register-
25                                   ; register adds in the loop
26           mov     cx,TEST_LENGTH  ;# of bytes to add
27   SumArrayLoop:
```

```
28          add     al,[bx+si]      ;add in the next byte
29          adc     ah,dl           ; to the 16-bit sum
30          inc     si              ;point to next byte
31          loop    SumArrayLoop
32          call    ZTimerOff
```

```
1    ;
2    ; *** Listing 7-11 ***
3    ;
4    ; Adds up the elements of a byte-sized array using
5    ; base-only addressing inside the loop.
6    ;
7            jmp     Skip
8    ;
9    ARRAY_LENGTH        equ     1000
10   TestArray           db      ARRAY_LENGTH dup (1)
11   TEST_START_OFFSET equ     200     ;we'll add elements 200-299
12   TEST_LENGTH         equ     100     ; of TestArray
13   ;
14   Skip:
15           call    ZTimerOn
16           mov     bx,offset TestArray+TEST_START_OFFSET
17                                   ;build the array start
18                                   ; offset right into the
19                                   ; base so we can use
20                                   ; base addressing, with no
21                                   ; displacement
22           sub     ax,ax           ;initialize sum
23           sub     dl,dl           ;store 0 in DL so we can use
24                                   ; it for faster register-
25                                   ; register adds in the loop
26           mov     cx,TEST_LENGTH  ;# of bytes to add
27   SumArrayLoop:
28           add     al,[bx]         ;add in the next byte
29           adc     ah,dl           ; to the 16-bit sum
30           inc     bx              ;point to next byte
31           loop    SumArrayLoop
32           call    ZTimerOff
```

mod-reg-rm Addressing: Slow, but Not Quite as Slow as You Think

There's no doubt about it: *mod-reg-rm* addressing is slow. Still, relative to register operands, *mod-reg-rm* operands might not be quite as slow as you think, for an unexpected reason—the prefetch queue. *mod-reg-rm* addressing executes so slowly that it allows time for quite a few instruction bytes to be prefetched, and that means that instructions that use *mod-reg-rm* addressing often run at pretty much their official speed.

Consider this: **mov al,bl** is a 2-byte, 2-cycle instruction. String a few such instructions together and the prefetch queue empties, making the actual execution time 8 cycles, the time it takes to fetch the instruction bytes.

By contrast, **mov al,[bx]** is a 2-byte, 13-cycle instruction. Counting both the memory access needed to read the operand pointed to by BX and the two instruction fetches, only three memory accesses are incurred by this instruction. Since three memory accesses take only 12 cycles, the 13-cycle official execution time of **mov al,[bx]** is a fair reflection of the instruction's true execution time.

That doesn't mean that **mov al,[bx]** is *faster* than **mov al,bl**, or that memory-accessing instructions are faster than register-only instructions—they're not. Under any circumstances, **mov al,bl** is at least about 50 percent faster than **mov al,[bx]**. What it does mean is that memory-accessing instructions tend to suffer less from the prefetch queue cycle eater than do register-only instructions, because the considerably longer execution times of memory-accessing instructions often allow a good deal of prefetching per instruction byte executed. As a result, the performance difference between the two is often not quite so great as official execution times indicate.

In short, memory-accessing instructions, especially those that use *mod-reg-rm* addressing, generally have a better balance between overall memory access time and execution time than register-only instructions, and consequently run closer to their rated speeds. That's a mixed blessing, since it's a side effect of the slow speed of memory-accessing instructions, but it does make memory access—which is, after all, a necessary evil—somewhat less unappealing than it might seem.

Let me emphasize that the basic reason that instructions that use *mod-reg-rm* memory accesses suffer less from the prefetch queue cycle eater than do equivalent register-only instructions is that both sorts of instructions have *mod-reg-rm* bytes. True, register-only *mod-reg-rm* instructions don't have EA calculation times, but they do have at least 2 bytes, making them as long as the shortest *mod-reg-rm* memory-accessing instructions. (A number of non–*mod-reg-rm* instructions are just 1 byte long; we'll meet them in the next few chapters.) Since register-only instructions are much faster than memory-accessing instructions, it's just common sense that if they're the same length in bytes they can be hit much harder by the prefetch queue cycle eater.

Still and all, register-only *mod-reg-rm* instructions are *never* longer than memory-accessing *mod-reg-rm* instructions, and are shorter than memory-accessing instructions that use displacements. What's more, since memory-accessing instructions must by definition access memory at least once apart from fetching instruction bytes, register-only *mod-reg-rm* instructions must be at least 50 percent faster than their memory-accessing equivalents

(100 percent when word-sized operands are used). To sum up, register-only instructions are always much faster and often smaller than equivalent *mod-reg-rm* memory-accessing instructions. (Register-only instructions are also faster than, although not necessarily shorter than or even as short as, non–*mod-reg-rm* instructions, including the string instructions.)

Avoid memory. Use the registers as much as you possibly can.

The Importance of Addressing Well

When you do use *mod-reg-rm* addressing, use it efficiently. As we've discussed, that means using base- or index-only addressing whenever possible and avoiding displacements when you can, especially inside loops. If you're going to access a memory location only once and you don't have a pointer to that location already loaded into BX, BP, SI, or DI, just use direct addressing; base- and index-only addressing aren't so much faster than direct addressing that it pays to load a pointer. As we've seen, however, don't use direct addressing inside a loop if you can load a pointer register outside the loop and then use base- or index-only addressing inside the loop.

It's often surprising how much more efficient than direct addressing base- and index-only addressing are. Consider this simple bit of code:

```
mov   dl,[ByteVar]
and   dl,0fh
mov   [ByteVar],dl
```

You wouldn't think that this code could be improved upon by *adding* an instruction, but we can cut the code's size from 11 to 10 bytes by using base-only addressing:

```
mov   bx,offset ByteVar
mov   dl,[bx]
and   dl,0fh
mov   [bx],dl
```

The cycle count is 2 higher for the latter version, but a 1-byte advantage in instruction fetching could well overcome that.

The point is not that base-only addressing is always the best solution. In fact, the latter example could be made much more efficient simply by anding 0Fh directly with memory, as in

```
and   [ByteVar],0fh
```

(Always bear in mind that memory can serve as the destination operand as well as the source operand. When only one modification is involved, it's always faster to modify a memory location directly, as in the last example, than it is to load a register, modify the register, and store the register back to memory. However, the scales tip when two or more modifications to a memory operand are involved, as we'll see in Chapter 8.) The special accumulator-specific direct-addressing instructions that we'll discuss in the next chapter make direct addressing more desirable in certain circumstances as well.

The point is that, for repeated accesses to the same memory location, you should arrange your code so that the most efficient possible instruction can be used—base-only, a string instruction, whatever fills the bill. In the last example, base-only addressing was superior to direct addressing when just two accesses to the same byte were involved. Multiply the number of accesses by 10, or 100, or 1000, as is often the case in a tight loop, and you'll get a feel for the importance of selecting the correct memory-addressing mode in your time-critical code.

The 8088 Is Faster at Memory Address Calculations than You Are

You may recall that we found earlier that when you must access a word-sized memory operand, it is better to let the 8088 access the second byte than to do it with a separate instruction; the 8088 is simply faster at accessing two adjacent bytes than any two instructions can be. Much the same is true of *mod-reg-rm* addressing; the 8088 is faster at performing memory address calculations than you are. If you must add registers and/or constant values to address memory, the 8088 can do it faster during EA calculations than you can with separate instructions.

Suppose that we have to initialize a doubleword of memory pointed to by BX to zero. We could do that with

```
mov    word ptr [bx],0
inc    bx
inc    bx
mov    word ptr [bx],0
```

However, it's better to let the 8088 do the addressing calculations, as follows:

```
mov word ptr [bx],0
mov word ptr [bx+2],0
```

True, the latter version involves a 1-byte displacement, but that displacement is smaller than the 2 bytes required to advance BX in the first version. Since the incremental cost of base+displacement addressing over base-only addressing is 4 cycles, exactly the same number of cycles as two **inc** instructions, the code that uses base+displacement addressing is clearly superior.

Similarly, you're invariably better off letting EA calculations add one register to another than you are using **add**. For example, consider two approaches to scanning an array pointed to by BX+SI for the byte in AL:

```
        mov dx,bx       ;set aside the base address
ScanLoop:
        mov bx,dx       ;get back the base address
        add bx,si       ;add in the index
        cmp [bx],al     ;is this a match?
        jz   ScanFound  ;yes, we're done
        inc  si         ;advance the index to the next byte
        jmp  ScanLoop   ;scan the next byte
ScanFound:
```

and

```
ScanLoop:
        cmp [bx+si],al  ;is this a match?
        jz   ScanFound  ;yes, we're done
        inc  si         ;advance the index to the next byte
        jmp  ScanLoop   ;scan the next byte
ScanFound:
```

It should be pretty clear that the approach that lets the 8088 add the two memory components together is far superior.

While the point is perhaps a little exaggerated—I seriously doubt anyone would use the first approach—it is nonetheless valid. The 8088 can add BX to SI in just 2 extra cycles as part of an EA calculation, and at the cost of no extra bytes at all. What's more, EA calculations leave all registers unchanged. By contrast, at least one register must be changed to hold the final memory address when you perform memory calculations yourself. That's what makes the first version above so inefficient; we have to reload BX from DX every time through the loop because it's altered by the memory-address calculation.

I hope you noticed that neither example above is particularly efficient. We'd be better off simply adding the two memory components outside the loop and using base- or index-only addressing inside the loop. (We'd be even better off using string instructions, but we'll save that for another chapter.) To wit,

```
        add   si,bx         ;add together the memory address components
                            ; outside the loop
ScanLoop:
        cmp   [si],al       ;is this a match?
        jz    ScanFound     ;yes, we're done
        inc   si            ;point to the next byte
        jmp   ScanLoop      ;scan the next byte
ScanFound:
```

Although EA calculations can add faster than separate instructions can, it's faster still not to add at all. *Whenever you can, perform your calculations outside loops.*

Which brings us to **lea**.

Calculating Effective Addresses with lea

As the only *mod-reg-rm* memory-addressing instruction that doesn't access memory, **lea** is something of an odd bird. **lea** calculates the offset of the memory operand . . . and then just loads that offset into one of the 8 general-purpose registers, without accessing memory at all. Basically, **lea** is nothing more than a means by which to load the result of an EA calculation into a register.

For example, **lea bx,[MemVar]** loads the offset of **MemVar** into BX. Now, we wouldn't generally want to use **lea** to load simple offsets, since **mov** can do that more efficiently; **mov bx,offset MemVar** is 1 byte shorter and 4 cycles faster than **lea bx,[MemVar]**. (Since **lea** involves EA calculation, it's not particularly fast; however, it's faster than any *mod- reg-rm* memory-accessing instruction, taking only 2 cycles plus the EA calculation time.)

It's when you need to load a register with a complex memory address, preferably without disturbing any of the registers that make up the memory address, that **lea** shines. Suppose that we want to push the address of an array element that's indexed by BP+SI. We could use

```
mov   ax,offset TestArray
add   ax,bp
add   ax,si
push  ax
```

which is 8 bytes long. On the other hand, we could simply use

```
lea   ax,[TestArray+bp+si]
push ax
```

which is at most 5 bytes long. One of the principal uses of **lea** is in loading offsets of variables in stack frames, because such variables are addressed with base+displacement addressing.

Refer back to the example we examined in the previous section. Suppose that we wanted to scan memory without disturbing either BX or SI. In that case, we could use DI, with an assist from **lea**; thus:

```
         lea   di,[bx+si]   ;add together the memory address components
                           ; outside the loop
ScanLoop:
         cmp   [di],al      ;is this a match?
         jz    ScanFound    ;yes, we're done
         inc   di           ;point to the next byte
         jmp   ScanLoop     ;scan the next byte
ScanFound:
```

lea is particularly handy in this case because it can add two registers, BX and SI, and place the result in a third register, DI. That enables us to replace the two instructions

```
mov  di,bx
add   di,si
```

with a single **lea**.

The operation of **lea** should make it clear that offsets are just 16-bit numbers. Adding offsets stored in BX and SI together with **lea** is no different from adding any two 16-bit numbers together with **add**, because offsets are just 16-bit numbers.

Zero is a valid offset, so if we execute

```
sub  bx,bx        ;load BX with 0
mov  al,[bx]      ;load AL with the byte at offset 0 in DS
```

we'll read the byte at offset 0 in the segment pointed to by DS. It's important that you understand that offsets are just numbers and that you can manipulate offsets every bit as flexibly as any other values.

The flip side is that you could, if you wished, add two registers and/or a constant value together with **lea** and place the result in a third register. Of course, the source registers would have to be BX or BP and SI or DI, but since offsets and numbers are one and the same, there's no reason that **lea** couldn't be used for arithmetic under the right circumstances. For example, here's one way to add two memory variables and 52 together and store the result in DX:

```
mov    bx,[MemVar1]
mov    si,[MemVar2]
lea    dx,[bx+si+52]
```

That's not to say this is a *good* way to perform this particular task; the following is faster and uses fewer registers:

```
mov    dx,[MemVar1]
add    dx,[MemVar2]
add    dx,52
```

Nonetheless, the first approach does serve to illustrate the flexibility of **lea** and the equivalence of offsets and numbers.

Offset Wrapping at the Ends of Segments

Before we take leave of *mod-reg-rm* addressing, I'd like to repeat a point made earlier that may have slipped past unnoticed. That point is that offsets wrap at the ends of segments. Offsets are 16-bit entities, so they're limited to the range 0 to 64 K-1. However, it is possible to use two or three *mod-reg-rm* address components that together add up to a number that's larger than 64 K. For example, the sum of the memory-addressing components in the following code is 18000h:

```
mov    bx,4000h
mov    di,8000h
mov    ax,[bx+di+0c000h]
```

What happens in such a case? We found earlier that segments are limited to 64 Kb in length; is this a clever way to enlarge the effective size of a segment?

Alas, no. If the sum of two offset components won't fit in 16 bits, bits 16 and above of the sum are simply ignored. In other words, *mod-reg-rm* address calculations are always performed modulo 64 K (that is, modulo 10000h), as shown in Figure 7.11. As a result, the last example will access not the word at offset 18000h but the word at offset 8000h. Likewise, the following will access the byte at offset 0:

```
mov   bx,0ffffh
mov   dl,[bx+1]
```

The same rule holds for all memory-accessing instructions, *mod-reg-rm* or otherwise: *offsets are 16-bit values; any additional bits that result from address calculations are ignored.*

Put another way, memory addresses that reach past the end of a segment's 64-K limit wrap back to the start of the segment. This allows the use of negative displacements, and is the reason a displacement can always reach anywhere in a segment, including addresses lower than those in the base and/or index registers, as in **mov ax,[bx-1]**.

7.7 ◆ Non–*mod-reg-rm* Memory Addressing

mod-reg-rm addressing is the most flexible memory addressing mode of the 8088, and the most widely used as well, but it's certainly not the *only* addressing mode. The 8088 also offers a number of specialized addressing modes, including stack addressing and the addressing supported by the string instructions. These addressing modes are supported by fewer instructions than *mod-reg-rm* instructions and are considerably more restrictive about the operands they'll accept—but they're also more compact and/or faster than the *mod-reg-rm* instructions.

Why are instructions that use the non–*mod-reg-rm* addressing modes generally superior to *mod-reg-rm* instructions? Simply because by being less flexible than *mod-reg-rm* instructions they have fewer possible operands to specify, so fewer instruction bits are needed. Non–*mod-reg-rm* instructions also don't require any EA calculation time, because they don't support the many addressing modes of the *mod-reg-rm* byte.

We'll discuss five sorts of non–*mod-reg-rm* memory-addressing instructions next: special forms of common instructions, string instructions, immediate-addressing instructions, stack-oriented instructions, and **xlat**, which is in a category all its own. For all these sorts of instructions, the rule is that if they're well matched to your application, they're almost

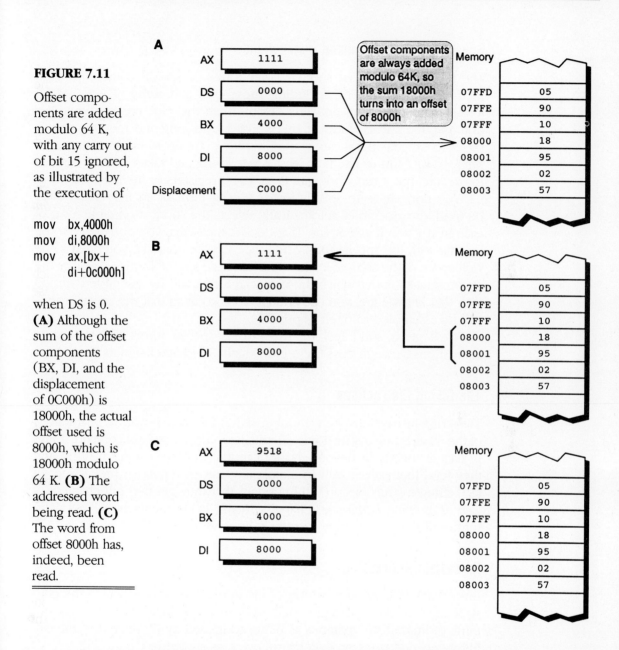

FIGURE 7.11

Offset components are added modulo 64 K, with any carry out of bit 15 ignored, as illustrated by the execution of

```
mov   bx,4000h
mov   di,8000h
mov   ax,[bx+
      di+0c000h]
```

when DS is 0. **(A)** Although the sum of the offset components (BX, DI, and the displacement of 0C000h) is 18000h, the actual offset used is 8000h, which is 18000h modulo 64 K. **(B)** The addressed word being read. **(C)** The word from offset 8000h has, indeed, been read.

surely worth using in preference to *mod-reg-rm* addressing. Some of the non–*mod-reg-rm* instructions, especially the string instructions, are so much faster than *mod-reg-rm* instructions that they're worth going out of your way for, as we'll see throughout *Zen of Assembly Language*.

Special Forms of Common Instructions

The 8088 offers special shorter, faster forms of several commonly used *mod-reg-rm* instructions, including **mov**, **inc**, and **xchg**. These special forms are both shorter and less flexible than the *mod-reg-rm* forms. For example, the special form of **inc** is just 1 byte long and requires only 2 cycles to execute, but it can work only with 16-bit registers. By contrast, the *mod-reg-rm* form of **inc** is at least 2 bytes long and takes at least 3 cycles to execute, but it can work with 8- or 16-bit registers or memory locations.

You don't have to specify that a special form of an instruction is to be used; the assembler automatically selects the shortest possible form of each instruction it assembles. That doesn't mean that you don't need to be familiar with the special forms, however. On the contrary, you need to be well aware of the sorts of instructions that have special forms, as well as the circumstances under which those special forms will be assembled. Armed with that knowledge, you can arrange your code so that the special forms will be assembled as often as possible.

We'll get a solid feel for the various special forms of *mod-reg-rm* instructions as we discuss them individually in Chapters 8 and 9.

The String Instructions

The string instructions are without question the most powerful instructions of the 8088. String instructions can initialize, copy, scan, and compare arrays of data at speeds far beyond those of mortal *mod-reg-rm* instructions, and they lend themselves well to almost any sort of repetitive processing. In fact, string instructions are so important that they get two full chapters of *Zen of Assembly Language* (Chapters 10 and 11) to themselves. We'll defer further discussion of these extremely important instructions until then.

Immediate Addressing

Immediate addressing is a form of memory addressing in which the constant value of one operand is built right in to the instruction. You should think of immediate operands as being addressed by IP, since they directly follow opcode bytes or *mod-reg-rm* bytes, as shown in Figure 7.12.

Instructions that use immediate addressing are clearly faster than instructions that use *mod-reg-rm* addressing. In fact, according to official execution times, immediate addressing would seem to be *much* faster than *mod-reg-rm* addressing. For example, **add ax,1** is a 4-cycle instruction, while **add ax,[bx]** is an 18-cycle instruction. What's more, **add *reg,immed***

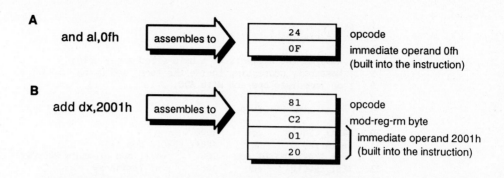

A

and al,0fh   assembles to →

| 24 | opcode |
| 0F | immediate operand 0fh (built into the instruction) |

B

add dx,2001h   assembles to →

81	opcode
C2	mod-reg-rm byte
01	immediate operand 2001h
20	(built into the instruction)

FIGURE 7.12   Immediate operands are built right in to instructions, coming immediately after opcode bytes or *mod-reg-rm* bytes. **(A)** The immediate operand 0Fh follows the opcode byte in **and al,0fh**. **(B)** The immediate operand 2001h follows the *mod-reg-rm* byte in **add dx,2001h**.

is just 1 cycle slower than **add *reg,reg***, so immediate addressing seems to be nearly as fast as register addressing.

The official cycle counts are misleading, however. Although immediate addressing is certainly faster than *mod-reg-rm* addressing, it is by no means as fast as register-only addressing, and the reason is a familiar one, the prefetch queue cycle eater. You see, immediate operands are instruction bytes. When we use an immediate operand, we increase the size of that instruction, and that increases the number of cycles needed to fetch the instruction's bytes.

Looked at another way, immediate operands need to be fetched from the memory location pointed to by IP, so immediate addressing could be considered a memory-addressing mode. Granted, immediate addressing is an efficient memory-addressing mode, with no EA calculation time or the like—but memory accesses are nonetheless required, at the inescapable 4 cycles per byte.

The upshot is simply that register operands are superior to immediate operands in loops and time-critical code, although immediate operands are still much better than *mod-reg-rm* memory operands.

Back in Listing 7-11, we set DL to 0 outside the loop so we could use register-register **adc** inside the loop. That approach allowed the code to run in 0.95 msec. Listing 7-12 is similar to Listing 7-11, but is modified to use an immediate operand of 0 rather than a register operand containing 0. Even though the immediate operand is only byte-sized, Listing 7-12 slows

```
1    ;
2    ; *** Listing 7-12 ***
3    ;
4    ; Adds up the elements of a byte-sized array using
5    ; base-only addressing inside the loop, and using
6    ; an immediate operand with ADC.
7    ;
8            jmp     Skip
9    ;
10   ARRAY_LENGTH      equ     1000
11   TestArray         db      ARRAY_LENGTH dup (1)
12   TEST_START_OFFSET equ     200     ;we'll add elements 200-299
13   TEST_LENGTH       equ     100     ; of TestArray
14   ;
15   Skip:
16           call    ZTimerOn
17           mov     bx,offset TestArray+TEST_START_OFFSET
18                                   ;build the array start
19                                   ; offset right into the
20                                   ; base so we can use
21                                   ; base+index addressing,
22                                   ; with no displacement
23           sub     ax,ax           ;initialize sum
24           mov     cx,TEST_LENGTH  ;# of bytes to add
25   SumArrayLoop:
26           add     al,[bx]         ;add in the next byte
27           adc     ah,0            ; to the 16-bit sum
28           inc     bx              ;point to next byte
29           loop    SumArrayLoop
30           call    ZTimerOff
```

down to 1.02 msec. In other words, the need to fetch just 1 immediate operand byte every time through the loop slowed the entire loop by about 7%. What's more, the performance loss would have been approximately twice as great if we had used a word-sized immediate operand.

On the other hand, immediate operands are certainly preferable to memory operands. Listing 7-13, which adds the constant value 0 from memory, runs in 1.26 msec. (I should hope you'll never use code as obviously inefficient as Listing 7-13; I'm just presenting it for illustrative purposes.)

```
1    ;
2    ; *** Listing 7-13 ***
3    ;
4    ; Adds up the elements of a byte-sized array using
5    ; base-only addressing inside the loop, and using
6    ; a memory operand with ADC.
7    ;
8            jmp     Skip
9    ;
10   ARRAY_LENGTH      equ     1000
11   TestArray         db      ARRAY_LENGTH dup (1)
12   TEST_START_OFFSET equ     200     ;we'll add elements 200-299
```

```
13   TEST_LENGTH      equ     100       ; of TestArray
14   MemZero          db      0         ;the constant value 0
15   ;
16   Skip:
17            call    ZTimerOn
18            mov     bx,offset TestArray+TEST_START_OFFSET
19                              ;build the array start
20                              ; offset right into the
21                              ; base so we can use
22                              ; base+index addressing,
23                              ; with no displacement
24            sub     ax,ax     ;initialize sum
25            mov     cx,TEST_LENGTH ;# of bytes to add
26   SumArrayLoop:
27            add     al,[bx]        ;add in the next byte
28            adc     ah,[MemZero]   ; to the 16-bit sum
29            inc     bx             ;point to next byte
30            loop    SumArrayLoop
31            call    ZTimerOff
```

To sum up: when speed matters, use register operands rather than immediate operands if you can. If registers are at a premium, however, immediate operands are reasonably fast and are certainly better than memory operands. If bytes rather than cycles are at a premium, immediate operands are excellent, for it takes fewer bytes to use an immediate operand than it does to load a register with a constant value and then use that register. For example

```
LoopTop:
      or   byte ptr [bx],80h
      loop LoopTop
```

is 1 byte shorter than

```
      mov   al,80h
LoopTop:
      or   [bx],al
      loop LoopTop
```

However, the latter, register-only version is faster, because it moves 1 byte out of the loop.

There are many circumstances in which we can substitute register-only instructions for instructions that use immediate operands *without* adding extra instructions. The commonest of these cases involve testing for 0. There's almost never a need to compare a register with 0; instead, we can simply **and** or **or** the register with itself and check the resulting flags. We'll discuss ways to handle zero in the next two chapters, and we'll see similar cases in which immediate operands can be eliminated throughout *Zen of Assembly Language*.

By the way, you should be aware that you can use an immediate operand even when the other operand is a memory variable rather than a register. For example, **add [MemVar],16** is a valid instruction, as is **mov [MemVar],52**. As I mentioned earlier, we're better off performing single operations directly to memory than we are loading from memory into a register, operating on the register, and storing the result back to memory. However, we're generally better off working with a register when multiple operations are involved.

Ideally, we'd load a memory value into a register, perform multiple operations on it there, store the result back to memory, and then have some additional use for the value left in the register, thereby getting double use out of our memory accesses. For example, suppose that we want to perform the equivalent of the C statement

```
i = ++j + k;
```

We could do this as follows:

```
inc    [j]
mov    ax,[j]
add    ax,[k]
mov    [i],ax
```

However, we can eliminate a memory access by incrementing **j** in a register:

```
mov    ax,[j]
inc    ax
mov    [j],ax
add    ax,[k]
mov    [i],ax
```

While the latter version is one instruction longer than the original, it's actually faster and requires the same number of bytes. One reason for this is that we get double use out of loading **j** into AX; we increment **j** in AX and store the result to memory, then immediately use the incremented value left in AX as part of the calculation being performed.

The other reason the second example above is superior to the original version is that it uses two of the special, more efficient instruction forms: the accumulator-specific direct-addressing form of **mov** and the 16-bit register-only form of **inc**. We'll study these instructions in detail in Chapters 8 and 9.

Sign extension of immediate operands.

I've already noted that immediate operands tend to make for compact code. One key to this property is that, like displacements in *mod-reg-rm* addressing, word-sized immediate operands can be stored as a byte and then extended to a word by replicating bit 7 as bits 15 to 8; that is, word-sized immediate operands can be sign extended. Almost all instructions that support immediate operands allow word-sized operands in the range -128 to $+127$ to be stored as single bytes. That means that while **and dx,1000h** is a 4-byte instruction (1 opcode byte, 1 *mod-reg-rm* byte, and a 2-byte immediate operand) **and dx,0fffeh** is just 3 bytes long; since the signed value of the immediate operand 0FFFEh is -2, 0FFFEh is stored as the single immediate operand byte 0FEh.

Not all values of the form 000*nn*h and 0FF*nn*h (where *nn* is any two hex digits) can be stored as a single byte and sign extended. The value 0007Fh can be stored as a single byte; 00080h cannot; 0FF80h can be stored as a single byte; 0FF7Fh cannot. Watch out for cases where you're using a word-sized immediate operand that can't be stored as a byte when a byte-sized immediate operand would serve as well.

For example, suppose we want to set the lower 8 bits of DX to 0. **and dx,0ff00h** is a 4-byte instruction that accomplishes the desired result—but **and dl,000h** produces the same result in just 3 bytes. (Of course, **sub dl,dl** does the same thing in just 2 bytes. There are *many* ways to skin a cat in assembler.) Recognizing when a word-sized immediate operand can be handled as a byte-sized operand is also important when using accumulator-specific immediate-operand instructions, which we'll explore in the next chapter.

mov doesn't sign extend immediate operands.

Along the same lines, **or bh,0ffh** does the same thing as **or bx,0ff00h** and is shorter, while **mov bh,0ffh** is also equivalent and is shorter still. That brings us to the one instruction that cannot sign extend immediate operands: **mov**. Word-sized operands to **mov** are always stored as words, no matter what size they are; however, there's a compensating factor, and that's that there's a special, non–*mod-reg-rm* form of **mov** *reg,immed* that's 1 byte shorter than the *mod-reg-rm* form.

Let me put it this way: **and dx,1000h** is a 4-byte instruction, with 1 opcode byte, 1 *mod-reg-rm* byte, and a 2-byte immediate operand. On the other hand, **mov dx,1000h** is only 3 bytes long. There's a special form of the **mov** instruction, used only when a register is loaded with an immediate value, that requires just the 1 opcode byte in addition to the immediate value.

There's also the standard *mod-reg-rm* form of **mov**, which is 4 bytes long for word-sized immediate operands. This form does exactly the same thing as the special form but is a different instruction, with a different opcode and a *mod-reg-rm* byte. The 8088 offers a number of duplicate instructions, as we'll see in the next chapter. Don't worry about selecting the right form of **mov**, however; the assembler does that for you automatically.

In short, you're no worse off—and often better off—moving immediate values into registers than you are using immediate operands with instructions such as **add** and **xor**. It takes just 2 or 3 bytes, for byte- or word-sized registers, respectively, to load a register with an immediate operand. Actually, **mov al,2** is the same size (2 bytes) as **mov al,bl**, although the official execution time of the register-only **mov** is 2 cycles shorter.

On balance, immediate operands used with **mov *reg,immed*** perform at nearly the speed of register operands, especially when the register is byte sized; consequently, there's less need to avoid immediate operands with **mov** than with other instructions. Nonetheless, register-only instructions are never slower, so you won't go wrong using register rather than immediate operands.

Don't mov immediate operands to memory if you can help it. One final note, and then we're done with immediate addressing. There is *no* special form of **mov** for moving an immediate operand to a memory operand; the special form is limited to register operands. What's more, **mov [*mem16*],*immed16*** has no sign extension capability. This double whammy means that storing immediate values to memory is the single least desirable way to use immediate operands. Over the next few chapters, we'll explore several ways to set memory operands to given values. The one thing that the various approaches have in common is that they all improve performance by avoiding immediate operands to **mov**.

Don't move immediate values to memory unless you have no choice.

Stack Addressing

While SP can't be used to point to memory by *mod-reg-rm* instructions, it is nonetheless a memory-addressing register. After all, SP is used to address the top of the stack. Surely you know how the stack works, so I'll simply note that SP points to the data item most recently pushed onto the top of the stack that has not yet been popped off the stack. Consequently, stack data can be accessed only in last in, first out (LIFO) order via SP (that is, the order in which data is popped off the stack is the reverse of the order in which it was pushed on). However, other addressing modes (in particular *mod-reg-rm* BP-based addressing) can be used to access stack data in non–LIFO order, as we'll see when we discuss stack frames.

What's so great about the stack? Simply put, the stack is terrific for temporary storage. Each named memory variable, as in

```
MemVar    dw  0
```

takes up 1 or more bytes of memory for the duration of the program. That's not the case with stack data, however; when data is popped from the stack, the space it occupied is freed up for other use. In other words, stack memory is a reusable resource. This makes the stack an excellent place to store temporary data, especially when large data elements such as buffers and structures are involved.

Space allocated on the stack is also unique for each invocation of a given subroutine, which is useful for any subroutine that needs to be capable of being called directly or indirectly from itself. Stack-based storage is how C implements automatic (dynamic) variables, which are unique for each invocation of a given subroutine. In fact, stack-based storage is the heart of the parameter-passing mechanism used by most C implementations as well as the mechanism used for automatic variables, as we'll see shortly.

Don't underestimate the flexibility of the stack. I've heard of programs that actually compile code right into a buffer on the stack, then execute that code in place, *on the stack.* While that's a strange concept, stack memory is memory like any other, and instruction bytes are data; obviously, those programs needed a temporary place in which to compile code, run it, and discard it, and the stack fits those requirements nicely.

Similarly, suppose that we need to pass a pointer to a variable from an assembler program to a C subroutine but there's no variable to point to in the assembler code because we keep the variable in a register. Suppose also that the C subroutine actually modifies the variable pointed to, so we need to retrieve the altered value after the call. The stack is admirably suited to the job; at the beginning of the following code, the variable of interest is in DX, and that's just where the modified result is at the end of the code

```
;
; Calls:   int CSubroutine(int *Count, char *BufferPointer).
;
```

```
mov  dx,MAX_COUNT  ;store the maximum # of bytes to handle
                   ; in the count variable
push dx            ;store the count variable on the stack
                   ; for the duration of the call
mov  dx,sp         ;put a pointer to the just-pushed temporary
                   ; count variable in DX
mov  ax,offset TestBuffer
push ax            ;pass the buffer pointer parameter
push dx            ;pass the count pointer parameter
call CSubroutine   ;do the count
add  sp,4          ;clear the parameter bytes from the stack
pop  dx            ;get the actual count back into DX
```

The important point in the code above is that we created a temporary memory variable on the stack as we needed it. Then, when the call was over, we simply popped the variable back into DX, and its space on the stack was freed up for other use. The code is compact, and not a single byte of memory storage had to be reserved permanently.

Compact code without the need for permanent memory space is the hallmark of stack-based code. It's often possible to write amazingly complex code without using *mod-reg-rm* addressing or named variables simply by pushing and popping registers. The code tends to be compact because **push** *reg16* and **pop** *reg16* are each only 1 byte long. These two instructions are so compact because they don't need to support the complex memory-addressing options of *mod-reg-rm* addressing; there are only eight possible register operands, and each instruction can address only one location, by way of the stack pointer, at any one time. (**push** *mem16* and **pop** *mem16* are *mod-reg-rm* instructions, so they're 2 to 4 bytes long; **push** *reg16* and **pop** *reg16*, and **push** *segreg* and **pop** *segreg* as well, are special, shorter forms of **push** and **pop**.)

For once, though, shorter isn't necessarily better. You see, **push** and **pop** are memory-accessing instructions, and although they don't require EA calculation time, they're still slow, like all instructions that access memory. They're fast considering that they are word-sized memory-accessing instructions (**push** takes 15 cycles, **pop** takes just 12), and they make for good prefetching, as only three memory accesses (including instruction fetches) are performed during an official execution time of 12 to 15 cycles. Nonetheless, they're clearly slower than register-only instructions. This is basically the same case we studied when we looked into copying segments; it's faster but takes more bytes and requires a free register to preserve a register by copying it to another register:

```
    mov   dx,ax
          :
    mov   ax,dx
```

than it is to preserve it by pushing and popping it:

```
    push  ax
          :
    pop   ax
```

What does all this mean to you? Simply this: use a free register for temporary storage if speed is of the essence, and **push** and **pop** if code size is your primary concern, if speed is not an issue, or if no registers happen to be free. In any case, it's faster and far more compact to store register values temporarily by pushing and popping them than it is to store them to memory with *mod-reg-rm* instructions. So use **push** and **pop**—but remember that they come with substantial performance overhead relative to register-only instructions.

An example of avoiding push and pop.   Let's quickly look at an example of improving performance by using register-only instructions rather than **push** and **pop**. When copying images into display memory, it's common to use code such as this:

```
;
; Copies an image into display memory.
;
;
; Input:
;     BX = width of image in bytes
;     DX = height of image in lines
;     BP = number of bytes from the start of one line to the
;             start of the next
;     DS:SI = pointer to image to draw
;     ES:DI = display memory address at which to draw image
;     Direction flag must be cleared on entry
;
; Output:
;     none
;
DrawLoop:
      push di            ;remember where the line starts
```

```
      mov  cx,bx        ;# of bytes per line
      rep  movsb        ;copy the next line
      pop  di           ;get back the line start offset
      add  di,bp        ;point to the next line in display memory
      dec  dx           ;repeat if there are any more lines
      jnz  DrawLoop
```

That's fine, but 1 **push** and 1 **pop** are performed per line, which seems a shame, all the more so given that we can eliminate those pushes and pops altogether, as follows:

```
;
; Copies an image into display memory.
;
; Input:
;     BX = width of image in bytes
;     DX = height of image in lines
;     BP = number of bytes from the start of one line to the
;            start of the next
;     DS:SI = pointer to image to draw
;     ES:DI = display memory address at which to draw image
;     Direction flag must be cleared on entry
;
; Output:
;     none
;
      sub  bp,bx        ;# of bytes from the end of 1 line of the
                        ; image in display memory to the start of
                        ; the next line of the image
DrawLoop:
      mov  cx,bx        ;# of bytes per line
      rep  movsb        ;copy the next line
      add  di,bp        ;point to the next line in display memory
      dec  dx           ;repeat if there are any more lines
      jnz  DrawLoop
```

Do you see what we've done? By converting an obvious solution (advancing one full line at a time) to a less obvious but fully equivalent solution (advancing only the remaining portion of the line), we've saved about 27 cycles per loop—*at no cost.* Given inputs like the width of the screen and instructions like **push** and **pop**, we tend to use them; it's just human nature to frame solutions in familiar terms. By rethinking problems just a little, however, we can often find simpler, better solutions.

Saving 27 cycles not by knowing more instructions but by *not* using two powerful instructions is an excellent example indeed of the Zen of assembly language.

Miscellaneous notes about stack addressing.   Before we proceed to stack frames, I'd like to take a moment to review a few important points about stack addressing.

SP always points to the next item to be popped from the stack. When you push a value onto the stack, SP is first decremented by 2, and then the value is stored at the location pointed to by SP. When you pop a value off of the stack, the value is read from the location pointed to by SP, and then SP is incremented by 2. It's useful to know this whenever you need to point to data stored on the stack, as we did when we created and pointed to a temporary variable on the stack a few sections back, and as we will need to do when we work with stack frames.

push and **pop** can work with *mod-reg-rm*-addressed memory variables as easily as with registers, albeit more slowly and with more instruction bytes. The instruction **push [WordVar]** is perfectly legitimate, as is **pop word ptr [bx+si+100h]**. Bear in mind, however, that only 16-bit values can be pushed and popped; **push bl** won't work, and neither will **pop byte ptr [bx]**.

Finally, please remember that once you've popped a value from the stack, it's gone from memory. It's tempting to look at the way the stack pointer works and think that the data is still in memory at the address just below the new stack pointer, but that's simply not the case, as shown in Figure 7.13. Sure, *sometimes* the data is still there—but whenever an interrupt occurs, it uses the top of the stack, wiping out the values that were popped most recently. Interrupts can happen at any time, so unless you're willing to disable interrupts, accessing popped stack memory is a sure way to get intermittent bugs.

Even if interrupts are disabled, it's really not a good idea to access popped stack data. Why bother, when stack frames give you the same sort of access to stack data, but in a straightforward, risk-free way? Not coincidentally, stack frames are our next topic, but first let me emphasize: once you've popped data off the stack, it's gone from memory. Vanished. Kaput. Extinct. For all intents and purposes, that data is nonexistent.

Don't access popped stack memory. Period.

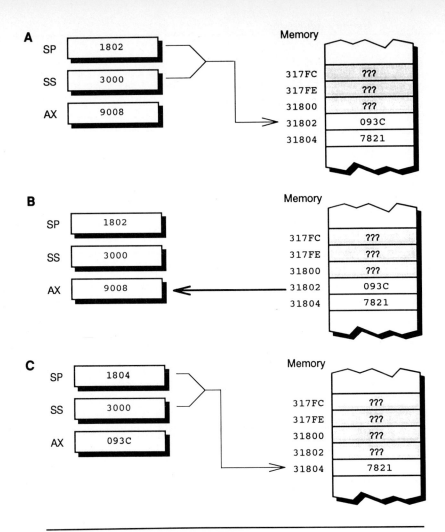

FIGURE 7.13

It might appear that popped data still exists in memory, since **pop** merely adds 2 to the stack pointer without altering memory in any way, but that's not the case. When a value is popped off the stack, it can no longer be relied on to exist in memory, because interrupts may occur any time, expanding the stack and wiping out any data lying around the area of memory just past the top of the stack. **(A)** The stack just before a pop, with the value 93Ch stored at address 31802, the top of the stack. **(B)** The value on top of the stack being popped into AX. **(C)** The completed pop, with SP pointing 2 bytes higher in memory and with the value 93Ch no longer shown at 31802. In truth, that value *may* still be there—but it may also have been wiped out by an interrupt, and there's no way to know which is the case at any given time. Note that all data past the top of the stack is shaded in all three figures, indicating that such data may change at any time.

Stack Frames

Stack frames are transient data structures, usually local to specific subroutines, that are stored on the stack. Two sorts of data normally are stored in stack frames: parameters that are passed from the calling routine by being pushed on the stack and variables that are local to the subroutine using the stack frame.

Why use stack frames? Well, as we discussed earlier, the stack is an excellent place to store temporary data, a category into which both passed parameters and local storage fall. The instructions **push** and **pop** aren't good for accessing stack frames, which often contain many variables and which aren't generally accessed in LIFO order; however, there are several *mod-reg-rm*–addressing modes that are perfect for accessing stack frames—the *mod-reg-rm* addressing modes involving BP. (We can't use SP for two reasons: it can't serve as a memory pointer with *mod-reg-rm*–addressing modes and it changes constantly during code execution, making offsets from SP hard to calculate.)

If you'll recall, BP-based addressing modes are the only *mod-reg-rm*–addressing modes that don't access DS by default. BP-based addressing modes access SS by default, and now we can see why: in order to access stack frames. Typically, BP is set to equal the stack pointer at the start of a subroutine and is then used to point to data in the stack frame for the remainder of the subroutine, as in

```
push  bp          ;save caller's BP
mov   bp,sp       ;point to stack frame
mov   ax,[bp+4]   ;retrieve a parameter
      :
pop   bp          ;restore caller's BP
ret
```

If temporary local storage is needed, SP is moved to allocate the necessary room:

```
push  bp          ;save caller's BP
mov   bp,sp       ;point to stack frame
sub   sp,10       ;allocate 10 bytes of local storage
mov   ax,[bp+4]   ;retrieve a parameter
mov   [bp-2],ax   ;save it in local storage
      :
mov   sp,bp       ;dump the temporary storage
```

```
pop   bp        ;restore caller's BP
ret
```

I'm not going to spend a great deal of time on stack frames for one simple reason: they're not all that terrific in assembler code. Stack frames are ideal for high level languages, because they allow regular parameter-passing schemes and support dynamically allocated local variables. For assembler code, however, stack frames are quite limiting, because they require a single consistent parameter-passing convention and the presence of code to create and destroy stack frames at the beginning and end of each subroutine. In particular, the ability of assembler code to pass pointers and variables in registers (which is much more efficient than pushing them on the stack) is constrained by standard stack frame conventions. In addition, the BP register, which is dedicated to pointing to stack frames, normally cannot be used for other purposes when stack frames are used; the loss of one of a mere seven generally available 16-bit registers is not insignificant.

High level language stack frame conventions also generally mandate the preservation of several registers—always BP, usually DS, and often SI and DI as well—and that requires time-consuming pushes and pops. Finally, while stack frame addressing is compact (owing to the heavy use of **bp+ *disp*** addressing with 1-byte displacements), it is rather inefficient, even as memory-accessing instructions go; **mov ax,[bp+*disp8*]** is only 3 bytes long but takes 21 cycles to execute.

In short, stack frames are powerful and useful—but they don't make for the best possible 8088 code. The best *compiled* code, yes, but not the best assembler code.

What's more, compilers handle stack frames very efficiently. If you're going to work within the constraints of stack frames, you may have a difficult time out-coding compilers, which rarely miss a trick in terms of generating efficient stack frame code. Handling stack frames well is not so simple as it might seem; you have to be sure *not* to insert unneeded stack frame–related code, such as code to load BP when there is no stack frame, and you need to be sure that you always preserve the proper registers when they're altered, but not otherwise. It's not hard, but it's tedious, and it's easy to make mistakes that either waste bytes or lead to bugs as a result of registers that should be preserved but aren't.

When you work with stack frames, you're trying to out-compile a compiler while playing by its rules, and that's hard to do. In pure assembler code, I generally recommend against the use of stack frames, although there are surely exceptions to this rule. Personally, I often use C for the sort of code that requires stack frames, building only the subroutines that do the time-critical work in pure assembler. Why not let a compiler do the dirty work while you focus your efforts on the code that really makes a difference?

When stack frames are useful.   That's not to say that stack frames aren't useful in assembler. They're not only useful but mandatory when assembler subroutines are called from high level language code, since the stack frame approach is the sole parameter-passing mechanism for most high level language implementations.

Assembler subroutines for use with high level languages are most useful; together, assembler subroutines and high level languages provide relatively good performance and fast development time. The *best* code is written in assembler, but the best code within a reasonable time frame is often written in a mixture of high level language and assembler code. Then, too, high level languages are generally better than assembler for managing the complexities of very large applications.

In short, stack frames are generally useful in assembler when assembler is interfaced to a high level language. High level language interfacing and stack frame organization vary from one language to another, however, so I'm not going to cover stack frames in detail, although I will offer a few tips about using stack frames in the next section. Before I do that, I'd like to point out an excellent way to mix assembler with high-level language code: in-line assembler. Many compilers offer the option of embedding assembler code directly in high level language code; in many cases, high level language and assembler variables and parameters can even be shared. For example, here's a Turbo C subroutine to set the video mode:

```
void SetVideoMode(unsigned char ModeNumber){
    asm   mov ah,0
    asm   mov al,byte ptr [ModeNumber]
    asm   int   10h
}
```

What makes in-line assembler so terrific is that it lets the compiler handle all the messy details of stack frames while freeing you to use assembler. In the example above, we didn't have to worry about defining and accessing the stack frame; Turbo C handled all that for us, saving and setting up BP and substituting the appropriate BP+*disp* value for **ModeNumber**. In-line assembler is harder to use than pure assembler for large tasks, but in most cases where the power of assembler is needed in a high level language, in-line assembler is a very good compromise.

One warning: many compilers turn off some or all code optimization in subroutines that contain in-line assembler. For that reason, it's often a good idea *not* to mix high level language and in-line assembler statements when performance matters. Write your time-critical code either entirely in in-line assembler or entirely in pure assembler; don't let the compiler insert code of uncertain quality when every cycle counts.

Still and all, when you need to create the fastest or tightest code, try to avoid stack frames except when you must interface your assembler code to a high level language. When you must use stack frames, bear in mind that assembler is infinitely flexible; there are more ways to handle stack frames than are dreamt of in high level languages. In Chapter 16 we'll see an unusual but remarkably effective way to handle stack frames in a Pascal-callable assembler subroutine.

Tips on stack frames.   Before we go on to **xlat**, I'm going to skim over a few items that you may find useful should you need to use stack frames in assembler code.

MASM provides the **struc** directive for defining data structures. Such data structures can be used to access stack frames, as in:

```
Parms     struc
     dw   ?      ;pushed BP
     dw   ?      ;return address
X    dw   ?      ;X coordinate parameter
Y    dw   ?      ;Y coordinate parameter
Parms     end
          :
DrawXY    proc near
     push bp          ;save caller's stack frame pointer
     mov  bp,sp       ;point to stack frame
     mov  cx,[bp+X]   ;get X coordinate
     mov  dx,[bp+Y]   ;get Y coordinate
          :
     pop  bp
     ret
DrawXY    endp
```

MASM structures have a serious drawback when used with stack frames, however: they don't allow for negative displacements from BP, which are generally used to access local variables stored on the stack. While it is possible to access local storage by accessing all variables in the stack frames at positive offsets from BP, as in

```
Parms      struc
Temp dw    ?      ;temporary storage
OldBP dw   ?      ;pushed BP
      dw   ?      ;return address
X      dw  ?      ;X coordinate parameter
Y      dw  ?      ;Y coordinate parameter
Parms      end
           :
DrawXY     proc near
     push bp               ;save caller's stack frame pointer
     sub  sp,OldBP         ;make room for temp storage
     mov  bp,sp            ;point to stack frame
     mov  cx,[bp+X]        ;get X coordinate
     mov  dx,[bp+Y]        ;get Y coordinate
     mov  [bp+Temp],dx ;set aside  Y  coordinate
           :
     add  sp,OldBP         ;dump temp storage space
     pop  bp
     ret
DrawXY     endp
```

this approach has two disadvantages. First, it prevents us from dumping temporary storage with **mov sp,bp**, requiring instead that we use the less efficient **add sp,OldBP**. Second, and more important, it makes it more likely that parameters will be accessed with a 2-byte displacement.

Why? Remember that a 1-byte displacement can address memory in the range −128 to +127 bytes away from BP. If our entire stack frame is addressed at positive offsets from BP, then we've lost the use of fully half of the addresses that we can access with 1-byte displacements.

Now, we *can* use negative stack frame offsets in assembler; it's just a bit more trouble than we'd like. There are many possible solutions, ranging from a variety of ways to use equated symbols for stack frame variables, as in

```
Temp equ -2    ;temporary storage
X     equ 4    ;X coordinate parameter
Y     equ 6    ;Y coordinate parameter
```

and

```
Temp equ -2    ;temporary storage
X     equ 4    ;X coordinate parameter
Y     equ X+2 ;Y coordinate parameter
```

to ways to get the assembler to adjust structure offsets for us. See my "On Graphics" column in the July 1987 issue of *Programmer's Journal* (issue 5.4) for an elegant solution, provided by John Navas. (Incidentally, TASM provides special directives, **arg** and **local**, that handle many of the complications of stack frame addressing and allow negative offsets.)

While we're discussing stack frame displacements, allow me to emphasize that you should strive to use 1-byte displacements into stack frames as much as possible. If you have so many parameters or local variables that 2-byte displacements must be used, make an effort to put the least frequently used variables at those larger displacements. Alternatively, you may want to put large data elements such as arrays and structures in the stack frame areas that are addressed with 2-byte displacements, since such data elements are often accessed by way of pointer registers such as BX and SI rather than directly via **bp+*disp*** addressing. Finally, you should avoid forward references to structures; if you refer to elements of a structure before the structure itself is defined in the code, you'll always get 2-byte displacements, as we'll see in Chapter 14.

Whenever you're uncertain whether 1- or 2-byte displacements are being used, simply generate a listing file, or look at your code with a debugger.

By the way, it's worth examining the size of your stack frame displacements even in high level languages. If you can figure out the order in which your compiler organizes data in a stack frame, you can often speed up and shrink your code simply by reorganizing your local variable declarations so that arrays and structures are at 2-byte offsets, allowing most variables to be addressed with 1-byte offsets.

Stack frames are often in DS. Although it's not always the case, often enough the stack segment pointed to by SS and the default data segment pointed to by DS are one and the same. This is true in most high level language memory models, and is standard for COM programs.

If DS and SS are the same, the implication is clear: *all mod-reg-rm–* addressing modes can be used to point to stack frames. That's a real advantage if you need to scan stack frame arrays and the like, because SI or DI can be loaded with the array start address and used to address the array without the need for segment override prefixes. Similarly, BX could be set to point to a stack frame structure, which could then be accessed by way of **bx+*disp*** addressing without a segment override. In short, be sure to take advantage of the extra stack frame addressing power that you have at your disposal when SS equals DS.

Use BP as a normal register if you must. When stack frame addressing is in use, BP is normally dedicated to addressing the current stack frame. That doesn't mean you can't use BP as a normal register in a tight loop, though, and use it as a normal register you should; registers are too scarce to let even one go to waste when performance matters. Just push BP, use it however you wish in the loop, then pop it when you're done, as in

```
        push bp                ;preserve stack frame pointer
        mov  bp,LOOP_COUNT ;get # of times to repeat loop
LoopTop:
             :
        dec  bp                ;count off loops
        loop LoopTop
        pop  bp                ;restore stack frame pointer
```

Of course, the stack frame can't be accessed while BP is otherwise occupied, but you don't want to be accessing memory inside a tight loop anyway if you can help it.

Using BP as a normal register in a tight loop can make the difference between a register-only loop and one that accesses memory operands, and that can translate into quite a performance improvement. Also, don't forget that BP can be used in *mod-reg-rm* addressing even when stack frames aren't involved, so BP can come in handy as a memory-addressing register when BX, SI, and DI are otherwise engaged. In that use, however, bear in mind that there is no BP-only memory-addressing mode; either a 1- or 2-byte displacement or an index register (SI or DI) or both is always involved.

The many ways of specifying *mod-reg-rm* addressing. There are, it seems, more ways of specifying an operand addressed with *mod-reg-rm* addressing than you can shake a stick at. For example, **[bp+MemVar+si]**, **MemVar[bp+si]**, **MemVar[si][bp]**, and **[bp][MemVar+si]** are all equivalent. Now stack frame addressing introduces us to a new form involving the dot operator: **[bp.MemVar.si]**. What's the story with all these *mod-reg-rm* forms?

It's actually fairly simple. The dot operator does the same thing as the plus operator: it adds two memory addressing components together. Any memory-addressing component enclosed in brackets is also added into the memory address. The order of the operands doesn't matter, because everything resolves to a *mod-reg-rm* byte in the end; **mov al,[bx+si]** assembles to exactly the same instruction as **mov al,[si+bx]**. All the constant values and symbols (variable names and equated values) in an address are added together into a single displacement, and that's used with whatever memory addressing registers are present (from among BX, BP, SI, and DI) to form a *mod-reg-rm* address. (Of course, only valid combinations—those listed in Figure 7.6—will assemble.) Last, if memory addressing registers are present, they must be inside square brackets, but that's optional for constant values and symbols.

There are a few other rules about constructing memory-addressing operands, but I avoid those complications by making it a practice to use a single simple *mod-reg-rm* memory address notation. As I said at the start of this chapter, I prefer to put square brackets around all memory operands, and I also prefer to use only the plus operator. There are three reasons for this: it's not complicated; it reminds me that I'm programming in assembler, not in a high level language where complexities such as array element size are automatically taken care of; and it reminds me that I'm accessing a memory operand rather than a register operand, thereby losing performance and gaining bytes.

You can use whatever *mod-reg-rm* addressing notation you wish. I do suggest, however, that you choose a single notation and stick with it. Why confuse yourself?

xlat

At long last, we come to the final addressing mode of the 8088. This addressing mode is unique to the **xlat** instruction, an odd and rather limited instruction that can nonetheless outperform every other 8088 memory-addressing instruction under the proper circumstances.

The operation of **xlat** is simple: AL is loaded from the offset addressed by the sum of BX and AL, as shown in Figure 7.14. DS is the default data segment, but a segment override prefix may be used.

As you can see, **xlat** bears no resemblance to any of the other addressing modes. It's certainly limited, and it always wipes out one of the two registers it uses to address memory (AL). In fact, the first thought that leaps to mind is, why would we *ever* want to use **xlat**?

If **xlat** were slow and large, the answer would be that we never would want to use it. However, **xlat** is just 1 byte long, and, at 11 cycles, is as fast at accessing a memory operand as any 8088 instruction. As a result, **xlat** is excellent for a small but often time-critical category of tasks.

xlat excels when byte values must be translated from one representation to another. The most common example occurs when one character set must be translated to another, as for example when the ASCII charac-

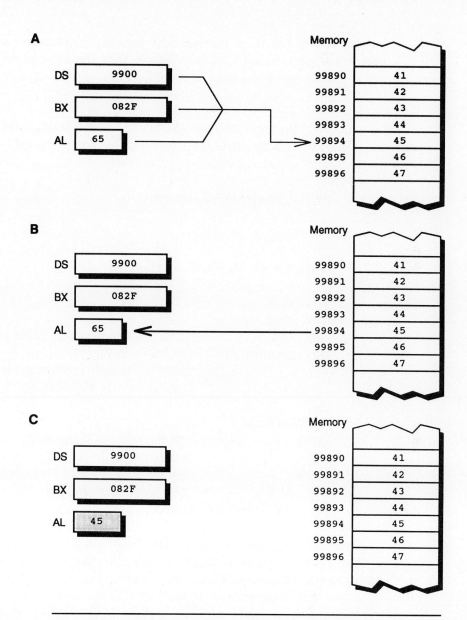

FIGURE 7.14   The operation of **xlat**. **(A)** **xlat** addresses memory by using the sum of BX and AL to form an offset, which points
into the DS segment by default. **(B)** The addressed byte
being read (**xlat** works only with byte-sized operands).
(C) The addressed byte was read into AL, as is always the
case with **xlat**.

ter set used by the PC is translated to the EBCDIC character set used by IBM mainframes. In such a case **xlat** can form the heart of an extremely efficient loop, along the lines of the following:

```
;
; Converts the contents of an ASCII buffer to an EBCDIC buffer.
; Stops when a zero byte is encountered, but copies the zero byte.
;
; Input:
;     DS:SI = pointer to ASCII buffer.
;
; Output: none
;
; Registers altered: AL, BX, SI, DI, ES
;
        mov   di,ds
        mov   es,di
        mov   di,si             ;point ES:DI to the ASCII buffer as well
        mov   bx,offset ASCIIToEBCDICTable
                                ;point to the table containing the EBCDIC
                                ; equivalents of ASCII codes
        cld
ASCIIToEBCDICLoop:
        lodsb                   ;get the next ASCII character
        xlat                    ;convert it to EBCDIC
        stosb                   ;put the result back in the buffer
        and   al,al             ;zero byte is the last byte
        jnz   ASCIIToEBCDICLoop
```

Besides being small and fast, **xlat** has an advantage in that byte-sized look-up values don't need to be converted to words before they can be used to address memory. (Remember, *mod-reg-rm*-addressing modes allow only word-sized registers to be used to address memory.) If we were to implement the look-up in the last example with *mod-reg-rm* instructions, the code would become a good deal less efficient, no matter how carefully we set up for *mod-reg-rm* addressing:

```
sub   bh,bh       ;for use in converting a byte in BL
                  ; to a word in BX
mov   si,offset ASCIIToEBCDICTable
                  ;point to the table containing the EBCDIC
                  ; equivalents of ASCII codes
```

```
ASCIIToEBCDICLoop:
    lodsb              ;get the next ASCII character
    mov   bl,al        ;get the character into BX, where
                       ; we can use it to address memory
    mov   al,[si+bx]   ;convert it to EBCDIC
    stosb              ;put the result back in the buffer
    and   al,al        ;zero byte is the last byte
    jnz   ASCIIToEBCDICLoop
```

In short, **xlat** is clearly superior when a byte-sized look-up is performed, so long as it's possible to put both the look-up value and the result in AL. Shortly, we'll see how **xlat** can be used to good effect in a case where it certainly isn't the obvious choice.

Memory Is Cheap: You Could Look It Up

Simply put, **xlat** is a table look-up instruction. A table look-up occurs whenever you use an index value to look up a result in an array, or table, of data. A rough analogy might be using the number on a ballplayer's uniform to look up his name in a program.

Look-up tables are a superb way to improve performance. The basic premise of look-up tables is that it's faster to precalculate results, either by letting the assembler do the work or by calculating the results yourself and inserting them in the source code, than it is to have the 8088 calculate them at run time. The key factor is this: the 8088 is relatively fast at looking up data in tables and slow at performing almost any kind of calculation. Given that, why not perform your calculations before run time, when speed doesn't matter, and let the 8088 do what it does best at run time?

Now, look-up tables do have a significant disadvantage—they require extra memory. This is a trade-off we'll see again and again in *Zen of Assembly Language:* cycles for bytes. If you're willing to expend more memory, you can almost always improve the performance of your code. One trick to generating top-notch code is knowing when that trade is worth making.

Let's look at an example that illustrates the power of look-up tables. In the process, we'll see an unusual but effective use of **xlat**; we'll also see that there are many ways to approach any programming task, and we'll get a firsthand look at the cycles-for-bytes tradeoff that arises so often in assembler programming.

Five ways to double bits.   The example we're about to study is based on the article "Optimizing for Speed," by Michael Hoyt, which appeared in *Programmer's Journal* in March 1986 (issue 4.2). This is the article I referred to back in Chapter 2 as an example of a programmer operating without full knowledge of code performance on the PC. By no means am I denigrating Mr. Hoyt; his article simply happens to be an excellent starting point for examining both look-up tables and the hazards of the prefetch queue cycle eater.

The goal of Mr. Hoyt's article was to expand a byte to a word by doubling each bit, for the purpose of converting display memory pixels to printer pixels in order to perform a screen dump. So, for example, the value 01h (00000001b) would become 0003h (0000000000000011b), the value 02h (00000010b) would become 000Ch (0000000000001100b), and the value 5Ah (01011010b) would become 33CCh (0011001111001100b). Now, in general this isn't a particularly worthy pursuit, given that the speed of the printer is likely to be the limiting factor; however, speed could matter if the screen dump code is used by a background print spooler. At any rate, bit doubling is an ideal application for look-up tables, so we're going to spend some time studying it.

Mr. Hoyt started his article with code that doubled each bit by testing that bit and branching accordingly to set the appropriate doubled bit values. He then optimized the code by eliminating branches entirely, instead using fast shift and rotate instructions in a manner similar to that used by Listing 7-14.

```
1   ;
2   ; *** Listing 7-14 ***
3   ;
4   ; Performs bit-doubling of a byte in AL to a word in AX
5   ; by using doubled shifts, one from each of two source
6   ; registers. This approach avoids branching and is very
7   ; fast according to official instruction timings, but is
8   ; actually quite slow due to instruction prefetching.
9   ;
10  ; (Based on an approach used in "Optimizing for Speed,"
11  ; by Michael Hoyt, Programmer's Journal 4.2, March, 1986.)
12  ;
13  ; Macro to double each bit in a byte.
14  ;
15  ; Input:
16  ;       AL = byte to bit-double
17  ;
18  ; Output:
19  ;       AX = bit-doubled word
20  ;
21  ; Registers altered: AX, BX
22  ;
23  DOUBLE_BYTE     macro
24          mov     ah,al   ;put the byte to double in two
25                          ; registers
26          mov     bx,ax
27          rept    8
```

```
28              shr     bl,1    ;get the next bit to double
29              rcr     ax,1    ;move it into the msb...
30              shr     bh,1    ;...then get the bit again...
31              rcr     ax,1    ;...and replicate it
32              endm
33              endm
34      ;
35              call    ZTimerOn
36      BYTE_TO_DOUBLE=0
37              rept    100
38              mov     al,BYTE_TO_DOUBLE
39              DOUBLE_BYTE
40      BYTE_TO_DOUBLE=BYTE_TO_DOUBLE+1
41              endm
42              call    ZTimerOff
```

Eliminating branches isn't a bad idea in general, since, as we'll see in Chapter 12, branching is very slow; however, as we saw in Chapter 4, instruction fetching is also very slow . . . and the code in Listing 7-14 requires a *lot* of instruction fetching. Seventy instruction bytes must be fetched for each byte that's doubled, meaning that this code can't possibly run in less than about 280 (70 × 4) cycles per byte doubled, even though its official EU execution time is scarcely 70 cycles.

The Zen timer confirms our calculations, reporting that Listing 7-14 runs in 6.34 msec, or about 300 cycles per byte doubled. (The excess cycles are the result of DRAM refresh.) As a result of this intensive instruction fetching, Mr. Hoyt's optimized shift-and-rotate code actually ran slower than his original test-and-jump code, as discussed in my article "More Optimizing for Speed," *Programmer's Journal,* July 1986 (issue 4.4).

So far, all we've done is confirm that the prefetch queue cycle eater can cause code to run much more slowly than the official execution times would indicate. This is, of course, not news to us. In fact, I haven't even bothered to show the test-and-jump code and contrast it with the shift-and-rotate code, since that would just restate what we already know. What's interesting is not that Mr. Hoyt's optimization didn't make his code faster but rather that a look-up table approach can make the code *much* faster. So let's plunge headlong into look-up tables, and see what we can do with this code.

Table look-ups to the rescue.   Bit doubling is beautifully suited to an approach based on look-up tables. There are only 256 possible input values, all byte sized, and only 256 possible output values, all word sized. Better yet, each input value maps to one and only one output value, and all the input values are consecutive, covering the range 0 to 255, inclusive.

Given those parameters, it should be clear that we can create a table of

256 words, one corresponding to each possible byte to be bit doubled. We can then use each byte to be doubled as a look-up index into that table, retrieving the appropriate bit-doubled word with just a few instructions. Granted, 512 bytes would be needed to store the table, but the 50 or so instruction bytes we would save would partially compensate for the size of the table. Besides, surely the performance improvement from eliminating all those shifts, rotates, and especially instruction fetches would justify the extra bytes, wouldn't it?

It would indeed. Listing 7-15, which uses the table look-up approach I've just described, runs in just 1.32 msec—*more than four times as fast as Listing 7-14!* When performance matters, trading less than 500 bytes for a more than fourfold speed increase is quite a deal. Listing 7-15 is so fast that it's faster than Listing 7-14 would be even if there were no prefetch queue cycle eater. In other words, the official execution time of Listing 7-15 is faster than that of Listing 7-14. Factor in instruction fetch time, though, and you have a fine example of the massive performance improvement that look-up tables can offer.

```
 1   ;
 2   ; *** Listing 7-15 ***
 3   ;
 4   ; Performs very fast bit-doubling of a byte in AL to a
 5   ; word in AX by using a look-up table.
 6   ; This approach avoids both branching and the severe
 7   ; instruction-fetching penalty of the shift-based approach.
 8   ;
 9   ; Macro to double each bit in a byte.
10   ;
11   ; Input:
12   ;       AL = byte to bit-double
13   ;
14   ; Output:
15   ;       AX = bit-doubled word
16   ;
17   ; Registers altered: AX, BX
18   ;
19   DOUBLE_BYTE     macro
20           mov     bl,al   ;move the byte to look up to BL,
21           sub     bh,bh   ; make a word out of the value,
22           shl     bx,1    ; and double the value so we can
23                           ; use it as a pointer into the
24                           ; table of word-sized doubled byte
25                           ; values
26           mov     ax,[DoubledByteTable+bx]
27                           ;look up the doubled byte value
28           endm
29   ;
30           jmp     Skip
31   DOUBLED_VALUE=0
```

```
32   DoubledByteTable        label    word
33          dw       00000h,00003h,0000ch,0000fh,00030h,00033h,0003ch,0003fh
34          dw       000c0h,000c3h,000cch,000cfh,000f0h,000f3h,000fch,000ffh
35          dw       00300h,00303h,0030ch,0030fh,00330h,00333h,0033ch,0033fh
36          dw       003c0h,003c3h,003cch,003cfh,003f0h,003f3h,003fch,003ffh
37          dw       00c00h,00c03h,00c0ch,00c0fh,00c30h,00c33h,00c3ch,00c3fh
38          dw       00cc0h,00cc3h,00ccch,00ccfh,00cf0h,00cf3h,00cfch,00cffh
39          dw       00f00h,00f03h,00f0ch,00f0fh,00f30h,00f33h,00f3ch,00f3fh
40          dw       00fc0h,00fc3h,00fcch,00fcfh,00ff0h,00ff3h,00ffch,00fffh
41   ;
42          dw       03000h,03003h,0300ch,0300fh,03030h,03033h,0303ch,0303fh
43          dw       030c0h,030c3h,030cch,030cfh,030f0h,030f3h,030fch,030ffh
44          dw       03300h,03303h,0330ch,0330fh,03330h,03333h,0333ch,0333fh
45          dw       033c0h,033c3h,033cch,033cfh,033f0h,033f3h,033fch,033ffh
46          dw       03c00h,03c03h,03c0ch,03c0fh,03c30h,03c33h,03c3ch,03c3fh
47          dw       03cc0h,03cc3h,03ccch,03ccfh,03cf0h,03cf3h,03cfch,03cffh
48          dw       03f00h,03f03h,03f0ch,03f0fh,03f30h,03f33h,03f3ch,03f3fh
49          dw       03fc0h,03fc3h,03fcch,03fcfh,03ff0h,03ff3h,03ffch,03fffh
50   ;
51          dw       0c000h,0c003h,0c00ch,0c00fh,0c030h,0c033h,0c03ch,0c03fh
52          dw       0c0c0h,0c0c3h,0c0cch,0c0cfh,0c0f0h,0c0f3h,0c0fch,0c0ffh
53          dw       0c300h,0c303h,0c30ch,0c30fh,0c330h,0c333h,0c33ch,0c33fh
54          dw       0c3c0h,0c3c3h,0c3cch,0c3cfh,0c3f0h,0c3f3h,0c3fch,0c3ffh
55          dw       0cc00h,0cc03h,0cc0ch,0cc0fh,0cc30h,0cc33h,0cc3ch,0cc3fh
56          dw       0ccc0h,0ccc3h,0cccch,0cccfh,0ccf0h,0ccf3h,0ccfch,0ccffh
57          dw       0cf00h,0cf03h,0cf0ch,0cf0fh,0cf30h,0cf33h,0cf3ch,0cf3fh
58          dw       0cfc0h,0cfc3h,0cfcch,0cfcfh,0cff0h,0cff3h,0cffch,0cfffh
59   ;
60          dw       0f000h,0f003h,0f00ch,0f00fh,0f030h,0f033h,0f03ch,0f03fh
61          dw       0f0c0h,0f0c3h,0f0cch,0f0cfh,0f0f0h,0f0f3h,0f0fch,0f0ffh
62          dw       0f300h,0f303h,0f30ch,0f30fh,0f330h,0f333h,0f33ch,0f33fh
63          dw       0f3c0h,0f3c3h,0f3cch,0f3cfh,0f3f0h,0f3f3h,0f3fch,0f3ffh
64          dw       0fc00h,0fc03h,0fc0ch,0fc0fh,0fc30h,0fc33h,0fc3ch,0fc3fh
65          dw       0fcc0h,0fcc3h,0fccch,0fccfh,0fcf0h,0fcf3h,0fcfch,0fcffh
66          dw       0ff00h,0ff03h,0ff0ch,0ff0fh,0ff30h,0ff33h,0ff3ch,0ff3fh
67          dw       0ffc0h,0ffc3h,0ffcch,0ffcfh,0fff0h,0fff3h,0fffch,0ffffh
68   ;
69   Skip:
70          call     ZTimerOn
71   BYTE_TO_DOUBLE=0
72          rept     100
73          mov      al,BYTE_TO_DOUBLE
74          DOUBLE_BYTE
75   BYTE_TO_DOUBLE=BYTE_TO_DOUBLE+1
76          endm
77          call     ZTimerOff
```

The key to Listing 7-15, of course, is that I precalculated all the doubled bit patterns when I wrote the program. As a result, the code doesn't have to perform any calculation more complex than looking up a precalculated bit pattern at run time. In a little while, we'll see how MASM can often perform look-up table calculations at assembly time, relieving us of the drudgery of precalculating results.

There are many ways to approach any task. Never assume that there's only one way, or even one best way, to approach a programming task. There are always many ways to solve any given programming problem in assembler, and different solutions may well be superior in different situations.

Suppose, for example, that we're writing bit-doubling code in a situation where size is more important than speed, perhaps because we're writing a memory-resident program or perhaps because the code will be used in a very large program that's squeezed for space. We'd like to improve our speed, if we can, but not at the expense of a single byte. In this case, Listing 7-14 is preferable to Listing 7-15—but is Listing 7-14 the best we can do?

Not by a long shot.

What we'd like to do is somehow shrink Listing 7-15 a good deal. Well, Listing 7-15 is so large only because it has a 512-byte table that's used to look up the bit-doubled words that can be selected by the 256 values that can be stored in a byte. We can shrink the table a great deal simply by converting it to a 16-byte table that's used to look up the bit-doubled *bytes* that can be selected by the 16 values that can be stored in a *nybble* (4 bits), and performing two look-ups into that table, one for each half of the byte being doubled.

Listing 7-16 shows this double table look-up solution in action. This listing requires only 23 bytes of code for each byte doubled, and even if you add the 16-byte size of the table, the total size of 39 bytes is still considerably smaller than the 70 bytes needed to bit double each byte in Listing 7-14. What's more, the table only needs to appear once in any program, so practically speaking Listing 7-16 is *much* more compact than Listing 7-14.

```
 1   ;
 2   ; *** Listing 7-16 ***
 3   ;
 4   ; Performs fast, compact bit-doubling of a byte in AL
 5   ; to a word in AX by using two nibble look-ups rather
 6   ; than a byte look-up.
 7   ;
 8   ; Macro to double each bit in a byte.
 9   ;
10   ; Input:
11   ;       AL = byte to bit-double
12   ;
13   ; Output:
14   ;       AX = bit-doubled word
15   ;
16   ; Registers altered: AX, BX, CL
17   ;
18   DOUBLE_BYTE     macro
```

```
19              mov     bl,al    ;move the byte to look up to BL
20              sub     bh,bh    ; and make a word out of the value
21              mov     cl,4     ;make a look-up pointer out of the
22              shr     bx,cl    ; upper nibble of the byte
23              mov     ah,[DoubledNibbleTable+bx]
24                       ;look up the doubled upper nibble
25              mov     bl,al    ;get the byte to look up again,
26              and     bl,0fh   ; and make a pointer out of the
27                       ; lower nibble this time
28              mov     al,[DoubledNibbleTable+bx]
29                       ;look up the doubled lower nibble
30              endm
31      ;
32              jmp     Skip
33      DOUBLED_VALUE=0
34      DoubledNibbleTable      label   byte
35              db      000h, 003h, 00ch, 00fh
36              db      030h, 033h, 03ch, 03fh
37              db      0c0h, 0c3h, 0cch, 0cfh
38              db      0f0h, 0f3h, 0fch, 0ffh
39      ;
40      Skip:
41              call    ZTimerOn
42      BYTE_TO_DOUBLE=0
43              rept    100
44              mov     al,BYTE_TO_DOUBLE
45              DOUBLE_BYTE
46      BYTE_TO_DOUBLE=BYTE_TO_DOUBLE+1
47              endm
48              call    ZTimerOff
```

Listing 7-16 also is more than twice as fast as Listing 7-14, clocking at 2.52 msec. Of course, Listing 7-16 is nearly twice as *slow* as Listing 7-15—but then, it's much more compact.

There's that choice again: cycles or bytes.

In truth, there are both cycles and bytes yet to be saved in Listing 7-16. If we apply our knowledge of *mod-reg-rm* addressing to Listing 7-16, we'll realize that it's a waste to use base+displacement addressing with the same displacement twice in a row; we can save a byte and a few cycles by loading SI with the displacement and using base+index addressing instead. Listing 7-17, which incorporates this optimization, runs in 2.44 msec, a little faster than Listing 7-16.

```
1       ;
2       ; *** Listing 7-17 ***
3       ;
4       ; Performs fast, compact bit-doubling of a byte in AL
5       ; to a word in AX by using two nibble look-ups. Overall
6       ; code length and performance are improved by
7       ; using base indexed addressing (bx+si) rather than base
8       ; direct addressing (bx+DoubleNibbleTable). Even though
9       ; an additional 3-byte MOV instruction is required to load
```

```
10   ; SI with the offset of DoubleNibbleTable, each access to
11   ; DoubleNibbleTable is 2 bytes shorter thanks to the
12   ; elimination of mod-reg-rm displacements.
13   ;
14   ; Macro to double each bit in a byte.
15   ;
16   ; Input:
17   ;       AL = byte to bit-double
18   ;
19   ; Output:
20   ;       AX = bit-doubled word
21   ;
22   ; Registers altered: AX, BX, CL, SI
23   ;
24   DOUBLE_BYTE       macro
25           mov       bl,al    ;move the byte to look up to BL
26           sub       bh,bh    ; and make a word out of the value
27           mov       cl,4     ;make a look-up pointer out of the
28           shr       bx,cl    ; upper nibble of the byte
29           mov       si,offset DoubledNibbleTable
30           mov       ah,[si+bx]
31                              ;look up the doubled upper nibble
32           mov       bl,al    ;get the byte to look up again,
33           and       bl,0fh   ; and make a pointer out of the
34                              ; lower nibble this time
35           mov       al,[si+bx]
36                              ;look up the doubled lower nibble
37           endm
38   ;
39           jmp       Skip
40   DOUBLED_VALUE=0
41   DoubledNibbleTable        label     byte
42           db        000h, 003h, 00ch, 00fh
43           db        030h, 033h, 03ch, 03fh
44           db        0c0h, 0c3h, 0cch, 0cfh
45           db        0f0h, 0f3h, 0fch, 0ffh
46   ;
47   Skip:
48           call      ZTimerOn
49   BYTE_TO_DOUBLE=0
50           rept      100
51           mov       al,BYTE_TO_DOUBLE
52           DOUBLE_BYTE
53   BYTE_TO_DOUBLE=BYTE_TO_DOUBLE+1
54           endm
55           call      ZTimerOff
```

There's yet another optimization to be made, and this one brings us full circle, back to the start of our discussion of look-up tables. Think about it: Listing 7-17 basically does nothing more than use two nybble values as look-up indices into a table of byte values. Sound familiar? It should—that's an awful lot like a description of **xlat** (**xlat** can handle byte look-up values, but this task is just a subset of that).

Listing 7-18 shows an **xlat**-based version of our bit-doubling code. This code runs in just 1.94 msec, still about 50% slower than the single–look-up approach, but a good deal faster than anything else we've seen. Better yet, this approach takes just 17 instruction bytes per bit-doubled byte (33, if you count the table), which makes this by far the shortest approach we've seen. Comparing Listing 7-18 to Listing 7-14 reveals that we've improved the code to an astonishing degree: Listing 7-18 runs more than three times as fast as Listing 7-14, and yet it requires less than one-fourth as many instruction bytes per bit-doubled byte.

There are many lessons here. First, **xlat** is extremely efficient at performing the limited category of tasks it can manage; when you need to use a byte index into a byte-sized look-up table, **xlat** is often your best bet. Second, the official execution times aren't a particularly good guide to writing high-performance code. (Of course, you already knew *that*!) Third, there is no such thing as the best code, because the fastest code is rarely the smallest code, and vice versa.

Finally, there are an awful lot of solutions to any given programming problem on the 8088. Don't fall into the trap of thinking that the obvious solution is the best one. In fact, we'll see yet another solution to the bit-doubling problem in Chapter 9; this solution, based on the **sar** instruction, isn't like *any* of the solutions we've seen so far.

We'll see look-up tables again in Chapter 14, in the form of jump tables.

```
1    ;
2    ; *** Listing 7-18 ***
3    ;
4    ; Performs fast, compact bit-doubling of a byte in AL
5    ; to a word in AX by using two nibble look-ups. Overall
6    ; code length and performance are improved by
7    ; using XLAT to look up the nibbles.
8    ;
9    ; Macro to double each bit in a byte.
10   ;
11   ; Input:
12   ;       AL = byte to bit-double
13   ;
14   ; Output:
15   ;       AX = bit-doubled word
16   ;
17   ; Registers altered: AX, BX, CL
18   ;
19   DOUBLE_BYTE     macro
20           mov     ah,al   ;set aside the byte to look up
21           mov     cl,4    ;make a look-up pointer out of the
22           shr     al,cl   ; upper nibble of the byte (XLAT
23                           ; uses AL as an index pointer)
24           mov     bx,offset DoubledNibbleTable
25                           ;XLAT uses BX as a base pointer
26           xlat            ;look up the doubled value of the
27                           ; upper nibble
28           xchg    ah,al   ;store the doubled upper nibble in AH
```

```
29                            ; and get back the value to double
30              and    al,0fh ;make a look-up pointer out of the
31                            ; lower nibble of the byte
32              xlat          ;look up the doubled value of the
33                            ; lower nibble of the byte
34              endm
35      ;
36              jmp    Skip
37      DOUBLED_VALUE=0
38      DoubledNibbleTable    label    byte
39              db     000h, 003h, 00ch, 00fh
40              db     030h, 033h, 03ch, 03fh
41              db     0c0h, 0c3h, 0cch, 0cfh
42              db     0f0h, 0f3h, 0fch, 0ffh
43      ;
44      Skip:
45              call   ZTimerOn
46      BYTE_TO_DOUBLE=0
47              rept   100
48              mov    al,BYTE_TO_DOUBLE
49              DOUBLE_BYTE
50      BYTE_TO_DOUBLE=BYTE_TO_DOUBLE+1
51              endm
52              call   ZTimerOff
```

7.8 ♦ Initializing Memory

Assembler offers excellent data-definition capabilities, and look-up tables can benefit greatly from those capabilities. No high level language even comes close to assembler so far as flexible definition of data is concerned, both in terms of arbitrarily mixing different data types and in terms of letting the assembler perform calculations at assembly time. Given that, why not let the assembler generate your look-up tables for you?

For example, consider the multiplication of a word-sized value by 80, a task often performed in order to calculate row offsets in display memory. Listing 7-19 does this with the compact but slow **mul** instruction, at a pace of 30.17 μsec per multiply. Listing 7-20 improves to 15.08 μsec per multiply by using a faster shift-and-add approach; however, the performance of the shift-and-add approach is limited by the prefetch queue cycle eater. Listing 7-21, which looks up the multiplication results in a table, is considerably faster yet, at 12.26 μsec per multiply. Once again, the look-up approach is faster even than tight register-only code, but that's not what's most interesting here.

What's really interesting about Listing 7-21 is that it's the assembler, not the programmer, that generates the look-up table of multiples of 80. Back

```
1    ;
2    ; *** Listing 7-19 ***
3    ;
4    ; Measures the performance of multiplying by 80 with
5    ; the MUL instruction
6    ;
7            sub     ax,ax
8            call    ZTimerOn
9            rept    1000
10           mov     ax,10   ;so we have a constant value to
11                           ; multiply by
12           mov     dx,80   ;amount to multiply by
13           mul     dx
14           endm
15           call    ZTimerOff
```

```
1    ;
2    ; *** Listing 7-20 ***
3    ;
4    ; Measures the performance of multiplying by 80 with
5    ; shifts and adds.
6    ;
7            sub     ax,ax
8            call    ZTimerOn
9            rept    1000
10           mov     ax,10   ;so we have a constant value to
11                           ; multiply by
12           mov     cl,4
13           shl     ax,cl   ;times 16
14           mov     cx,ax   ;set aside times 16
15           shl     ax,1    ;times 32
16           shl     ax,1    ;times 64
17           add     ax,cx   ;times 80 (times 64 + times 16)
18           endm
19           call    ZTimerOff
```

```
1    ;
2    ; *** Listing 7-21 ***
3    ;
4    ; Measures the performance of multiplying by 80 with
5    ; a table look-up.
6    ;
7            jmp     Skip
8    ;
9    ; Table of multiples of 80, covering the range 80 times 0
10   ; to 80 times 479.
11   ;
12   Times80Table    label   word
13   TIMES_80_SUM=0
14           rept    480
15           dw              TIMES_80_SUM
16   TIMES_80_SUM=TIMES_80_SUM+80
17           endm
18   ;
19   Skip:
```

```
20          sub     ax,ax
21          call    ZTimerOn
22          rept    1000
23          mov     ax,10   ;so we have a constant value to
24                          ; multiply by
25          mov     bx,ax   ;put the factor where we can use it
26                          ; for a table look-up
27          shl     bx,1    ;times 2 for use as an index in a
28                          ; word-sized look-up table
29          mov     ax,[Times80Table+bx]
30                          ;look up the answer
31          endm
32          call    ZTimerOff
```

in Listing 7-15, I had to calculate and type each entry in the look-up table myself. In Listing 7-21, however, I've used the **rept** and = directives to instruct the assembler to build the table automatically. That's even more convenient than you might think. Not only does it save a lot of tedious typing, but it avoids the sort of typos that inevitably creep in whenever a lot of typing is involved.

Another area in which assembler's data-definition capabilities lend themselves to good code is in constructing and using mini-interpreters, which are nothing less than task-specific minilanguages that are easily created and used in assembler. We'll discuss mini-interpreters at length in Volume II of *Zen of Assembly Language*.

You can also take advantage of assembler's data definition capabilities by assigning initial values to variables when they're defined, rather than initializing them with code. In other words,

```
MemVar     dw  0
```

takes no time at all at run time; **MemVar** simply *is* 0 when the program starts. By contrast,

```
MemVar     dw  ?
           :
      mov  [MemVar],0
```

takes 20 cycles at run time and adds 6 bytes to the program as well.

In general, the rule is: *calculate results and initialize data at or before assembly time if you can, rather than at run time.* What makes look-up tables so powerful is simply that they provide an easy way to shift the overhead of calculations from run time to assembly time.

7.9 ◆ A Brief Note on I/O Addressing

You may wonder why we've spent so much time on memory addressing but none on input/output (I/O) addressing. The answer is simple: I/O addressing is so limited that there's not much to know about it. There aren't any profound performance implications or optimizations associated with I/O addressing simply because there are only two ways to perform it.

The **out** instruction, which writes data to a port, always uses the accumulator for the source operand: AL when writing to byte-sized ports, AX when writing to word-sized ports. The destination port address may be specified either by a constant value in the range 0 to 255 (basically direct port addressing with a byte-sized displacement) or by the value in DX (basically indirect port addressing). Here are the two possible ways to send the value 5Ah to port 99:

```
mov   al,5ah
out   99,al
mov   dx,99
out   dx,al
```

Likewise, **in**, which reads data from a port, always uses AL or AX for the destination operand and may use either a constant port value between 0 and 255 or the port pointed to by DX as the source operand. Here are the two ways to read a value from port 255 into AL:

```
in    al,0ffh
mov   dx,0ffh
in    al,dx
```

And that just about does it for I/O addressing. As you can see, there's not much flexibility or opportunity for Zen here. All I/O data must pass through the accumulator, and if you want to access a port address greater than 255, you *must* address the port with DX. What's more, there are no substitutes for the I/O instructions; when you need to perform I/O, what we've just seen is all there is.

Although the I/O instructions are a bit awkward, at least they aren't particularly slow, at 8 (DX-indirect) or 10 (direct-addressed) cycles apiece, with no EA calculation time. Neither are the I/O instructions particularly lengthy; in fact, **in** and **out** are considerably more compact than the memory-addressing instructions, which shouldn't be surprising given that the I/O instructions provide such limited functionality. The DX-indirect forms of both **in** and **out** are just 1 byte long, and the direct-addressed forms are 2 bytes long.

Each I/O access takes over the bus and thereby briefly prevents prefetching, much as each memory access does. However, the ratio of total bus accesses (including instruction byte fetches) to execution time for **in** and **out** isn't bad. In fact, byte-sized DX-indirect I/O instructions, which are only 1 byte long and perform only one I/O access, should actually run in close to the advertised 8 cycles per out.

Among our limited repertoire of I/O instructions, which is best? It doesn't make all *that* much difference, but given the choice between DX-indirect I/O instructions and direct-addressed I/O instructions for heavy I/O, choose DX-indirect, which is slightly faster and more compact. For one-shot I/O to ports in the 0 to 255 range, use direct-addressed I/O instructions, because it takes 3 bytes and 4 cycles to set up DX for a DX-indirect I/O instruction.

On balance, though, don't worry about I/O—just do it when you must. Rare indeed is the program that spends an appreciable amount of its time performing I/O, and given the paucity of I/O addressing modes, there's not much to be done about performance in such cases anyway.

Video Programming and I/O

I'd like to make one final point about I/O addressing. This section won't mean much to you if you haven't worked with video programming, and I'm not going to explain it further now; we'll return to the topic when we discuss video programming in Volume II. For those of you who are involved with video programming, however, here goes.

Word-sized **out** instructions—**out dx,ax**—unquestionably provide the fastest way to set the indexed video registers of the CGA, EGA, and VGA. Just put the index of the video register you're setting in AL and the value you're setting the register to in AH, and **out dx,ax** sets both the index and the register in a single instruction. Using byte-sized **out** instructions, we'd have to do all this to achieve the same results:

```
out   dx,al
inc   dx
xchg  ah,al
out   dx,al
dec   dx
xchg  ah,al
```

(Sometimes you can leave off the final **dec** and **xchg**, but the word-sized approach is still much more efficient.)

However, there's a potential pitfall to the use of word-sized **out** instructions to set indexed video registers. The 8088 can't actually perform word-sized I/O accesses, since the bus is only 8 bits wide. Consequently, the 8088 breaks 16-bit I/O accesses into two 8-bit accesses, one sending AL to the addressed port and a second one sending AH to the addressed port plus one. (If you think about it, you'll realize that this is exactly how the 8088 handles word-sized memory accesses, too.)

All well and good. Unfortunately, on computers built around the 8086, the 80286, and the like, the processors do not automatically break up word-sized I/O accesses, since they're fully capable of outputting 16 bits at once. Consequently, when word-sized accesses are made to 8-bit adapters like the EGA by code running on such computers, it's the bus, not the processor, that breaks up those accesses. Generally, that works perfectly well, but on certain PC-compatible computers, the bus outputs the byte in AH to the addressed port plus one first and *then* sends the byte in AL to the addressed port. The correct values go to the correct ports, but here sequence is critical; **out dx,ax** to an indexed video register relies on the index in AL being output before the data in AH, and that simply doesn't happen. As a result, the data goes to the wrong video register, and the video programming works incorrectly, sometimes with disastrous results.

You may protest that any computer that gets the sequencing of word-sized **out** instructions wrong isn't truly PC compatible, and I suppose that's so. Nonetheless, if a computer runs *everything* except your code that uses word-sized **out** instructions, you're going to have a tough time selling that explanation. Consequently, I recommend using byte-sized **out** instructions to indexed video registers whenever you can't be sure of the particular PC-compatible models on which your code will run.

Avoid Memory!

We've come to the end of our discussion of memory addressing. Memory addressing on the 8088 is no trivial matter, is it? Now that we've familiarized ourselves with the registers and memory-addressing capabilities of the 8088, we'll start exploring the instruction set, a journey that will occupy most of the rest of this volume.

Before we leave the realm of memory addressing, let me repeat: *avoid memory.* Use the registers to the hilt; register-only instructions are shorter and faster. If you must access memory, try not to use *mod-reg-rm* addressing; the special memory-accessing instructions, such as the string instructions and **xlat**, are generally shorter and faster. When you do use *mod-reg-rm* addressing, try not to use displacements, especially 2-byte displacements.

Last but not least, choose your spots. Don't waste time optimizing noncritical code; focus on loops and other chunks of code in which every cycle counts. Assembler programming is not some sort of game where the object is to save cycles and bytes blindly. Rather, the goal is a dual one: to produce whole programs that perform well and *to produce those programs as quickly as possible.* The key to doing that is knowing how to optimize code and then doing so in time-critical code and *only* in time-critical code.

Chapter 8

Strange Fruit of the 8080

8.1   The 8080 Legacy

8.2   Accumulator-Specific Instructions

8.3   Pushing and Popping the 8080 Flags

8.4   A Brief Digression on Optimization

For of all sad words of tongue or pen
The saddest are these: "It might have been!"

John Greenleaf Whittier

With this chapter we start our exploration of the 8088's instruction set. What better place to begin than with the roots of that instruction set, which trace all the way back to the dawn of the microcomputer age?

If you're a veteran programmer, you probably remember the years Before IBM, when state-of-the-art micros were built around the 8-bit 8080 processor and its derivatives. In today's era of ever mightier 16- and 32-bit processors, you no doubt think you've seen the last of the venerable but not particularly powerful 8080.

Not a chance.

The 8080 lingers on in the instruction set and architecture of the 8088, which were designed with an eye toward making it easy to port 8080 programs to the 8088. Although it may seem strange that the design of an advanced processor would be influenced by the architecture of a less capable one, that practice is actually quite common and makes excellent marketing sense. For example, the 80286 and 80386 processors provide complete 8088 compatibility, and would certainly not have been as successful were they not 8088-compatible. In fact, one of the great virtues of the 80386 is its ability to emulate several 8088s at once, and it is well known that the designers of the 80386 went to considerable trouble to maintain that link with the past.

Less well known, perhaps, is the degree to which the designers of the 8088 were guided by the past as well. (Actually, as discussed in Chapter 3, the 8086 was designed first and the 8088 was spun off from it, but we'll refer simply to the 8088 from now on, since that's our focus and since the two processors share the same instruction set.)

8.1 ◆ The 8080 Legacy

At the time the 8088 was designed, the Intel 8080, an 8-bit processor, was an industry standard, along with the more powerful but 8080-compatible Zilog Z80 and Intel 8085 chips. The 8080 had spawned CP/M, a widely used operating system, and with it a variety of useful programs, including word processing, spreadsheet, and database software.

New processors are *always*—without fail—more powerful than their predecessors. Nonetheless, processors that lack compatibility with any previous generation are generally not widely used for several years—if ever—because software developers don't come fully up to speed on new processors for several years, and it's a broad software base that makes a processor useful and therefore popular. In the interim, relatively few programs are available to run on that processor, and sales languish. One solution to this problem is to provide complete compatibility with an earlier standard, as the Z80 and 8085 did. Indeed, today the NEC V20 processor, which is fully 8088-compatible, has the equivalent of an 8080 built in, and can readily switch between 8088- and 8080-compatible modes.

Unfortunately, chip space was at a premium during the 1970s, and presumably Intel couldn't afford to put both 8088 and 8080 functionality into a single package. What Intel could and did do was design the 8088 so that it would be relatively easy to port 8080 programs (especially assembler programs, since most programs were written in assembler in those days) to run on the 8088 and so that those ported programs would perform reasonably well.

The designers of the 8088 provided such source level compatibility by making the 8088's register set similar to the 8080's, by implementing directly analogous (although not identical) 8088 instructions for most 8080 instructions and by providing special speedy, compact forms of key 8080 instructions. As a result, the 8088's architecture bears a striking similarity to that of the 8080.

For example, the 8088's 16-bit AX, BX, CX, and DX registers can also be accessed as paired 8-bit registers, making it possible for the 8088 to mimic the seven 8-bit program-accessible registers and the 8-bit flags register of the 8080, as shown in Figure 8.1. In particular, the 8088's BH and BL registers can be used together as the BX register to address memory, just as the 8080's HL register pair can.

The register correspondence between the 8080 and 8088 is not perfect. For one thing, neither CX nor DX can be used to address memory as can the 8080's BC and DE register pairs; however, the 8088's **xchg** instruction and/or index registers can readily be used to compensate for this. Similarly, the 8080 can push both the flags and the accumulator onto the stack with a single instruction, while the 8088 cannot. As we'll see later in this chapter, though, the designers of the 8088 provided two instructions, **lahf** and **sahf**, to take care of that very problem.

All in all, while the 8080 and 8088 certainly aren't twins, they're unmistakably related.

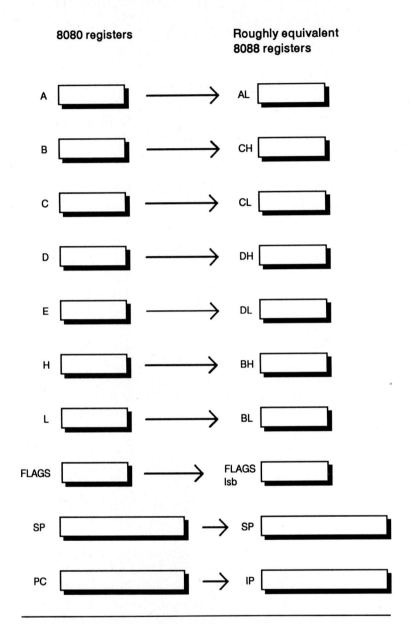

8080 registers

Roughly equivalent 8088 registers

A → AL

B → CH

C → CL

D → DH

E → DL

H → BH

L → BL

FLAGS → FLAGS lsb

SP → SP

PC → IP

FIGURE 8.1   The general correspondence of 8080 registers to 8088 registers indicates the strong influence of the 8080 on the design of the 8088.

More Than a Passing Resemblance

In general, the 8088's instruction set reflects the influence of the 8080 fairly strongly. Although the 8088's instruction set is a considerable superset of the 8080's, there are few 8080 instructions that can't be emulated by one (or at most two) 8088 instructions, and there are several 8088 instructions that most likely would not exist were it not for the 8080 legacy. Also, although it's only speculation, it certainly seems possible that the segmented memory architecture of the 8088 is at least partially the result of needing to reconcile the 1-Mb address space of the 8088 with the 8- and 16-bit nature of the registers the 8088 inherited from the 8080. (Segmentation does allow some types of code to be more compact than they would be if the 8088 had an unsegmented address space, so let's not blame segmentation entirely on the 8080.)

The 8088 is without question a more powerful processor than the 8080, with far more flexible registers and addressing modes, but it is nonetheless merely a 16-bit extension of the 8080 in many ways, rather than a processor designed from scratch. We can only speculate as to what the capabilities of an 8088 built without regard for the 8080 might have been, but a glance at the 68000's 16-Mb linear address space and large 32-bit register set gives us a glimpse of that future that never was.

At any rate, the 8088 *was* designed with the 8080 in mind, and the orientation of the 8088's instruction set toward porting 8080 programs seems to have served its purpose. Many 8080 programs, including WordStar and VisiCalc, were ported to the 8088, and those ported programs helped generate the critical mass of software that catapulted the 8088 to a position of dominance in the microcomputer world. How much of the early success of the 8088 was due to ported 8080 software and how much resulted from the letters *IBM* on the nameplate of the PC is arguable, but ported 8080 software certainly sold well for some time.

Today the need for 8080 source level compatibility is long gone, but that 8080-oriented instruction set is with us still, and seems likely to survive well into the 21st century in the silicon of the 80386 and its successors. (Every processor in Figure 3.5 that's newer than the 8088 provides 8088 compatibility, and it's a safe bet that future generations will be compatible as well. In fact, although it hasn't happened as of this writing, it appears that some *non-Intel* manufacturers may build 8088-compatible subprocessors into their chips!)

The 8080 flavor of the 8088's instruction set is both a curse and a blessing. It's a curse because it limits the performance of average 8088 code and a blessing because it provides great opportunity for assembler code to shine. In particular, the 8080-specific instructions occupy valuable space in the 8088 opcode set, arguably causing native 8088 code (as opposed to ported 8080 code) to be larger and slower than it would otherwise be—and that is, by and large, one of the less appealing aspects of the 8088. For the assembler programmer, however, the 8080-specific instructions can be an asset. Since those instructions are faster and more compact than their general-purpose counterparts, they can often be used to create significantly better code. Next, we'll examine the 8080-specific instructions in detail.

8.2 ◆ Accumulator-Specific Instructions

The accumulator is a rather special register on the 8080. For one thing, the 8080 requires that the accumulator be the destination for most arithmetic and logical operations. For another, the accumulator is the register generally used as source and destination for memory accesses that use direct addressing. (Refer to Chapter 7 for a discussion of addressing modes.)

Not so with the 8088. In the 8088's instruction set, the accumulator (AL for 8-bit operations, AX for 16-bit operations) is a special register for some operations, such as multiplication and division, but is, by and large, no different from any other general-purpose register. With the 8088, any of the eight general-purpose registers can be the source or destination for logical operations, addition, subtraction, and memory accesses as readily as the accumulator can.

Although the 8088's instructions are far more flexible than the 8080's instructions, that flexibility has a price. The price is an extra instruction byte, the *mod-reg-rm* byte, which encodes the 8088's many addressing modes and source/destination combinations, as we learned in Chapter 7. Thanks to the *mod-reg-rm* byte, 8088 instructions are normally 1 byte longer than equivalent 8080 instructions; however, several 8080-inspired 8088 instructions, which require that the accumulator be one of the operands and accept only a few possibilities for the other operand, are the same length as their 8080 counterparts. (Not all the special instructions have exact 8080 counterparts, but that doesn't make them any less useful.) While these accumulator-specific instructions lack the flexibility of their native 8088 counterparts, they are also smaller and faster, so it's desirable to use them whenever possible.

The accumulator-specific 8088 instructions fall into two categories: instructions involving direct addressing of memory and instructions involving immediate arithmetic and logical operands. We'll look at accumulator-specific memory accesses first.

Accumulator-Specific Direct-Addressing Instructions

The 8088 lets you address memory operands in a great many different ways—16 ways, to be precise, as we saw in Chapter 7. This flexibility is one of the strengths of the 8088 and is one area in which the 8088 far exceeds the 8080. There's a price for that flexibility, though, and that's the *mod-reg-rm* byte, which we encountered in Chapter 7. To recap briefly, the *mod-reg-rm* byte is a second instruction byte, immediately following the opcode byte of most instructions that access memory, that specifies which of 32 possible addressing modes are to be used to select the source and/or destination for the instruction. (Eight of the addressing modes are used to select the eight general-purpose registers as operands, and eight addressing modes differ only in the size of the displacement field, hence the discrepancy between the 32 addressing modes and the 16 ways to address memory operands.) Together, the *mod-reg-rm* byte and the 16-bit displacement required for direct addressing mean that any instruction that uses *mod-reg-rm* direct addressing must be at least 4 bytes long, as shown in Figure 8.2.

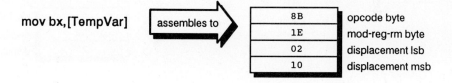

FIGURE 8.2   Together, the *mod-reg-rm* byte and the 16-bit displacement required by direct addressing mean that instructions that use direct addressing are a minimum of 4 bytes long. Above, the instruction

         mov   bx,[TempVar]

with **TempVar** located at offset 1002h in the data segment, can be seen to consist of an opcode byte, a *mod-reg-rm* byte, and a 16-bit displacement, for a total of 4 bytes.

Direct addressing is used whenever you simply want to refer to a memory location by name, with no pointing or indexing. For example, a counter named **Count** could be incremented with direct addressing as follows:

inc [Count]

Direct addressing is intuitive and convenient, and is one of the most heavily used addressing modes of the 8088.

Since direct addressing is one of the very few addressing modes of the 8080, and since the 8088's designers needed to make sure that ported 8080 code ran reasonably well on the 8088, there are 8088 instructions that do nothing more than load and store the accumulator from and to memory via direct addressing. These instructions are only 3 bytes long, as shown in Figure 8.3; better yet, they execute in just 10 cycles, rather than the 14 (memory read) or 15 (memory write) cycles required by *mod-reg-rm* memory accesses that use direct addressing. (Those cycle counts are for byte-sized accesses; add 4 cycles to both forms of **mov** for word-sized accesses.)

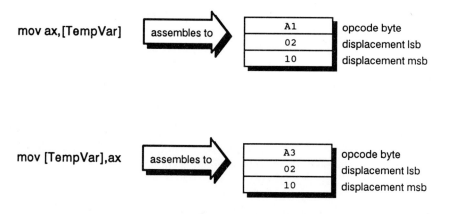

FIGURE 8.3   The accumulator-specific direct-addressing instructions are each only 3 bytes long, 1 byte shorter (and 4 to 5 cycles faster) than the equivalent instructions that use *mod-reg-rm* direct addressing.

Looks Aren't Everything

One odd aspect of the accumulator-specific direct-addressing instructions is that in assembler form they don't *look* any different from the more general form of the **mov** instruction; the difference between the two versions becomes apparent only in machine language. So, for example, although

        mov   al,[Count]

and

        mov   dl,[Count]

look as if they refer to the same instruction, the machine code assembled from the two differs greatly, as shown in Figure 8.4; the first instruction is a byte shorter and 4 cycles faster than the second.

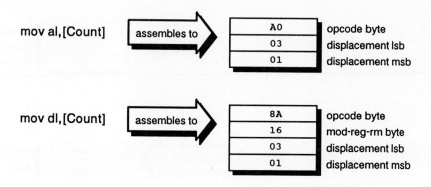

FIGURE 8.4   While the assembler lines

        mov   al,[Count]

and

        mov   dl,[Count]

look like two forms of the same instruction, the two lines actually assemble to two very different instructions; the accumulator-specific version is 1 byte shorter and 4 cycles faster than the *mod-reg-rm* version. In this example, **Count** is at offset 103h in the data segment.

Odder still, there are actually *two* legitimate machine language forms of the assembler code for each of the accumulator-specific direct-addressing instructions (and, indeed, for all the accumulator-specific instructions discussed in this chapter), as shown in Figure 8.5. Any 8088 assembler worth its salt automatically assembles the shorter form, of course, so the longer, general-purpose versions of the accumulator-specific instructions aren't used. Still, the mere existence of two forms of the accumulator-specific instructions points up the special nature of these instructions and the general irregularity of the 8088's instruction set.

How Fast Are They?

How much difference does the use of the accumulator-specific direct-addressing instructions make? Generally, less difference than the official timings in Appendix A would indicate, but a significant difference

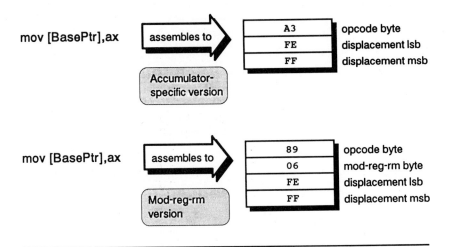

FIGURE 8.5   There are two valid forms of the instruction

> mov   [BasePtr],ax

The shorter form uses accumulator-specific direct addressing, and the longer form uses *mod-reg-rm* direct addressing. A good 8088 assembler will automatically assemble the shorter form whenever possible. In this example, **BasePtr** is at offset 0FFFEh in the data segment.

nonetheless—and you save a byte every time you use an accumulator-specific direct-addressing instruction as well.

Suppose you want to copy the value of one byte-sized memory variable to another byte-sized memory variable. A common way to perform this simple task is to read the value of the first variable into a register, then write the value from the register to the other variable. Listing 8-1 shows a code fragment that performs such a byte copy 1000 times by way of the AH register. As the accumulator is neither source nor destination in Listing 8-1, the 4-byte *mod-reg-rm* direct-addressing form of **mov** is assembled for each instruction; consequently, 8 bytes of code are assembled in order to copy each byte via AH, as shown in Figure 8.6. (Remember that AH is not considered to be the accumulator. For 8-bit operations, AL is the accumulator, and for 16-bit operations, AX is the accumulator, but AH by itself is just another general-purpose register.)

```
1    ;
2    ; *** Listing 8-1 ***
3    ;
4    ; Copies a byte via AH, with memory addressed with
5    ; mod-reg-rm direct addressing.
6    ;
7            jmp         Skip
8    ;
9    SourceValue     db      1
10   DestValue       db      0
11   ;
12   Skip:
13           call        ZTimerOn
14           rept        1000
15           mov         ah,[SourceValue]
16           mov         [DestValue],ah
17           endm
18           call        ZTimerOff
```

Plugged into the Zen timer test program, Listing 8-1 yields an average time per byte copied of 10.06 μsec, or about 48 cycles per byte copied. That's considerably longer than the 29 cycles per byte copied you'd expect from adding up the official cycle times given in Appendix A; the difference is the result of the prefetch queue and dynamic RAM refresh cycle eaters. We can't cover all the aspects of code performance at once, so for the moment let's just discuss the implications of the times reported by the Zen timer. Remember, no matter how much theory of code performance you've mastered, there's still only one reliable way to know how fast PC code really is: measure it!

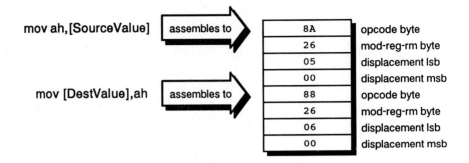

FIGURE 8.6   Eight bytes of code are generated in order to copy a byte
from one direct-addressed memory location to another
by way of AH. Note that *mod-reg-rm* addressing is used
because AH is not the 8-bit accumulator (AL is).

Listing 8-2 performs the same 1000 byte copies as Listing 8-1, but
does so by way of the 8-bit accumulator AL. In Listing 8-2, 6 bytes of
code are assembled in order to copy each byte by way of AL, as shown
in Figure 8.7. Each **mov** instruction in Listing 8-2 is a byte shorter than
the corresponding instruction in Listing 8-1, thanks to the 3-byte size of
the accumulator-specific direct-addressing **mov** instructions. The Zen timer
reports that copying by way of the accumulator reduces the average time per
byte copied to 7.55 µsec, which works out to about 36 cycles per byte—a
33 percent improvement in performance over Listing 8-1.

Enough said.

```
1     ;
2     ; *** Listing 8-2 ***
3     ;
4     ; Copies a byte via AL, with memory addressed with
5     ; accumulator-specific direct addressing.
6     ;
7             jmp     Skip
8     ;
9     SourceValue     db      1
10    DestValue       db      0
11    ;
12    Skip:
13            call    ZTimerOn
14            rept    1000
15            mov     al,[SourceValue]
16            mov     [DestValue],al
17            endm
18            call    ZTimerOff
```

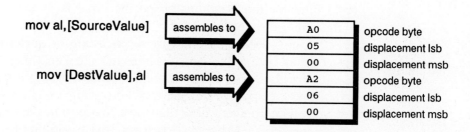

mov al,[SourceValue]   assembles to

A0	opcode byte
05	displacement lsb
00	displacement msb
A2	opcode byte
06	displacement lsb
00	displacement msb

mov [DestValue],al   assembles to

FIGURE 8.7   Six bytes of code are generated in order to copy a byte from one direct-addressed memory location to another by way of AL, the 8-bit accumulator.

When Should You Use Them?

The implication of accumulator-specific direct addressing is obvious: whenever you need to read or write a direct-addressed memory operand, do so via the accumulator if at all possible. You can take this a step further by running unorthodox applications of accumulator-specific direct addressing through the Zen timer to see whether they're worth using. For example, one common use of direct addressing is checking whether a flag or count is 0 with an instruction sequence such as

```
cmp    [NumberOfShips],0   ;5 bytes/20 cycles
jz     NoMoreShips         ;2 bytes/16 or 4 cycles
```

In this example, **NumberOfShips** is accessed with *mod-reg-rm* direct addressing. We'd like to use accumulator-specific direct addressing, but because this is a **cmp** instruction rather than a **mov** instruction, it would seem that accumulator-specific direct addressing can't help us.

Even here, however, accumulator-specific direct addressing can speed things up a bit. Because we're interested only in whether or not **NumberOfShips** is 0, we can load it into the accumulator and then **and** the accumulator with itself to set the zero flag (ZF) appropriately, as in

```
mov    ax,[NumberOfShips]   ;3 bytes/14 cycles
and    ax,ax                ;2 bytes/3 cycles
jz     NoMoreShips          ;2 bytes/16 or 4 cycles
```

While the accumulator-specific version is longer in terms of instructions, what really matters is that both code sequences are 7 bytes long and that the cycle time for the accumulator-specific code is 3 cycles less according to the timings in Appendix A.

Of course, we trust only what we measure for ourselves, so we'll run the code in Listings 8-3 and 8-4 through the Zen timer. The Zen timer reports that the accumulator-specific means of testing a memory location and setting the appropriate zero/non-zero status executes in 6.34 μsec per test, more than 6 percent faster than the 6.76 μsec time per test of the standard test-for-zero code. Although 6 percent isn't a vast improvement, it *is* an improvement, and that boost in performance comes at no cost in code size. In addition, the accumulator-specific form leaves the variable's value available in the accumulator after the test is completed, allowing for even faster code if you need to manipulate or test that value further. The flip side is that the accumulator-specific direct-addressing approach *requires* that the test value be loaded into the accumulator, so if you've got something stored in the accumulator that you don't want to lose, by all means use the *mod-reg-rm* **cmp** instruction.

```
1    ;
2    ; *** Listing 8-3 ***
3    ;
4    ; Tests the zero/non-zero status of a variable via
5    ; the direct-addressing mod-reg-rm form of CMP.
6    ;
7              jmp      Skip
8    ;
9    TestValue      dw      ?
10   ;
11   Skip:
12             call     ZTimerOn
13             rept     1000
14             cmp      [TestValue],0
15             endm
16             call     ZTimerOff
```

```
1    ;
2    ; *** Listing 8-4 ***
3    ;
4    ; Tests the zero/non-zero status of a variable via
5    ; the accumulator-specific form of MOV followed by a
6    ; register-register AND.
7    ;
8              jmp      Skip
9    ;
10   TestValue      dw      ?
11   ;
12   Skip:
13             call     ZTimerOn
14             rept     1000
15             mov      ax,[TestValue]
16             and      ax,ax
17             endm
18             call     ZTimerOff
```

Don't get hung up on using nifty tricks for their own sake. The object is simply to select the best instructions for the task at hand, and it matters not in the least whether those instructions happen to be dazzlingly clever or perfectly straightforward.

Don't expect that unorthodox uses of accumulator-specific direct addressing will always pay off, either, but try them out anyway; they *might* speed up your code, and even if they don't, your experiments might well lead to something else worth knowing. For instance, based on the official execution times in Appendix A it appears that

```
mov   ax,1                  ;3 bytes/4 cycles
mov   [InitialValue],ax     ;3 bytes/14 cycles
```

should be faster than

```
mov   [InitialValue],1      ;6 bytes/20 cycles
```

Running Listings 8-5 and 8-6 through the Zen timer, however, we find that both versions take exactly 7.54 μsec per initialization. The execution time in both cases is determined by the number of memory accesses rather than by execution unit (EU) execution time, and both versions perform eight memory accesses per initialization (six instruction byte fetches and one word-sized memory operand access).

Although that particular trick didn't work out, it does suggest another possibility. Suppose that we want to initialize the variable **InitialValue** to the specific value of 0; now we can modify Listing 8-5 to

```
sub   ax,ax                 ;2 bytes/3 cycles
mov   [InitialValue],ax     ;3 bytes/14 cycles
```

```
1    ;
2    ; *** Listing 8-5 ***
3    ;
4    ; Initializes a variable to 1 by setting AX to 1, then
5    ; using the accumulator-specific form of MOV to store
6    ; that value to a direct-addressed operand.
7    ;
8             jmp       Skip
9    ;
10   InitialValue    dw        ?
11   ;
12   Skip:
13            call      ZTimerOn
14            rept      1000
15            mov       ax,1
16            mov       [InitialValue],ax
17            endm
18            call      ZTimerOff
```

```
1    ;
2    ; *** Listing 8-6 ***
3    ;
4    ; Initializes a variable to 1 via the direct-addressing
5    ; mod-reg-rm form of MOV.
6    ;
7            jmp     Skip
8    ;
9    InitialValue    dw      ?
10   ;
11   Skip:
12           call    ZTimerOn
13           rept    1000
14           mov     [InitialValue],1
15           endm
16           call    ZTimerOff
```

which is both 1 byte shorter and 3 cycles faster than the *mod-reg-rm* instruction

```
mov   word ptr [InitialValue],0     ;6 bytes/20 cycles
```

Code that's shorter in both bytes and cycles (remember, we're talking about official cycles, as listed in Appendix A) almost always provides superior performance, and Listing 8-7 does indeed clock the accumulator-specific initialize-to-0 approach at 6.76 μsec per initialization, more than 11 percent faster than Listing 8-6.

```
1    ;
2    ; *** Listing 8-7 ***
3    ;
4    ; Initializes a variable to 0 via a register-register SUB,
5    ; followed by the accumulator-specific form of MOV to a
6    ; direct-addressed operand.
7    ;
8            jmp     Skip
9    ;
10   InitialValue    dw      ?
11   ;
12   Skip:
13           call    ZTimerOn
14           rept    1000
15           sub     ax,ax
16           mov     [InitialValue],ax
17           endm
18           call    ZTimerOff
```

Actively pursue the possibilities in your assembler code. You never know where they might lead.

Accumulator-Specific Immediate-Operand Instructions

The 8088 also offers special accumulator-specific versions of a number of arithmetic and logical instructions—**adc**, **add**, **and**, **cmp**, **or**, **sub**, **sbb**, and **xor**—when these instructions are used with one register operand and one immediate operand. (Remember that an immediate operand is a constant operand that is built right into an instruction.) The *mod-reg-rm* immediate-addressing versions of the above instructions, when used with a register as the destination operand, are 3 bytes long for byte comparisons and 4 bytes long for word comparisons, as shown in Figure 8.8. The accumulator-specific immediate-addressing versions, on the other hand, are 2 bytes long for byte comparisons and 3 bytes long for word comparisons, as shown in Figure 8.9. Although the official cycle counts listed in Appendix A for the immediate-addressing forms of these instructions, accumulator-specific or otherwise, are all 4 when used with a register as the destination, shorter is generally faster, thanks to the prefetch queue cycle eater.

Let's see how much faster the accumulator-specific immediate-addressing form of **cmp** is than the *mod-reg-rm* version. (The results will hold true for all eight accumulator-specific immediate-addressing instructions, as they all have the same sizes and execution times.) The Zen timer

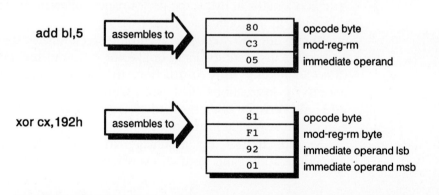

FIGURE 8.8   The *mod-reg-rm* immediate-addressing versions of **adc**, **add**, **and**, **cmp**, **or**, **sub**, **sbb**, and **xor**, when used with a register as the destination operand, are 3 bytes long for byte-sized comparisons and 4 bytes long for word-sized comparisons.

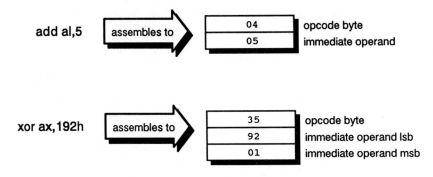

FIGURE 8.9   The accumulator-specific immediate-addressing versions of
adc, **add**, **and**, **cmp**, **or**, **sub**, **sbb**, and **xor**, when used
with a register as the destination operand, are 2 bytes long
for byte-sized comparisons and 3 bytes long for word-
sized comparisons, 1 byte shorter than the *mod-reg-rm*
equivalents.

reports that each accumulator-specific **cmp** in Listing 8-8 takes 1.81 μsec,
making it 50 percent faster than the *mod-reg-rm* version in Listing 8-9, which
clocks in at 2.71 μsec per comparison. It is not in the least coincidental
that the ratio of the execution times, 3:2, is the same as the ratio of instruction lengths in bytes; the performance difference is entirely due to the
difference in instruction lengths.

There are two *caveats* regarding accumulator-specific immediate-
addressing instructions. First, unlike the accumulator-specific form of the
direct-addressing **mov** instruction, the accumulator-specific immediate-
addressing instructions can't work with memory operands. For instance,
add al,[Temp] assembles to a *mod-reg-rm* instruction, not to an
accumulator-specific instruction.

Second, there's no advantage to using the accumulator-specific
immediate-addressing instructions when they're used with word-sized im-

```
1    ;
2    ; *** Listing 8-8 ***
3    ;
4    ; The accumulator-specific immediate-addressing form of CMP.
5    ;
6            call    ZTimerOn
7            rept    1000
8            cmp     al,1
9            endm
10           call    ZTimerOff
```

```
1   ;
2   ; *** Listing 8-9 ***
3   ;
4   ; The mod-reg-rm immediate-addressing form of CMP with a
5   ; register as the destination operand.
6   ;
7           call    ZTimerOn
8           rept    1000
9           cmp     bl,1
10          endm
11          call    ZTimerOff
```

mediate operands in the range −128 to +127 (inclusive), although there's no disadvantage, either. This is true because the word-sized *mod-reg-rm* equivalents of the accumulator-specific instructions can store immediate values in this range as bytes and then sign extend them to words at execution time, while the accumulator-specific immediate-addressing instructions cannot, as shown in Figure 8.10. Consequently, both word-sized forms of these instructions are 3 bytes long when used with immediate operands in the range −128 to +127.

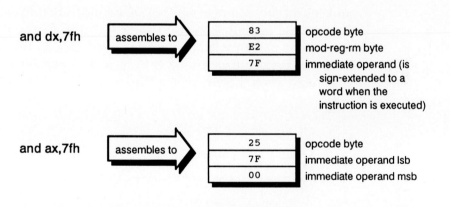

FIGURE 8.10   The word-sized *mod-reg-rm* immediate-addressing versions of **adc**, **add**, **and**, **cmp**, **or**, **sub**, **sbb**, and **xor**, when used with a register as the destination operand, can store values in the range −128 to +127 (inclusive) as bytes, then sign extend them to words at run time, while the accumulator-specific immediate-addressing versions of those instructions cannot. Consequently, there's no advantage or disadvantage to using the accumulator-specific versions with operands in the range −128 to +127.

An important note: some 8088 references indicate that immediate operands to arithmetic instructions can be sign extended but immediate operands to logical instructions—**xor, and,** and **or**—cannot. Not true! Immediate operands to logical instructions *can* be sign extended, and MASM does so automatically whenever possible.

Remember, if you're not sure exactly what instructions the assembler is generating from your source code, you can always look at the instructions directly with a debugger. Alternatively, you can look at the assembled hex bytes at the left side of the assembly listing.

An Accumulator-Specific Example

Let's look at a real-world example of saving bytes and cycles with accumulator-specific instructions. We're going to force the adapter-select bits—bits 5 and 4 of the BIOS equipment flag variable at 0000:0410—to the setting for an 80-column color adapter. This involves setting bit 5 to 1 and bit 4 to 0.

The simplest approach to setting the equipment flag to 80-column color text mode is shown in Listing 8-10; this code uses one *mod-reg-rm* **and** instruction and one *mod-reg-rm* **or** instruction to set the equipment flag in 18.86 μsec. By contrast, Listing 8-11 uses four accumulator-specific instructions to set the equipment flag. Even though Listing 8-11 uses two more instructions than Listing 8-10, it is 12.5 percent faster, taking only 16.76 μsec to set the equipment flag.

```
1    ;
2    ; *** Listing 8-10 ***
3    ;
4    ; Sets the BIOS equipment flag to select an 80-column
5    ; color monitor.
6    ; Uses mod-reg-rm AND and OR instructions.
7    ;
8            call    ZTimerOn
9            rept    1000
10           sub     ax,ax
11           mov     es,ax           ;point ES to the segment at 0
12           and     byte ptr es:[410h],not 30h
13                                   ;mask off the adapter bits
14           or      byte ptr es:[410h],20h
15                                   ;set the adapter bits to select
16                                   ; 80-column color
17           endm
18           call    ZTimerOff
```

```
1    ;
2    ; *** Listing 8-11 ***
3    ;
4    ; Sets the BIOS equipment flag to select an 80-column
```

```
 5    ; color monitor.
 6    ; Uses accumulator-specific MOV, AND, and OR instructions.
 7    ;
 8            call    ZTimerOn
 9            rept    1000
10            sub     ax,ax
11            mov     es,ax           ;point ES to the segment at 0
12            mov     al,es:[410h]    ;get the equipment flag
13            and     al,not 30h      ;mask off the adapter bits
14            or      al,20h          ;set the adapter bits to select
15                                    ; 80-column color
16            mov     es:[410h],al    ;set the new equipment flag
17            endm
18            call    ZTimerOff
```

Other Accumulator-Specific Instructions

Two more instructions have accumulator-specific versions: **test** and **xchg**. Although these instructions have no direct equivalents in the 8080 instruction set, we'll cover them now, while we're on the topic of accumulator-specific instructions. (Although the 8080 does offer some exchange instructions, the 8088's accumulator-specific form of **xchg** doesn't correspond directly to any of those 8080 instructions.)

The Accumulator-Specific Version of test

The instruction **test** sets the flags as if an **and** had taken place, but does not modify the destination. As with **and**, there's an accumulator-specific immediate-addressing version of **test** that's a byte shorter than the *mod-reg-rm* immediate version. (Unlike **and**, the accumulator-specific version of **test** is also a cycle faster than the *mod-reg-rm* version.)
So, for example,

    test al,1

is a byte shorter and a cycle faster than

    test dh,1

The AX-Specific Version of xchg

In its general form, **xchg** swaps the values of two registers or of a register and a memory location. The *mod-reg-rm* register-register interchange form of **xchg** is 2 bytes long and executes in 4 cycles. There is, however, a special form of **xchg** specifically for interchanging AX (not AL) with any of the eight general-purpose registers. This AX-specific form is just 1 byte long and executes in a mere 3 cycles. So, for example,

```
xchg ax,bx
```

is 1 byte and 1 cycle shorter than

```
xchg al,bl
```

as shown in Figure 8.11. In fact,

```
xchg ax,bx
```

is 1 byte shorter (albeit 1 cycle slower) than

```
mov   ax,bx
```

so the AX-specific form of **xchg** can be an attractive alternative to **mov** when you don't require that the copied value remain in the source register after the copy.

When else might the AX-specific version of **xchg** be useful? Suppose that we've got a loop in which we need to add together elements from two arrays, subtract from that sum a value from a third array, and store the result in a fourth array. Suppose further that we can't use BP, perhaps because it's dedicated to maintaining a stack frame. What's more, the pointers to the arrays are passed in, so we can't just use one pointer register as an array subscript by way of displacement+base addressing. Now we've got a bit

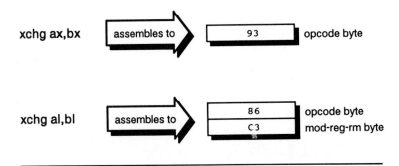

FIGURE 8.11   The AX-specific form of **xchg** is 1 byte shorter and 1 cycle faster than the *mod-reg-rm* form.

of a problem: only three registers other than BP are capable of addressing memory, but we need pointers to four arrays. We could, of course, load two or more of the pointers from memory each time through the loop, but that would slow processing considerably. We could also store two of the pointers in other registers and copy them into, say, BX as we need them, but that would require us to use three registers to maintain two pointers, and, as it happens, we don't have a register to spare.

The solution is to keep one pointer in BX and one in AX and to swap them as needed via the AX-specific form of **xchg**. (As usual, the assembler automatically uses the most efficient possible form of **xchg**; you don't have to worry about explicitly selecting it.) Listing 8-12 shows an implementation that uses the AX-specific form of **xchg** to handle our four-array case without accessing memory or using BP.

```
1   ;
2   ; *** Listing 8-12 ***
3   ;
4   ; Adds together bytes from two arrays, subtracts a byte from
5   ; another array from the sum, and stores the result in a fourth
6   ; array, for all elements in the arrays.
7   ; Uses the AX-specific form of XCHG.
8   ;
9           jmp     Skip
10  ;
11  ARRAY_LENGTH    equ     1000
12  Array1  db      ARRAY_LENGTH dup (3)
13  Array2  db      ARRAY_LENGTH dup (2)
14  Array3  db      ARRAY_LENGTH dup (1)
15  Array4  db      ARRAY_LENGTH dup (?)
16  ;
17  Skip:
18          mov     ax,offset Array1        ;set up array pointers
19          mov     bx,offset Array2
20          mov     si,offset Array3
21          mov     di,offset Array4
22          mov     cx,ARRAY_LENGTH
23          call    ZTimerOn
24  ProcessingLoop:
25          xchg    ax,bx           ;point BX to Array1,
26                                  ; point AX to Array2
27          mov     dl,[bx]         ;get next byte from Array1
28          xchg    ax,bx           ;point BX to Array2,
29                                  ; point AX to Array1
30          add     dl,[bx]         ;add Array2 element to Array1
31          sub     dl,[si]         ;subtract Array3 element
32          mov     [di],dl         ;store result in Array4
33          inc     ax              ;point to next element of each array
34          inc     bx
35          inc     si
36          inc     di
37          loop    ProcessingLoop  ;do the next element
38          call    ZTimerOff
```

Listing 8-12 is intentionally constructed to allow us to use the AX-specific form of **xchg**. It's natural to choose AL, not DL, as the register used for adding and moving data, but if we had done that, then the **xchg** would have become **xchg dx,bx**, which is the 2-byte *mod-reg-rm* version. Listing 8-13 shows this less efficient version of Listing 8-12. Thanks solely to the AX-specific form of **xchg**, Listing 8-12 executes in 21.12 μsec per array element, 7 percent faster than the 22.63 μsec per array element of Listing 8-13. (By the way, we could revamp Listing 8-13 to run considerably faster by using the **lodsb** and **stosb** string instructions, but for the moment we're focusing on the AX-specific form of **xchg**. Nonetheless, there's a lesson here: be careful not to become fixated on a particular trick to the point where you miss other, and possibly better, approaches.)

```
1    ;
2    ; *** Listing 8-13 ***
3    ;
4    ; Adds together bytes from two arrays, subtracts a byte from
5    ; another array from the sum, and stores the result in a fourth
6    ; array, for all elements in the arrays.
7    ; Uses the mod-reg-rm form of XCHG.
8    ;
9            jmp     Skip
10   ;
11   ARRAY_LENGTH    equ     1000
12   Array1  db      ARRAY_LENGTH dup (3)
13   Array2  db      ARRAY_LENGTH dup (2)
14   Array3  db      ARRAY_LENGTH dup (1)
15   Array4  db      ARRAY_LENGTH dup (?)
16   ;
17   Skip:
18           mov     dx,offset Array1
19           mov     bx,offset Array2
20           mov     si,offset Array3
21           mov     di,offset Array4
22           mov     cx,ARRAY_LENGTH
23           call    ZTimerOn
24   ProcessingLoop:
25           xchg    dx,bx           ;point BX to Array1,
26                                   ; point DX to Array2
27           mov     al,[bx]         ;get next byte from Array1
28           xchg    dx,bx           ;point BX to Array2,
29                                   ; point DX to Array1
30           add     al,[bx]         ;add Array2 element to Array1
31           sub     al,[si]         ;subtract Array3 element
32           mov     [di],al         ;store result in Array4
33           inc     dx              ;point to next element of each array
34           inc     bx
35           inc     si
36           inc     di
37           loop    ProcessingLoop  ;do the next element
38           call    ZTimerOff
```

The important point is that in 8088 assembler it often matters which registers and which forms of various instructions you select. Two seemingly similar code sequences, such as Listings 8-12 and 8-13, can actually have quite different performance characteristics.

Yet another aspect of the Zen of assembly language.

8.3 ◆ Pushing and Popping the 8080 Flags

Finally, we come to the strangest part of the 8080 legacy, the **lahf** and **sahf** instructions. The **lahf** instruction loads AH with the lower byte of the 8088's flags register, as shown in Figure 8.12. Not coincidentally, the lower byte of the flags register contains the 8088 equivalents of the 8080's flags, and those flags are located in precisely the same bit positions in the lower byte of the 8088's flags register as they are in the 8080's flags register. The **sahf** instruction reverses the action of **lahf**, loading the 8080-compatible flags into the 8088's flags register by copying AH to the lower byte of the 8088's flags register, as shown in Figure 8.13.

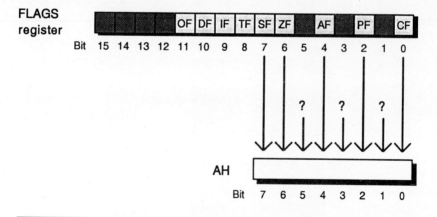

FIGURE 8.12   The **lahf** instruction copies the lower byte of the 8088's flags register to the AH register. This byte contains the 8088 equivalents of the 8080's flags, located in the same bit positions as in the 8080's flags register. Note that the values of the bits of AH copied from unused bits of the flags register (bits 5, 3, and 1) are undefined; that is, those bits are not guaranteed to have any particular values.

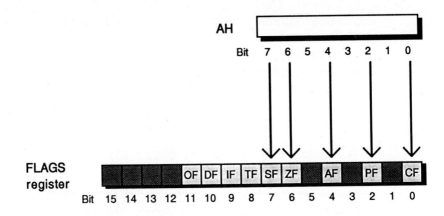

FIGURE 8.13 The **sahf** instruction copies the AH register to the lower byte of the 8088's flags register, reversing the action of **lahf**.

Why do these odd instructions exist? Simply to allow the 8088 to emulate efficiently the 8080's **push psw** and **pop psw** instructions, which transfer both the 8080's accumulator and flags to and from the stack as a single word. The 8088 sequence

```
lahf
push   ax
```

is equivalent to the 8080 sequence

```
push   psw
```

and the 8088 sequence

```
pop   ax
sahf
```

is equivalent to the 8080 sequence

```
pop   psw
```

While it's a pretty safe bet that nobody is writing code that uses **lahf** and **sahf** to emulate 8080 instructions any more, there are nonetheless a few interesting tricks to be played with these instructions. The key is that **lahf** and **sahf** give us a compact (1 byte) and fast (4 cycles) way to save and load the flags we're generally most interested in testing without disturbing the direction (DF) and interrupt (IF) flags. (Note that the overflow flag (OF) also is not saved or restored by these instructions.) By contrast, **pushf** and **popf**, the standard instructions for saving and restoring the flags, take 14 and 12 cycles, respectively, and affect all the flags. What's more, **lahf** and **sahf**, unlike **pushf** and **popf**, avoid the potential complications of accessing the stack.

All in all, **lahf** and **sahf** run faster and tend to cause fewer complications than **pushf** and **popf**. This means that these instructions are attractive whenever you generate a status but don't want to check it right away. This is particularly true if you can't be sure the stack pointer will point to the same place when you finally do check the status, since **pushf** and **popf** wouldn't work in such a case.

By the way, **sahf** is also useful for handling certain status flags of the 8087 numeric coprocessor. The 8087's flags can't be tested directly; they must be stored to memory by the 8087 and then tested by the 8088. One good way to do this for testing certain 8087 statuses, such as greater-than/less-than results from comparisons, is by storing the 8087's flags to memory, loading AH from the stored flags, and executing **sahf** to copy the flags into the 8088's flags register, where they can be used to control conditional jumps.

lahf and sahf: An Example

Let's look at **lahf** and **sahf** in action. Suppose we have a loop in which a value stored in AL is added to each element of a byte array, with the loop ending only when the result of any addition exceeds 7Fh, causing the sign flag (SF) to be set. Unfortunately, the array pointer must be incremented after the addition, wiping out SF, which we need to test at the bottom of the loop, so we need some way to preserve SF during execution of the instruction that increments the array pointer.

Listing 8-14 solves this problem by using **pushf** and **popf** to preserve SF. The Zen timer reports that with this approach it takes 16.45 msec to process 1000 array elements, or 16.45 μsec per element. Astoundingly, Listing 8-15, which is exactly the same as Listing 8-14 except that it uses **lahf** and **sahf** instead of **pushf** and **popf**, takes only 11.31 msec, or 11.31 μsec per array element—a performance improvement of 45 percent! (That's a 45 percent improvement in the *whole loop;* the performance advantage of just **lahf** and **sahf** versus **pushf** and **popf** in this loop is far greater, in the neighborhood of 200 percent.)

```
1    ;
2    ; *** Listing 8-14 ***
3    ;
4    ; Adds AL to each element in an array until the result
5    ; of an addition exceeds 7Fh.
6    ; Uses PUSHF and POPF.
7    ;
8            jmp     Skip
9    ;
10   Data    db      999 dup (0),7fh
11   ;
12   Skip:
13           mov     bx,offset Data
14           mov     al,2    ;we'll add 2 to each array element
15           call    ZTimerOn
16   AddLoop:
17           add     [bx],al ;add the value to this element
18           pushf           ;save the sign flag
19           inc     bx      ;point to the next array element
20           popf            ;get back the sign flag
21           jns     AddLoop ;do the next element, if any
22           call    ZTimerOff
```

```
1    ;
2    ; *** Listing 8-15 ***
3    ;
4    ; Adds AL to each element in an array until the result
5    ; of an addition exceeds 7Fh.
6    ; Uses LAHF and SAHF.
7    ;
8            jmp     Skip
9    ;
10   Data    db      999 dup (0),7fh
11   ;
12   Skip:
13           mov     bx,offset Data
14           mov     al,2    ;we'll add 2 to each array element
15           call    ZTimerOn
16   AddLoop:
17           add     [bx],al ;add the value to this element
18           lahf            ;save the sign flag
19           inc     bx      ;point to the next array element
20           sahf            ;get back the sign flag
21           jns     AddLoop ;do the next element, if any
22           call    ZTimerOff
```

8.4 ◆ A Brief Digression on Optimization

As is always the case, there are other solutions to the programming task at
hand than those shown in Listings 8-14 and 8-15. For example, SF could
be tested immediately after the addition, as shown in Listing 8-16. The

```
1  ;
2  ; *** Listing 8-16 ***
3  ;
4  ; Adds AL to each element in an array until the result
5  ; of an addition exceeds 7Fh.
6  ; Uses two jumps in the loop, with a final INC to adjust
7  ; BX for the last addition.
8  ;
9          jmp      Skip
10 ;
11 Data    db       999 dup (0),7fh
12 ;
13 Skip:
14         mov      bx,offset Data
15         mov      al,2     ;we'll add 2 to each array element
16         call     ZTimerOn
17 AddLoop:
18         add      [bx],al ;add the value to this element
19         js       EndAddLoop ;done if Sign flag set
20         inc      bx       ;point to the next array element
21         jmp      AddLoop ;do the next element
22 EndAddLoop:
23         inc      bx       ;adjust BX for the final addition
24         call     ZTimerOff
```

approach of Listing 8-16 is exactly equivalent to that of Listings 8-14 and 8-15 but eliminates the need to preserve the flags. Listing 8-16 executes in 10.78 μsec per array element, a slight improvement over Listing 8-15.

Let's look at the code in Listing 8-16 for a moment more, as it's often true that with a little effort even heavily optimized code can be made to yield a bit more performance. What's looks less than optimal about Listing 8-16? The **add** instruction is pretty clearly indispensable, as is **inc**. However, there are two jumps inside the loop. If we could manage with one jump, things should speed up somewhat. With a bit of ingenuity, it is indeed possible to get by with one jump, as shown in Listing 8-17.

The key to Listing 8-17 is that the **inc** instruction that points BX to the next memory location is moved ahead of the addition, allowing us to put the conditional jump at the bottom of the loop without the necessity of preserving the flags for several instructions (as is done in Listings 8-14 and 8-15). Listing 8-17 appears to be much faster than Listing 8-16; after all, it's a full instruction and 2 bytes shorter in the loop. Still, we trust only what we measure, so let's compare actual performance.

Incredibly, the Zen timer reports that Listing 8-17 executes in 10.78 μsec per array element—*no faster than Listing 8-16!* Why isn't Listing 8-17 faster? To be honest, I don't know. Listing 8-17 probably wastes some prefetches

```
 1    ;
 2    ; *** Listing 8-17 ***
 3    ;
 4    ; Adds AL to each element in an array until the result
 5    ; of an addition exceeds 7Fh.
 6    ; Uses one jump in the loop, with a predecrement before
 7    ; the loop, an INC before the ADD in the loop, and a final
 8    ; INC to adjust BX for the last addition.
 9    ;
10            jmp     Skip
11    ;
12    Data  db      999 dup (0),7fh
13    ;
14    Skip:
15            mov     bx,offset Data
16            mov     al,2    ;we'll add 2 to each array element
17            call    ZTimerOn
18            dec     bx      ;compensate for the initial INC
19    AddLoop:
20            inc     bx      ;point to the next array element
21            add     [bx],al ;add the value to this element
22            jns     AddLoop ;do the next element, if any
23    EndAddLoop:
24            inc     bx      ;adjust BX for the final addition
25            call    ZTimerOff
```

at the bottom of the loop, where **add [bx],al** (a slow, short instruction that allows the prefetch queue to fill) is followed by a jump that flushes the queue. There may also be interaction between the memory operand accesses of the **add** instruction and prefetching that works to the relative benefit of Listing 8-16. Synchronization with DRAM refresh may be taking place as well.

I could hook up the hardware I used in Chapter 5 to find the answer, but that takes considerable time and money and simply isn't worth the effort. As we've established in earlier chapters, we'll never understand the exact operation of 8088 code; that's why we have to use the Zen timer to monitor performance. The important points of this exercise in optimization are these: we created shorter, faster code by examining a programming problem from a new perspective, and we measured that code and found that it actually ran no faster than the old code.

Bring your knowledge and creativity to bear on improving your code. Then use the Zen timer to make sure you've really improved the code!

Interesting optimizations aside, **lahf** and **sahf** are always preferred to **pushf** and **popf** whenever you can spare AH and don't need to save IF, OF, and DF, all the more so when you don't *want* to save those flags or don't want to have to use the stack to store flag states. Who would ever have thought that two warmed-over 8080 instructions could be so useful?

Onward through the Instruction Set

Given the extent to which the 8080 influenced the decidedly unusual architecture and instruction set of the 8088, it is interesting (although admittedly pointless) to wonder what might have happened had the 8080 been less successful, allowing Intel to make a clean break with the past when the 8088 was designed. Still, the 8088 is what it is, so it's on to the rest of the instruction set for us.

Chapter 9

Around and about the Instruction Set

9.1	Shortcuts for Handling Zero and Constants
9.2	inc and dec
9.3	Carrying Results along in a Flag
9.4	Byte-to-Word and Word-to-Doubleword Conversion
9.5	xchg Is Handy When Registers Are Tight
9.6	Destination: Register
9.7	neg and not
9.8	Rotates and Shifts
9.9	ASCII and Decimal Adjust
9.10	Mnemonics That Cover Multiple Instructions

So far, we've covered assembler programming in a fairly linear fashion, with one topic leading neatly to the next and with related topics grouped by chapter. Alas, assembler programming isn't so easily compartmentalized. For one thing, the relationships among the many facets of assembler programming are complex; consider how often I've already mentioned the string instructions, which we have yet to discuss formally. For another, certain aspects of assembler stand alone, and are not particularly closely related to any other assembler topic.

Some interesting members of the 8088's instruction set fall into the category of stand-alone topics, as do unusual applications of a number of instructions. For example, while the knowledge that **inc ax** is a byte shorter than **inc al** doesn't have any far-reaching implications, that knowledge can save a byte and a few cycles when applied properly. Likewise, the use of **cbw** to convert certain unsigned byte values to word values is a self-contained programming technique.

Over the last few chapters, we've covered the 8088's registers, memory addressing, and 8080-influenced instructions. In this chapter, we'll touch on more 8088 instructions. Not all the instructions, by any means (remember, I'm assuming you already know 8088 assembler), but rather those with subtle, useful idiosyncrasies. These instructions fall into the class described above—well worth knowing but unrelated to one another—so this chapter will be a potpourri of assembler topics, and I will leap from one instruction to another.

In the next chapter we'll return to a more linear format as we discuss the string instructions. After that we'll get into branching, look-up tables, and more. For now, though, hold on to your hat as we bound through the instruction set.

9.1 ◆ Shortcuts for Handling Zero and Constants

The instruction set of the 8088 can perform any of a number of logical and arithmetic operations on byte- and word-sized, signed and unsigned integer values. What's more, those values may be stored either in registers or in memory. Much of the complexity of the 8088's instruction set results from this flexibility, and so does the slow performance of many of the 8088's instructions. However, some of the 8088's instructions can be used in a less flexible—but far speedier—fashion. Nowhere is this more apparent than in handling 0.

Zero pops up everywhere in assembler programs. Up counters are initialized to 0. Down counters are counted down to 0. Flag bytes are compared with 0. Parameters of value 0 are passed to subroutines. Zero is surely the most commonly used value in assembler programming—and the easiest value to handle, as well.

Making Zero

For starters, there is almost never any reason to assign the immediate value 0 to a register. Why assign 0 to a register when **sub** *reg,reg* or **xor** *reg,reg* always zeros the register in fewer cycles (and also in fewer bytes for 16-bit registers)? The only time you should assign the value 0 to a register rather than clearing the register with **sub** or **xor** is when you need to preserve the flags, since **mov** doesn't affect the flags but **sub** and **xor** do.

Initializing Constants from the Registers

As we discussed in the last chapter, it pays to clear a direct-addressed memory variable by zeroing AL or AX and storing that register to the memory variable. If you're setting two or more direct-addressed variables to any specific value (and here we're talking about *any* value, not just 0), it's worth storing that value in the accumulator and then storing the accumulator to the memory variables. (When initializing large blocks of memory, **rep stos** works better still, as we'll see in Chapter 10.) The basic principle is this: *avoid extra immediate-operand bytes by storing frequently used constants in registers and using the registers as operands.*

Listing 9-1 provides an example of initializing multiple memory variables to the same value. This listing, which stores 0FFFFh in AX and then stores AX to three memory variables, executes in 17.60 μsec per three-word initialization. That's more than 28 percent faster than the 22.63 μsec per

```
1   ;
2   ; *** Listing 9-1 ***
3   ;
4   ; An example of initializing multiple memory variables
5   ; to the same value by placing the value in a register,
6   ; then storing the register to each of the variables.
7   ; This avoids the overhead that's incurred when using
8   ; immediate operands.
9   ;
10          jmp     Skip
11  ;
12  MemVar1 dw      ?
13  MemVar2 dw      ?
14  MemVar3 dw      ?
15  ;
```

```
16    Skip:
17              call     ZTimerOn
18              rept     1000
19              mov      ax,0ffffh        ;place the initial value in
20                                        ; AX
21              mov      [MemVar1],ax     ;store AX to each memory
22              mov      [MemVar2],ax     ; variable to be initialized
23              mov      [MemVar3],ax
24              endm
25              call     ZTimerOff
```

initialization of Listing 9-2, which stores the immediate value 0FFFFh to each of the three words. Listing 9-1 is that much faster than Listing 9-2, *even though Listing 9-1 is one instruction longer per initialization.* The difference? Each of the three **mov** instructions in Listing 9-2 is 3 bytes longer than the corresponding **mov** in Listing 9-1: 2 bytes are taken up by the immediate value 0FFFFh, and 1 extra byte is required because the accumulator-specific direct-addressing form of **mov** isn't used. That's a to-tal of 9 extra bytes for the three **mov** instructions of Listing 9-2, more than offsetting the 3 bytes required by the extra instruction **mov ax,0ffffh** of Listing 9-1. (Remember, the 8088 doesn't sign extend immediate operands to **mov**.) As always, those extra bytes take 4 cycles each to fetch.

Shorter is better.

```
1     ;
2     ; *** Listing 9-2 ***
3     ;
4     ; An example of initializing multiple memory variables
5     ; to the same value by making the value an immediate
6     ; operand to each instruction. Immediate operands
7     ; increase instruction size by 1 to 2 bytes, and preclude
8     ; use of the accumulator-specific direct-addressing
9     ; form of MOV.
10    ;
11              jmp      Skip
12    ;
13    MemVar1 dw    ?
14    MemVar2 dw    ?
15    MemVar3 dw    ?
16    ;
17    Skip:
18              call     ZTimerOn
19              rept     1000
20              mov      [MemVar1],0ffffh ;store 0ffffh to each memory
21              mov      [MemVar2],0ffffh ; variable as an immediate
22              mov      [MemVar3],0ffffh ; operand
23              endm
24              call     ZTimerOff
```

If you're initializing more than one register to 0, you can save 1 cycle per additional register by initializing just one of the registers and copying it to the others, as follows:

```
sub    si,si      ;point to offset 0 in DS
mov    di,si      ;point to offset 0 in ES
mov    dx,si      ;initialize counter to 0
```

While **mov** *reg,reg* is 2 bytes long, the same as **sub** *reg,reg*, according to the official specs **mov** is the faster of the two by 1 cycle. Whether this translates into any performance advantage depends on the code mix: if the prefetch queue is empty, code-fetching time will dominate and **mov** will have no advantage—but it can't hurt and *might* help.

Similarly, if you're initializing multiple 8-bit registers to the same nonzero value, you can save up to 2 cycles per additional register by initializing one of the registers and copying it to the other(s). Although **mov** *reg,immed8* is 2 cycles slower than **mov** *reg,reg*, both instructions are the same size.

Finally, if you're initializing multiple 16-bit registers to the same nonzero value, it *always* pays to initialize one register and copy it to the other(s). The reason: **mov** *reg,immed16*, 3 bytes long, is 1 byte longer (and 2 cycles slower) than **mov** *reg,reg*.

Initializing Two Bytes with a Single mov

While we're on the topic of initializing registers and variables, let's take a quick look at initializing paired bytes. Suppose we want to initialize AH to 16h and AL to 1. The obvious solution is to set each register to the desired value:

```
mov    ah,16h
mov    al,1
```

However, a better solution is to set the pair of registers with a single **mov**:

```
mov    ax,1601h
```

The paired-register initialization is a byte shorter and four cycles faster— *and it does exactly the same thing as the separate initializations!*

A trick that makes it easier to initialize paired 8-bit registers is to shift the value for the upper register by 8 bits. For example, the last initialization could be performed as

```
mov    ax,(16h shl 8) + 1
```

This method has two benefits. First, it's easy to distinguish between the values for the upper and lower registers; 16 and 1 are easy to pick out in the above example. Second, it's much simpler to handle nonhexadecimal values by shifting and adding. You must admit that

```
mov   dx,(201 shl 8) + 'A'
```

is easier to write and understand than

```
mov   dx,0c941h ;DH=201, DL='A'
```

You need not limit paired-byte initializations to registers. Adjacent byte-sized memory variables can be initialized with a single word access as well. If you do use paired-byte initializations of memory variables, though, be sure to place prominent comments around the memory variables; otherwise, you or someone else might accidentally separate the pair at a later date, ruining the initialization.

More Fun with Zero

What else can we do with 0? Well, we can test the zero or nonzero status of a register with either **and reg,reg** or **or reg,reg**. Both of these instructions set the zero flag (ZF) just as **cmp reg,0** would, and they execute faster and are anywhere from 0 to 2 bytes shorter than **cmp**. (Both **and reg,reg** and **or reg,reg** are guaranteed to be at least 1 byte shorter than **cmp reg,0** except when **reg** is AL, in which case all three instructions are the same length.) Listing 9-3, which uses **and dx,dx** to test for the zero status of DX, clocks in at 3.62 μsec per test. That's 25 percent faster than the 4.53 μsec per test of Listing 9-4, which uses **cmp dx,0**.

```
1    ;
2    ; *** Listing 9-3 ***
3    ;
4    ; An example of using AND reg,reg to test for the
5    ; zero/non-zero status of a register. This is faster
6    ; (and usually shorter) than CMP reg,0.
7    ;
8            sub     dx,dx    ;set DX to 0, so we don't jump
9            call    ZTimerOn
10           rept    1000
11           and     dx,dx    ;is DX 0?
12           jnz     $+2      ;just jumps to the next line if
13                            ; Z is not set (never jumps)
14           endm
15           call    ZTimerOff
```

```
1    ;
2    ; *** Listing 9-4 ***
3    ;
4    ; An example of using CMP reg,0 to test for the
5    ; zero/non-zero status of a register.
6    ;
7            sub     dx,dx     ;set DX to 0, so we don't jump
8            call    ZTimerOn
9            rept    1000
10           cmp     dx,0      ;is DX 0?
11           jnz     $+2       ;just jumps to the next line if
12                             ; Z is not set (never jumps)
13           endm
14           call    ZTimerOff
```

As described in the previous chapter, it is (surprisingly) faster to load the accumulator from a direct-addressed memory variable and to **and** or **or** the accumulator with itself in order to test whether that memory variable is 0 than it is to simply compare the memory variable with an immediate operand. For instance,

```
mov   al,[ByteFlag]
and   al,al
jnz   FlagNotZero
```

is equivalent to and faster than

```
cmp   [ByteFlag],0
jnz   FlagNotZero
```

Finally, in some cases tests that are really not zero-nonzero tests can be converted to tests for 0. For example, consider a test to check whether or not DX is 0FFFFh. We could use **cmp dx,0ffffh**, which is 3 bytes long and takes 4 cycles to execute. On the other hand, if we don't need to preserve DX (that is, if we're performing a one-time-only test) we could simply use **inc dx**, which is only 1 byte long and takes just 2 cycles to execute, and then test for a zero-nonzero status. So, if we don't mind altering DX in the course of the test,

```
cmp   dx,0ffffh
jnz   NotFFFF
```

and

```
inc   dx
jnz   NotFFFF
```

are functionally the same—the latter version is much smaller and faster.

A similar case of turning a test into a zero-nonzero test occurs when testing a value for membership in a short sequence of consecutive numbers—the equivalent of a C switch construct with just a few cases consisting of consecutive values. (Longer and/or nonconsecutive sequences should be handled with look-up tables.) For example, suppose that you want to perform one action if CX is 4, another if CX is 3, a third action if CX is 2, and yet another if CX is 1. Listing 9-5, which uses four **cmp** instructions to test for the four cases of interest, runs in 17.01 μsec per switch handled. That's a good 4.94 μsec slower per switch than the 12.07 μsec of Listing 9-6, so Listing 9-5 runs at less than 75 percent of the speed of Listing 9-6. Listing 9-6 gets its speed boost by using the 1-byte **dec cx** instruction instead of the 3-byte **cmp cx,*immed8*** instruction to test for each of the four cases, thereby turning all the tests into zero-nonzero tests.

```
1    ;
2    ; *** Listing 9-5 ***
3    ;
4    ; An example of performing a switch statement with just a
5    ; few cases, all consecutive, by using CMP to test for each
6    ; of the cases.
7    ;
8    ; Macro to perform switch statement. This must be a macro
9    ; rather than code inside the REPT block because MASM
10   ; doesn't handle LOCAL declarations properly inside REPT
11   ; blocks, but it does handle them properly inside macros.
12   ;
13   HANDLE_SWITCH    macro
14            local   ValueWas1, ValueWas2, ValueWas3, ValueWas4
15            cmp     cx,1
16            jz      ValueWas1
17            cmp     cx,2
18            jz      ValueWas2
19            cmp     cx,3
20            jz      ValueWas3
21            cmp     cx,4
22            jz      ValueWas4
23   ;        <none of the above>
24   ValueWas1:
25   ValueWas2:
26   ValueWas3:
27   ValueWas4:
28            endm
29   ;
30            call    ZTimerOn
31   TEST_VALUE = 1
32            rept    1000
33            mov     cx,TEST_VALUE    ;set the test value
34            HANDLE_SWITCH            ;perform the switch test
35   TEST_VALUE = (TEST_VALUE MOD 5)+1 ;cycle the test value from
36                                     ; 1 to 4
37            endm
38            call    ZTimerOff
```

```
 1    ;
 2    ; *** Listing 9-6 ***
 3    ;
 4    ; An example of performing a switch statement with just a
 5    ; few cases, all consecutive, by using DEC to test for each
 6    ; of the cases.
 7    ;
 8    ; Macro to perform switch statement. This must be a macro
 9    ; rather than code inside the REPT block because MASM
10    ; doesn't handle LOCAL declarations properly inside REPT
11    ; blocks, but it does handle them properly inside macros.
12    ;
13    HANDLE_SWITCH    macro
14            local    ValueWas1, ValueWas2, ValueWas3, ValueWas4
15            dec      cx
16            jz       ValueWas1
17            dec      cx
18            jz       ValueWas2
19            dec      cx
20            jz       ValueWas3
21            dec      cx
22            jz       ValueWas4
23    ;       <none of the above>
24    ValueWas1:
25    ValueWas2:
26    ValueWas3:
27    ValueWas4:
28            endm
29    ;
30            call     ZTimerOn
31    TEST_VALUE = 1
32            rept     1000
33            mov      cx,TEST_VALUE   ;set the test value
34            HANDLE_SWITCH            ;perform the switch test
35    TEST_VALUE = (TEST_VALUE MOD 5)+1 ;cycle the test value from
36                                      ; 0 to 3
37            endm
38            call     ZTimerOff
```

Unorthodox, yes—but very effective. The moral is clear: *even when the 8088 has an instruction that's clearly intended to perform a given task (such as **cmp** for comparing), don't assume that instruction is the best way to perform that task under all conditions.*

9.2 ◆ inc and dec

The **inc** and **dec** instructions are simple, unpretentious—and more powerful than you might imagine. Since **inc** and **dec** require only one operand (the immediate value 1 that's added or subtracted is implied by the instruction), they are among the shortest (1 to 4 bytes) and fastest (2 to 3 cycles for a register operand, but up to 35 for a word-sized memory operand—keep your operands in registers!) instructions of the 8088. In particular, when working with 16-bit register operands, **inc** and **dec** are the fastest arithmetic instructions of the 8088, with an execution time of 2 cycles paired with a length of just 1 byte.

How much difference does it make to use **inc** or **dec** rather than **add** or **sub**? When you're manipulating a register, the answer is, a *lot*. In fact, it's actually better to use *two* **inc** instructions to add 2 to a 16-bit register than to add 2 with a single **add**, because a single **add** with an immediate operand of 2 is 3 bytes long, three times the length of a 16-bit register **inc.** (Remember, shorter is better, thanks to the prefetch queue cycle eater.)

The same is true of **dec** versus **sub** as of **inc** versus **add**. For example, the code in Listing 9-7, which uses a 16-bit register **dec** instruction, clocks in at 5.03 μsec per loop, 33 percent faster than the 6.70 μsec of the code in Listing 9-8, which uses a **sub** instruction to decrement DX.

```
1   ;
2   ; *** Listing 9-7 ***
3   ;
4   ; Times the performance of a 16-bit register DEC.
5   ;
6           mov     dx,1000
7           call    ZTimerOn
8   TestLoop:
9           dec     dx        ;16-bit register DEC
10                            ; (1 byte long, uses 16-bit-
11                            ; register-specific form of DEC)
12          jnz     TestLoop
13          call    ZTimerOff
```

```
1   ;
2   ; *** Listing 9-8 ***
3   ;
4   ; Times the performance of a 16-bit subtraction
5   ; of an immediate value of 1.
6   ;
7           mov     dx,1000
8           call    ZTimerOn
9   TestLoop:
10          sub     dx,1      ;decrement DX by subtracting 1 from
11                            ; it (3 bytes long, uses sign-
12                            ; extended mod-reg-rm form of SUB)
13          jnz     TestLoop
14          call    ZTimerOff
```

The difference between the times of Listings 9-7 and 9-8 is attributable primarily to the 8 cycles required to fetch the 2 extra bytes of the **sub** instruction. To illustrate that point, consider Listing 9-9, which decrements

```
1    ;
2    ; *** Listing 9-9 ***
3    ;
4    ; Times the performance of two 16-bit register DEC
5    ; instructions.
6    ;
7            mov     dx,2000
8            call    ZTimerOn
9    TestLoop:
10           dec     dx        ;subtract 2 from DX by decrementing
11           dec     dx        ; it twice (2 bytes long, uses
12                             ; 2 16-bit-register-specific DECs)
13           jnz     TestLoop
14           call    ZTimerOff
```

DX twice per loop. Listing 9-9 executes in 5.80 μsec per loop, approximately halfway between the times of Listings 9-7 and 9-8. That's just what we'd expect, since the loop in Listing 9-9 is 1 byte longer than the loop in Listing 9-7 and 1 byte shorter than the loop in Listing 9-8.

*Use **inc** or **dec** in preference to **add** or **sub** whenever possible.*

(Actually, when SP is involved there's an exception to this rule for code that will run on 80286- or 80386-based computers. Such code should use **add**, **sub**, **push**, and **pop** to alter SP in preference to **inc** and **dec**, because an odd stack pointer is highly undesirable on 16- and 32-bit processors. I'll cover this topic in detail in Chapter 15.)

I'd like to pause at this point to emphasize that the 16-bit register versions of **inc** and **dec** are different beasts from the run-of-the-mill **inc** and **dec** instructions. As with the 16-bit register **xchg**-with-AX instructions we discussed in the previous chapter, there are actually two separate **inc** instructions on the 8088, one of which is a superset of the other. (The same is true of **dec**, but we'll just discuss **inc** for now.)

Figure 9.1 illustrates the two forms of **inc**. Although the special form is limited to 16-bit register operands, it has the advantage of being a byte shorter and a cycle faster than the *mod-reg-rm* register form, even when both instructions operate on the same register. As you'd expect, 8088 assemblers automatically use the more efficient special version whenever possible, so you don't need to select between the two forms explicitly; however, it's up to you to use 16-bit register **inc** (and **dec**) instructions whenever you possibly can, because only then can the assembler assemble the more efficient form of those instructions.

For example, Listing 9-7, which uses the 1-byte-long 16-bit register form of **dec** to decrement the 16-bit DX register, executes in 5.03 μsec per loop, 15 percent faster than Listing 9-10, which uses the 2-byte-long *mod-reg-rm* form of **dec** to decrement the 8-bit DL register and executes in 5.79 μsec per loop.

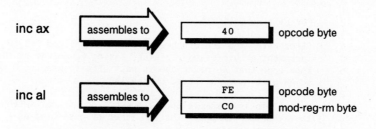

FIGURE 9.1 The 16-bit register-only versions of **inc** and **dec** are only 1 byte long and execute in just 2 cycles. By contrast, the *mod-reg-rm* versions of **inc reg** and **dec reg** are 2 bytes long and execute in 3 cycles.

```
1    ;
2    ; *** Listing 9-10 ***
3    ;
4    ; Times the performance of an 8-bit register DEC.
5    ;
6            mov     dl,100
7            call    ZTimerOn
8    TestLoop:
9            dec     dl      ;8-bit register DEC
10                           ; (2 bytes long, uses mod-reg-rm
11                           ; form of DEC)
12           jnz     TestLoop
13           call    ZTimerOff
```

Using 16-Bit inc and dec Instructions for 8-Bit Operations

If you're clever, you can sometimes use the 16-bit form of **inc** or **dec** even when you only want to affect an 8-bit register. Consider Listing 9-11, which uses AL to count from 0 to 8. Since AL will never pass 0FFh and turn over (the only circumstance in which **inc ax** modifies AH), it's perfectly safe to use **inc ax** rather than **inc al**. In this case, both instructions always produce the same result; however, **inc ax** produces that result considerably more rapidly than **inc al**. If you do use such a technique, however, remember that the flags are set on the basis of the *whole operand*. For example, **dec ax** will set ZF only when both AH and AL—not AL alone—go to 0. This seems obvious, but if you're thinking of AL as the working register, as in Listing 9-11, it's easy to forget that **dec ax** sets the flags to reflect the status of AX, not AL.

```
1   ;
2   ; *** Listing 9-11 ***
3   ;
4   ; Illustrates the use of the efficient word-sized INC to
5   ; increment a byte-sized register, taking advantage of the
6   ; knowledge that AL never counts past 0FFh to wrap to 0 and
7   ; so AH will never affected by the INC.
8   ;
9   ; Note: This is a sample code fragment, and is not intended
10  ; to either be run under the Zen timer or assembled as a
11  ; standalone program.
12  ;
13          sub     al,al   ;count up from 0
14  TestLoop:
15          inc     ax      ;AL will never turn over, so AH
16                          ; will never be affected
17          cmp     al,8    ;count up to 8
18          jbe     TestLoop
```

To carry the quest for **inc** and **dec** efficiency to the limit, suppose we're constructing code that contains nested countdown loops. Suppose further that all registers but CX are in use, so all we've got available for counters are CH and CL. Normally, we would expect to use two 8-bit **dec** instructions here. However, we know that the counter for the inner loop is 0 after the loop is completed, so we've got an opportunity to perform a 16-bit **dec** for the outer loop if we play our cards right.

Listing 9-12 shows how this trick works. CH is the counter for the inner loop, and we are indeed stuck with an 8-bit **dec** for this loop. However, by the time we get around to using CL as a counter, CH is guaranteed to be 0, so we can use a 16-bit **dec cx** for the outer loop. Granted, it would be preferable to place the 16-bit **dec** in the time-critical inner loop, and if that loop were long enough, we might well do that by pushing CX for the duration of the inner loop. Nonetheless, a 16-bit **dec** is preferable in any loop, and in Listing 9-12 we get the benefits of a 16-bit **dec** at no cost other than a bit of careful register use.

```
1   ;
2   ; *** Listing 9-12 ***
3   ;
4   ; Illustrates the use of a word-sized DEC for the outer
5   ; loop, taking advantage of the knowledge that the counter
6   ; for the inner loop is always 0 when the outer loop is
7   ; counted down. This code uses no registers other than
8   ; CX, and would be used when registers are in such short
9   ; supply that no other registers are available. Otherwise,
10  ; word-sized DECs would be used for both loops. (Ideally,
11  ; a LOOP would also be used instead of DEC CX/JNZ.)
12  ;
13  ; Note: This is a sample code fragment, and is not intended
14  ; to either be run under the Zen timer or assembled as a
```

```
15   ; standalone program.
16   ;
17          mov     cl,5     ;outer loop is performed 5 times
18   OuterLoop:
19          mov     ch,10    ;inner loop is performed 10 times
20                           ; each time through the outer loop
21   InnerLoop:
22   ;<<<working code goes here>>>
23          dec     ch       ;count down inner loop
24          jnz     InnerLoop
25          dec     cx       ;CH is always 0 at this point, so
26                           ; we can use the shorter & faster
27                           ; word DEC to count down CL
28          jnz     OuterLoop
```

By the way, you've likely noticed that Listing 9-12 fairly begs for a **loop** instruction at the bottom of the outer loop. That's certainly the most efficient code in this case; I've broken the **loop** into a **dec** and a **jnz** for illustrative purposes.

How inc and add (and dec and sub) Differ— and Why

The instructions **inc** and **dec** are not *exactly* the same as **add 1** and **sub 1**. Unlike addition and subtraction, **inc** and **dec** don't affect the carry flag (CF). This can often be a nuisance, but there is a good use for this quirk of **inc** and **dec** in adding or subtracting multi-word memory values.

Multi-word memory values are values longer than 16 bits that are stored in memory. On the 8088 such values can be added together only by a series of 16- and/or 8-bit additions. The first addition—of the least significant words—must be performed with **add**, or with **adc** with CF set to 0. Subsequent additions of successively more-significant words must be performed with **adc**, so that the carry out can be passed from one addition to the next via CF. The same is true of **sub**, **sbb**, and borrow for subtraction of multi-word memory variables.

Some way is needed to address each of the words in a multi-word memory value in turn, so that each part of the value may be used as an operand. Consequently, multi-word memory values are often pointed to by registers (BP or BX and/or SI or DI), which can be advanced to point to successively more-significant portions of the values as addition or subtraction proceeds. If, however, there were no way to advance a memory-addressing register without modifying CF, then **adc** and **sbb** would work properly only if we preserved CF around the **inc** instructions, with **pushf** and **popf** or **lahf** and **sahf**.

The instructions **inc** and **dec** don't affect CF, however, and that greatly simplifies the process of adding multi-word memory variables. The code in Listing 9-13, which adds together two 64-bit memory variables (one pointed to by SI and the other pointed to by DI) works only because the **inc** instructions that advance the pointers don't affect the CF values that join the additions of the various parts of the variables. (It's equally important that **loop** doesn't affect any flags, as we'll see in Chapter 14.)

```
1    ;
2    ; *** Listing 9-13 ***
3    ;
4    ; Adds together two 64-bit memory variables, taking
5    ; advantage of the fact that neither INC nor LOOP affects
6    ; the Carry flag.
7    ;
8    ; Note: This is a sample code fragment, and is not intended
9    ; to either be run under the Zen timer or assembled as a
10   ; standalone program.
11   ;
12           jmp     Skip
13   ;
14   MemVar1       db      2, 0, 0, 0, 0, 0, 0, 0
15   MEM_VAR_LEN   equ     ($-MemVar1)
16   MemVar2       db      0feh, 0ffh, 0ffh, 0ffh, 0, 0, 0, 0
17   ;
18   Skip:
19           mov     si,offset MemVar1 ;set up memory variable
20           mov     di,offset MemVar2 ; pointers
21           mov     ax,[si]           ;add the first words
22           add     [di],ax           ; together
23           mov     cx,(MEM_VAR_LEN/2)-1
24                                     ;we'll add together the
25                                     ; remaining 3 words in
26                                     ; each variable
27   AdditionLoop:
28           inc     si
29           inc     si                ;point to next word
30           inc     di                ; (doesn't affect Carry
31           inc     di                ; flag)
32           mov     ax,[si]           ;add the next words
33           adc     [di],ax           ; together-C flag still set
34                                     ; from last addition
35           loop    AdditionLoop      ;add the next word of each
36                                     ; variable together
```

9.3 ◆ Carrying Results along in a Flag

As mentioned in Chapter 6 and illustrated in the last section, many instructions don't affect all the flags, and some don't affect any flags at all. You can take advantage of this by carrying a status along in the flags register for several instructions before testing that status. Of course, if you do choose to carry a status along, all the instructions executed between setting the status and testing it must leave the status alone.

For example, the following code tests AL for a specific value, then sets AL to 0 before branching according to the results of the test:

```
cmp   al,RESET_FLAG   ;sets ZF to reflect test result
mov   al,0            ;set AL for the code following the
                      ; branch
                      ;*** NOTE: THIS INSTRUCTION MUST ***
                      ;*** NOT ALTER ZF!               ***
jz    IsReset         ;branch according to the ZF set
                      ; by CMP
```

In this example, AL must be set to 0 no matter which way the branch goes. If we were to set AL after the branch rather than before, two **mov al,0** instructions (one for each code sequence that might follow **jz IsReset**) would be needed. If we set AL before the **cmp** instruction, the test couldn't even be performed because the value under test in AL would be lost. In very specific cases such as this, clear advantages result from carrying a status flag along for a few instructions.

One caution when using the above approach: *never set a register to 0 via* **sub reg,reg** *or* **xor reg,reg** *while carrying a status along*. With time, you'll get in the habit of setting registers to 0 with **sub *reg,reg*** or **xor *reg,reg***, either of which is faster (and often smaller) than **mov *reg*,0**. Unfortunately, **sub** and **xor** affect the flags, while **mov** doesn't. For example,

```
cmp   al,RESET_FLAG   ;sets ZF to reflect status under test
sub   al,al           ;alters ZF, causing the code to
                      ; malfunction
jz    IsReset         ;won't jump properly
```

fails to preserve ZF between **cmp** and **jz** and wouldn't work properly. In cases such as this, always be sure to use **mov**.

The bugs that can arise from the use of a carried-along status that is accidentally wiped out are often hard to reproduce and difficult to track down, so all possible precautions should be taken whenever this technique is used. No more than a few instructions—and *no* branches—should occur between the setting and the testing of the status. The use of a carried-along status should always be clearly commented, as in the first example in this section. Careful commenting is particularly important in order to forestall trouble should you (or worse, someone else) alter the code at a later date without noticing that a status is being carried along.

If you do need to carry a status along for more than a few instructions, store the status with either **pushf** or **lahf**, then restore it later with **popf** or **sahf**, so there's no chance of the intervening code accidentally wiping out the status.

9.4 ◆ Byte-to-Word and Word-to-Doubleword Conversion

On the 8088 the need frequently arises to convert byte values to word values. A byte value might be converted to a word in order to add it to a 16-bit value or in order to use it as a pointer into a table. (Remember that only 16-bit registers can be used as pointers, with the sole exception of AL in the case of **xlat**.) Occasionally it's also necessary to convert word values to doubleword values. One application for word-to-doubleword conversion is the preparation of a 16-bit dividend for 32-bit by 16-bit division.

Unsigned values are converted to a larger data type by simply zeroing the upper portion of the desired data type. For example, an unsigned byte value in DL is converted to an unsigned word value in DX with

```
sub   dh,dh
```

Likewise, an unsigned byte value in AL can be converted to a doubleword value in DX:AX with

```
sub   dx,dx
mov   ah,dh
```

In principle, conversion of a signed value to a larger data type is more complex, because it requires replication of the high (or sign) bit of the original value throughout the upper portion of the desired data type. Fortunately, the 8088 provides two instructions that handle the complications of signed conversion for us: **cbw** and **cwd**. The instruction **cbw** sets all the bits of AH to the value of bit 7 of AL, performing signed byte-to-word conversion, whereas **cwd** sets all the bits of DX to the value of bit 15 of AX, performing signed word-to-doubleword conversion.

There's nothing tricky about **cbw** and **cwd**, and you're doubtless familiar with them already. What's particularly interesting about these instructions is that they're each only 1 byte long—1 byte *shorter* than **sub reg,reg**. What's more, the official execution time of **cbw** is only 2 cycles, so it's 1 cycle faster than **sub** as well. The official execution time of **cwd** is 5 cycles, but as it's shorter than **sub**, actually it often executes more rapidly than **sub**, thanks to the prefetch queue cycle eater.

What all this means is that **cbw** and **cwd** are the preferred means of converting values to larger data types and should be used whenever possible. In particular, you should use **cbw** to convert unsigned bytes in the range 0 to 7Fh to unsigned words. Though it may seem strange to use a signed type-conversion instruction to convert unsigned values, there's no distinction between unsigned bytes in the range 0 to 7Fh and signed bytes in the range 0 to +127, as they have the same values and have bit 7 set to 0.

Listing 9-14 illustrates the use of **cbw** to convert an array of unsigned byte values between 0 and 7Fh to an array of word values. Note that values are read from memory and written back to memory and that the loop counter is decremented, so this is a realistic use of **cbw** rather than an artificial situation designed to show the instruction in the best possible light. Despite all the other activity occurring in the loop, Listing 9-14 executes in 10.06 μsec per loop, 12 percent faster than Listing 9-15, which executes in 11.31 μsec per loop while using **sub ah,ah** to perform unsigned byte-to-word conversion.

```
 1   ;
 2   ; *** Listing 9-14 ***
 3   ;
 4   ; An illustration of the use of CBW to convert an
 5   ; array of unsigned byte values between 0 and 7Fh to an
 6   ; array of unsigned words. Note that this would not work
 7   ; if Array1 contained values greater than 7Fh.
 8   ;
 9           jmp     Skip
10   ;
11   ARRAY_LENGTH    equ     1000
12   ;
13   Array1  label   byte
14   ARRAY_VALUE=0
15           rept    ARRAY_LENGTH
16           db      ARRAY_VALUE
17   ARRAY_VALUE=(ARRAY_VALUE+1) and 07fh
18                                   ;cycle source array byte
19                                   ; values from 0-7Fh
20           endm
21   ;
22   Array2  dw      ARRAY_LENGTH dup (?)
23   ;
24   Skip:
25           mov     si,offset Array1 ;set up array pointers
```

```
26              mov     di,offset Array2
27              mov     ax,ds
28              mov     es,ax           ;copy to & from same segment
29              cld                     ;make string instructions
30                                      ; increment pointers
31              mov     cx,ARRAY_LENGTH
32              call    ZTimerOn
33      ProcessingLoop:
34              lodsb                   ;get the next element
35              cbw                     ;make it a word
36              stosw                   ;save the word value
37              loop    ProcessingLoop  ;do the next element
38              call    ZTimerOff
```

```
1       ;
2       ; *** Listing 9-15 ***
3       ;
4       ; An illustration of the use of SUB AH,AH to convert an
5       ; array of unsigned byte values between 0 and 7Fh to an
6       ; array of words. Note that this would work even if Array1
7       ; contained values greater than 7Fh.
8       ;
9               jmp     Skip
10      ;
11      ARRAY_LENGTH    equ     1000
12      ;
13      Array1 label    byte
14      ARRAY_VALUE=0
15              rept    ARRAY_LENGTH
16              db      ARRAY_VALUE
17      ARRAY_VALUE=(ARRAY_VALUE+1) and 07fh
18                                      ;cycle source array byte
19                                      ; values from 0-7Fh
20              endm
21      ;
22      Array2 dw       ARRAY_LENGTH dup (?)
23      ;
24      Skip:
25              mov     si,offset Array1 ;set up array pointers
26              mov     di,offset Array2
27              mov     ax,ds
28              mov     es,ax           ;copy to & from same segment
29              cld                     ;make string instructions
30                                      ; increment pointers
31              mov     cx,ARRAY_LENGTH
32              call    ZTimerOn
33      ProcessingLoop:
34              lodsb                   ;get the next element
35              sub     ah,ah           ;make it a word
36              stosw                   ;save the word value
37              loop    ProcessingLoop  ;do the next element
38              call    ZTimerOff
```

The instruction **cwd** can be used in a similar manner to speed up the conversion of unsigned word values in the range 0 to 7FFFh to doubleword values. Another clever use of **cwd** is as a more efficient way than **sub reg,reg** to set DX to 0 when you're certain that bit 15 of AX is 0 or as a better way than **mov *reg*,0FFFFh** to set DX to 0FFFFh when you're sure that bit 15 of AX is 1. Similarly, **cbw** can be used as a faster way to set AH to 0 whenever bit 7 of AL is 0 or to 0FFh when bit 7 of AL is 1.

Viewed objectively, there's no difference between using **cbw** to convert AL to a signed word, to set AH to 0 when bit 7 of AL is 0, and to set AH to 0FFh when bit 7 of AL is 1. In all three cases each bit of AH is set to the value of bit 7 of AL. Viewed *conceptually,* however, it can be useful to think of **cbw** as being capable of performing three distinct functions: converting a signed value in AL to a signed value in AX, setting AH to 0 when bit 7 of AL is 0, and setting AH to 0FFh when bit 7 of AL is 1. After all, an important aspect of the Zen of assembly language is the ability to view your resources (such as the instruction set) from the perspective best suited to your current needs. Rather than getting locked in to the limited functionality of the instruction set as it was intended to be used, you must tap into the functionality of the instruction set as it is *capable* of being used.

Listing 9-14 is an excellent example of how focusing too closely on a particular sort of optimization or getting too locked in to a particular meaning for an instruction can obscure a better approach. In Listing 9-14, aware that the values in the array are less than 80h, we cleverly use **cbw** to set AH to 0. This means that AH is set to 0 every time through the loop, even though AH never changes from one pass through the loop to the next! This makes sense only if you view each byte-to-word conversion in isolation. Listing 9-16 shows a more sensible approach, in which AH is set to 0 just once, outside the loop. In Listing 9-16, each byte value is automatically converted to a word value in AX simply by being loaded into AL.

```
1    ;
2    ; *** Listing 9-16 ***
3    ;
4    ; An illustration of the use of SUB AH,AH outside the
5    ; processing loop to convert an array of byte values
6    ; between 0 and 7Fh to an array of words. AH never changes
7    ; from one pass through the loop to the next, so there's no
8    ; need to continually set AH to 0.
9    ;
10            jmp      Skip
11   ;
12   ARRAY_LENGTH     equ      1000
13   ;
14   Array1  label    byte
15   ARRAY_VALUE=0
16           rept     ARRAY_LENGTH
17           db       ARRAY_VALUE
18   ARRAY_VALUE=(ARRAY_VALUE+1) and 07fh
19                                    ;cycle source array byte
20                                    ; values from 0-7Fh
21           endm
```

```
22    ;
23    Array2    dw        ARRAY_LENGTH dup (?)
24    ;
25    Skip:
26              mov       si,offset Array1 ;set up array pointers
27              mov       di,offset Array2
28              mov       ax,ds
29              mov       es,ax            ;copy to & from same segment
30              cld                        ;make string instructions
31                                         ; increment pointers
32              mov       cx,ARRAY_LENGTH
33              sub       ah,ah            ;set up to make each byte
34                                         ; read into AL a word in AX
35                                         ; automatically
36              call      ZTimerOn
37    ProcessingLoop:
38              lodsb                      ;get the next element
39              stosw                      ;save the word value
40              loop      ProcessingLoop   ;do the next element
41              call      ZTimerOff
```

In the particular case of Listing 9-16, it happens that moving the setting of AH to 0 outside the loop doesn't improve performance; Listing 9-16 runs at exactly the same speed as Listing 9-14, no doubt thanks to the prefetch queue and DRAM refresh cycle eaters. That's just a fluke, though; on average, an optimization such as the one in Listing 9-16 saves about 4 cycles. Don't let the quirks of the 8088 deter you from the pursuit of saving bytes and cycles—but do remember to always time your code to make sure you've improved it!

If for any reason AH *did* change each time through the loop, we could no longer use the method of Listing 9-16, and Listing 9-14 would be a good alternative. That's why there are no hard and fast rules that produce the best assembler code. Instead, you must respond flexibly to the virtually infinite variety of assembler coding situations that arise. The bigger your bag of tricks, the better off you'll be.

9.5 ◆ xchg Is Handy When Registers Are Tight

One key to good assembler code is avoiding memory and using the registers as much as possible. When you start juggling registers in order to get the maximum mileage from them, you'll find that **xchg** is a good friend.

Why? Because the 8088's general-purpose registers are actually fairly special purpose. BX is used to point to memory, CX is used to count, SI is used with **lods**, and so on. As a result, you may want to use a specific register for two different purposes in a tight loop. The **xchg** instruction makes that possible.

Consider the case in which you need to handle both a loop count and a shift count. Ideally, you would want to use CX to store the loop count and CL to store the shift count. Listing 9-17 uses CX for both purposes by pushing and popping the loop count around the use of the shift count. However, this solution is less than ideal because **push** and **pop** are relatively slow instructions. Instead, we can use **xchg** to swap the lower byte of the loop count with the shift count, giving each a turn in CL, as shown in Listing 9-18. Listing 9-18 runs in 15.08 μsec per byte processed, versus the 20.11 μsec time of Listing 9-17. *That's a 33 percent improvement from a seemingly minor change!* The secret is that **push** and **pop** together take 27 cycles, while a register-register **xchg** takes no more than four cycles to execute once fetched and only eight cycles even when the prefetch queue is empty.

```
1    ;
2    ; *** Listing 9-17 ***
3    ;
4    ; Supports the use of CX to store a loop count and CL
5    ; to store a shift count by pushing and popping the loop
6    ; count around the use of the shift count.
7    ;
8            jmp     Skip
9    ;
10   ARRAY_LENGTH    equ     1000
11   Array1  db      ARRAY_LENGTH dup (3)
12   Array2  db      ARRAY_LENGTH dup (2)
13   ;
14   Skip:
15           mov     si,offset Array1 ;point to the source array
16           mov     di,offset Array2 ;point to the dest array
17           mov     ax,ds
18           mov     es,ax           ;copy to & from same segment
19           mov     cx,ARRAY_LENGTH ;the loop count
20           mov     dl,2            ;the shift count
21           call    ZTimerOn
22   ProcessingLoop:
23           lodsb                   ;get the next byte
24           push    cx              ;save the loop count
25           mov     cl,dl           ;get the shift count into CL
26           shl     al,cl           ;shift the byte
27           pop     cx              ;get back the loop count
28           stosb                   ;save the modified byte
29           loop    ProcessingLoop
30           call    ZTimerOff


1    ;
2    ; *** Listing 9-18 ***
3    ;
4    ; Supports the use of CX to store a loop count and CL
```

```
 5     ; to store a shift count by using XCHG to swap the
 6     ; contents of CL as needed.
 7     ;
 8             jmp       Skip
 9     ;
10     ARRAY_LENGTH    equ       1000
11     Array1  db        ARRAY_LENGTH dup (3)
12     Array2  db        ARRAY_LENGTH dup (2)
13     ;
14     Skip:
15             mov       si,offset Array1 ;point to the source array
16             mov       di,offset Array2 ;point to the dest array
17             mov       ax,ds
18             mov       es,ax            ;copy to & from same segment
19             mov       cx,ARRAY_LENGTH  ;the loop count
20             mov       dl,2             ;the shift count
21             call      ZTimerOn
22     ProcessingLoop:
23             lodsb                      ;get the next byte
24             xchg      cl,dl            ;get the shift count into CL
25                                        ; and save the low byte of
26                                        ; the loop count in DL
27             shl       al,cl            ;shift the byte
28             xchg      cl,dl            ;put the shift count back
29                                        ; into DL and restore the
30                                        ; low byte of the loop count
31                                        ; to CL
32             stosb                      ;save the modified byte
33             loop      ProcessingLoop
34             call      ZTimerOff
```

Neither Listing 9-17 nor Listing 9-18 is the most practical solution to this particular problem. A better solution would be to simply store the loop count in a register other than CX and to use **dec/jnz** rather than **loop**. The object of this exercise wasn't to produce ideal code but to illustrate that **xchg** gives you both speed and flexibility when you need to use a single register for more than one purpose.

The instruction **xchg** is also useful when you need more memory pointers in a loop than there are registers that can point to memory. (See Chapter 8 for an example of the use of **xchg** to allow BX to point to two arrays.) As the example in Chapter 8 also points out, the form of **xchg** used to swap AX with another general-purpose register is 1 byte shorter than the standard form of **xchg**.

Finally, **xchg** is useful for getting and setting a memory variable at the same time. For example, suppose that we're maintaining a flag that's used by an interrupt handler. One way to get the current flag setting and force the flag to 0 is

```
cli              ;turn interrupts off
mov   al,[Flag]  ;get the current flag value
```

```
mov    [Flag],0   ;set the flag to 0
sti               ;turn interrupts on
```

(It's necessary to disable interrupts to ensure that the interrupt handler doesn't access **Flag** between the instruction that reads the flag and the instruction that resets it.)

With **xchg**, however, we can do the same thing with just two instructions:

```
sub    al,al    ;set AL to 0
xchg   [Flag],al ;get the current flag value and
                 ; set the flag to 0
```

Best of all, we don't need to disable interrupts in the **xchg**-based code, since interrupts can occur only between instructions, not during them. (Interrupts *can* occur between repetitions of a repeated string instruction, but that's because a single string instruction is actually executed multiple times when it's repeated. We'll discuss repeated string instructions at length in Chapters 10 and 11.)

9.6 ◆ Destination: Register

Many arithmetic and logical operations can be performed with a register as one operand and a memory location as the other, with either one being the source and the other serving as the destination. For example, both of the following forms of **sub** are valid:

```
sub   [bx],al
sub   al,[bx]
```

The two instructions are not the same, of course. Memory is the destination in the first case, while AL is the destination in the second case. That's not the only distinction between the two instructions, however. There's also a major difference in the area of performance.

Consider this. A non-**mov** instruction, such as **sub**, with a register source operand and a memory destination operand must access memory twice: once to fetch the destination operand prior to performing an operation and once to store the result of the operation to the destination operand. By contrast, the same instruction with a memory source operand and a register destination operand must access memory just once, in order to fetch the source value from memory. Consequently, having a memory operand as the destination imposes an immediate penalty of at least 4 cycles per instruction, since each memory access takes a minimum of 4 cycles.

As it turns out, however, the extra time required to access destination memory operands with such instructions—which include **adc**, **add**, **and**, **or**, **sbb**, **sub**, and **xor**—is not 4, but 7 cycles, according to the official specs in Appendix A. We can measure the actual difference by timing the code in Listings 9-19 and 9-20. As it turns out, the code with AL as the destination takes just 5.03 μsec per instruction. That's 1.00 μsec (4.77 cycles) or nearly 20 percent faster than the code with memory as the destination operand, which takes 6.03 μsec per instruction.

```
1    ;
2    ; *** Listing 9-19 ***
3    ;
4    ; Times the performance of SUB with a register as the
5    ; destination operand and memory as the source operand.
6    ;
7            jmp     Skip
8    ;
9    Dest    db      0
10   ;
11   Skip:
12           call    ZTimerOn
13           rept    1000
14           sub     al,[Dest]       ;subtract [Dest] from AL
15                                   ; Only 1 memory access
16                                   ; is performed
17           endm
18           call    ZTimerOff
```

```
1    ;
2    ; *** Listing 9-20 ***
3    ;
4    ; Times the performance of SUB with memory as the
5    ; destination operand and a register as the source operand.
6    ;
7            jmp     Skip
8    ;
9    Dest    db      0
10   ;
11   Skip:
12           call    ZTimerOn
13           rept    1000
14           sub     [Dest],al       ;subtract AL from [Dest]
15                                   ; Two memory accesses are
16                                   ; performed
17           endm
18           call    ZTimerOff
```

The moral of the story? Keep those operands that tend to be destination operands most frequently—counters, pointers, and the like—in registers whenever possible. The ideal situation is one in which both destination and source operands are in registers.

By the way, remember that an instruction with a word-sized memory operand requires an additional 4 cycles per memory access to access the second byte of the word. Consequently,

```
add   [si],dx    ;performs 2 word-sized accesses
                 ; (= 4 byte-sized accesses)
```

takes 8 cycles longer than

```
add   [si],dl    ;performs 2 byte-sized accesses
```

However

```
add   dx,[si]    ;performs 1 word-sized access
                 ; (= 2 byte-sized accesses)
```

takes only four cycles longer than

```
add   dl,[si]    ;performs 1 byte-sized access
```

A final note: at least one 8088 reference lists **cmp** as requiring the same 7 additional cycles as **sub** when used with a memory operand that is the destination rather than the source. Not so: **cmp** requires the same time no matter which operand is a memory operand. That makes sense, since **cmp** doesn't actually modify the destination operand and so has no reason to perform a second memory access. The same is true for **test**, which doesn't modify the destination operand.

9.7 ◆ neg and not

The instructions **neg** and **not** are short, fast, and sometimes undeservedly overlooked. Each is 2 bytes long and executes in just 3 cycles when used with a register operand, and each can often replace a longer instruction or several instructions.

The instruction **not** *mem/reg* is similar to **xor** *mem/reg*,**0ffffh** (or

xor *mem/reg*,**0ffh** for 8-bit operands) but is usually 1 byte shorter and 1 cycle faster. (If *mem/reg* is AL, **not** and **xor** are the same length, but **not** is still 1 cycle faster.) Another difference between the two instructions is that unlike **xor**, **not** doesn't affect any of the status flags. This can be useful for, say, toggling the state of a flag byte without disturbing the statuses that an earlier operation left in the flags register.

The instruction **neg** negates a signed value in a register or memory variable. You can think of **neg** as subtracting the operand from 0 and storing the result back in the operand. The flags are set to reflect this subtraction from 0, so **neg ax** sets the flags as if

```
mov   dx,ax
mov   ax,0
sub   ax,dx
```

had been performed.

One interesting consequence of the way in which **neg** sets the flags is that CF is set in every case except when the operand was originally 0. (That's because in every other case a value larger than 0 is being subtracted from 0, resulting in a borrow.) This is very handy for negating 32-bit operands quickly. In the following example, DX:AX contains a 32-bit operand to be negated:

```
neg   dx
neg   ax
sbb   dx,0
```

Although it's not obvious, the above code does indeed negate DX:AX, and does so very quickly indeed. (You might well think that there couldn't possibly be a faster way to negate a 32-bit value, but in Chapter 13 we'll see a decidedly unusual approach that's faster still. Beware of thinking you've found the fastest possible code for any task!)

How does the above negation code work? Well, normally we would want to perform a two's complement negation by flipping all bits of the operand and then adding 1 to it, as follows:

```
not   dx    ;flip all bits...
not   ax    ;...of the operand
add   ax,1  ;remember, INC doesn't set the carry flag!
adc   dx,0  ;then add 1 to finish the two's complement
```

However, this code is 10 bytes long, 3 bytes longer than our optimized negation code. In the optimized code, the first negation word flips all bits of DX and adds 1 to that result, and the second negation flips all bits of AX and adds 1 to that result. At this point, we've got a perfect two's complement result, except that 1 has been added to DX. That's incorrect, unless AX was originally 0.

Aha! Thanks to the way **neg** sets the flags, CF is always set *except when the operand was originally 0*. Consequently, we need only subtract from DX the carry-out from **neg ax** and we've got a 32-bit two's-complement negation—in just 7 bytes!

By the way, 32-bit negation can also be performed with the three instruction, 7-cycle sequence

```
not   dx
neg   ax
sbb   dx,-1
```

If you can understand why this sequence works, you've got a good handle on **neg**, **not**, and two's complement arithmetic. (Hint: the underlying principle in the last sequence is exactly the same as with the **neg/neg/sbb** approach we just discussed.) If not, wait until Chapter 13, in which we'll explore the workings of 32-bit negation in considerable detail.

The instruction **neg** is also handy for generating differences without using **sub** and without using other registers. For example, suppose that we're scanning a list for a match with AL. The instruction **repnz scasb**, which we'll discuss further in Chapter 10, is ideal for such an application. However, after **repnz scasb** has found a match, CX contains the number of entries in the list that weren't scanned, not the number that *were* scanned, and it's the latter number that we want in CX. Fortunately, we can use **neg** to convert the entries-remaining count in CX into an entries-scanned count, as follows:

```
; The value to search for is already in AL, and ES:DI
; already points to the list to scan.
      mov   cx,[NumberOfEntries] ;# of entries to scan
      cld                        ;make SCASB count up
      repnz scasb                ;look for the value
      jnz   ValueNotFound        ;the value is not in the list
      neg   cx                   ;the # of entries not scanned
                                 ; times −1
```

```
add    cx,[NumberOfEntries] ;total # of entries − # of
                            ; entries not scanned = # of
                            ; entries scanned
```

Thanks to **neg**, this replaces the longer code sequence

```
; The value to search for is already in AL, and ES:DI
; already points to the list to scan.
    mov    cx,[NumberOfEntries] ;# of entries to scan
    cld                         ;make SCASB count up
    repnz  scasb                ;look for the value
    jnz    ValueNotFound        ;the value is not in the list
    mov    ax,[NumberOfEntries] ;total # of entries
    sub    ax,cx                ;total # of entries − # of
                                ; entries not scanned = # of
                                ; entries scanned
    mov    cx,ax                ;put the result back in CX
```

Another advantage of **neg** in the above example is that it lets us generate the entries-remaining count without using another register. By contrast, the alternative approach requires the use of a 16-bit register for temporary storage. When registers are in short supply, as is usually the case, the register-conserving nature of **neg** can be most useful.

9.8 ◆ Rotates and Shifts

Next, we're going to spend some time going over interesting aspects of the various shift and rotate instructions. To my mind, the single most fascinating thing about these instructions is their ability to shift or rotate by either 1 bit or the number of bits specified by CL; in particular, it's most informative to examine the relative performance of the two approaches for multi-bit operations.

It's much more desirable than you might think to perform multi-bit shifts and rotates by repeating the shift or rotate CL times than to use multiple 1-bit shift or rotate instructions. As is so often the case, the cycle counts in Appendix A are misleading in this regard. As it turns out, shifting or rotating multiple bits by repeating an instruction CL times, as in

```
mov  cl,4
shr  ax,cl
```

is almost always faster than shifting by 1 bit repeatedly, as in

```
shr   ax,1
shr   ax,1
shr   ax,1
shr   ax,1
```

This is true even though the official specs in Appendix A indicate that the latter approach is more than twice as fast.

Shifting or rotating by CL also requires fewer instruction bytes for shifts of more than 2 bits. In fact, that reduced instruction byte count is precisely the reason the shift/rotate by CL approach is faster. As we saw in Chapter 4, fetching the instruction bytes of **shr ax,1** takes up to 4 cycles per byte; each shift or rotate instruction is 2 bytes long, so **shr ax,1** can take as long as 8 cycles per bit shifted. By contrast, only 4 instruction bytes in total need to be fetched in order to load CL and execute **shr ax,cl**. Once those bytes are fetched, **shr ax,cl** runs at its EU speed of 4 cycles per bit shifted, since no additional instruction fetching is needed. Better yet, the *next* instruction's bytes can be prefetched while a shift or rotate by CL executes.

The point is not that shifts and rotates by CL are faster than you'd expect but rather that 1-bit shifts and rotates are *slower* than you'd expect, courtesy of the prefetch queue cycle eater. The question is, of course, at what point does it become faster to shift or rotate by CL instead of using multiple 1-bit shift or rotate instructions?

To answer that, I've timed the two approaches, shown in Listings 9-21 and 9-22, for shifts ranging from 1 to 7 bits, by altering the equated value of BITS_TO_SHIFT accordingly. The results are shown in Table 9.1.

```
1    ;
2    ; *** Listing 9-21 ***
3    ;
4    ; Times shifts performed by shifting CL times.
5    ;
6    BITS_TO_SHIFT    equ     1
7             call    ZTimerOn
8             rept    100
9             mov     cl,BITS_TO_SHIFT
10            shl     ax,cl
11            endm
12            call    ZTimerOff
```

```
1    ;
2    ; *** Listing 9-22 ***
3    ;
```

```
4      ; Times shifts performed by using multiple 1-bit shift
5      ; instructions.
6      ;
7      BITS_TO_SHIFT    equ    1
8               call    ZTimerOn
9               rept    100
10              rept    BITS_TO_SHIFT
11              shl     ax,1
12              endm
13              endm
14              call    ZTimerOff
15
```

Astonishingly, it hardly *ever* pays to shift or rotate by multiple bit places with separate 1-bit instructions. The prefetch queue cycle eater exacts such a price on 1-bit shifts and rotates that it pays to shift or rotate by CL for shifts of 3 or more bits. Actually, the choice is not entirely clear cut for 3- to 5-bit shifts or rotates, since the 1-bit-at-a-time approach can become relatively faster if the prefetch queue is full when the shift or rotate sequence begins. Still, there's no question that shifting or rotating by CL is as good as or superior to using multiple 1-bit shifts for most multi-bit shifts.

By the way, you should be aware that the contents of CL are not changed when CL is used to supply the count for a shift or rotate instruction. This allows you to load CL once and then use it to control multiple shift and/or rotate instructions.

Shifting and Rotating Memory

One feature of the 8088 that for some reason is often overlooked is the ability to shift or rotate a memory variable. True, the 8088 doesn't shift or rotate memory variables very *rapidly,* but the capability is there should you

TABLE 9.1   Comparison of bit-shifting approaches

Bits shifted (BITS_TO_SHIFT)	Time taken to shift by CL (Listing 9-21)	Time taken to shift 1 bit at a time (Listing 9-22)
1	3.6 μsec	1.8 μsec
2	4.2 μsec	3.6 μsec
3	5.0 μsec	5.4 μsec
4	5.9 μsec	7.2 μsec
5	6.7 μsec	9.1 μsec
6	7.5 μsec	10.9 μsec
7	8.4 μsec	12.7 μsec

need it. If you do find the need to perform a multi-bit shift or rotate on a memory variable, for goodness sakes use a CL shift! Every 1-bit memory shift or rotate takes a *minimum* of 20 cycles. By contrast, a shift-by-CL memory shift or rotate takes a minimum of 25 cycles, but only 4 additional cycles per bit shifted. It doesn't take a genius to see that for, say, a 4-bit rotate, the 41 cycles taken by the CL shift would beat the stuffing out of the 80 cycles taken by the four 1-bit shifts.

Rotates. You should be well aware that there are two sorts of rotates. One category, made up of **rol** and **ror**, consists of rotates that simply rotate the bits in the operand, as shown in Figure 9.2. These instructions are useful for adjusting masks, swapping nybbles, and the like. For example,

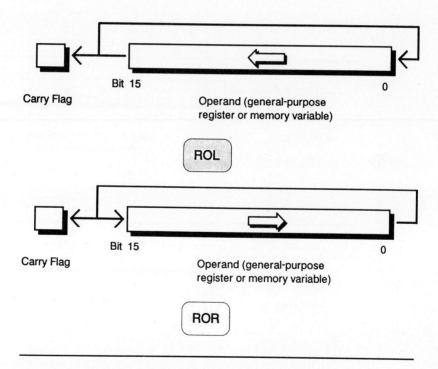

FIGURE 9.2 The instructions **rol** and **ror** shift the bits in the operand to the left and right, respectively, wrapping the bit shifted out around to the other end of the operand. The bit shifted out is copied to CF as well. This figure illustrates a 16-bit operation; 8-bit operands can be rotated as well.

```
mov   cl,4
ror   al,cl
```

swaps the high and low nybbles of AL. Note that these instructions don't rotate through CF. However, they *do* copy the bit wrapped around to the other end of the operand to CF as well.

The other rotate category, made up of **rcl** and **rcr**, consists of rotates that rotate the operand *through* CF, as shown in Figure 9.3. These instructions are useful for multi-word shifts and rotates. For example,

```
shr   dx,1
rcr   cx,1
rcr   bx,1
rcr   ax,1
```

shifts the 64-bit value in DX:CX:BX:AX right one bit.

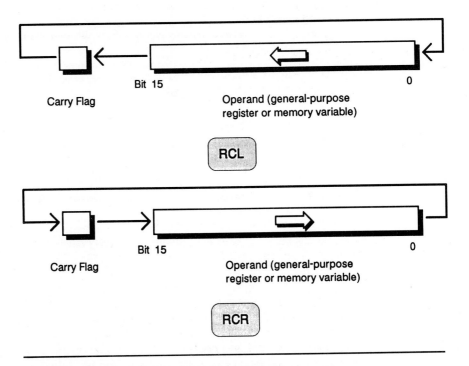

FIGURE 9.3   The instructions **rcl** and **rcr** shift the bits in the operand to the left and right, copying the bit shifted out to CF and shifting CF into the operand. This figure illustrates a 16-bit operation; 8-bit operands can be rotated as well.

The rotate instructions affect fewer flags than you might think, befitting their role as bit-manipulation rather than arithmetic instructions. None of the rotate instructions affect the sign, zero, auxiliary carry, or parity flags. On 1-bit left rotates the overflow flag (OF) is set to the exclusive-or of the value of the resulting CF and the most-significant bit of the result. On 1-bit right rotates OF is set to the exclusive-or of the two most significant bits of the result. (These OF settings indicate whether the rotate has changed the sign of the operand.) On rotates by CL the setting of OF is undefined.

Shifts. Similarly, there are two sorts of shift instructions. One category, made up of **shl** (also known as **sal**) and **shr**, consists of shifts that shift out to CF, shifting a 0 into the vacated bit of the operand, as shown in Figure 9.4. These instructions are used for moving masks and bits about and for performing fast unsigned division and multiplication by powers of 2. For example,

    shl   ax,1

multiplies AX, viewed as an unsigned value, by 2.

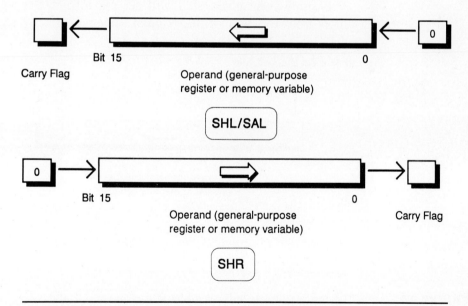

FIGURE 9.4   The **shl** (also known as **sal**) and **shr** instructions shift the bits in the operand to the left and right, respectively, copying the bit shifted out to CF and shifting a 0 bit into the operand. This figure illustrates a 16-bit operation; 8-bit operands can be shifted as well.

The other shift category contains only **sar**. This instruction performs the same shift right as does **shr**, except that the most significant bit of the operand is preserved rather than zeroed after the shift, as shown in Figure 9.5. This preserves the sign of the operand, useful for performing fast signed division by powers of 2. For example,

```
sar   ax,1
```

divides AX, viewed as a signed value, by 2.

The shift instructions affect the arithmetic = oriented flags that the rotate instructions leave alone, which makes sense since the shift instructions can perform certain types of multiplication and division. Unlike the rotate instructions, the shift instructions modify the sign, zero, and parity flags in the expected ways. The setting of the auxiliary carry flag is undefined. The setting of OF by the shift instructions is identical to the overflow settings of the rotate instructions. On 1-bit left shifts OF is set to the exclusive-or of the resulting CF and the most significant bit of the result. On 1-bit right shifts OF is set to the exclusive-or of the 2 most-significant bits of the result.

Basically, any given shift will set OF to 1 if the sign of the result differs from the sign of the original operand, thereby signalling that the

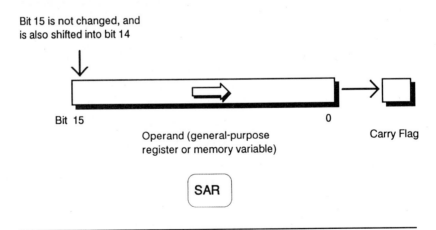

Bit 15 is not changed, and
is also shifted into bit 14

Bit 15   0

Operand (general-purpose   Carry Flag
register or memory variable)

SAR

FIGURE 9.5   The instruction **sar** shifts the bits in the operand to the right, copying the bit shifted out to CF. Nothing is shifted into the operand; the most-significant bit is left un-changed, and its value is shifted into the next most signif-icant bit as well. This figure illustrates a 16-bit operation; 8-bit operands can be shifted as well.

shift has not produced a valid signed multiplication or division result. The instruction **sar** always sets OF to 0, since **sar** can never change the sign of an operand. The instruction **shr** always sets OF to the high order bit of the original value, since the sign of the result is always positive. On shifts by CL the setting of OF is undefined.

Signed division with sar.
One tip if you do use **sar** to divide signed values: for negative dividends, **sar** rounds to the integer result of the next *largest* absolute value. This can be confusing, since for positive values **sar** rounds to the integer result of the next *smallest* absolute value, just as **shr** does. That is,

```
mov   ax,1
sar   ax,1
```

returns $1/2=0$, whereas

```
mov   ax,-1
sar   ax,1
```

doesn't return $-1/2=0$, but rather $-1/2=-1$. Similarly, **sar** insists that $-5/4=-2$, not -1. This is actually a tendency to round to the next integer value less than the actual result in all cases, which is exactly what **shr** also does. Although that may be consistent, it's nonetheless generally a nuisance, because we tend to expect that, say, $-1/2*-1$ should equal $1/2*1$, but with **sar** we actually get 1 for the former and 0 for the latter.

The solution? For a signed division by n of a negative number with **sar**, simply add $n-1$ to the dividend before shifting. This compensates exactly for the rounding **sar** performs. For example,

```
        mov   ax,−1      ;sample dividend
        and   ax,ax      ;is the dividend negative?
        jns   DoDiv      ;it's positive, so we're ready to divide
        add   ax,2−1     ;it's negative, so we need to compensate.
                         ; This is division by 2, so we'll
                         ; add n−1 = 2−1
DoDiv:
        sar   ax,1       ;signed divide by 2
```

returns 0, just what we'd expect from $-1/2$.

That's a quick look at what the shift and rotate instructions were designed to do. Now let's bring a little Zen of assembly language to bear in cooking up a use for **sar** that you can be fairly sure was never planned by the architects of the 8088.

Bit-doubling made easy.

Think back to the bit-doubling example of Chapter 7, where we found that a bit-doubling routine based on register-register instructions didn't run nearly as fast as it should have, thanks to the prefetch queue. We boosted the performance of the routine by performing a table look-up, and that's the best solution that I know of. There is, however, yet *another* bit-doubling technique, conceived by my friend Dan Illowsky, that's faster than the original shift-based approach. Interestingly enough, this new technique uses **sar**.

Let's consider **sar** as a bit-manipulation instruction rather than as a signed arithmetic instruction. What does **sar** really do? Well, it shifts all the bits of the operand 1 bit to the right, and it shifts bit 0 of the operand into CF. The most significant bit of the operand is left unchanged—*and it is also shifted 1 bit to the right.*

In other words, the most significant bit is doubled!

Once we've made the conceptual leap from **sar** as arithmetic instruction to **sar** as "bit twiddler," we've got an excellent tool for bit doubling. The code in Listing 7-14 placed the byte containing the bits to be doubled in two registers (BL and BH) and then doubled the bits with four instructions:

```
shr   bl,1
rcr   ax,1
shr   bh,1
rcr   ax,1
```

By contrast, the **sar** approach, illustrated in Listing 9-23, requires only one source register and doubles the bits with just three instructions:

```
shr   bl,1
rcr   ax,1
sar   ax,1
```

The **sar** approach requires only 75 percent as many code bytes as the approach in Listing 7-14. As instruction fetching dominates the execution time of Listing 7-14, the shorter **sar**-based code should be considerably faster, and indeed it is. Listing 9-23 doubles bits in 47.07 μsec per byte doubled, more than 34 percent faster than the 63.36 μsec of Listing 7-14.

```
1    ;
2    ; *** Listing 9-23 ***
3    ;
4    ; Performs bit-doubling of a byte in AL to a word in AX
5    ; by using SAR. This is not as fast as bit-doubling with
6    ; a look-up table, but it is faster than any other
7    ; shift-based approach.
8    ; (Conceived by Dan Illowsky.)
9    ;
10   DOUBLE_BYTE      macro
11           mov      bl,al
12           rept     8
13           shr      bl,1     ;get the next bit to double
14           rcr      ax,1     ;move it into the msb...
15           sar      ax,1     ;...and replicate it
16           endm
17           endm
18   ;
19           call     ZTimerOn
20   BYTE_TO_DOUBLE=0
21           rept     100
22           mov      al,BYTE_TO_DOUBLE
23           DOUBLE_BYTE
24   BYTE_TO_DOUBLE=(BYTE_TO_DOUBLE+1) and 0ffH
25           endm
26           call     ZTimerOff
```

(Note that the ratio of the execution times is almost exactly 3:4, which is the ratio of the code sizes of the two approaches. *Keep your code short!*)

Mind you, the **sar** approach of Listing 9-23 is still *much* slower than the look-up approach of Listing 7-15. What's more, the code in Listing 9-23 is both slower and larger than the **xlat**-based nybble look-up approach shown in Listing 7-18, so **sar** really isn't a preferred technique for doubling bits. The point of our discussion of bit doubling with **sar** is actually this: *all sorts of interesting possibilities open up once you start to view instructions in terms of what they do, rather than what they were designed to do.*

9.9 ◆ ASCII and Decimal Adjust

Now we come to the ASCII and decimal-adjust instructions: **daa**, **das**, **aaa**, **aas**, **aam**, and **aad**. To be honest, I'm covering these instructions only because many people have asked me what they are used for. In truth, they aren't useful very often, and there aren't any particularly nifty or nonobvious uses for them that I'm aware of, so I'm not going to cover them at great length, and you shouldn't spend too much time trying to understand them unless they fill a specific need of yours. Still, the ASCII and decimal-adjust instructions do have their purposes, so here goes.

daa, das, and Packed BCD Arithmetic

The instructions **daa** (decimal adjust AL after addition) and **das** (decimal adjust AL after subtraction) adjust AL to the correct value after addition of two packed binary coded decimal (BCD) operands. Packed BCD is a number-storage format wherein a digit between 0 and 9 is stored in each nybble, so the hex value 1000h interpreted in BCD is 1000 decimal, not 4096 decimal. (Unpacked BCD is similar to packed BCD, except that one digit, rather than two, is stored in each byte.)

Naturally, the addition of two BCD values with the **add** instruction doesn't produce the right result. The contents of AL after **add al,bl** is performed with 09h (9 decimal in BCD) in AL and 01h (1 decimal in BCD) in BL is 0Ah, which isn't even a BCD digit. What **daa** does is take the binary result of the addition of a packed BCD byte (two digits) in AL and adjust it to the correct sum. If, in the last example, **daa** had been performed after **add al,bl**, AL would have contained 10h, which is 10 in packed BCD, the correct answer.

The instruction **das** performs a similar adjustment after subtraction of packed BCD numbers. The mechanics of **daa** and **das** are a bit complex, and I won't go into them here, since I know of no use for the instructions save to adjust packed BCD results. Yes, I *do* remember that I told you to look at instructions for what they can do, not what they were designed to do. As far as I know, though, the two are one and the same for **daa** and **das**. I'll tell you what: look up the detailed operation of these instructions, find an unintended use for them, and let me know what it is. I'll be delighted to hear! One possible hint: these instructions are among the very few that pay attention to the auxiliary carry flag (AF).

I'm not going to spend any more time on **daa** and **das**, because they're just not used that often. BCD arithmetic is used primarily for working with on values to an exact number of decimal digits. (By contrast, normal binary arithmetic stores values to an exact number of *binary* digits, which can cause rounding problems with decimal calculations.) Consequently, BCD arithmetic is useful for accounting purposes but not much else. Moreover, BCD arithmetic is decidedly slow. If you're one of the few who need BCD arithmetic, the BCD-oriented instructions are there, and BCD arithmetic is discussed thoroughly in the literature—it's been around for decades, and some mainframes use it—so go to it. For the rest of you, don't worry that you're missing out on powerful and mysterious instructions—the BCD instructions are deservedly obscure.

aam, aad, and Unpacked BCD Arithmetic

The instructions **aam** and **aad** are BCD instructions of a slightly different flavor and a bit more utility. The **aam** (ASCII adjust AX after multiply) instruction adjusts the result in AL of the multiplication of two single-digit unpacked BCD values to a valid two-digit unpacked BCD value in AX. This is accomplished by dividing AL by 10 and storing the quotient in AH and the remainder in AL. (By contrast, **div** stores the quotient in AL and the remainder in AH.)

The instruction **aad** (ASCII adjust AL *before* division) converts a two-digit unpacked BCD value in AX into the binary equivalent in AX. This is performed by multiplying AH by 10, adding it to AL, and zeroing AH. The binary result of **aad** can then be divided by a single-digit BCD value to generate a single-digit BCD result.

By the way, "ASCII adjust" really means unpacked BCD for these instructions, since ASCII digits with the upper nybble zeroed are unpacked BCD digits. Shortly we'll discuss **aaa** and **aas**, which explicitly convert ASCII digits into unpacked BCD, but **aam** and **aad** require that you use **and** to zero the upper nybble of ASCII digits before performing multiplication and division.

The instruction **aam** can be used to implement multiplication of arbitrarily long unpacked BCD operands *one digit at a time*. That is, with **aam** you can multiply decimal numbers just the way we do it with a pencil and paper, multiplying one digit of each product together at a time and carrying the results along. Presumably, **aad** can be used similarly in the division of two BCD operands, although I've never found an example of the use of **aad**.

At any rate, the two instructions do have some small use apart from unpacked BCD arithmetic. They can save a bit of code space if you need to perform exactly the specified division by 10 of **aam** or multiplication by 10 and addition of **aad**, although you must be sure that the result can fit in a single byte. In particular, **aam** has an advantage over **div** in that a **div** by an 8-bit divisor requires a 16-bit dividend in AX, while **aam** uses only an 8-bit dividend in AL. The instruction **aam** has another advantage in that, unlike **div**, it doesn't require a register to store the divisor.

For example, Listing 9-24 shows code that converts a byte value to a three-digit ASCII string by way of **aam**. Listing 9-25, by contrast, converts

```
 1    ;
 2    ; *** Listing 9-24 ***
 3    ;
 4    ; Performs binary-to-ASCII conversion of a byte value
 5    ; by using AAM.
 6    ;
 7            jmp     Skip
 8    ;
 9    ResultString    db      3 dup (?)
10    ResultStringEnd label   byte
11            db      0       ;a zero to mark the string end
12    ;
13    Skip:
14    BYTE_VALUE=0
15            call    ZTimerOn
16            rept    100
17            std             ;make STOSB decrement DI
18            mov     ax,ds
19            mov     es,ax   ;for STOSB
20            mov     bl,'0'  ;used for converting to ASCII
21            mov     di,offset ResultStringEnd-1
22            mov     al,BYTE_VALUE
23            aam             ;put least significant decimal
24                            ; digit of BYTE_VALUE in AL,
25                            ; other digits in AH
26            add     al,bl   ;make it an ASCII digit
27            stosb           ;save least significant digit
28            mov     al,ah
29            aam             ;put middle decimal digit in AL
30            add     al,bl   ;make it an ASCII digit
31            stosb           ;save middle digit
32                            ;most significant decimal
33                            ; digit is in AH
34            add     ah,bl   ;make it an ASCII digit
35            mov     [di],ah ;save most significant digit
36    BYTE_VALUE=BYTE_VALUE+1
37            endm
38            call    ZTimerOff
```

a byte value to an ASCII string by using explicit division by 10 via **div**. Listing 9-24 is only 28 bytes long per byte converted, 2 bytes shorter than Listing 9-25. Listing 9-24 also executes in 54.97 μsec per conversion, 2.65 μsec faster than the 57.62 μsec of Listing 9-25. Normally, an improvement of 2.65 μsec would have us jumping up and down, but the lengthy execution times of both conversion routines mean that the speed advantage of Listing 9-24 is only about 5 percent. That's certainly an improvement—but painfully slow nonetheless.

The instructions **aam** and **aad** would be more interesting if they provided significantly faster ways than **div** and **mul** to divide and multiply by 10. Unfortunately, that's not the case, as the last results illustrate. The **aad** and **aam** instructions must use the 8088's general-purpose multiplication and division capabilities, for they are just about as slow as **mul** and **div**.

```
 1    ;
 2    ; *** Listing 9-25 ***
 3    ;
 4    ; Performs binary-to-ASCII conversion of a byte value
 5    ; by using DIV.
 6    ;
 7            jmp     Skip
 8    ;
 9    ResultString    db      3 dup (?)
10    ResultStringEnd label   byte
11            db      0       ;a zero to mark the string end
12    ;
13    Skip:
14    BYTE_VALUE=0
15            call    ZTimerOn
16            rept    100
17            mov     cx,(10 shl 8)+'0'
18                            ;CL='0', used for converting to ASCII
19                            ; CH=10, used for dividing by 10
20            mov     di,offset ResultString
21            mov     al,BYTE_VALUE
22            sub     ah,ah   ;prepare 16-bit dividend
23            div     ch      ;put least significant decimal
24                            ; digit of BYTE_VALUE in AH,
25                            ; other digits in AL
26            add     ah,cl   ;make it an ASCII digit
27            mov     [di+2],ah ;save least significant digit
28            sub     ah,ah   ;prepare 16-bit dividend
29            div     ch      ;put middle decimal digit in AL
30            add     ah,cl   ;make it an ASCII digit
31            mov     [di+1],ah ;save middle ASCII decimal digit
32                            ;most significant decimal
33                            ; digit is in AL
34            add     al,cl   ;make it an ASCII digit
35            mov     [di],al ;save most significant digit
36    BYTE_VALUE=BYTE_VALUE+1
37            endm
38            call    ZTimerOff
```

Of the two **aad** is the speedier at 60 cycles per execution; **aam** executes in 83 cycles.

Notes on mul and div

I'd like to take a moment to note some occasionally annoying characteristics of **mul** and **div**. The instruction **mul** (and **imul**, but I'll refer only to **mul** for brevity) has a tendency to surprise you by wiping out a register that you'd intuitively think it wouldn't, because the product is stored in twice as many bits as either factor. For example, **mul bl** stores the result in AX, not AL, and **mul cx** stores the result in DX:AX, not AX. Although this sounds simple enough, it's easy to forget in the heat of coding.

Similarly, it's easy to forget that **div** requires that the dividend be twice as large as the divisor and quotient. (The following discussion applies to **idiv** as well; again, I'll refer only to **div** for brevity.) In order to divide one 16-bit value by another, it's essential that the 16-bit dividend be extended to a 32-bit value, as in

```
mov    bx,[Divisor]
mov    ax,[Dividend]
sub    dx,dx           ;extend Dividend to an unsigned 32-bit value
div    bx
```

(The instruction **cwd** can be used for sign extension to a 32-bit value.) What's particularly tricky about 32-bit by 16-bit division is that it leaves the remainder in DX. That means that if you perform multiple 16-bit by 16-bit divisions in a loop, *you must zero DX every time through the loop*. For example, the following code to convert a binary number to five ASCII digits wouldn't work properly, because the dividend wouldn't be properly extended to 32 bits after the first division, which would leave the remainder in DL:

```
        mov    ax,[Count]     ;value to convert to ASCII
        sub    dx,dx          ;extend Count to an unsigned 32-bit value
        mov    bx,10          ;divide by 10 to convert to decimal
        mov    si,offset CountEnd-1 ;ASCII count goes here
        mov    cx,5           ;we want 5 ASCII digits
DivLoop:
        div    bx             ;divide by 10
        add    dl,'0'         ;convert this digit to ASCII
        mov    [si],dl        ;store the ASCII digit
        dec    si             ;point to the next most significant digit
        loop   DivLoop
```

On the other hand, the following code would work perfectly well, because it extends the dividend to 32 bits every time through the loop:

```
        mov    ax,[Count]     ;value to convert to ASCII
        mov    bx,10          ;divide by 10 to convert to decimal
        mov    si,offset CountEnd-1 ;ASCII count goes here
        mov    cx,5           ;we want 5 ASCII digits
DivLoop:
        sub    dx,dx          ;extend the dividend to an unsigned 32-bit value
```

```
div    bx            ;divide by 10
add    dl,'0'        ;convert this digit to ASCII
mov    [si],dl       ;store the ASCII digit
dec    si            ;point to the next most significant digit
loop   DivLoop
```

All this applies to 8-bit by 8-bit division as well, except that in that case it's the 8-bit dividend in AL that you must extend to a word in AX before each division.

There's another tricky point to **div**: **div** can crash a program by generating a divide-by-0 interrupt (interrupt 0) under certain circumstances. Obviously, this can happen if you divide by 0, but that's not the only way **div** can generate a divide-by-0 interrupt. If a division is attempted for which the quotient doesn't fit into the destination register (AX for 32-bit-by-16-bit divides, AL for 16-bit-by-8-bit divides), a divide-by-0 interrupt occurs. So, for example,

```
mov    ax,0ffffh
mov    dl,1
div    dl
```

results in a divide-by-0 interrupt.

Often, you know exactly what the dividend and divisor will be for a particular division, or at least in what range they'll be, and in those cases you don't have to worry about **div** causing a divide-by-0 interrupt. If you're not sure that the dividend and divisor are safe, however, you *must* guard against potential problems. One way to do this is by intercepting interrupt 0 and handling divide-by-0 interrupts. The alternative is to check the dividend and divisor before each division to make sure both that the divisor is nonzero and that the dividend isn't so much larger than the divisor that the result won't fit in 8 or 16 bits, whichever size the division happens to be.

This division-by-0 business is undeniably a nuisance to deal with—but it's absolutely necessary if you're going to perform division without knowing beforehand that the inputs can safely be used.

aaa, aas, and Decimal ASCII Arithmetic

Finally, we come to **aaa** and **aas**, which support addition and subtraction of decimal ASCII digits. Actually, **aaa** and **aas** support addition and subtraction of any two unpacked BCD digits, or indeed of any 2 bytes at all the lower nybbles of which contain digits in   ) to 9.

The instruction **aaa** (ASCII adjust after addition) adjusts AL to the correct decimal (unpacked BCD) result of the addition of two nybbles. Consider this: if you add two digits in the range 0 to 9, one of three things can happen. The result can be in the range 0 to 9, in which case no adjustment is needed and no decimal carry has occurred. Alternatively, the result can be in the range 0Ah to 0Fh, in which case the result can be corrected by adding 6 to the result, taking the result modulo 16 (decimal), and setting carry-out. Finally, the result can be in the range 10h to 12h, in which case the result can be corrected in exactly the same way as for results in the range 0Ah to 0Fh.

The 1-byte instruction **aaa** handles all three cases. **aaa** assumes that an **add** or **adc** instruction has just executed, with the auxiliary carry flag (AF) set appropriately. If AF is set (indicating a result in the range 10h to 12h) or if the lower nybble of AL is in the range 0Ah to 0Fh, then 6 is added to AL, AF and CF are set to 1, and AH is incremented. Finally, the upper nybble of AL is set to 0 in all cases.

What does all this mean? Obviously, it means that it's easy to add together unpacked BCD numbers. More important, though, is that **aaa** makes it fast (4 cycles per **aaa**) and easy to add together ASCII representations of decimal numbers. That's genuinely useful, because it takes a slew of cycles to convert a binary number to an ASCII representation; after all, a division by 10 is required for each digit to be converted. ASCII numbers are necessary for all sorts of data displays for which speed is important, ranging from game scores to instrumentation readouts. The instruction **aaa** makes possible the attractive alternative of keeping the numbers in displayable ASCII forms at all times, thereby avoiding the need for any sort of conversion at all.

Listing 9-26 shows the use of **aaa** in adding the value 1—stored as the ASCII decimal string "00001"—to an ASCII decimal count. Granted, it takes much longer to perform the ASCII decimal increment shown in Listing 9-26 than it does to execute an **inc** instruction, more than 100 times as long, in fact, at 93.00 μsec per ASCII decimal increment versus a maximum of 0.809 μsec per **inc**. However, Listing 9-26 maintains the count in instantly displayable ASCII form, and for frequently displayed but rarely changed numbers, a ready-to-display format can more than compensate for lengthier calculations.

```
1  ;
2  ; *** Listing 9-26 ***
3  ;
4  ; Performs addition of the ASCII decimal value "00001"
5  ; to an ASCII decimal count variable.
```

```
 6   ;
 7   DECIMAL_INCREMENT          macro
 8               local   DigitLoop
 9               std             ;we'll work from least-significant
10                               ; to most-significant
11               mov     si,offset ASCIIOne+VALUE_LENGTH-1
12               mov     di,offset Count+VALUE_LENGTH-1
13               mov     ax,ds
14               mov     es,ax   ;ES:DI points to Count for STOSB
15               mov     cx,VALUE_LENGTH
16               clc             ;there's no carry into the least-
17                               ; significant digit
18   DigitLoop:
19               lodsb           ;get the next increment digit
20               adc     al,[di] ;add it to the next Count digit
21               aaa             ;adjust to an unpacked BCD digit
22               lahf            ;save the carry, in case we just
23                               ; turned over 9
24               add     al,'0'  ;make it an ASCII digit
25               stosb
26               sahf            ;get back the carry for the next adc
27               loop    DigitLoop
28               endm
29   ;
30               jmp     Skip
31   ;
32   Count   db      '00000'
33   VALUE_LENGTH    equ     $-Count
34   ASCIIOne db     '00001'
35   ;
36   Skip:
37               call    ZTimerOn
38               rept    100
39               DECIMAL_INCREMENT
40               endm
41               call    ZTimerOff
```

If you do use **aaa**, remember that you have not two but three ways to use the carry-out that indicates that a decimal digit has counted from 9 back around to 0. CF is set on carry-out; that's what we use as the carry-out status in Listing 9-26. Similarly, AF is set on carry-out. In addition, though, AH is incremented by **aaa** whenever decimal carry-out occurs. It's certainly possible to get some extra mileage by putting the next-most-significant digit in AH before performing **aaa**, so that the carry-out is carried automatically. It's also conceivable that you could use **aaa** specifically to increment AH, depending on either the value in AL or the setting of AF, although I've never seen such an application. Since AF isn't testable by any conditional jump (or indeed by any instructions other than **daa**, **das**, **aaa**, and **aas**), **aaa** is perhaps the best hope for getting extra utility from that obscure flag.

The instruction **aas** (ASCII adjust after subtraction) is well and truly the mirror image of **aaa**; it is designed to be used after a **sub** or **sbb**, and operates by subtracting 6 from the result, decrementing AH, and setting CF and AF if the result in AL is not in the range 0 to 9, and zeroing the high nybble of AL in any case. You'll find that wherever **aaa** is useful, so too will be **aas**.

9.10 ◆ Mnemonics That Cover Multiple Instructions

As we've seen several times in this chapter and the previous one, 8088 assembler often uses a single mnemonic, such as **mov**, to name two or more instructions that perform the same operations but are quite different in size and execution speed. When the assembler encounters such a mnemonic in assembler source code, it automatically chooses the most efficient instruction that fills the bill.

For example, earlier in this chapter we learned that there's a special 16-bit register-only version of **inc** that's shorter and faster than the standard *mod-reg-rm* version. Whenever you use a 16-bit register **inc** in source code—for example, **inc ax**—the assembler uses the more efficient 16-bit register-only **inc**; otherwise, the assembler uses the standard version.

Naturally, you'd prefer to use the most efficient version of a given mnemonic whenever possible. The only way to do that is to know the various instructions described by each mnemonic and to strive to use the forms of the mnemonic that assemble to the most efficient instruction. For instance, consider the choice between **inc ax** and **inc al**. Without inside knowledge, there's no basis on which to choose between the two assembler instructions. In fact, there might be a temptation to choose the 8-bit form on the premise that an 8-bit operation can't *possibly* be slower than a 16-bit one. Actually, of course, it *can*—but you'll only know that the 16-bit **inc** is the one to pick if you're aware of the two instructions **inc** describes.

This section is a summary of mnemonics that cover multiple instructions, many of which we've covered in detail elsewhere in this book. The mnemonics that describe multiple instructions are

- ◆ **inc**, which has a *mod-reg-rm* version and a 16-bit register-only version, as described earlier in this chapter (the same applies to **dec**)
- ◆ **xchg**, which has a *mod-reg-rm* version and a 16-bit register exchange-with-AX-only version, as described in Chapter 8
- ◆ **add**, which has two *mod-reg-rm* versions (one for adding a register and a memory variable or a second register together, and another for adding immediate data to a register or memory variable) and an accumulator-specific immediate-addressing version, as described in Chapter 8 (the

same applies to **adc**, **and**, **cmp**, **or**, **sbb**, **sub**, **test**, and **xor**, also as described in Chapter 8)

♦ **push,** which has a *mod-reg-rm* version and a 16-bit register version, as described in Chapter 7.

♦ **mov**, which requires further explanation

The mnemonic **mov** covers several instructions, and it's worthwhile to understand each one. The basic form of **mov** is a *mod-reg-rm* form that copies one register or memory variable to another register or memory variable. (Memory-to-memory moves are not permitted, however.) There's also a *mod-reg-rm* form of **mov** that allows the copying of a segment register to a general-purpose register or a memory variable, and vice versa. Last among the *mod-reg-rm* versions of **mov**, there's a form of **mov** that supports the setting of a register or a memory variable to an immediate value.

There are two more versions of **mov**, both of which are non–*mod-reg-rm* forms of the instruction. There's an accumulator-specific version that allows the transfer of values between direct-addressed memory variables and the accumulator (AL or AX) faster and in fewer bytes than the *mod-reg-rm* instruction, as discussed in Chapter 8. There's also a register-specific form of **mov**, as we discussed in Chapter 7; I'd like to discuss that version of **mov** further, for it's an important version indeed.

Every *mod-reg-rm* instruction requires at least 2 bytes, one for the instruction opcode and one for the *mod-reg-rm* byte. Consequently, the *mod-reg-rm* version of **mov *mem/reg,immed8*** is 3 bytes long, since the immediate value takes another byte. However, there's a register-specific immediate-addressing form of **mov** that doesn't have a *mod-reg-rm* byte. Instead, the register selection is built right into the opcode, so only 1 byte is needed to both describe the instruction and select the destination. The result: the register-specific immediate-addressing form of **mov** allows **mov *reg,immed8*** to assemble to just 2 bytes and **mov *reg,immed16*** to assemble to just 3 bytes.

The presence of the register-specific immediate-addressing version of **mov** makes loading immediate values into registers quite reasonable in terms of code size and performance. For example, **mov al,0** assembles to a 2-byte instruction, exactly the same length as **sub al,al**. Granted, **sub al,al** is 1 cycle faster than **mov al,0**, and **sub ax,ax** is both 1 cycle faster and 1 byte shorter than **mov ax,0**, but the upshot is that registers can be loaded with immediate values fairly efficiently.

Be aware, however, that the same is *not* generally true of **add**, **sub**, or any of the logical or arithmetic instructions. The *mod-reg-rm* immediate-addressing forms of these instructions take a minimum of 3 bytes. As mentioned above, though, the accumulator-specific immediate-addressing forms of these instructions *are* fast and compact at 2 or 3 bytes.

While there is a special form of **mov** for loading registers with immediate data, there is no such form for loading memory variables. The shortest possible instruction for loading memory with an immediate value is 3 bytes, and such instructions can be as long as 6 bytes. In fact, thanks to the 8088's accumulator- and register-specific **mov** instructions,

```
mov   al,0
mov   [MemVar],al
```

is not only the same length as

```
mov   [MemVar],0
```

but is also 2 cycles faster!

Learn well those special cases in which a single mnemonic covers multiple instructions—and *use* them! They're one of the secrets of good 8088 assembler code.

On to the String Instructions

We've cut a wide swath through the 8088's instruction set in this chapter, but we have yet to touch on one important set of instructions: the string instructions. These instructions, which are perhaps the most important instructions the 8088 has to offer when it comes to high-performance programming, are coming up next. Stay tuned.

Late flash: As I read the page proofs for this chapter, I came across an article, "Tricks of the Trade," by Tim Paterson, scheduled to be printed in the March 1990 issue of Doctor Dobb's Journal, *that describes an excellent use for* **daa**, *along with a number of other nifty 8088 assembler tricks, many of which don't appear in* Zen of Assembly Language. *Never assume that you know all the tricks or have the best approach.*

Chapter 10

String Instructions: The Magic Elixir

10.1   A Quick Tour of the String Instructions

10.2   Hither and Yon with the String Instructions

The 8088's instruction set is flexible, full-featured, and a lot of fun to work with. On the whole, there's just one thing that seriously ails the 8088's instruction set, and that's lousy performance. Branches are slow, memory accesses are slow, and even register-only instructions are slowed by the prefetch queue cycle eater. Let's face it: most 8088 code just doesn't run very fast.

Don't despair, though. There's a sure cure for the 8088 performance blues: the magic elixir of the string instructions. The string instructions are like nothing else in the 8088's instruction set. They're compact—1 byte apiece—so they're not much affected by the prefetch queue cycle eater. A single string instruction can be repeated up to 65,535 times, avoiding both branching and instruction fetching. String instructions access memory faster than most 8088 instructions, and can advance pointers and decrement counters in the bargain. In short, string instructions can do more with fewer cycles than other 8088 instructions.

Of course, nothing is perfect in this imperfect world, and the string instructions are no exception. The major drawback to the string instructions is that there are just so darn *few* of them—five, to be exact. The only tasks that can be performed with string instructions are reading from memory, writing to memory, copying from memory to memory, comparing a byte or word to a block of memory, and comparing two blocks of memory. That may sound like a lot, but in truth it isn't. The many varieties of normal (nonstring) instructions can add constants to memory, shift memory, perform logical operations with memory operands, and much more, far exceeding the limited capabilities of the five string instructions. What's more, the normal instructions can work with a variety of registers and can address memory in all sorts of ways, whereas string instructions are very restrictive in terms of register use and memory addressing modes.

That doesn't mean that the string instructions have limited value—far from it, in fact. What it does mean is that your programs must be built around the capabilities of the string instructions if they are to run as fast as possible. As you learn to bring string instructions to bear on your programming tasks, you'll find that the performance of your code improves considerably.

In other words, use string instructions whenever you possibly can, and try to think of ways to use them even when it seems you can't.

10.1 ◆ A Quick Tour of the String Instructions

Odds are good that you're already at least somewhat conversant with the string instructions, so I'm not going to spend much time going over their basic functionality. I am going to summarize them briefly, however; I want to make sure that we're speaking the same language, and I also want you to be as knowledgeable as possible about these key instructions.

After we've discussed the individual string instructions, we'll cover a variety of important and often non-obvious facts, tips, and potential problems associated with the string instructions. Finally, in the next chapter we'll look at some powerful applications of the string instructions.

This chapter is a tour of the string instructions, not a tutorial. We'll be moving fast; while we'll hit the important points about the string instructions, we won't linger. At times I'll refer to some material that's not covered until later in this chapter or the next. Alas, that sort of forward reference is unavoidable with a topic as complex as the string instructions. Bear with me, though—by the end of the next chapter, I promise that everything will come together.

Reading Memory: lods

The **lodsb** (load string byte) instruction reads the byte addressed by DS:SI (the source operand) into AL and then either increments or decrements SI, depending on the setting of the Direction flag, as shown in Figure 10.1. The **lodsw** (load string word) instruction reads the word addressed by DS:SI into AX and then adds or subtracts 2 to or from SI, again depending on the state of the direction flag. In either case, the use of DS as the segment can be overridden, as we'll see later.

We'll discuss the direction flag in detail later on. For now, let's just refer to string instructions as "advancing" their pointers, with the understanding that advancing means either adding or subtracting 1 or 2, depending on the direction flag and the data size.

The instruction **lods** is particularly useful for reading the elements of an array or string sequentially, since SI is automatically advanced each time **lods** is executed.

The **lods** instruction is considerably more limited than, say, **mov** *reg8,*[*mem8*]. For instance, **lodsb** requires that AL be the destination and that SI point to the source operand, whereas the **mov** instruction allows

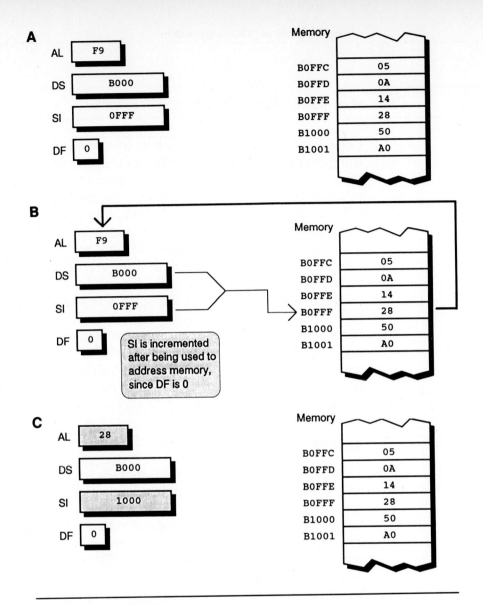

FIGURE 10.1 The operation of **lodsb** with DF set to 0. **(A)** The state of the PC before **lodsb** is executed. **(B)** The data and addressing paths as **lodsb** executes. (As usual, data movement is shown with heavy lines, while addressing is shown with light lines.) **(C)** The state of the PC after **lodsb** is finished, with altered registers shaded. Note that SI is decremented when DF is 1. The instructions **lodsw** and **lodsb** are identical, except that with **lodsw** AX, rather than AL, is loaded and SI is incremented or decremented by 2, rather than by 1.

any of the 8 general-purpose registers to be the destination and allows the use of any of the 16 addressing modes to address the source.

On the other hand, **lodsb** is shorter and a good deal faster than **mov**. The instruction **mov reg8,[mem8]** is between 2 and 4 bytes long, whereas **lodsb** is exactly 1 byte long. The instruction **lodsb** also advances SI, an action that requires a second instruction (albeit a fast one), **inc si**, when **mov** is used.

Let's compare **lodsb** and **mov** in action. Listing 10-1, which loads AL and advances SI 1000 times with **mov** and **inc**, executes in 3.77 msec. Listing 10-2, which uses **lodsb** to both load and advance in a single instruction, is 33 percent faster at 2.83 msec. When two code sequences perform the same task and one of them is 33 percent faster and one third as long, there can't be much doubt about which is better.

```
1    ;
2    ; *** Listing 10-1 ***
3    ;
4    ; Loads each byte in a 1000-byte array into AL, using
5    ; MOV and INC.
6    ;
7            jmp     Skip
8    ;
9    ARRAY_LENGTH    equ     1000
10   ByteArray       db      ARRAY_LENGTH dup (0)
11   ;
12   Skip:
13           call    ZTimerOn
14           mov     si,offset ByteArray
15                           ;point to the start of the array
16           rept    ARRAY_LENGTH
17           mov     al,[si] ;get this array byte
18           inc     si      ;point to the next byte in the array
19           endm
20           call    ZTimerOff
```

```
1    ;
2    ; *** Listing 10-2 ***
3    ;
4    ; Loads each byte in a 1000-byte array into AL, using
5    ; LODSB.
6    ;
7            jmp     Skip
8    ;
9    ARRAY_LENGTH    equ     1000
10   ByteArray       db      ARRAY_LENGTH dup (0)
11   ;
12   Skip:
13           call    ZTimerOn
14           mov     si,offset ByteArray
15                           ;point to the start of the array
```

```
16              cld             ;make LODSB increment SI
17              rept    ARRAY_LENGTH
18              lodsb               ;get this array byte & point to the
19                                  ; next byte in the array
20              endm
21              call    ZTimerOff
```

Even when the time required to advance SI is ignored, **lodsb** is superior
to **mov**. Suppose, for example, that you were to load SI with a pointer into
a look-up table. Would you be better off using **lods** or **mov** to perform
the look-up, given that it doesn't matter in this case whether SI advances
or not?

Use **lods**. Listing 10-3, which is Listing 10-1 modified to remove the
inc instructions, executes in 3.11 msec. Listing 10-2, which uses **lodsb**,
is one half the length of Listing 10-3 and 10 percent faster, even though
Listing 10-3 uses the shortest and fastest memory-accessing form of the
mov instruction and doesn't advance SI.

```
1       ;
2       ; *** Listing 10-3 ***
3       ;
4       ; Loads a byte into AL 1000 times via MOV, with no
5       ; INC performed.
6       ;
7                   jmp     Skip
8       ;
9       ARRAY_LENGTH    equ     1000
10      ByteArray       db      ARRAY_LENGTH dup (0)
11      ;
12      Skip:
13                  call    ZTimerOn
14                  mov     si,offset ByteArray
15                              ;point to the start of the array
16                  rept    ARRAY_LENGTH
17                  mov     al,[si] ;get this array byte but don't point
18                              ; to the next byte in the array
19                  endm
20                  call    ZTimerOff
```

Of course, if you specifically didn't *want* SI to advance, you'd be better
off with **mov**, because there's no way to stop **lods** from advancing SI.
(In fact, all the string instructions always advance their pointer registers,
whether you want them to or not.)

I'm not going to contrast the other string instructions with their nonstring equivalents in the next few sections; we'll get plenty of that later in
the chapter. The rule we just established applies to the other string instructions as well, though: it's often better to use a string instruction rather than
mov even when you don't need all the power of the string instruction.

While it can be a nuisance to set up the registers for the string instructions, it's still usually worth using the string instructions whenever you can do so without going through too many contortions. In general, the string instructions simply make for shorter, faster code than their **mov**-based equivalents.

Never assume, though: string instructions aren't superior in *all* cases. Always time your code!

Writing Memory: stos

The **stosb** (store string byte) instruction writes the value in AL to the byte addressed by ES:DI (the destination operand) and then either increments or decrements DI, depending on the setting of the direction flag. The **stosw** (store string word) instruction writes the value in AX to the word addressed by ES:DI and then adds or subtracts 2 to or from DI, again depending on the direction flag, as shown in Figure 10.2. The use of ES as the destination segment cannot be overridden.

The **stos** instruction is the preferred way to initialize arrays, strings, and other blocks of memory, especially when used with the **rep** prefix, which we'll discuss shortly. **stos** also works well with **lods** for tasks that require performing some sort of translation while copying arrays or strings, such as conversion of a text string to upper case. In this use, **lods** loads an array element into AL, the element is translated in AL, and **stos** stores the element to the new array. Put a loop around all that and you've got a compact, fast translation routine. We'll discuss this further in the next chapter.

Moving Memory: movs

The **movsb** (move string byte) instruction copies the value stored at the byte addressed by DS:SI (the source operand) to the byte addressed by ES:DI (the destination operand) and then either increments or decrements SI and DI, depending on the setting of the direction flag, as shown in Figure 10.3. The **movsw** (move string word) instruction copies the value stored at the word addressed by DS:SI to the word addressed by ES:DI and then adds or subtracts 2 to or from SI or DI, again depending on the direction flag. The use of DS as the source segment can be overridden, but the use of ES as the destination segment cannot.

Note that the accumulator is not affected by **movs**; each byte or word is copied directly from memory to memory, not by way of AL or AX.

The **movs** instruction is by far the 8088's best instruction for copying arrays, strings, and other blocks of data from one memory location to another.

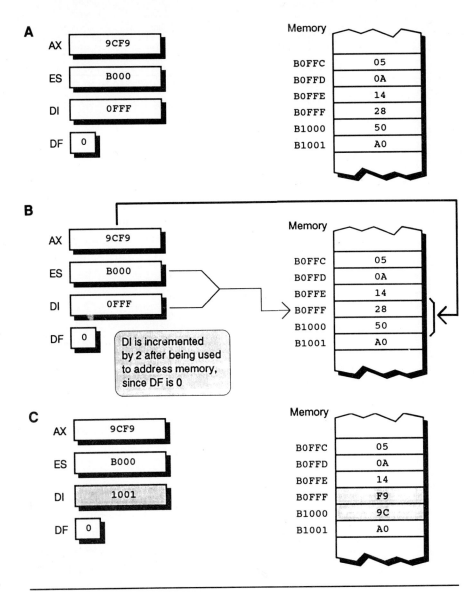

FIGURE 10.2   The operation of **stosw** with DF set to 0. **(A)** The state of the PC before **stosw** is executed. **(B)** The data and addressing paths as **stosw** executes. **(C)** The state of the PC after **stosw** is finished, with altered registers and memory locations shaded. Note that DI is decremented when DF is 1. The instruction **stosb** is identical to **stosw**, except that AL rather than AX is written to memory and DI is incremented or decremented by 1 rather than 2.

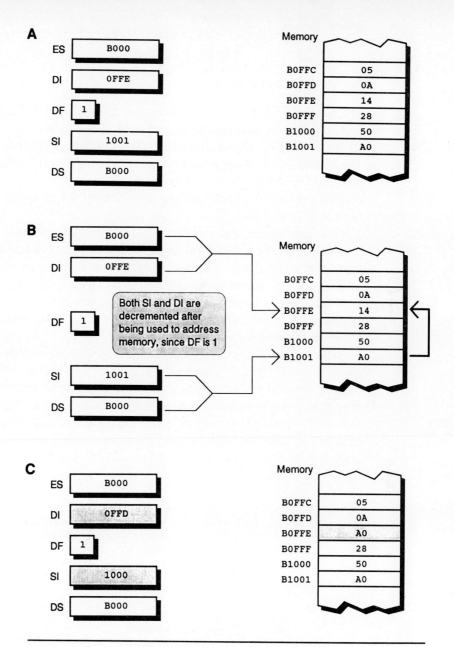

FIGURE 10.3 The operation of **movsb** with DF set to 1. **(A)** The state of the PC before **movsb** is executed. **(B)** The data and addressing paths as **movsb** executes. **(C)** The state of the PC after **movsb** is finished, with altered registers and memory locations shaded. Note that SI and DI are incremented when DF is 0. The instruction **movsw** is identical to **movsb**, except that a word rather than a byte of memory is copied and SI and DI are incremented or decremented by 2 rather than 1.

Scanning Memory: scas

The **scasb** (scan string byte) instruction compares AL to the byte addressed by ES:DI (the source operand) and then either increments or decrements DI, depending on the setting of the direction flag, as shown in Figure 10.4. The **scasw** (scan string word) instruction compares the value in AX to the word addressed by ES:DI and then adds or subtracts 2 to or from DI, again depending on the direction flag. The use of ES as the source segment cannot be overridden.

The instruction **scas** performs its comparison exactly as **cmp** does, by performing a trial subtraction of the memory location addressed by ES:DI from the accumulator without actually changing either the accumulator or the memory location. All the arithmetic flags—OF, SF, ZF, AF, PF, and CF—are affected by **scas**. That's easy to forget when you use **repz scas** or **repnz scas**, which can only terminate according to the status of ZF. (We'll cover all the repeated string instruction below.)

The **scas** instruction is excellent for searching strings and arrays for specific values, and is especially good for looking up values in tables. Many programmers get so used to using **repz scas** and **repnz scas** that they forget that nonrepeated **scas** instructions are more flexible than their repeated counterparts and can often be used when the repeated versions of **scas** can't. For example, suppose that we wanted to search a word-sized array for the first element greater than 10,000. Listing 10-4 shows code for

```
1      ;
2      ; *** Listing 10-4 ***
3      ;
4      ; Searches a word-sized array for the first element
5      ; greater than 10,000, using non-string instructions.
6      ;
7              jmp     Skip
8      ;
9      WordArray       dw      1000 dup (0), 10001
10     ;
11     Skip:
12             call    ZTimerOn
13             mov     di,offset WordArray-2
14                                     ;start 1 word early so the
15                                     ; first preincrement points
16                                     ; to the first element
17             mov     ax,10000        ;value we'll compare with
18     SearchLoop:
19             inc     di              ;point to the next element
20             inc     di
21             cmp     ax,[di]         ;compare the next element
22                                     ; to 10,000
23             jae     SearchLoop      ;if not greater than 10,000,
24                                     ; do the next element
25             call    ZTimerOff
```

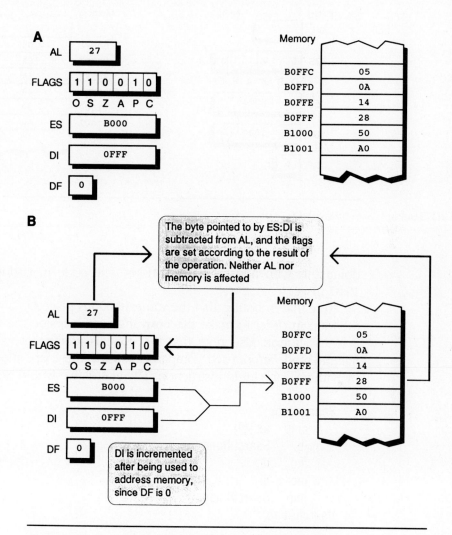

FIGURE 10.4 The operation of **scasb** with DF set to 0. **(A)** The state of the PC before **scasb** is executed. **(B)** The data and addressing paths as **scasb** executes. **(C)** The state of the PC after **scasb** is finished, with altered registers shaded. Note that DI is decremented when DF is 1. The instruction **scasw** is identical to **scasb**, except that AX rather than AL is compared to memory and DI is incremented or decremented by 2 rather than 1.

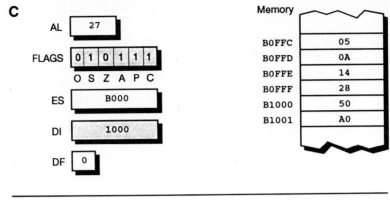

FIGURE 10.4   (*continued*)

doing this with nonstring instructions. The code in Listing 10-4 runs in 10.07 msec.

Note that in Listing 10-4 the value 10,000 is placed in a register outside the loop in order to make the **cmp** instruction inside the loop faster and 2 bytes shorter. Also note that the code is arranged so that DI can be incremented *before* each comparison inside the loop, allowing us to get by with just one jump instruction. The alternative would be

```
SearchLoop:
      cmp   ax,[di]
      jb    SearchDone
      inc   di
      inc   di
      jmp   SearchLoop
SearchDone:
```

While this works perfectly well, it has not only the four instructions of the loop in Listing 10-4 but also an additional jump instruction, so it's bound to be slower.

Listing 10-5 is functionally equivalent to Listing 10-4 but uses **scasw** rather than **cmp** and **inc**. That slight difference allows Listing 10-5 to run in 8.25 msec, 22 percent faster than Listing 10-4. While **scasw** works beautifully in this application, **rep scasw** would not have worked at all, because **rep scasw** can only check for equality/nonequality relationships. If we had been thinking in terms of **rep scasw**, we might well have missed the superior **scasw** implementation. The moral: although repeated string

```
1    ;
2    ; *** Listing 10-5 ***
3    ;
4    ; Searches a word-sized array for the first element
5    ; greater than 10,000, using SCASW.
6    ;
7            jmp     Skip
8    ;
9    WordArray       dw      1000 dup (0), 10001
10   ;
11   Skip:
12           call    ZTimerOn
13           mov     di,seg WordArray
14           mov     es,di    ;SCASW always uses ES:SI as a
15                            ; memory pointer
16           mov     di,offset WordArray
17           mov     ax,10000 ;value we'll compare with
18           cld              ;make SCASW add 2 to DI after
19                            ; each execution
20   SearchLoop:
21           scasw            ;compare the next element to 10,000
22           jae     SearchLoop ;if not greater than 10,000, do
23                            ; the next element
24           dec     di       ;point back to the matching word
25           dec     di
26           call    ZTimerOff
```

instructions are the most powerful instructions of the 8088, don't forget that nonrepeated string instructions are nearly as powerful and generally more flexible.

As another example, Listing 10-6 shows a **lodsw**-based version of Listing 10-4. While this straightforward approach is faster than Listing 10-4 (it executes in 9.07 msec), it is clearly inferior to the **scasw**-based implementation of Listing 10-5. When you set out to tackle a programming problem, always think of the string instructions first—and think of *all* the string instructions. The obvious solution is not necessarily the best.

```
1    ;
2    ; *** Listing 10-6 ***
3    ;
4    ; Searches a word-sized array for the first element
5    ; greater than 10,000, using LODSW & CMP.
6    ;
7            jmp     Skip
8    ;
9    WordArray       dw      1000 dup (0), 10001
10   ;
11   Skip:
12           call    ZTimerOn
13           mov     si,offset WordArray
14                            ;array to search
15           mov     dx,10000 ;value we'll compare with
16           cld              ;make LODSW add 2 to SI after each
```

```
17                              ; execution
18   SearchLoop:
19           lodsw            ;get the next element
20           cmp     dx,ax    ;compare the element to 10,000
21           jae     SearchLoop ;if not greater than 10,000, do
22                            ; the next element
23           dec     di       ;point back to the matching word
24           dec     di
25           call    ZTimerOff
```

Notes on Loading Segments for String Instructions

You may have noticed that in Listing 10-5 I chose to use DI to load ES with the target segment. This is a useful practice to follow when setting up pointers in ES:DI for string instructions; since you know you're going to load DI with the target offset next, you can be sure that you won't accidentally wipe out any important data in that register. It's more common to use AX to load segment registers, since AX is the most general purpose of registers, but why use AX, which *might* contain something useful, when DI is guaranteed to be free?

Similarly, I make a practice of using SI to load DS for string instructions, loading the offset into SI immediately after setting DS.

Along the same lines, I load the segment into DI in Listing 10-5 with the **seg** operator. You may prefer to load the name of the segment instead (for example, **mov di,DataSeg**). That's okay too, but consider this: you can't go wrong with the **seg** operator when you're loading a segment in order to access a specific named variable. Even if you change the name of the segment containing the array in Listing 10-5, the code will still assemble properly. The same cannot be said for loading DI with the name of the segment. The choice is yours, but personally I prefer to make my code as immune as possible to errors induced by later changes.

It may have occurred to you that in Listing 10-5 it would be faster to load DI with the target segment from DS rather than with a constant. That is,

```
mov  di,ds
mov  es,di
```

is shorter and faster than

```
mov  di,seg WordArray
mov  es,di
```

True enough, and you should use the first approach whenever you can. I've chosen to use the latter approach in the listings in this chapter in order to make the operation of the string instructions clear and to illustrate the most general case. After all, in many cases the destination segment for a string instruction won't be DS.

Comparing Memory: cmps

The **cmpsb** (compare string byte) instruction compares the byte addressed by DS:SI (the destination operand) to the byte addressed by ES:DI (the source operand) and then either increments or decrements SI and DI, depending on the setting of the direction flag. The **cmpsw** (compare string word) instruction compares the value stored at the word addressed by DS:SI to the word addressed by ES:DI and then adds or subtracts 2 to or from SI and DI, again depending on the direction flag, as shown in Figure 10.5. The use of DS as the destination segment can be overridden, but the use of ES as the source segment cannot.

The instruction **cmps** performs its comparison as **cmp** does, by performing a trial subtraction of the memory location addressed by ES:DI from the memory location addressed by DS:SI without actually changing either location. As with **scas**, all six arithmetic flags are affected by **cmps**. The key difference between **scas** and **cmps** is that **scas** compares the accumulator to memory whereas **cmps** compares two memory locations directly. The accumulator is not affected by **cmps** in any way; the comparison is performed directly from one memory operand to the other, not by way of AL or AX.

For comparing arrays, strings, and other blocks of memory data, **cmps** is in a class by itself.

10.2 ◆ Hither and Yon with the String Instructions

That does it for our quick tour of the individual string instructions. Now it's on to a variety of useful items about string instructions in general.

Data Size, Advancing Pointers, and the Direction Flag

Each string instruction advances its associated pointer register (or registers) by one memory location each time it executes: **lods** advances SI, **stos** and **scas** advance DI, and **movs** and **cmps** advance both SI and DI. As we've seen, that's a very handy bonus of using the string instructions:

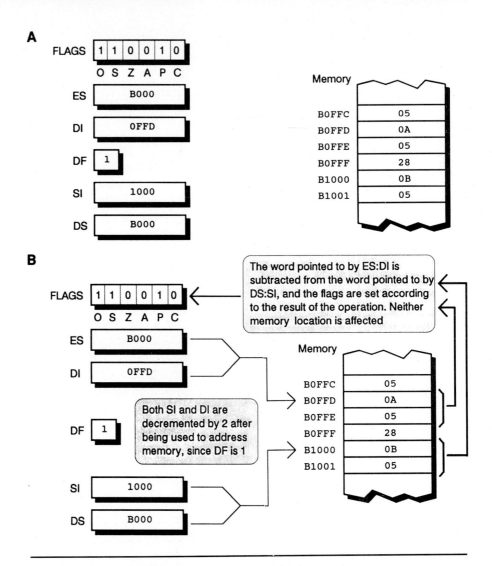

FIGURE 10.5   The operation of **cmpsw** with DF set to 1. **(A)** The state of the PC before **cmpsw** is executed. **(B)** The data and addressing paths as **cmpsw** executes. **(C)** The state of the PC after **cmpsw** is finished, with altered registers and memory locations shaded. Note that SI and DI are incremented when DF is 0. The instruction **cmpsb** is identical to **cmpsw**, except that bytes rather than words of memory are compared and SI and DI are incremented or decremented by 1 rather than 2.

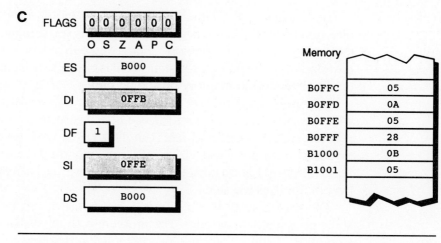

FIGURE 10.5 (*continued*)

not only do they access memory rapidly, they also advance pointers in that same short time. String instructions advance their pointer registers just once per execution; however, any string instruction prefixed with **rep** can execute—and consequently advance its pointer or pointers—thousands of times.

All that seems straightforward enough. There are complications, though: both the definition of "one memory location" and the direction in which the pointer or pointers advance can vary.

String instructions can operate on either byte- or word-sized data. We've already seen one way to choose data size: by putting the suffix **b** or **w** on the end of a string instruction's mnemonic. For example, **lodsb** loads a byte, and **cmpsw** compares two words. Later in the chapter we'll see another way to specify data size, along with ways to specify segment overrides for string instructions that access memory via SI.

When working with byte-sized data, string instructions advance their pointers by 1 byte per memory access, and when working with word-sized data, they advance their pointers by one word per memory access. So "one memory location" means 1 byte or 1 word—whichever is the data size of the instruction. That makes perfect sense given that the idea of using string instructions is to advance sequentially through the elements of a byte- or word-sized array.

Ah, but what exactly does "advance" mean? Do the pointer registers used by string instructions move to the next location higher in memory or to the next location lower in memory?

Both, actually. Or, rather, either one, depending on the setting of the direction flag (DF) in the flags register. If DF is set, string instructions move their pointers down in memory, subtracting either 1 or 2, whichever is the data size, from the pointer registers. If DF is cleared, string instructions move their pointers up in memory by adding either 1 or 2.

DF can be explicitly set with the **std** (set DF) instruction and cleared with the **cld** (clear DF) instruction. Other instructions that load the flags register, such as **popf** and **iret**, can alter DF as well. Be aware, however, that **sahf** does not affect DF; **sahf** loads only the lower byte of the flags register from AH, and a glance at Figure 6.2 shows that DF resides in the upper byte of the flags register.

DF doesn't seem like a big deal, but in fact it can be responsible for some particularly nasty bugs. The problem with DF is that it allows a given string instruction to produce two completely different results under what appear to be the same circumstances—the same register settings, memory contents, and so on. In other words, DF makes string instructions modal, and the instruction that controls that mode at any given time—the **cld** or **std** that selected the string direction—may have occurred long ago in a subroutine far, far away. A string instruction that runs perfectly most of the time can mysteriously crash the system every so often because a different DF state was selected by seemingly unrelated code that ran thousands of cycles earlier.

What's the solution? Well, usually you'll want your string instructions to move their pointers up in memory, since that's the way arrays and strings are stored. (It's also the way people tend to think about memory, with storage running from low to high addresses.) There are good uses for counting down, such as copying overlapping source and destination blocks and searching for the last element in an array, but those are not the primary applications for string instructions. Given that, it makes sense to leave DF cleared at all times except when you explicitly need to move pointers down rather than up in memory. That way you can always count on your string instructions to move their pointers up unless you specify otherwise.

Unfortunately, that solution can be used only when you've written all the code in a program yourself and have done so in pure assembler. Since you have no control over the code generated by compilers or the code in third-party libraries, you can't rely on such code to leave DF cleared. I know of one compiler with library functions that do indeed leave DF set occasionally, and I've no doubt that there are others. What to do here?

The solution is obvious, though a bit painful: whenever you can't be sure of the state of DF, you absolutely *must* put it in a known state before using any of the string instructions. This causes your code to be sprinkled with **cld** and **std** instructions, and that makes your programs a bit bigger and slower. Fortunately, though, **cld** and **std** are 1-byte, 2-cycle instructions, so they have minimal impact on size and performance. As with so much else about the 8088, it would have been nice if Intel had chosen to build direction into the opcode bytes of the string instructions, as they did with data size. Alas, Intel chose not to do so—so be sure DF is in the proper state each and every time you use a string instruction.

That doesn't mean you have to put a **cld** or **std** before *every* string instruction. Just be sure you know the state of DF when each string instruction is executed. For example, in Listing 10-5 **cld** is performed just once, outside the loop. Because nothing inside the loop changes DF, there's no need to set the flag again.

An important tip: *always* put DF in a known state in interrupt-handling code. Interrupts can occur at any time, while any code is executing, including BIOS and DOS code, over which you have no control. Consequently, DF may be in any state when an interrupt handler is invoked, even if your program always keeps DF cleared.

The rep Prefix

Taken by themselves, the string instructions are superior instructions: they're shorter and faster than the average memory-accessing instruction, and advance pointer registers too. It's in conjunction with the **rep** prefix that string instructions really shine, though.

As you may recall from Chapter 7, a prefix is an instruction byte that modifies the operation of the following instruction. For example, segment override prefixes can cause many instructions to access memory in segments other than their default segments.

The prefix **rep** modifies the operation of the string instructions (and only the string instructions). The **rep** prefix is exactly 1 byte long, so it effectively doubles the 1-byte length of the string instruction it prefixes. Put another way, **movsb** is a 1-byte instruction, while **rep movsb** is effectively a 2-byte instruction, although it actually consists of a 1-byte prefix and a 1-byte instruction. What **rep** does to justify the expenditure of an extra byte is simple enough: it instructs the following string instruction to execute the number of times specified by CX.

Sounds familiar, doesn't it? It should—it's a lot like the repeat-CL-times capability of the shift and rotate instructions that we discussed in the previous chapter. There is a difference, however. Because **rep** causes instructions to be repeated CX times, any string instruction can be repeated up to 65,535 times, rather than the paltry 255 times a shift or rotate can be repeated. Of course, there's really no reason to want to repeat a shift or rotate more than 16 times, but there's plenty of reason to want to do so with a string instruction. A single string instruction, repeated CX times, can, if necessary, access every word in an entire segment. That's one—count it, *one*—string instruction!

The above description makes it sound as if string instruction repetitions are free. They aren't. A string instruction repeated *n* times takes about *n* times longer to execute than a single non-repeated instance of that instruction, as measured in execution unit (EU) cycles. There's some start-up time for repeated string instructions, and some of the string instructions take a cycle more or less per execution when repeated than when run singly. Nonetheless, the execution time of a repeated string instruction is generally proportional to the number of repetitions.

That's okay, though, because repeated string instructions do the next best thing to running in no time at all: *they beat the prefetch queue cycle eater.* How? By performing multiple repetitions of an instruction with just one instruction fetch. When you repeat a string instruction, you're basically executing multiple instances of that instruction without having to fetch the extra instruction bytes. For instance, as shown in Figure 10.6, the **rep** prefix lets this:

```
sub    di,di
mov    ax,0a000h
mov    es,ax
sub    ax,ax
mov    cx,10
cld
rep    stosw
```

replace this:

```
sub    di,di
mov    ax,0a000h
mov    es,ax
sub    ax,ax
cld
stosw
stosw
stosw
stosw
stosw
```

```
stosw
stosw
stosw
stosw
stosw
```

The **rep**-based version takes a bit more set-up, but it's worth it. Because **rep stosw** (requiring one 2-byte instruction fetch) replaces 10 **stosw** instructions (requiring 10 1-byte instruction fetches), we can replace 20 instruction bytes with 15 instruction bytes. The instruction fetching benefits should be obvious.

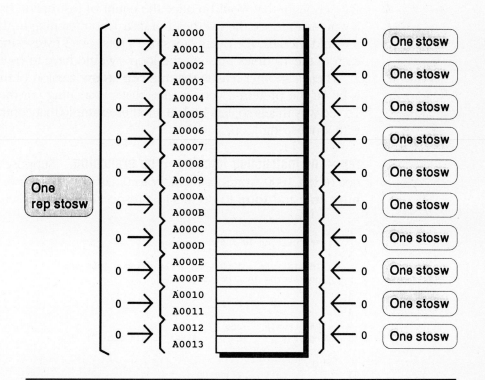

FIGURE 10.6   Here **rep stosw** clears 10 words of memory, with one 2-byte prefix/instruction pair doing what would otherwise take ten 1-byte **stosw** instructions. The **rep** prefix is capable of much more; a single repeated string instruction can be executed up to 64 K−1 times.

No doubt you'll look at the last example and think that it would be easy to reduce the number of instruction bytes by using a loop, such as:

```
        sub   di,di
        mov   ax,0a000h
        mov   es,ax
        sub   ax,ax
        cld
        mov   cx,10
ClearLoop:
        stosw
        loop  ClearLoop
```

True enough, that would reduce the count of instruction bytes to 16—but it wouldn't reduce the overhead of instruction fetching in the least. In fact, it would *increase* the overhead, since a total of 43 bytes—including 3 bytes each of the 10 times through the loop—would have to be fetched.

There's another reason that the **rep stosw** version of the last example is by far the preferred version, and that's branching (or the lack thereof). To see why this is so, lets look at another example that contrasts **rep stosw** with a nonstring loop.

rep = no instruction fetching + no branching.

Suppose we want to set not 10 but 1000 words of memory to 0. Listing 10-7 shows code that uses **mov**, **inc**, and **loop** to do this in a respectable 10.06 msec.

```
1    ;
2    ; *** Listing 10-7 ***
3    ;
4    ; Initializes a 1000-word array using a loop and
5    ; non-string instructions.
6    ;
7            jmp     Skip
8    ;
9    ARRAY_LENGTH    equ     1000
10   WordArray       dw      ARRAY_LENGTH dup (?)
11   ;
12   Skip:
13           call    ZTimerOn
14           mov     di,offset WordArray
15                           ;point to array to fill
16           sub     ax,ax   ;we'll fill with the value zero
17           mov     cx,ARRAY_LENGTH ;# of words to fill
18   ZeroLoop:
19           mov     [di],ax ;zero one word
20           inc     di      ;point to the next word
21           inc     di
22           loop    ZeroLoop
23           call    ZTimerOff
```

By contrast, Listing 10-8 initializes the same 1000 words to 0 with one repeated **stosw** instruction—*and no branches*. The result: the 1000 words are set to 0 in just 3.03 msec. Listing 10-8 is over *three times* as fast as Listing 10-7, a staggeringly large difference between two well-written assembler routines.

```
1    ;
2    ; *** Listing 10-8 ***
3    ;
4    ; Initializes a 1000-word array using a single
5    ; repeated STOSW.
6    ;
7            jmp     Skip
8    ;
9    ARRAY_LENGTH    equ     1000
10   WordArray       dw      ARRAY_LENGTH dup (?)
11   ;
12   Skip:
13           call    ZTimerOn
14           mov     di,seg WordArray
15           mov     es,di
16           mov     di,offset WordArray
17                           ;point ES:DI to the array to
18                           ; fill, since STOSW must
19                           ; use that segment:offset combo
20                           ; as a memory pointer
21           sub     ax,ax   ;we'll fill with the value zero
22           mov     cx,ARRAY_LENGTH ;# of words to fill
23           cld             ;make STOSW add 2 to DI after each
24                           ; execution
25           rep     stosw   ;fill the array
26           call    ZTimerOff
```

Now you know why it's worth going out of your way to use string instructions.

Why is there so large a difference in performance between Listings 10-7 and 10-8? It's not because of instruction execution speed. Sure, **stos** is faster than **mov**, but a repeated **stosw** takes 14 cycles to write each word, whereas **mov [di],ax** takes 18 cycles, hardly a threefold difference.

The real difference lies in instruction fetching and branching. When Listing 10-7 runs, the 8088 must fetch 6 instruction bytes and write 2 data bytes per loop, which means that each loop takes at least 32 cycles (4 cycles per memory byte accessed times 8 bytes) no matter what.

By contrast, because the 8088 simply holds a repeated string instruction inside the chip while executing it over and over, the loop-equivalent code in Listing 10-8 requires no instruction fetching at all after the 2 bytes of **rep stosw** are fetched. What's more, since the 8 cycles required to write the 2 data bytes fit neatly within the 14-cycle official execution time of a repeated **stosw**, that 14-cycle official execution time should be close to the actual execution time, apart from any effects DRAM refresh may have. Indeed, dividing 3.03 msec by 1000 repetitions reveals that each **stosw** takes 14.5 cycles (3.03 μsec) to execute, which works out nicely as 14 cycles plus about 4 percent DRAM refresh overhead.

Let's look at this from a different perspective. The 8088 must fetch 6000 instruction bytes (6 bytes per loop times 1000 loops, as shown in Figure 10.7) when the loop in Listing 10-7 executes. The **rep stosw** instruction in Listing 10-8, on the other hand, requires the fetching of exactly 2 instruction bytes *in total*, as shown in Figure 10.8—quite a difference!

Better still, the prefetch queue can fill completely whenever a string instruction is repeated a few times. Fast as string instructions are, they don't keep the bus busy all the time. Because repetitions of string instructions require no additional instruction fetching, there's plenty of time for the instruction bytes of the following instructions to be fetched while string instructions repeat. On balance, then, repeated string instructions not only require very little fetching for a great many executions but also allow the prefetch queue to fill with the bytes of the following instructions.

There's more to the difference between Listings 10-7 and 10-8 than just prefetching, however. The 8088 not only must fetch the bytes of the instructions in the loop in Listing 10-7 over and over but must also perform one **loop** instruction per word written to memory, and that's costly indeed. Although **loop** is the 8088's most efficient instruction for repeating code by branching, it's slow nonetheless, as we'll see in Chapter 12. Each **loop** instruction in Listing 10-7 takes at least 17 cycles to execute. That means that the code in Listing 10-7 spends more time looping than the code in Listing 10-8 spends *in total* to initialize each word!

Used properly, repeated string instructions are truly the magic elixir of the PC. Alone among the 8088's instructions, they can cure the most serious performance ills of the PC, the prefetch queue cycle eater and slow branching. The flip side is that repeated string instructions are much less flexible than normal instructions. For example, you can do whatever you want inside a loop terminated with **loop**, but all you can do during a repeated string instruction is the single action of which that instruction is capable. Even so, the performance advantages of repeated string instructions are so great that you should try to use them at every opportunity.

repz and repnz

Two special forms of **rep**—**repz** and **repnz**—are designed specifically for use with **scas** and **cmps**. The notion behind these prefixes is that when you repeat one of the comparison string instructions, you want the repeated

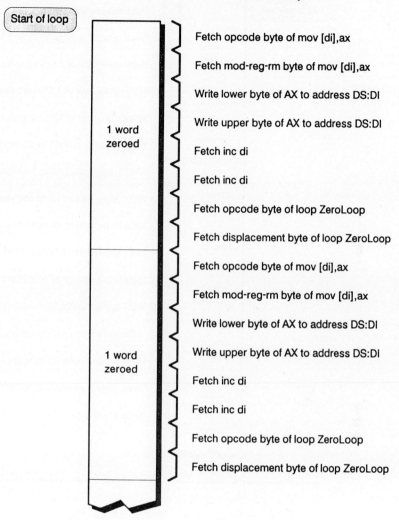

FIGURE 10.7 Bus activity as the loop in Listing 10-7 executes. Instruction prefetching dominates because the 6 bytes in the loop must be fetched once for each word written to memory. Given the eight memory accesses required each time through the loop, there is no way a pass through the loop can take less than 32 cycles (8 bytes at 4 cycles per byte). Note that this figure is only an illustrative approximation of bus activity and does not necessarily represent the actual sequence of bus accesses as the code in Listing 10-7 executes.

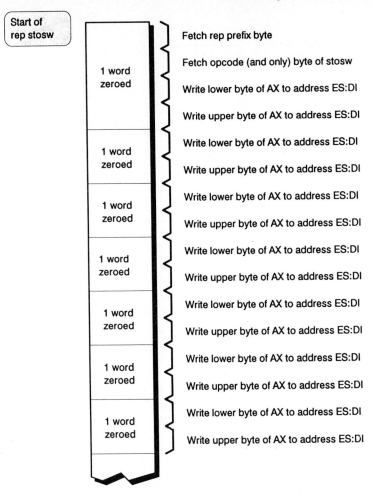

FIGURE 10.8   Bus activity as the **rep stosw** in Listing 10-8 executes. Instruction fetching is not required for the duration of **rep stosw** after the 2 bytes of that instruction are fetched, since the 8088 holds repeated string instructions internally and does not require them to be fetched again as they're repeated. (In fact, 4 instruction bytes will be prefetched as **stosw** repeats, giving the next few instructions a head start when **rep stosw** finishes.) The lack of instruction fetching means that only 8 cycles (2 bytes times 4 cycles) are required to complete the bus accesses for each **stosw**. This allows **rep stosw** to run at about its official speed of 14 cycles per repetition. Note that this figure is only an illustrative approximation of bus activity and does not necessarily represent the actual sequence of bus accesses as the code in Listing 10-8 executes.

comparison to end either the first time a specified match does occur or the first time that match *doesn't* occur.

The **repnz** (repeat while not ZF) prefix causes the following **scas** or **cmps** to repeat until either the string instruction sets ZF (indicating a match) or CX counts down to 0. For instance, the following compares **ByteArray1** to **ByteArray2** until either a position at which the two arrays are the same is found or 100 bytes have been checked:

```
mov   si,seg ByteArray1
mov   ds,si
mov   si,offset ByteArray1
mov   di,seg ByteArray2
mov   es,di
mov   di,offset ByteArray2
mov   cx,100
cld
repnz cmpsb
```

The **repnz** prefix also goes by the name of **repne**; the two are interchangeable.

The **repz** (repeat while ZF) prefix causes the following **scas** or **cmps** to repeat until either the string instruction resets ZF (indicating a nonmatch) or CX counts down to 0. For instance, the following scans **WordArray** until either a nonzero word is found or 1000 words have been checked:

```
mov   di,seg WordArray
mov   es,di
mov   di,offset WordArray
sub   ax,ax
mov   cx,1000
cld
repz  scasw
```

The **repz** prefix is also known as **repe**.

How do you know whether a repeated **scas** or **cmps** has found its termination condition (match or nonmatch) or has simply run out of repetitions? By way of ZF, of course. If—and only if—ZF is set after a **repnz scas** or **repnz cmps**, then the desired match was found. Likewise, if and only if ZF is cleared after a **repz scas** or **repz cmps** was the desired nonmatch found.

As I pointed out earlier, repeated **scas** and **cmps** instructions are not as flexible as their unrepeated counterparts. When used singly, **scas** and **cmps** set all the arithmetic flags, which can be tested with the appropriate conditional jumps. Although these instructions still set all the arithmetic flags when repeated, they can then terminate only according to the state of ZF.

Beware of accidentally using just plain **rep** with **scas** or **cmps**. MASM will accept a dubious construct such as **rep scasw** without complaint and will dutifully generate a **rep** prefix byte. Unfortunately, the same byte that MASM generates for **rep** with **movs**, **lods**, and **stos** means **repz** when used with **scas** and **cmps**. Of course, **repz** may not have been at all what you had in mind, and because **rep scas** and **rep cmps** *look* all right and assemble without warning, this can lead to some difficult debugging. It's unfortunate that MASM doesn't at least generate a warning when it encounters **rep scas** or **rep cmps**, but it doesn't, so you'll just have to watch out for such cases yourself.

(Don't expect too much from MASM, which not only accepts a number of dubious assembler constructs, as we'll see again later in this chapter, but also has some out-and-out bugs. If something just doesn't seem to assemble properly, no matter what you do, then the problem is most likely a bug in MASM. This can often be confirmed by running the malfunctioning code through TASM, which generally has far fewer bugs than MASM—and my experience is that the bugs it does have are present to afford MASM compatibility!)

The **repnz** prefix is ideal for all sort of searches and look-ups, as we'll see at the end of the chapter. Although it is less generally useful, **repz** can serve to find the first location at which a sequence of repeated values ends. For example, suppose you want to find the last nonblank character in a buffer padded to the end with blanks. You could set DF, point ES:DI to the last byte of the buffer, set CX to the length of the buffer, and load AL with a space character. A fairly elaborate set-up sequence, true, but a single **rep scasb** will then find the last nonblank character for you. We'll look at this application in more detail in the next chapter.

rep is a prefix, not an instruction.

I'd like to take a moment to point out that **rep**, **repz**, and **repnz** are prefixes, not instructions. When you see code like

```
cld
rep    stosw
jmp    Test
```

you may well get the impression that **rep** is an instruction and that **stosw** is some sort of operand. Not so—**rep** is a prefix, and **stosw** is an instruction. A more appropriate way to show a repeated **stosw** might be

```
    cld
rep stosw
    jmp  Test
```

which makes it clear that **rep** is a prefix by putting it to the left of the instruction field. However, MASM considers both forms to be the same, and as it has become the convention in the PC world to put **rep** in the mnemonic column, I'll do the same in *Zen of Assembly Language*. Bear in mind, though, that **rep** is not an instruction.

Also remember that **rep** works only with string instructions. Lines like

```
rep  mov  [di],al
```

don't do anything out of the ordinary. If you think about it, you'll realize that that's no great loss; there really isn't any reason to want to repeat a nonstring instruction. Without the automatically advanced pointers that only the string instructions offer, the action of a repeated nonstring instruction would simply be repeated over and over, to no useful end. At any rate, like it or not, the repeat prefix serves no useful end with nonstring instructions.

Of Counters and Flags

When you use CL as a count for a shift or rotate instruction, CL is left unchanged by the instruction. Not so with CX and **rep**. Repeated string instructions decrement CX once for each repetition. CX always contains 0 after repeated **lods**, **stos**, and **movs** instructions finish, because those instructions simply execute until CX counts down to 0.

The situation is a bit more complex with **scas** and **cmps** instructions. When repeated, these instructions can terminate either when CX counts down to 0 or when a match or nonmatch, as selected with **repz** or **repnz**, becomes true. As a result, **scas** and **cmps** instructions can leave CX with any value between 0 and $n-1$, where n is the value loaded into CX when the repeated instruction began. The value $n-1$ is left in CX if the termination condition for the repeated **scas** or **cmps** occurred on the first byte or word. CX counts down by 1 for each additional byte or word checked, ending up at 0 if the instruction was repeated the full number of times initially specified by CX.

Point number 1, then: CX is always altered by repeated string instructions.

By the way, although both repeated and unrepeated string instructions alter pointer registers, it's only *repeated* string instructions that alter CX. For example, after the following code is executed:

```
mov    di,0b800h
mov    es,di
mov    di,1000h
mov    cx,1
sub    al,al
cld
stosb
```

DI will contain 1001h but CX will still contain 1. However, if we add a **rep** prefix, as follows:

```
mov    di,0b800h
mov    es,di
mov    di,1000h
mov    cx,1
sub    al,al
cld
rep stosb
```

DI will contain 1001h and CX will contain 0 after the code is executed.

As we saw earlier, repeated **scas** and **cmps** instructions count CX down to 0 if they complete without encountering the terminating match or nonmatch condition. As a result, you may be tempted to test whether CX is 0—perhaps with the compact **jcxz** instruction—to see whether a repeated **scas** or **cmps** instruction found its match or nonmatch condition. *Don't do it!*

It's true that repeated **scas** and **cmps** instructions count CX down to 0 if the termination condition isn't found—but this is a case of "if but *not* only if." These instructions also count CX down to 0 if the termination condition is found on the last possible execution. That is, if CX was initially set to 10 and a **repz scasb** instruction is about to repeat for the tenth time, CX will be equal to 1. The next repetition will be performed, decrementing CX, regardless of whether the next byte scanned matches AL or not, so CX will surely be 0 when the **repz scasb** ends, no matter what the outcome.

In short, always use ZF, *not* CX, to determine whether a **scas** or **cmps** instruction found its termination condition.

There's another point to be made here. We've established that the flags set by a repeated **scas** or **cmps** instruction reflect the result of the last repetition of **scas** or **cmps**. Given that, it would seem that the flags can't very well reflect the result of decrementing CX too. (After all, there's only one set of flags, and it's already spoken for.) That is indeed the case: the changes made to CX during a repeated string instruction never affect the flags. In fact, **movs**, **lods**, and **stos**, whether repeated or not, never affect the flags at all, while **scas** and **cmps** set the flags to reflect the comparison performed (the last comparison, when repeated).

There's a certain logic to this. The **loop** instruction, which **rep** resembles, doesn't affect any flags, even though it decrements CX and may branch on the result. You can view both **loop** and **rep** as program flow control instructions rather than counting instructions; as such, there's really no reason for them to set the flags. You set CX for a certain number of repetitions, and those repetitions occur in due course; where's the need for a status? Anyway, whether you agree with the philosophy or not, that's the way both **rep** and **loop** work.

Of data size and counters.   We said earlier that CX specifies the number of times that a string instruction preceded by a **rep** prefix should be repeated. Be aware that CX literally controls the number of repeated executions of a string instruction, not the number of memory accesses. Although that seems easy enough to remember, consider the case where you want to set every element of an array containing 1000 8-bit values to 1. The obvious approach to setting the array is shown in Listing 10-9, which sets the array in 2.17 msec.

```
1    ;
2    ; *** Listing 10-9 ***
3    ;
4    ; Sets every element of a 1000-byte array to 1 by
5    ; repeating STOSB 1000 times.
6    ;
7            jmp     Skip
8    ;
9    ARRAY_LENGTH    equ     1000
10   ByteArray       db      ARRAY_LENGTH dup (?)
11   ;
12   Skip:
13           call    ZTimerOn
14           mov     di,seg ByteArray
15           mov     es,di   ;point ES:DI to the array to fill
16           mov     di,offset ByteArray
17           mov     al,1    ;we'll fill with the value 1
18           mov     cx,ARRAY_LENGTH ;# of bytes to fill
```

```
19          cld               ;make STOSB increment DI after
20                            ; each execution
21          rep     stosb     ;initialize the array
22          call    ZTimerOff
```

While Listing 10-9 is certainly fast, it is not the ideal way to initialize this array. It would be far better to repeat **stos** half as many times, writing 2 bytes at a time with **stosw** rather than 1 byte at a time with **stosb**. Why? Well, recall that way back in Chapter 4 we found that the 8088 handles the second byte of a word-sized memory access in just 4 cycles. That's faster than any normal instruction can handle that second byte, and, as it turns out, it's faster than **rep stosb** can handle a second byte as well. Whereas **rep stosw** can write the second byte of a word access in just 4 cycles, for a total time per word written of 14 cycles, **rep stosb** requires 10 cycles for each byte, for a total time per word of 20 cycles. The same holds true across the board: you should use string instructions with word-sized data whenever possible.

Listing 10-10 illustrates the use of word-sized data to initialize the same array to the same values as in Listing 10-9. As expected, Listing 10-10 is considerably faster than Listing 10-9, finishing in just 1.52 msec. In fact, the ratio of the execution time of Listing 10-9 to that of Listing 10-10 is 1.43, which happens to be a ratio of 10:7, or 20:14. That should ring a bell: since it's the ratio of the execution time of two **rep stosb** instructions to one **rep stosw** instruction.

```
1   ;
2   ; *** Listing 10-10 ***
3   ;
4   ; Sets every element of a 1000-byte array to 1 by
5   ; repeating STOSW 500 times.
6   ;
7           jmp     Skip
8   ;
9   ARRAY_LENGTH    equ     1000
10  WordArray       db      ARRAY_LENGTH dup (?)
11  ;
12  Skip:
13          call    ZTimerOn
14          mov     di,seg WordArray
15          mov     es,di    ;point ES:DI to the array to fill
16          mov     di,offset WordArray
17          mov     ax,(1 shl 8) + 1
18                           ;fill each byte with the value 1
19          mov     cx,ARRAY_LENGTH/2 ;# of words to fill
20          cld              ;make STOSW add 2 to DI on each
21                           ; execution
22          rep     stosw    ;fill a word at a time
23          call    ZTimerOff
```

All well and good, but we didn't set out to compare the performance of word- and byte-sized string instructions. The important point in Listing 10-10 is that, since we're using **rep stosw**, CX is loaded with **ARRAY_LENGTH/2**, the array length in words, rather than **ARRAY_LENGTH**, the array length in bytes. Of course, it is **ARRAY_LENGTH**, not **ARRAY_LENGTH/2**, that's the actual length of the array as measured in byte-sized array elements. When you're thinking of a **rep stosw** instruction as clearing a byte array of length **ARRAY_LENGTH**, as we are in Listing 10-10, it's *very* easy to slip and load CX with **ARRAY_LENGTH** rather than **ARRAY_LENGTH/2**. The end result is unpredictable but almost surely unpleasant, as you'll wipe out the contents of the **ARRAY_LENGTH** bytes immediately following the array.

The lesson is simple: whenever you use a repeated word-sized string instruction, make sure that the count you load into CX is a count in words, not in bytes.

Pointing Back to the Last Element

Sometimes it's a little tricky figuring out where your pointers are after a string instruction finishes. That's because each string instruction advances its pointer or pointers only *after* performing its primary function, so pointers are always one location past the last byte or word processed, as shown in Figures 10.9 and 10.10. This is definitely a convenience with **lods**, **stos**, and **movs**, since it always leaves the pointers ready for the next operation. However, it can be a nuisance with **scas** and **cmps**, because it complicates the process of calculating exactly where a match or nonmatch occurred.

Along the same lines, CX counts down one time more than you might expect when repeated **scas** and **cmps** instructions find their termination conditions. Suppose, for instance, that a **repnz scasb** instruction is started with CX equal to 100 and DI equal to 0. If the very first byte, byte 0, is a match, the **repnz scasb** instruction will terminate; however, CX will contain 99, not 100, and DI will contain 1, not 0.

We'll return to this topic in the next chapter. For now, just remember that string instructions never leave their pointers pointing at the last byte or word processed, and repeated **scas** and **cmps** instructions count down CX one more time than you'd expect.

Handling Very Small and Very Large Blocks

The repeated string instructions have some interesting boundary conditions. One of those boundary conditions occurs when a repeated string instruction is executed with CX equal to 0.

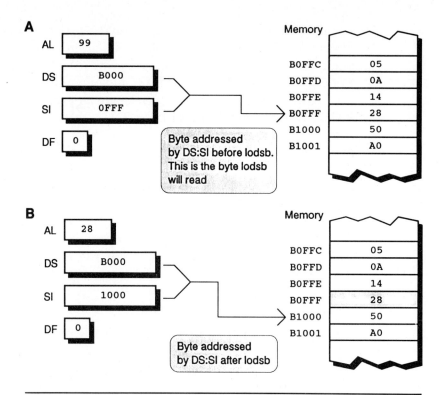

A

AL `99`

DS `B000`

SI `0FFF`

DF `0`

Byte addressed by DS:SI before lodsb. This is the byte lodsb will read

Memory

BOFFC	05
BOFFD	0A
BOFFE	14
BOFFF	28
B1000	50
B1001	A0

B

AL `28`

DS `B000`

SI `1000`

DF `0`

Byte addressed by DS:SI after lodsb

Memory

BOFFC	05
BOFFD	0A
BOFFE	14
BOFFF	28
B1000	50
B1001	A0

FIGURE 10.9   String instructions leave their pointers pointing one location past the last byte or word accessed. **(A)** The state of the PC before **lodsb** executes. **(B)** The state of the PC after **lodsb** executes. The byte read by **lodsb** is shaded. It's clear that **lodsb** advances SI to point 1 byte past the location read, because DS:SI does not point to the shaded location but rather to the adjacent memory address.

When CX is 0, the analogy of **rep** to **loop** breaks down. A **loop**-based loop entered with CX equal to 0 will execute 64 K times, as CX decrements from 0 to 0FFFFh and then all the way back down to 0. However, a repeated instruction executed with CX equal to 0 won't even execute once! That actually can be a useful feature, because it saves you from having to guard against a 0 repeat count, as you do with **loop**.

(Be aware that if you repeat **scas** or **cmps** with CX equal to 0, no comparisons will be performed *and no flags will be changed*. This means that when CX could possibly be set to 0, you must actively check for that case and skip the comparison if CX is indeed 0, as follows:

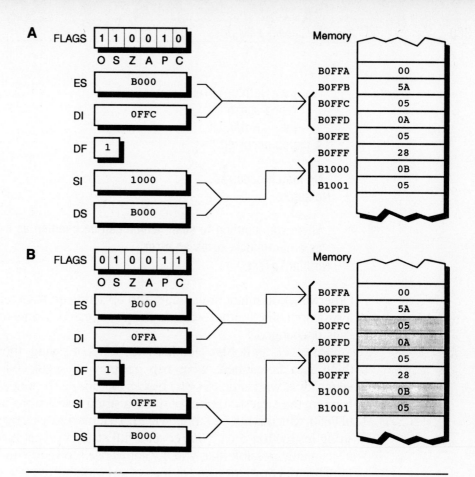

FIGURE 10.10   Another example of a string instruction advancing its pointers past the last location accessed. **(A)** The state of the PC before **cmpsw** executes. **(B)** The state of the PC after **cmpsw** executes. The words that are compared are shaded. You can see that **cmpsw** advances both SI and DI 1 word past the locations compared. Because DF is 1, SI and DI point to the start of the word *preceding* the words that were compared. When DF is 0, the pointers used by word-sized string instructions advance to the addresses immediately following (1 byte after) the words accessed. If DF had been 0 in this figure, DS:SI would have advanced to B000:1002 and ES:DI would have advanced to B000:0FFE, as those are the locations immediately above the words accessed. However, when DF is 1, as in this figure, the pointers advance to the addresses *2 bytes* before the words accessed. This is an inevitable result of the memory storage scheme of the 8088, whereby words are stored with the low byte at address *n* and the high byte at address *n*+1, with pointers aimed at the low byte.

```
      jcxz NothingToTest
      repnz scasb
      jnz   NoMatch
; A match occurred.
         :
; No match occurred.
NoMatch:
         :
; There was nothing to scan, which can be handled as a match,
; as a non-match, or as an error.
NothingToTest:
```

Otherwise, you might unwittingly end up acting on flags set by some earlier instruction, since either **scas** or **cmps** repeated 0 times will leave those flags unchanged.)

However, as Robert Heinlein was fond of saying, there ain't no such thing as a free lunch. What **rep** giveth with small (0-length) blocks it taketh away with large (64-Kb) blocks. Because a 0 count causes nothing to happen, the largest number of times a string instruction can be repeated is 0FFFFh, which is not 64 K but 64 K−1. That means that a byte-sized repeated string instruction can't *quite* cover a full segment. That can be a bother, as it's certainly possible that you'll want to use repeated string instructions to initialize or copy arrays and strings of any length from 0 to 64 K bytes. What to do?

First of all, let me point out that covering large blocks with *word-sized* repeated string instructions is never a problem. A mere 8000h repetitions of any word-sized string instruction will suffice to cover an entire segment; additional repetitions are useless. That brings us to another interesting point about string instructions: they can handle a maximum of 64 K bytes, but only *within a single segment.*

You'll surely recall that string instructions advance pointer registers. Those pointer registers are SI, DI, or both SI and DI. Notice that we didn't mention anything about advancing DS, ES, or any other segment register. That's because the string instructions don't affect the segment registers. The implication should be pretty obvious: like all the memory-addressing instructions of the 8088, the string instructions can access only those bytes that lie within the 64-Kb ranges of their associated segment registers, as shown in Figure 10.11. (We'll discuss the relationships between the segment registers and the string instructions in detail shortly.) Granted, **movs** and **cmps** can access source bytes in one 64-Kb block and destination bytes in another 64-Kb block, but each pointer register has a maximum range of 64 K, and that's that.

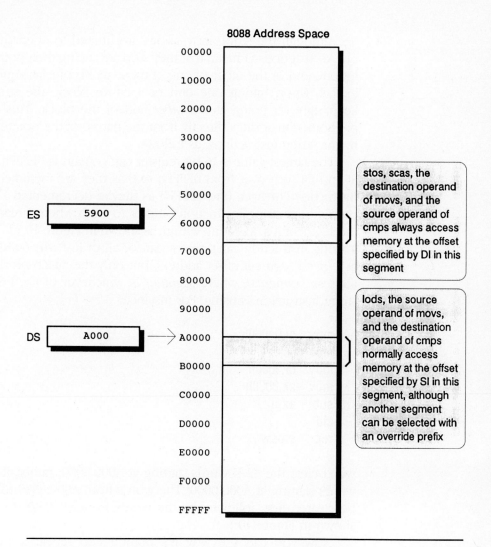

8088 Address Space

ES 5900

DS A000

stos, scas, the destination operand of movs, and the source operand of cmps always access memory at the offset specified by DI in this segment

lods, the source operand of movs, and the destination operand of cmps normally access memory at the offset specified by SI in this segment, although another segment can be selected with an override prefix

FIGURE 10.11   A given string instruction pointer register can access only memory locations lying within one of the four 64-Kb blocks pointed to by the segment registers. This is true no matter how many times a string instruction is repeated or what initial offset a string instruction's pointer or pointers are set to. Note that **stos**, **scas**, the destination operand of **movs**, and the source operand of **cmps** can access memory only within the segment pointed to by ES. However, **lods**, the source operand of **movs**, and the destination operand of **cmps** can access memory within any one of the four segments with the help of a segment override prefix, although they default to accessing the segment pointed to by DS.

Although the string instructions are limited to operating within 64-Kb blocks, that doesn't mean that they stop advancing their pointers when they hit one end or the other of one of those 64-Kb blocks—quite the contrary, in fact. Upon hitting one end of a 64-Kb block, the string instructions keep right on going at the *other* end of the block. This somewhat odd phenomenon springs directly from the nature of the pointer registers used by the string instructions, as follows.

The largest value a 16-bit register can contain is 0FFFFh. Consequently, SI and DI turn over from 0FFFFh to 0 as they are incremented by a string instruction (or from 0 to 0FFFFh as they're decremented.) This effectively causes each string instruction pointer to wrap when it reaches the end of the segment it's operating within, as shown in Figure 10.12. This means that a string instruction can't access part or all of just *any* 64-Kb block starting at a given segment:offset address, but only the 64-Kb block starting at the address *segment*:0, where *segment* is whichever of CS, DS, ES, or SS the string instruction is using. For instance,

```
mov    di,0a000h
mov    es,di
mov    di,8000h
mov    cx,8000h
sub    ax,ax
cld
rep    stosw
```

won't clear the 32 K words starting at A000:8000; rather, it clears the 32 K words starting at A000:0000. The words from A000:8000 to A000:FFFE will be cleared first, followed by the words from A000:0000 to A000:7FFE, as shown in Figure 10.13.

Now you can see why it's pointless to repeat a word-sized string instruction more than 8000h times. Repetitions after 8000h simply access the same addresses as the first 8000h repetitions, as shown in Figure 10.14.

That brings us back to the original problem of handling both 0-length and 64-Kb blocks that consist of byte-sized elements. It should be clear that there's no way that a single block of code can handle both 0-length and 64-Kb blocks unless the block length is stored in something larger than a 16-bit register. Handling both the 0-length and 64-Kb cases and everything in between takes 64 K+1 possible counter values, one more than the 64 K values that can be stored in 16 bits. Simply put, if CX is 0, that can mean *handle 0 bytes* or *handle 64 K bytes,* but it can't mean both.

If you want to take CX equal to 0 to mean *handle 0 bytes,* you're all set;

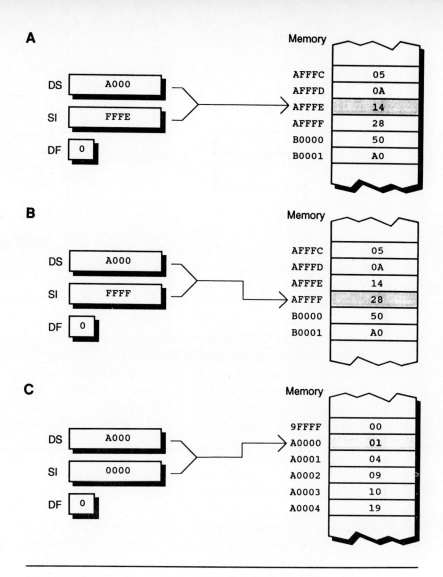

FIGURE 10.12   As a string instruction accesses memory at the end of
a segment with a pointer register, it wraps that register
to point back to the start of the segment. **(A)** A **lodsb**
instruction accessing memory 1 byte from the end of
the segment pointed to by DS. (In this and all other
parts of this figure, the memory location being accessed
is shaded.) **(B)** The next **lodsb** accessing the last byte
in the segment. **(C)** SI has advanced from 0FFFFh to 0,
wrapping back to the start of the segment, with the third
lodsb accessing the byte at offset 0. **(D)** The fourth **lodsb**
accessing the second byte in the segment, continuing on
normally from the start of the segment after the wrap.

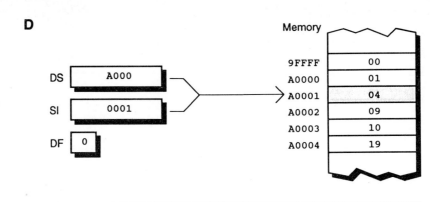

that's exactly how repeated string instructions work, as described above. For example, the subroutine **BlockClear** in Listing 10-11 clears a block of memory between 0 and 64 K-1 bytes in length; as called in Listing 10-11, **BlockClear** clears a 1000-byte block in 2.18 msec. If you want to take CX equal to 0 to mean *handle 64 K bytes,* however, you have to do a bit of work, but there's an opportunity for better performance there as well.

The obvious way to handle 64 K bytes with a single repeated string instruction is to perform 32 K word-sized operations. Now, that's fine for blocks that are exactly 64 K bytes long, but what about blocks from 1 to 64 K-1 bytes long? The length of such blocks may be an odd number of bytes, so we can't just divide the count by 2 and perform a word-sized repeated string instruction.

What we can do, however, is divide the byte count by 2, perform a word-sized repeated string instruction, and then make up the odd byte (if there is one) with a byte-sized unrepeated string instruction. The subroutine **BlockClear64** in Listing 10-12 does exactly that. Listing 10-12 divides the count by 2 with a **rcr** instruction, converting 0 counts into 32 K-word counts in the process. Next, **BlockClear64** clears memory in word-sized chunks with **rep stosw**. Finally, one extra **stosb** is performed if there was a carry from the **rcr** (that is, if the array is an odd number of bytes in length), in order to clear the last byte of the array.

Listing 10-12, unlike Listing 10-11, is capable of handling blocks between 1 and 64 K bytes long. The more interesting thing about Listing 10-12, however, is that it's *fast,* clocking in at 1.55 msec, about 41 percent faster than Listing 10-11. Why? Well, as we found earlier, we're better off using word-sized rather than byte-sized repeated string instructions. A side effect of Listing 10-12 is that initialization of byte-sized data is done almost entirely with word-sized string instructions, and that pays off handsomely.

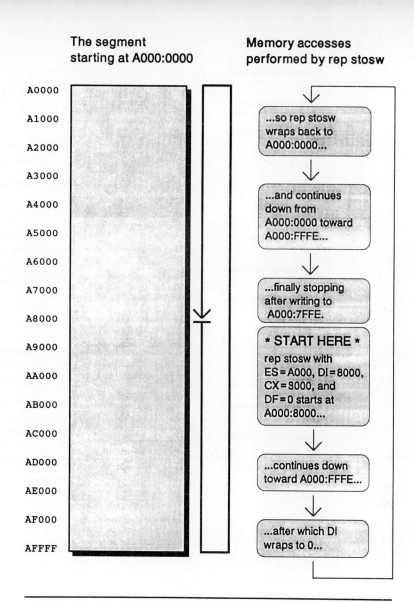

The segment starting at A000:0000

A0000
A1000
A2000
A3000
A4000
A5000
A6000
A7000
A8000
A9000
AA000
AB000
AC000
AD000
AE000
AF000
AFFFF

Memory accesses performed by rep stosw

...so rep stosw wraps back to A000:0000...

...and continues down from A000:0000 toward A000:FFFE...

...finally stopping after writing to A000:7FFE.

* START HERE *
rep stosw with ES=A000, DI=8000, CX=3000, and DF=0 starts at A000:8000...

...continues down toward A000:FFFE...

...after which DI wraps to 0...

FIGURE 10.13   Regardless of the offset within a segment at which a repeated string instruction starts, only the 64 K bytes starting at offset 0 within that segment can be accessed by that string instruction. Here **stosw** is repeated 8000h times starting at offset 8000h. After 4000h repetitions, DI reaches the end of the segment pointed to by ES and wraps back to the start of the segment. DI ultimately winds up right back at the same offset—8000h—at which it started, and it is the 64-Kb block starting at ES:0 that is accessed by **rep stosw**, rather than the 64-Kb block starting at A000:8000, the address to which ES:DI initially pointed.

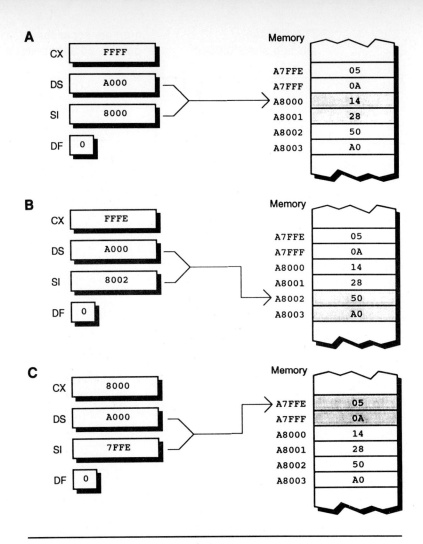

FIGURE 10.14 It's pointless to repeat a word-sized string instruction more than 8000h times, because the pointers will simply wrap back to addresses that were accessed earlier. **(A)** The first of 64 K−1 repetitions of **rep lodsw**, which accesses address A000:8000. (In this and all other parts of this figure, the memory location being accessed is shaded.) **(B)** The second repetition, which accesses address A000:8002. **(C)** Repetition 8000h, which accesses address A000:7FFE. **(D)** Repetition 8001h, which accesses address A000:8000 for the second time. There's not much point in accessing a memory location twice with a single repeated string instruction! (Yes, I know—there's also not much point to repeating **lodsw** 8000h times, or even twice. I'm doing it here only to illustrate a point, which I'll state again: word-sized string instructions repeated more than 8000h times do double duty for no good reason.)

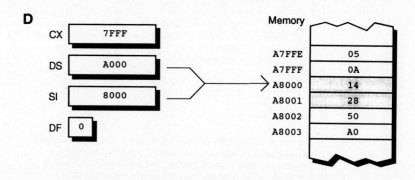

FIGURE 10.14 (*continued*)

```
1    ;
2    ; *** Listing 10-11 ***
3    ;
4    ; Clears a 1000-byte block of memory via BlockClear,
5    ; which handles blocks between 0 and 64K-1 bytes in
6    ; length.
7    ;
8            jmp     Skip
9    ;
10   ARRAY_LENGTH    equ     1000
11   ByteArray       db      ARRAY_LENGTH dup (?)
12   ;
13   ; Clears a block of memory CX bytes in length. A value
14   ; of 0 means "clear zero bytes," so the maximum length
15   ; that can be cleared is 64K-1 bytes and the minimum
16   ; length is 0 bytes.
17   ;
18   ; Input:
19   ;       CX = number of bytes to clear
20   ;       ES:DI = start of block to clear
21   ;
22   ; Output:
23   ;       none
24   ;
25   ; Registers altered: AL, CX, DI
26   ;
27   ; Direction flag cleared
28   ;
29   BlockClear:
30           sub     al,al   ;fill with zero
31           cld             ;make STOSB move DI up
32           rep     stosb   ;clear the block
33           ret
34   ;
35   Skip:
36           call    ZTimerOn
37           mov     di,seg ByteArray
38           mov     es,di   ;point ES:DI to the array to clear
```

```
39          mov     di,offset ByteArray
40          mov     cx,ARRAY_LENGTH ;# of bytes to clear
41          call    BlockClear      ;clear the array
42          call    ZTimerOff
```

```
1   ;
2   ; *** Listing 10-12 ***
3   ;
4   ; Clears a 1000-byte block of memory via BlockClear64,
5   ; which handles blocks between 1 and 64K bytes in
6   ; length. BlockClear64 gains the ability to handle
7   ; 64K blocks by using STOSW rather than STOSB to
8   ; the greatest possible extent, getting a performance
9   ; boost in the process.
10  ;
11          jmp     Skip
12  ;
13  ARRAY_LENGTH      equ     1000
14  ByteArray         db      ARRAY_LENGTH dup (?)
15  ;
16  ; Clears a block of memory CX bytes in length. A value
17  ; of 0 means "clear 64K bytes," so the maximum length
18  ; that can be cleared is 64K bytes and the minimum length
19  ; is 1 byte.
20  ;
21  ; Input:
22  ;       CX = number of bytes to clear
23  ;       ES:DI = start of block to clear
24  ;
25  ; Output:
26  ;       none
27  ;
28  ; Registers altered: AX, CX, DI
29  ;
30  ; Direction flag cleared
31  ;
32  BlockClear64:
33          sub     ax,ax   ;fill with zero a word at a time
34          stc             ;assume the count is zero-setting
35                          ; the Carry flag will give us 8000h
36                          ; after the RCR
37          jcxz    DoClear ;the count is zero
38          clc             ;it's not zero
39  DoClear:
40          rcr     cx,1    ;divide by 2, copying the odd-byte
41                          ; status to the Carry flag and
42                          ; shifting a 1 into bit 15 if and
43                          ; only if the count is zero
44          cld             ;make STOSW move DI up
45          rep     stosw   ;clear the block
46          jnc     ClearDone
47                          ;the Carry status is still left over
48                          ; from the RCR. If we had an even #
49                          ; of bytes, we're done
50          stosb           ;clear the odd byte
51  ClearDone:
52          ret
```

```
53        ;
54        Skip:
55                call     ZTimerOn
56                mov      di,seg ByteArray
57                mov      es,di   ;point ES:DI to the array to clear
58                mov      di,offset ByteArray
59                mov      cx,ARRAY_LENGTH ;# of bytes to clear
60                call     BlockClear64     ;clear the array
61                call     ZTimerOff
```

You need not be copying full 64-Kb blocks in order to use the approach of Listing 10-12. It's worth converting any byte-sized string instruction that's repeated more than a few times to use a word-sized string instruction followed by a final conditional byte-sized instruction. For instance, Listing 10-13 is functionally identical to Listing 10-11, but is 5 bytes longer and executes in just 1.54 msec, thanks to the use of a word-sized **rep stos**. That's the same 41 percent improvement that we got in Listing 10-12, which isn't surprising considering that Listings 10-12 and 10-13 both spend virtually all their time performing repeated **stosw** instructions. I'm sure you'll agree that a 41 percent speed increase is quite a return for the expenditure of 5 bytes.

Once again: *use word-sized rather than byte-sized repeated string instructions whenever you can.*

```
 1        ;
 2        ; *** Listing 10-13 ***
 3        ;
 4        ; Clears a 1000-byte block of memory via BlockClearW,
 5        ; which handles blocks between 0 and 64K-1 bytes in
 6        ; length. BlockClearW uses STOSW rather than STOSB to
 7        ; the greatest possible extent in order to improve
 8        ; performance.
 9        ;
10                jmp      Skip
11        ;
12        ARRAY_LENGTH      equ      1000
13        ByteArray         db       ARRAY_LENGTH dup (?)
14        ;
15        ; Clears a block of memory CX bytes in length. A value
16        ; of 0 means "clear zero bytes," so the maximum length
17        ; that can be cleared is 64K-1 bytes and the minimum
18        ; length is 0 bytes.
19        ;
20        ; Input:
21        ;       CX = number of bytes to clear
22        ;       ES:DI = start of block to clear
23        ;
24        ; Output:
25        ;       none
26        ;
27        ; Registers altered: AX, CX, DI
28        ;
```

```
29    ; Direction flag cleared
30    ;
31    BlockClearW:
32            sub     ax,ax   ;we'll fill with the value 0
33            shr     cx,1    ;divide by 2, copying the odd-byte
34                            ; status to the Carry flag
35            cld             ;make STOSW move DI up
36            rep     stosw   ;clear the block
37            jnc     ClearDone
38                            ;the Carry status is still left over
39                            ; from the SHR. If we had an even #
40                            ; of bytes, we're done
41            stosb           ;clear the odd byte
42    ClearDone:
43            ret
44    ;
45    Skip:
46            call    ZTimerOn
47            mov     di,seg ByteArray
48            mov     es,di   ;point ES:DI to the array to clear
49            mov     di,offset ByteArray
50            mov     cx,ARRAY_LENGTH ;# of bytes to clear
51            call    BlockClearW     ;clear the array
52            call    ZTimerOff
```

Words of Caution

Before we take our leave of the issue of byte- versus word-sized repeated string instructions, I'd like to give you a couple of warnings about the use of word-sized string instructions.

You must exercise additional caution when using word-sized string instructions on the 8086, 80286, and 80386 processors. The 8086 and 80286 processors access word-sized data that start at an even address (word-aligned data) twice as fast as they do word-sized data that start at an odd address. This means that code such as that in Listing 10-13 would run at only half speed on an 8086 or 80286 if the array happened to start at an odd address. This can be solved by altering the code to detect whether arrays start at odd or even addresses and then performing byte moves as needed to ensure that the bulk of the operation—performed with a repeated word-sized instruction—is word-aligned.

The 80386 has similar constraints involving doubleword alignment. We'll discuss the issue of word and doubleword alignment in detail in Chapter 15. For now just be aware that although the word-sized string instruction rule for the 8088 is simple—use word-sized string instructions whenever possible—there are additional considerations involving alignment for the other members of the 8086 family.

The second warning concerns the use of word-sized string instructions to access EGA and VGA display memory in modes 0Dh, 0Eh, 0Fh, 10h, and

12h. In each of these modes it's possible to copy 4 bytes of video data at once (1 byte from each of the four planes) by loading the 4 bytes into four special latches in the adapter with a single read and then storing the contents of all four latches back to display memory with a single write, as shown in Figure 10.15. Use of the latches can greatly speed graphics code; for example, copying via the latches can improve the performance of tasks that require block copies from one part of display memory to another, such as scrolling, by a factor of four over normal byte-at-a-time copying techniques.

Unfortunately, because each latch can store only 1 byte, the latches work properly only with byte-sized string instructions. Word-sized string instructions cause the latches to be loaded twice per word-sized read from display memory: once for the lower byte of each word, then again for the upper byte, wiping out the data read from the lower byte. Consequently, only half of each word is really transferred. The end result is that half the data you'd expect to copy is missing, and the other half is copied twice.

The EGA/VGA latches are complex, and now is not the time to describe them in detail. We'll return to the latches in Volume II of *Zen of Assembly Language*. For now, remember this: don't use word-sized string instructions to copy data from one area to another of EGA/VGA display memory via the latches.

Segment Overrides: Sometimes You Can, Sometimes You Can't

We've said that string instructions advance only their pointer registers, not their segment registers, so they can access memory only within the 64-Kb block addressed by a given segment register. That raises the questions of which segments the string instructions access by default and when the default segment selections can be overridden.

The rules for default segments are simple. String instructions that use DI as a pointer register (**stos** and **movs** for the destination operand and **scas** and **cmps** for the source operand) use DI as an offset in the ES segment. String instructions that use SI as a pointer register (**lods** and **movs** for the source operand, and **cmps** for the destination operand) use SI as an offset in the DS segment.

The rule for segment overrides is equally simple. Accesses via DI must go to the ES segment; that cannot be overridden. Accesses via SI default to the DS segment, but that default can be overridden. In other words, the source segment for **lods** and **movs** and the destination segment for **cmps**

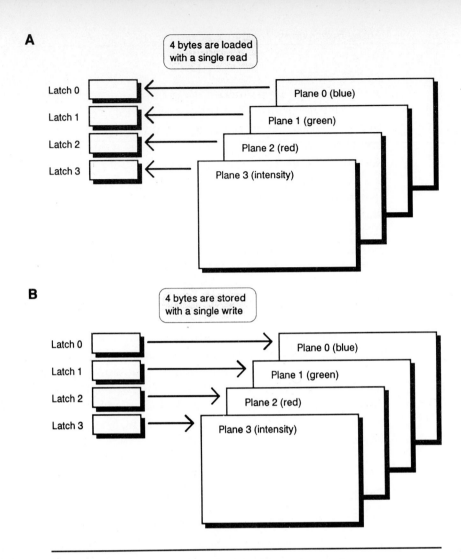

A

4 bytes are loaded
with a single read

Latch 0 ← Plane 0 (blue)

Latch 1 ← Plane 1 (green)

Latch 2 ← Plane 2 (red)

Latch 3 ← Plane 3 (intensity)

B

4 bytes are stored
with a single write

Latch 0 → Plane 0 (blue)

Latch 1 → Plane 1 (green)

Latch 2 → Plane 2 (red)

Latch 3 → Plane 3 (intensity)

FIGURE 10.15 The internal latches of the EGA and VGA can be used to copy 4 bytes from one display memory location to another with a single byte-sized read followed by a single byte-sized write, effectively quadrupling the speed at which blocks of display memory copy be copied. **(A)** A single byte-sized read can load all four latches at once, with each latch receiving 1 byte from the corresponding plane. **(B)** A single byte-sized write can then store the contents of all four latches back to the corresponding planes. Unfortunately, each latch can only store a byte, so word-sized string instructions (or, for that matter, word-sized memory accesses of any sort) don't work properly when the latches are used.

can be any of the four segments, but the destination segment for **stos** and **movs** and the source segment for **scas** and **cmps** must be ES.

How do we tell MASM to override the segment for those string instructions that allow segment overrides? While we're at it, how do we specify the size—word or byte—of a string instruction's data? Both answers lie in the slightly unusual way in which string instructions are coded in 8088 assembler.

String instructions are odd in that operands are optional. The **stosb** instruction with no operands means *perform a byte-sized **stos***, and the **cmpsw** instruction with no operands means *perform a word-sized **cmps**.* There really isn't any need for explicit operands to string instructions, because the memory operands are always specified by the contents of the SI, DI, and segment registers.

However, MASM is a strongly typed assembler, meaning that MASM considers named memory operands to have inherent types—byte, word, and so on. Consequently, MASM lets you provide operands to string instructions, *even though those operands have no effect on the memory location actually accessed!* MASM uses operands to string instructions to check segment accessibility (by way of the **assume** directive, which is a bit of a kludge—but that's another story), to decide whether to assemble byte- or word-sized string instructions, and to decide whether to perform segment overrides—and that's all.

For example, the following is a valid **movs** instruction that copies **SourceWord** to **DestWord**:

```
SourceWord      dw  1
DestWord        dw  ?
        :
        mov  si,seg SourceWord
        mov  ds,si
        mov  si,offset SourceWord
        mov  di,seg DestWord
        mov  es,di
        mov  di,offset DestWord
        movs es:[DestWord],[SourceWord]
```

There's something strange here, though, and that's that the operands to **movs** have *nothing* to do with the source and destination addresses.

Why? String instructions don't explicitly specify addresses at all; they're only 1 byte long, so there isn't room for a *mod-reg-rm* byte, let alone a displacement. Instead, string instructions use whatever addresses are already in DS:SI and ES:DI. By providing operands to **movs** in the last example, you've simply told the assembler to *assume* that DS:SI points to **SourceWord** and ES:DI points to **DestWord**. The assembler uses that information only to decide to assemble a **movsw** rather than a **movsb**, as the operands are word sized. If you had set up SI or DI to point to a different variable, the assembler would never have known, and the **movs** operands would only have served to confuse you when you tried to debug the program. For example,

```
SourceWord      dw   1
DestWord        dw   ?
        :
    mov   di,seg SourceWord
    mov   es,di
    mov   di,offset SourceWord
    mov   si,seg DestWord
    mov   ds,si
    mov   si,offset DestWord
    movs  es:[DestWord],[SourceWord]
```

actually copies **DestWord** to **SourceWord**, despite the operands to **movs**. Seems pretty silly, doesn't it? That's MASM, though.

(Actually, that's not the worst of it. Try assembling

```
movs byte ptr es:[bx],byte ptr [di]
```

which features not one but *two* memory-addressing modes that can't be used by **movs**. MASM cheerfully assembles this line without complaint; it already knows the addressing modes used by **movs**, so it pays little attention to the modes you specify.)

In short, operands to string instructions can be misleading and don't really provide any data-type information that the simple suffixes **b** and **w** on string instructions don't. Consequently, I prefer to steer clear of string instruction operands in favor of autonomous string instructions such as **scasb** and **lodsw**. However, there's one case where operands are quite useful, and that's when you want to force a segment override.

Recall from Chapter 7 that a prefix like **ES:** can be placed on a memory operand in order to force a segment override on that memory access. Segment overrides work in just the same way with string instructions. For instance, we can modify our ongoing example to copy **SourceWord** to **DestWord**, with both operands accessed in ES, as follows:

```
SourceWord      dw  1
DestWord        dw  ?
        :
    mov  si,seg SourceWord
    mov  es,si
    mov  si,offset SourceWord
    mov  di,offset DestWord
    movs es:[DestWord],es:[SourceWord]
```

The segment override on **SourceWord** forces the 8088 to access the source operand at ES:SI rather than the default of DS:SI.

This is a less-than-ideal approach, however. For one thing, I'm still not fond of using meaningless and potentially misleading memory operands with string instructions. For another, there are many cases where SI and/or DI are passed to a subroutine that uses a string instruction, or where SI and/or DI can be set to point to any one of a number of memory locations before a string instruction is executed. In these cases, there simply isn't any single memory variable name that can legitimately be assigned to an operand.

Fortunately, there's an easy solution: specify the memory operands to string instructions as consisting of only the pointer registers in the form **[SI]** and **[DI]**. Here's our ongoing example with the pointer-register approach:

```
SourceWord      dw  1
DestWord        dw  ?
        :
    mov  si,seg SourceWord
    mov  es,si
    mov  si,offset SourceWord
    mov  di,offset DestWord
    movs word ptr es:[di],word ptr es:[si]
```

This code is acceptable, as the operands to **movs** merely confirm what we already know, that **movs** copies the data pointed to by SI to the location pointed to by DI. Note that the operator **word ptr** is required because the **movsw** form of **movs** doesn't accept operands (yet another quirk of MASM).

Now that we have a decent solution to the problem of generating segment overrides to string instructions, let's review what we've learned. The entire point of our discussion of operands to string instructions is simply that such operands make it possible to perform segment overrides with string instructions. If you don't need to perform segment overrides, I strongly suggest that you skip the operands altogether. Here's my preferred version of the first example in this section:

```
SourceWord      dw  1
DestWord        dw  ?
        :
    mov si,seg SourceWord
    mov ds,si
    mov si,offset SourceWord
    mov di,seg DestWord
    mov es,di
    mov di,offset DestWord
    movsw
```

A final note. You may be tempted to try something like

```
movs    byte ptr ds:[di],byte ptr [si]
```

After all, it would be awfully convenient if string instruction accesses via DI didn't always have to be in ES. Go right ahead and try it, if you wish—but it won't work. It won't even assemble. (The same goes for trying to use registers or addressing modes other than those I've shown as operands to string instructions; MASM either ignores the operands or spits them out with an error message.)

Segment overrides on string instruction accesses via DI don't assemble because the ES segment must *always* be used when string instructions access operands addressed by DI. Why? There is no particular reason: that's just the way the 8088 works. The 8088 doesn't have to make sense; inside the universe of PC programming, the quirks of the 8088 become laws of nature. Understanding those laws and making the best possible use of them is what the Zen of assembly language is all about.

Then, too, if you had to choose one segment to be stuck with, it would certainly be ES. CS and SS can't be changed freely, and DS is often dedicated to maintaining a near data segment, but ES is usually free to point anywhere in memory. Remember also that the segments of all SI operands to string instructions can be overridden, so string instructions can access *any* operand—source, destination, or both—via the ES segment if that becomes necessary.

The good and the bad of segment overrides.   Should you use segment overrides with string instructions? That depends on the situation. Segment override prefixes take up 1 byte and take 2 cycles to execute, so you're better off without them if that's possible. When you use a string instruction repeatedly within a loop, you should generally set up the segment registers outside the loop in such a way that the string instruction can use its default segment or segments. If, on the other hand, you're using a string instruction to perform a single memory access, a segment override prefix is preferable to all the code required to set up the default segment registers for that instruction.

For example, suppose that we're calculating the 8-bit checksum of a 1000-byte array residing in a far segment. Listing 10-14, which reads the 1000 elements via a **lods** with an **ES:** prefix, runs in 9.06 msec. In contrast, Listing 10-15, which juggles the registers so that DS points to the array's segment for the duration of the loop, runs in just 7.56 msec.

```
1  ;
2  ; *** Listing 10-14 ***
3  ;
4  ; Generates the 8-bit checksum of a 1000-byte array
5  ; using LODS with an ES: override.
6  ;
7          jmp      Skip
8  ;
9  FarSeg  segment  para
10 ARRAY_LENGTH     equ      1000
11 ByteArray        db       ARRAY_LENGTH dup (0)
12 FarSeg  ends
13 Skip:
14          call     ZTimerOn
15          mov      si,seg ByteArray
16          mov      es,si    ;point ES:SI to the array to
17                            ; checksum
18          mov      si,offset ByteArray
19          mov      cx,ARRAY_LENGTH ;# of bytes to checksum
20          sub      ah,ah    ;zero the checksum counter
21          cld               ;make LODS move the pointer up
22 ChecksumLoop:
23          lods     byte ptr es:[si]
24                            ;get the next byte to checksum
25          add      ah,al    ;add the byte into the checksum
26          loop     ChecksumLoop
27          call     ZTimerOff
```

```
1  ;
2  ; *** Listing 10-15 ***
3  ;
4  ; Generates the 8-bit checksum of a 1000-byte array
5  ; using LODS without a segment override, by setting
6  ; DS up to point to the far segment for the duration
7  ; of the loop.
8  ;
9          jmp      Skip
10 ;
```

```
11    FarSeg  segment para
12    ARRAY_LENGTH    equ     1000
13    ByteArray       db      ARRAY_LENGTH dup (0)
14    FarSeg  ends
15    Skip:
16            call    ZTimerOn
17            push    ds      ;preserve the normal DS setting
18            mov     si,seg ByteArray
19            mov     ds,si   ;point DS to the far segment for
20                            ; the duration of the loop-we
21                            ; won't need the normal DS setting
22                            ; until the loop is done
23            mov     si,offset ByteArray
24            mov     cx,ARRAY_LENGTH
25            sub     ah,ah   ;zero the checksum counter
26            cld             ;make LODSB move the pointer up
27    ChecksumLoop:
28            lodsb           ;get the next byte to checksum
29            add     ah,al   ;add the byte into the checksum
30            loop    ChecksumLoop
31            pop     ds      ;retrieve the normal DS setting
32            call    ZTimerOff
```

Now suppose that we're reading a single memory location—also located in a far segment—with **lods**. Listing 10-16, which does this by loading ES and using an **ES:** override, runs in 10.35 μsec per byte read. Listing 10-17, which first preserves DS, then loads DS and reads the memory location via DS, the default segment for **lods**, and finally pops DS, runs in a considerably more leisurely 15.06 μsec per byte read. In this situation it pays to use the segment override.

```
1     ;
2     ; *** Listing 10-16 ***
3     ;
4     ; Reads a single byte stored in a far segment by
5     ; using a segment override prefix.
6     ;
7             jmp     Skip
8     ;
9     FarSeg  segment para
10    MemVar  db      0       ;this variable resides in a
11                            ; far segment
12    FarSeg  ends
13    ;
14    Skip:
15            call    ZTimerOn
16            rept    100
17            mov     si,seg MemVar
18            mov     es,si
19            mov     si,offset MemVar ;point ES:SI to MemVar
20            lods    byte ptr es:[si] ;read MemVar
21            endm
22            call    ZTimerOff
```

```
1   ;
2   ; *** Listing 10-17 ***
3   ;
4   ; Reads a single byte stored in a far segment by
5   ; temporarily pointing DS to the far segment.
6   ;
7           jmp       Skip
8   ;
9   FarSeg  segment para
10  MemVar  db        0         ;this variable resides in a
11                              ; far segment
12  FarSeg  ends
13  ;
14  Skip:
15          call      ZTimerOn
16          rept      100
17          push      ds        ;preserve the normal data segment
18          mov       si,seg MemVar
19          mov       ds,si
20          mov       si,offset MemVar ;point DS:SI to MemVar
21          lodsb               ;read MemVar
22          pop       ds        ;retrieve the normal data segment
23          endm
24          call      ZTimerOff
```

By the way, there's an opportunity for tremendous performance improvement in Listing 10-16. The trick: just leave ES set for as long as necessary. Listing 10-18 performs exactly the same task as Listing 10-16, except that ES is loaded only once, at the start of the program. The result: an execution time of just 5.87 msec per byte read, a 76 percent improvement over Listing 10-16. What that means is that you should . . .

```
1   ;
2   ; *** Listing 10-18 ***
3   ;
4   ; Reads a single byte stored in a far segment by
5   ; using a segment override prefix. Loads ES just
6   ; once and then leaves ES set to point to the far
7   ; segment at all times.
8   ;
9           jmp       Skip
10  ;
11  FarSeg  segment para
12  MemVar  db        0         ;this variable resides in a
13                              ; far segment
14  FarSeg  ends
15  ;
16  Skip:
17          call      ZTimerOn
18          mov       si,seg MemVar
19          mov       es,si     ;point ES to the far segment for
20                              ; the remainder of the test
21          rept      100
22          mov       si,offset MemVar ;point ES:SI to MemVar
23          lods      byte ptr es:[si] ;read MemVar
24          endm
25          call      ZTimerOff
```

Leave ES and/or DS Set for as Long as Possible

When you're accessing far data, leave ES and/or DS (whichever you're using) set for as long as possible. This rule may seem impractical, as it prevents the use of those registers to point to any other area of memory, but properly applied it has tremendous benefits.

For example, you can leave DS set for the duration of a loop that scans a far data array, as we did in Listing 10-15. This is one of the areas in which you can outshine any compiler. Typically, compilers reload both the segment and offset portions of far pointers on every use, even inside a loop. Listing 10-19, which is the sort of code a high level language compiler would generate for the task of Listing 10-15, takes 25.14 msec to execute. Listing 10-15 is *232 percent* faster than Listing 10-19, and the difference is due entirely to the superior ability of the assembler programmer to deal with string instructions and segments. (Actually, Listing 10-19 is *more* efficient than the code generated by most high-level language compilers would be, since it keeps the checksum in a byte-sized register rather than in a memory variable and uses a **loop** instruction rather than decrementing a counter stored in memory.)

```
1    ;
2    ; *** Listing 10-19 ***
3    ;
4    ; Generates the 8-bit checksum of a 1000-byte array
5    ; by loading both segment and offset from a far
6    ; pointer each time through the loop and without
7    ; using string instructions, as the code generated
8    ; by a typical high-level language compiler would.
9    ;
10           jmp     Skip
11   ;
12   FarSeg  segment para
13   ARRAY_LENGTH    equ       1000
14   ByteArray       db        ARRAY_LENGTH dup (0)
15                                     ;this array resides in a
16                                     ; far segment
17   FarSeg  ends
18   ;
19   FarPtr  dd        ByteArray       ;a far pointer to the array
20   ;
21   Skip:
22           call    ZTimerOn
23           mov     cx,ARRAY_LENGTH ;# of bytes to checksum
24           sub     ah,ah           ;zero the checksum counter
25   ChecksumLoop:
26           les     bx,[FarPtr]     ;load both segment and
27                                   ; offset from the far
28                                   ; pointer
29           inc     word ptr [FarPtr]
30                                   ;advance the offset portion
```

```
31                                ; of the far pointer
32          add      ah,es:[bx]   ;add the next byte to the
33                                ; checksum
34          loop     ChecksumLoop
35          call     ZTimerOff
```

As an example of leaving ES set for as long as possible, I once wrote and sold a game in which ES contained the display memory segment 0B800h for the entire duration of the game. My program spent so much of its time drawing that it was worth dedicating ES to a single area of memory in order to save the cycles that would otherwise have been expended on preserving and reloading ES during each call to the video driver. I'm not saying this is generally a good idea (in fact, it's not, because it sharply restricts the use of the most flexible segment register), but rather that this is the sort of unusual approach that's worth considering when you're looking to turbocharge your code.

rep and Segment Prefixes Don't Mix

One case in which you should exercise extreme caution when using segment overrides is in conjunction with repeated string instructions. The reason: the 8088 has the annoying habit of remembering a maximum of 1 prefix byte when a string instruction is interrupted by a hardware interrupt and then continues after an **iret**. Because **rep** is a prefix byte, and segment overrides are prefix bytes, a repeated string instruction with a segment override has two prefix bytes—and that's one too many. You're pretty much guaranteed to have erratic and unreproducible bugs in any code that uses instructions such as

```
rep   movs byte ptr es:[di],byte ptr es:[si]
```

If you have some time-critical task that absolutely requires the use of a repeated string instruction with a segment override, you must turn off interrupts before executing the instruction. With interrupts disabled, there's no chance that the repeated string instruction will be messed up by an interrupt and subsequent **iret**. However, this technique should be used only as a last resort, because it involves disabling interrupts for the potentially lengthy duration of a repeated string instruction. If interrupts are kept disabled for too long, then keystrokes, mouse actions, and serial data can be lost or corrupted. The preferred solution is to reduce the 2 prefix bytes to just one—the **rep** prefix—by juggling the segments so that the repeated string instruction can use its default segments.

On to String Instruction Applications

We haven't covered *everything* there is to know about the string instructions, but we have touched on the important points. Now we're ready to see the string instructions in action. To an assembler programmer, that's a pleasant sight indeed.

Chapter 11

String Instruction Applications

11.1   String Handling with lods and stos

11.2   Block Handling with movs

11.3   Searching with scas

11.4   Comparing Memory with Memory Using cmps

11.5   A Note about Returning Values

11.6   Putting String Instructions to Work in Unlikely Places

11.7   A Note on Handling Blocks Larger Than 64 K Bytes

Now that we've got a solid understanding of what the string instructions do, let's look at a few applications to get a sense of what they're particularly good for. The applications we'll look at include copying arrays, searching strings for characters, looking up entries in tables, comparing strings, and animation.

There's a lot of meat in this chapter, and a lot of useful code. The code isn't fully fleshed out, as I'm trying to illustrate basic principles rather than provide you with a library from A to Z, but that's actually all to the good. You can build on this code to meet your specific needs or write your own code from scratch once you understand the ins and outs of the string instructions. In either case, you'll be better off with code customized to suit your purposes than you would be using any one-size-fits-all code I could provide.

I'll frequently contrast the string instruction–based implementations with versions built around nonstring instructions. This should give you a greater appreciation for the string instructions and may shed new light on the nonstring instructions as well. I'll tell you ahead of time how the comparisons will turn out: in almost every case the string instructions will prove to be vastly superior. The lesson we learned in the last chapter holds true: *use the string instructions to the hilt!* There's nothing like them under the 8088 sun.

Contrasting string and nonstring implementations also reinforces an important point. There are many, many ways to accomplish any given task on the 8088. It's knowing which approach to choose that separates the journeyman programmer from the guru.

11.1 ◆ String Handling with lods and stos

The **lods** instruction is an odd bird among string instructions, being the only one that doesn't benefit in the least from **rep**. While **rep** does work with **lods**, in that it causes **lods** to repeat multiple times, the combination of the two is nonetheless totally impractical. What good could it possibly do to load AL twice (to say nothing of 64 K−1 times)? Without **rep**, **lods** is still better than **mov**, but not *that* much better; **lods** certainly doesn't generate the quantum jump in performance that **rep stos** and **rep movs** do. So, when *does* **lods** really shine?

It turns out that **lods** is what might be called a synergistic instruction; it is at its best when used with **stos** (or sometimes **scas** or even nonstring instructions) in a loop. Together, **lods** and **stos** let you load an array or string element into AL, test and/or modify it, and then write the element back to either the original array or a new one, as shown in Figure 11.1. You might think of the **lods**-process-**stos** combination as being a sort of meta-**movs** with which you can whip up customized memory-to-memory moves as needed. Of course, **lods/stos** is slower than **movs** (especially **rep movs**), but by the same token **lods/stos** is far more flexible. Besides, **lods/stos** isn't *that* slow—*all* the 8088's memory-accessing instructions suffer by comparison with **movs**. Placed inside a loop, the **lods/stos** combination makes for fairly speedy array and string processing.

For example, Listing 11-1 copies a string to a new location, converting all characters to upper case in the process, by using a loop containing **lods** and **stos**. Listing 11-1 takes just 773 μsec to copy and convert. By contrast, Listing 11-2, which uses nonstring instructions to perform the same task, takes 921 μsec to perform the copy and conversion.

By the way, Listing 11-1 could just as easily have converted **Source-String** to upper case in place, rather than copying the converted text to **DestString**. This would be accomplished simply by loading both DS:SI and ES:DI to point to **SourceString**, as shown in Listing 11-3, which changes nothing else from Listing 11-1.

Why is this interesting? It's interesting because two pointers—DS:SI and ES:DI—are used to point to a single array. It's often faster to maintain two pointers and use **lods** and **stos** than it is to use a single pointer with nonstring instructions, as in Listing 11-4. Listing 11-3 runs in 771 μsec, about the same as Listing 11-1 (after all, they're virtually identical). However, Listing 11-4 takes 838 μsec, even though it uses only one pointer to point to the array being converted to upper case.

The **lods/stos** pair lies somewhere between the repeated string instructions and the nonstring instructions in terms of performance and flexibility. It isn't as fast as any of the repeated string instructions, both because two instructions are involved and because it can't be used with a **rep** prefix but must instead be placed in a loop. However, **lods/stos** is a good deal more flexible than any repeated string instruction, because once a memory operand is loaded into AL or AX it can be tested and manipulated easily (and often quickly as well, thanks to the accumulator-specific instructions).

On the other hand, the **lods/stos** pair is certainly faster than nonstring instructions, as Listings 11-1 through 11-4 illustrate. However, **lods/stos** is not as flexible as the nonstring instructions, because DS:SI and ES:DI must be used as pointer registers and only the accumulator can be loaded from and stored to memory.

On balance, the **lods/stos** pair overcomes some but not all of the limitations of repeated string instructions and does so at a substantial

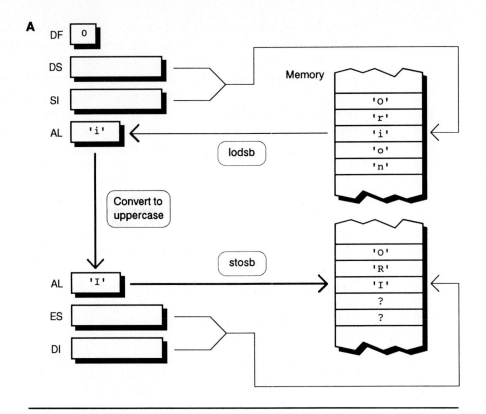

FIGURE 11.1   Together, **lods** and **stos** provide fast, flexible array and
string handling. This figure illustrates that principle by
showing the use of **lodsb** and **stosb** to copy an array,
converting all lower case characters to upper case in the
process, with the following code:

```
        cld
LoopTop:
        lodsb           ;get the next character
        cmp   al,'a'    ;is it below the lowercase range?
        jb    IsUpper   ;yes-we're all set
        cmp   al,'z'    ;is it above the lowercase range?
        ja    IsUpper   ;yes-we're all set
        and   al,not 20h ;it's lowercase-make it uppercase
IsUpper
        stosb           ;save the uppercase character to
                        ; the destination
        loop  LoopTop   ;copy & convert the next character
```

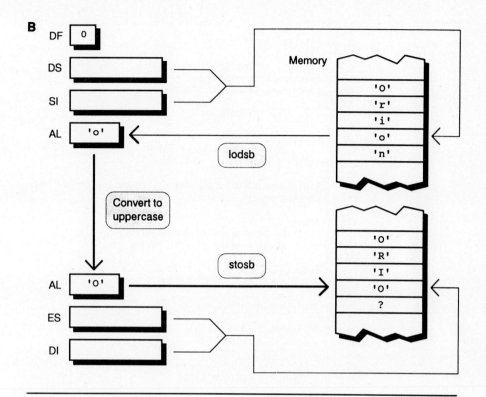

(A) The copying and conversion of the third character in the array. (B) The copying and conversion of the fourth character. These two figures illustrate a significant advantage of using **lods/stos** for array and string processing, which is that, like all string instructions, **lods** and **stos** automatically advance their pointers.

You could think of the step labelled *Convert to uppercase* in each figure as a sort of black box between **lodsb** and **stosb**. Once **lods** has loaded a source value into AL or AX, any sort of testing or conversion can be performed before **stos** stores the result to the destination string or array. This gives the **lods/stos** pair unparalleled flexibility among the string instructions, albeit at a price in performance.

FIGURE 11.1   (*continued*)

```
1    ;
2    ; *** Listing 11-1 ***
3    ;
4    ; Copies a string to another string, converting all
5    ; characters to uppercase in the process, using a loop
6    ; containing LODSB and STOSB.
7    ;
8            jmp     Skip
9    ;
10   SourceString    label   word
11           db      'This space intentionally left not blank',0
12   DestString      db      100 dup (?)
13   ;
14   ; Copies one zero-terminated string to another string,
15   ; converting all characters to uppercase.
16   ;
17   ; Input:
18   ;       DS:SI = start of source string
19   ;       ES:DI = start of destination string
20   ;
21   ; Output:
22   ;       none
23   ;
24   ; Registers altered: AL, BX, SI, DI
25   ;
26   ; Direction flag cleared
27   ;
28   ; Note: Does not handle strings that are longer than 64K
29   ;       bytes or cross segment boundaries. Does not handle
30   ;       overlapping strings.
31   ;
32   CopyStringUpper:
33           mov     bl,'a'  ;set up for fast register-register
34           mov     bh,'z'  ; comparisons
35           cld
36   StringUpperLoop:
37           lodsb           ;get the next character and
38                           ; point to the following character
39           cmp     al,bl   ;below 'a'?
40           jb      IsUpper ;yes, not lowercase
41           cmp     al,bh   ;above 'z'?
42           ja      IsUpper ;yes, not lowercase
43           and     al,not 20h ;is lowercase-make uppercase
44   IsUpper:
45           stosb           ;put the uppercase character into
46                           ; the new string and point to the
47                           ; following character
48           and     al,al   ;is this the zero that marks the
49                           ; end of the string?
50           jnz     StringUpperLoop ;no, do the next character
51           ret
52   ;
53   Skip:
54           call    ZTimerOn
55           mov     si,offset SourceString  ;point DS:SI to the
56                                           ; string to copy from
57           mov     di,seg DestString
58           mov     es,di                   ;point ES:DI to the
59           mov     di,offset DestString    ; string to copy to
```

```
60              call    CopyStringUpper         ;copy & convert to
61                                              ; uppercase
62              call    ZTimerOff


1       ;
2       ; *** Listing 11-2 ***
3       ;
4       ; Copies a string to another string, converting all
5       ; characters to uppercase in the process, using a loop
6       ; containing non-string instructions.
7       ;
8               jmp     Skip
9       ;
10      SourceString    label   word
11              db      'This space intentionally left not blank',0
12      DestString      db      100 dup (?)
13      ;
14      ; Copies one zero-terminated string to another string,
15      ; converting all characters to uppercase.
16      ;
17      ; Input:
18      ;       DS:SI = start of source string
19      ;       ES:DI = start of destination string
20      ;
21      ; Output:
22      ;       none
23      ;
24      ; Registers altered: AL, BX, SI, DI
25      ;
26      ; Note: Does not handle strings that are longer than 64K
27      ;       bytes or cross segment boundaries.
28      ;
29      CopyStringUpper:
30              mov     bl,'a'  ;set up for fast register-register
31              mov     bh,'z'  ; comparisons
32      StringUpperLoop:
33              mov     al,[si] ;get the next character
34              inc     si      ;point to the following character
35              cmp     al,bl   ;below 'a'?
36              jb      IsUpper ;yes, not lowercase
37              cmp     al,bh   ;above 'z'?
38              ja      IsUpper ;yes, not lowercase
39              and     al,not 20h ;is lowercase-make uppercase
40      IsUpper:
41              mov     es:[di],al ;put the uppercase character into
42                              ; the new string
43              inc     di      ;point to the following character
44              and     al,al   ;is this the zero that marks the
45                              ; end of the string?
46              jnz     StringUpperLoop ;no, do the next character
47              ret
48      ;
49      Skip:
50              call    ZTimerOn
51              mov     si,offset SourceString  ;point DS:SI to the
52                                              ; string to copy from
53              mov     di,seg DestString
```

```
54              mov     es,di                   ;point ES:DI to the
55              mov     di,offset DestString    ; string to copy to
56              call    CopyStringUpper         ;copy & convert to
57                                              ; uppercase
58              call    ZTimerOff
```

```
 1      ;
 2      ; *** Listing 11-3 ***
 3      ;
 4      ; Converts all characters in a string to uppercase,
 5      ; using a loop containing LODSB and STOSB and using
 6      ; two pointers.
 7      ;
 8              jmp     Skip
 9      ;
10      SourceString    label   word
11              db              'This space intentionally left not blank',0
12      ;
13      ; Copies one zero-terminated string to another string,
14      ; converting all characters to uppercase.
15      ;
16      ; Input:
17      ;       DS:SI = start of source string
18      ;       ES:DI = start of destination string
19      ;
20      ; Output:
21      ;       none
22      ;
23      ; Registers altered: AL, BX, SI, DI
24      ;
25      ; Direction flag cleared
26      ;
27      ; Note: Does not handle strings that are longer than 64K
28      ;       bytes or cross segment boundaries.
29      ;
30      CopyStringUpper:
31              mov     bl,'a'  ;set up for fast register-register
32              mov     bh,'z'  ; comparisons
33              cld
34      StringUpperLoop:
35              lodsb           ;get the next character and
36                              ; point to the following character
37              cmp     al,bl   ;below 'a'?
38              jb      IsUpper ;yes, not lowercase
39              cmp     al,bh   ;above 'z'?
40              ja      IsUpper ;yes, not lowercase
41              and     al,not 20h ;is lowercase-make uppercase
42      IsUpper:
43              stosb           ;put the uppercase character into
44                              ; the new string and point to the
45                              ; following character
46              and     al,al   ;is this the zero that marks the
47                              ; end of the string?
48              jnz     StringUpperLoop ;no, do the next character
49              ret
50      ;
51      Skip:
```

```
52              call    ZTimerOn
53              mov     si,offset SourceString  ;point DS:SI to the
54                                              ; string to convert
55              mov     di,ds
56              mov     es,di             ;point ES:DI to the
57              mov     di,si             ; same string
58              call    CopyStringUpper   ;convert to
59                                        ; uppercase in place
60              call    ZTimerOff
```

```
1       ;
2       ; *** Listing 11-4 ***
3       ;
4       ; Converts all characters in a string to uppercase,
5       ; using a loop containing non-string instructions
6       ; and using only one pointer.
7       ;
8               jmp     Skip
9       ;
10      SourceString    label   word
11              db      'This space intentionally left not blank',0
12      ;
13      ; Converts a string to uppercase.
14      ;
15      ; Input:
16      ;       DS:SI = start of string
17      ;
18      ; Output:
19      ;       none
20      ;
21      ; Registers altered: AL, BX, SI
22      ;
23      ; Note: Does not handle strings that are longer than 64K
24      ;       bytes or cross segment boundaries.
25      ;
26      StringToUpper:
27              mov     bl,'a'  ;set up for fast register-register
28              mov     bh,'z'  ; comparisons
29      StringToUpperLoop:
30              mov     al,[si] ;get the next character
31              cmp     al,bl   ;below 'a'?
32              jb      IsUpper ;yes, not lowercase
33              cmp     al,bh   ;above 'z'?
34              ja      IsUpper ;yes, not lowercase
35              and     al,not 20h ;is lowercase-make uppercase
36      IsUpper:
37              mov     [si],al ;put the uppercase character back
38              inc     si      ; into the string and point to the
39                              ; following character
40              and     al,al   ;is this the zero that marks the
41                              ; end of the string?
42              jnz     StringToUpperLoop ;no, do the next character
43              ret
44      ;
45      Skip:
46              call    ZTimerOn
47              mov     si,offset SourceString  ;point to the string
```

```
48                                     ; to convert
49              call    StringToUpper  ;convert it to
50                                     ; uppercase
51              call    ZTimerOff
```

performance cost *vis à vis* the repeated string instructions. One thing that **lods/stos** doesn't do particularly well is modify memory directly. For example, suppose that we want to set the high bit of every byte in a 1000-byte array. We could of course do this with **lodsb** and **stosb**, setting the high bit of each word while it's loaded into AL. Listing 11-5, which does exactly that, takes 10.07 μsec per word.

```
1       ;
2       ; *** Listing 11-5 ***
3       ;
4       ; Sets the high bit of every element in a byte
5       ; array using LODSB and STOSB.
6       ;
7               jmp     Skip
8       ;
9       ;
10      ARRAY_LENGTH    equ     1000
11      ByteArray       db      ARRAY_LENGTH dup (?)
12      ;
13      Skip:
14              call    ZTimerOn
15              mov     si,offset ByteArray     ;point to the array
16              mov     di,ds                   ; as both source and
17              mov     es,di                   ; destination
18              mov     di,si
19              mov     cx,ARRAY_LENGTH
20              mov     ah,80h                  ;bit pattern to OR
21              cld
22      SetHighBitLoop:
23              lodsb                           ;get the next byte
24              or      al,ah                   ;set the high bit
25              stosb                           ;save the byte
26              loop    SetHighBitLoop
27              call    ZTimerOff
```

However, we could also use a plain old **or** instruction working directly with a memory operand to do the same thing, as shown in Listing 11-6. Listing 11-6 is just as fast as Listing 11-5 at 10.06 μsec per word, and it's also considerably shorter, at 13 rather than 21 bytes, with 1 fewer byte inside the loop. In this case **lods/stos** isn't *disastrously* worse, but it certainly isn't the preferred solution, and there are plenty of other situations in which **lods/stos** is less than ideal.

For instance, when registers are tight, the extra pointer register **lods/stos** takes can be sorely missed. If the accumulator is reserved for some specific purpose and can't be modified, **lods/stos** can't very well be

```
1    ;
2    ; *** Listing 11-6 ***
3    ;
4    ; Sets the high bit of every element in a byte
5    ; array by ORing directly to memory.
6    ;
7            jmp     Skip
8    ;
9    ;
10   ARRAY_LENGTH    equ     1000
11   ByteArray       db      ARRAY_LENGTH dup (?)
12   ;
13   Skip:
14           call    ZTimerOn
15           mov     si,offset ByteArray     ;point to the array
16           mov     cx,ARRAY_LENGTH
17           mov     al,80h                  ;bit pattern to OR
18   SetHighBitLoop:
19           or      [si],al                 ;set the high bit
20           inc     si                      ;point to the next
21                                           ; byte
22           loop    SetHighBitLoop
23           call    ZTimerOff
```

used. If a pointer to far data is needed by other instructions in the same routine, the limitation of **stos** to operating in the ES segment would become a burden. In other words, although the **lods/stos** pair is more flexible than the repeated string instructions, its limitations are significant nonetheless.

The point is not simply that the **lods/stos** pair is not as flexible as the nonstring instructions. The real point is that you shouldn't assume you've come up with the best solution just because you've used string instructions. Yes, I know that I've been touting string instructions as the greatest thing since sliced bread, and by and large that's true. However, because the string instructions have a sharply limited repertoire and often require a good deal of preliminary setup, you must consider your alternatives before concluding that a string instruction–based implementation is best.

11.2 ◆ Block Handling with movs

Simply put, **movs** is the king of the block copy. There's no other 8088 instruction that can hold a candle to **movs** when it comes to copying blocks of data from one area of memory to another. It does take several instructions to set up for **movs**, so if you're moving only a few bytes and DS:SI and ES:DI don't happen to be pointing to your source and destination, you might want to use a regular **mov**. Whenever you want to move more than a few bytes, though, **movs**—or better yet **rep movs**—is the ticket.

Let's look at the archetypal application for **movs**, a subroutine that copies a block of memory from one memory area to another. What's special about the subroutine we'll look at is that it handles copying a block when the destination of the copy overlaps the source. This is a bit tricky because the direction in which the copy must proceed—from the start of the block toward the end, or vice versa—depends on the direction of overlap.

If the destination block overlaps the source block and starts at a lower memory address than the source block, then the copy can proceed in the normal direction, from lower to higher addresses, as shown in Figure 11.2. If the destination block overlaps the source block and starts at a *higher* address, however, the block must be copied starting at its highest address and proceeding toward the low end, as shown in Figure 11.3. Otherwise, the first data copied to the destination block would wipe out source data that had yet to be copied, resulting in a corrupted copy, as shown in Figure 11.4. Finally, if the blocks don't overlap, the copy can proceed in either direction, since the two blocks can't conflict.

The block copy subroutine **BlockCopyWithOverlap** shown in Listing 11-7 handles potential overlap problems exactly as described above. In

```
1     ;
2     ; *** Listing 11-7 ***
3     ;
4     ; Copies overlapping blocks of memory with MOVS.
5     ; To the greatest possible extent, the copy is
6     ; performed a word at a time.
7     ;
8             jmp     Skip
9     ;
10    TEST_LENGTH1    equ     501        ;sample copy length #1
11    TEST_LENGTH2    equ     1499       ;sample copy length #2
12    TestArray       db      1500 dup (0)
13    ;
14    ; Copies a block of memory CX bytes in length. A value
15    ; of 0 means "copy zero bytes," since it wouldn't make
16    ; much sense to copy one 64K block to another 64K block
17    ; in the same segment, so the maximum length that can
18    ; be copied is 64K-1 bytes and the minimum length
19    ; is 0 bytes. Note that both blocks must be in DS. Note
20    ; also that overlap handling is not guaranteed if either
21    ; block wraps at the end of the segment.
22    ;
23    ; Input:
24    ;       CX = number of bytes to clear
25    ;       DS:SI = start of block to copy
26    ;       DS:DI = start of destination block
27    ;
28    ; Output:
29    ;       none
30    ;
31    ; Registers altered: CX, DX, SI, DI, ES
```

```
32      ;
33      ; Direction flag cleared
34      ;
35      BlockCopyWithOverlap:
36              mov     dx,ds       ;source and destination are in the
37              mov     es,dx       ; same segment
38              cmp     si,di       ;which way do the blocks overlap, if
39                                  ; they do overlap?
40              jae     LowToHigh
41                                  ;source is not below destination, so
42                                  ; we can copy from low to high
43
44                                  ;source is below destination, so we
45                                  ; must copy from high to low
46              add     si,cx       ;point to the end of the source
47              dec     si          ; block
48              add     di,cx       ;point to the end of the destination
49              dec     di          ; block
50              std                 ;copy from high addresses to low
51              shr     cx,1        ;divide by 2, copying the odd-byte
52                                  ; status to the Carry flag
53              jnc     CopyWordHighToLow ;no odd byte to copy
54              movsb               ;copy the odd byte
55      CopyWordHighToLow:
56              dec     si          ;point one word lower in memory, not
57              dec     di          ; one byte
58              rep     movsw       ;move the rest of the block
59              cld
60              ret
61      ;
62      LowToHigh:
63              cld                 ;copy from low addresses to high
64              shr     cx,1        ;divide by 2, copying the odd-byte
65                                  ; status to the Carry flag
66              jnc     CopyWordLowToHigh       ;no odd byte to copy
67              movsb               ;copy the odd byte
68      CopyWordLowToHigh:
69              rep     movsw       ;move the rest of the block
70              ret
71      ;
72      Skip:
73              call    ZTimerOn
74      ;
75      ; First run the case where the destination overlaps & is
76      ; higher in memory.
77      ;
78              mov     si,offset TestArray
79              mov     di,offset TestArray+1
80              mov     cx,TEST_LENGTH1
81              call    BlockCopyWithOverlap
82      ;
83      ; Now run the case where the destination overlaps & is
84      ; lower in memory.
85      ;
86              mov     si,offset TestArray+1
87              mov     di,offset TestArray
88              mov     cx,TEST_LENGTH2
89              call    BlockCopyWithOverlap
90              call    ZTimerOff
```

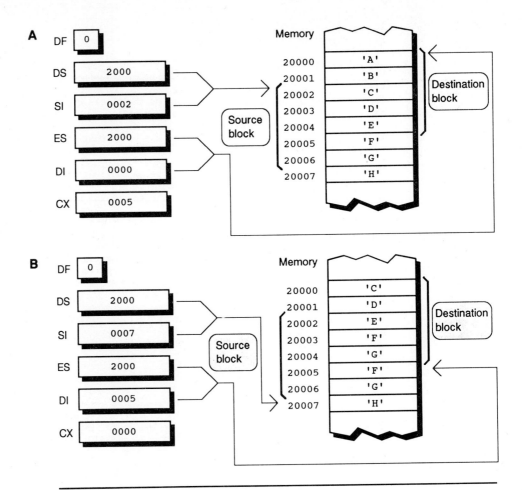

FIGURE 11.2   When overlapping blocks are the source and destination
for **rep movsb**, the direction in which the copy must
proceed depends on the direction of overlap. In this
figure the source block starts at a higher address than
the destination block, so the copy must proceed from
lower addresses to higher addresses. This is the mode
of operation of the string instructions when DF is equal
to 0, as it normally is. **(A)** The state of the PC before **rep
movsb** is executed to copy such an overlapping block.
(B) The state of the PC after the copy is completed.

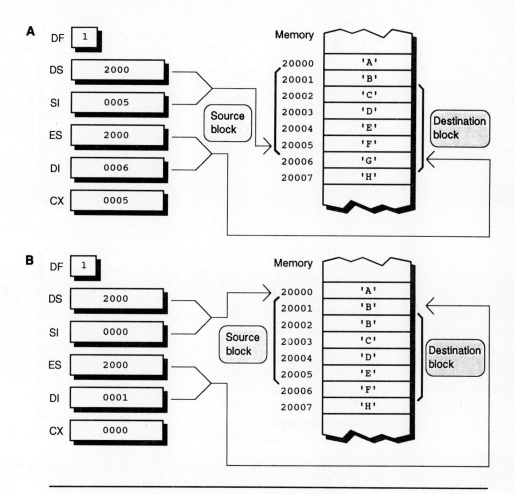

FIGURE 11.3 When the source block in a block copy overlaps the destination block and starts at a lower address than the destination block, the copy must proceed from higher addresses to lower addresses. When string instructions are used, DF must be set to 1 in order to handle this overlap case properly. **(A)** The state of the PC before **rep movsb** is executed to copy such an overlapping block. **(B)** The state of the PC after the copy is completed.

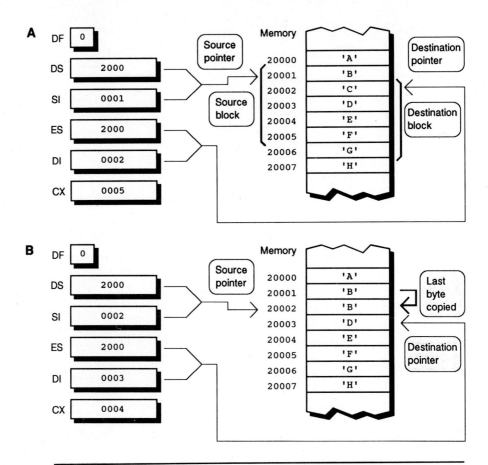

FIGURE 11.4   When the source block in a block copy overlaps the destination block and starts at a lower address than the destination block, the data will be corrupted as it's copied if DF is set to 0. **(A)** The state of the PC before such a copy is performed. **(B)** The state of the PC after the first repetition of **rep movsb** is completed. As expected, the character *B*, which is the first element of the source block, has been copied to the first element of the destination block. Notice, though, that the first element of the destination block *is also the second element of the source block*. In other words, an as yet uncopied element of the source block has just been altered.

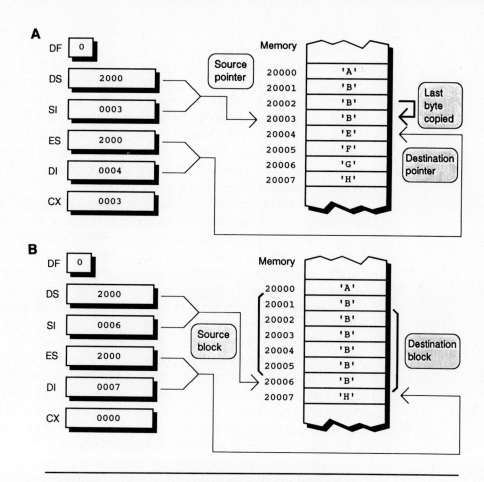

(C) The effect of this modification of the source block, as the *B* that was just copied is copied again to the second element of the destination block. Given the original source block of **(A)**, a *C* should have been copied to this position in the destination block. In fact, *B* is copied by *every* repetition of **rep movsb** in this case.
(D) Ultimately every byte of the destination block is set to *B*.

DF must be set to 1 for this sort of block copy, with the copy proceeding from higher to lower addresses. Refer to Figure 11.3 for an illustration of the proper operation of this particular block copy.

FIGURE 11.4   (*continued*)

cases where the destination block starts at a higher address than the source block, **BlockCopyWithOverlap** performs an **std** and uses **movs** to copy the source block starting at the high end and proceeding to the low end. Otherwise, the source block is copied from the low end to the high end with **cld/movs**. **BlockCopyWithOverlap** is both remarkably compact and very fast, clocking in at 5.57 msec for the cases tested in Listing 11-7. The subroutine could actually be more compact still, but I've chosen to improve performance at the expense of a few bytes by copying as much of the block as possible a word (rather than a byte) at a time.

There are two points of particular interest in Listing 11-7. First, **BlockCopyWithOverlap** handles only blocks that reside in the same segment, and only if neither block wraps around the end of the segment. Although it would certainly be possible to write a version of the subroutine that properly handled both potentially overlapping copies between different segments and segment wrapping, neither of those features is usually necessary, and the additional code would reduce overall performance. If you need such a routine, write it, but as a general practice don't write extra, slower code just to handle cases that you can readily avoid.

Second, **BlockCopyWithOverlap** nicely illustrates a nasty aspect of the use of word-sized string instructions when the direction flag is set to 1. The basic problem is this: if you point to the last byte of a block of memory and perform a word-sized operation, the byte *after* the end of the memory block will be accessed along with the last byte of the block, rather than the last 2 bytes of the block, as shown in Figure 11.5.

This problem of accessing the byte after the end of a memory block can occur with all word-sized instructions, not just string instructions. However, it's especially liable to happen with a word-sized string instruction that's moving its pointer or pointers backward (with the direction flag equal to 1), because the temptation is to point to the end of the block, set the direction flag, and let the string instruction do its stuff in repeated word-sized chunks for maximum performance. To avoid this problem, you must always be sure to point to the last *word,* rather than byte, when you point to the last element in a memory block and then access memory with a word-sized instruction.

Matters get even more dicey when byte- and word-sized string instructions are mixed when the direction flag is set to 1. This is done in Listing 11-7 in order to use **rep movsw** to move the largest possible portion of odd-length memory blocks. The problem here is that when a string instruction moves its pointer or pointers from high addresses to low, the address of the next byte that we want to access (with **lodsb**, for example) and the address of the next word that we want to access (with **lodsw**, for exam-

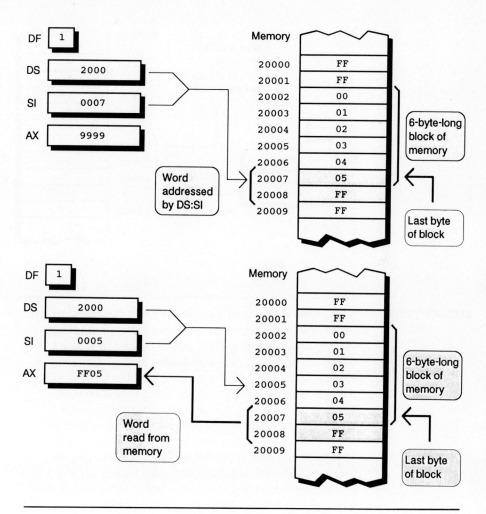

FIGURE 11.5   When a pointer is set to point to the last byte of a memory block and a word-sized access to that address is performed, the last word of the block is *not* read. Rather, the last *byte* of the block is read, along with the byte immediately following the block.

ple) differ, as shown in Figure 11.6. For a byte-sized string instruction such as **lodsb**, we *do* want to point to the end of the array. After that **lodsb** has executed with the direction flag equal to 1, though, where do the pointers point? To the address 1 byte—not 1 word—lower in memory. Then what happens when **lodsw** is executed as the next instruction, with the intent

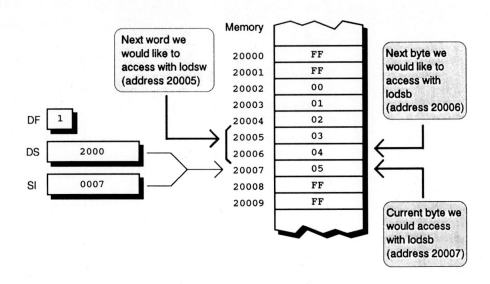

FIGURE 11.6   After **lodsb** is executed with DF set to 1 (causing SI to
decrement), the address of the next byte we would want
to access with **lodsb** and the address of the next word
we would want to access with **lodsw** are not the same.
This figure shows that after reading the byte at 2000:0007,
the next byte we would want to access is at 2000:0006,
whereas the next word we would want to access is at
2000:0005. (Reading the *word* at 2000:0006 gets the byte
read by the initial **lodsb**—the byte at 2000:0007—again,
along with the byte at 2000:0006. What we want are the
bytes at 2000:0005 and 2000:0006, which form the word
immediately preceding the byte at 2000:0007 that was read
with the initial **lodsb**.) This can cause problems when
byte- and word-sized string instructions are mixed when
DF is set to 1.

of accessing the word just above the last byte of the array? Why, the last
byte of the array is incorrectly accessed again, as shown in Figure 11.7.

The solution, as shown in Listing 11-7, is fairly simple. We must perform
the initial **movsb** and then adjust the pointers to point 1 byte lower in
memory—to the start of the next *word*. Only then can we go ahead with a
movsw, as shown in Figure 11.8.

Mind you, all this applies *only* when the direction flag is 1. When the
direction flag is 0, **movsb** and **movsw** can be mixed freely, because the

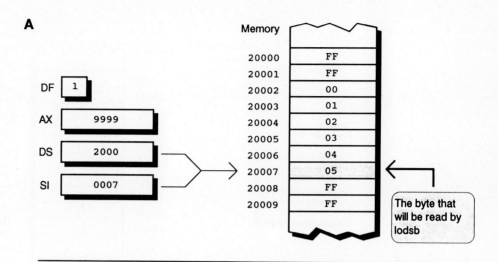

A

FIGURE 11.7 When DF is 1, problems can occur when byte- and word-sized string instructions are mixed, since the address of the next byte is not the same as the address of the next word. This figure shows that the last 3 bytes of a memory block are read incorrectly with the following code:

```
std
lodsb
lodsw
```

(A) The byte that will be read by the initial **lodsb**. This is indeed the last byte of the block, as intended. **(B)** The word that will be read by the following **lodsw**. This word does not contain the 2 bytes immediately preceding the last byte of the block; rather, it contains the last byte of the block again, along with the next-to-last byte of the block. Also, **(B)** shows the word that we want **lodsw** to read, which is clearly not the word it will read. The discrepancy arises because **lodsb** leaves DS:SI pointing to the preceding byte, not the preceding word. **(C)** The instruction **lodsw** does indeed load the wrong word from the block, placing the value 0504h, rather than the correct value of 0403h, in AX.

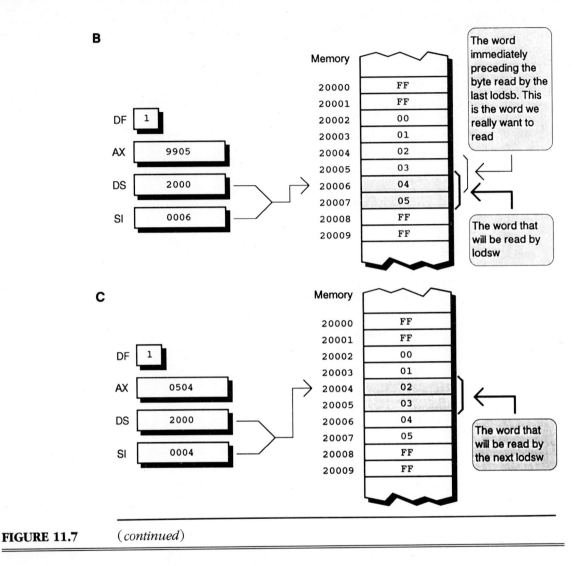

FIGURE 11.7   (*continued*)

address of the next byte is the same as the address of the next word when we're counting from low addresses to high, as shown in Figure 11.9. Listing 11-7 reflects this, since the pointer adjustments are made only when the direction flag is 1.

Listing 11-8 contains a version of **BlockCopyWithOverlap** that does exactly what the version in Listing 11-7 does, but does so without string instructions. While Listing 11-8 doesn't *look* all that much different from

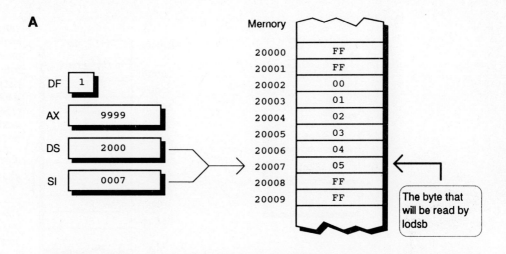

FIGURE 11.8 When DF is 1, adjustments must be made when switching between byte- and word-sized string instructions. Since the address of the next byte is not the same as the address of the next word, incorrect data will be read if adjustments are not made, as illustrated by Figure 11.7. This figure shows that the last 3 bytes of a memory block are read correctly with the following code:

```
std
lodsb
dec  si
lodsw
```

(A) The last byte of the block will be read by the initial **lodsb**. **(B)** The word that **lodsb** leaves DS:SI pointing to is not the word preceding the byte just read, but rather the last word of the block, which includes the byte just read. **(C)** The instruction **dec si** corrects SI to point to the desired word. **(D)** After the adjustment **lodsw** does indeed load the correct word from the block, placing the value 0403h in AX.

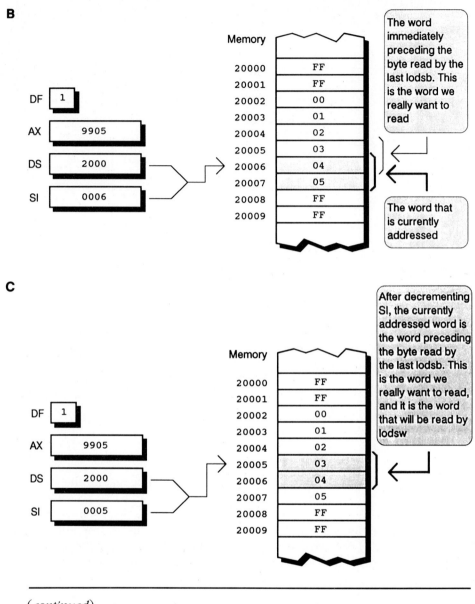

B

The word immediately preceding the byte read by the last lodsb. This is the word we really want to read

The word that is currently addressed

C

After decrementing SI, the currently addressed word is the word preceding the byte read by the last lodsb. This is the word we really want to read, and it is the word that will be read by lodsw

FIGURE 11.8   (*continued*)

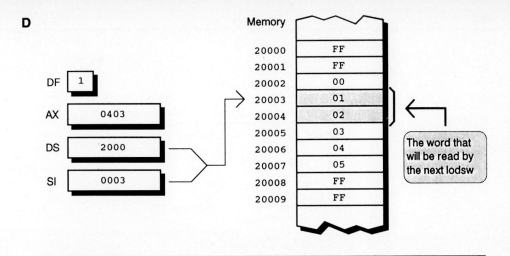

D

FIGURE 11.8   (*continued*)

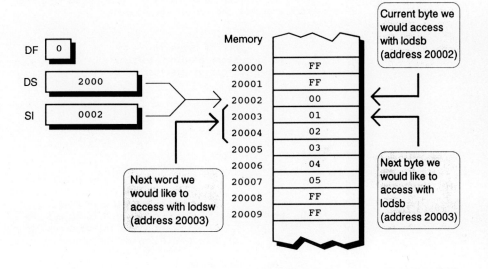

FIGURE 11.9   After **lodsb** is executed with DF set to 0 (causing SI to increment), the address of the next byte we would want to access with **lodsb** and the address of the next word we would want to access with **lodsw** are exactly the same. In this figure, after the byte at 2000:0002 is read, both the next byte and the next word are at 2000:0003. (Reading the word at 2000:0003 gets the bytes at 2000:0003 and 2000:0004, which are the bytes immediately following the byte at 2000:0002 that was read with the initial **lodsb**.) As a result, no nasty problems result from mixing byte- and word-sized string instructions when DF is 0. As we've seen over the last few figures, the same is most decidedly not true when DF is 1.

```
1    ;
2    ; *** Listing 11-8 ***
3    ;
4    ; Copies overlapping blocks of memory with
5    ; non-string instructions. To the greatest possible
6    ; extent, the copy is performed a word at a time.
7    ;
8             jmp     Skip
9    ;
10   TEST_LENGTH1    equ     501      ;sample copy length #1
11   TEST_LENGTH2    equ     1499     ;sample copy length #2
12   TestArray       db      1500 dup (0)
13   ;
14   ; Copies a block of memory CX bytes in length. A value
15   ; of 0 means "copy zero bytes," since it wouldn't make
16   ; much sense to copy one 64K block to another 64K block
17   ; in the same segment, so the maximum length that can
18   ; be copied is 64K-1 bytes and the minimum length
19   ; is 0 bytes. Note that both blocks must be in DS. Note
20   ; also that overlap handling is not guaranteed if either
21   ; block wraps at the end of the segment.
22   ;
23   ; Input:
24   ;        CX = number of bytes to clear
25   ;        DS:SI = start of block to copy
26   ;        DS:DI = start of destination block
27   ;
28   ; Output:
29   ;        none
30   ;
31   ; Registers altered: AX, CX, DX, SI, DI
32   ;
33   BlockCopyWithOverlap:
34           jcxz    BlockCopyWithOverlapDone
35                           ;guard against zero block size,
36                           ; since LOOP will execute 64K times
37                           ; when started with CX=0
38           mov     dx,2     ;amount by which to adjust the
39                           ; pointers in the word-copy loop
40           cmp     si,di    ;which way do the blocks overlap, if
41                           ; they do overlap?
42           jae     LowToHigh
43                           ;source is not below destination, so
44                           ; we can copy from low to high
45
46                           ;source is below destination, so we
47                           ; must copy from high to low
48           add     si,cx    ;point to the end of the source
49           dec     si       ; block
50           add     di,cx    ;point to the end of the destination
51           dec     di       ; block
52           shr     cx,1     ;divide by 2, copying the odd-byte
53                           ; status to the Carry flag
54           jnc     CopyWordHighToLow ;no odd byte to copy
55           mov     al,[si]  ;copy the odd byte
56           mov     [di],al
57           dec     si       ;advance both pointers
58           dec     di
59   CopyWordHighToLow:
```

```
60              dec     si      ;point one word lower in memory, not
61              dec     di      ; one byte
62      HighToLowCopyLoop:
63              mov     ax,[si] ;copy a word
64              mov     [di],ax
65              sub     si,dx   ;advance both pointers 1 word
66              sub     di,dx
67              loop    HighToLowCopyLoop
68              ret
69      ;
70      LowToHigh:
71              shr     cx,1    ;divide by 2, copying the odd-byte
72                              ; status to the Carry flag
73              jnc     LowToHighCopyLoop       ;no odd byte to copy
74              mov     al,[si] ;copy the odd byte
75              mov     [di],al
76              inc     si      ;advance both pointers
77              inc     di
78      LowToHighCopyLoop:
79              mov     ax,[si] ;copy a word
80              mov     [di],ax
81              add     si,dx   ;advance both pointers 1 word
82              add     di,dx
83              loop    LowToHighCopyLoop
84      BlockCopyWithOverlapDone:
85              ret
86      ;
87      Skip:
88              call    ZTimerOn
89      ;
90      ; First run the case where the destination overlaps & is
91      ; higher in memory.
92      ;
93              mov     si,offset TestArray
94              mov     di,offset TestArray+1
95              mov     cx,TEST_LENGTH1
96              call    BlockCopyWithOverlap
97      ;
98      ; Now run the case where the destination overlaps & is
99      ; lower in memory.
100     ;
101             mov     si,offset TestArray+1
102             mov     di,offset TestArray
103             mov     cx,TEST_LENGTH2
104             call    BlockCopyWithOverlap
105             call    ZTimerOff
```

Listing 11-7, it takes a full 15.16 msec to run—quite a difference from the time of 5.57 msec we measured for Listing 11-7. Think about it: Listing 11-7 is nearly *three times* as fast as Listing 11-8, thanks to **movs**, and it's shorter, too.

Enough said.

11.3 ◆ Searching with scas

The **scas** instruction is often (but not always, as we shall see) the preferred way to search for either a given value or the absence of a given value in an array. When **scas** is well suited to the task at hand, it is the best choice by a wide margin. For example, suppose that we want to count the number of times the letter *A* appears in a text array. Listing 11-9, which uses nonstring instructions, counts the number of occurrences of *A* in the sample array in 475 μsec. Listing 11-10, which does exactly the same thing with **repnz scasb**, finishes in just 203 μsec. That, my friends, is an improvement of 134 percent. What's more, Listing 11-10 is shorter than Listing 11-9.

```
 1  ;
 2  ; *** Listing 11-9 ***
 3  ;
 4  ; Counts the number of times the letter 'A'
 5  ; appears in a byte-sized array, using non-string
 6  ; instructions.
 7  ;
 8           jmp       Skip
 9  ;
10  ByteArray        label     byte
11           db        'ARRAY CONTAINING THE LETTER ''A'' 4 TIMES'
12  ARRAY_LENGTH     equ       ($-ByteArray)
13  ;
14  ; Counts the number of occurrences of the specified byte
15  ; in the specified byte-sized array.
16  ;
17  ; Input:
18  ;       AL = byte of which to count occurrences
19  ;       CX = array length (0 means 64K)
20  ;       DS:DI = array to count byte occurrences in
21  ;
22  ; Output:
23  ;       DX = number of occurrences of the specified byte
24  ;
25  ; Registers altered: CX, DX, DI
26  ;
27  ; Note: Does not handle arrays that are longer than 64K
28  ;       bytes or cross segment boundaries.
29  ;
30  ByteCount:
31           sub       dx,dx           ;set occurrence counter to 0
32           dec       di              ;compensate for the initial
33                                     ; upcoming INC DI
34           and       cx,cx           ;64K long?
35           jnz       ByteCountLoop   ;no
36           dec       cx              ;yes, so handle first byte
37                                     ; specially, since JCXZ will
38                                     ; otherwise conclude that
39                                     ; we're done right away
40           inc       di              ;point to first byte
```

```
41              cmp      [di],al           ;is this byte the value
42                                         ; we're looking for?
43              jz       ByteCountCountOccurrence
44                                         ;yes, so count it
45      ByteCountLoop:
46              jcxz     ByteCountDone     ;done if we've checked all
47                                         ; the bytes in the array
48              dec      cx                ;count off the byte we're
49                                         ; about to check
50              inc      di                ;point to the next byte to
51                                         ; check
52              cmp      [di],al           ;see if this byte contains
53                                         ; the value we're counting
54              jnz      ByteCountLoop     ;no match
55      ByteCountCountOccurrence:
56              inc      dx                ;count this occurrence
57              jmp      ByteCountLoop     ;check the next byte, if any
58      ByteCountDone:
59              ret
60      ;
61      Skip:
62              call     ZTimerOn
63              mov      al,'A'            ;byte of which we want a
64                                         ; count of occurrences
65              mov      di,offset ByteArray
66                                         ;array we want a count for
67              mov      cx,ARRAY_LENGTH ;# of bytes to check
68              call     ByteCount         ;get the count
69              call     ZTimerOff
```

```
1       ;
2       ; *** Listing 11-10 ***
3       ;
4       ; Counts the number of times the letter 'A'
5       ; appears in a byte-sized array, using REPNZ SCASB.
6       ;
7               jmp      Skip
8       ;
9       ByteArray        label    byte
10               db       'ARRAY CONTAINING THE LETTER ''A'' 4 TIMES'
11      ARRAY_LENGTH     equ      ($-ByteArray)
12      ;
13      ; Counts the number of occurrences of the specified byte
14      ; in the specified byte-sized array.
15      ;
16      ; Input:
17      ;       AL = byte of which to count occurrences
18      ;       CX = array length (0 means 64K)
19      ;       DS:DI = array to count byte occurrences in
20      ;
21      ; Output:
22      ;       DX = number of occurrences of the specified byte
23      ;
24      ; Registers altered: CX, DX, DI, ES
25      ;
26      ; Direction flag cleared
27      ;
```

```
28   ; Note: Does not handle arrays that are longer than 64K
29   ;       bytes or cross segment boundaries. Does not handle
30   ;       overlapping strings.
31   ;
32   ByteCount:
33           push    ds
34           pop     es                  ;SCAS uses ES:DI
35           sub     dx,dx               ;set occurrence counter to 0
36           cld
37           and     cx,cx               ;64K long?
38           jnz     ByteCountLoop       ;no
39           dec     cx                  ;yes, so handle first byte
40                                       ; specially, since JCXZ will
41                                       ; otherwise conclude that
42                                       ; we're done right away
43           scasb                       ;is first byte a match?
44           jz      ByteCountCountOccurrence
45                                       ;yes, so count it
46   ByteCountLoop:
47           jcxz    ByteCountDone       ;if there's nothing left to
48                                       ; search, we're done
49           repnz   scasb               ;search for the next byte
50                                       ; occurrence or the end of
51                                       ; the array
52           jnz     ByteCountDone       ;no match
53   ByteCountCountOccurrence:
54           inc     dx                  ;count this occurrence
55           jmp     ByteCountLoop       ;check the next byte, if any
56   ByteCountDone:
57           ret
58   ;
59   Skip:
60           call    ZTimerOn
61           mov     al,'A'              ;byte of which we want a
62                                       ; count of occurrences
63           mov     di,offset ByteArray
64                                       ;array we want a count for
65           mov     cx,ARRAY_LENGTH     ;# of bytes to check
66           call    ByteCount           ;get the count
67           call    ZTimerOff
```

Incidentally, Listing 11-10 illustrates the subtlety of the pitfalls associated with forgetting that **scas** repeated 0 times (with CX equal to 0) doesn't alter the flags. If the **jcxz** instruction in Listing 11-10 were to be removed, the code would still work perfectly—except when the array being scanned was exactly 64 K bytes long and *every* byte in the array matched the byte being searched for. In that one case, CX would be 0 when **repnz scasb** was restarted after the last match, causing **repnz scasb** to drop through without altering the flags. The zero flag (ZF) would be 0 as a result of DX previously incrementing from 0FFFFh to 0, and so the **jnz** branch would not be taken. Instead, DX would be incremented again, causing a nonexistent match to be counted. The result would be that 1 rather than 64 K matches would be returned as the match count, an error of considerable magnitude.

If you could be sure that no array longer than 64 K−1 bytes would ever be passed to **ByteCount**, you *could* eliminate the **jcxz** and speed the code considerably. Trimming the fat from your code until it's matched exactly to an application's needs is one key to performance.

scas and Zero-Terminated Strings

Clearly, then, when you want to find a given byte or word value in a buffer, table, or array of a known fixed length, it's often best to load up the registers and let a repeated **scas** do its stuff. However, the same is not always true of searching tasks that require multiple comparisons for each byte or word, such as a loop that ends when either the letter *A or* a 0 byte is found. Alas, **scas** can perform just one comparison per memory location, and **repz** or **repnz** can terminate only on the basis of the ZF setting after that one comparison. This is unfortunate, because multiple comparisons are exactly what we need to handle C-style strings, which are of no fixed length and are terminated with 0s. The **rep scas** instruction can still be used in such situations, but its power is diluted by the workarounds needed to allow it to function more flexibly than it is normally capable of doing. The choice between repeated **scas** instructions and other approaches then must be made on a case-by-case basis, according to the balance between the extra overhead needed to coax **scas** into doing what is needed and the inherent speed of the instruction.

For example, suppose we need a subroutine that returns either the offset in a string of the first instance of a selected byte value or the value 0 if a 0 byte (marking the end of the string) is encountered before the desired byte is found. There's no simple way to do this with **scasb**, for in this application we have to compare each memory location first to the desired byte value and then to 0. The **scasb** instruction can perform one comparison or the other, but not both.

Now, we *could* use **repnz scasb** to find the 0 byte at the end of the string, so we'd know how long the string was, and then use **repnz scasb** again with CX set to the length of the string to search for the selected byte value. Unfortunately, that involves processing *every* byte in the string once before even beginning the search. On average, this double-search approach would read every element of the string being searched once and would then read one half of the elements again, as shown in Figure 11.10. By contrast, an approach that reads each byte and immediately compares it with both the desired value *and* 0 would read only one half of the elements in the string, as shown in Figure 11.11. Powerful as repeated **scasb** is, could it

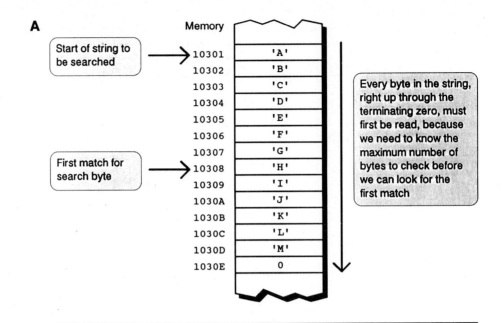

A

Memory

Start of string to be searched → 10301 'A'

10302 'B'

10303 'C'

10304 'D'

10305 'E'

10306 'F'

10307 'G'

First match for search byte → 10308 'H'

10309 'I'

1030A 'J'

1030B 'K'

1030C 'L'

1030D 'M'

1030E 0

Every byte in the string, right up through the terminating zero, must first be read, because we need to know the maximum number of bytes to check before we can look for the first match

FIGURE 11.10   When repeated **scas** is used to find a given character in a 0-terminated string, a double-search method must be used. **(A)** Every byte in the string must first be read in order to find the terminating 0. This gives us the length of the string, so we know the maximum number of bytes to search in the second step. **(B)** The second step involves searching again from the beginning of the string, this time looking for the desired byte. If all the bytes read in the first step are read again in the second step without finding the desired byte, then we know the desired byte isn't present in the string.

With this double-search approach, each byte in the string is read at least once and the first byte is always read twice, that being the minimum case that occurs only when the desired byte is the first byte of the string. Each byte is read twice at most, that being the case if the desired byte isn't found. On average, the entire string is read one and one half times.

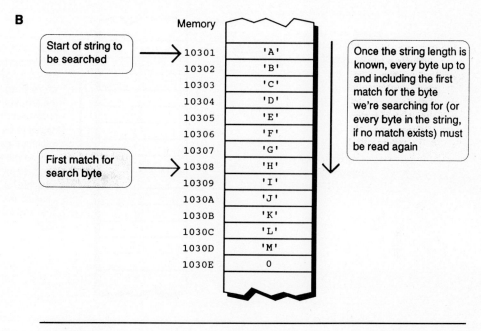

FIGURE 11.10 (*continued*)

possibly run fast enough to allow the double-search approach to outperform an approach that accesses memory only one third as many times?

The answer is yes . . . conditionally. The double-search approach actually *is* slightly faster than a **lodsb**-based single-search string-searching approach for the average case. The double-search approach performs relatively more poorly if matches tend to occur most frequently in the first half of the strings being searched and relatively better if matches tend to occur in the second half of the strings. Also, the more flexible **lodsb**-based approach rapidly becomes the solution of choice if the termination condition becomes more complex, as when a case-insensitive search is desired. The same is true when modification as well as searching of the string is desired, as when the string is converted to upper case.

Listing 11-11 shows **lodsb**-based code that searches a zero-terminated string for the character *z*. For the sample string, which has the first match right in the middle of the string, Listing 11-11 takes 375 μsec to find the match. Listing 11-12 shows **repnz scasb**-based code that uses the double-search approach. For the same sample string as Listing 11-11, Listing 11-12 takes just 340 μsec to find the match, despite having to perform about three times as many memory accesses as Listing 11-11—a tribute to the raw

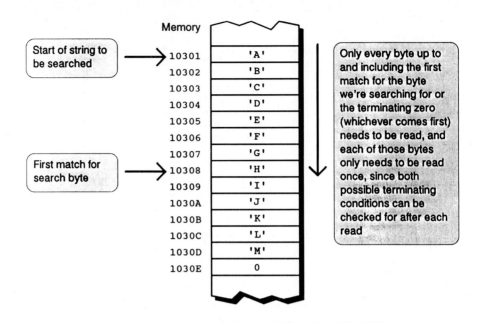

FIGURE 11.11   When **lods** and **cmp** are used to search a string for a
given byte, both the desired byte and the 0 that terminates
the string can be checked for at once, since **lods** reads
each byte into the accumulator, where multiple tests can
be performed easily and quickly. With this approach, only
those bytes in the string up to and including the desired
byte or the terminating 0 (whichever comes first) are
read. At a minimum, 1 byte must be read (if the desired
byte is the first byte of the string); at most, every byte
in the string must be read once (if the desired byte isn't
present). On average, the entire string will be read one
half time.

```
1    ;
2    ; *** Listing 11-11 ***
3    ;
4    ; Finds the first occurrence of the letter 'z' in
5    ; a zero-terminated string, using LODSB.
6    ;
7          jmp     Skip
8    ;
9    TestString    label   byte
10         db      'This is a test string that is '
11         db      'z'
12         db      'terminated with a zero byte...',0
13   ;
```

```
14      ; Finds the first occurrence of the specified byte in the
15      ; specified zero-terminated string.
16      ;
17      ; Input:
18      ;       AL = byte to find
19      ;       DS:SI = zero-terminated string to search
20      ;
21      ; Output:
22      ;       SI = pointer to first occurrence of byte in string,
23      ;               or 0 if the byte wasn't found
24      ;
25      ; Registers altered: AX, SI
26      ;
27      ; Direction flag cleared
28      ;
29      ; Note: Do not pass a string that starts at offset 0 (SI=0),
30      ;       since a match on the first byte and failure to find
31      ;       the byte would be indistinguishable.
32      ;
33      ; Note: Does not handle strings that are longer than 64K
34      ;       bytes or cross segment boundaries.
35      ;
36      FindCharInString:
37              mov     ah,al   ;we'll need AL since that's the
38                              ; only register LODSB can use
39              cld
40      FindCharInStringLoop:
41              lodsb           ;get the next string byte
42              cmp     al,ah   ;is this the byte we're
43                              ; looking for?
44              jz      FindCharInStringDone
45                              ;yes, so we're done
46              and     al,al   ;is this the terminating zero?
47              jnz     FindCharInStringLoop
48                              ;no, so check the next byte
49              sub     si,si   ;we didn't find a match, so return
50                              ; 0 in SI
51              ret
52      FindCharInStringDone:
53              dec     si      ;point back to the matching byte
54              ret
55      ;
56      Skip:
57              call    ZTimerOn
58              mov     al,'z'          ;byte value to find
59              mov     si,offset TestString
60                              ;string to search
61              call    FindCharInString ;search for the byte
62              call    ZTimerOff


1       ;
2       ; *** Listing 11-12 ***
3       ;
4       ; Finds the first occurrence of the letter 'z' in
5       ; a zero-terminated string, using REPNZ SCASB in a
6       ; double-search approach, first finding the terminating
7       ; zero to determine the string length, and then searching
8       ; for the desired byte.
```

```
 9    ;
10            jmp     Skip
11    ;
12    TestString      label   byte
13            db      'This is a test string that is '
14            db      'z'
15            db      'terminated with a zero byte...',0
16    ;
17    ; Finds the first occurrence of the specified byte in the
18    ; specified zero-terminated string.
19    ;
20    ; Input:
21    ;       AL = byte to find
22    ;       DS:SI = zero-terminated string to search
23    ;
24    ; Output:
25    ;       SI = pointer to first occurrence of byte in string,
26    ;               or 0 if the byte wasn't found
27    ;
28    ; Registers altered: AH, CX, SI, DI, ES
29    ;
30    ; Direction flag cleared
31    ;
32    ; Note: Do not pass a string that starts at offset 0 (SI=0),
33    ;       since a match on the first byte and failure to find
34    ;       the byte would be indistinguishable.
35    ;
36    ; Note: If the search value is 0, will not find the
37    ;       terminating zero in a string that is exactly 64K
38    ;       bytes long. Does not handle strings that are longer
39    ;       than 64K bytes or cross segment boundaries.
40    ;
41    FindCharInString:
42            mov     ah,al   ;set aside the byte to be found
43            sub     al,al   ;we'll search for zero
44            push    ds
45            pop     es
46            mov     di,si   ;SCAS uses ES:DI
47            mov     cx,0ffffh ;long enough to handle any string
48                            ; up to 64K-1 bytes in length, and
49                            ; will handle 64K case except when
50                            ; the search value is the terminating
51                            ; zero
52            cld
53            repnz   scasb   ;find the terminating zero
54            not     cx      ;length of string in bytes, including
55                            ; the terminating zero except in the
56                            ; case of a string that's exactly 64K
57                            ; long including the terminating zero
58            mov     al,ah   ;get back the byte to be found
59            mov     di,si   ;point to the start of the string again
60            repnz   scasb   ;search for the byte of interest
61            jnz     FindCharInStringNotFound
62                            ;the byte isn't present in the string
63            dec     di      ;we've found the desired value. Point
64                            ; back to the matching location
65            mov     si,di   ;return the pointer in SI
66            ret
```

```
67    FindCharInStringNotFound:
68            sub     si,si       ;return a 0 pointer indicating that
69                                ; no match was found
70            ret
71    ;
72    Skip:
73            call    ZTimerOn
74            mov     al,'z'          ;byte value to find
75            mov     si,offset TestString
76                                ;string to search
77            call    FindCharInString ;search for the byte
78            call    ZTimerOff
```

power of repeated **scas**. Finally, Listing 11-13, which performs the same
search using nonstring instructions, takes 419 μsec to find the match.

It is apparent from Listings 11-11 and 11-12 that the performance margin
between **scas**-based string searching and other approaches is considerably
narrower than it was for array searching, owing to the more complex termination conditions. Given a still more complex termination condition, **lods**
would likely become the preferred solution, due to its greater flexibility.
In fact, if we're willing to expend a few bytes, the greater flexibility of **lods**
can be translated into higher performance for Listing 11-11, as follows.

```
1     ;
2     ; *** Listing 11-13 ***
3     ;
4     ; Finds the first occurrence of the letter 'z' in
5     ; a zero-terminated string, using non-string instructions.
6     ;
7             jmp     Skip
8     ;
9     TestString      label   byte
10            db      'This is a test string that is '
11            db      'z'
12            db      'terminated with a zero byte...',0
13    ;
14    ; Finds the first occurrence of the specified byte in the
15    ; specified zero-terminated string.
16    ;
17    ; Input:
18    ;       AL = byte to find
19    ;       DS:SI = zero-terminated string to search
20    ;
21    ; Output:
22    ;       SI = pointer to first occurrence of byte in string,
23    ;               or 0 if the byte wasn't found
24    ;
25    ; Registers altered: AH, SI
26    ;
27    ; Note: Do not pass a string that starts at offset 0 (SI=0),
28    ;       since a match on the first byte and failure to find
29    ;       the byte would be indistinguishable.
30    ;
```

```
31    ; Note: Does not handle strings that are longer than 64K
32    ;         bytes or cross segment boundaries.
33    ;
34    FindCharInString:
35    FindCharInStringLoop:
36          mov     ah,[si] ;get the next string byte
37          cmp     ah,al   ;is this the byte we're
38                          ; looking for?
39          jz      FindCharInStringDone
40                          ;yes, so we're done
41          inc     si      ;point to the following byte
42          and     ah,ah   ;is this the terminating zero?
43          jnz     FindCharInStringLoop
44                          ;no, so check the next byte
45          sub     si,si   ;we didn't find a match, so return
46                          ; 0 in SI
47    FindCharInStringDone:
48          ret
49    ;
50    Skip:
51          call    ZTimerOn
52          mov     al,'z'          ;byte value to find
53          mov     si,offset TestString
54                                  ;string to search
55          call    FindCharInString ;search for the byte
56          call    ZTimerOff
```

Listing 11-14 shows an interesting variation on Listing 11-11. Here **lodsw** rather than **lodsb** is used, and AL and AH, respectively, are checked for the termination conditions. This technique uses a bit more code, but the replacement of two **lodsb** instructions with a single **lodsw** and the elimination of every other branch pays off handsomely, as Listing 11-14 runs in just 325 μsec, 15 percent faster than Listing 11-11 and 5 percent faster than Listing 11-12. The key here is that **lods** allows us leeway in designing code to work around the slow memory access and slow branching of the 8088, while **scas** allows little leeway of any sort. In truth, the flexibility of **lods** can make for better performance still through in-line code—but that's a story for the next few chapters.

```
1     ;
2     ; *** Listing 11-14 ***
3     ;
4     ; Finds the first occurrence of the letter 'z' in
5     ; a zero-terminated string, using LODSW and checking
6     ; 2 bytes per read.
7     ;
8             jmp     Skip
9     ;
10    TestString      label   byte
11            db      'This is a test string that is '
12            db      'z'
13            db      'terminated with a zero byte...',0
14    ;
```

```
15      ; Finds the first occurrence of the specified byte in the
16      ; specified zero-terminated string.
17      ;
18      ; Input:
19      ;       AL = byte to find
20      ;       DS:SI = zero-terminated string to search
21      ;
22      ; Output:
23      ;       SI = pointer to first occurrence of byte in string,
24      ;            or 0 if the byte wasn't found
25      ;
26      ; Registers altered: AX, BL, SI
27      ;
28      ; Direction flag cleared
29      ;
30      ; Note: Do not pass a string that starts at offset 0 (SI=0),
31      ;       since a match on the first byte and failure to find
32      ;       the byte would be indistinguishable.
33      ;
34      ; Note: Does not handle strings that are longer than 64K
35      ;       bytes or cross segment boundaries.
36      ;
37      FindCharInString:
38              mov     bl,al   ;we'll need AX since that's the
39                              ; only register LODSW can use
40              cld
41      FindCharInStringLoop:
42              lodsw           ;get the next 2 string bytes
43              cmp     al,bl   ;is the first byte the byte we're
44                              ; looking for?
45              jz      FindCharInStringDoneAdjust
46                              ;yes, so we're done after we adjust
47                              ; back to the first byte of the word
48              and     al,al   ;is the first byte the terminating
49                              ; zero?
50              jz      FindCharInStringNoMatch ;yes, no match
51              cmp     ah,bl   ;is the second byte the byte we're
52                              ; looking for?
53              jz      FindCharInStringDone
54                              ;yes, so we're done
55              and     ah,ah   ;is the second byte the terminating
56                              ; zero?
57              jnz     FindCharInStringLoop
58                              ;no, so check the next 2 bytes
59      FindCharInStringNoMatch:
60              sub     si,si   ;we didn't find a match, so return
61                              ; 0 in SI
62              ret
63      FindCharInStringDoneAdjust:
64              dec     si      ;adjust to the first byte of the
65                              ; word we just read
66      FindCharInStringDone:
67              dec     si      ;point back to the matching byte
68              ret
69      ;
70      Skip:
71              call    ZTimerOn
72              mov     al,'z'          ;byte value to find
```

```
73              mov     si,offset TestString
74                              ;string to search
75              call    FindCharInString ;search for the byte
76              call    ZTimerOff
```

More on scas and Zero-Terminated Strings

Although repeated **scas** instructions aren't ideally suited to string searches involving complex conditions, they *do* work nicely with strings whenever brute force scanning comes into play. One such application is finding the offset of the *last* element of some sort in a string. For example, Listing 11-15, which finds the last nonblank element of a string by using **lodsw** and remembering the offset of the most recent nonblank character encountered, takes 907 μsec to find the last nonblank character of the sample string, which has the last nonblank character in the middle of the string. Listing 11-16, which does the same thing by using **repnz scasb** to find the end of the string and then **repz scasw** with the direction flag set to 1 to find the first nonblank character scanning backward from the end of the string, runs in just 386 μsec.

```
1   ;
2   ; *** Listing 11-15 ***
3   ;
4   ; Finds the last non-blank character in a string, using
5   ; LODSW and checking 2 bytes per read.
6   ;
7           jmp     Skip
8   ;
9   TestString      label   byte
10          db      'This is a test string with blanks....'
11          db      '                                    ',0
12  ;
13  ; Finds the last non-blank character in the specified
14  ; zero-terminated string.
15  ;
16  ; Input:
17  ;       DS:SI = zero-terminated string to search
18  ;
19  ; Output:
20  ;       SI = pointer to last non-blank character in string,
21  ;               or 0 if there are no non-blank characters in
22  ;               the string
23  ;
24  ; Registers altered: AX, BL, DX, SI
25  ;
26  ; Direction flag cleared
27  ;
28  ; Note: Do not pass a string that starts at offset 0 (SI=0),
29  ;       since a return pointer to the first byte and failure
30  ;       to find a non-blank character would be
31  ;       indistinguishable.
```

```
32    ;
33    ; Note: Does not handle strings that are longer than 64K
34    ;       bytes or cross segment boundaries.
35    ;
36    FindLastNonBlankInString:
37            mov     dx,1    ;so far we haven't found a non-blank
38                            ; character
39            mov     bl,' '  ;put our search character, the space
40                            ; character, in a register for speed
41            cld
42    FindLastNonBlankInStringLoop:
43            lodsw           ;get the next 2 string bytes
44            and     al,al   ;is the first byte the terminating
45                            ; zero?
46            jz      FindLastNonBlankInStringDone
47                            ;yes, we're done
48            cmp     al,bl   ;is the second byte a space?
49            jz      FindLastNonBlankInStringNextChar
50                            ;yes, so check the next character
51            mov     dx,si   ;remember where the non-blank was
52            dec     dx      ;adjust back to first byte of word
53    FindLastNonBlankInStringNextChar:
54            and     ah,ah   ;is the second byte the terminating
55                            ; zero?
56            jz      FindLastNonBlankInStringDone
57                            ;yes, we're done
58            cmp     ah,bl   ;is the second byte a space?
59            jz      FindLastNonBlankInStringLoop
60                            ;yes, so check the next 2 bytes
61            mov     dx,si   ;remember where the non-blank was
62            jmp     FindLastNonBlankInStringLoop
63                            ;check the next 2 bytes
64    FindLastNonBlankInStringDone:
65            dec     dx      ;point back to the last non-blank
66                            ; character, correcting for the
67                            ; 1-byte overrun of LODSW
68            mov     si,dx   ;return pointer to last non-blank
69                            ; character in SI
70            ret
71    ;
72    Skip:
73            call    ZTimerOn
74            mov     si,offset TestString    ;string to search
75            call    FindLastNonBlankInString ;search for the byte
76            call    ZTimerOff
```

That's an *amazing* improvement given our earlier results involving the relative speeds of **lodsw** and repeated **scas** in string applications. The reason that repeated **scas** outperforms **lodsw** by a tremendous amount in this case but underperformed it earlier is simple. The **lodsw**-based code always has to check every character in the string—right up to the terminating 0—when searching for the last nonblank character, as shown in Figure 11.12. While the **scasb**-based code also has to access every character in the string, and then some, as shown in Figure 11.13, the worst case is that

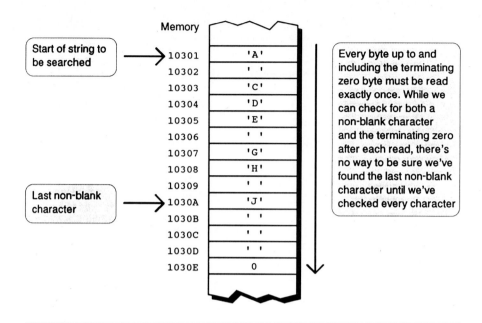

FIGURE 11.12   When **lods** and **cmp** are used to find the last non-blank character in a 0-terminated string, every byte in the string must always be read. Although each byte can be loaded into the accumulator and tested at once both for blank/nonblank status and for being the 0 that terminates the string, it is nonetheless necessary to read every byte right up through the terminating 0; we're looking for the *last* nonblank character, and we can't be sure we've found it without reading the last character as well as every character that precedes it. Under all circumstances, the entire string is read exactly one time.

Listing 11-16 accesses string elements no more than twice as many times as Listing 11-15. In our earlier example, the *best* case was a 2:1 ratio. The timing results for Listings 11-15 and 11-16 show that the superior speed, lack of prefetching, and lack of branching associated with repeated **scas** far outweigh any performance loss resulting from a memory access ratio of less than 2:1.

By the way, Listing 11-16 is an excellent example of the need to correct for pointer overrun when using the string instructions. No matter which direction we scan in, it's necessary to undo the last advance of DI performed by **scas** in order to point to the byte on which the comparison ended.

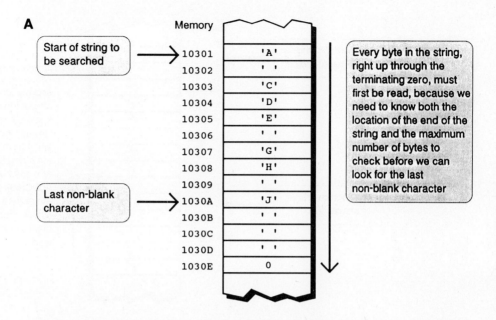

A

Memory

Start of string to be searched	→	10301	'A'
		10302	' '
		10303	'C'
		10304	'D'
		10305	'E'
		10306	' '
		10307	'G'
		10308	'H'
		10309	' '
Last non-blank character	→	1030A	'J'
		1030B	' '
		1030C	' '
		1030D	' '
		1030E	0

Every byte in the string, right up through the terminating zero, must first be read, because we need to know both the location of the end of the string and the maximum number of bytes to check before we can look for the last non-blank character

FIGURE 11.13 When repeated **scas** is used to find the last non-blank character in a 0-terminated string, a double-search method must be used. **(A)** Every byte in the string must first be read in order to find the terminating 0. This gives us the length of the string, so we know the maximum number of bytes to search in the second step. This first step also tells us where to start our search for the last nonblank character, because we'll use **scas** with DF set to 1 to search backward from the end of the string. **(B)** The second step consists of the backward search, which continues until a nonblank character is found or until the number of bytes found in the first step have been searched without finding a nonblank character.

With this double-search approach, each byte in the string is read at least once and the byte preceding the terminating 0 is always read twice, that being the minimum case that occurs only when the last nonblank character is the last byte of the string. Each byte (except for the terminating 0) is read at most twice, that being the case if the entire string consists of blanks. On average, the entire string will be read one and one half times.

B

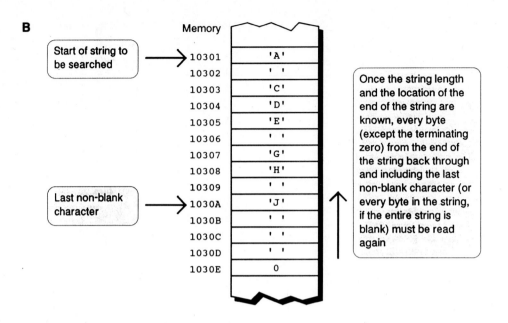

Start of string to
be searched → 10301   'A'

10302   ' '

10303   'C'

10304   'D'

10305   'E'

10306   ' '

10307   'G'

10308   'H'

10309   ' '

Last non-blank
character → 1030A   'J'

1030B   ' '

1030C   ' '

1030D   ' '

1030E   0

Memory

Once the string length
and the location of the
end of the string are
known, every byte
(except the terminating
zero) from the end of
the string back through
and including the last
non-blank character (or
every byte in the string,
if the entire string is
blank) must be read
again

FIGURE 11.13   (*continued*)

```
1    ;
2    ; *** Listing 11-16 ***
3    ;
4    ; Finds the last non-blank character in a string, using
5    ; REPNZ SCASB to find the end of the string and then using
6    ; REPZ SCASW from the end of the string to find the last
7    ; non-blank character.
8    ;
9            jmp      Skip
10   ;
11   TestString     label    byte
12           db       'This is a test string with blanks....'
13           db       '                            ',0
14   ;
15   ; Finds the last non-blank character in the specified
16   ; zero-terminated string.
17   ;
18   ; Input:
19   ;       DS:SI = zero-terminated string to search
20   ;
21   ; Output:
22   ;       SI = pointer to last non-blank character in string,
23   ;               or 0 if there are no non-blank characters in
24   ;               the string
25   ;
26   ; Registers altered: AX, CX, SI, DI, ES
27   ;
28   ; Direction flag cleared
29   ;
```

```
30    ; Note: Do not pass a string that starts at offset 0 (SI=0),
31    ;       since a return pointer to the first byte and failure
32    ;       to find a non-blank character would be
33    ;       indistinguishable.
34    ;
35    ; Note: If there is no terminating zero in the first 64K-1
36    ;       bytes of the string, it is assumed without checking
37    ;       that byte #64K-1 (the 1 byte in the segment that
38    ;       wasn't checked) is the terminating zero.
39    ;
40    ; Note: Does not handle strings that are longer than 64K
41    ;       bytes or cross segment boundaries.
42    ;
43    FindLastNonBlankInString:
44            push    ds
45            pop     es
46            mov     di,si   ;SCAS uses ES:DI
47            sub     al,al   ;first we'll search for the
48                            ; terminating zero
49            mov     cx,0ffffh ;we'll search the longest possible
50                            ; string
51            cld
52            repnz   scasb   ;find the terminating zero
53            dec     di      ;point back to the zero
54            cmp     [di],al ;make sure this is a zero.
55                            ; (Remember, ES=DS)
56            jnz     FindLastNonBlankInStringSearchBack
57                            ; not a zero. The string must be
58                            ; exactly 64K bytes long, so we've
59                            ; come up 1 byte short of the zero
60                            ; that we're assuming is at byte
61                            ; 64K-1. That means we're already
62                            ; pointing to the byte before the
63                            ; zero
64            dec     di      ;point to the byte before the zero
65            inc     cx      ;don't count the terminating zero
66                            ; as one of the characters we've
67                            ; searched through (and have to
68                            ; search back through)
69    FindLastNonBlankInStringSearchBack:
70            std             ;we'll search backward
71            not     cx      ;length of string, not including
72                            ; the terminating zero
73            mov     ax,2020h ;now we're looking for a space
74            shr     cx,1    ;divide by 2 to get a word count
75            jnc     FindLastNonBlankInStringWord
76            scasb           ;see if the odd byte is the last
77                            ; non-blank character
78            jnz     FindLastNonBlankInStringFound
79                            ;it is, so we're done
80    FindLastNonBlankInStringWord:
81            jcxz    FindLastNonBlankInStringNoMatch
82                            ;if there's nothing left to check,
83                            ; there are no non-blank characters
84            dec     di      ;point back to the start of the
85                            ; next word, not byte
86            repz    scasw   ;find the first non-blank character
87            jz      FindLastNonBlankInStringNoMatch
```

```
88                               ;there is no non-blank character in
89                               ; this string
90              inc     di       ;undo 1 byte of SCASW's overrun, so
91                               ; this looks like SCASB's overrun
92              cmp     [di+2],al ;which of the 2 bytes we just
93                               ; checked was the last non-blank
94                               ; character?
95              jz      FindLastNonBlankInStringFound
96              inc     di       ;the byte at the higher address was
97                               ; the last non-blank character, so
98                               ; adjust by 1 byte
99      FindLastNonBlankInStringFound:
100             inc     di       ;point to the non-blank character
101                              ; we just found, correcting for
102                              ; overrun of SCASB running from high
103                              ; addresses to low
104             mov     si,di    ;return pointer to the last
105                              ; non-blank in SI
106             cld
107             ret
108     FindLastNonBlankInStringNoMatch:
109             sub     si,si    ;return that we didn't find a
110                              ; non-blank character
111             cld
112             ret
113     ;
114     Skip:
115             call    ZTimerOn
116             mov     si,offset TestString     ;string to search
117             call    FindLastNonBlankInString ;search for the
118                                              ; last non-blank
119                                              ; character
120             call    ZTimerOff
```

Listing 11-16 also shows the use of **jcxz** to guard against the case where CX is 0. As you'll recall from the last chapter, repeated **scas** doesn't alter the flags when started with CX equal to 0. Consequently, we must test for the case of CX equal to 0 before performing **repz scasw**, and we must treat that case as if we had never found the terminating condition (a nonblank character). Otherwise, the leftover flags from an earlier instruction might give us a false result following a **repz scasw** that doesn't change the flags because it is repeated 0 times. In Listing 11-21 we'll see that we need to do the same with repeated **cmps** as well.

Bear in mind, however, that there are several ways to solve any problem in assembler. For example, in Listing 11-16 I've chosen to use **jcxz** to guard against the case where CX is 0, thereby compensating for the fact that **scas** repeated 0 times doesn't change the flags. Rather than thinking defensively, however, we could actually take advantage of that particular property of repeated **scas**. How? We could set ZF to 1 (the match state) by placing **sub dx,dx** before **repz scasw**. Then if **repz scasw** is repeated 0 times because CX is 0, the following conditional jump will reach the proper conclusion—that the desired nonmatch (a nonblank character) wasn't found.

As it happens, **sub dx,dx** isn't particularly faster than **jcxz**, so there's not much to choose from between the two solutions. With **sub dx,dx** the code is 3 cycles faster when CX isn't 0 but is the same number of bytes in length and is considerably slower when CX is 0. (There's really no reason to worry about performance here when CX is 0, however, since that's a rare case that's always handled relatively quickly. Rather, our focus should be on losing as little performance as possible to the test for CX being 0 in the more common case, when CX *isn't* 0.) In another application, though, the desired ZF setting might fall out of the code preceding the repeated **cmps**, and no extra code at all would be required for the test for CX equal to 0. Listing 11-24, which we'll come to shortly, is such a case.

What's interesting here is that it's instinctive to use **jcxz**, which is after all a specialized and fast instruction that is clearly present in the 8088's instruction set for just such a purpose as protecting against repeating a string comparison 0 times. The idea of presetting a flag and letting the comparison drop through without changing the flag, on the other hand, is anything but intuitive, but it is just about as effective as **jcxz**, more so under certain circumstances.

Don't let your mind be constrained by intentions of the designers of the 8088. Think in terms of what instructions *do* rather than what they were *intended* to do.

Using Repeated scasw on Byte-Sized Data

Listing 11-16 is also a fine example of how to use repeated **scasw** on byte-sized data. You'll recall that one of the rules of repeated string instruction utilization is that word-sized string instructions should be used wherever possible, owing to their faster overall speed. It turns out, however, that it's rather tricky to apply this rule to **scas**.

For starters, there's hardly ever any use for **repnz scasw** when searching for a specific byte value in memory. Why? Well, although we could load up both AH and AL with the byte we're looking for and then use **repnz scasw**, we'd find only cases where the desired byte occurs at least twice in a row, and then we'd find only such 2-byte cases that didn't span word boundaries. Unfortunately, there's no way to use **repnz scasw** to check whether either AH or AL—but not necessarily both—matched their respective bytes. With **repnz scasw**, if AX doesn't match all 16 bits of memory, the search will continue, and individual byte matches will be missed.

On the other hand, we *can* use **repz scasw** to search for the first *nonmatch*, as in Listing 11-16. Why is it all right to search a word at a time for nonmatches but not for matches? Because if *either* byte of each word compared with **repz scasw** doesn't match the byte of interest (which is stored in both AH and AL), then **repz scasw** will stop, which is what we want. Of course, there's a bit of cleaning up to do in order to figure out which of the 2 bytes was the first nonmatch, as illustrated by Listing 11-16. Yes, it is a bit complex and does add a few bytes, but it also speeds things up, and that's what we're after.

In short, **repz scasw** can be used to boost performance when scanning for nonmatching byte-sized data. However, **repnz scasw** is generally useless when scanning for matching byte-sized data.

scas and Look-Up Tables

One common application for table searching is to get an element number or an offset into a table that can be used to look up related data or a jump address in another table. We saw look-up tables in Chapter 7, and we'll see them again, for they're a potent performance tool.

The **scas** instruction is often excellent for look-up code, but the pointer and counter overrun characteristic of all string instructions make it a bit of a nuisance to calculate offsets and/or element numbers after repeated **scas** instructions. Listing 11-17 shows a subroutine that calculates the offset of a match in a word-sized table in the process of jumping to the associated routine from a jump table. Notice that it's necessary to subtract the 2-byte overrun from the difference between the final value of DI and the start of the table. The calculation would be the same for a byte-sized table scanned with **scasb**, except that **scasb** has only a 1-byte overrun and so only 1 would be subtracted from the difference between DI and the start of the table.

```
 1   ;
 2   ; *** Listing 11-17 ***
 3   ;
 4   ; Demonstrates the calculation of the offset of the word
 5   ; matching a keystroke in a look-up table when SCASW is
 6   ; used, where the 2-byte overrun of SCASW must be
 7   ; compensated for. The offset in the look-up table is used
 8   ; to look up the corresponding address in a second table;
 9   ; that address is then jumped to in order to handle the
10   ; keystroke.
11   ;
12   ; This is a standalone program, not to be used with PZTIME
13   ; but rather assembled, linked, and run by itself.
14   ;
15   stack   segment para stack 'STACK'
16           db       512 dup (?)
17   stack   ends
```

```
18      ;
19      code    segment para public 'CODE'
20              assume  cs:code, ds:nothing
21      ;
22      ; Main loop, which simply calls VectorOnKey until one of the
23      ; key handlers ends the program.
24      ;
25      start   proc    near
26              call    VectorOnKey
27              jmp     start
28      start   endp
29      ;
30      ; Gets the next 16-bit key code from the BIOS, looks it up
31      ; in KeyLookUpTable, and jumps to the corresponding routine
32      ; according to KeyJumpTable. When the jumped-to routine
33      ; returns, is will return to the code that called
34      ; VectorOnKey. Ignores the key if the key code is not in the
35      ; look-up table.
36      ;
37      ; Input: none
38      ;
39      ; Output: none
40      ;
41      ; Registers altered: AX, CX, DI, ES
42      ;
43      ; Direction flag cleared
44      ;
45      ; Table of 16-bit key codes this routine handles.
46      ;
47      KeyLookUpTable  label   word
48              dw      0011bh  ;Esc to exit
49              dw      01c0dh  ;Enter to beep
50      ;*** Additional key codes go here ***
51      KEY_LOOK_UP_TABLE_LENGTH_IN_WORDS equ (($-KeyLookUpTable)/2)
52      ;
53      ; Table of addresses to jump to when corresponding key codes
54      ; in KeyLookUpTable are found.
55      ;
56      KeyJumpTable    label   word
57              dw      EscHandler
58              dw      EnterHandler
59      ;*** Additional addresses go here ***
60      ;
61      VectorOnKey     proc    near
62      WaitKeyLoop:
63              mov     ah,1    ;BIOS key status function
64              int     16h     ;invoke BIOS to see if
65                              ; a key is pending
66              jz      WaitKeyLoop     ;wait until key comes along
67              sub     ah,ah   ;BIOS get key function
68              int     16h     ;invoke BIOS to get the key
69              push    cs
70              pop     es
71              mov     di,offset KeyLookUpTable
72                              ;point ES:DI to the table of keys
73                              ; we handle, which is in the same
74                              ; segment as this code
75              mov     cx,KEY_LOOK_UP_TABLE_LENGTH_IN_WORDS
76                              ;# of words to scan
```

```
77              cld
78              repnz   scasw   ;look up the key
79              jnz     WaitKeyLoop   ;it's not in the table, so
80                              ; ignore it
81              jmp     cs:[KeyJumpTable+di-2-offset KeyLookUpTable]
82                              ;jump to the routine for this key
83                              ; Note that:
84                              ;   DI-2-offset KeyLookUpTable
85                              ; is the offset in KeyLookUpTable of
86                              ; the key we found, with the -2
87                              ; needed to compensate for the
88                              ; 2-byte (1-word) overrun of SCASW
89      VectorOnKey     endp
90      ;
91      ; Code to handle Esc (ends the program).
92      ;
93      EscHandler      proc    near
94              mov     ah,4ch  ;DOS terminate program function
95              int     21h     ;exit program
96      EscHandler      endp
97      ;
98      ; Code to handle Enter (beeps the speaker).
99      ;
100     EnterHandler    proc    near
101             mov     ax,0e07h ;AH=0E is BIOS print character
102                             ; function, AL=7 is bell (beep)
103                             ; character
104             int     10h     ;tell BIOS to beep the speaker
105             ret
106     EnterHandler    endp
107     ;
108     code    ends
109             end     start
```

Finding the element number is a slightly different matter. After a repeated **scas**, CX contains the number of elements that weren't scanned. Since CX counts down just once each time **scas** is repeated, there's no difference between **scasw** and **scasb** in this respect.

Well, if CX contains the number of elements that weren't scanned, then subtracting CX from the table length in elements must yield the number of elements that *were* scanned. Subtracting 1 from that value gives us the number of the last element scanned. (The first element is element number 0, the second element is element number 1, and so on.) Listing 11-18 illustrates the calculation of the element number found in a look-up table as a step in the process of jumping to the associated routine from a jump table, much as in Listing 11-17.

```
1       ;
2       ; *** Listing 11-18 ***
3       ;
4       ; Demonstrates the calculation of the element number in a
5       ; look-up table of a byte matching the ASCII value of a
```

```
 6      ; keystroke when SCASB is used, where the 1-count
 7      ; overrun of SCASB must be compensated for. The element
 8      ; number in the look-up table is used to look up the
 9      ; corresponding address in a second table; that address is
10      ; then jumped to in order to handle the keystroke.
11      ;
12      ; This is a standalone program, not to be used with PZTIME
13      ; but rather assembled, linked, and run by itself.
14      ;
15      stack   segment para stack 'STACK'
16              db      512 dup (?)
17      stack   ends
18      ;
19      code    segment para public 'CODE'
20              assume  cs:code, ds:nothing
21      ;
22      ; Main loop, which simply calls VectorOnASCIIKey until one
23      ; of the key handlers ends the program.
24      ;
25      start   proc    near
26              call    VectorOnASCIIKey
27              jmp     start
28      start   endp
29      ;
30      ; Gets the next 16-bit key code from the BIOS, looks up just
31      ; the 8-bit ASCII portion in ASCIIKeyLookUpTable, and jumps
32      ; to the corresponding routine according to
33      ; ASCIIKeyJumpTable. When the jumped-to routine returns, it
34      ; will return directly to the code that called
35      ; VectorOnASCIIKey. Ignores the key if the key code is not
36      ; in the look-up table.
37      ;
38      ; Input: none
39      ;
40      ; Output: none
41      ;
42      ; Registers altered: AX, CX, DI, ES
43      ;
44      ; Direction flag cleared
45      ;
46      ; Table of 8-bit ASCII codes this routine handles.
47      ;
48      ASCIIKeyLookUpTable      label   word
49              db      02h     ;Ctrl-B to beep
50              db      18h     ;Ctrl-X to exit
51      ;*** Additional ASCII codes go here ***
52      ASCII_KEY_LOOK_UP_TABLE_LENGTH equ ($-ASCIIKeyLookUpTable)
53      ;
54      ; Table of addresses to jump to when corresponding key codes
55      ; in ASCIIKeyLookUpTable are found.
56      ;
57      ASCIIKeyJumpTable        label   word
58              dw      Beep
59              dw      Exit
60      ;*** Additional addresses go here ***
61      ;
62      VectorOnASCIIKey         proc    near
63      WaitASCIIKeyLoop:
64              mov     ah,1     ;BIOS key status function
```

```
65              int     16h       ;invoke BIOS to see if
66                                ; a key is pending
67              jz      WaitASCIIKeyLoop ;wait until key comes along
68              sub     ah,ah     ;BIOS get key function
69              int     16h       ;invoke BIOS to get the key
70              push    cs
71              pop     es
72              mov     di,offset ASCIIKeyLookUpTable
73                                ;point ES:DI to the table of keys
74                                ; we handle, which is in the same
75                                ; segment as this code
76              mov     cx,ASCII_KEY_LOOK_UP_TABLE_LENGTH
77                                ;# of bytes to scan
78              cld
79              repnz   scasb     ;look up the key
80              jnz     WaitASCIIKeyLoop ;it's not in the table, so
81                                ; ignore it
82              mov     di,ASCII_KEY_LOOK_UP_TABLE_LENGTH-1
83              sub     di,cx     ;calculate the # of the element we
84                                ; found in ASCIIKeyLookUpTable.
85                                ; The -1 is needed to compensate for
86                                ; the 1-count overrun of SCAS
87              shl     di,1      ;multiply by 2 in order to perform
88                                ; the look-up in word-sized
89                                ; ASCIIKeyJumpTable
90              jmp     cs:[ASCIIKeyJumpTable+di]
91                                ;jump to the routine for this key
92  VectorOnASCIIKey      endp
93  ;
94  ; Code to handle Ctrl-X (ends the program).
95  ;
96  Exit    proc    near
97          mov     ah,4ch    ;DOS terminate program function
98          int     21h       ;exit program
99  Exit    endp
100 ;
101 ; Code to handle Ctrl-B (beeps the speaker).
102 ;
103 Beep    proc    near
104         mov     ax,0e07h  ;AH=0E is BIOS print character
105                           ; function, AL=7 is bell (beep)
106                           ; character
107         int     10h       ;tell BIOS to beep the speaker
108         ret
109 Beep    endp
110 ;
111 code    ends
112         end     start
```

Consider Your Options

Don't assume that **scas** is the ideal choice, even for all memory-searching tasks in which the search length is known. Suppose that we simply want to know whether a given character is any of, say, four characters: *A, Z, 3,* or *!.* We could do this with **repnz scasb**, as shown in Listing 11-19. Alternatively, we could simply do it with four comparisons and conditional

```
1    ;
2    ; *** Listing 11-19 ***
3    ;
4    ; Tests whether several characters are in the set
5    ; {A,Z,3,!} by using REPNZ SCASB.
6    ;
7            jmp     Skip
8    ;
9    ; List of characters in the set.
10   ;
11   TestSet db      "AZ3!"
12   TEST_SET_LENGTH equ     ($-TestSet)
13   ;
14   ; Determines whether a given character is in TestSet.
15   ;
16   ; Input:
17   ;       AL = character to check for inclusion in TestSet
18   ;
19   ; Output:
20   ;       Z if character is in TestSet, NZ otherwise
21   ;
22   ; Registers altered: DI, ES
23   ;
24   ; Direction flag cleared
25   ;
26   CheckTestSetInclusion:
27           push    ds
28           pop     es
29           mov     di,offset TestSet
30                           ;point ES:DI to the set in which to
31                           ; check inclusion
32           mov     cx,TEST_SET_LENGTH
33                           ;# of characters in TestSet
34           cld
35           repnz   scasb   ;search the set for this character
36           ret             ;the success status is already in
37                           ; the Zero flag
38   ;
39   Skip:
40           call    ZTimerOn
41           mov     al,'A'
42           call    CheckTestSetInclusion    ;check 'A'
43           mov     al,'Z'
44           call    CheckTestSetInclusion    ;check 'Z'
45           mov     al,'3'
46           call    CheckTestSetInclusion    ;check '3'
47           mov     al,'!'
48           call    CheckTestSetInclusion    ;check '!'
49           mov     al,' '
50           call    CheckTestSetInclusion    ;check space, so
51                                            ; we get a failed
52                                            ; search
53           call    ZTimerOff
```

jumps, as shown in Listing 11-20. Even with the prefetch queue cycle eater doing its worst, each compare and conditional jump pair takes no more than 16 cycles when the jump isn't taken (the jump is taken at most once, on a match), which stacks up pretty well against the 15 cycles

```
1    ;
2    ; *** Listing 11-20 ***
3    ;
4    ; Tests whether several characters are in the set
5    ; {A,Z,3,!} by using the compare-and-jump approach.
6    ;
7             jmp     Skip
8    ;
9    ; Determines whether a given character is in the set
10   ; {A,Z,3,!}.
11   ;
12   ; Input:
13   ;       AL = character to check for inclusion in the set
14   ;
15   ; Output:
16   ;       Z if character is in TestSet, NZ otherwise
17   ;
18   ; Registers altered: none
19   ;
20   CheckTestSetInclusion:
21           cmp     al,'A'  ;is it 'A'?
22           jz      CheckTestSetInclusionDone ;yes, we're done
23           cmp     al,'Z'  ;is it 'Z'?
24           jz      CheckTestSetInclusionDone ;yes, we're done
25           cmp     al,'3'  ;is it '3'?
26           jz      CheckTestSetInclusionDone ;yes, we're done
27           cmp     al,'!'  ;is it '!'?
28   CheckTestSetInclusionDone:
29           ret             ;the success status is already in
30                           ; the Zero flag
31   ;
32   Skip:
33           call    ZTimerOn
34           mov     al,'A'
35           call    CheckTestSetInclusion    ;check 'A'
36           mov     al,'Z'
37           call    CheckTestSetInclusion    ;check 'Z'
38           mov     al,'3'
39           call    CheckTestSetInclusion    ;check '3'
40           mov     al,'!'
41           call    CheckTestSetInclusion    ;check '!'
42           mov     al,' '
43           call    CheckTestSetInclusion    ;check space, so
44                                            ; we get a failed
45                                            ; search
46           call    ZTimerOff
```

per comparison and 9-cycle setup time of **repnz scasb**. What's more, the compare-and-jump approach requires no setup instructions. In other words, the less sophisticated approach might well be better in this case.

The Zen timer bears this out. Listing 11-19, which uses **repnz scasb**, takes 183 μsec to perform five checks; Listing 11-20, which uses the compare-and-jump approach, takes just 119 μsec to perform the same five checks. Listing 11-20 is not only 54 percent faster than Listing 11-19 but is also 1 byte shorter. (Don't forget to count the look-up table bytes in Listing 11-19.)

Of course, the compare-and-jump approach is less flexible than the look-up approach, since the table length and contents can't be passed as parameters or changed as the program runs. The compare-and-jump approach also becomes unwieldy when more entries need to be checked, since 4 bytes are needed for each additional compare-and-jump entry where the **repnz scasb** approach needs just 1. The compare-and-jump approach finally falls apart when it's no longer possible to short jump out of the comparison/jump code and jumps around jumps must be used, as in

```
cmp    al,'Z'
jnz    $+5
jmp    CharacterFound
cmp    al,'3'
```

When jumps around jumps are used, the comparison time per character goes from 16 to 24 cycles and **rep scasb** emerges as the clear favorite.

Nonetheless, Listings 11-19 and 11-20 illustrate two important points. Point number 1: the repeated string instructions tend to have a greater advantage when they're repeated many times, allowing their speed and compact size to offset the overhead in setup time and code they require. Point number 2: specialized as the string instructions are, there are ways to program the 8088 that are more specialized still. In certain cases, those specialized approaches can even outperform the string instructions. Sure, the specialized approaches, such as the compare-and-jump approach we just saw, are limited and inflexible—but when you don't need the flexibility, why pay for it in lost performance?

11.4 ◆ Comparing Memory with Memory Using cmps

When **cmps** does exactly what you need done it can't be beat, although to an even greater extent than with **scas** the cases in which that is true are relatively few. The **cmps** instruction is used for applications in which byte-for-byte or word-for-word comparisons between two memory blocks of a known length are performed, most notably array comparisons and substring searching. Like **scas**, **cmps** is not flexible enough to work at full power on other comparison tasks, such as case-insensitive substring searching or the comparison of 0-terminated strings, although with a bit of thought **cmps** can be made to serve adequately in some such applications.

The **cmps** instruction does just one thing, but it does that thing far better than any other 8088 instruction or combination of instructions. The one transcendent ability of **cmps** is the direct comparison of two fixed-length blocks of memory. The obvious use of **cmps** is in determining whether two memory arrays or blocks of memory are the same, and if not, where they differ. Listing 11-21, which runs in 685 μsec, illustrates **repz cmpsw** in action. Listing 11-22, which performs exactly the same task as Listing 11-21 but uses **lodsw** and **scasw** instead of **cmpsw**, runs in 1298 μsec. Finally, Listing 11-23, which uses nonstring instructions, takes a leisurely 1798 μsec to complete the task. As you can see, **cmps** blows away not only nonstring instructions but also other string instructions under the right circumstances. (As I've said before, there are many, many different sequences of assembler code that will work for any given task. It's the choice of implementation that makes the difference between adequate code and great code.)

```
1    ;
2    ; *** Listing 11-21 ***
3    ;
4    ; Compares two word-sized arrays of equal length to see
5    ; whether they differ, and if so where, using REPZ CMPSW.
6    ;
7            jmp     Skip
8    ;
9    WordArray1      dw      100 dup (1), 0, 99 dup (2)
10   ARRAY_LENGTH_IN_WORDS   equ     (($-WordArray1)/2)
11   WordArray2      dw      100 dup (1), 100 dup (2)
12   ;
13   ; Returns pointers to the first locations at which two
14   ; word-sized arrays of equal length differ, or zero if
15   ; they're identical.
16   ;
17   ; Input:
18   ;       CX = length of the arrays (they must be of equal
19   ;               length)
20   ;       DS:SI = the first array to compare
21   ;       ES:DI = the second array to compare
22   ;
23   ; Output:
24   ;       DS:SI = pointer to the first differing location in
25   ;               the first array if there is a difference,
26   ;               or SI=0 if the arrays are identical
27   ;       ES:DI = pointer to the first differing location in
28   ;               the second array if there is a difference,
29   ;               or DI=0 if the arrays are identical
30   ;
31   ; Registers altered: SI, DI
32   ;
33   ; Direction flag cleared
34   ;
35   ; Note: Does not handle arrays that are longer than 32K
36   ;       words or cross segment boundaries.
37   ;
38   FindFirstDifference:
39           cld
40           jcxz    FindFirstDifferenceSame
41                                   ;if there's nothing to
```

```
42                                         ; check, we'll consider the
43                                         ; arrays to be the same.
44                                         ; (If we let REPZ CMPSW
45                                         ; execute with CX=0, we
46                                         ; may get a false match
47                                         ; because CMPSW repeated
48                                         ; zero times doesn't alter
49                                         ; the flags)
50          repz    cmpsw               ;compare the arrays
51          jz      FindFirstDifferenceSame ;they're identical
52          dec     si                  ;the arrays differ, so
53          dec     si                  ; point back to first
54          dec     di                  ; difference in both arrays
55          dec     di
56          ret
57  FindFirstDifferenceSame:
58          sub     si,si               ;indicate that the strings
59          mov     di,si               ; are identical
60          ret
61  ;
62  Skip:
63          call    ZTimerOn
64          mov     si,offset WordArray1    ;point to the two
65          mov     di,ds                   ; arrays to be
66          mov     es,di                   ; compared
67          mov     di,offset WordArray2
68          mov     cx,ARRAY_LENGTH_IN_WORDS
69                                          ;# of words to check
70          call    FindFirstDifference ;see if they differ
71          call    ZTimerOff
```

```
1   ;
2   ; *** Listing 11-22 ***
3   ;
4   ; Compares two word-sized arrays of equal length to see
5   ; whether they differ, and if so where, using LODSW and
6   ; SCASW.
7   ;
8           jmp     Skip
9   ;
10  WordArray1      dw      100 dup (1), 0, 99 dup (2)
11  ARRAY_LENGTH_IN_WORDS   equ     (($-WordArray1)/2)
12  WordArray2      dw      100 dup (1), 100 dup (2)
13  ;
14  ; Returns pointers to the first locations at which two
15  ; word-sized arrays of equal length differ, or zero if
16  ; they're identical.
17  ;
18  ; Input:
19  ;       CX = length of the arrays (they must be of equal
20  ;            length)
21  ;       DS:SI = the first array to compare
22  ;       ES:DI = the second array to compare
23  ;
24  ; Output:
25  ;       DS:SI = pointer to the first differing location in
26  ;               the first array if there is a difference,
```

```
27    ;              or SI=0 if the arrays are identical
28    ;     ES:DI = pointer to the first differing location in
29    ;              the second array if there is a difference,
30    ;              or DI=0 if the arrays are identical
31    ;
32    ; Registers altered: AX, SI, DI
33    ;
34    ; Direction flag cleared
35    ;
36    ; Note: Does not handle arrays that are longer than 32K
37    ;       words or cross segment boundaries.
38    ;
39    FindFirstDifference:
40            cld
41            jcxz    FindFirstDifferenceSame
42                                    ;if there's nothing to
43                                    ; check, we'll consider the
44                                    ; arrays to be the same.
45                                    ; (If we let LOOP
46                                    ; execute with CX=0, we'll
47                                    ; get 64 K repetitions)
48    FindFirstDifferenceLoop:
49            lodsw
50            scasw                   ;compare the next two words
51            jnz     FindFirstDifferenceFound
52                                    ;the arrays differ
53            loop    FindFirstDifferenceLoop
54                                    ;the arrays are the
55                                    ; same so far
56    FindFirstDifferenceSame:
57            sub     si,si           ;indicate that the strings
58            mov     di,si           ; are identical
59            ret
60    FindFirstDifferenceFound:
61            dec     si              ;the arrays differ, so
62            dec     si              ; point back to first
63            dec     di              ; difference in both arrays
64            dec     di
65            ret
66    ;
67    Skip:
68            call    ZTimerOn
69            mov     si,offset WordArray1    ;point to the two
70            mov     di,ds                   ; arrays to be
71            mov     es,di                   ; compared
72            mov     di,offset WordArray2
73            mov     cx,ARRAY_LENGTH_IN_WORDS
74                                    ;# of words to check
75            call    FindFirstDifference     ;see if they differ
76            call    ZTimerOff
```

```
1     ;
2     ; *** Listing 11-23 ***
3     ;
4     ; Compares two word-sized arrays of equal length to see
5     ; whether they differ, and if so, where, using non-string
```

```
 6    ; instructions.
 7    ;
 8              jmp     Skip
 9    ;
10    WordArray1        dw        100 dup (1), 0, 99 dup (2)
11    ARRAY_LENGTH_IN_WORDS   equu    ' (($-WordArray1)/2)
12    WordArray2        dw        100 dup (1), 100 dup (2)
13    ;
14    ; Returns pointers to the first locations at which two
15    ; word-sized arrays of equal length differ, or zero if
16    ; they're identical.
17    ;
18    ; Input:
19    ;         CX = length of the arrays (they must be of equal
20    ;                  length)
21    ;         DS:SI = the first array to compare
22    ;         ES:DI = the second array to compare
23    ;
24    ; Output:
25    ;         DS:SI = pointer to the first differing location in
26    ;                  the first array if there is a difference,
27    ;                  or SI=0 if the arrays are identical
28    ;         ES:DI = pointer to the first differing location in
29    ;                  the second array if there is a difference,
30    ;                  or DI=0 if the arrays are identical
31    ;
32    ; Registers altered: AX, SI, DI
33    ;
34    ; Note: Does not handle arrays that are longer than 32K
35    ;          words or cross segment boundaries.
36    ;
37    FindFirstDifference:
38              jcxz    FindFirstDifferenceSame
39                                      ;if there's nothing to
40                                      ; check, we'll consider the
41                                      ; arrays to be the same
42    FindFirstDifferenceLoop:
43              mov     ax,[si]
44              cmp     es:[di],ax      ;compare the next two words
45              jnz     FindFirstDifferenceFound ;the arrays differ
46              inc     si
47              inc     si              ;point to the next words to
48              inc     di              ; compare
49              inc     di
50              loop    FindFirstDifferenceLoop ;the arrays are the
51                                      ; same so far
52    FindFirstDifferenceSame:
53              sub     si,si           ;indicate that the strings
54              mov     di,si           ; are identical
55    FindFirstDifferenceFound:
56              ret
57    ;
58    Skip:
59              call    ZTimerOn
60              mov     si,offset WordArray1    ;point to the two
61              mov     di,ds                   ; arrays to be
62              mov     es,di                   ; compared
63              mov     di,offset WordArray2
64              mov     cx,ARRAY_LENGTH_IN_WORDS
```

```
65                                              ;# of words to check
66              call    FindFirstDifference     ;see if they differ
67              call    ZTimerOff
```

By the way, in Listings 11-21 though 11-23 I've used **jcxz** to make sure
the correct result is returned if 0-length arrays are compared. If you use this
routine in your code and you can be sure that 0-length arrays will never
be passed as parameters, however, you can save a few bytes and cycles by
eliminating the **jcxz** check. After all, what sense does it make to compare
0-length arrays—and what sense does it make to waste precious bytes and
cycles guarding against a contingency that can never arise?

Make the comparison a bit more complex, however, and **cmps** comes
back to the pack. Consider the comparison of two 0-terminated strings
rather than two fixed-length arrays. As with **scas** in the last section, **cmps**
can be made to work in this application by first performing a **scasb** pass to
determine one string length and then comparing the strings with **cmpsw**,
but the double pass negates much of the superior performance of **cmps**.
Listing 11-24 shows an implementation of this approach, which runs in 364
μsec for the test strings.

```
 1      ;
 2      ; *** Listing 11-24 ***
 3      ;
 4      ; Determines whether two zero-terminated strings differ, and
 5      ; if so where, using REP SCASB to find the terminating zero
 6      ; to determine one string length, and then using REPZ CMPSW
 7      ; to compare the strings.
 8      ;
 9              jmp     Skip
10      ;
11      TestString1     label   byte
12              db      'This is a test string that is '
13              db      'z'
14              db      'terminated with a zero byte...',0
15      TestString2     label   byte
16              db      'This is a test string that is '
17              db      'a'
18              db      'terminated with a zero byte...',0
19      ;
20      ; Compares two zero-terminated strings.
21      ;
22      ; Input:
23      ;       DS:SI = first zero-terminated string
24      ;       ES:DI = second zero-terminated string
25      ;
26      ; Output:
27      ;       DS:SI = pointer to first differing location in
28      ;               first string, or 0 if the byte wasn't found
29      ;       ES:DI = pointer to first differing location in
30      ;               second string, or 0 if the byte wasn't found
31      ;
```

```
32      ; Registers altered: AL, CX, DX, SI, DI
33      ;
34      ; Direction flag cleared
35      ;
36      ; Note: Does not handle strings that are longer than 64K
37      ;       bytes or cross segment boundaries.
38      ;
39      ; Note: If there is no terminating zero in the first 64K-1
40      ;       bytes of a string, the string is treated as if byte
41      ;       64K is a zero without checking, since if it isn't
42      ;       the string isn't zero-terminated at all.
43      ;
44      CompareStrings:
45              mov     dx,di   ;set aside the start of the second
46                              ; string
47              sub     al,al   ;we'll search for zero in the second
48                              ; string to see how long it is
49              mov     cx,0ffffh ;long enough to handle any string
50                              ; up to 64K-1 bytes in length. Any
51                              ; longer string will be treated as
52                              ; if byte 64K is zero
53              cld
54              repnz   scasb   ;find the terminating zero
55              not     cx      ;length of string in bytes, including
56                              ; the terminating zero except in the
57                              ; case of a string that's exactly 64K
58                              ; long including the terminating zero
59              mov     di,dx   ;get back the start of the second
60                              ; string
61              shr     cx,1    ;get count in words
62              jnc     CompareStringsWord
63                              ;if there's no odd byte, go directly
64                              ; to comparing a word at a time
65              cmpsb           ;compare the odd bytes of the
66                              ; strings
67              jnz     CompareStringsDifferentByte
68                              ;we've already found a difference
69      CompareStringsWord:
70                              ;there's no need to guard against
71                              ; CX=0 here, since we know that if
72                              ; CX=0 here, the preceding CMPSB
73                              ; must have successfully compared
74                              ; the terminating zero bytes of the
75                              ; strings (which are the only bytes
76                              ; of the strings), and the Zero flag
77                              ; setting of 1 from CMPSB will be
78                              ; preserved by REPZ CMPSW if CX=0,
79                              ; resulting in the correct
80                              ; conclusion that the strings are
81                              ; identical
82              repz    cmpsw   ;compare the rest of the strings a
83                              ; word at a time for speed
84              jnz     CompareStringsDifferent ;they're not the same
85              sub     si,si   ;return 0 pointers indicating that
86              mov     di,si   ; the strings are identical
87              ret
88      CompareStringsDifferent:
89                              ;the strings are different, so we
90                              ; have to figure which byte in the
```

```
91                                 ; word just compared was the first
92                                 ; difference
93              dec     si         ;point back to the second byte of
94              dec     di         ; the differing word in each string
95              dec     si         ;point back to the differing byte in
96              dec     di         ; each string
97              lodsb
98              scasb              ;compare that first byte again
99              jz      CompareStringsDone
100                                ;if the first bytes are the same,
101                                ; then it must have been the second
102                                ; bytes that differed. That's where
103                                ; we're pointing, so we're done
104    CompareStringsDifferentByte:
105             dec     si         ;the first bytes differed, so point
106             dec     di         ; back to them
107    CompareStringsDone:
108             ret
109    ;
110    Skip:
111             call    ZTimerOn
112             mov     si,offset TestString1 ;point to one string
113             mov     di,seg TestString2
114             mov     es,di
115             mov     di,offset TestString2 ;point to other string
116             call    CompareStrings  ;and compare the strings
117             call    ZTimerOff
```

We found earlier that **lods** works well for string searching when multiple termination conditions must be dealt with. That is true of string comparison as well, particularly as there we can benefit from the combination of **scas** and **lods**. The **lodsw/scasw** approach, shown in Listing 11-25, runs in just 306 μsec—19 percent faster than the **repnz scasb/repz cmpsw**-based Listing 11-24. For once, I won't bother with a nonstring instruction–based implementation, as it's perfectly obvious that replacing **lodsw** and **scasw** with nonstring sequences such as

```
mov    ax,[si]
inc    si
inc    si
```

and

```
cmp    [di],ax
       :
inc    di
inc    di
```

can only reduce performance.

```
1     ;
2     ; *** Listing 11-25 ***
3     ;
4     ; Determines whether two zero-terminated strings differ, and
5     ; if so where, using LODS/SCAS.
6     ;
7              jmp      Skip
8     ;
9     TestString1    label    byte
10            db       'This is a test string that is '
11            db       'z'
12            db       'terminated with a zero byte...',0
13    TestString2    label    byte
14            db       'This is a test string that is '
15            db       'a'
16            db       'terminated with a zero byte...',0
17    ;
18    ; Compares two zero-terminated strings.
19    ;
20    ; Input:
21    ;        DS:SI = first zero-terminated string
22    ;        ES:DI = second zero-terminated string
23    ;
24    ; Output:
25    ;        DS:SI = pointer to first differing location in
26    ;                first string, or 0 if the byte wasn't found
27    ;        ES:DI = pointer to first differing location in
28    ;                second string, or 0 if the byte wasn't found
29    ;
30    ; Registers altered: AX, SI, DI
31    ;
32    ; Direction flag cleared
33    ;
34    ; Note: Does not handle strings that are longer than 64K
35    ;       bytes or cross segment boundaries.
36    ;
37    CompareStrings:
38            cld
39    CompareStringsLoop:
40            lodsw              ;get the next 2 bytes
41            and      al,al     ;is the first byte the terminating
42                               ; zero?
43            jz       CompareStringsFinalByte
44                               ;yes, so there's only one byte left
45                               ; to check
46            scasw              ;compare this word
47            jnz      CompareStringsDifferent ;the strings differ
48            and      ah,ah     ;is the second byte the terminating
49                               ; zero?
50            jnz      CompareStringsLoop ;no, continue comparing
51                               ;the strings are the same
52    CompareStringsSame:
53            sub      si,si     ;return 0 pointers indicating that
54            mov      di,si     ; the strings are identical
55            ret
56    CompareStringsFinalByte:
57            scasb              ;does the terminating zero match in
58                               ; the 2 strings?
59            jz       CompareStringsSame ;yes, the strings match
```

```
60              dec     si      ;point back to the differing byte
61              dec     di      ; in each string
62              ret
63      CompareStringsDifferent:
64                              ;the strings are different, so we
65                              ; have to figure which byte in the
66                              ; word just compared was the first
67                              ; difference
68              dec     si
69              dec     si      ;point back to the first byte of the
70              dec     di      ; differing word in each string
71              dec     di
72              lodsb
73              scasb           ;compare that first byte again
74              jz      CompareStringsDone
75                              ;if the first bytes are the same,
76                              ; then it must have been the second
77                              ; bytes that differed. That's where
78                              ; we're pointing, so we're done
79              dec     si      ;the first bytes differed, so point
80              dec     di      ; back to them
81      CompareStringsDone:
82              ret
83      ;
84      Skip:
85              call    ZTimerOn
86              mov     si,offset TestString1 ;point to one string
87              mov     di,seg TestString2
88              mov     es,di
89              mov     di,offset TestString2 ;point to other string
90              call    CompareStrings  ;and compare the strings
91              call    ZTimerOff
```

The **cmps** instruction and even the **scas** instruction become still less suitable if a highly complex operation such as case-insensitive string comparison is required. Because both source and destination must be converted to the same case before being compared, both must be loaded into the registers for manipulation, and only **lods** among the string instructions will do us any good at all. Listing 11-26 shows code that performs case-insensitive string comparison. Listing 11-26 takes 869 μsec to run, which is not very fast by comparison with Listings 11-21 through 11-25. That's to be expected, though, given the flexibility required for this comparison. The more flexibility required for a given task, the less likely we are to be able to bring the full power of the highly specialized string instructions to bear on that task. That doesn't mean that we shouldn't try to do so, just that we won't always succeed.

If we're willing to expend 200 extra bytes or so, we can speed up Listing 11-26 considerably with a clever trick. Making sure a character is upper case takes a considerable amount of time even when all calculations are done in the registers, as is the case in Listing 11-26. Fast as the instructions in the

```
 1      ;
 2      ; *** Listing 11-26 ***
 3      ;
 4      ; Determines whether two zero-terminated strings differ
 5      ; ignoring case-only differences, and if so where, using
 6      ; LODS.
 7      ;
 8              jmp     Skip
 9      ;
10      TestString1     label   byte
11              db      'THIS IS A TEST STRING THAT IS '
12              db      'Z'
13              db      'TERMINATED WITH A ZERO BYTE...',0
14      TestString2     label   byte
15              db      'This is a test string that is '
16              db      'a'
17              db      'terminated with a zero byte...',0
18      ;
19      ; Macro to convert the specified register to uppercase if
20      ; it is lowercase.
21      ;
22      TO_UPPER macro  REGISTER
23              local   NotLower
24              cmp     REGISTER,ch     ;below 'a'?
25              jb      NotLower        ;yes, not lowercase
26              cmp     REGISTER,cl     ;above 'z'?
27              ja      NotLower        ;yes, not lowercase
28              and     REGISTER,bl     ;lowercase-convert to uppercase
29      NotLower:
30              endm
31      ;
32      ; Compares two zero-terminated strings, ignoring differences
33      ; that are only uppercase/lowercase differences.
34      ;
35      ; Input:
36      ;       DS:SI = first zero-terminated string
37      ;       ES:DI = second zero-terminated string
38      ;
39      ; Output:
40      ;       DS:SI = pointer to first case-insensitive differing
41      ;               location in first string, or 0 if the byte
42      ;               wasn't found
43      ;       ES:DI = pointer to first case-insensitive differing
44      ;               location in second string, or 0 if the byte
45      ;               wasn't found
46      ;
47      ; Registers altered: AX, BL, CX, DX, SI, DI
48      ;
49      ; Direction flag cleared
50      ;
51      ; Note: Does not handle strings that are longer than 64K
52      ;       bytes or cross segment boundaries.
53      ;
54      CompareStringsNoCase:
55              cld
56              mov     cx,'az' ;for fast register-register
57                              ; comparison in the loop
58              mov     bl,not 20h ;for fast conversion to
59                              ; uppercase in the loop
```

```
60   CompareStringsLoop:
61           lodsw           ;get the next 2 bytes
62           mov     dx,es:[di] ; from each string
63           inc     di      ;point to the next word in the
64           inc     di      ; second string
65           TO_UPPER al      ;convert the first byte from each
66           TO_UPPER dl      ; string to uppercase
67           cmp     al,dl   ;do the first bytes match?
68           jnz     CompareStringsDifferent1 ;the strings differ
69           and     al,al   ;is the first byte the terminating
70                           ; zero?
71           jz      CompareStringsSame
72                           ;yes, we're done with a match
73           TO_UPPER ah      ;convert the second byte from each
74           TO_UPPER dh      ; string to uppercase
75           cmp     ah,dh   ;do the second bytes match?
76           jnz     CompareStringsDifferent ;the strings differ
77           and     ah,ah   ;is the second byte the terminating
78                           ; zero?
79           jnz     CompareStringsLoop
80                           ;no, do the next 2 bytes
81   CompareStringsSame:
82           sub     si,si   ;return 0 pointers indicating that
83           mov     di,si   ; the strings are identical
84           ret
85   CompareStringsDifferent1:
86           dec     si      ;point back to the second byte of
87           dec     di      ; the word we just compared
88   CompareStringsDifferent:
89           dec     si      ;point back to the first byte of the
90           dec     di      ; word we just compared
91           ret
92   ;
93   Skip:
94           call    ZTimerOn
95           mov     si,offset TestString1 ;point to one string
96           mov     di,seg TestString2
97           mov     es,di
98           mov     di,offset TestString2 ;point to other string
99           call    CompareStringsNoCase    ;and compare the
100                          ; strings without
101                          ; regard for case
102          call    ZTimerOff
```

macro **TO_UPPER** in Listing 11-26 are, two to five of them are executed every time a byte is made upper case, and a time-consuming conditional jump may also be performed.

So what's better than two to five register-only instructions with at most one jump? A look-up table, that's what. Listing 11-27 is a modification of Listing 11-26 that looks up the upper case version of each character in **ToUpperTable** with a single instruction, the extremely fast and compact **xlat** instruction. (It's possible that **mov** could be used instead of **xlat** to make an even faster version of Listing 11-27, as **mov** can reference any general-purpose register whereas **xlat** can load only AL. As I've said, there

```
1    ;
2    ; *** Listing 11-27 ***
3    ;
4    ; Determines whether two zero-terminated strings differ
5    ; ignoring case-only differences, and if so where, using
6    ; LODS, with an XLAT-based table look-up to convert to
7    ; uppercase.
8    ;
9            jmp     Skip
10   ;
11   TestString1     label   byte
12           db      'THIS IS A TEST STRING THAT IS '
13           db      'Z'
14           db      'TERMINATED WITH A ZERO BYTE...',0
15   TestString2     label   byte
16           db      'This is a test string that is '
17           db      'a'
18           db      'terminated with a zero byte...',0
19   ;
20   ; Table of conversions between characters and their
21   ; uppercase equivalents. (Could be just 128 bytes long if
22   ; only 7-bit ASCII characters are used.)
23   ;
24   ToUpperTable    label   word
25   CHAR=0
26           rept    256
27   if (CHAR lt 'a') or (CHAR gt 'z')
28           db      CHAR    ;not a lowercase character
29   else
30           db      CHAR and not 20h
31                           ;convert in the range 'a'-'z' to
32                           ; uppercase
33   endif
34   CHAR=CHAR+1
35           endm
36   ;
37   ; Compares two zero-terminated strings, ignoring differences
38   ; that are only uppercase/lowercase differences.
39   ;
40   ; Input:
41   ;       DS:SI = first zero-terminated string
42   ;       ES:DI = second zero-terminated string
43   ;
44   ; Output:
45   ;       DS:SI = pointer to first case-insensitive differing
46   ;               location in first string, or 0 if the byte
47   ;               wasn't found
48   ;       ES:DI = pointer to first case-insensitive differing
49   ;               location in second string, or 0 if the byte
50   ;               wasn't found
51   ;
52   ; Registers altered: AX, BX, DX, SI, DI
53   ;
54   ; Direction flag cleared
55   ;
56   ; Note: Does not handle strings that are longer than 64K
57   ;       bytes or cross segment boundaries.
58   ;
59   CompareStringsNoCase:
```

```
60              cld
61              mov     bx,offset ToUpperTable
62      CompareStringsLoop:
63              lodsw               ;get the next 2 bytes
64              mov     dx,es:[di] ; from each string
65              inc     di      ;point to the next word in the
66              inc     di      ; second string
67              xlat                ;convert the first byte in the
68                                  ; first string to uppercase
69              xchg    dl,al   ;set aside the first byte &
70              xlat                ; convert the first byte in the
71                                  ; second string to uppercase
72              cmp     al,dl   ;do the first bytes match?
73              jnz     CompareStringsDifferent1 ;the strings differ
74              and     al,al   ;is this the terminating zero?
75              jz      CompareStringsSame
76                                  ;yes, we're done, with a match
77              mov     al,ah
78              xlat                ;convert the second byte from the
79                                  ; first string to uppercase
80              xchg    dh,al   ;set aside the second byte &
81              xlat                ; convert the second byte from the
82                                  ; second string to uppercase
83              cmp     al,dh   ;do the second bytes match?
84              jnz     CompareStringsDifferent ;the strings differ
85              and     ah,ah   ;is this the terminating zero?
86              jnz     CompareStringsLoop
87                                  ;no, do the next 2 bytes
88      CompareStringsSame:
89              sub     si,si   ;return 0 pointers indicating that
90              mov     di,si   ; the strings are identical
91              ret
92      CompareStringsDifferent1:
93              dec     si      ;point back to the second byte of
94              dec     di      ; the word we just compared
95      CompareStringsDifferent:
96              dec     si      ;point back to the first byte of the
97              dec     di      ; word we just compared
98              ret
99      ;
100     Skip:
101             call    ZTimerOn
102             mov     si,offset TestString1 ;point to one string
103             mov     di,seg TestString2
104             mov     es,di
105             mov     di,offset TestString2 ;point to other string
106             call    CompareStringsNoCase    ;and compare the
107                                  ; strings without
108                                  ; regard for case
109             call    ZTimerOff
```

are many ways to do anything in assembler.) For most characters there is no upper case version, and the same character that we started with is looked up in **ToUpperTable**. For the 26 lower case characters, however, the character looked up is the upper case equivalent.

You may well be thinking that it doesn't make much sense to try to speed up code by *adding* a memory access, and normally you'd be right. However, **xlat** is very fast—a 1-byte instruction that executes in 10 cycles—and it saves us the trouble of fetching the many instruction bytes of **TO‑UPPER**. (Remember, instruction fetches are memory accesses too.) What's more, **xlat** eliminates the need for conditional jumps in the upper case-conversion process.

Sounds good in theory, doesn't it? It works just as well in the real world, too. Listing 11-27 runs in just 638 μsec, a 36 percent improvement over Listing 11-26. Of course, Listing 11-27 is also a good deal larger than Listing 11-26, owing to the look-up table, and that's a dilemma the assembler programmer faces frequently on the PC: the choice between speed and size. More memory, in the form of look-up tables and in-line code, often means better performance. It's actually relatively easy to speed up most code by throwing memory at it. The hard part is knowing where to strike the balance between performance and size.

Although both look-up tables and in-line code are discussed elsewhere in this volume, a broad discussion of the issue of memory versus performance will have to wait until Volume II of *Zen of Assembly Language*. The mechanics of translating memory into performance—the knowledge aspect, if you will—is quite simple, but understanding when that tradeoff can and should be made is more complex and properly belongs in the discussion of the flexible mind.

String Searching

Perhaps the single finest application of **cmps** is in searching for a sequence of bytes within a data buffer. In particular, **cmps** is excellent for finding a particular text sequence in a buffer full of text, as is the case when implementing a find-string capability in a text editor.

One way to implement such a searching capability is by simply starting **repz cmps** at each byte of the buffer until either a match is found or the end of the buffer is reached, as shown in Figure 11.14. Listing 11-28, which employs this approach, runs in 2995 μsec for the sample search sequence and buffer.

That's not bad, but there's a better way to go. Suppose we load the first byte of the search string into AL and use **repnz scasb** to find the next candidate for the full **repz cmps** comparison, as shown in Figure 11.15. By so doing we could use a fast repeated string instruction to disqualify most of the potential strings, rather than having to loop and start up **repz cmps** at each byte in the buffer. Would that make a difference?

It would indeed! Listing 11-29, which uses the hybrid **repnz**

A

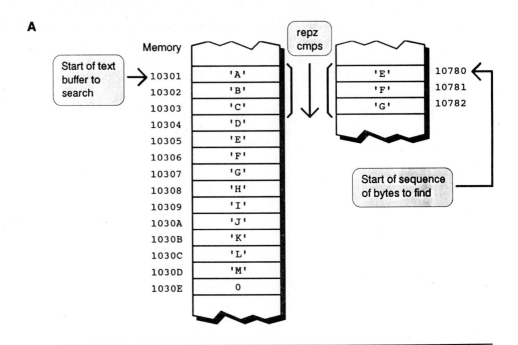

FIGURE 11.14   One way to search for a fixed-length sequence of bytes
in a text buffer is by starting **repz cmps** at each byte of
the buffer that is at least sequence-length number of bytes
away from the end of the buffer. In other words, we could
start **repz cmps** at every byte of the buffer that could
conceivably start the sequence. **(A)** The check of the first
byte of the buffer. **(B)** The check of the second byte of
the buffer. While this approach works, it requires one loop
for each potential sequence-starting byte and also incurs
the start-up overhead of **repz cmps** at each character. In
this figure, five loops, each starting a new **repz cmps**,
would be required to find the matching sequence starting
at 10305.

```
1   ;
2   ; *** Listing 11-28 ***
3   ;
4   ; Searches a text buffer for a sequence of bytes by checking
5   ; for the sequence with CMPS starting at each byte of the
6   ; buffer that potentially could start the sequence.
7   ;
8           jmp     Skip
9   ;
```

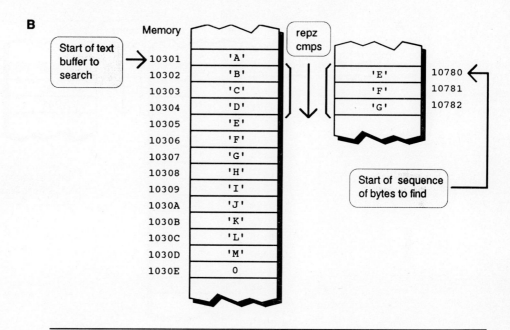

FIGURE 11.14 (*continued*)

```
10      ; Text buffer that we'll search.
11      ;
12      TextBuffer      label   byte
13              db      'This is a sample text buffer, suitable '
14              db      'for a searching text of any sort... '
15              db      'ABCDEFGHIJKLMNOPQRSTUVWXYZ0123456789 '
16              db      'End of text... '
17      TEXT_BUFFER_LENGTH      equ     ($-TextBuffer)
18      ;
19      ; Sequence of bytes that we'll search for.
20      ;
21      SearchSequence  label   byte
22              db      'text...'
23      SEARCH_SEQUENCE_LENGTH  equ     ($-SearchSequence)
24      ;
25      ; Searches a buffer for the first occurrence of a specified
26      ; sequence of bytes.
27      ;
28      ; Input:
29      ;       CX = length of sequence of bytes to search for
30      ;       DX = length of buffer to search in
31      ;       DS:SI = start of sequence of bytes to search for
32      ;       ES:DI = start of buffer to search
33      ;
34      ; Output:
35      ;       ES:DI = pointer to start of first occurrence of
36      ;               desired sequence of bytes in the buffer, or
```

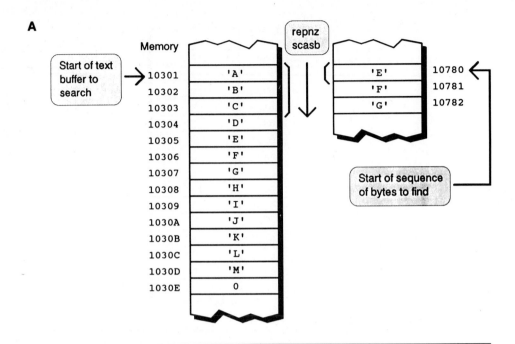

FIGURE 11.15   We can speed up the search for a fixed-length sequence of bytes in a text buffer considerably by using **repnz scasb** to eliminate many buffer locations as potential sequence-starting locations. This is accomplished by using **repnz scasb** to search the text buffer for the first character of the sequence, and then using **repz cmps** to check only those potential sequences that have been prequalified by **repnz scasb**. **(A)** The use of **repnz scasb** to eliminate the first 4 bytes of the buffer as potential sequence-starting bytes. **(B)** The single **repz cmps** needed to compare the remainder of the match found by **repnz scasb**. This approach eliminates the need to expend loops and executions of **repz cmps** on those buffer locations that don't begin with the sequence-starting byte and therefore can't possibly start the desired sequence. In this figure, just one **repnz scasb** and one **repz cmps** would be required to find the matching sequence starting at 10305.

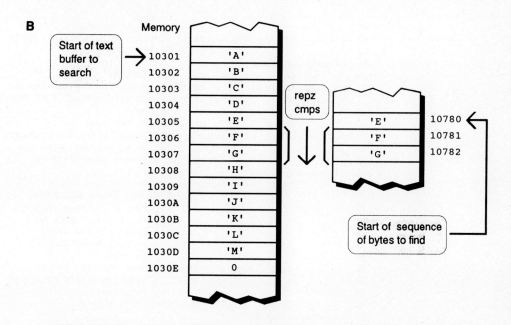

FIGURE 11.15 (*continued*)

```
37    ;                       0:0 if the sequence wasn't found
38    ;
39    ; Registers altered: AX, BX, CX, DX, SI, DI, BP
40    ;
41    ; Direction flag cleared
42    ;
43    ; Note: Does not handle search sequences or text buffers
44    ;       that are longer than 64K bytes or cross segment
45    ;       boundaries.
46    ;
47    ; Note: Assumes non-zero length of search sequence (CX > 0),
48    ;       and search sequence shorter than 64K (CX <= 0ffffh).
49    ;
50    ; Note: Assumes buffer is longer than search sequence
51    ;       (DX > CX). Zero length of buffer is taken to mean
52    ;       that the buffer is 64K bytes long.
53    ;
54    FindSequence:
55         cld
56         mov     bp,si   ;set aside the sequence start
57                         ; offset
58         mov     ax,di   ;set aside the buffer start offset
59         mov     bx,cx   ;set aside the sequence length
60         sub     dx,cx   ;difference between buffer and
```

```
 61                           ; search sequence lengths
 62          inc     dx       ;# of possible sequence start bytes
 63                           ; to check in the buffer
 64   FindSequenceLoop:
 65          mov     cx,bx    ;sequence length
 66          shr     cx,1     ;convert to word for faster search
 67          jnc     FindSequenceWord ;do word search if no odd
 68                           ; byte
 69          cmpsb            ;compare the odd byte
 70          jnz     FindSequenceNoMatch ;odd byte doesn't match,
 71                           ; so we havent' found the
 72                           ; search sequence here
 73   FindSequenceWord:
 74          jcxz    FindSequenceFound
 75                               ;since we're guaranteed to
 76                               ; have a non-zero length,
 77                               ; the sequence must be 1
 78                               ; byte long and we've
 79                               ; already found that it
 80                               ; matched
 81          repz    cmpsw        ;check the rest of the
 82                               ; sequence a word at a time
 83                               ; for speed
 84          jz      FindSequenceFound ;it's a match
 85   FindSequenceNoMatch:
 86          mov     si,bp    ;point to the start of the search
 87                           ; sequence again
 88          inc     ax       ;advance to the next buffer start
 89                           ; search location
 90          mov     di,ax    ;point DI to the next buffer start
 91                           ; search location
 92          dec     dx       ;count down the remaining bytes to
 93                           ; search in the buffer
 94          jnz     FindSequenceLoop
 95          sub     di,di    ;return 0 pointer indicating that
 96          mov     es,di    ; the sequence was not found
 97          ret
 98   FindSequenceFound:
 99          mov     di,ax    ;point to the buffer location at
100                           ; which the first occurrence of the
101                           ; sequence was found
102          ret
103   ;
104   Skip:
105          call    ZTimerOn
106          mov     si,offset SearchSequence
107                               ;point to search sequence
108          mov     cx,SEARCH_SEQUENCE_LENGTH
109                               ;length of search sequence
110          mov     di,seg TextBuffer
111          mov     es,di
112          mov     di,offset TextBuffer
113                               ;point to buffer to search
114          mov     dx,TEXT_BUFFER_LENGTH
115                               ;length of buffer to search
116          call    FindSequence     ;search for the sequence
117          call    ZTimerOff
```

```
 1    ;
 2    ; *** Listing 11-29 ***
 3    ;
 4    ; Searches a text buffer for a sequence of bytes by using
 5    ; REPNZ SCASB to identify bytes in the buffer that
 6    ; potentially could start the sequence and then checking
 7    ; only starting at those qualified bytes for a match with
 8    ; the sequence by way of REPZ CMPS.
 9    ;
10            jmp     Skip
11    ;
12    ; Text buffer that we'll search.
13    ;
14    TextBuffer      label   byte
15            db      'This is a sample text buffer, suitable '
16            db      'for a searching text of any sort... '
17            db      'ABCDEFGHIJKLMNOPQRSTUVWXYZ0123456789 '
18            db      'End of text... '
19    TEXT_BUFFER_LENGTH      equ     ($-TextBuffer)
20    ;
21    ; Sequence of bytes that we'll search for.
22    ;
23    SearchSequence  label   byte
24            db      'text...'
25    SEARCH_SEQUENCE_LENGTH equ     ($-SearchSequence)
26    ;
27    ; Searches a buffer for the first occurrence of a specified
28    ; sequence of bytes.
29    ;
30    ; Input:
31    ;       CX = length of sequence of bytes to search for
32    ;       DX = length of buffer to search in
33    ;       DS:SI = start of sequence of bytes to search for
34    ;       ES:DI = start of buffer to search
35    ;
36    ; Output:
37    ;       ES:DI = pointer to start of first occurrence of
38    ;               desired sequence of bytes in the buffer, or
39    ;               0:0 if the sequence wasn't found
40    ;
41    ; Registers altered: AL, BX, CX, DX, SI, DI, BP
42    ;
43    ; Direction flag cleared
44    ;
45    ; Note: Does not handle search sequences or text buffers
46    ;       that are longer than 64K bytes or cross segment
47    ;       boundaries.
48    ;
49    ; Note: Assumes non-zero length of search sequence (CX > 0),
50    ;       and search sequence shorter than 64K (CX <= 0ffffh).
51    ;
52    ; Note: Assumes buffer is longer than search sequence
53    ;       (DX > CX). Zero length of buffer (DX = 0) is taken
54    ;       to mean that the buffer is 64K bytes long.
55    ;
56    FindSequence:
57            cld
```

```
 58          lodsb                 ;get the first byte of the search
 59                                ; sequence, which we'll leave in AL
 60                                ; for faster searching
 61          mov     bp,si         ;set aside the sequence start
 62                                ; offset plus one
 63          dec     cx            ;we don't need to compare the first
 64                                ; byte of the sequence with CMPS,
 65                                ; since we'll do it with SCAS
 66          mov     bx,cx         ;set aside the sequence length
 67                                ; minus 1
 68          sub     dx,cx         ;difference between buffer and
 69                                ; search sequence lengths plus 1
 70                                ; (# of possible sequence start
 71                                ; bytes to check in the buffer)
 72          mov     cx,dx         ;put buffer search length in CX
 73          jnz     FindSequenceLoop ;start normally if the
 74                                ; buffer isn't 64Kb long
 75          dec     cx            ;the buffer is 64K bytes long-we
 76                                ; have to check the first byte
 77                                ; specially since CX = 0 means
 78                                ; "do nothing" to REPNZ SCASB
 79          scasb                 ;check the first byte of the buffer
 80          jz      FindSequenceCheck ;it's a match for 1 byte,
 81                                ; at least-check the rest
 82  FindSequenceLoop:
 83          repnz   scasb         ;search for the first byte of the
 84                                ; search sequence
 85          jnz     FindSequenceNotFound
 86                                ;it's not found, so there are no
 87                                ; possible matches
 88  FindSequenceCheck:
 89                                ;we've got a potential (first byte)
 90                                ; match-check the rest of this
 91                                ; candidate sequence
 92          push    di            ;remember the address of the next
 93                                ; byte to check in case it's needed
 94          mov     dx,cx         ;set aside the remaining length to
 95                                ; search in the buffer
 96          mov     si,bp         ;point to the rest of the search
 97                                ; sequence
 98          mov     cx,bx         ;sequence length (minus first byte)
 99          shr     cx,1          ;convert to word for faster search
100          jnc     FindSequenceWord ;do word search if no odd
101                                ; byte
102          cmpsb                 ;compare the odd byte
103          jnz     FindSequenceNoMatch
104                                ;odd byte doesn't match,
105                                ; so we haven't found the
106                                ; search sequence here
107  FindSequenceWord:
108          jcxz    FindSequenceFound
109                                ;since we're guaranteed to have
110                                ; a non-zero length, the
111                                ; sequence must be 1 byte long
112                                ; and we've already found that
113                                ; it matched
114          repz    cmpsw         ;check the rest of the sequence a
115                                ; word at a time for speed
116          jz      FindSequenceFound ;it's a match
```

```
117     FindSequenceNoMatch:
118             pop     di          ;get back the pointer to the next
119                                 ; byte to check
120             mov     cx,dx       ;get back the remaining length to
121                                 ; search in the buffer
122             and     cx,cx       ;see if there's anything left to
123                                 ; check
124             jnz     FindSequenceLoop ;yes-check next byte
125     FindSequenceNotFound:
126             sub     di,di       ;return 0 pointer indicating that
127             mov     es,di       ; the sequence was not found
128             ret
129     FindSequenceFound:
130             pop     di          ;point to the buffer location at
131             dec     di          ; which the first occurrence of the
132                                 ; sequence was found (remember that
133                                 ; earlier we pushed the address of
134                                 ; the byte after the potential
135                                 ; sequence start)
136             ret
137     ;
138     Skip:
139             call    ZTimerOn
140             mov     si,offset SearchSequence
141                                     ;point to search sequence
142             mov     cx,SEARCH_SEQUENCE_LENGTH
143                                     ;length of search sequence
144             mov     di,seg TextBuffer
145             mov     es,di
146             mov     di,offset TextBuffer
147                                     ;point to buffer to search
148             mov     dx,TEXT_BUFFER_LENGTH
149                                     ;length of buffer to search
150             call    FindSequence    ;search for the sequence
151             call    ZTimerOff
```

scasb/**repz cmps** technique, runs in just 719 μsec for the same search sequence and buffer as Listing 11-28. Now, the margin between the two techniques could vary considerably, depending on the contents of the buffer and the search sequence. Nonetheless, we've just seen an improvement of more than 300 percent over already fast string instruction–based code! That improvement is due primarily to the use of **repnz scasb** to eliminate most of the instruction fetches and branches of Listing 11-28.

Even when you're using string instructions, stretch your mind to think of still better approaches . . .

As for nonstring implementations, Listing 11-30, which performs the same task as do Listings 11-28 and 11-29 but does so with nonstring instructions, takes a full 3812 μsec to run. It should be very clear that nonstring instructions should be used in searching applications only when their greater flexibility is absolutely required.

```
1      ;
2      ; *** Listing 11-30 ***
3      ;
4      ; Searches a text buffer for a sequence of bytes by checking
5      ; for the sequence with non-string instructions starting at
6      ; each byte of the buffer that potentially could start the
7      ; sequence.
8      ;
9              jmp     Skip
10     ;
11     ; Text buffer that we'll search.
12     ;
13     TextBuffer      label    byte
14             db      'This is a sample text buffer, suitable '
15             db      'for a searching text of any sort... '
16             db      'ABCDEFGHIJKLMNOPQRSTUVWXYZ0123456789 '
17             db      'End of text... '
18     TEXT_BUFFER_LENGTH     equ     ($-TextBuffer)
19     ;
20     ; Sequence of bytes that we'll search for.
21     ;
22     SearchSequence  label    byte
23             db      'text...'
24     SEARCH_SEQUENCE_LENGTH equ     ($-SearchSequence)
25     ;
26     ; Searches a buffer for the first occurrence of a specified
27     ; sequence of bytes.
28     ;
29     ; Input:
30     ;       CX = length of sequence of bytes to search for
31     ;       DX = length of buffer to search in
32     ;       DS:SI = start of sequence of bytes to search for
33     ;       ES:DI = start of buffer to search
34     ;
35     ; Output:
36     ;       ES:DI = pointer to start of first occurrence of
37     ;               desired sequence of bytes in the buffer, or
38     ;               0:0 if the sequence wasn't found
39     ;
40     ; Registers altered: AX, BX, CX, DX, SI, DI, BP
41     ;
42     ; Note: Does not handle search sequences or text buffers
43     ;       that are longer than 64K bytes or cross segment
44     ;       boundaries.
45     ;
46     ; Note: Assumes non-zero length of search sequence (CX > 0),
47     ;       and search sequence shorter than 64K (CX <= 0ffffh).
48     ;
49     ; Note: Assumes buffer is longer than search sequence
50     ;       (DX > CX). Zero length of buffer is taken to mean
51     ;       that the buffer is 64K bytes long.
52     ;
53     FindSequence:
54             mov     bp,si   ;set aside the sequence start
55                             ; offset
56             mov     bx,cx   ;set aside the sequence length
57             sub     dx,cx   ;difference between buffer and
58                             ; search sequence lengths
59             inc     dx      ;# of possible sequence start bytes
```

```
60                                   ; to check in the buffer
61      FindSequenceLoop:
62              push    di      ;remember the address of the current
63                              ; byte in case it's needed
64              mov     cx,bx   ;sequence length
65              shr     cx,1    ;convert to word for faster search
66              jnc     FindSequenceWord ;do word search if no odd
67                                       ; byte
68              mov     al,[si]
69              cmp     es:[di],al      ;compare the odd byte
70              jnz     FindSequenceNoMatch ;odd byte doesn't match,
71                                      ; so we havent' found the
72                                      ; search sequence here
73              inc     si              ;odd byte matches, so point
74              inc     di              ; to the next byte in the
75                                      ; buffer and sequence
76      FindSequenceWord:
77              jcxz    FindSequenceFound
78                                      ;since we're guaranteed to
79                                      ; have a non-zero length,
80                                      ; the sequence must be 1
81                                      ; byte long and we've
82                                      ; already found that it
83                                      ; matched
84      FindSequenceWordCompareLoop:
85              mov     ax,[si]         ;compare the remainder of
86              cmp     es:[di],ax      ; the search sequence to
87              jnz     FindSequenceNoMatch ; this part of the
88              inc     si              ; buffer a word at a time
89              inc     si              ; for speed
90              inc     di
91              inc     di
92              loop    FindSequenceWordCompareLoop
93      FindSequenceFound:      ;it's a match
94              pop     di      ;point to the buffer location at
95                              ; which the first occurrence of the
96                              ; sequence was found (remember that
97                              ; earlier we pushed the address of
98                              ; the potential sequence start)
99              ret
100     FindSequenceNoMatch:
101             pop     di      ;get back the pointer to the current
102                             ; byte
103             inc     di      ;point to the next buffer start
104                             ; search location
105             mov     si,bp   ;point to the start of the search
106                             ; sequence again
107             dec     dx      ;count down the remaining bytes to
108                             ; search in the buffer
109             jnz     FindSequenceLoop
110             sub     di,di   ;return 0 pointer indicating that
111             mov     es,di   ; the sequence was not found
112             ret
113     ;
114     Skip:
115             call    ZTimerOn
116             mov     si,offset SearchSequence
117                             ;point to search sequence
118             mov     cx,SEARCH_SEQUENCE_LENGTH
```

```
119                                       ;length of search sequence
120             mov     di,seg TextBuffer
121             mov     es,di
122             mov     di,offset TextBuffer
123                                       ;point to buffer to search
124             mov     dx,TEXT_BUFFER_LENGTH
125                                       ;length of buffer to search
126             call    FindSequence      ;search for the sequence
127             call    ZTimerOff
```

Make no mistake, there's more to searching performance than simply using the right combination of string instructions. The right choice of algorithm is critical. For a list of several thousand sorted items, a poorly coded binary search might well beat the pants off a slick **repnz scasb/repz cmps** implementation. On the other hand, the **repnz scasb/repz cmps** approach is excellent for searching free-form data of the sort that's found in text buffers.

The key to searching performance lies in choosing a good algorithm for your application *and* implementing it with the best possible code. Either the searching algorithm or the implementation may be the factor that limits performance. Ideally, a searching algorithm would be chosen with an eye toward using the strengths of the 8088—and that usually means the string instructions.

cmps without rep

In the last chapter I pointed out that **scas** and **cmps** are slower but more flexible when they're not repeated. Although **repz** and **repnz** allow termination only according to the state of ZF, **scas** and **cmps** actually set all the status flags, and we can take advantage of that when **scas** and **cmps** aren't repeated. Of course, we should use **repz** or **repnz** whenever we can, but nonrepeated **scas** and **cmps** let us tap the power of string instructions when **repz** and **repnz** simply won't do.

For instance, suppose that we're comparing two arrays that contain signed 16-bit values representing signal measurements. Suppose further that we want to find the first point at which the waves represented by the arrays cross. That is, if wave A starts out above wave B, we want to know when wave A becomes less than or equal to wave B, as shown in Figure 11.16. If wave B starts out above wave A, then we want to know when wave B becomes less than or equal to wave A.

There's no way to perform this comparison with repeated **cmps**, since greater-than/less-than comparisons aren't in the limited repertoire of the **rep** prefix; however, plain old unrepeated **cmpsw** is up to the task, as

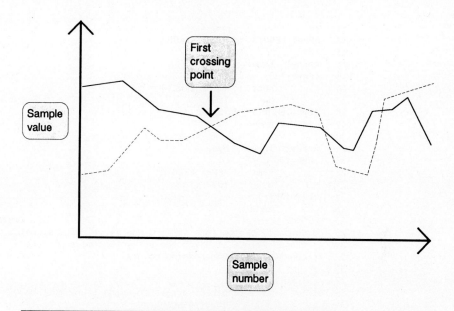

FIGURE 11.16   Given two arrays containing data samples, the first crossing point is defined as the first sample at which the array
that started out on top (with the higher value for sample
0) isn't greater than the corresponding sample from the
other array.

shown in Listing 11-31, which runs in 1232 μsec. As shown in Listing 11-31,
we must initially determine which array starts out on top, in order to set
SI to point to the initially greater array and DI to point to the other array.
Once that's done, all we need do is perform a **cmpsw** on each data point
and check whether that point is still greater with **jng**. The **loop** instruction
repeats the comparison for however many data points there are—and that's
the whole routine in a very compact package! The 3-instruction, 5-byte loop
of Listing 11-31 is hard to beat for this fairly demanding task.

```
 1   ;
 2   ; *** Listing 11-31 ***
 3   ;
 4   ; Compares two arrays of 16-bit signed values in order to
 5   ; find the first point at which the arrays cross, using
 6   ; non-repeated CMPSW.
 7   ;
 8           jmp     Skip
 9   ;
10   ; The two arrays that we'll compare.
```

```
11      ;
12      ARRAY_LENGTH    equ     200
13      ;
14      Array1  label   byte
15      TEMP=-100
16              rept    ARRAY_LENGTH
17              dw      TEMP
18      TEMP=TEMP+1
19              endm
20      ;
21      Array2  label   byte
22      TEMP=100
23              rept    ARRAY_LENGTH
24              dw      TEMP
25      TEMP=TEMP-1
26              endm
27      ;
28      ; Compares two buffers to find the first point at which they
29      ; cross. Points at which the arrays become equal are
30      ; considered to be crossing points.
31      ;
32      ; Input:
33      ;       CX = length of arrays in words (they must be of
34      ;               equal length)
35      ;       DS:SI = start of first array
36      ;       ES:DI = start of second array
37      ;
38      ; Output:
39      ;       DS:SI = pointer to crossing point in first array,
40      ;               or SI=0 if there is no crossing point
41      ;       ES:DI = pointer to crossing point in second array,
42      ;               or DI=0 if there is no crossing point
43      ;
44      ; Registers altered: AX, CX, SI, DI
45      ;
46      ; Direction flag cleared
47      ;
48      ; Note: Does not handle arrays that are longer than 64K
49      ;       bytes or cross segment boundaries.
50      ;
51      FindCrossing:
52              cld
53              jcxz    FindCrossingNotFound
54                              ;if there's nothing to compare, we
55                              ; certainly can't find a crossing
56              mov     ax,[si] ;compare the first two points to
57              cmp     ax,es:[di] ; make sure that the first array
58                              ; doesn't start out below the second
59                              ; array
60              pushf           ;remember the original relationship
61                              ; of the arrays, so we can put the
62                              ; pointers back at the end (can't
63                              ; use LAHF because it doesn't save
64                              ; the Overflow flag)
65              jnl     FindCrossingLoop ;the first array is above
66                                      ; the second array
67              xchg    si,di   ;swap the array pointers so that
68                              ; SI points to the initially-
69                              ; greater array
```

```
70    FindCrossingLoop:
71            cmpsw               ;compare the next element in each
72                                ; array
73            jng     FindCrossingFound ;if SI doesn't point to a
74                                     ; greater value, we've found
75                                     ; the first crossing
76            loop    FindCrossingLoop ;check the next element in
77                                     ; each array
78    FindCrossingNotFound:
79            popf                ;clear the flags we pushed earlier
80            sub     si,si       ;return 0 pointers to indicate that
81            mov     di,si       ; no crossing was found
82            ret
83    FindCrossingFound:
84            dec     si
85            dec     si          ;point back to the crossing point
86            dec     di          ; in each array
87            dec     di
88            popf                ;get back the original relationship
89                                ; of the arrays
90            jnl     FindCrossingDone
91                                ;SI pointed to the initially-
92                                ; greater array, so we're all set
93            xchg    si,di       ;SI pointed to the initially-
94                                ; less array, so swap SI and DI to
95                                ; undo our earlier swap
96    FindCrossingDone:
97            ret
98    ;
99    Skip:
100           call    ZTimerOn
101           mov     si,offset Array1 ;point to first array
102           mov     di,seg Array2
103           mov     es,di
104           mov     di,offset Array2 ;point to second array
105           mov     cx,ARRAY_LENGTH ;length to compare
106           call    FindCrossing    ;find the first crossing, if
107                                   ; any
108           call    ZTimerOff
```

By contrast, Listing 11-32, which performs the same crossing search but does so with nonstring instructions, has 6 instructions and 13 bytes in the loop and takes considerably longer (1821 μsec) to complete the sample crossing search. Although we were unable to use repeated **cmps** for this particular task, we were nonetheless able to improve performance a great deal by using the string instruction in its nonrepeated form.

```
1    ;
2    ; *** Listing 11-32 ***
3    ;
4    ; Compares two arrays of 16-bit signed values in order to
5    ; find the first point at which the arrays cross, using
6    ; non-string instructions.
7    ;
8            jmp     Skip
```

```
 9   ;
10   ; The two arrays that we'll compare.
11   ;
12   ARRAY_LENGTH    equ     200
13   ;
14   Array1 label    byte
15   TEMP=-100
16           rept    ARRAY_LENGTH
17           dw      TEMP
18   TEMP=TEMP+1
19           endm
20   ;
21   Array2 label    byte
22   TEMP=100
23           rept    ARRAY_LENGTH
24           dw      TEMP
25   TEMP=TEMP-1
26           endm
27   ;
28   ; Compares two buffers to find the first point at which they
29   ; cross. Points at which the arrays become equal are
30   ; considered to be crossing points.
31   ;
32   ; Input:
33   ;       CX = length of arrays in words (they must be of
34   ;               equal length)
35   ;       DS:SI = start of first array
36   ;       ES:DI = start of second array
37   ;
38   ; Output:
39   ;       DS:SI = pointer to crossing point in first array,
40   ;               or SI=0 if there is no crossing point
41   ;       ES:DI = pointer to crossing point in second array,
42   ;               or DI=0 if there is no crossing point
43   ;
44   ; Registers altered: BX, CX, DX, SI, DI
45   ;
46   ; Note: Does not handle arrays that are longer than 64K
47   ;       bytes or cross segment boundaries.
48   ;
49   FindCrossing:
50           jcxz    FindCrossingNotFound
51                           ;if there's nothing to compare, we
52                           ; certainly can't find a crossing
53           mov     dx,2    ;amount we'll add to the pointer
54                           ; registers after each comparison,
55                           ; kept in a register for speed
56           mov     bx,[si] ;compare the first two points to
57           cmp     bx,es:[di] ; make sure that the first array
58                           ; doesn't start out below the second
59                           ; array
60           pushf           ;remember the original relationship
61                           ; of the arrays, so we can put the
62                           ; pointers back at the end (can't
63                           ; use LAHF because it doesn't save
64                           ; the Overflow flag)
65           jnl     FindCrossingLoop ;the first array is above
66                                    ; the second array
67           xchg    si,di   ;swap the array pointers so that
68                           ; SI points to the initially-
```

```
69                              ; greater array
70      FindCrossingLoop:
71              mov     bx,[si]         ;compare the next element in
72              cmp     bx,es:[di]      ; each array
73              jng     FindCrossingFound ;if SI doesn't point to a
74                                      ; greater value, we've found
75                                      ; the first crossing
76              add     si,dx           ;point to the next element
77              add     di,dx           ; in each array
78              loop    FindCrossingLoop ;check the next element in
79                                      ; each array
80      FindCrossingNotFound:
81              popf                    ;clear the flags we pushed earlier
82              sub     si,si           ;return 0 pointers to indicate that
83              mov     di,si           ; no crossing was found
84              ret
85      FindCrossingFound:
86              popf                    ;get back the original relationship
87                                      ; of the arrays
88              jnl     FindCrossingDone
89                                      ;SI pointed to the initially-
90                                      ; greater array, so we're all set
91              xchg    si,di           ;SI pointed to the initially-
92                                      ; less array, so swap SI and DI to
93                                      ; undo our earlier swap
94      FindCrossingDone:
95              ret
96      ;
97      Skip:
98              call    ZTimerOn
99              mov     si,offset Array1 ;point to first array
100             mov     di,seg Array2
101             mov     es,di
102             mov     di,offset Array2 ;point to second array
103             mov     cx,ARRAY_LENGTH ;length to compare
104             call    FindCrossing    ;find the first crossing, if
105                                     ; any
106             call    ZTimerOff
```

11.5 ◆ A Note about Returning Values

Throughout this chapter I've been returning "not found" statuses by passing zero pointers (pointers set to 0) back to the calling routine. This is a commonly used and very flexible means of returning such statuses, because the same registers that are used to return pointers when searches are successful can be used to return 0 when searches are not successful. The success or failure of a subroutine can then be tested with code such as

```
call    FindCharInString
and     si,si
jz      CharNotFound
```

Returning failure statuses as zero pointers is particularly popular in high level languages such as C, although C returns pointers in AX, DX:AX, or memory, rather than in SI or DI.

There are, however, many other ways of returning statuses in assembler. One particularly effective approach is that of returning success or failure in either ZF or CF, so that the calling routine can immediately jump conditionally upon return from the subroutine, without the need for any **and**ing, **or**ing, or comparing of any sort. This works out especially well when the proper setting of a flag falls out of the normal functioning of a subroutine. For example, consider the following subroutine, which returns ZF set to 1 if the character in AL is white space:

```
Whitespace:
     cmp   al,' '      ;space
     jz    WhitespaceDone
     cmp   al,9        ;tab
     jz    WhitespaceDone
     and   al,al       ;zero byte
WhitespaceDone:
     ret
```

The key point here is that ZF is set automatically by the comparisons preceding the **ret**. Any test for white space would have to perform the same comparisons, so practically speaking we didn't have to write a single extra line of code to return the subroutine's status in ZF. Because the return status is in a flag rather than a register, **Whitespace** could be called and the outcome handled with a very short sequence of instructions, as follows:

```
mov   al,[Char]
call  Whitespace
jnz   NotWhitespace
```

The particular example isn't important here. What is important is that you realize that in assembler (unlike high level languages) there are many ways to return statuses and that it's possible to save a great deal of code and/or time by taking advantage of that. Now is not the time to pursue the topic further, but we'll return to the issues of passing values and statuses both to and from assembler subroutines in Volume II of *Zen of Assembly Language*.

11.6 ◆ Putting String Instructions to Work in Unlikely Places

I've said several times that string instructions are so powerful that you should try to use them even when they don't seem especially well-matched to a particular application. Now I'm going to back that up with an unlikely application in which the string instructions have served me well over the years: animation.

This section is actually a glimpse into the future. Volume II of *Zen of Assembly Language* will take up the topic of animation in much greater detail, as animation truly falls in the category of the flexible mind rather than knowledge. Still, animation is such a wonderful example of what the string instructions can do that we'll spend a little time on it here and now. It'll be a whirlwind look, with few details and nothing more than a quick glance at theory, for the focus isn't on animation per se. What's important is not that you understand how animation works but rather that you get a feel for the miracles string instructions can perform in places where you wouldn't think they could serve at all.

Animation Basics

Animation involves erasing and redrawing one or more images quickly enough to fool the eye into perceiving motion, as shown in Figure 11.17. Animation is a marginal application for the PC, by which I mean that the 8088 has barely enough horsepower to support decent animation under the best of circumstances. What that means is that the Zen of assembly language is an absolute must for PC animation.

Traditionally, microcomputer animation has been performed by **xor**ing images into display memory; that is, by drawing images by inserting the bits that control their pixels into display memory with the **xor** instruction. When an image is first **xor**ed into display memory at a given location, that image becomes visible. A second **xor**ing of the image at the same location then erases it. Why? That's simply the nature of the **xor** operation.

Consider this. When you **xor** a 1 bit with another bit once, the other bit is flipped. When you **xor** the same 1 bit with that other bit again, the other bit is flipped again—*right back to its original state,* as shown in Figure 11.18. After all, a bit has only two possible states, so a double flip must restore the bit back to the state in which it started. Since **xor**ing a 0 bit with another bit never affects the other bit, **xor**ing a target bit twice with either a 1 bit or a 0 bit always leaves the target bit in its original state.

Why is **xor**ing so popular for animation? Simply because no matter how

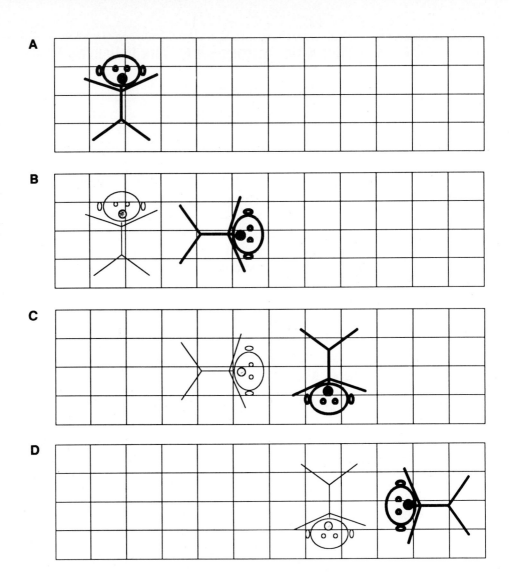

FIGURE 11.17   Animation is nothing more than the process of erasing, moving, and redrawing an image in a sequence that fools the eye into perceiving motion. **(A-D)** Four steps in the animation of what would appear to be a cartwheeling stick figure if the steps were repeated rapidly enough. The erased figure at the last location is shown with light lines in **(B-D)**; the figure drawn at the current location is shown with heavy lines in all four steps. This erase-move-redraw approach is used by animation based on **xor**ing.

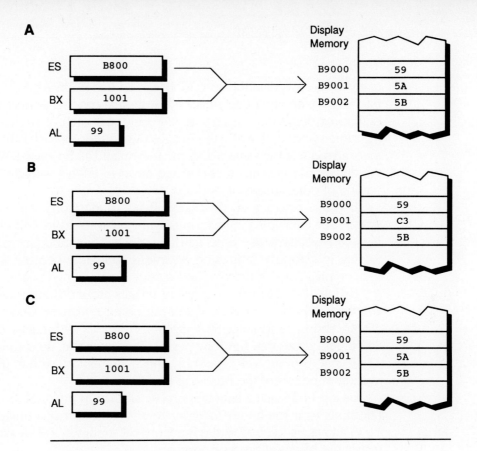

FIGURE 11.18   If the same value is **xor**ed twice with a given byte of
memory, the effects of the first **xor** operation are can-
celled completely and the byte of memory shows no signs
that either **xor** ever took place. **(A)** The state of the PC
before any **xor** operation is performed. **(B)** The state of
the PC after one **xor** is performed with **xor es:[bx],al**.
Note that the bits of B800:1001 that correspond to 1 bits
in AL are flipped, whereas the bits of that memory location that correspond to 0 bits in AL remain unchanged.
(C) The state of the PC after another **xor es:[bx],al** is
performed. Again, the bits of B800:1001 that correspond
to 1 bits in AL are flipped; the bits corresponding to 0
bits remain unchanged. What's noteworthy here is that
the second **xor** of the value 99h with B800:1001 returns
B800:1001 to exactly the state that was shown in **(A)**, before either **xor** was performed. This perfect reversibility of
the **xor** operation makes **xor**ing very convenient for animation applications, because any image drawn by being
xored into display memory can be erased by being **xor**ed
a second time into the same display memory location.

many images overlap, the second **xor** of an image always erases it without interfering with any other images. In other words, the perfect reversibility of the **xor** operation means that you could **xor** each of 10 images once at the same location, drawing the images right on top of each other, then **xor** them all again at the same place, and they would all be erased. With **xor**ing, the drawing or erasing of one image never interferes with the drawing or erasing of other images it overlaps.

If you're catching all this, great. If not, don't worry. I'm not going to spend time explaining animation now. Better we should wait until Volume II, when we have the time to do it right. The important point is that **xor**ing is a popular animation technique, primarily because it eliminates the complications of drawing and erasing overlapping images.

Listing 11-33, which bounces 10 images around the screen, illustrates animation based on **xor**ing. When run on an Enhanced Graphics Adapter (EGA), Listing 11-33 takes 30.29 seconds to move and redraw every image 500 times. (Note that the long-period Zen timer was used to time Listing 11-33, because we can't perform much animation within the 54-msec maximum period of the precision Zen timer.)

Listing 11-33 isn't a general-purpose animation program. I've kept complications to a minimum in order to show basic **xor** animation. Listing 11-33 allows us to observe the fundamental strengths and weaknesses (primarily the latter) of the **xor** approach.

```
1    ;
2    ; *** Listing 11-33 ***
3    ;
4    ; Illustrates animation based on exclusive-oring.
5    ; Animates 10 images at once.
6    ; Not a general animation implementation, but rather an
7    ; example of the strengths and weaknesses of exclusive-or
8    ; based animation.
9    ;
10   ; Make with LZTIME.BAT, since this program is too long to be
11   ; handled by the precision Zen timer.
12   ;
13          jmp     Skip
14   ;
15   DELAY   equ     0               ;set to higher values to
16                                   ; slow down for closer
17                                   ; observation
18   REPETITIONS equ 500             ;# of times to move and
19                                   ; redraw the images
20   DISPLAY_SEGMENT equ     0b800h  ;display memory segment
21                                   ; in 320x200 4-color
22                                   ; graphics mode
23   SCREEN_WIDTH    equ     80      ;# of bytes per scan line
24   BANK_OFFSET     equ     2000h   ;offset from the bank
25                                   ; containing the even-
26                                   ; numbered lines on the
```

```
27                                        ; screen to the bank
28                                        ; containing the odd-
29                                        ; numbered lines
30     ;
31     ; Used to count down # of times images are moved.
32     ;
33     RepCount        dw      REPETITIONS
34     ;
35     ; Complete info about one image that we're animating.
36     ;
37     Image    struc
38     XCoord          dw      ?       ;image X location in pixels
39     XInc            dw      ?       ;# of pixels to increment
40                                     ; location by in the X
41                                     ; direction on each move
42     YCoord          dw      ?       ;image Y location in pixels
43     YInc            dw      ?       ;# of pixels to increment
44                                     ; location by in the Y
45                                     ; direction on each move
46     Image    ends
47     ;
48     ; List of images to animate.
49     ;
50     Images   label   Image
51             Image   <64,4,8,4>
52             Image   <144,0,56,2>
53             Image   <224,-4,104,0>
54             Image   <64,4,152,-2>
55             Image   <144,0,8,-4>
56             Image   <224,-4,56,-2>
57             Image   <64,4,104,0>
58             Image   <144,0,152,2>
59             Image   <224,-4,8,4>
60             Image   <64,4,56,2>
61     ImagesEnd       label   Image
62     ;
63     ; Pixel pattern for the one image this program draws,
64     ; a 32x32 3-color square.
65     ;
66     TheImage        label   byte
67             rept    32
68             dw      0ffffh, 05555h, 0aaaah, 0ffffh
69             endm
70     IMAGE_HEIGHT    equ     32      ;# of rows in the image
71     IMAGE_WIDTH     equ     8       ;# of bytes across the image
72     ;
73     ; Exclusive-ors the image of a 3-color square at the
74     ; specified screen location. Assumes images start on
75     ; even-numbered scan lines and are an even number of
76     ; scan lines high. Always draws images byte-aligned in
77     ; display memory.
78     ;
79     ; Input:
80     ;       CX = X coordinate of upper left corner at which to
81     ;            draw image (will be adjusted to nearest
82     ;            less-than or equal-to multiple of 4 in order
83     ;            to byte-align)
84     ;       DX = Y coordinate of upper left corner at which to
85     ;            draw image
```

```
 86   ;          ES = display memory segment
 87   ;
 88   ; Output: none
 89   ;
 90   ; Registers altered: AX, CX, DX, SI, DI, BP
 91   ;
 92   XorImage:
 93            push     bx          ;preserve the main loop's pointer
 94            shr      dx,1        ;divide the row # by 2 to compensate
 95                                 ; for the 2-bank nature of 320x200
 96                                 ; 4-color mode
 97            mov      ax,SCREEN_WIDTH
 98            mul      dx          ;start offset of top row of image in
 99                                 ; display memory
100            shr      cx,1        ;divide the X coordinate by 4
101            shr      cx,1        ; because there are 4 pixels per
102                                 ; byte
103            add      ax,cx       ;point to the offset at which the
104                                 ; upper left byte of the image will
105                                 ; go
106            mov      di,ax
107            mov      si,offset TheImage
108                                 ;point to the start of the one image
109                                 ; we always draw
110            mov      bx,BANK_OFFSET-IMAGE_WIDTH
111                                 ;offset from the end of an even line
112                                 ; of the image in display memory to
113                                 ; the start of the next odd line of
114                                 ; the image
115            mov      dx,IMAGE_HEIGHT/2
116                                 ;# of even/odd numbered row pairs to
117                                 ;  draw in the image
118            mov      bp,IMAGE_WIDTH/2
119                                 ;# of words to draw per row of the
120                                 ; image. Note that IMAGE_WIDTH must
121                                 ; be an even number since we XOR
122                                 ; the image a word at a time
123   XorRowLoop:
124            mov      cx,bp       ;# of words to draw per row of the
125                                 ; image
126   XorColumnLoopEvenRows:
127            lodsw                ;next word of the image pattern
128            xor      es:[di],ax      ;XOR the next word of the
129                                     ; image into the screen
130            inc      di          ;point to the next word in display
131            inc      di          ; memory
132            loop     XorColumnLoopEvenRows
133            add      di,bx       ;point to the start of the next
134                                 ; (odd) row of the image, which is
135                                 ; in the second bank of display
136                                 ; memory
137            mov      cx,bp       ;# of words to draw per row of the
138                                 ; image
139   XorColumnLoopOddRows:
140            lodsw                ;next word of the image pattern
141            xor      es:[di],ax      ;XOR the next word of the
142                                     ; image into the screen
143            inc      di          ;point to the next word in display
144            inc      di          ; memory
```

```
145              loop     XorColumnLoopOddRows
146              sub      di,BANK_OFFSET-SCREEN_WIDTH+IMAGE_WIDTH
147                               ;point to the start of the next
148                               ; (even) row of the image, which is
149                               ; in the first bank of display
150                               ; memory
151              dec      dx      ;count down the row pairs
152              jnz      XorRowLoop
153              pop      bx      ;restore the main loop's pointer
154              ret
155      ;
156      ; Main animation program.
157      ;
158      Skip:
159      ;
160      ; Set the mode to 320x200 4-color graphics mode.
161      ;
162              mov      ax,0004h        ;AH=0 is mode select fn
163                                       ;AL=4 selects mode 4,
164                                       ; 320x200 4-color mode
165              int      10h             ;invoke the BIOS video
166                                       ; interrupt to set the mode
167      ;
168      ; Point ES to display memory for the rest of the program.
169      ;
170              mov      ax,DISPLAY_SEGMENT
171              mov      es,ax
172      ;
173      ; We'll always want to count up.
174      ;
175              cld
176      ;
177      ; Start timing.
178      ;
179              call     ZTimerOn
180      ;
181      ; Draw all the images initially.
182      ;
183              mov      bx,offset Images        ;list of images
184      InitialDrawLoop:
185              mov      cx,[bx+XCoord]  ;X coordinate
186              mov      dx,[bx+YCoord]  ;Y coordinate
187              call     XorImage        ;draw this image
188              add      bx,size Image   ;point to next image
189              cmp      bx,offset ImagesEnd
190              jb       InitialDrawLoop ;draw next image, if
191                                       ; there is one
192      ;
193      ; Erase, move, and redraw each image in turn REPETITIONS
194      ; times.
195      ;
196      MainMoveAndDrawLoop:
197              mov      bx,offset Images        ;list of images
198      ImageMoveLoop:
199              mov      cx,[bx+XCoord]  ;X coordinate
200              mov      dx,[bx+YCoord]  ;Y coordinate
201              call     XorImage        ;erase this image (it's
202                                       ; already drawn at this
203                                       ; location, so this XOR
```

```
204                                          ; erases it)
205             mov     cx,[bx+XCoord]   ;X coordinate
206             cmp     cx,4             ;at left edge?
207             ja      CheckRightMargin ;no
208             neg     [bx+XInc]        ;yes, so bounce
209     CheckRightMargin:
210             cmp     cx,284           ;at right edge?
211             jb      MoveX            ;no
212             neg     [bx+XInc]        ;yes, so bounce
213     MoveX:
214             add     cx,[bx+XInc]     ;move horizontally
215             mov     [bx+XCoord],cx   ;save the new location
216             mov     dx,[bx+YCoord]   ;Y coordinate
217             cmp     dx,4             ;at top edge?
218             ja      CheckBottomMargin ;no
219             neg     [bx+YInc]        ;yes, so bounce
220     CheckBottomMargin:
221             cmp     dx,164           ;at bottom edge?
222             jb      MoveY            ;no
223             neg     [bx+YInc]        ;yes, so bounce
224     MoveY:
225             add     dx,[bx+YInc]     ;move horizontally
226             mov     [bx+YCoord],dx   ;save the new location
227             call    XorImage         ;draw the image at its
228                                      ; new location
229             add     bx,size Image    ;point to the next image
230             cmp     bx,offset ImagesEnd
231             jb      ImageMoveLoop    ;move next image, if there
232                                      ; is one
233
234     if DELAY
235             mov     cx,DELAY         ;slow down as specified
236             loop    $
237     endif
238             dec     [RepCount]       ;animate again?
239             jnz     MainMoveAndDrawLoop ;yes
240     ;
241             call    ZTimerOff        ;done timing
242     ;
243     ; Return to text mode.
244     ;
245             mov     ax,0003h         ;AH=0 is mode select fn
246                                      ;AL=3 selects mode 3,
247                                      ; 80x25 text mode
248             int     10h              ;invoke the BIOS video
249                                      ; interrupt to set the mode
```

When you run Listing 11-33, you'll see why **xor**ing is less than ideal. Even though overlapping images don't interfere with each other insofar as drawing and erasing go, they do produce some unattractive effects onscreen. In particular, unintended colors and patterns often result when multiple images are **xor**ed into the same bytes of display memory. Another problem is that **xor**ed images flicker because they're constantly being erased and redrawn. (Each image could instead be redrawn at its new location before being erased at the old location, but the overlap color effects characteristic of **xor**ing would still cause flicker.) That's not all, though. There's a still more serious problem with **xor**-based animation . . .

It's slow.

The problem isn't that the **xor** instruction itself is particularly slow; rather, it's that **xor** isn't a string instruction. It can't be repeated with **rep**, it doesn't advance its pointers automatically, and it just isn't as speedy as, say, **movs**. Still, neither **movs** nor any other string instruction can perform **xor** operations, so it would seem we're stuck.

We're hardly stuck, though. On the contrary, we're bound for glory!

String Instruction–Based Animation

If string instructions can't **xor**, then we'll just have to figure out a way to animate without **xor**. As it turns out, there's a *very* nice way to do this. I learned this approach from Dan Illowsky, who developed it before string instructions even existed, way back in the early days of the Apple II.

First, we'll give each image a small blank fringe. Then we'll make it a rule never to move an image by more than the width of its fringe before redrawing it. Finally we'll draw images by simply copying them to display memory, destroying whatever they overwrite, as shown in Figure 11.19. Now, what does that do for us?

Amazing things. For starters, each image will, as it is redrawn, automatically erase its former incarnation. That means that there's no flicker, since images are never really erased but are only drawn over themselves. There are also no color effects when images overlap, as only the image that was drawn most recently at any given pixel is visible.

In short, this sort of animation (which I'll call block-move animation) actually looks considerably better than animation based on **xor**. That's just frosting on the cake, though—the big payoff is speed. With block-move animation we suddenly don't need to **xor** anymore. In fact, **rep movs** works beautifully to draw a whole line of an image in a single instruction. We also don't need to draw each image twice per move, once to erase the image at its old location and once to draw it at its new location, as we did with **xor**, because the act of drawing the image at a new location serves to erase the old image as well.

But wait, there's more! The **xor** instruction accesses a given byte of memory twice per draw, once to read the original byte and once to write the modified byte back to memory. With block-move animation, on the other hand, we simply write each byte of an image to memory once and we're done with that byte. In other words, between the elimination of a

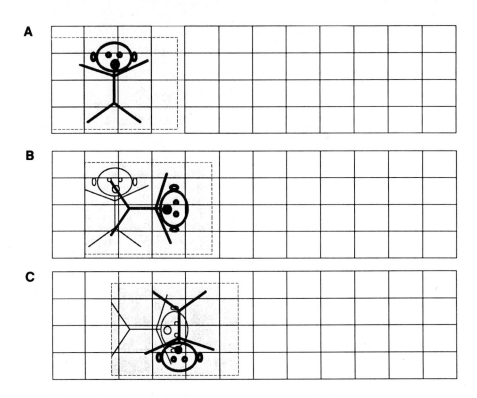

FIGURE 11.19   Block-move animation uses a fundamentally different principle than animation based on **xor**ing. In block-move animation, an image is drawn by simply writing its bytes to a rectangular area of display memory. Each image includes a blank fringe wide enough to cover the longest distance that image ever moves at one time. Given that restriction, as each image is moved and redrawn at its new location it automatically erases itself from the old location; no separate drawing step is required. **(A-D)** Four steps in the block move animation of a cartwheeling stick figure; the animated image is shown with heavy lines and the blank fringe is shaded gray. Each time the figure is drawn at a new location, the blank fringe completely erases the image at the last location. (The erased image is shown with light lines.) Note that this restricts the maximum movement of the figure to the width of the fringe. By contrast, images that are explicitly erased and then redrawn, as shown in Figure 11-17, can move any distance at all.

D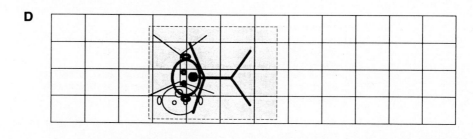

FIGURE 11.19   (*continued*)

separate erasing step and the replacement of read-**xor**-write with a single write, block move animation accesses display memory only about one third as many times as **xor** animation. (The ratio isn't quite 1:4 because the blank fringe makes block-move animation images somewhat larger.)

Are alarm bells going off in your head? They should be. Think back to our journey beneath the programming interface. Think of the cycle eaters. Ah, you've got it! *The **xor** animation approach loses about three times as much performance to the display adapter cycle eater as does block-move animation.* What's more, block-move animation uses the blindingly fast **movs** instruction. To top it off, block-move animation loses almost nothing to the prefetch queue cycle eater or the 8088's slow branching speed, thanks to the **rep** prefix.

Sounds almost too good to be true, doesn't it? It is true, though: block-move animation relies almost exclusively on one of the two most powerful instructions of the 8088 (**cmps** being the other) and avoids the gaping maws of the prefetch queue and display adapter cycle eaters in the process. Which leaves only one question . . .

How fast *is* block-move animation?

Remember, theory is fine, but we don't trust any code until we've timed it. Listing 11-34 performs the same animation as Listing 11-33, but with block-move rather than **xor** animation. Happily, Listing 11-34 lives up to its advance billing, finishing in just 10.35 seconds when run on an EGA. *Block-move animation is close to three times as fast as **xor** in this application*—and it looks better, too. (You can slow down the animation in order to observe the differences between the two approaches more closely by setting **DELAY** to a higher value in each listing.)

Let's not underplay the appearance issue just because the performance advantage of block-move animation is so great. If you possibly can, enter and run Listings 11-33 and 11-34. The visual impact of block-move animation's flicker-free, high-speed animation is startling. It's hard to imagine that

```
1   ;
2   ; *** Listing 11-34 ***
3   ;
4   ; Illustrates animation based on block moves.
5   ; Animates 10 images at once.
6   ; Not a general animation implementation, but rather an
7   ; example of the strengths and weaknesses of block-move
8   ; based animation.
9   ;
10  ; Make with LZTIME.BAT, since this program is too long to be
11  ; handled by the precision Zen timer.
12  ;
13          jmp     Skip
14  ;
15  DELAY    equ     0              ;set to higher values to
16                                  ; slow down for closer
17                                  ; observation
18  REPETITIONS equ 500             ;# of times to move and
19                                  ; redraw the images
20  DISPLAY_SEGMENT equ    0b800h   ;display memory segment
21                                  ; in 320x200 4-color
22                                  ; graphics mode
23  SCREEN_WIDTH    equ     80      ;# of bytes per scan line
24  BANK_OFFSET     equ     2000h   ;offset from the bank
25                                  ; containing the even-
26                                  ; numbered lines on the
27                                  ; screen to the bank
28                                  ; containing the odd-
29                                  ; numbered lines
30  ;
31  ; Used to count down # of times images are moved.
32  ;
33  RepCount        dw      REPETITIONS
34  ;
35  ; Complete info about one image that we're animating.
36  ;
37  Image    struc
38  XCoord          dw      ?       ;image X location in pixels
39  XInc            dw      ?       ;# of pixels to increment
40                                  ; location by in the X
41                                  ; direction on each move
42  YCoord          dw      ?       ;image Y location in pixels
43  YInc            dw      ?       ;# of pixels to increment
44                                  ; location by in the Y
45                                  ; direction on each move
46  Image    ends
47  ;
48  ; List of images to animate.
49  ;
50  Images   label   Image
51           Image   <60,4,4,4>
52           Image   <140,0,52,2>
53           Image   <220,-4,100,0>
54           Image   <60,4,148,-2>
55           Image   <140,0,4,-4>
56           Image   <220,-4,52,-2>
57           Image   <60,4,100,0>
58           Image   <140,0,148,2>
59           Image   <220,-4,4,4>
```

```
60                   Image        <60,4,52,2>
61      ImagesEnd         label     Image
62      ;
63      ; Pixel pattern for the one image this program draws,
64      ; a 32x32 3-color square.  There's a 4-pixel-wide blank
65      ; fringe around each image, which makes sure the image at
66      ; the old location is erased by the drawing of the image at
67      ; the new location.
68      ;
69      TheImage          label     byte
70              rept      4
71              dw        5 dup (0)          ;top blank fringe
72              endm
73              rept      32
74              db        00h                ;left blank fringe
75              dw        0ffffh, 05555h, 0aaaah, 0ffffh
76              db        00h                ;right blank fringe
77              endm
78              rept      4
79              dw        5 dup (0)          ;bottom blank fringe
80              endm
81      IMAGE_HEIGHT      equ       40       ;# of rows in the image
82                                           ; (including blank fringe)
83      IMAGE_WIDTH       equ       10       ;# of bytes across the image
84                                           ; (including blank fringe)
85      ;
86      ; Block-move draws the image of a 3-color square at the
87      ; specified screen location. Assumes images start on
88      ; even-numbered scan lines and are an even number of
89      ; scan lines high. Always draws images byte-aligned in
90      ; display memory.
91      ;
92      ; Input:
93      ;       CX = X coordinate of upper left corner at which to
94      ;            draw image (will be adjusted to nearest
95      ;            less-than or equal-to multiple of 4 in order
96      ;            to byte-align)
97      ;       DX = Y coordinate of upper left corner at which to
98      ;            draw image
99      ;       ES = display memory segment
100     ;
101     ; Output: none
102     ;
103     ; Registers altered: AX, CX, DX, SI, DI, BP
104     ;
105     BlockDrawImage:
106             push      bx         ;preserve the main loop's pointer
107             shr       dx,1       ;divide the row # by 2 to compensate
108                                  ; for the 2-bank nature of 320x200
109                                  ; 4-color mode
110             mov       ax,SCREEN_WIDTH
111             mul       dx         ;start offset of top row of image in
112                                  ; display memory
113             shr       cx,1       ;divide the X coordinate by 4
114             shr       cx,1       ; because there are 4 pixels per
115                                  ; byte
116             add       ax,cx      ;point to the offset at which the
117                                  ; upper left byte of the image will
118                                  ; go
```

```
119              mov      di,ax
120              mov      si,offset TheImage
121                                ;point to the start of the one image
122                                ; we always draw
123              mov      ax,BANK_OFFSET-SCREEN_WIDTH+IMAGE_WIDTH
124                                ;offset from the end of an odd line
125                                ; of the image in display memory to
126                                ; the start of the next even line of
127                                ; the image
128              mov      bx,BANK_OFFSET-IMAGE_WIDTH
129                                ;offset from the end of an even line
130                                ; of the image in display memory to
131                                ; the start of the next odd line of
132                                ; the image
133              mov      dx,IMAGE_HEIGHT/2
134                                ;# of even/odd numbered row pairs to
135                                ;  draw in the image
136              mov      bp,IMAGE_WIDTH/2
137                                ;# of words to draw per row of the
138                                ; image. Note that IMAGE_WIDTH must
139                                ; be an even number since we draw
140                                ; the image a word at a time
141      BlockDrawRowLoop:
142              mov      cx,bp    ;# of words to draw per row of the
143                                ; image
144              rep      movsw    ;draw a whole even row with this one
145                                ; repeated instruction
146              add      di,bx    ;point to the start of the next
147                                ; (odd) row of the image, which is
148                                ; in the second bank of display
149                                ; memory
150              mov      cx,bp    ;# of words to draw per row of the
151                                ; image
152              rep      movsw    ;draw a whole odd row with this one
153                                ; repeated instruction
154              sub      di,ax
155                                ;point to the start of the next
156                                ; (even) row of the image, which is
157                                ; in the first bank of display
158                                ; memory
159              dec      dx       ;count down the row pairs
160              jnz      BlockDrawRowLoop
161              pop      bx       ;restore the main loop's pointer
162              ret
163      ;
164      ; Main animation program.
165      ;
166      Skip:
167      ;
168      ; Set the mode to 320x200 4-color graphics mode.
169      ;
170              mov      ax,0004h          ;AH=0 is mode select fn
171                                         ;AL=4 selects mode 4,
172                                         ; 320x200 4-color mode
173              int      10h               ;invoke the BIOS video
174                                         ; interrupt to set the mode
175      ;
176      ; Point ES to display memory for the rest of the program.
177      ;
```

```
178             mov     ax,DISPLAY_SEGMENT
179             mov     es,ax
180     ;
181     ; We'll always want to count up.
182     ;
183             cld
184     ;
185     ; Start timing.
186     ;
187             call    ZTimerOn
188     ;
189     ; There's no need to draw all the images initially with
190     ; block-move animation.
191     ;
192     ; Move and redraw each image in turn REPETITIONS times.
193     ; Redrawing automatically erases the image at the old
194     ; location, thanks to the blank fringe.
195     ;
196     MainMoveAndDrawLoop:
197             mov     bx,offset Images        ;list of images
198     ImageMoveLoop:
199             mov     cx,[bx+XCoord]  ;X coordinate
200             cmp     cx,0            ;at left edge?
201             ja      CheckRightMargin ;no
202             neg     [bx+XInc]       ;yes, so bounce
203     CheckRightMargin:
204             cmp     cx,280          ;at right edge?
205             jb      MoveX           ;no
206             neg     [bx+XInc]       ;yes, so bounce
207     MoveX:
208             add     cx,[bx+XInc]    ;move horizontally
209             mov     [bx+XCoord],cx  ;save the new location
210             mov     dx,[bx+YCoord]  ;Y coordinate
211             cmp     dx,0            ;at top edge?
212             ja      CheckBottomMargin ;no
213             neg     [bx+YInc]       ;yes, so bounce
214     CheckBottomMargin:
215             cmp     dx,160          ;at bottom edge?
216             jb      MoveY           ;no
217             neg     [bx+YInc]       ;yes, so bounce
218     MoveY:
219             add     dx,[bx+YInc]    ;move horizontally
220             mov     [bx+YCoord],dx  ;save the new location
221             call    BlockDrawImage  ;draw the image at its
222                                     ; new location
223             add     bx,size Image   ;point to the next image
224             cmp     bx,offset ImagesEnd
225             jb      ImageMoveLoop   ;move next image, if there
226                                     ; is one
227
228     if DELAY
229             mov     cx,DELAY        ;slow down as specified
230             loop    $
231     endif
232             dec     [RepCount]      ;animate again?
233             jnz     MainMoveAndDrawLoop ;yes
234     ;
235             call    ZTimerOff       ;done timing
236     ;
```

```
237    ; Return to text mode.
238    ;
239            mov     ax,0003h        ;AH=0 is mode select fn
240                                    ;AL=3 selects mode 3,
241                                    ; 80x25 text mode
242            int     10h             ;invoke the BIOS video
243                                    ; interrupt to set the mode
```

any programmer would go back to **xor** after seeing block-move animation in action.

That's not to say that block-move animation is perfect. Unlike **xor**, block-move animation wipes out the background unless the just-uncovered portion of the background is explicitly redrawn after each image is moved. Block-move animation does produce flicker and fringe effects when images overlap, and it also limits to the width of the fringe the distance an image can move before it's redrawn.

If block-move animation isn't perfect, however, it's *much* better than **xor**. What's really noteworthy, however, is that we looked at an application (animation) without preconceived ideas about the best implementation and came up with an approach that merged the application's needs with one of the strengths of the PC (the string instructions) while avoiding the cycle eaters. In the end, we not only improved performance remarkably but also got better animation, in the process turning an apparent liability—the limitations of the string instructions—into a big asset. All in all, we've just seen the full range of the Zen of assembly language: knowledge, flexible mind, and implementation.

Try to use the string instructions for all your time-critical code, even when you think they just don't fit. Sometimes they don't, but you can never be sure unless you try—and if they *can* be made to fit, it will pay off *big*.

Notes on the Animation Implementations

Spend as much time as you wish perusing Listings 11-33 and 11-34, but *do not worry* if they don't make complete sense to you right now. The point of this exercise was to illustrate the use of the string instructions in an unusual application, not to get you started with animation. In Volume II of *Zen of Assembly Language* we'll return to animation in a big way.

The animation listings are not full-featured, flexible implementations, nor were they meant to be. My intent in creating these programs was to contrast the basic operation and raw performance of **xor** and block-move animation. Consequently, I've structured the two listings along much the same lines, and while the code is fast, I've avoided further optimizations (notably the use of in-line code) that would have complicated matters. We'll see those additional optimizations in Volume II.

One interesting point to be made about the animation listings is that I've assumed in the drawing routines that images always start on even rows of the screen and are always an even number of rows in height. Many people would consider the routines to be incomplete, since they lack the extra code needed to handle the complications of odd start rows and odd heights in 320-by-200 four-color graphics mode. Of course, that extra code would slow performance and increase program size, but it would nonetheless be deemed necessary in any "full" animation implementation.

Is the handling of odd start rows and odd heights really necessary, though? Not if you can structure your application so that images can always start on even rows and can always be of even heights, and that's actually easy to do. No one will ever notice whether images move 1 or 2 pixels at a time; the nature of animation is such that the motion of an image appears just as smooth in either case. And why should there be a need for odd image heights? If necessary, images of odd heights could be padded out with an extra line. In fact, an extra line can often be used to improve the appearance of an image.

In short, "full" animation implementations not only run slower than the implementation in Listings 11-33 and 11-34 but may not even yield any noticeable benefits. The lesson is this: add features that slow your code only when you're sure you need them. High-performance assembler programming is partly an art of eliminating everything but the essentials.

By the way, Listings 11-33 and 11-34 move images a full 4 pixels at a time horizontally, and that's a bit *too* far. Two pixels is a far more visually attractive distance by which to move animated images, especially those that move slowly. However, because each byte of 320-by-200 four-color mode display memory controls 4 pixels, alignment of images to start in columns that aren't multiples of four is more difficult, although not really that hard once you get the hang of it. Because our goal in this section was to contrast block-move and **xor** animation, I didn't add the extra code and complications required to bit align the images. We will discuss bit alignment of images at length in Volume II, however.

11.7 ◆ A Note on Handling Blocks Larger Than 64 K Bytes

All the string instruction–based code we've seen in this chapter handles only blocks or strings that are 64 K bytes in length or shorter. There's a very good reason for this, of course—the infernal segmented architecture of the 8088—but there are nonetheless times when larger memory blocks are needed.

I'm going to save the topic of handling blocks larger than 64 K bytes for Volume II of *Zen of Assembly Language*. Why? Well, the trick with code that handles larger memory blocks isn't getting it to work; that's relatively easy if you're willing to perform 32-bit arithmetic and reload the segment registers before each memory access. No, the trick is getting code that handles large memory blocks to work reasonably fast.

We've seen that a key to assembler programming lies in converting difficult problems from approaches ill-suited to the 8088 to ones that the 8088 can handle well, and this is no exception. In this particular application, we need to convert the task at hand from one of independently addressing every byte in the 8088's 1-megabyte address space to one of handling a series of blocks that are each no larger than 64 K bytes, so that we can process up to 64 K bytes at a time very rapidly without touching the segment registers.

The concept is simple, but the implementation is not so simple and requires the flexible mind, and that's why the handling of memory blocks larger than 64 K bytes will have to wait until Volume II.

Conclusion

This chapter had two objectives. First, I wanted you to get a sense of how and when the string instructions can best be applied. Second, I wanted you to heighten your regard for these instructions, which are the best the 8088 has to offer. With any luck, this chapter has both broadened your horizons for string instruction applications and increased your respect for these unique and uniquely powerful members of the 8088's instruction set.

Chapter 12

Don't Jump!

12.1   How Slow Is It?

12.2   Branching and Calculation of the Target Address

12.3   Branching and the Prefetch Queue

12.4   Branching and the *Second* Byte of the Instruction Branched To

Don't jump!

Sounds crazy, doesn't it? After all, a computer is at heart a decision-making machine that decides by branching, and any programmer worthy of the name knows that jumps, calls, interrupts, and loops are integral to any program of substance. I've led you into some mighty strange places, including unlikely string instruction applications and implausible regions of the 8088's instruction set, to say nothing of the scarcely comprehensible cycle eaters. Is it possible that I've finally tipped over the edge into sheer lunacy?

No such luck—I'm merely indulging in a bit of overstatement in a good cause. Of course you'll need to branch, but since branching is slow—make that *very* slow—on the 8088, you'll want to branch as little as possible. If you're clever, you can often manage to eliminate virtually all branching in the most time-critical portions of your code. Sometimes avoiding branching is merely a matter of rearranging code, and sometimes it involves a few extra bytes and some unusual code. Either way, code that's branch-free (or nearly so) is one key to high performance.

This business of avoiding branching—a term that covers jumps, subroutine calls, subroutine returns, and interrupts—is as much a matter of the flexible mind as of pure knowledge. You may have noticed that in recent chapters we've discussed ways to use instructions more effectively as much as we've discussed the instructions themselves. For example, much of the last chapter was about how to put the string instructions to work in unorthodox but effective ways, not about how the string instructions work per se. It's inevitable that as we've accumulated a broad base of knowledge about the 8088 and gained a better sense of how to approach high-performance coding, we've developed an itch to put that hard-won knowledge to work developing superior code. That's the flexible mind, and we'll see plenty of it over the next three chapters. Ultimately, we're building toward Volume II, which will focus on the flexible mind and implementation.

This chapter is emphatically *not* going to be a comprehensive discussion of all the ways to branch on the 8088. I started this book with the assumption that you were already familiar with assembly language, and we've spent many pages since then expanding your assembler knowledge. Chapter 6 discussed the flags that are tested by the various conditional jumps, and the last chapter used branching instructions in a variety of situations. By now I trust you know that **jz** branches if ZF is set to 1 and that **call** pushes the address of the next instruction on the stack and branches to the specified destination. If not, get a good reference book and study the various branching instructions carefully. There's nothing Zen in their functionality; they do what they're advertised to do, and that's that.

On the other hand, there is much Zen in the way the various branching instructions *perform*. In Chapter 13 we'll talk about ways to branch as little as possible, and in Chapter 14 we'll talk about ways to make branches perform as well as possible when you must use them. Right now, let's find out why branching as little as possible is a desirable goal.

12.1 ◆ How Slow Is It?

We want to avoid branching for one simple reason: it's slow. There's nothing inherently slow about branching; it just happens to suffer from a slow implementation on the 8088. Even the venerable Z80 branches about 50 percent faster than the 8088.

So how slow *is* branching on the 8088? Well, the answer varies from one type of branch to another, so let's pick a commonly used jump—say, **jmp**—and see what we find. The official execution time of **jmp** is 15 cycles. Listing 12-1, which measures the performance of 1000 **jmp** instructions in a row, reports that **jmp** actually takes 3.77 μsec (18 cycles) to execute. (Listing 12-1 actually uses **jmp short** rather than **jmp**, since the jumps don't cover much distance. We'll discuss the distinction between the two in a little while.)

```
1    ;
2    ; *** Listing 12-1 ***
3    ;
4    ; Measures the performance of JMP.
5    ;
6            call    ZTimerOn
7            rept    1000
8            jmp     short $+2       ;we'll do a short jump,
9                                    ; since the next instruction
10                                   ; can be reached with a
11                                   ; 1-byte displacement
12           endm
13           call    ZTimerOff
```

Eighteen cycles is a long time in anybody's book; that's long enough to copy a byte from one memory location to another and increment both SI and DI with **movsb**, long enough to add two 32-bit values together, and long enough to increment a 16-bit register at least 4 times. How could it possibly take the 8088 so long just to load a value into the instruction pointer? (Think about it: all a branch really consists of is setting IP, and sometimes CS, to point to the desired instruction.) Well, let's round up the usual suspects, the cycle eaters, and figure out what's going on. In the process, we'll surely acquire some knowledge that we can put to good use in creating high performance code.

12.2 ◆ Branching and Calculation of the Target Address

Of the 18 cycles **jmp** takes to execute in Listing 12-1, 4 cycles seem to be used to calculate the target offset. I can't state this with absolute certainty, since Intel doesn't make the inner workings of its instructions public, but it's most likely true. You see, most of the 8088's **jmp** instructions don't have the form *load the Instruction Pointer with offset* xxxx, where the **jmp** instruction specifies the exact offset to branch to. (This sort of jump is known as an *absolute* branch, since the destination offset is specified as a fixed, or absolute, offset in the code segment. Figure 12.1 shows one of the few jump instructions that does use absolute branching.) Rather, most of the 8088's **jmp** instructions have the form *add* nnnn *to the contents of the instruction pointer,* where the byte or word following the **jmp** opcode specifies the distance from the current IP to the offset to branch to, as shown in Figure 12.2.

Jumps that use displacements are known as *relative* branches, because the destination offset is specified relative to the offset of the current instruction. Relative branches are actually performed by adding a displacement to the value in the instruction pointer, and there's a bit of a trick there.

By the time a relative branching instruction actually gets around to branching, IP points to the byte *after* the last byte of the instruction, since IP has already been used to read in all the bytes of the branching instruction and has advanced to point to the next instruction. As shown in Figure 12.2, relative branches work by adding a displacement to the IP after it has advanced to point to the byte after the branching instruction, *not* by adding a displacement to the offset of the branching instruction itself.

So, to sum up, most **jmp** instructions contain a field that specifies a displacement from the current IP to the target address rather than a field that specifies the target address directly. (Jumps that *don't* use relative branching include **jmp** *reg16*, **jmp** *mem16*, and all far jumps. All conditional jumps use relative branching.)

There are definite advantages to the use of relative rather than absolute branches. First, code that uses relative branching will work properly no matter where in memory it is loaded, since relative branch destinations aren't tied to specific memory offsets. If a block of code is moved to another

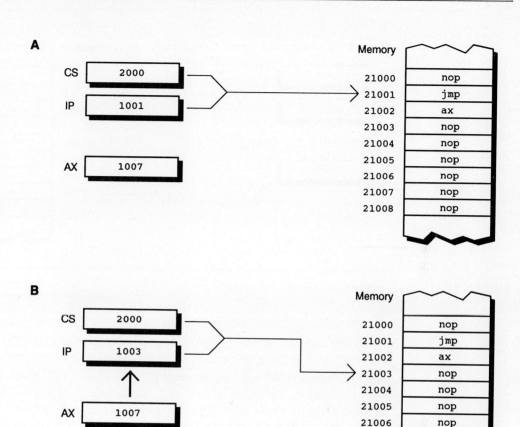

FIGURE 12.1 The **jmp *reg16*** instruction is one of the few jump instructions that performs an absolute branch—that is, a branch to a specific offset in the code segment. Instead, most of the 8088's jump instructions use relative branching (as shown in Figure 12.2). This figure shows the steps that occur as **jmp ax** branches, with the thin lines showing how IP advances as the execution of **jmp ax** progresses. **(A)** Here, **jmp ax** is just starting. **(B)** AX is copied into IP after IP has advanced past (and allowed the fetching of) the last byte of the **jmp** instruction, the *mod-reg-rm* byte that specifies AX as the source register. **(C)** The branch is complete, with IP pointing to the branched-to instruction.

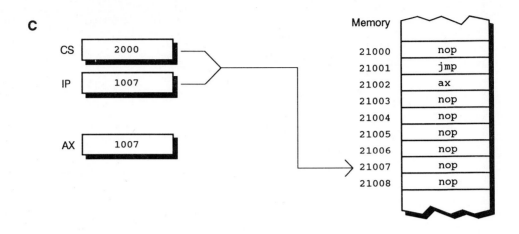

C

	Memory	
	21000	nop
	21001	jmp
	21002	ax
	21003	nop
	21004	nop
	21005	nop
	21006	nop
	21007	nop
	21008	nop

CS 2000
IP 1007
AX 1007

FIGURE 12.1   (*continued*)

area of memory, the relative displacements between the instructions remain the same, and so relative branching instructions still work properly. This property makes relative branches useful in any code that must be moved about in memory, although by and large such code isn't needed very often.

Second (and more important), when relative branches are used, any branch whose target is within −128 to +127 bytes of the byte after the end of the branching instruction can be specified in a more compact form, with a 1-byte rather than 1-word displacement, as shown in Figure 12.3. The key, of course, is that −128 to +127 decimal is equivalent to 0FF80h to 007Fh hexadecimal, which is the range of values that can be specified with a single signed byte. The short jumps to which I referred earlier are such 1 byte–displacement short branches, in contrast to normal jumps, which use full 2-byte displacements. The smaller displacement allows short jump instructions to squeeze into 2 bytes, 1 byte less than a normal jump.

By definition, then, short branches take 1 less instruction byte than normal relative branches. The tradeoff is that short jumps can reach offsets only within the aforementioned 256-address range, while the 1-word displacement of normal branches allows them to reach any offset in the current code segment.

Since most branches are in fact to nearby addresses, the availability of short (1 displacement byte) branches can produce significant savings in code size. In fact, the 8088's conditional jumps can *only* use 1-byte displacements, and while that's sometimes a nuisance when long conditional jumps need to be made, it does indeed help to keep code size down.

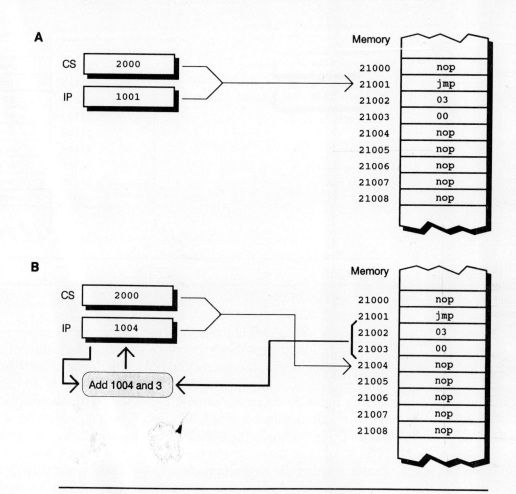

FIGURE 12.2   Most of the 8088's jump instructions use relative branching, where the destination address is specified as a displacement from the offset pointed to by the current instruction pointer. This figure shows the steps that occur as
a **jmp**, which performs a relative branch to offset 1007h
executes, with the thin lines showing how IP advances as
the execution of the **jmp** progresses. **(A)** Here, **jmp** is
just starting. **(B)** The branch is taking place, with IP having advanced past the opcode and displacement bytes as
they're fetched; the displacement is added to IP *after* IP
has advanced past the last byte of the instruction. **(C)** The
branch is complete, with IP pointing to the branched-to
instruction.

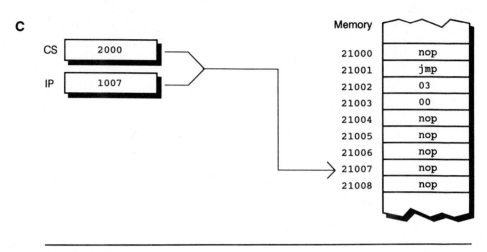

c

FIGURE 12.2   (*continued*)

There's also a definite disadvantage to the use of relative branches, and it's the usual drawback: speed, or rather the lack thereof. Adding a jump displacement to the instruction pointer is similar to adding a constant value to a register, a task that takes the 8088 4 cycles. By all appearances, it takes the 8088 about the same 4 cycles to add a jump displacement to the instruction pointer. Indeed, although there's no way to be sure exactly what's going on inside the 8088 during a **jmp**, it does make sense that the 8088 would use the same internal logic to add a constant to a register no matter whether the instruction causing the addition is a **jmp** or an **add**.

What's the evidence that the 8088 takes about 4 cycles to add a displacement to IP? Item 1: **jmp *reg16***, an instruction that branches directly to the offset (not displacement) stored in a register, executes in just 11 cycles, 4 cycles faster than a normal **jmp**. Item 2: **jmp *segment:offset***, the 8088's far jump that loads both CS and IP at once, executes at the same 15-cycles per execution speed as **jmp**. Although a far jump requires that CS be loaded, it doesn't involve any displacement arithmetic. The addition of the displacement to IP pretty clearly takes longer than simply loading an offset into IP; otherwise it seems that a near jump would *have* to be faster than a far jump, by virtue of not having to load CS.

By the way, in this one instance it's acceptable to speculate on the basis of official execution times rather than times reported by the Zen timer. Why? Because we're theorizing as to what's going on inside the 8088, and that's most accurately reflected by the official execution times, which ignore external data bus activity. Actual execution times include

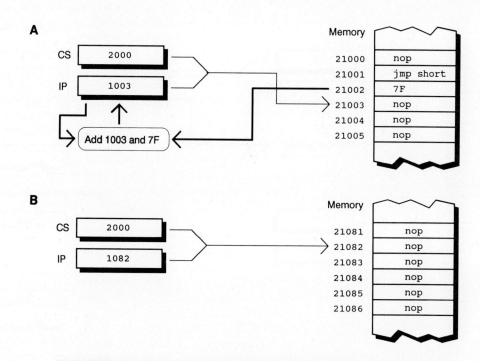

FIGURE 12.3 Relative branches within the range of −128 to +127 bytes of the current instruction pointer setting can be specified with 1 byte rather than 1 word, saving code space.

(A) A relative branch of 7Fh (+127) bytes is performed with a 1-byte displacement. **(B)** The completion of the branch.

(C) How a relative branch of +128 bytes is performed with a 2-byte displacement. A 2-byte rather than 1-byte displacement is necessary because a branch of 128 bytes is outside the range of −128 to +127 that can be specified with a single signed byte. **(D)** The completion of the branch.

(E) Why a relative branch of +128 bytes can't be performed with a 1-byte displacement. A 1-byte displacement of 80h is not interpreted as +128; instead, because single-byte displacements are treated as signed values and sign-extended to words, 80h is interpreted as 0FF80h, or −128. **(F)** The completion of the branch.

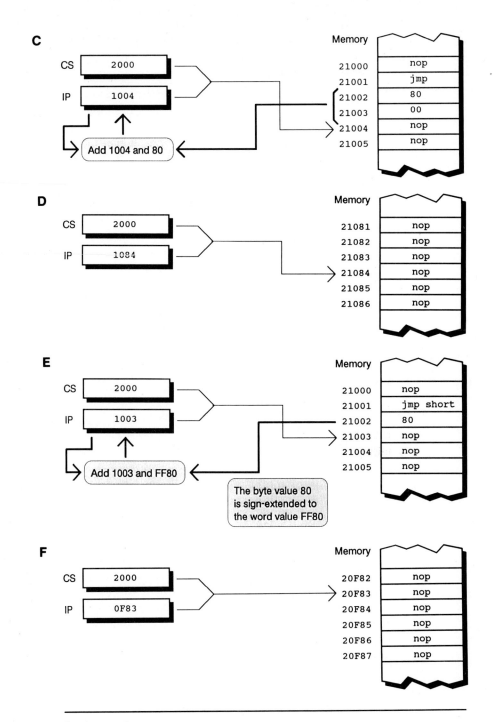

FIGURE 12.3   (*continued*)

instruction fetching time, and as far jumps are 2 to 3 bytes longer than near jumps, the prefetch queue cycle eater would obscure the comparison between the internal operations of near versus far jumps that we're trying to make. However, when it comes to evaluating real code performance (as opposed to speculating about the 8088's internal operations) you should *always* measure with the Zen timer.

Near subroutine calls (except **call *reg16***) also use displacements, and, like near jumps, near calls seem to spend several cycles performing displacement arithmetic. On the other hand, return instructions, which pop into IP offsets previously pushed on the stack by calls, do not perform displacement arithmetic, nor do far calls. Interrupts don't perform displacement arithmetic either; as we will see, however, interrupts have their own performance problems.

Displacement arithmetic accounts for about 4 of the 18 cycles **jmp** takes to execute. That leaves 14 cycles, still an awfully long time. What else is **jmp** doing to keep itself busy?

12.3 ◆ Branching and the Prefetch Queue

Since the actual execution time of **jmp** in Listing 12-1 is 3 cycles longer than its official execution time, one or more of the cycle eaters must be taking those cycles. If experience is any guide, it's a pretty good bet that the prefetch queue cycle eater is rearing its ugly head once again. The DRAM refresh cycle eater may also be taking some cycles (it usually does), but the 20 percent discrepancy between the official and actual execution times is far too large to be explained by DRAM refresh alone. In any case, let's measure the execution time of **jmp** with **imul** instructions interspersed so that the prefetch queue is full when it comes time for each **jmp** to execute.

First, let's figure out the execution time of **imul** when it's used to calculate the 32-bit product of two 16-bit 0 factors. Later, that will allow us to determine how much of the combined execution time of **imul** and **jmp** is due to **imul** alone. (By the way, we're using **imul** rather than **mul** because when I tried **mul** and **jmp** together, overall execution synchronized with DRAM refresh, distorting the results. Each **mul/jmp** pair executed in exactly 144 cycles, with DRAM refresh adding 6 of those cycles by holding up instruction fetching right after the jump. Here we have yet another example of why you should always time code in context. Be careful about generalizing from artificial tests like Listing 12-2!) The Zen

```
1   ;
2   ; *** Listing 12-2 ***
3   ;
4   ; Measures the performance of IMUL when used to calculate
5   ; the 32-bit product of two 16-bit factors each with a value
6   ; of zero.
7   ;
8           sub     ax,ax   ;we'll multiply zero times zero
9           call    ZTimerOn
10          rept    1000
11          imul    ax
12          endm
13          call    ZTimerOff
```

timer reports that the 1000 **imul** instructions in Listing 12-2 execute in 26.82 msec, or 26.82 μsec (128 cycles) per **imul**.

Given that, we can determine how long **jmp** takes to execute when started with the prefetch queue full. Listing 12-3, which measures the execution time of alternating **imul** and **jmp** instructions, runs in 31.18 msec. That's 31.18 μsec (148.8 cycles) per **imul**/**jmp** pair, or 20.8 cycles per **jmp**.

```
1   ;
2   ; *** Listing 12-3 ***
3   ;
4   ; Measures the performance of JMP when the prefetch queue
5   ; is full when it comes time for each JMP to run.
6   ;
7           sub     ax,ax   ;we'll multiply zero times zero
8           call    ZTimerOn
9           rept    1000
10          imul    ax        ;let the prefetch queue fill
11          jmp     short $+2   ;we'll do a short jump,
12                              ; since the next instruction
13                              ; is less than 127 bytes
14                              ; away
15          endm
16          call    ZTimerOff
```

Wait one minute! The **jmp** instruction takes more than 2 cycles *longer* when started with the prefetch queue full in Listing 12-3 than it did in Listing 12-1. Instructions don't slow down when the prefetch queue is allowed to fill before they start—if anything, they speed up. Yet a slowdown is just what we've found.

What the heck is going on?

The Prefetch Queue Empties When You Branch

It's true that the prefetch queue is full when it comes time for each **jmp** to start in Listing 12-3, but *it's also true that the prefetch queue is empty* *when **jmp** ends.* To understand why that is and what the implications are, we must consider the nature of the prefetch queue.

We learned way back in Chapter 3 that the bus interface unit (BIU) of the 8088 reads the bytes immediately following the current instruction into the prefetch queue whenever the external data bus isn't otherwise engaged. This is done in an attempt to anticipate the next few instruction-byte requests that the execution unit (EU) will issue. Every time the EU requests an instruction byte and the BIU has guessed right by prefetching that byte, 4 cycles are saved that would otherwise have to be expended on fetching the requested byte while the EU waited, as shown in Figure 12.4.

What happens if the BIU guesses wrong? Nothing disastrous. Since the prefetched bytes are no help in fulfilling the EU's request, the requested instruction byte must be fetched from memory at a cost of 4 cycles, just as if prefetching had never occurred.

That leaves us with an obvious question. *When* does the BIU guess wrong? In one case and one case only:

Whenever a branch occurs.

Think of it this way. The BIU prefetches bytes sequentially, starting with the byte after the instruction being executed. So long as no branches occur, those prefetched bytes *must* be the bytes the EU will want next, since the instruction pointer simply marches along from low addresses to high addresses.

When a branch occurs, however, the bytes immediately following the instruction bytes for the branch instruction are no longer necessarily the next bytes the EU will want, as shown in Figure 12.5. If they aren't, the BIU has no choice but to throw away those bytes and start fetching bytes again at the location branched to. In other words, if the BIU gambles that the EU will request instruction bytes sequentially and loses that gamble because of a branch, all pending prefetches of the instruction bytes following the branch instruction in memory are wasted.

That doesn't make prefetching undesirable. The BIU prefetches only during idle times, so prefetching—even wasted prefetching—doesn't slow down execution. (At worst, prefetching might slow things down a bit by postponing memory accesses by a cycle or two, but whether and how often that happens, only Intel knows, since it's a function of the internal logic of the 8088. At any rate, wasted prefetching shouldn't greatly affect performance.) All that's lost when you branch is the performance bonus obtained when the 8088 manages to coprocess by prefetching and executing at the same time.

The 8088 could have been designed so that whenever a branch occurs any bytes in the prefetch queue that are still usable are kept, while other,

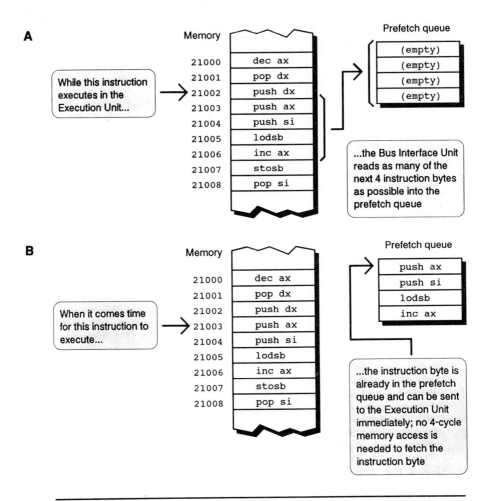

FIGURE 12.4   While the execution unit executes an instruction, the bus interface unit prefetches up to 4 of the instruction bytes immediately following the current instruction in memory. This often allows the BIU to have the next instruction byte immediately available when the EU requests it, thereby avoiding the 4 or more EU idle cycles that result when the BIU has to read memory in order to fill an EU request.

(A) The instruction bytes that the 8088 tries to read into the prefetch queue while **push dx** executes. In reality, the 8088 couldn't fetch 4 bytes during one **push dx**, but for illustrative purposes we'll assume 4 bytes are prefetched.

C

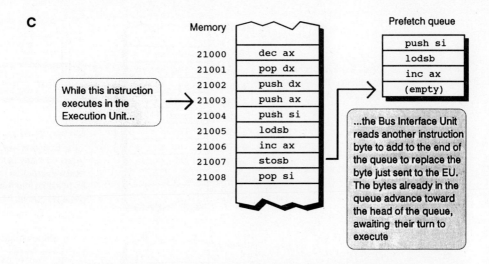

Memory

Prefetch queue

push si
lodsb
inc ax
(empty)

21000	dec ax
21001	pop dx
21002	push dx
21003	push ax
21004	push si
21005	lodsb
21006	inc ax
21007	stosb
21008	pop si

While this instruction executes in the Execution Unit...

...the Bus Interface Unit reads another instruction byte to add to the end of the queue to replace the byte just sent to the EU. The bytes already in the queue advance toward the head of the queue, awaiting their turn to execute

FIGURE 12.4
(*continued*)

(B) The instruction following **push dx**, **push ax**, is waiting in the prefetch queue when **push dx** ends and the EU requests the next instruction byte, and so the 4 cycles that would otherwise have been used to fetch that byte are saved.

(C) The remaining instructions in the prefetch queue advance toward the head of the queue, while the BIU does its best to prefetch another instruction byte to replace **push ax**.

This figure is for illustrative purposes only and is not intended to show the exact workings of the prefetch queue.

now useless bytes are discarded. That would speed processing of code such as

```
        jz    Skip
        jmp   DistantLabel
Skip:
```

in the case where **jz** jumps, because the instruction byte at the label **Skip** might well be in the prefetch queue when the branch occurs. The 8088 could also have been designed to prefetch from both possible next instructions at a branch, so that the prefetch queue wouldn't be empty no matter which way the branch went.

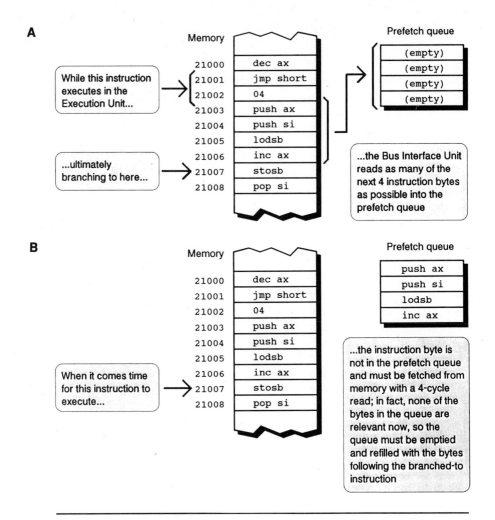

FIGURE 12.5 When the EU performs a branch, the prefetch queue is always emptied.

(A) The instruction bytes that the 8088 tries to get into the prefetch queue while **jmp short** executes. In reality, the 8088 couldn't fetch 4 bytes during one **jmp short**, but for illustrative purposes we'll assume 4 bytes are fetched. (Note that the byte following **jmp short**, the value 4, is the jump displacement, specifying a branch to address 21007.)

(B) The instruction following **jmp short**, **push ax**, is waiting in the prefetch queue when **jmp short** ends—because of the branch, however, that waiting byte is not the instruction to be executed next. Four or more cycles

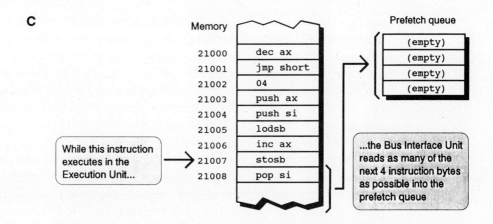

Memory

21000	dec ax
21001	jmp short
21002	04
21003	push ax
21004	push si
21005	lodsb
21006	inc ax
21007	stosb
21008	pop si

Prefetch queue

(empty)
(empty)
(empty)
(empty)

C

While this instruction executes in the Execution Unit...

...the Bus Interface Unit reads as many of the next 4 instruction bytes as possible into the prefetch queue

FIGURE 12.5 (*continued*)

must be used to fetch the branched-to instruction, **stosb**, as it is not in the prefetch queue. (Actually, branched-to instructions must always be fetched, even when they're already in the prefetch queue, because branches always empty the prefetch queue.)

(C) The prefetch queue is empty after the branch, so the BIU must once again refill it from scratch.

This figure is for illustrative purposes only and is not intended to show the exact workings of the prefetch queue.

The 8088 could have been designed to do all that and more—but it wasn't. The BIU simply prefetches sequentially forward from the current instruction byte. Whenever a branch occurs, the prefetch queue is *always* emptied, even if the instruction branched to is in the queue, and instruction fetching is started again at the new location, as illustrated by Figure 12.5. While that sounds innocent enough, it has far-reaching implications. After all, what does an empty prefetch queue mean? Right you are . . .

Branching always—and I do mean *always*—awakens the prefetch queue cycle eater.

Branching Instructions Do Prefetch

Things aren't quite as bad as they might seem, however. As you'll recall, we decided back in Chapters 4 and 5 that the true execution time of an instruction is the interval from the time when the first byte of the instruction reaches the EU until the time when the first byte of the next instruction reaches the EU. Because branches always empty the prefetch queue, there obviously must be a 4-cycle delay from the time the branch is completed until the time when the first byte of the branched-to instruction reaches the EU, as that instruction byte must always be fetched from memory. In fact, the 8088 passes the first instruction byte fetched after a branch straight through to the EU as quickly as possible, because the EU is without question ready and waiting to execute that byte.

The designers of the 8088 seem to have agreed with our definition of true execution time. I pointed out previously that Intel's official execution time for a given instruction doesn't include the time required to fetch the bytes of that instruction. That's not because Intel is hiding anything, but rather because the fetch time for a given instruction can vary considerably depending on the code preceding the instruction, as we've seen time and again. That's not quite the case with branching, however. Whenever a branch occurs, we can be quite certain that the prefetch queue will be emptied and that at least one prefetch will occur before anything else happens.

What that means is that the 4 cycles required to fetch the first byte of the instruction branched to can reliably be counted as part of the execution time of a branch, and that's exactly what Intel does. Although I've never seen documentation that explicitly states as much, official execution times that involve branches clearly include an extra 4 cycles for the fetching of the first byte of the instruction branched to.

What evidence is there for this phenomenon? Well, Listing 12-1 is solid evidence. Listing 12-1 shows that a branching instruction (**jmp**) with an official execution time of 15 cycles actually executes in 18 cycles. If the official execution time didn't include the fetch time for the first byte of the instruction branched to, repeated **jmp** instructions would take a minimum of 19 cycles to execute, consisting of 15 cycles of EU execution time followed by 4 cycles of BIU fetch time for the first byte of the next **jz**. In other words, the 18-cycle time that we actually measured could not happen if the 15-cycle execution time didn't include the 4 cycles required to fetch the first instruction byte at the location branched to.

Ironically, branching instructions would superficially appear to be excellent candidates to *improve* the state of the prefetch queue. After all, **jmp** takes 15 cycles to execute but accesses memory just once, to fetch the first byte of the instruction branched to. Normally, such an instruction would allow 2 or 3 bytes to be prefetched, and, in fact, it's quite possible that 2 or 3 bytes *are* prefetched while **jmp** executes—but if that's true, then those prefetches are wasted. Any bytes that are prefetched during a **jmp** are thrown away at the end of the instruction, when the prefetch queue is emptied and the first byte of the instruction at the address branched to is fetched.

So, the time required to fetch the instruction branched to accounts for 4 cycles of the unusually long time the 8088 requires to branch. Once again, we've fingered the prefetch queue cycle eater as a principal contributor to poor performance. You might think that for once the 8-bit bus isn't a factor; after all, the same emptying of the prefetch queue during each branch would occur on an 8086, wouldn't it?

The prefetch queue would indeed be emptied on an 8086—but it would refill much more rapidly. Remember, instructions are fetched one word at a time on the 16-bit 8086. In particular, one half of the time the 4 cycles expended on the critical first fetch after a branch would fetch not 1 but 2 bytes on an 8086 (1 byte if the address branched to is odd, 2 bytes if it is even, since the 8086 can only read words that start at even addresses). By contrast, the 8088 can fetch only 1 byte during the final 4 cycles of a branch, and therein lies the answer to our mystery of how code could possibly slow down when started with the prefetch queue full.

12.4 ◆ Branching and the *Second* Byte of the Instruction Branched To

Although the execution time of each branch includes the 4 cycles required to fetch the first byte of the instruction branched to, that's not the end of the impact of branching on instruction fetching. When a branch instruction ends, the EU is just starting to execute the first byte of the instruction branched to, the BIU is just starting to fetch the following instruction byte, and *the prefetch queue is empty*. In other words, the single instruction fetch built into the execution time of each branch doesn't fully account for the prefetch queue cycle eater consequences of branching, but merely defers them for one byte. No matter how you look at it, the prefetch queue is flat-out empty after every branch.

Now, sometimes the prefetch queue doesn't eat a single additional cycle after a branching instruction fetches the first byte of the instruction branched to. That happens when the 8088 doesn't need a second instruction byte for at least 4 cycles after the branch finishes, thereby giving the BIU enough time to fetch the second instruction byte. For example, consider Listing 12-4, which shows **jmp** (actually, **jmp short**, but we'll just use **jmp** for simplicity) instructions alternating with **push ax** instructions.

What's interesting about **push ax** is that it's a 1-byte instruction that takes 15 cycles to execute but accesses memory only twice, using just 8 cycles in the process. That means that after each branch, in the time during which **push ax** executes, there are 7 cycles free for prefetching the instruction bytes of the next **jmp**. That's long enough to fetch the opcode byte for **jmp** and most of the displacement byte as well, and when **jmp** starts to execute, the BIU can likely finish fetching the displacement byte before it's needed. In Listing 12-4, in other words, the prefetch queue should never slow down the EU either before or after **jmp** is executed, and that should make for faster execution.

```
1    ;
2    ; *** Listing 12-4 ***
3    ;
4    ; Measures the performance of JMP when 1) the prefetch queue
5    ; is full when it comes time for each JMP to run and 2) the
6    ; prefetch queue is allowed to fill faster than the
7    ; instruction bytes after the JMP are requested by the EU,
8    ; so the EU doesn't have to wait for instruction bytes.
9    ;
10            call    ZTimerOn
11            rept    1000
12            push    ax        ;let the prefetch queue fill while
13                              ; the first instruction byte after
14                              ; each branch executes
15            jmp     short $+2 ;we'll do a short jump,
16                              ; since the next instruction
17                              ; is less than 127 bytes
18                              ; away
19            endm
20            call    ZTimerOff
```

Incidentally, **push** is a good instruction to start a subroutine with, in light of the beneficial prefetch queue effects described above. Why? Because **push** allows the 8088 to recover partially from the emptying of the prefetch queue caused by subroutine calls. By happy chance, pushing registers in order to preserve them is a common way to start a subroutine.

At any rate, let's try out our theories in the real world. Listing 12-4 runs in 6704 μsec, or 32 cycles per **push ax/jmp** pair. The instruction **push ax** officially runs in 15 cycles, and as it's a "prefetch-positive" instruction—the prefetch queue tends to be more full when **push ax** finishes than when **push ax** starts—15 cycles should prove to be the actual execution time as well. Listing 12-5 confirms this, running in 3142 μsec, or exactly 15 cycles per **push ax**.

Quick subtraction reveals that each **jmp** in Listing 12-4 takes 17 cycles. That's 1 cycle better than the execution time of **jmp** in Listing 12-1, and more than 3 cycles better than the execution time of **jmp** in Listing 12-3,

```
1   ;
2   ; *** Listing 12-5 ***
3   ;
4   ; Measures the performance of PUSH AX.
5   ;
6           call    ZTimerOn
7           rept    1000
8           push    ax
9           endm
10          call    ZTimerOff
```

confirming our speculations about post-branch prefetching. It seems that we have indeed found the answer to the mystery of how **jmp** can run slower when the prefetch queue is allowed to fill before **jmp** is started: because the prefetch queue is emptied after a branch, one or more instructions following a branch can suffer from reduced performance at the hands of the prefetch queue cycle eater. The fetch time for the first instruction byte after the branch is built into the branch, but not the fetch time for the second byte or the bytes after that.

So exactly what happens when Listing 12-3 runs to slow performance by 3-plus cycles relative to Listing 12-4? I can only speculate, but it seems likely that when the first byte of an **imul** instruction is fetched, the EU is ready for the second byte of the **imul**, the *mod-reg-rm* byte, after just 1 cycle, as shown in Figure 12.6. After all, the EU can't do much processing of a multiplication until the source and destination are known, so it makes sense that the *mod-reg-rm* byte would be needed right away. Unfortunately, the branch preceding each **imul** in Listing 12-3 empties the prefetch queue, so the EU must wait for several cycles while the *mod-reg-rm* byte is fetched from memory.

In Listing 12-4, on the other hand, the first byte fetched after each branch is the instruction byte for **push ax**. That's the only byte of the instruction, so the EU can proceed right through to completion of the instruction without requiring additional instruction bytes, affording ample time for the BIU to fetch at least the first byte of the next **jmp**, as shown in Figure 12.7. As a result, the prefetch queue cycle eater has little or no impact on the performance of this code.

Finally, the code in Listing 12-1 falls somewhere between Listings 12-3 and 12-4 in regard to post-branch prefetching. Presumably, the EU has a more immediate need for the *mod-reg-rm* byte when executing **imul** than it does for the displacement byte when executing **jmp**.

Each **push ax**/**jmp** pair in Listing 12-4 still takes 2 cycles longer than it should according to the official execution times, so at least one cycle eater must still be active. Perhaps the prefetch queue cycle eater is still taking 2

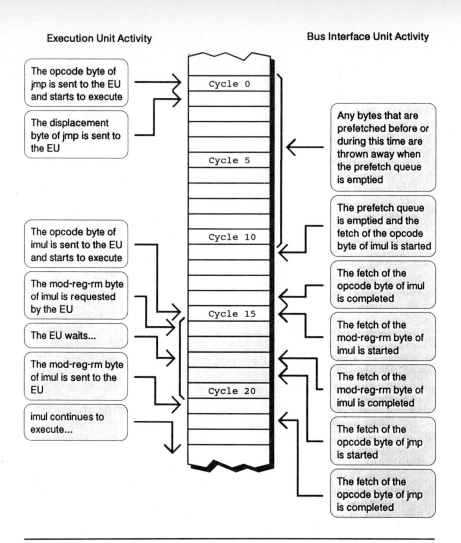

Execution Unit Activity

The opcode byte of jmp is sent to the EU and starts to execute

The displacement byte of jmp is sent to the EU

The opcode byte of imul is sent to the EU and starts to execute

The mod-reg-rm byte of imul is requested by the EU

The EU waits...

The mod-reg-rm byte of imul is sent to the EU

imul continues to execute...

Bus Interface Unit Activity

Any bytes that are prefetched before or during this time are thrown away when the prefetch queue is emptied

The prefetch queue is emptied and the fetch of the opcode byte of imul is started

The fetch of the opcode byte of imul is completed

The fetch of the mod-reg-rm byte of imul is started

The fetch of the mod-reg-rm byte of imul is completed

The fetch of the opcode byte of jmp is started

The fetch of the opcode byte of jmp is completed

Cycle 0
Cycle 5
Cycle 10
Cycle 15
Cycle 20

FIGURE 12.6   Because branches empty the prefetch queue, the prefetch queue cycle eater often takes cycles immediately following a branch. In this figure, the **jmp** instruction ends by fetching the opcode byte of **imul**, which immediately starts to execute. After 1 cycle, the EU requests the *mod-reg-rm* byte of **imul**, which is needed in order to perform any further processing. Unfortunately, the prefetch queue is empty, thanks to the branch, and the BIU has just started the 4-cycle process of fetching the *mod-reg-rm* byte. The EU must wait for the 5 cycles that are shaded before the *mod-reg-rm* byte is fetched and delivered; during that time, the EU is effectively idled. As a result, 5 cycles are lost to the prefetch queue cycle eater, even though **imul** allows the prefetch queue to fill before each **jmp**.

This figure is for illustrative purposes only and is not intended to show the exact timings of 8088 operations.

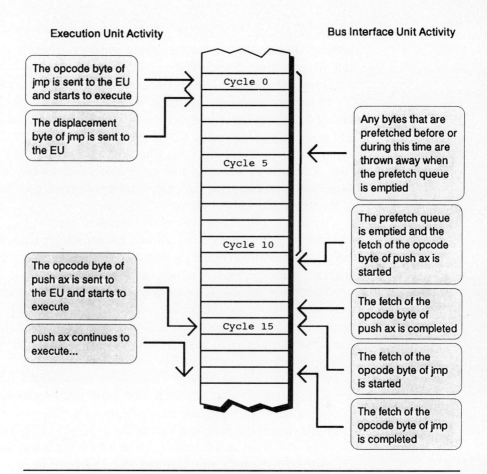

Execution Unit Activity

The opcode byte of jmp is sent to the EU and starts to execute

The displacement byte of jmp is sent to the EU

Cycle 0

Cycle 5

Cycle 10

The opcode byte of push ax is sent to the EU and starts to execute

push ax continues to execute...

Cycle 15

Bus Interface Unit Activity

Any bytes that are prefetched before or during this time are thrown away when the prefetch queue is emptied

The prefetch queue is emptied and the fetch of the opcode byte of push ax is started

The fetch of the opcode byte of push ax is completed

The fetch of the opcode byte of jmp is started

The fetch of the opcode byte of jmp is completed

FIGURE 12.7   Under the right circumstances, the prefetch queue cycle eater doesn't take any cycles after a branch. In this figure, the **jmp** instruction ends by fetching the opcode byte of **push ax**, which immediately starts to execute. The instruction **push ax** takes 15 cycles to execute but uses only 8 of those cycles to access memory, leaving 7 cycles free for instruction prefetching. As a result, the BIU is able to prefetch at least the opcode byte of the following **jmp** instruction, allowing that instruction to start without any instruction-fetch delay.

This figure is for illustrative purposes only and is not intended to show the exact timings of 8088 operations.

cycles, or perhaps the DRAM refresh cycle eater is taking 1 cycle and the prefetch queue cycle eater is taking another. There's really no way to tell where those 2 cycles are going without getting out hardware and watching the 8088 run—and it's not worth worrying about anyway.

In the grand scheme of things, it matters not a whit which cycle eater is taking what portion of the cycles in Listings 12-1, 12-3, and 12-4. Even if it did matter, there's no point to trying to understand exactly how the prefetch queue behaves after branching. The detailed behavior of the cycle eaters is highly variable in real code and is extremely difficult to pin down precisely. Moreover, that behavior depends on the internal logic of the 8088, which is forever hidden from our view.

What *is* important is that you understand that the true execution times of branching instructions are almost always longer than the official times because the prefetch queue is *guaranteed* to be empty after each and every branch. True, the fetch time for the first instruction byte after a branch is accounted for in official branching execution times (making those times very slow). However, the prefetch queue is still empty after that first byte is fetched and begins execution, and the time the EU usually spends waiting for subsequent bytes to arrive is not accounted for in the official execution times.

Sometimes, as in Listing 12-4, there may be no further instruction fetch penalty following a branch, but those circumstances are few and far between, since they require that a branch be followed by an instruction byte that causes the 8088 not to require another instruction byte for at least 4 cycles. The truth of the matter is that it took me a bit of searching to find an instruction (**push ax**) that met that criterion. In real code, branching almost always incurs a delayed prefetch penalty.

It's this simple. Branches empty the prefetch queue. Many of the 8088's fastest instructions run well below their maximum speed when the prefetch queue is empty, and most instructions slow down at least a little. It stands to reason, then, that branches reduce the performance of the code branched to, the reduction being most severe for the sort of high-performance code we're most interested in writing.

Don't Jump!

Slow as they seem from the official execution times, branches are actually even slower than that, because they put the PC in just the right state for the prefetch queue cycle eater to do its worst. Every time you branch, you expend at least 11 cycles (usually more) and then you're left with an empty prefetch queue. Is that the sort of instruction you want mucking up your time-critical code? Hardly. I'll say it again:

Don't jump!

Now That We Know Why Not to Branch

We've accounted for 11 of the 18 cycles that **jmp** takes to execute in Listing 12-1: 4 cycles to perform displacement arithmetic, 4 cycles to fetch the first byte of the next **jmp**, and 3 cycles lost to the prefetch queue cycle eater after the branch empties the queue. (Some of that 3-cycle loss may be due to DRAM refresh as well.)

That leaves us with 7 cycles unaccounted for. One of those cycles goes to decoding the instruction, but frankly I'm not certain where the other 6 go. The 8088 has to load IP with the target address and empty the prefetch queue, but I wouldn't expect that to take 6 cycles; more like 1 cycle, or 2 at most. Several additional cycles may go to calculating the 20-bit address at which to fetch the first byte of the instruction branched to. In fact, that's a pretty good bet: the 8088 takes a minimum of 5 cycles to perform effective address calculations, which would neatly account for most of the remaining 6 cycles. However, I don't know for sure that that's the case, and I probably never will.

No matter. We've established where the bulk of the time goes when a **jmp** occurs, and in the process we've found that branches are slow indeed—even slower than documented, thanks to the prefetch queue cycle eater. In other words, we've learned why it's desirable not to branch in high-performance code. Now it's time to find out how to go about that unusual but essential task.

Chapter 13

Not-Branching

13.1	Think Functionally
13.2	rep: Looping without Branching
13.3	Look-up Tables: Calculating without Branching
13.4	Take the Branch Less Travelled By
13.5	Yes, Virginia, There *Is* a Faster 32-Bit Negate!
13.6	Arrange Your Code to Eliminate Branches
13.7	loop May Not Be Bad, but Lord Knows It's Not Good: In-Line Code
13.8	A Note on Self-Modifying Code

Now we know *why* we don't want to branch, but we haven't a clue as to *how* to manage that trick. After all, decisions still have to be made, loops still have to be iterated through, and so on. Branching is the way we've always performed those tasks, and it's certainly not obvious what the alternatives are, or, for that matter, that alternatives even exist.

Although alternatives to branching do indeed exist, they are anything but obvious. Programming without branches—*not-branching*, in Zenspeak—is without question one of the stranger arts you must master in your growth as a Zen programmer.

Strange, but most rewarding. So let's get to it!

13.1 ♦ Think Functionally

The key to not-branching lies in understanding each programming task strictly in terms of what that task needs to do, not in terms of how the task will ultimately be implemented. Put another way, you should not consider how you might implement a task, even in a general way, until you have a clear picture of exactly what results the implementation must produce.

Once you've separated the objective from the implementation, you're free to bring to bear all the capabilities of the 8088, in their limitless combinations and permutations, in designing the implementation, rather than the limited subset of programming techniques you've grown accustomed to using. This is one of the areas in which assembler programmers have a vast advantage over compilers, which can use only the small and inflexible set of techniques their designers built in. Compilers operate by translating human-oriented languages to machine language along a few fixed paths; there's no way such a rigid code-generation mechanism can properly address the boundless possibilities of the 8088.

Of course, separating the objective and the implementation is more easily said than done, especially given an instruction set in which almost every instruction seems to have been designed for a specific purpose. For example, it's hard not to think of the **loop** instruction when you need to **xor** together all the bytes in a block of memory 64 bytes long and do so as quickly as possible. (Such a cumulative **xor** might be used as a check against corrupted data in a block of data about to be transmitted or stored. The speed at which the cumulative **xor** could be generated might well determine the maximum error checked transfer rate supported by the program.)

In this case, as in many others, the objective (a fast cumulative **xor**) and the implementation (64 loops by way of the **loop** instruction, with each loop **xor**ing 1 byte into the cumulative result) are inseparable to the experienced non-Zen programmer.

Why? Consider the solution shown in Listing 13-1. Listing 13-1 is obviously well-matched to the task of generating the cumulative **xor** for a block of 64 bytes. In fact, it's so well-matched that few programmers would even bother to consider alternatives. The code in the listing works, it's easy to write, and it runs in just 503 μsec. Surely that's just about as fast as the 8088 can manage to perform this task. After all, the loop involves just three instructions: one **lodsb** (string instructions are the fastest around), one register-register **xor** (register-register instructions are short and fast), and one **loop** (the 8088's special, fast-looping instruction). Who would ever think that performance could be nearly doubled by literally duplicating the code inside the loop 64 times and executing that code sequentially, thereby eliminating branching *entirely?*

```
1      ;
2      ; *** Listing 13-1 ***
3      ;
4      ; Generates the cumulative exclusive-or of all bytes in a
5      ; 64-byte block of memory by using the LOOP instruction to
6      ; repeat the same code 64 times.
7      ;
8              jmp     Skip
9      ;
10     ; The 64-byte block for which to generate the cumulative
11     ; exclusive-or.
12     ;
13     X=1
14     ByteArray       label   byte
15             rept    64
16             db      X
17     X=X+1
18             endm
19     ;
20     ; Generates the cumulative exclusive-or of all bytes in a
21     ; 64-byte memory block.
22     ;
23     ; Input:
24     ;       SI = pointer to start of 64-byte block for which to
25     ;                   calculate cumulative exclusive-or
26     ;
27     ; Output:
28     ;       AH = cumulative exclusive-or of all bytes in the
29     ;                   64-byte block
30     ;
31     ; Registers altered: AX, CX, SI
32     ;
33     CumulativeXor:
34             cld
```

```
35              sub     ah,ah    ;initialize our cumulative XOR to 0
36              mov     cx,64    ;number of bytes to XOR together
37   XorLoop:
38              lodsb            ;get the next byte and
39              xor     ah,al    ; XOR it into the cumulative result
40              loop    XorLoop
41              ret
42   ;
43   Skip:
44              call    ZTimerOn
45              mov     si,offset ByteArray
46                               ;point to the 64-byte block
47              call    CumulativeXor   ;get the cumulative XOR
48              call    ZTimerOff
```

Only a Zen programmer would even consider the possibility, for not-branching simply has no counterpart in non-Zen programming. Not-branching just plain feels *wrong* at first to any programmer raised on high level languages. Not-branching goes against the grain and intent of both the 8088 instruction set and virtually all computer science teachings and high level languages. That's only to be expected; language designers and computer science teachers are concerned with the form of programs, for they're most interested in making programming more amenable to people; that is, matching implementations to the way people think.

By contrast, Zen programmers are concerned with the functionality of programs. Zen programmers focus on performance and/or program size and are most interested in matching implementations to the way *computers* think. The desired application is paramount, but the true Zen comes in producing the necessary result (the functionality) in the best possible way given the computer's resources.

Zen programmers understand that the objective in generating the cumulative **xor** of 64 bytes actually has nothing whatsoever to do with looping. The objective is simply to **xor** together the 64 bytes in whatever way the PC can most rapidly accomplish the task, and looping is just one of many possible means to that end. Most programmers have seen and solved similar problems so many times, however, that they instinctively—almost unconsciously—select the **loop** instruction from their bag of tricks the moment they see the problem. To these programmers, repetitive processing and **loop** are synonymous.

Zen programmers have a bigger bag of tricks, however, and a more flexible view of the world. Listing 13-2 shows a Zen solution to the array-sum problem. Listing 13-2 performs no branches at all, thanks to the use of in-line code, which we'll discuss in detail later in this chapter.

Functionally, there's not much difference between Listings 13-1 and 13-2. Both listings leave the same cumulative result in AH, leave the same

```
1    ;
2    ; *** Listing 13-2 ***
3    ;
4    ; Generates the cumulative exclusive-or of all bytes in a
5    ; 64-byte block of memory by replicating the exclusive-or
6    ; code 64 times and then executing all 64 instances in a
7    ; row without branching.
8    ;
9            jmp     Skip
10   ;
11   ; The 64-byte block for which to generate the cumulative
12   ; exclusive-or.
13   ;
14   X=1
15   ByteArray       label   byte
16           rept    64
17           db      X
18   X=X+1
19           endm
20   ;
21   ; Generates the cumulative exclusive-or of all bytes in a
22   ; 64-byte memory block.
23   ;
24   ; Input:
25   ;       SI = pointer to start of 64-byte block for which to
26   ;               calculate cumulative exclusive-or
27   ;
28   ; Output:
29   ;       AH = cumulative exclusive-or of all bytes in the
30   ;               64-byte block
31   ;
32   ; Registers altered: AX, SI
33   ;
34   CumulativeXor:
35           sub     ah,ah   ;initialize our cumulative XOR to 0
36           rept    64
37           lodsb           ;get the next byte and
38           xor     ah,al   ; XOR it into the cumulative result
39           endm
40           ret
41   ;
42   Skip:
43           call    ZTimerOn
44           cld
45           mov     si,offset ByteArray
46                           ;point to the 64-byte block
47           call    CumulativeXor   ;get the cumulative XOR
48           call    ZTimerOff
```

value in SI, and even leave the flags set to the same values. There is a difference in that Listing 13-1 leaves CX set to 0 and Listing 13-2 doesn't touch CX, but that's really a point in favor of Listing 13-2 and could, in any case, be remedied simply by placing a **sub cx,cx** at the start of Listing 13-2 if necessary.

No, there's not much to choose from between the two listings—until you see them in action. Listing 13-2 calculates the 64-byte cumulative **xor** value in just 275 μsec—more than 82 percent faster than Listing 13-1. A 5 percent increase might not be worth worrying about, but we're talking about nearly *doubling* the performance of a well-coded three-instruction loop! Clearly, there's something to this business of Zen programming.

You may object that Listing 13-2 is many bytes longer than Listing 13-1, and indeed it is: 184 bytes, to be exact. If you need speed, though, a few hundred bytes is a small price to pay for nearly doubling performance; it's certainly preferable to requiring a more powerful (and expensive) processor, such as an 80286. You may also object that Listing 13-2 can handle only blocks that are exactly 64 bytes long, whereas the loop in Listing 13-1 can be made to handle blocks of any size simply by loading CX with different values. That, too, is true—but you're missing the point.

Listing 13-2 is constructed to meet a specific goal as well as possible on the PC. If the goal were different, then Listing 13-2 would be different. If blocks of different sizes were required, then we would modify our approach accordingly, possibly by jumping into the series of **xor** operations at the appropriate place. If space were tight, perhaps we would use partial in-line code (which we'll discuss later in this chapter), combining the space-saving qualities of loops with the speed of in-line code. If space were at a premium and performance were not an issue, we might well decide that **loop** was the best solution after all. The point is that the Zen programmer has a wide range of approaches to choose from, and in most cases at least one of those choices will handily outperform any standard, one-size-fits-all solution.

In the context of not-branching (which is after all how we got into all this), Zen programming means replicating the functionality of branches without branching. That's certainly not a goal we'd want to achieve all the time—in many cases branches really are the best (or only) choice—but you'll be surprised at how often it's possible to find good substitutes for branches in time-critical code.

For all their reputation as number-crunching machines, computers typically spend most of their time moving data, scanning data, and branching. In Chapters 10 and 11 we learned how to minimize the time spent moving and scanning data. Now we're going to attack the other part of the performance equation by learning how to minimize branching.

13.2 ◆ rep: Looping without Branching

It's a popular misconception that **loop** is the 8088's fastest instruction for looping. Not so. In truth, it's **rep** that supports far and away the most powerful looping possible on the 8088. In Chapters 10 and 11 we saw again and again that repeated string instructions perform repetitive tasks much, much faster than normal loops do. Not only do repeated string instructions not empty the prefetch queue on every repetition, as **loop** and other branching instructions do, but they actually eliminate the prefetch queue cycle eater altogether, since no instruction fetching at all is required while a string instruction repeats.

As we saw in Chapter 9, shifts and rotates by CL also eliminate the prefetch queue cycle eater, although those instructions don't pack quite the punch that repeated string instructions do, both because they perform relatively specialized tasks and because there's not much point to repeating a shift or rotate more than 16 times.

We've already discussed repeated string instructions and repeated shifts and rotates in plenty of detail, so I'm not going to spend much more time on them here. However, I would like to offer one hint about using shifts and rotates by CL. As we found in Chapter 9, repeated shifts and rotates are generally faster than individual shifts and rotates when a shift or rotate of 3 or more bits is required. Repeated shifts and rotates are also *much* faster than shifting 1 bit at a time in a loop; the sequence

```
BitShiftLoop:
     shr  ax,1
     loop BitShiftLoop
```

is far inferior to **shr ax,cl**.

Nonetheless, repeated shifts and rotates still aren't *fast.* Instead, you might think of them as less slow than the alternatives. It's easy to think that shifts and rotates by CL are so fast that they can be used with impunity, as they avoid looping and prefetching, but that's just not true. A repeated shift or rotate takes 8 cycles just to start and then takes 4 cycles per bit shifted. Even a 4-bit shift by CL takes 24 cycles, which is not insignificant, and a 16-bit shift by CL takes a full 72 cycles. Use shifts and rotates by CL sparingly, and keep them out of loops whenever you can. Look-up tables, our next topic, are often a faster alternative to multi-bit shifts and rotates.

13.3 ◆ Look-up Tables: Calculating without Branching

Like the use of repeated string instructions, the use of look-up tables is a familiar technique that can help avoid branching. Whenever you're using branching code to perform a calculation, see whether you can't use a look-up table instead; tight as your branching code may be, look-up tables are usually faster still. Listings 11-26 and 11-27 pit a five-instruction sequence that branches no more than once against an equivalent table look-up; you can't get branching code that's much tighter than that, and yet the table look-up is much faster.

In short, if you have a calculation to make, even a simple one, see whether it wouldn't be faster to precalculate the answer at assembly time and just look it up at run time.

13.4 ◆ Take the Branch Less Travelled By

One of the best ways to avoid branching is to arrange your code so that conditional jumps rarely jump. Usually you can guess which way a given conditional test will most often go, and if that's the case, you can save a good deal of branching simply by arranging your code so that the conditional jump will fall through—that is, not branch—in the more common case. Sometimes the choice is made on the basis of which case is most time-critical rather than which is most common, but the principle remains the same.

Why is falling through conditional jumps desirable? Simple: none of the horrendous speed loss associated with branching applies to conditional jumps that fall through, *because conditional jumps don't branch when they fall through*.

Let's look at the statistics. It always takes a conditional jump at least 16 cycles to branch, and the total cost in cycles is usually somewhat greater because the prefetch queue is emptied. On the other hand, it takes a conditional jump a maximum of just 8 cycles *not* to jump, that being the case if the prefetch queue is empty and both bytes of the instruction must be fetched before they can be executed. The official execution time of a conditional jump that doesn't branch is just 4 cycles, so it is particularly fast to fall through a conditional jump if both bytes of the instruction are waiting in the prefetch queue when it comes time to execute them.

In other words, falling through a conditional jump can be anywhere from 2 to 8 times faster than branching, depending on the exact state and behavior of the prefetch queue. As you might imagine, it's worth going out of your way to reap cycle savings of that magnitude, and that's why you should arrange your conditional jumps so that they fall through as often as possible.

For example, you'll recall that in Chapter 11—in Listing 11-20, to be precise—we tested several characters for inclusion in a small set via repeated **cmp/jz** instruction pairs. We arranged the conditional jumps so that a jump occurred only when a match was made, meaning that at most one branch was performed during any given inclusion test. Put another way, we branched out of the mainstream of the subroutine on the less common condition.

You may not have thought much of it at the time, but the arrangement of branches in Listing 11-20 was no accident. Tests for four potential matches are involved when testing for inclusion in a set of four characters, and no more than one of those matches can occur during any given test. Given an even distribution of match characters, matching is clearly less common than not matching. If we jumped whenever we *didn't* get a match (the more common condition), we'd end up branching as many as three times during a single test, with significantly worse performance the likely result.

Listing 13-3 shows Listing 11-20 modified to branch on nonmatches rather than on matches. The original branch-on-match version ran in 119 μsec, and, as predicted, that's faster than Listing 13-3, which runs in 133 μsec. That's not the twofold or threefold performance improvement we've grown accustomed to seeing (my, how jaded we've become!), but it's significant nonetheless, especially because we're talking about a very small number of conditional jumps. We'd see a more dramatic difference if we were dealing with a long series of tests.

```
 1    ;
 2    ; *** Listing 13-3 ***
 3    ;
 4    ; Tests whether several characters are in the set
 5    ; {A,Z,3,!} by using the compare-and-jump approach,
 6    ; branching each time a match isn't found.
 7    ;
 8            jmp     Skip
 9    ;
10    ; Determines whether a given character is in the set
11    ; {A,Z,3,!}.
12    ;
13    ; Input:
14    ;       AL = character to check for inclusion in the set
15    ;
16    ; Output:
17    ;       Z if character is in TestSet, NZ otherwise
18    ;
19    ; Registers altered: none
20    ;
21    CheckTestSetInclusion:
22            cmp     al,'A'  ;is it 'A'?
23            jnz     CheckTestSetZ
24            ret             ;yes, we're done
25    CheckTestSetZ:
```

```
26              cmp     al,'Z'  ;is it 'Z'?
27              jnz     CheckTestSet3
28              ret             ;yes, we're done
29   CheckTestSet3:
30              cmp     al,'3'  ;is it '3'?
31              jnz     CheckTestSetEx
32              ret             ;yes, we're done
33   CheckTestSetEx:
34              cmp     al,'!'  ;is it '!'?
35              ret             ;the success status is already in
36                              ; the Zero flag
37   ;
38   Skip:
39              call    ZTimerOn
40              mov     al,'A'
41              call    CheckTestSetInclusion   ;check 'A'
42              mov     al,'Z'
43              call    CheckTestSetInclusion   ;check 'Z'
44              mov     al,'3'
45              call    CheckTestSetInclusion   ;check '3'
46              mov     al,'!'
47              call    CheckTestSetInclusion   ;check '!'
48              mov     al,' '
49              call    CheckTestSetInclusion   ;check space, so
50                                              ; we've got a failed
51                                              ; search
52              call    ZTimerOff
```

Another relevant point is that the *worst-case* performance of Listing 13-3 is much worse than that of Listing 11-20. Listing 13-3 actually has a shorter best-case time than Listing 11-20, because no branches at all are performed when the test character is *A*. On the other hand, Listing 13-3 performs three branches when the test character is *!* or is not in the set, and that's two branches more than Listing 11-20 ever performs. When you're trying to make sure that code always responds within a certain time, worst-case performance can matter more than average performance.

Then, too, if the characters tested are often not in the set, as may well be the case with such a small set, the branching out approach of Listing 11-20 will far outperform the branch-branch-branch approach of Listing 13-3. When Listing 11-20 is modified so that none of the five test characters is in the set, its overall execution time scarcely changes, rising by just 8 μsec, to 127 μsec. When Listing 13-3 is modified similarly, however, its overall execution time increases by a considerably greater amount—26 μsec—to 159 μsec. This neatly illustrates the potential worst-case problem of repeated branching that we just discussed.

There are two lessons here. The first and obvious lesson is that you should arrange your conditional jumps so that they fall through as often as possible. The second lesson is that you must understand the conditions under which your code will operate before you can truly optimize it.

For instance, there's no way you can evaluate the relative merits of the versions of **CheckTestSetInclusion** in Listings 11-20 and 13-3 until you know the mix of characters that will be tested. There's no such beast as an absolute measure of code speed, only code speed in context. You've heard that before as it relates to instruction mix and the prefetch queue, but here we're dealing with a different aspect of performance. What I mean now is that you must understand the typical and worst-case conditions under which a block of code will run before you can get a handle on its performance and consider possible alternatives.

Your ability to understand and respond to the circumstances under which your assembler code will run gives you a big leg up on high level language compilers. There's no way for a compiler to know the typical and/or worst-case conditions under which code will run, let alone which of those conditions is more important in your application.

For instance, suppose that we have one loop that repeats 10 times on average and another loop that repeats 10,000 times on average, with both loops executed a variable (not constant) number of times. A C compiler couldn't know that cycles saved in the second loop would have a payoff 1000 times greater than cycles saved in the first loop, so it would have to approach both loops in the same way, generating the same sort of code in both cases. What this means is that compiled code is designed for reasonable performance under all conditions, hardly the ticket for greatness.

Put the Load on the Unimportant Case

When arranging branching code to branch on the less critical case, don't be afraid to heap the cycles on that case if that will help the more critical case.

For example, suppose that you need to test whether CX is 0 at the start of a long subroutine and return if CX is in fact 0. You'd normally do that with something like this:

```
LongSubroutine proc near
      jcxz  LongSubroutineEnd
         :
; *** Body of subroutine ***
         :
LongSubroutineEnd:
      ret
LongSubroutine endp
```

Now, however, assume that the body of the subroutine is more than 127 bytes long. In that case, the 1-byte displacement of **jcxz** can't reach **LongSubroutineEnd**, so the last bit of code won't work.

Well, then, the obvious alternative is

```
LongSubroutine proc near
        and   cx,cx
        jnz   DoLongSubroutine
        jmp   LongSubroutineEnd
DoLongSubroutine:
        :
; *** Body of subroutine ***
        :
LongSubroutineEnd:
        ret
LongSubroutine endp
```

There's a problem here, though. Every time CX *isn't* 0 we end up branching, and that's surely wrong. The case where CX is 0 is most likely rare, and is probably of no real interest to us anyway, since it's a do-nothing case for the subroutine. (At any rate, for the purposes of this example we'll assume that the CX equal to 0 case is rare and uninteresting.) What's more, whether the CX equal to 0 case is rare or not, the body of the subroutine is skipped when CX is 0, so that case is bound to be much faster than the other cases. That means that the CX equal to 0 case is not only unimportant but also doesn't affect the worst-case performance of the subroutine. Yet here we are, adding an extra branch to every single invocation of this subroutine simply to protect against the quick and unimportant case of CX equal to 0.

The tail is wagging the dog.

Instead, let's heap the branches on the CX equal to 0 case, sparing the other, more important cases as much as possible. One solution is

```
LongSubroutineExit     proc near
        ret
LongSubroutineExit     endp
;
LongSubroutine proc   near
        jcxz  LongSubroutineExit
        :
```

```
; *** Body of subroutine ***
              :
       ret
LongSubroutine endp
```

This restores the code to its original, saner state, where the shortest possible time—6 cycles for a single **jcxz** that falls through—is used to guard against the case of CX equal to 0.

If you prefer that your subroutines be exited only from the end, as is necessary, for example, when a stack frame must be deallocated, there's another solution:

```
LongSubroutineExit       proc near
       jmp   LongSubroutineEnd
LongSubroutineExit       endp
;
LongSubroutine proc     near
       jcxz   LongSubroutineExit
              :
; *** Body of subroutine ***
              :
LongSubroutineEnd:
       ret
LongSubroutine endp
```

Now we've *really* put the load on the CX equal to 0 case, for two branches must be performed in that case. So what? As far as we're concerned, the CX equal to 0 case can take as long as it pleases, so long as it doesn't slow down the real work of the subroutine, which is done when CX isn't equal to 0.

13.5   ◆ Yes, Virginia, There *Is* a Faster 32-Bit Negate!

In Chapter 9 we came across an extremely fast and compact way to negate 32-bit values:

```
neg   dx
neg   ax
sbb   dx,0
```

This very short sequence involves two register-only negations, one constant-from-register subtraction—and no branches. At the time, I told you that, fast as that code was, at some later point we'd run across a still faster way to negate a 32-bit value.

That time has come. Incredibly, we're going to speed up 32-bit negates by using a branching instruction. Yes, I know that I've been telling you to avoid branching like the plague, but there's a trick here: we're not really going to branch. The branching instruction we're going to use is a conditional jump, and we're going to fall through the jump almost every time.

There's a bit of history to this trick, and it's worth reviewing for the lesson about the Zen of assembly language it contains. The story goes as follows:

Having worked out to my satisfaction how the above 32-bit negation worked, I (somewhat egotistically, I admit) asked Dan Illowsky if *he* knew how to negate a 32-bit value in three instructions.

Well, it took him a while, but he did come up with a working three-instruction solution. Interestingly enough, it wasn't the solution I had found. Instead, he derived the second solution I mentioned in Chapter 9:

```
not  dx
neg  ax
sbb  dx,-1
```

This solution is equivalent to the first solution in functionality, length, and cycle count.

That's not the end of the tale, however. Taken aback because Dan had come up with a different and equally good solution (demonstrating that my solution wasn't so profound after all), I commented that although he had managed to *match* my solution, he surely could never *surpass* it.

Ha!

If there's one word that should set any Zen programmer off like a rocket, it's *never*. The 8088 instruction set is so rich and varied that there are dozens of ways to do just about anything. For any but the simplest task several of those approaches—and not necessarily the obvious ones—are bound to be good. Whenever you think that you've found the best possible solution for anything more complex than incrementing a register, you're most likely in for a humbling experience.

At any rate, that *never* certainly set Dan off. He got a thoughtful look on his face, walked off, and came back 5 minutes later with a faster implementation. Here it is:

```
        not  dx
        neg  ax
        jnc  Negate32BitsCarry
Negate32BitsDone:
        :
Negate32BitsIncDX:
        inc  dx
        jmp  short Negate32BitsDone
```

where the code at **Negate32BitsCarry** is somewhere—anywhere—within a 1-byte displacement (+127 to −128 bytes) of the byte after the **jnc** instruction.

It may not *look* like working 32-bit negation code, but working code it is, believe me. *Brilliant* working code.

How 32-Bit Negation Works

In order to understand the brilliance of Dan's code, we first need to get a firm grasp on the mechanics of 32-bit negation. The basic principle of two's complement negation is that the value to be negated is **not**ted (that is, all its bits are flipped from 1 to 0 or 0 to 1) and then incremented. For a 32-bit value stored in DX:AX, negation would ideally follow one of the two sequences shown in Figure 13.1, with all operations performed 32 bits at a time.

Unfortunately, the 8088 can handle data only 16 bits at a time, so we must perform negation with a series of 16-bit operations such as:

```
not  dx
neg  ax
sbb  dx,-1
```

as shown in Figure 13.2. The purpose of the first operation (**not**ting DX with the **not** instruction) is obvious enough: flipping all the bits in the high word of the value. The purpose of the second operation, negating AX, is equally obvious: negating the low word of the value with the **neg** instruction, which both **not**s AX and increments it all at once.

After two instructions, we've successfully **not**ted the entire 32-bit value in DX:AX, and we've incremented AX as well. All that remains to be done is to complete the full 32-bit increment by incrementing DX if necessary.

When does DX need to be incremented? In one case only—when AX is originally 0, is **not**ted to 0FFFFh, and is incremented back to 0, with a carry

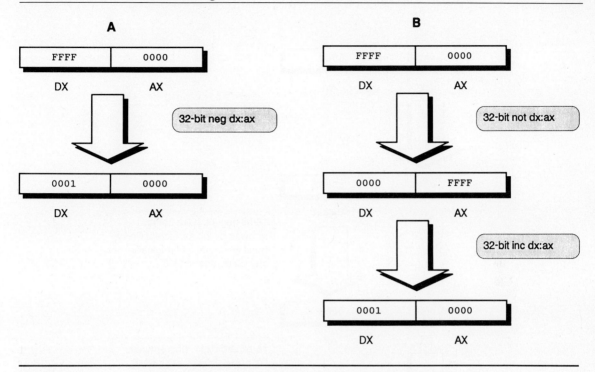

FIGURE 13.1   Ideally, a 32-bit negate would be performed with 32-bit instructions. **(A)** How a 32-bit **neg** instruction could perform a 32-bit negate in a single step. **(B)** How a 32-bit **not** followed by a 32-bit **inc** could perform a 32-bit negate in two steps.

out from bit 15 of AX indicating that AX has turned over to 0 and so the **not**ted value in DX must be incremented as well, as shown in Figure 13.3. In all other cases, incrementing the 32-bit **not**ted value in DX:AX doesn't alter DX at all, because incrementing AX doesn't cause a carry out of bit 15 unless AX is 0FFFFh.

However, owing to the way that **neg** sets the carry flag (CF)—as if subtraction from 0 had occurred—CF is set by **neg** in all cases *except* the one case in which DX needs to be incremented. Consequently, after **neg ax** we subtract −1 from DX with borrow, with the 1 value of the CF normally offsetting the −1, resulting in a subtraction of 0 from DX. In other words, DX remains unchanged when **neg ax** sets CF to 1, which is to say in all cases except when AX is originally 0. That's just what we want; in all those cases the 32-bit negation was actually complete after the first two

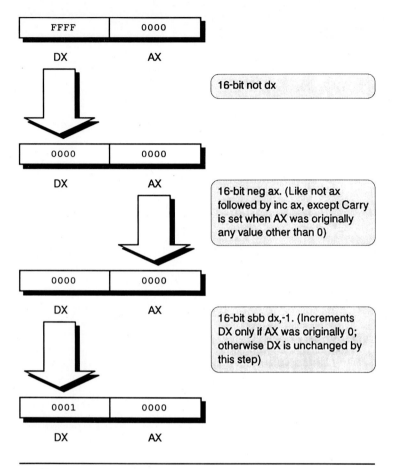

FFFF	0000

DX   AX

16-bit not dx

0000	0000

DX   AX

16-bit neg ax. (Like not ax followed by inc ax, except Carry is set when AX was originally any value other than 0)

0000	0000

DX   AX

16-bit sbb dx,-1. (Increments DX only if AX was originally 0; otherwise DX is unchanged by this step)

0001	0000

DX   AX

FIGURE 13.2   The 8088 has no 32-bit instructions, so 32-bit negates must be performed as a series of 16-bit operations. This figure illustrates the operation of a 32-bit negate performed with

```
not   dx
neg   ax
sbb   dx,-1
```

instructions, because the increment of the notted 32-bit value doesn't affect DX, as shown in Figure 13.4.

In the case where AX is originally 0, on the other hand, **neg ax** doesn't set CF. This is the one case in which DX must be incremented. In this one case only, **sbb dx,−1** succeeds in subtracting −1 from DX, since CF is 0.

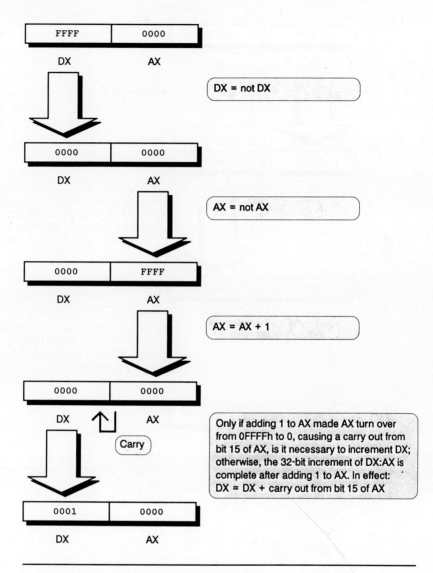

FIGURE 13.3 In most cases, a 32-bit negate performed with

```
not   dx
neg   ax
sbb   dx,-1
```

is complete after **neg ax**.

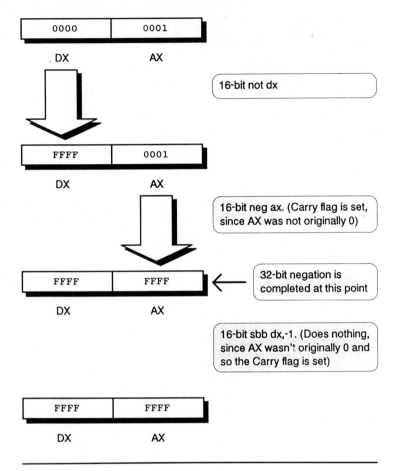

FIGURE 13.4   When performing a 32-bit negate with

```
not   dx
neg   ax
sbb   dx,-1
```

sbb dx,-1 does nothing when AX is not initially 0.

Again, that's what we want; in this one case DX is affected when the 32-bit value is incremented, so incrementing DX completes the 32-bit negation, as shown in Figure 13.5.

How Fast 32-Bit Negation Works

Now that we understand what our code has to do, we're in a position to think about optimizations. We'll do just what Dan did—look at negation

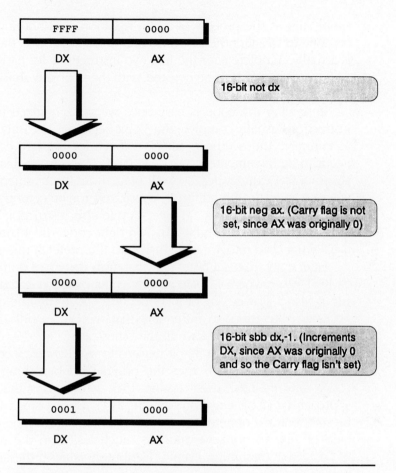

FIGURE 13.5   When performing a 32-bit negate with

```
not   dx
neg   ax
sbb   dx,-1
```

sbb dx,-1 increments DX if and only if AX is initially 0.

from a functional perspective, understanding exactly what needs to be done and tailoring our code to do precisely that and nothing more.

The breakthrough in Dan's thinking was the realization that DX needs to be incremented only when AX originally is 0, which normally happens only once in a blue moon (once out of every 64 K evenly distributed values, to be exact). For all other original values of AX, the bits in DX simply flip in the process of 32-bit negation, and nothing more needs to be done to DX after the initial **not**. As we found above, the 32-bit negation is actually complete after the first two instructions for 64 K—1 out of every 64 K possible values to be negated, with the final **sbb** almost always leaving DX unchanged.

Improving the code is easy once we've recognized that the first two instructions usually complete the 32-bit negation. The only question is how to minimize the overhead taken to check for the rare case in which DX needs to be incremented. A once-in-64 K case is more than rare enough to absorb a few extra cycles, so we'll branch out to increment DX in the case where it needs to be adjusted. The payoff for branching in that one case is that in all other cases a 3-byte, 4-cycle **sbb** instruction is replaced by a 2-byte, 4-cycle fall-through of **jnc**. In tight code, the 1-byte difference will usually translate into 4 cycles, thanks to the prefetch queue cycle eater.

Essentially, **jnc** is a faster way than **sbb dx,—1** of doing nothing in the 64 K—1 cases where DX:AX already contains the negated value. Granted, **jnc** is also a slower way of incrementing DX in the one case where that's necessary, but that's so infrequent that we can readily trade those extra cycles for the cycles we save in the other cases.

Let's try out the two 32-bit negates to see how they compare in actual use. Listing 13-4, which uses the original nonbranching 32-bit negation code, runs in 2264 μsec. Listing 13-5, which uses the branch-on-0-AX approach to 32-bit negation, runs in 2193 μsec. A small improvement, to be sure, but it is nonetheless an improvement, and as the test code's 100:1 ratio of zero to nonzero values is much less than the real world's ratio of 64 K—1:1 (assuming evenly distributed values), the superiority of the branch-on-0-AX approach is somewhat greater than this test indicates.

```
1   ;
2   ; *** Listing 13-4 ***
3   ;
4   ; Negates several 32-bit values with non-branching code.
5   ;
6           jmp     Skip
7   ;
8   ; Negates a 32-bit value.
9   ;
10  ; Input:
11  ;       DX:AX = 32-bit value to negate
12  ;
13  ; Output:
14  ;       DX:AX = negated 32-bit value
15  ;
16  ; Registers altered: AX, DX
17  ;
18  Negate32Bits:
```

```
19              neg     dx
20              neg     ax
21              sbb     dx,0
22              ret
23      ;
24      Skip:
25              call    ZTimerOn
26      ; First, negate zero.
27              sub     dx,dx
28              mov     ax,dx    ;0
29              call    Negate32Bits
30      ; Next, negate 1 through 50.
31      X=1
32              rept    50
33              sub     dx,dx
34              mov     ax,X
35              call    Negate32Bits
36      X=X+1
37              endm
38      ; Finally, negate -1 through -50.
39      X=-1
40              rept    50
41              mov     dx,0ffffh
42              mov     ax,X
43              call    Negate32Bits
44      X=X-1
45              endm
46              call    ZTimerOff


1       ;
2       ; *** Listing 13-5 ***
3       ;
4       ; Negates several 32-bit values using the branch-on-zero-AX
5       ; approach.
6       ;
7               jmp     Skip
8       ;
9       ; Negates a 32-bit value.
10      ;
11      ; Input:
12      ;       DX:AX = 32-bit value to negate
13      ;
14      ; Output:
15      ;       DX:AX = negated 32-bit value
16      ;
17      ; Registers altered: AX, DX
18      ;
19      ;-------------------------------------------------------------
20      ; Branching-out exit for Negate32Bits when AX negates to
21      ; zero, necessitating an increment of DX.
22      ;
23      Negate32BitsIncDX:
24              inc     dx
25              ret
26      ;
27      Negate32Bits:
28              not     dx
29              neg     ax
```

```
30              jnc     Negate32BitsIncDX
31              ret
32      ;
33      Skip:
34              call    ZTimerOn
35      ; First, negate zero.
36              sub     dx,dx
37              mov     ax,dx    ;0
38              call    Negate32Bits
39      ; Next, negate 1 through 50.
40      X=1
41              rept    50
42              sub     dx,dx
43              mov     ax,X
44              call    Negate32Bits
45      X=X+1
46              endm
47      ; Finally, negate -1 through -50.
48      X=-1
49              rept    50
50              mov     dx,0ffffh
51              mov     ax,X
52              call    Negate32Bits
53      X=X-1
54              endm
55              call    ZTimerOff
```

By itself, speeding the negation of 32-bit values by a few cycles isn't particularly noteworthy. On the other hand, you must surely realize that if it turned out to be possible to speed up even the three-instruction, nonbranching sequence that we started off with, then it must be possible to speed up just about any code, and that perception is important indeed.

Code for almost *any* task can be implemented in many different ways and in the process can usually be made faster than it currently is. It's not always worth the cost in programming time and/or bytes to speed up code—you must pick your spots carefully, concentrating on loops and other time-critical code—but it can almost always be done. The key to improved performance lies in understanding exactly what the task at hand requires and the context in which the code performs, then matching that understanding to the resources of the PC.

My own experience is that no matter how many times I study a time-critical sequence of, say, 20 to 100 instructions, I can always save at least a few more cycles—and sometimes many more—by viewing the code differently and reworking it to match more closely the capabilities of the 8088. That's why way back in Chapter 2 I said that *optimize* was not a word to be used lightly. When programming in assembler for the PC, only fools and geniuses consider their code optimized. As for the rest of us . . . well, we'll just have to keep working on our time-critical code, trying new approaches and timing the results, with the attitude that our code is good and getting better.

And have we finally found the fastest possible code for 32-bit negation, never to be topped? Lord knows I don't expect to come across anything faster in the near future. But *never?*

Don't bet on it.

13.6 ◆ Arrange Your Code to Eliminate Branches

There are many, many ways to arrange your code to eliminate branches. I'm going to discuss a few here, but don't consider this anything like an exhaustive list. Whenever you use branching instructions where performance matters, take it as a challenge to arrange those instructions for maximum performance and minimum code size.

Preloading the Less Common Case

One of my favorite ways to eliminate jumps comes up when a register must be set to one of two values based on a test condition. For example, suppose that we want to set AL to 0 if DL is less than or equal to 10 and set AL to 1 if DL is greater than 10.

The obvious solution is

```
        cmp    dl,10             ;is DL greater than 10?
        ja     DLGreaterThan10   ;yes, so set AL to 1
        sub    al,al             ;DL is less than or equal to 10
        jmp    short DLCheckDone
DLGreaterThan10:
        mov    al,1              ;DL is greater than 10
DLCheckDone:
```

Here we either branch or don't branch to reach the code that sets AL to the appropriate value; after setting AL, we rejoin the main flow of the code, branching if necessary. Whether DL is greater than 10 or not, a branch is always performed.

Now let's try this out:

```
        sub    al,al             ;assume DL will not be greater than 10
        cmp    dl,10             ;is DL greater than 10?
```

```
        jbe     DLCheckDone    ;no, so AL is already correct
        mov     al,1           ;DL is greater than 10
DLCheckDone:
```

Here we've loaded AL with one of the two possible results *before* the test. In one of the two possible cases, we've guessed right and AL is already correct, so a single branch ends the test-and-set code. In the other possible case, we've guessed wrong, so the conditional jump falls through and AL is set properly. (By the way, **inc ax** would be faster than and logically equivalent to **mov al,1** in the above code. Right now, though, we're focusing on a different sort of optimization, and I've opted for clarity rather than maximum speed; I also want you to see that the preload approach is inherently faster, whether or not tricks like **inc ax** are used.)

I'll admit that it's more than a little peculiar to go out of our way to set AL twice in some cases; the previous example set AL just once per test-and-set, and that would logically seem to be the faster approach. Although we do sometimes set AL an extra time with the preload approach, we also avoid a good bit of branching, and that's more than enough to compensate for the extra times AL is set.

Consider this. If DL is less than or equal to 10, then the first example (the "normal" test-and-branch code) performs a **cmp dl,10** (4 cycles/2 bytes), a **ja DLGreaterThan10** that falls through (4 cycles/2 bytes), a **sub al,al** (3 cycles/2 bytes), and a **jmp short DLCheckDone** (15 cycles/2 bytes). The grand total: 26 cycles, 8 instruction bytes and one branch, as shown in Figure 13.6A.

On the other hand, the preload code of the second example handles the same case with a **sub al,al** (3 cycles/2 bytes), a **cmp dl,10** (4 cycles/2 bytes), and a **jbe DLCheckDone** that branches (16 cycles/2 bytes). The total: 23 cycles, 6 instruction bytes, and one branch, as shown in Figure 13.7A. That's not much faster than the normal approach, but it is faster.

Now let's look at the case where DL is greater than 10. Here the test-and-branch code of the first example performs a **cmp dl,10** (4 cycles/2 bytes), a **ja DLGreaterThan10** that branches (16 cycles/2 bytes), and a **mov al,1** (4 cycles/2 bytes), for a total of 24 cycles, 6 instruction bytes, and one branch, as shown in Figure 13.6B.

The preload code of the second example handles the same DL greater than 10 case with a **sub al,al** (3 cycles/2 bytes), a **cmp dl,10** (4 cycles/2 bytes), a **jbe DLCheckDone** that doesn't branch (4 cycles/2 bytes), and a **mov al,1** (4 cycles/2 bytes). The total: 8 instruction bytes—2 bytes more than the test-and-branch code—but just 15 cycles . . . and *no branches*, as shown in Figure 13.7B. The lack of a prefetch queue-flushing branch

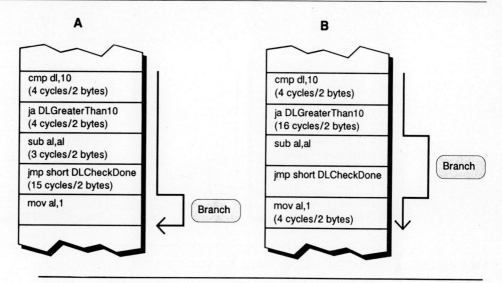

FIGURE 13.6   The two possible instruction sequences that can be executed by

```
        cmp   dl,10
        ja    DLGreaterThan10
        sub   al,al
        jmp   short DLCheckDone
DLGreaterThan10:
        mov   al,1
DLCheckDone:
```

(A) The instructions executed when DL is less than or equal to 10. **(B)** The instructions executed when DL is greater than 10.

should more than compensate for the two additional instruction bytes that must be fetched.

In other words, the preload code is either 3 or 9 cycles faster than the more familiar test-and-branch code, is 2 bytes shorter overall, and sometimes branches less but never branches more. That's a clean sweep for the preload code, all because always performing one extra register load made it possible to do away with a branch.

Let's run the two approaches through the Zen timer. Listing 13-6, which times the test-and-branch code when DL is 10 (causing AL to be set to 0), runs in 10.06 μsec per test-and-branch. By contrast, Listing 13-7, which times the preload code for the same case, runs in just 8.62 μsec.

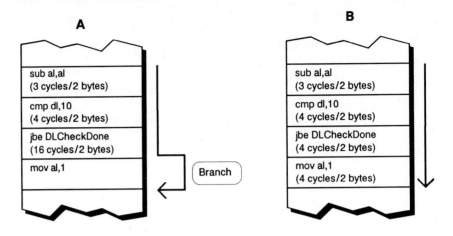

FIGURE 13.7   The two possible instruction sequences that can be executed by

```
        sub    al,al
        cmp    dl,10
        jbe    DLCheckDone
        mov    al,1
DLCheckDone:
```

(A) The instructions executed when DL is less than or equal to 10. **(B)** The instructions executed when DL is greater than 10.

```
1  ;
2  ; *** Listing 13-6 ***
3  ;
4  ; Measures the time needed to set AL, based on the contents
5  ; of DL, with test-and-branch code (a branch is required no
6  ; matter what value DL contains).
7  ;
8  ;--------------------------------------------------------------
9  ; Macro to perform the test of DL and setting of AL.
10 ; It's necessary to use a macro because the LOCAL directive
11 ; doesn't work properly inside REPT blocks with MASM.
12 ;
13 TEST_DL_AND_SET_AL        macro
14              local    DLGreaterThan10, DLCheckDone
15              cmp      dl,10              ;is DL greater than 10?
16              ja       DLGreaterThan10    ;yes, so set AL to 1
17              sub      al,al              ;DL is <= 10
18              jmp      short DLCheckDone
19 DLGreaterThan10:
20              mov      al,1               ;DL is greater than 10
```

```
21      DLCheckDone:
22              endm
23      ;
24              mov     dl,10   ;AL will always be set to 0
25              call    ZTimerOn
26              rept    1000
27              TEST_DL_AND_SET_AL
28              endm
29              call    ZTimerOff
```

```
1       ;
2       ; *** Listing 13-7 ***
3       ;
4       ; Measures the time needed to set AL, based on the contents
5       ; of DL, with preload code (a branch is required in only one
6       ; of the two possible cases).
7       ;
8       ;-----------------------------------------------------------
9       ; Macro to perform the test of DL and setting of AL.
10      ; It's necessary to use a macro because the LOCAL directive
11      ; doesn't work properly inside REPT blocks with MASM.
12      ;
13      TEST_DL_AND_SET_AL      macro
14              local   DLCheckDone
15              sub     al,al           ;assume DL <= 10
16              cmp     dl,10           ; is DL greater than 10?
17              jbe     DLCheckDone     ;no, so AL is already set
18              mov     al,1            ;DL is greater than 10
19      DLCheckDone:
20              endm
21      ;
22              mov     dl,10   ;AL will always be set to 0
23              call    ZTimerOn
24              rept    1000
25              TEST_DL_AND_SET_AL
26              endm
27              call    ZTimerOff
```

That's a healthy advantage for the preload code, but perhaps things will change if we test a case where AL is set to 1, by altering Listings 13-6 and 13-7 to set DL to 11 rather than 10 prior to the tests.

Things do indeed change when DL is set to 11. Listing 13-6 speeds up to 8.62 msec per test, matching the performance of Listing 13-7 when DL was 10. When DL is 11, however, Listing 13-7 speeds up to 8.15 μsec, again comfortably outperforming Listing 13-6.

In short, the preload approach is superior in every respect. Although it's counterintuitive to think that by loading a register an extra time we can actually speed up code, it does work, and that sort of unorthodox but effective technique is what the Zen of assembly language is all about.

A final note on the preload approach: arrange your preload code so that the more common case is *not* preloaded. Once again this is counterintuitive, as it seems that we're going out of our way to guess wrong about the outcome of the test. Remember, however, that it's much faster to fall through a conditional jump, and you'll see why preloading the less common value makes sense. It's actually faster to fall through the conditional jump and load a value than it is just to branch at the conditional jump, even if the correct value is already loaded.

The results from the two executions of Listing 13-7 confirm this. The case where the value preloaded into AL is correct actually runs a good bit more slowly than the case where the conditional jump falls through and a new value must be loaded.

Think of your assembler programs not just in terms of their logic but also in terms of how that logic can best be expressed—in terms of cycles and/or bytes—in the highly irregular language of the 8088. The first example in this section—the "normal" approach—seems at first glance to be the ideal expression of the desired test-and-set sequence in 8088 assembler. However, the poor performance of branching instructions renders the normal approach inferior to the preload approach on the 8088, even though preloading is counter to common sense and to most programming experience. In short, the best 8088 code can be arrived at only by thinking in terms of the 8088; superior 8088 solutions often seem to be lunacy in other logic systems.

Thinking in terms of the 8088 can be particularly difficult for those of us used to high level languages, in which programs are pure abstractions far removed from the ugly details of the processor. When programming in a high level language, it would seem to be faster to preload the correct value and test than to preload an incorrect value, test, and load the correct value. In fact, in any high level language it would seem most efficient to use an **if...then...else** structure to handle a test-and-set case such as the one above.

That's not the way it works on the 8088, though, because not all tests are created equal. Tests that branch are much slower than tests that fall through. When you're programming the 8088 in assembler, the maddening and fascinating capabilities of the processor must become part of your logic system, however illogical the paths down which that perspective leads may seem at times to be.

Use the Carry Flag to Replace Some Branches

Unlike the other flags, the carry flag (CF) can serve as a direct operand to some arithmetic instructions, such as **rcr** and **adc**. This gives CF a unique property—it can sometimes be used to alter the value in a register conditionally *without branching.*

For instance, suppose that we want to count the number of negative values in a 1000-word array, maintaining the count in DX. One way to do this is shown in Listing 13-8, which runs in 12.29 msec. In this code, each value is **and**ed with itself. The resulting setting of the sign flag (SF) indicates whether the value is positive or negative. With the help of a conditional jump, the sign flag (SF) setting controls whether DX is incremented or not.

```
1   ;
2   ; *** Listing 13-8 ***
3   ;
4   ; Counts the number of negative values in a 1000-word array,
5   ; by comparing each element to 0 and branching accordingly.
6   ;
7           jmp     Skip
8   ;
9   WordArray       label   word
10  X=-500
11          rept    1000
12          dw      X
13  X=X+1
14          endm
15  WORD_ARRAY_LENGTH       equ     ($-WordArray)
16  ;
17  ; Counts the number of negative values in a word-sized
18  ; array.
19  ;
20  ; Input:
21  ;       CX = length of array in words
22  ;       DS:SI = pointer to start of array
23  ;
24  ; Output:
25  ;       DX = count of negative values in array
26  ;
27  ; Registers altered: AX, CX, DX, SI
28  ;
29  ; Direction flag cleared
30  ;
31  ; Note: Does not handle arrays that are longer than 32K
32  ;       words or cross segment boundaries.
33  ;
34  CountNegativeWords:
35          cld
36          sub     dx,dx   ;initialize the count to 0
37  CountNegativeWordsLoop:
38          lodsw           ;get the next word from the array
39          and     ax,ax   ;is the word negative?
40          jns     CountNegativeWordsLoopBottom
41                          ;not negative-do the next element
42          inc     dx      ;word is negative, so increment the
43                          ; negative-word counter
44  CountNegativeWordsLoopBottom:
```

```
45              loop    CountNegativeWordsLoop
46              ret
47      ;
48      Skip:
49              call    ZTimerOn
50              mov     si,offset WordArray
51                          ;point to the array to count
52                          ; the # of negative words in...
53              mov     cx,WORD_ARRAY_LENGTH/2
54                          ;...set the # of words to check...
55              call    CountNegativeWords
56                          ;...and count the negative words
57              call    ZTimerOff
```

Speedy and compact as it is, Listing 13-8 *does* involve a conditional jump that branches about half the time, and by now you should be developing a distinct dislike for branching. By using CF to eliminate branching entirely, we can speed things up quite a bit.

```
1       ;
2       ; *** Listing 13-9 ***
3       ;
4       ; Counts the number of negative values in a 1000-word array,
5       ; by adding the Sign bit of each array element directly to
6       ; the register used for counting.
7       ;
8               jmp     Skip
9       ;
10      WordArray       label   word
11      X=-500
12              rept    1000
13              dw      X
14      X=X+1
15              endm
16      WORD_ARRAY_LENGTH       equ     ($-WordArray)
17      ;
18      ; Counts the number of negative values in a word-sized
19      ; array.
20      ;
21      ; Input:
22      ;       CX = length of array in words
23      ;       DS:SI = pointer to start of array
24      ;
25      ; Output:
26      ;       DX = count of negative values in array
27      ;
28      ; Registers altered: AX, BX, CX, DX, SI
29      ;
30      ; Direction flag cleared
31      ;
32      ; Note: Does not handle arrays that are longer than 32K
33      ;       words or cross segment boundaries.
34      ;
35      CountNegativeWords:
36              cld
```

```
37              sub     dx,dx   ;initialize the count to 0
38              mov     bx,dx   ;store the constant 0 in BX to speed
39                              ; up ADC in the loop
40      CountNegativeWordsLoop:
41              lodsw           ;get the next word from the array
42              shl     ax,1    ;put the sign bit in the Carry flag
43              adc     dx,bx   ;add the sign bit (via the Carry
44                              ; flag) to DX, since BX is 0
45      CountNegativeWordsLoopBottom:
46              loop    CountNegativeWordsLoop
47              ret
48      ;
49      Skip:
50              call    ZTimerOn
51              mov     si,offset WordArray
52                              ;point to the array to count
53                              ; the # of negative words in...
54              mov     cx,WORD_ARRAY_LENGTH/2
55                              ;...set the # of words to check...
56              call    CountNegativeWords
57                              ;...and count the negative words
58              call    ZTimerOff
```

Listing 13-9 does just that, shifting the sign bit of each tested value into CF and then adding it—along with 0, because **adc** requires two source operands—to DX, as shown in Figure 13.8. (Note that the constant 0 is stored in BX for speed; **adc dx,bx** is 1 byte shorter and 1 cycle faster than **adc dx,0**.) The result is that DX is incremented only when the sign bit of the value being tested is 1; that is, only when the value being tested is negative, which is exactly what we want.

Listing 13-9 runs in 10.80 msec. That's about 14 percent faster than Listing 13-8, even though the instruction that increments DX in Listing 13-9 (**adc dx,bx**) is actually 1 byte longer and 1 cycle slower than its counterpart in Listing 13-8 (**inc dx**). The key to the improved performance is, once again, avoiding branching. In this case that's made possible by recognizing that a CF-based operation can accomplish a task that we'd usually perform with a conditional jump. You wouldn't normally think to substitute **shl/adc** for **and/jns/inc**—they certainly don't *look* the least bit similar—but in this particular context the two instruction sequences are equivalent.

The many and varied parts of the 8088's instruction set are surprisingly interchangeable. Don't hesitate to mix and match them in unusual ways.

Never Use Two Jumps When One Will Do

Don't use a conditional jump followed by an unconditional jump when the conditional jump can do the job by itself. Generally, a conditional jump should be paired with an unconditional jump only when the 1-byte

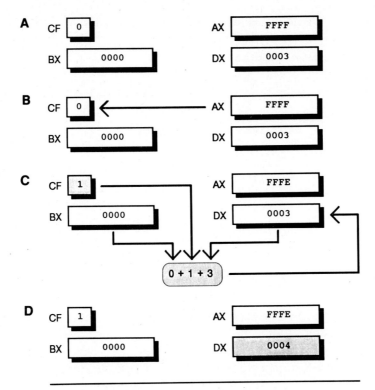

FIGURE 13.8   CF can be used to increment DX conditionally, depending on the sign of AX, without branching by way of the following code:

```
shl   ax,1
adc   dx,bx
```

where BX contains 0. **(A)** Sample initial states of the relevant registers. **(B)** How **shl ax,1** moves the sign bit of AX into CF. **(C)** How the sign bit that was transferred into CF is added to DX. **(D)** The final states of the registers; since AX was initially negative, DX has been incremented.

displacement of the conditional jump can't reach the desired offset—that is, when the offset to be branched to is more than −128 to +127 bytes away.

For example,

```
jz   IsZero
```

works fine unless **IsZero** is more than −128 or +127 bytes away from the first byte of the instruction immediately following the **jz** instruction. (You'll recall that we found in the previous chapter that conditional jumps, like all jumps that use displacements, actually branch relative to the offset of the start of the following instruction.) If, however, **IsZero** *is* more than −128 or +127 bytes away, the polarity of the conditional jump must be reversed, and the conditional jump must be used to skip around the unconditional jump:

```
        jnz   NotZero
        jmp   IsZero
NotZero:
```

When the conditional jump falls through (in the case that resulted in a branch in the first example), the 2-byte displacement of the unconditional jump can be used to jump to **IsZero**, no matter where in the code segment **IsZero** may be.

Logically, the two examples we've just covered are equivalent, branching in exactly the same cases. There's an obvious difference in the way the two examples *run,* though. The first example branches in only one of the two cases; the second example always branches, and is larger too.

In this case, it's pretty clear which is the code of choice (at least, I *hope* it is!). You'd use a conditional jump around an unconditional jump only when a conditional jump alone can't reach the target label. However, paired jumps can also be eliminated in a number of less obvious situations.

For example, suppose that you want to scan a string until you come to either a character that matches the character in AH or a 0 byte, whichever comes first. You might conceptualize the solution as follows:

1. Get the next byte.
2. If the next byte matches the desired byte, we've got a match and we're done.
3. If the next byte is 0, we're done without finding a match.
4. Repeat 1.

That sort of thinking is likely to produce code like that shown in Listing 13-10, which is a faithful line-by-line reproduction of the above sequence.

Listing 13-10 works perfectly well, finishing in 431 μsec; however, the loop in Listing 13-10 ends with a conditional jump followed by an unconditional jump. With a little code rearrangement, the conditional jump

```
1    ;
2    ; *** Listing 13-10 ***
3    ;
4    ; Finds the first occurrence of the letter 'z' in
5    ; a zero-terminated string, with a less-than-ideal
6    ; conditional jump followed by an unconditional jump at
7    ; the end of the loop.
8    ;
9            jmp     Skip
10   ;
11   TestString      label   byte
12           db      'This is a test string that is '
13           db      'z'
14           db      'terminated with a zero byte...',0
15   ;
16   ; Finds the first occurrence of the specified byte in the
17   ; specified zero-terminated string.
18   ;
19   ; Input:
20   ;       AL = byte to find
21   ;       DS:SI = zero-terminated string to search
22   ;
23   ; Output:
24   ;       SI = pointer to first occurrence of byte in string,
25   ;               or 0 if the byte wasn't found
26   ;
27   ; Registers altered: AX, SI
28   ;
29   ; Direction flag cleared
30   ;
31   ; Note: Do not pass a string that starts at offset 0 (SI=0),
32   ;       since a match on the first byte and failure to find
33   ;       the byte would be indistinguishable.
34   ;
35   ; Note: Does not handle strings that are longer than 64K
36   ;       bytes or cross segment boundaries.
37   ;
38   FindCharInString:
39           mov     ah,al   ;we'll need AL since that's the
40                           ; only register LODSB can use
41           cld
42   FindCharInStringLoop:
43           lodsb           ;get the next string byte
44           cmp     al,ah   ;is this the byte we're
45                           ; looking for?
46           jz      FindCharInStringFound
47                           ;yes, so we're done with a match
48           and     al,al   ;is this the terminating zero?
49           jz      FindCharInStringNotFound
50                           ;yes, so we're done with no match
51           jmp     FindCharInStringLoop
52                           ;check the next byte
53   FindCharInStringFound:
54           dec     si      ;point back to the matching byte
55           ret
56   FindCharInStringNotFound:
57           sub     si,si   ;we didn't find a match, so return
58                           ; 0 in SI
59           ret
```

```
60    ;
61    Skip:
62            call    ZTimerOn
63            mov     al,'z'          ;byte value to find
64            mov     si,offset TestString
65                                    ;string to search
66            call    FindCharInString ;search for the byte
67            call    ZTimerOff
```

can be made to handle both the test-for-0 and repeat-loop functions, and the unconditional jump can be done away with entirely. All we need do is put the no-match handling code right after the conditional jump and change the polarity of the jump from **jz** to **jnz**, so that the one conditional jump can either fall through if the terminating 0 is found or repeat the loop otherwise.

Listing 11-11 features just such rearranged code. (Listing 13-10 is actually Listing 11-11 modified to illustrate the perils of using two jumps when one will do.) Listing 11-11 runs in just 375 μsec; not only is it faster than Listing 13-10, it's also shorter by 2 bytes—the length of the eliminated jump.

Look to streamline your code whenever you see a short unconditional jump paired with a conditional jump. Of course, it's not always possible to eliminate paired jumps, but you'd be surprised at how often loops can be compacted and speeded up with a little rearrangement.

Jump to the Land of No Return

It's not uncommon that the last action before returning at the end of a subroutine is to call another subroutine, as follows:

```
        call SaveNewSymbol
        ret
PromptForSymbol         endp
```

What's wrong with this picture? That's easy: there's a branch to a branch here. The **ret** that ends **SaveNewSymbol** branches directly to the **ret** that follows the call to **SaveNewSymbol** at the end of **PromptForSymbol**. Surely there's a better way!

Indeed there is a better way, and that is to end **PromptForSymbol** by jumping to **SaveNewSymbol** rather than calling it. To wit,

```
        jmp  SaveNewSymbol
PromptForSymbol         endp
```

The **ret** at the end of **SaveNewSymbol** will serve perfectly well to return to the code that called **PromptForSymbol**, and by doing this we'll save one complete **ret** plus the performance difference between **jmp** and **call**—all without changing the logic of the code in the least.

One *caveat* regarding **jmp** in the place of **call/ret**: make sure that the types—near or far—of the two subroutines match. If **SaveNewSymbol** is near-callable but **PromptForSymbol** happens to be far-callable, then the **ret** instructions at the ends of the two subroutines are *not* equivalent, because near and far **ret** instructions perform distinctly different actions. Mismatch **ret** instructions in this way and you'll unbalance the stack, in the process most likely crashing your program, so exercise caution when replacing **call/ret** with **jmp**.

Don't Be Afraid to Duplicate Code

Whenever you use an unconditional jump, ask yourself, "Do I *really* need that jump?" Often the answer is yes—but not always.

What are unconditional jumps used for? Generally, they're used to allow a conditionally executed section of code to rejoin the main flow of program execution. For example, consider the following:

```
;
; Subroutine to set AH to 1 if AL contains the
; character 'Y', AH to 0 otherwise.
;
; Input:
;     AL = character to check
;
; Output;
;     AH = 1 if AL contains 'Y', 0 otherwise
;
; Registers altered: AH
;
CheckY      proc near
        cmp   al,'Y'
        jnz   CheckYNo
        mov   ah,1      ;it is indeed 'Y'
        jmp   short CheckYDone
CheckYNo:
        sub   ah,ah     ;it's not 'Y'
```

```
CheckYDone:
     ret
CheckY      endp
```

(You'll instantly recognize that the whole subroutine could be speeded up simply by preloading one of the values, as we learned a few sections back. In this particular case, however, we have a still better option available.) You'll notice that **jmp short CheckYDone**, the one unconditional jump in the above subroutine, doesn't actually serve much purpose. Sure, it rejoins the rest of the code after handling the case where AL is *Y*, but all that happens at that point is a return to the calling code. Surely it doesn't make sense to expend the time and 2 bytes required by a **jmp short** just to get to a **ret** instruction. Far better to simply replace the **jmp short** with a **ret**:

```
CheckY      proc near
     cmp    al,'Y'
     jnz    CheckYNo
     mov    ah,1       ;it is indeed 'Y'
     ret
CheckYNo:
     sub    ah,ah      ;it's not 'Y'
CheckYDone:
     ret
CheckY      endp
```

The net effect: the code is 1 byte shorter, the time required for a branch is saved about half the time, *and there is absolutely no change in the logic of the code.* It's important that you understand that **jmp short** was basically a **nop** instruction in the first example, because all it did was branch unconditionally to another branching instruction, as shown in Figure 13.9. We removed the unconditional jump simply by replacing it with a copy of the code that it branched to.

The basic principle here is duplicating code. Many unconditional jumps can be eliminated by replacing the jump with a copy of the code at the jump destination. (Unconditional jumps used for looping are an exception. As we found earlier, however, unconditional jumps used to end loops can often be replaced by conditional jumps, improving both performance and code size in the process.) Often the destination code is many bytes long, and in such cases code duplication doesn't pay. However, in many other cases, such as the example shown above, code duplication is an unqualified winner, saving both cycles and bytes.

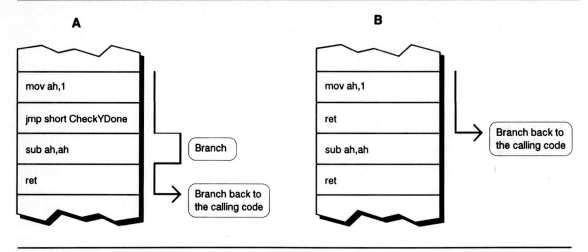

FIGURE 13.9   In the code

```
        mov   ah,1
        jmp   short CheckYDone
CheckYNo:
        sub   ah,ah
CheckYDone:
        ret
```

jmp short CheckYDone does nothing but waste cycles, as it unconditionally branches to a branch **(A)**. **(B)** Replacing **jmp short CheckYDone** with **ret** not only eliminates a branch but also saves a byte.

There are also cases where code duplication saves cycles but costs bytes, and then you'll have to decide which of the two matters more on a case-by-case basis. For instance, suppose that the last example required that AL be **and**ed with 0DFh (**not** 20h) after the test for *Y*. The standard code would be

```
;
; Subroutine to set AH to 1 if AL contains the
; character 'Y', AH to 0 otherwise. AL is then forced to
; uppercase. (AL must be a letter.)
;
```

```
;   Input;
;       AL = character to check (must be a letter)
;
; Output;
;       AH = 1 if AL contains 'Y', 0 otherwise
;       AL = character to check forced to uppercase
;
; Registers altered: AX
;
CheckY      proc near
        cmp     al,'Y'
        jnz     CheckYNo
        mov     ah,1            ;it is indeed 'Y'
        jmp     shortCheckYDone
CheckYNo:
        sub     ah,ah           ;it's not 'Y'
CheckYDone:
        and     al,not 20h      ;make it uppercase
        ret
CheckY      endp
```

The duplicate-code implementation would be

```
CheckY      proc near
        cmp     al,'Y'
        jnz     CheckYNo
        mov     ah,1        ;it is indeed 'Y'
        and     al,not 20h  ;make it uppercase
        ret
CheckYNo:
        sub     ah,ah       ;it's not 'Y'
CheckYDone:
        and     al,not 20h  ;make it uppercase
        ret
CheckY      endp
```

with both **and** and **ret** duplicated at the end of each of the two possible paths through the subroutine.

The decision as to which of the two above implementations is preferable is by no means cut and dried. The duplicated-code implementation is certainly faster, since it still avoids a branch in half the cases. On the other hand, the duplicated-code implementation is also 1 byte longer, since a 2-byte **jmp short** is replaced with a 3-byte sequence of **and** and **ret**. Neither sequence is superior on all counts, so the choice between the two depends on context and your own preferences.

Duplicated code is counter to all principles of structured programming. As we've learned, that's not inherently a bad thing—when you need performance, it can be most useful to discard conventions and look for fresh approaches.

Nonetheless, it's certainly possible to push the duplicated-code approach too far. As the code to be duplicated becomes longer and/or more complex, the duplicated-code approach becomes less appealing. In addition to the bytes that duplicating longer code can cost, there's also the risk that you'll modify the code at only one of the duplicated locations as you alter the program. For this reason, duplicated code sequences longer than a **ret** and perhaps one other instruction should be used only when performance is at an absolute premium.

Inside Loops Is Where Branches Really Hurt

Branches always hurt performance, but where they really hurt is inside loops. There, the performance loss incurred by a single branching instruction is magnified by the number of loop repetitions. It's important that you understand that not all branches are created equal, so that you can focus on eliminating or at least reducing the branches that most affect performance—and those branches are usually inside loops.

How can we apply this knowledge? By making every effort to use techniques such as duplicated code, in-line code (which we'll see shortly), and preloading values inside loops, and by simply moving decision making out of loops whenever we can. Let's take a look at an example of using duplicated code within a loop in order to see how easily cycle saving inside a loop can pay off.

Two loops can be better than one.   Suppose that we want to determine whether there are more negative or nonnegative values in an array of 8-bit signed values. Listing 13-11 does that in 3.60 msec for the sample array by using a straightforward and compact test-and-branch approach.

There's nothing wrong with Listing 13-11, but there *is* an unconditional jump. We'd just as soon do away with that unconditional jump, especially since it's in a loop. Unfortunately, the instruction the unconditional jump branches to isn't a simple **ret**—it's a **loop** instruction, and we all know that loops must end in one place, at the loop bottom.

```
 1      ;
 2      ; *** Listing 13-11 ***
 3      ;
 4      ; Determines whether there are more non-negative or negative
 5      ; elements in an array of 8-bit signed values, using a
 6      ; standard test-and-branch approach and a single LOOP
 7      ; instruction.
 8      ;
 9              jmp     Skip
10      ;
11      ARRAY_LENGTH    equ     256
12      ByteArray       label   byte
13      X=0
14              rept    ARRAY_LENGTH
15              db      X
16      X=X+1
17              endm
18      ;
19      ; Determines whether there are more non-negative or
20      ; negative elements in the specified array of 8-bit
21      ; signed values.
22      ;
23      ; Input:
24      ;       CX = length of array
25      ;       DS:SI = array to check
26      ;
27      ; Output:
28      ;       DX = signed count of the number of non-negative
29      ;               elements found in the array minus the number
30      ;               of negative elements found. (Zero if there
31      ;               are the same number of each type of element.
32      ;               Otherwise, sign bit set if there are more
33      ;               negative elements than non-negative
34      ;               elements, cleared if there are more
35      ;               non-negative elements than negative
36      ;               elements)
37      ;
38      ; Registers altered: AL, CX, DX, SI
39      ;
40      ; Direction flag cleared
41      ;
42      ; Note: Only useful if the surplus of non-negative
43      ;       elements over negative elements is less than
44      ;       32K, or if the surplus of negative elements
45      ;       over non-negative elements is less than or
46      ;       equal to 32K. Otherwise, the signed count
47      ;       returned in DX overflows.
48      ;
49      ; Note: Does not handle arrays that are longer than 64K
50      ;       bytes or cross segment boundaries.
51      ;
52      CountNegPos:
53              cld
54              sub     dx,dx   ;initialize the count to zero
55      CountNegPosLoop:
56              lodsb           ;get the next byte to check
57              and     al,al   ;see if it's negative or
58                              ; non-negative
59              js      CountNeg ;it's negative
```

```
60              inc     dx        ;count off one non-negative element
61              jmp     short CountNegPosLoopBottom
62      CountNeg:
63              dec     dx        ;count off one negative element
64      CountNegPosLoopBottom:
65              loop    CountNegPosLoop
66              ret
67      ;
68      Skip:
69              call    ZTimerOn
70              mov     si,offset ByteArray      ;array to check
71              mov     cx,ARRAY_LENGTH          ;# of bytes to check
72              call    CountNegPos              ;see whether there
73                                               ; are more negative
74                                               ; or non-negative
75                                               ; elements
76              call    ZTimerOff
```

Hmmmm. Why must loops end in one place? There's no particular reason that I can think of, apart from habit, so let's try duplicating some code and ending the loop in *two* places. Listing 13-12, which does exactly that, runs in just 3.05 msec. That's an improvement of 18 percent—quite a return for the 1 byte the duplicated-code approach adds.

It's evident that eliminating branching instructions inside loops can result in handsome performance gains for relatively little effort. That's why I urge you to focus your optimization efforts on loops. While we're on this important topic, let's look at another way to eliminate branches inside loops.

```
1       ;
2       ; *** Listing 13-12 ***
3       ;
4       ; Determines whether there are more non-negative or negative
5       ; elements in an array of 8-bit signed values, using
6       ; duplicated code with two LOOP instructions and two RET
7       ; instructions.
8       ;
9               jmp     Skip
10      ;
11      ARRAY_LENGTH    equ     256
12      ByteArray       label   byte
13      X=0
14              rept    ARRAY_LENGTH
15              db      X
16      X=X+1
17              endm
18      ;
19      ; Determines whether there are more non-negative or
20      ; negative elements in the specified array of 8-bit
21      ; signed values.
22      ;
23      ; Input:
24      ;       CX = length of array
```

```
25   ;          DS:SI = array to check
26   ;
27   ; Output:
28   ;          DX = signed count of the number of non-negative
29   ;               elements found in the array minus the number
30   ;               of negative elements found. (Zero if there
31   ;               are the same number of each type of element.
32   ;               Otherwise, sign bit set if there are more
33   ;               negative elements than non-negative
34   ;               elements, cleared if there are more
35   ;               non-negative elements than negative
36   ;               elements)
37   ;
38   ; Registers altered: AL, CX, DX, SI
39   ;
40   ; Direction flag cleared
41   ;
42   ; Note: Only useful if the surplus of non-negative
43   ;       elements over negative elements is less than
44   ;       32K, or if the surplus of negative elements
45   ;       over non-negative elements is less than or
46   ;       equal to 32K. Otherwise, the signed count
47   ;       returned in DX overflows.
48   ;
49   ; Note: Does not handle arrays that are longer than 64K
50   ;       bytes or cross segment boundaries.
51   ;
52   CountNegPos:
53           cld
54           sub     dx,dx    ;initialize the count to zero
55   CountNegPosLoop:
56           lodsb            ;get the next byte to check
57           and     al,al    ;see if it's negative or
58                            ; non-negative
59           js      CountNeg ;it's negative
60           inc     dx       ;count off one non-negative element
61           loop    CountNegPosLoop
62           ret
63   CountNeg:
64           dec     dx       ;count off one negative element
65           loop    CountNegPosLoop
66           ret
67   ;
68   Skip:
69           call    ZTimerOn
70           mov     si,offset ByteArray    ;array to check
71           mov     cx,ARRAY_LENGTH        ;# of bytes to check
72           call    CountNegPos            ;see whether there
73                                          ; are more negative
74                                          ; or non-negative
75                                          ; elements
76           call    ZTimerOff
```

Make up your mind once and for all. If you find yourself making a decision inside a loop, for heaven's sake see if you can manage to make that decision *before* the loop. Why decide every time through the loop when you can decide just once at the outset?

Consider Listing 13-13, in which the contents of DL are used to decide whether to convert each character to upper case while copying one string to another string. Listing 13-13, which runs in 3.03 msec for the sample string, is representative of the situation in which a parameter passed to a subroutine selects between different modes of operation.

```
1    ;
2    ; *** Listing 13-13 ***
3    ;
4    ; Copies a zero-terminated string to another string,
5    ; optionally converting characters to uppercase. The
6    ; decision as to whether to convert to uppercase is made
7    ; once for each character.
8    ;
9           jmp     Skip
10   ;
11   SourceString    label   byte
12           db      'This is a sample string, consisting of '
13           db      'both uppercase and lowercase characters.'
14           db      0
15   DestinationString       label   byte
16           db      100 dup (?)
17   ;
18   ; Copies a zero-terminated string to another string,
19   ; optionally converting characters to uppercase.
20   ;
21   ; Input:
22   ;       DL = 1 if conversion to uppercase during copying is
23   ;               desired, 0 otherwise
24   ;       DS:SI = source string
25   ;       ES:DI = destination string
26   ;
27   ; Output: none
28   ;
29   ; Registers altered: AL, SI, DI
30   ;
31   ; Direction flag cleared
32   ;
33   ; Note: Does not handle strings that are longer than 64K
34   ;       bytes or cross segment boundaries.
35   ;
36   CopyAndConvert:
37           cld
38   CopyAndConvertLoop:
39           lodsb                           ;get the next byte
40                                           ; to check
41           and     dl,dl                   ;conversion to
42                                           ; uppercase desired?
43           jz      CopyAndConvertUC        ;no
44           cmp     al,'a'                  ;less than 'a'?
45           jb      CopyAndConvertUC        ;yes, not lowercase
46           cmp     al,'z'                  ;greater than 'z'?
47           ja      CopyAndConvertUC        ;yes, not lowercase
48           and     al,not 20h              ;make it uppercase
49   CopyAndConvertUC:
50           stosb                           ;put the byte in the
```

```
51                                           ; destination string
52          and       al,al                  ;was that the
53                                            ; terminating zero?
54          jnz       CopyAndConvertLoop      ;no, do next byte
55          ret
56  ;
57  Skip:
58          call      ZTimerOn
59  ;
60  ; First, copy without converting to uppercase.
61  ;
62          mov       di,seg DestinationString
63          mov       es,di
64          mov       di,offset DestinationString
65                        ;ES:DI points to the destination
66          mov       si,offset SourceString
67                        ;DS:SI points to the source
68          sub       dl,dl   ;don't convert to uppercase
69          call      CopyAndConvert  ;copy without converting
70                            ; to uppercase
71  ;
72  ; Now copy and convert to uppercase.
73  ;
74          mov       di,offset DestinationString
75                        ;ES:DI points to the destination
76          mov       si,offset SourceString
77                        ;DS:SI points to the source
78          mov       dl,1    ;convert to uppercase this time
79          call      CopyAndConvert  ;copy and convert to
80                            ; uppercase
81          call      ZTimerOff
```

The failing of Listing 13-13 is that the decision as to whether to convert to upper case is made over and over, once for each character. We'd be much better off if we could make the decision just once at the start of the subroutine, moving the decision making (particularly the branching) out of the loop.

There are a number of ways to do this. One is shown in Listing 13-14. Here, a single branch outside the loop is used to force the test for inclusion in the lower case to function also as the test for whether conversion is desired. If conversion isn't desired, AH, which normally contains the start of the lower case range, is set to 0FFh. This has the effect of causing the lower case test always to fail on the first conditional jump if conversion isn't desired, just as was the case in Listing 13-13. Consequently, performance stays just about the same when conversion to upper case isn't desired.

```
1  ;
2  ; *** Listing 13-14 ***
3  ;
4  ; Copies a zero-terminated string to another string,
5  ; optionally converting characters to uppercase. The
```

```
 6     ; decision as to whether to convert to uppercase is made
 7     ; once at the beginning of the subroutine; if conversion
 8     ; is not desired, the register containing the value of the
 9     ; start of the lowercase range is simply set to cause all
10     ; tests for lowercase to fail. This avoids one test in the
11     ; case where conversion to uppercase is desired, since the
12     ; single test for the start of the lowercase range is able
13     ; to perform both that test and the test for whether
14     ; conversion is desired.
15     ;
16             jmp     Skip
17     ;
18     SourceString    label   byte
19             db      'This is a sample string, consisting of '
20             db      'both uppercase and lowercase characters.'
21             db      0
22     DestinationString       label   byte
23             db      100 dup (?)
24     ;
25     ; Copies a zero-terminated string to another string,
26     ; optionally converting characters to uppercase.
27     ;
28     ; Input:
29     ;       DL = 1 if conversion to uppercase during copying is
30     ;               desired, 0 otherwise
31     ;       DS:SI = source string
32     ;       ES:DI = destination string
33     ;
34     ; Output: none
35     ;
36     ; Registers altered: AX, SI, DI
37     ;
38     ; Direction flag cleared
39     ;
40     ; Note: Does not handle strings that are longer than 64K
41     ;       bytes or cross segment boundaries.
42     ;
43     CopyAndConvert:
44             cld
45             mov     ah,0ffh ;assume conversion to uppercase is
46                             ; not desired. In that case, this
47                             ; value will cause the initial
48                             ; lowercase test to fail (except
49                             ; when the character is 0FFh, but
50                             ; that's rare and will be rejected
51                             ; by the second lowercase test
52             and     dl,dl   ;is conversion to uppercase desired?
53             jz      CopyAndConvertLoop      ;no, AH is all set
54             mov     ah,'a'  ;set the proper lower limit of the
55                             ; lowercase range
56     CopyAndConvertLoop:
57             lodsb                           ;get the next byte
58                                             ; to check
59             cmp     al,ah                   ;less than 'a'?
60                                             ; (If conversion
61                                             ; isn't desired,
62                                             ; AH is 0FFh, and
63                                             ; this fails)
64             jb      CopyAndConvertUC        ;yes, not lowercase
```

```
65              cmp     al,'z'                  ;greater than 'z'?
66              ja      CopyAndConvertUC        ;yes, not lowercase
67              and     al,not 20h              ;make it uppercase
68      CopyAndConvertUC:
69              stosb                           ;put the byte in the
70                                              ; destination string
71              and     al,al                   ;was that the
72                                              ; terminating zero?
73              jnz     CopyAndConvertLoop      ;no, do next byte
74              ret
75      ;
76      Skip:
77              call    ZTimerOn
78      ;
79      ; First, copy without converting to uppercase.
80      ;
81              mov     di,seg DestinationString
82              mov     es,di
83              mov     di,offset DestinationString
84                      ;ES:DI points to the destination
85              mov     si,offset SourceString
86                      ;DS:SI points to the source
87              sub     dl,dl   ;don't convert to uppercase
88              call    CopyAndConvert  ;copy without converting
89                                      ; to uppercase
90      ;
91      ; Now copy and convert to uppercase.
92      ;
93              mov     di,offset DestinationString
94                      ;ES:DI points to the destination
95              mov     si,offset SourceString
96                      ;DS:SI points to the source
97              mov     dl,1    ;convert to uppercase this time
98              call    CopyAndConvert  ;copy and convert to
99                                      ; uppercase
100             call    ZTimerOff
```

However, when lower case conversion *is* desired, Listing 13-14 performs one fewer test each time through the loop than does Listing 13-13, because a separate test to find out whether conversion is desired is no longer needed. We've already performed the test for whether conversion is desired at the start of the subroutine—outside the loop—so the code inside the loop can sail through the copy-and-convert process at full speed. The result is that Listing 13-14 runs in 2.76 msec, significantly faster than Listing 13-13.

In Listing 13-14, we've really moved the test of whether conversion is desired out of the loop only in the case where conversion is indeed desired. When conversion isn't desired, a branch is still performed every time through the loop, just as in Listing 13-13. If we're willing to duplicate a bit of code, we can also move the branch out of the loop when conversion isn't desired, as shown in Listing 13-15. There's a cost in size for this optimization—7 bytes—but execution time is cut to just 2.35 μsec, a 29 percent improvement over Listing 13-13.

```
1    ;
2    ; *** Listing 13-15 ***
3    ;
4    ; Copies a zero-terminated string to another string,
5    ; optionally converting characters to uppercase. The
6    ; decision as to whether to convert to uppercase is made
7    ; once at the beginning of the subroutine, with separate
8    ; code executed depending on whether conversion is desired
9    ; or not.
10   ;
11          jmp     Skip
12   ;
13   SourceString    label    byte
14          db      'This is a sample string, consisting of '
15          db      'both uppercase and lowercase characters.'
16          db      0
17   DestinationString        label    byte
18          db      100 dup (?)
19   ;
20   ; Copies a zero-terminated string to another string,
21   ; optionally converting characters to uppercase.
22   ;
23   ; Input:
24   ;       DL = 1 if conversion to uppercase during copying is
25   ;               desired, 0 otherwise
26   ;       DS:SI = source string
27   ;       ES:DI = destination string
28   ;
29   ; Output: none
30   ;
31   ; Registers altered: AL, SI, DI
32   ;
33   ; Direction flag cleared
34   ;
35   ; Note: Does not handle strings that are longer than 64K
36   ;       bytes or cross segment boundaries.
37   ;
38   CopyAndConvert:
39          cld
40          and     dl,dl           ;is conversion desired?
41          jz      CopyLoop        ;no, so just copy the string
42   ;
43   ; Copy the string, converting to uppercase.
44   ;
45   CopyAndConvertLoop:
46          lodsb                           ;get the next byte
47                                          ; to check
48          cmp     al,'a'                  ;less than 'a'?
49          jb      CopyAndConvertUC        ;yes, not lowercase
50          cmp     al,'z'                  ;greater than 'z'?
51          ja      CopyAndConvertUC        ;yes, not lowercase
52          and     al,not 20h              ;make it uppercase
53   CopyAndConvertUC:
54          stosb                           ;put the byte in the
55                                          ; destination string
56          and     al,al                   ;was that the
57                                          ; terminating zero?
58          jnz     CopyAndConvertLoop      ;no, do next byte
59          ret
60   ;
```

```
61     ; Copy the string without conversion to uppercase.
62     ;
63     CopyLoop:
64             lodsb                   ;get the next byte to check
65             stosb                   ;copy the byte
66             and     al,al           ;was that the terminating 0?
67             jnz     CopyLoop        ;no, do next byte
68             ret
69     ;
70     Skip:
71             call    ZTimerOn
72     ;
73     ; First, copy without converting to uppercase.
74     ;
75             mov     di,seg DestinationString
76             mov     es,di
77             mov     di,offset DestinationString
78                     ;ES:DI points to the destination
79             mov     si,offset SourceString
80                     ;DS:SI points to the source
81             sub     dl,dl   ;don't convert to uppercase
82             call    CopyAndConvert  ;copy without converting
83                             ; to uppercase
84     ;
85     ; Now copy and convert to uppercase.
86     ;
87             mov     di,offset DestinationString
88                     ;ES:DI points to the destination
89             mov     si,offset SourceString
90                     ;DS:SI points to the source
91             mov     dl,1    ;convert to uppercase this time
92             call    CopyAndConvert  ;copy and convert to
93                             ; uppercase
94             call    ZTimerOff
```

Moreover, Listing 13-15 could easily be speeded up further by using the word-at-a-time or **scas/movs** techniques we encountered in Chapter 11. Why is it easier to do this to Listing 13-15 than to Listing 13-13? It's easier because we've completely separated the instruction sequences for the two modes of operation of the subroutine, so we have fewer instructions and simpler code to optimize in whichever case we try to speed up.

Remember, not all branches are created equal. If you have a choice between branching once before a loop and branching once every time through the loop, it's really like choosing between one branch and dozens or hundreds (however many times the loop is repeated) of branches. Even when it costs a few extra bytes, that's not a particularly hard choice to make, is it?

Don't Come Calling

Jumps aren't the 8088's only branching instructions. Calls, returns, and interrupts branch as well. Interrupts aren't usually repeated unnecessarily inside loops, although you should try to handle data obtained through DOS interrupts in large blocks, rather than a character at a time, as we'll see in the next chapter.

By definition, returns can't be executed repeatedly inside loops, since a return branches out of a loop back to the calling code.

That leaves calls—and calls in loops are in fact among the great cycle wasters of the 8088.

Consider what the **call** instruction does. First it pushes the instruction pointer onto the stack, and then it branches. That's like pairing a **push** and a **jmp**—a gruesome prospect from a performance perspective. Actually, things aren't *that* bad; the official execution time of **call**, at 23 cycles, is only 8 cycles longer than that of **jmp**. Nonetheless, you should cast a wary eye on any instruction that takes 23 cycles to execute *and* empties the prefetch queue.

The cycles spent executing **call** aren't the end of the performance loss associated with calling a subroutine, however. Once you're done with a subroutine, you have to branch back to the calling code. The instruction that does that, **ret**, takes another 20 cycles and empties the prefetch queue again. On balance, then, a subroutine call expends 43 cycles on overhead operations and empties the prefetch queue not once but *twice!*

Fine, you say, but what's the alternative? After all, subroutines are fundamental to good programming—we can't just do away with them altogether.

By and large, that's true, but inside time-critical loops there's no reason why we can't eliminate calls simply by moving the called code into the loop. Replacing the subroutine call with a macro is the simplest way to do this. For example, suppose that we have a subroutine called **IsPrintable**, which tests whether the character in AL is a printable character (in the range 20h to 7Eh). Listing 13-16 shows a loop that calls this subroutine in the process of copying only printable characters from one string to another string. Call and all, Listing 13-16 runs in 3.48 msec for the test string.

```
1    ;
2    ; *** Listing 13-16 ***
3    ;
4    ; Copies a zero-terminated string to another string,
5    ; filtering out non-printable characters by means of a
6    ; subroutine that performs the test.
7    ;
8              jmp     Skip
9    ;
10   SourceString    label   byte
11           db      'This is a sample string, consisting of '
12   X=1
13           rept    31
```

```
14          db      X
15    X=X+1
16          endm
17          db      7fh
18          db      'both printable and non-printable '
19          db      'characters', 0
20    DestinationString      label      byte
21          db      200 dup (?)
22    ;
23    ; Determines whether a character is printable (in the range
24    ; 20h through 7Eh).
25    ;
26    ; Input:
27    ;       AL = character to check
28    ;
29    ; Output:
30    ;       Zero flag set to 1 if character is printable,
31    ;               set to 0 otherwise
32    ;
33    ; Registers altered: none
34    ;
35    IsPrintable:
36          cmp     al,20h
37          jb      IsPrintableDone ;not printable
38          cmp     al,7eh
39          ja      IsPrintableDone ;not printable
40          cmp     al,al    ;set the Zero flag to 1, since the
41                           ; character is printable
42    IsPrintableDone:
43          ret
44    ;
45    ; Copies a zero-terminated string to another string,
46    ; filtering out non-printable characters.
47    ;
48    ; Input:
49    ;       DS:SI = source string
50    ;       ES:DI = destination string
51    ;
52    ; Output: none
53    ;
54    ; Registers altered: AL, SI, DI
55    ;
56    ; Direction flag cleared
57    ;
58    ; Note: Does not handle strings that are longer than 64K
59    ;       bytes or cross segment boundaries.
60    ;
61    CopyPrintable:
62          cld
63    CopyPrintableLoop:
64          lodsb                   ;get the next byte to copy
65          call    IsPrintable     ;is it printable?
66          jnz     NotPrintable    ;nope, don't copy it
67          stosb                   ;put the byte in the
68                                  ; destination string
69          jmp     CopyPrintableLoop ;the character was
70                                  ; printable, so it couldn't
71                                  ; possibly have been 0. No
72                                  ; need to check whether it
```

```
73                                      ; terminated the string
74    NotPrintable:
75              and     al,al           ;was that the
76                                      ; terminating zero?
77              jnz     CopyPrintableLoop ;no, do next byte
78              stosb                    ;copy the terminating zero
79              ret                      ;done
80    ;
81    Skip:
82              call    ZTimerOn
83              mov     di,seg DestinationString
84              mov     es,di
85              mov     di,offset DestinationString
86                      ;ES:DI points to the destination
87              mov     si,offset SourceString
88                      ;DS:SI points to the source
89              call    CopyPrintable   ;copy the printable
90                                      ; characters
91              call    ZTimerOff
```

Listing 13-17 is functionally identical to Listing 13-16. In Listing 13-17, however, the call to the subroutine **IsPrintable** has been converted to the expansion of the macro **IS_PRINTABLE**, eliminating the **call** and **ret** instructions. How much difference does that change from call to macro expansion make? Listing 13-17 runs in 2.21 msec, 57 percent faster than Listing 13-16. *Listing 13-16 spends over one third of its entire execution time simply calling **IsPrintable** and returning from that subroutine!*

```
1     ;
2     ; *** Listing 13-17 ***
3     ;
4     ; Copies a zero-terminated string to another string,
5     ; filtering out non-printable characters by means of a
6     ; macro that performs the test.
7     ;
8              jmp     Skip
9     ;
10    SourceString    label   byte
11              db      'This is a sample string, consisting of '
12    X=1
13              rept    31
14              db      X
15    X=X+1
16              endm
17              db      7fh
18              db      'both printable and non-printable '
19              db      'characters', 0
20    DestinationString       label   byte
21              db      200 dup (?)
22    ;
23    ; Macro that determines whether a character is printable (in
24    ; the range 20h through 7Eh).
25    ;
26    ; Input:
```

```
27    ;         AL = character to check
28    ;
29    ; Output:
30    ;         Zero flag set to 1 if character is printable,
31    ;                 set to 0 otherwise
32    ;
33    ; Registers altered: none
34    ;
35    IS_PRINTABLE    macro
36            local   IsPrintableDone
37            cmp     al,20h
38            jb      IsPrintableDone ;not printable
39            cmp     al,7eh
40            ja      IsPrintableDone ;not printable
41            cmp     al,al    ;set the Zero flag to 1, since the
42                             ; character is printable
43    IsPrintableDone:
44            endm
45    ;
46    ; Copies a zero-terminated string to another string,
47    ; filtering out non-printable characters.
48    ;
49    ; Input:
50    ;         DS:SI = source string
51    ;         ES:DI = destination string
52    ;
53    ; Output: none
54    ;
55    ; Registers altered: AL, SI, DI
56    ;
57    ; Direction flag cleared
58    ;
59    ; Note: Does not handle strings that are longer than 64K
60    ;         bytes or cross segment boundaries.
61    ;
62    CopyPrintable:
63            cld
64    CopyPrintableLoop:
65            lodsb                   ;get the next byte to copy
66            IS_PRINTABLE            ;is it printable?
67            jnz     NotPrintable    ;nope, don't copy it
68            stosb                   ;put the byte in the
69                                    ; destination string
70            jmp     CopyPrintableLoop ;the character was
71                                    ; printable, so it couldn't
72                                    ; possibly have been 0. No
73                                    ; need to check whether it
74                                    ; terminated the string
75    NotPrintable:
76            and     al,al           ;was that the
77                                    ; terminating zero?
78            jnz     CopyPrintableLoop ;no, do next byte
79            stosb                   ;copy the terminating zero
80            ret                     ;done
81    ;
82    Skip:
83            call    ZTimerOn
84            mov     di,seg DestinationString
85            mov     es,di
```

```
86              mov     di,offset DestinationString
87                          ;ES:DI points to the destination
88              mov     si,offset SourceString
89                          ;DS:SI points to the source
90              call    CopyPrintable   ;copy the printable
91                              ; characters
92              call    ZTimerOff
```

While the superior performance of Listing 13-17 clearly illustrates the price paid for subroutine calls, that listing by no means applies all of the optimizations made possible by the elimination of the calls that plagued Listing 13-16. It's true that the macro **IS_PRINTABLE** eliminates the subroutine call, but there are still internal branches in **IS_PRINTABLE**, and there's still a **cmp** instruction that sets the zero flag (ZF) on success. In other words, Listing 13-17 hasn't taken full advantage of moving the code into the loop; it has simply taken the call and return overhead out of determining whether a character is printable.

Listing 13-18 does take full advantage of moving the test code into the loop, by eliminating the macro and thereby eliminating the need to place a return status in ZF. Instead, Listing 13-18 branches directly to **NotPrintable** if a character is found to be nonprintable, eliminating the intermediate conditional jump that Listing 13-17 performed. It's also no longer necessary to test ZF to see whether the character is printable before storing it in the destination array, since any character that passes the two comparisons for inclusion in the printable range must be printable. The upshot is that Listing 13-18 runs in just 1.74 msec, 27 percent faster than Listing 13-17 and 100 percent faster than Listing 13-16.

```
1   ;
2   ; *** Listing 13-18 ***
3   ;
4   ; Copies a zero-terminated string to another string,
5   ; filtering out non-printable characters by means of
6   ; carefully customized code that performs the test
7   ; directly in the loop.
8   ;
9               jmp     Skip
10  ;
11  SourceString    label   byte
12              db      'This is a sample string, consisting of '
13  X=1
14              rept    31
15              db      X
16  X=X+1
17              endm
18              db      7fh
19              db      'both printable and non-printable '
20              db      'characters', 0
21  DestinationString       label   byte
```

```
22              db       200 dup (?)
23      ;
24      ; Copies a zero-terminated string to another string,
25      ; filtering out non-printable characters.
26      ;
27      ; Input:
28      ;       DS:SI = source string
29      ;       ES:DI = destination string
30      ;
31      ; Output: none
32      ;
33      ; Registers altered: AL, SI, DI
34      ;
35      ; Direction flag cleared
36      ;
37      ; Note: Does not handle strings that are longer than 64K
38      ;       bytes or cross segment boundaries.
39      ;
40      CopyPrintable:
41              cld
42      CopyPrintableLoop:
43              lodsb                       ;get the next byte to copy
44              cmp      al,20h
45              jb       NotPrintable       ;not printable
46              cmp      al,7eh
47              ja       CopyPrintableLoop  ;not printable
48              stosb                       ;put the byte in the
49                                          ; destination string
50              jmp      CopyPrintableLoop  ;the character was
51                                          ; printable, so it couldn't
52                                          ; possibly have been 0. No
53                                          ; need to check whether it
54                                          ; terminated the string
55      NotPrintable:
56              and      al,al              ;was that the
57                                          ; terminating zero?
58              jnz      CopyPrintableLoop  ;no, do next byte
59              stosb                       ;copy the terminating zero
60              ret                         ;done
61      ;
62      Skip:
63              call     ZTimerOn
64              mov      di,seg DestinationString
65              mov      es,di
66              mov      di,offset DestinationString
67                          ;ES:DI points to the destination
68              mov      si,offset SourceString
69                          ;DS:SI points to the source
70              call     CopyPrintable    ;copy the printable
71                                         ; characters
72              call     ZTimerOff
```

Listing 13-18 illustrates two useful optimizations in the case where a character is found to be printable. First, there's no need to branch to the bottom of the loop just to branch back to the top of the loop, so Listing 13-18 just branches directly to the top of the loop after storing each printable character. The same is done when a nonprintable character greater than 7Eh is detected. The point here is that it's fine to branch back to the top of a loop from multiple places. Second, there's no way that a printable character can end a string (0 isn't a printable character), so we don't bother testing for the terminating 0 after storing a printable character; again, the same is true for nonprintable characters greater than 7Eh. When you duplicate code, it's not necessary to duplicate any portion of the code that performs no useful function in the new location.

Whenever you use a subroutine or a macro, you're surrendering some degree of control over your code in exchange for ease of programming. In particular, the use of subroutines involves a direct tradeoff of decreased performance for reduced code size and greater modularity. In general, ease of programming, reduced code size, and modularity are highly desirable attributes—but in time-critical code performance is paramount.

Try to eliminate calls from your tight loops and time-critical code. If the code called is large, that may not be possible, but then you have to ask yourself what such a large subroutine is doing in your time-critical code in the first place. It may also be beneficial to eliminate macros in time-critical code; whether that's the case depends on the nature of the macros, but at least make sure you understand what code you're really writing. In this pursuit, it can be useful to generate a listing file in order to see the code the assembler is actually generating.

As I mentioned above, there are three objections to moving subroutines into loops: size, modularity, and ease of programming. Let's quickly address each of these points.

Sure, code gets bigger when you move subroutines into loops: performance is often a balancing of program size and performance. That's why you should concentrate on applying the techniques in this chapter (and, indeed, all the performance-enhancing techniques presented in *Zen of Assembly Language*) to time-critical code, where a few extra bytes can buy a great many cycles.

On the other hand, code doesn't really have to be less modular when subroutines are moved into loops. Macros are just as modular as subroutines, in the sense that in your code both are one-line entries that perform a well-defined set of actions. In any case, in discussing moving subroutine code into loops we're generally talking about moving relatively few instructions into any given loop, because the call/return overhead becomes proportionately less significant for longer subroutines (although never insignificant, if you're really squeezed for cycles). Modularity shouldn't be a big issue with short instruction sequences.

Finally, as to ease of programming: if you want easy programming, program in C or Pascal, or, better yet, COBOL. Assembler subroutine and macro libraries are fine for run-of-the-mill code, but when it comes to the high-performance, time-critical parts of your programs, it's your ability to write the difficult assembler code that will set you apart. Assembler isn't easy, but any competent programmer can eventually get almost any application to work in assembler. The Zen of assembly language lies not in making an application work but in making it work as well as it possibly can, given the strengths and limitations of the PC.

Smaller Isn't *Always* Better

You've no doubt noticed that this chapter seems to have repeatedly violated the rule that smaller is better. Not so, given the true meaning of the rule. *Smaller is better* applies to instruction prefetching, where fewer bytes to be fetched means less time waiting for instruction bytes. Subroutine calls don't fall into this category, even though they reduce overall program size.

Subroutines merely allow you to run the same instructions from multiple places in a program. That reduces program size, as the code needs to appear in only one place, but there are no fewer bytes to be fetched on any given call than if the code of the subroutine were placed directly into the calling code. In fact, instruction fetching becomes *more* of a problem with subroutines, because the prefetch queue is emptied twice and the call and return instruction bytes must be fetched.

In short, although subroutines are great for reducing program size and have a host of other virtues as regards program design, modularity, and maintenance, they don't come under the smaller-is-better rule and are, in fact, lousy for performance. Much the same—smaller is slower—can be said of branches of many sorts. Of all the branching instructions, loops are perhaps the worst smaller-is-slower offender. We're going to close out this chapter with a discussion of the potent in-line code alternative to looping—yet another way to trade a few bytes for a great many cycles.

13.7   ◆ loop May Not Be Bad, but Lord Knows It's Not Good: In-Line Code

One of the great misconceptions of 8088 programming is that **loop** is a good instruction for looping. It's true that **loop** is designed especially for looping. It's also true that **loop** is the 8088's best looping instruction. But *good?*

No way.

You see, **loop** is a branching instruction, and not an especially fast branching instruction, at that. The official execution time of **loop** is 17 cycles, which makes it just 1 cycle faster than the similar construct **dec cx/jnz**, although **loop** is also 1 byte shorter. Like all branching instructions, **loop** empties the prefetch queue, so it is effectively even slower than it would appear to be. I don't see how you can call an instruction that takes in the neighborhood of 20 cycles just to repeat a loop "good." Better than the obvious alternatives, sure, and pleasantly compact and easy to use if you don't much care about speed—but not *good*.

Look at it this way. Suppose you have a program containing a loop that zeroes the high bit of each byte in a 100-byte array, as shown in Listing 13-19, which runs in 1023 μsec. What percentage of that overall execution time do you suppose this program spends just decrementing CX and branching back to the top of the loop—that is, looping? Ten percent?

No.

Twenty percent?

No.

Thirty percent?

```
1    ;
2    ; *** Listing 13-19 ***
3    ;
4    ; Zeros the high-bit of each byte in a 100-byte array,
5    ; using the LOOP instruction.
6    ;
7            jmp     Skip
8    ;
9    ARRAY_LENGTH    equ     100
10   ByteArray       label   byte
11           db      ARRAY_LENGTH dup (80h)
12   ;
13   ; Clears the high bit of each byte in an array of
14   ; length ARRAY_LENGTH.
15   ;
16   ; Input:
17   ;       BX = pointer to the start of the array to clear
18   ;
19   ; Output: none
20   ;
21   ; Registers altered: AL, BX, CX
22   ;
23   ClearHighBits:
24           mov     cx,ARRAY_LENGTH    ;# of bytes to clear
25           mov     al,not 80h         ;pattern to clear
26                                      ; high bits with
27   ClearHighBitsLoop:
28           and     [bx],al            ;clear the high bit
29                                      ; of this byte
30           inc     bx                 ;point to the next
31                                      ; byte
```

```
32              loop       ClearHighBitsLoop      ;repeat until we're
33                                                ; out of bytes
34              ret
35      ;
36      Skip:
37              call       ZTimerOn
38              mov        bx,offset ByteArray
39                                         ;array in which to clear
40                                         ; high bits
41              call       ClearHighBits   ;clear the high bits of the
42                                         ; bytes
43              call       ZTimerOff
```

No, but you're getting warm . . . Listing 13-19 spends *45 percent* of the total execution time looping. (That figure was arrived at by comparing the execution time of Listing 13-20, which uses no branches and which we'll get to shortly, to the execution time of Listing 13-19.) Yes, you read that correctly—in a loop that accesses memory twice and that contains a second instruction in addition to the memory-accessing instruction, **loop** manages to take nearly one half of the total execution time. Appalling?

You bet.

```
1       ;
2       ; *** Listing 13-20 ***
3       ;
4       ; Zeros the high-bit of each byte in a 100-byte array,
5       ; using in-line code.
6       ;
7               jmp        Skip
8       ;
9       ARRAY_LENGTH    equ        100
10      ByteArray       label      byte
11              db         ARRAY_LENGTH dup (80h)
12      ;
13      ; Clears the high bit of each byte in an array of
14      ; length ARRAY_LENGTH.
15      ;
16      ; Input:
17      ;       BX = pointer to the start of the array to clear
18      ;
19      ; Output: none
20      ;
21      ; Registers altered: AL, BX
22      ;
23      ClearHighBits:
24              mov        al,not 80h              ;pattern to clear
25                                                 ; high bits with
26              rept       ARRAY_LENGTH            ;# of bytes to clear
27              and        [bx],al                 ;clear the high bit
28                                                 ; of this byte
29              inc        bx                      ;point to the next
30                                                 ; byte
31              endm
32              ret
```

```
33   ;
34   Skip:
35           call    ZTimerOn
36           mov     bx,offset ByteArray
37                                   ;array in which to clear
38                                   ; high bits
39           call    ClearHighBits   ;clear the high bits of the
40                                   ; bytes
41           call    ZTimerOff
```

Still, although **loop** may not be much faster than other branching instructions, it is nonetheless *somewhat* faster, and it's also more compact. We know we're losing a great deal of performance to the 8088's abysmal branching speed, but there doesn't seem to be much we can do about it.

But of course there is something we can do, as is almost always the case with the 8088. Let's look at exactly what **loop** is used for, and then let's see if we can produce the same functionality in a different way.

Well, **loop** is used to repeat a given sequence of instructions multiple times, and that's about all. What can we do with that job description?

Heck, that's *easy*. We'll eliminate branching and loop counting entirely by *literally* repeating the instructions, as shown in Figure 13.10. Instead of using **loop** to execute the same code, say, 10 times, we'll just line up 10 repetitions of the code inside the loop and then execute them one after another. This is known as *in-line code,* because the repetitions of the code are lined up in order rather than being separated by branches. (*In-line code* is sometimes used to refer to subroutine code that's brought into the main code, eliminating a call, a technique we discussed in the previous section. I'm going to use the phrase *in-line code* only to refer to code that's repeated by assembling multiple instances and running them back-to-back rather than in a loop.)

Listing 13-20 shows in-line code used to speed up Listing 13-19. The **loop** instruction is gone, replaced with a **rept** directive that creates 100 back-to-back instances of the code inside the loop of Listing 13-19. The performance improvement is dramatic: Listing 13-20 runs in 557 μsec, more than 83 percent faster than Listing 13-19.

Often-enormous improvement in performance is the good news about in-line code. Often-enormous increase in code size—depending on the number of repetitions and the amount of code in the loop—is the bad news. Listing 13-20 is nearly 300 bytes larger than Listing 13-19. On the other hand, we're talking about nearly doubling performance by adding those extra bytes. Yes, once again we've encountered the trade-off between bytes and cycles that pops up so often when we set out to improve performance: in-line code can be used to speed up just about any loop, but

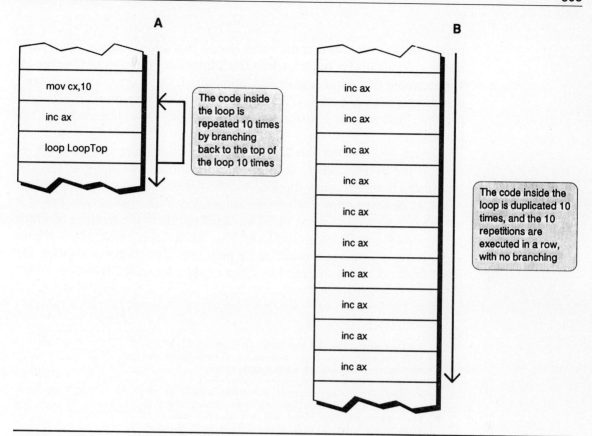

FIGURE 13.10   In-line code reproduces the functionality of loops without branching. This is accomplished by literally assembling the instructions inside a given loop however many times the loop repeats, then executing all of the multiple instances of the code one after another. **(A)** A loop that repeats 10 times. **(B)** An in-line version of that loop.

the cost in bytes ranges from modest to prohibitive. Still, when you need flat-out performance, in-line code is a tried and true way to get a sizable performance boost.

In-line code has another benefit beside eliminating branching. When in-line code is used, CX (or whatever register would otherwise have been used as a loop counter) is freed up. An extra 16-bit register is always welcome in high-performance code.

You may well object at this point that in-line code is fine when the number of repetitions of a loop is known in advance and is always the same, but how often is that the case? Not all that often, I admit, but it does happen. For example, think back to our animation examples in Chapter 11. The example that used **xor**-based animation looped once for each word **xor**ed into display memory, and always drew the same number of words per line. That sounds like an excellent candidate for in-line code, and in fact it is.

Listing 13-21 shows the **XorImage** subroutine from Listing 11-33 revised to use in-line code to draw each line without branching. Instead, the four instructions that draw the four words of the image are duplicated four times, in order to draw a whole line at a time. This frees up not only CX but also BP, which in Listing 11-33 was used to reload the number of words per line each time through the loop. That has a ripple effect which lets us avoid using BX, saving a **push** and a **pop**, and also allows us to store the offset from odd lines to even lines in a register for added speed.

```
 1     ;
 2     ; *** Listing 13-21 ***
 3     ;
 4     ; Replacement code for XorImage in Listing 11-33.
 5     ; This version uses in-line code to eliminate branching
 6     ; during the drawing of each image line.
 7     ;-------------------------------------------------------------
 8     ; Exclusive-ors the image of a 3-color square at the
 9     ; specified screen location. Assumes images start on
10     ; even-numbered scan lines and are an even number of
11     ; scan lines high. Always draws images byte-aligned in
12     ; display memory.
13     ;
14     ; Input:
15     ;       CX = X coordinate of upper left corner at which to
16     ;            draw image (will be adjusted to nearest
17     ;            less-than or equal-to multiple of 4 in order
18     ;            to byte-align)
19     ;       DX = Y coordinate of upper left corner at which to
20     ;            draw image
21     ;       ES = display memory segment
22     ;
23     ; Output: none
24     ;
25     ; Registers altered: AX, CX, DX, SI, DI, BP
26     ;
27     XorImage:
28             shr     dx,1    ;divide the row # by 2 to compensate
29                             ; for the 2-bank nature of 320x200
30                             ; 4-color mode
31             mov     ax,SCREEN_WIDTH
32             mul     dx      ;start offset of top row of image in
33                             ; display memory
34             shr     cx,1    ;divide the X coordinate by 4
35             shr     cx,1    ; because there are 4 pixels per
36                             ; byte
37             add     ax,cx   ;point to the offset at which the
```

```
38                        ; upper left byte of the image will
39                        ; go
40      mov     di,ax
41      mov     si,offset TheImage
42                        ;point to the start of the one image
43                        ; we always draw
44      mov     dx,BANK_OFFSET-IMAGE_WIDTH
45                        ;offset from the end of an even line
46                        ; of the image in display memory to
47                        ; the start of the next odd line of
48                        ; the image
49      mov     bp,BANK_OFFSET-SCREEN_WIDTH+IMAGE_WIDTH
50                        ;offset from the end of an odd line
51                        ; of the image in display memory to
52                        ; the start of the next even line of
53                        ; the image
54      mov     cx,IMAGE_HEIGHT/2
55                        ;# of even/odd numbered row pairs to
56                        ;  draw in the image
57  XorRowLoop:
58      rept    IMAGE_WIDTH/2
59      lodsw             ;next word of the image pattern
60      xor     es:[di],ax      ;XOR the next word of the
61                        ; image into the screen
62      inc     di      ;point to the next word in display
63      inc     di      ; memory
64      endm
65      add     di,dx   ;point to the start of the next
66                        ; (odd) row of the image, which is
67                        ; in the second bank of display
68                        ; memory
69      rept    IMAGE_WIDTH/2
70      lodsw             ;next word of the image pattern
71      xor     es:[di],ax      ;XOR the next word of the
72                        ; image into the screen
73      inc     di      ;point to the next word in display
74      inc     di      ; memory
75      endm
76      sub     di,bp   ;point to the start of the next
77                        ; (even) row of the image, which is
78                        ; in the first bank of display
79                        ; memory
80      loop    XorRowLoop      ;count down the row pairs
81      ret
```

The net effect of the in-line code in Listing 13-21 is far from trivial. When this version of **XorImage** is substituted for the version in Listing 11-33, execution time drops from 30.29 seconds to 24.21 seconds, a 25 percent improvement in overall performance. Put another way, the **loop** instructions in the two loops that draw the even and odd lines in Listing 11-33 take up about 1 out of every 5 cycles that the entire program uses! Bear in mind that we're not talking now about a program that zeros the high bits of bytes in three-instruction loops; we're talking about a program that performs complex animation and accesses display memory heavily . . .

in other words, a program that does many time-consuming things besides looping.

To drive the point home, let's modify Listing 11-34 to use in-line code, as well. Listing 11-34 uses **rep movsw** to draw each line, so there are no branches to get rid of during line drawing, and consequently no way to put in-line code to work there. There is, however, a loop that's used to repeat the drawing of each pair of rows in the image. That's not *nearly* so intensive a loop as the line-drawing loop was in Listing 11-33; instead of being repeated once for every word that's drawn, it's repeated just once every two lines, or 10 words.

Nonetheless, when the in-line version of **BlockDrawImage** shown in Listing 13-22 is substituted for the version in Listing 11-34, overall execution time drops from 10.35 seconds to 9.69 seconds, an improvement of nearly 7 percent. Not earth shaking—but in demanding applications such as animation, where every cycle counts, it's certainly worth expending a few hundred extra bytes to get that extra speed.

```
1    ;
2    ; *** Listing 13-22 ***
3    ;
4    ; Replacement code for BlockDrawImage in Listing 11-34.
5    ; This version uses in-line code to eliminate branching
6    ; entirely during the drawing of each image (eliminates
7    ; the branching between the drawing of each pair of lines.)
8    ;-----------------------------------------------------------
9    ; Block-move draws the image of a 3-color square at the
10   ; specified screen location. Assumes images start on
11   ; even-numbered scan lines and are an even number of
12   ; scan lines high. Always draws images byte-aligned in
13   ; display memory.
14   ;
15   ; Input:
16   ;       CX = X coordinate of upper left corner at which to
17   ;            draw image (will be adjusted to nearest
18   ;            less-than or equal-to multiple of 4 in order
19   ;            to byte-align)
20   ;       DX = Y coordinate of upper left corner at which to
21   ;            draw image
22   ;       ES = display memory segment
23   ;
24   ; Output: none
25   ;
26   ; Registers altered: AX, CX, DX, SI, DI, BP
27   ;
28   BlockDrawImage:
29           shr     dx,1    ;divide the row # by 2 to compensate
30                           ; for the 2-bank nature of 320x200
31                           ; 4-color mode
32           mov     ax,SCREEN_WIDTH
33           mul     dx      ;start offset of top row of image in
34                           ; display memory
35           shr     cx,1    ;divide the X coordinate by 4
```

```
36          shr     cx,1      ; because there are 4 pixels per
37                            ; byte
38          add     ax,cx     ;point to the offset at which the
39                            ; upper left byte of the image will
40                            ; go
41          mov     di,ax
42          mov     si,offset TheImage
43                            ;point to the start of the one image
44                            ; we always draw
45          mov     ax,BANK_OFFSET-SCREEN_WIDTH+IMAGE_WIDTH
46                            ;offset from the end of an odd line
47                            ; of the image in display memory to
48                            ; the start of the next even line of
49                            ; the image
50          mov     dx,BANK_OFFSET-IMAGE_WIDTH
51                            ;offset from the end of an even line
52                            ; of the image in display memory to
53                            ; the start of the next odd line of
54                            ; the image
55          mov     bp,IMAGE_WIDTH/2
56                            ;# of words to draw per row of the
57                            ; image. Note that IMAGE_WIDTH must
58                            ; be an even number since we XOR
59                            ; the image a word at a time
60          rept    IMAGE_HEIGHT/2
61          mov     cx,bp     ;# of words to draw per row of the
62                            ; image
63          rep     movsw     ;draw a whole even row with this one
64                            ; repeated instruction
65          add     di,dx     ;point to the start of the next
66                            ; (odd) row of the image, which is
67                            ; in the second bank of display
68                            ; memory
69          mov     cx,bp     ;# of words to draw per row of the
70                            ; image
71          rep     movsw     ;draw a whole odd row with this one
72                            ; repeated instruction
73          sub     di,ax
74                            ;point to the start of the next
75                            ; (even) row of the image, which is
76                            ; in the first bank of display
77                            ; memory
78          endm
79          ret
```

The 7-percent improvement we got with Listing 13-22 is more impressive when you consider that the bulk of the work in Listing 11-34 is done with **rep movsw**. If you take a moment to contemplate the knowledge that 7 percent of overall execution time in Listing 11-34 is used by just 20 **dec dx**/**jnz** pairs per image draw (and remember that cycle-eating display memory is accessed 400 times for every 20 **dec dx**/**jnz** pairs executed), you'll probably reach the conclusion that **loop** really isn't a very good instruction for high-performance looping.

And you'll be right.

Branched-to In-Line Code: Flexibility Needed and Found

What we've just seen is "pure" in-line code, where a loop that's always repeated a fixed number of times is converted to in-line code by simply repeating the contents of the loop however many times the loop was repeated. The above animation examples notwithstanding, pure in-line code isn't used very often. Why? Because loops rarely repeat a fixed number of times, and pure in-line code isn't flexible enough to handle a variable number of repetitions. With pure in-line code, if you put five repetitions of a loop in-line, you'll always get five repetitions, no more and no less. Most looping applications demand more flexibility than that.

As it turns out, however, it's no great trick to modify pure in-line code to replace loops that repeat a variable number of times, so long as you know the maximum number of times you'll ever want to repeat the loop. The basic concept is shown in Figure 13.11. The loop code is repeated in line as many times as the maximum possible number of loop repetitions. Then the specified repetition count is used to jump right into the in-line code at the distance from the end of the in-line code that will produce the desired number of repetitions. This mechanism, known as *branched-to in-line code,* is almost startlingly simple, but powerful nonetheless.

Let's convert the in-line code example of Listing 13-20 to use branched-to in-line code. Listing 13-23 shows this implementation. First, in-line code to support up to the maximum possible number of repetitions (in this case, 200) is created with **rept**. Then the start offset in the in-line code that will result in the desired number of repetitions is calculated by multiplying the number of instruction bytes per repetition by the desired number of repetitions and subtracting the result from the offset of the end of the table. As a result, Listing 13-23 can handle any number of repetitions between 0 and 200, and does so with just one branch, the **jmp cx** that branches into the in-line code.

The performance price for the flexibility of Listing 13-23 is small; the code runs in 584 μsec, just 27 μsec slower than Listing 13-20. Moreover, Listing 13-23 could be speeded up a little by multiplying by 3 with a shift-and-add sequence rather than the notoriously slow **mul** instruction; I used **mul** in order to illustrate the general case and because I didn't want to obscure the workings of branched-to in-line code.

Branched-to in-line code retains almost all of the performance advantages of in-line code without the inflexibility. Branched-to in-line code does everything **loop** does, and does it without branching inside the loop. Branched-to in-line code is sort of the poor man's **rep**, capable of repeating

A

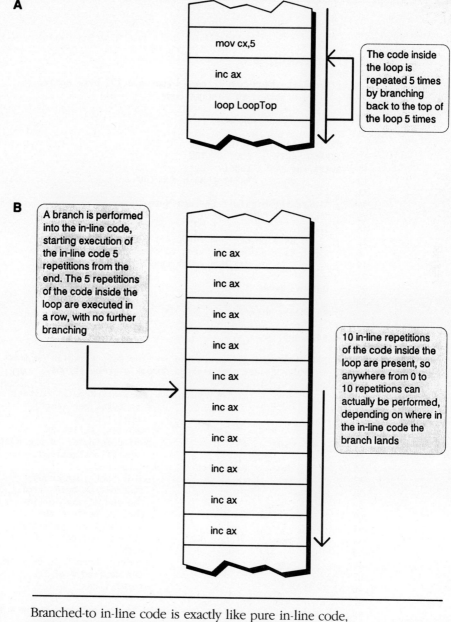

mov cx,5

inc ax

loop LoopTop

The code inside the loop is repeated 5 times by branching back to the top of the loop 5 times

B

A branch is performed into the in-line code, starting execution of the in-line code 5 repetitions from the end. The 5 repetitions of the code inside the loop are executed in a row, with no further branching

inc ax

inc ax

inc ax

inc ax

inc ax

inc ax

inc ax

inc ax

inc ax

inc ax

10 in-line repetitions of the code inside the loop are present, so anywhere from 0 to 10 repetitions can actually be performed, depending on where in the in-line code the branch lands

FIGURE 13.11   Branched-to in-line code is exactly like pure in-line code, except that the in-line code is not necessarily executed starting at the first in-line instruction. Instead, the in-line code is branched into at whatever location produces the desired number of repetitions. As a result, branched-to in-line code can handle variable repetition counts, unlike pure in-line code. **(A)** A loop that repeats five times. **(B)** A branched-to in-line version of that loop that repeats five times and is capable of handling up to 10 repetitions.

```
1    ;
2    ; *** Listing 13-23 ***
3    ;
4    ; Zeros the high-bit of each byte in a 100-byte array,
5    ; using branched-to in-line code.
6    ;
7            jmp     Skip
8    ;
9    MAXIMUM_ARRAY_LENGTH    equ     200
10   ARRAY_LENGTH   equ     100
11   ByteArray      label   byte
12           db      ARRAY_LENGTH dup (80h)
13   ;
14   ; Clears the high bit of each byte in an array.
15   ;
16   ; Input:
17   ;       BX = pointer to the start of the array to clear
18   ;       CX = number of bytes to clear (no greater than
19   ;               MAXIMUM_ARRAY_LENGTH)
20   ;
21   ; Output: none
22   ;
23   ; Registers altered: AX, BX, CX
24   ;
25   ClearHighBits:
26   ;
27   ; Calculate the offset in the in-line code to which to jump
28   ; in order to get the desired number of repetitions.
29   ;
30           mov     al,InLineBitClearEnd-SingleRepetitionStart
31                                   ;# of bytes per single
32                                   ; repetition of
33                                   ; AND [BX],AL/INC BX
34           mul     cl              ;# of code bytes in the # of
35                                   ; repetitions desired
36           mov     cx,offset InLineBitClearEnd
37           sub     cx,ax           ;point back just enough
38                                   ; instruction bytes from
39                                   ; the end of the in-line
40                                   ; code to perform the
41                                   ; desired # of repetitions
42           mov     al,not 80h      ;pattern to clear high bits
43                                   ; with
44           jmp     cx              ;finally, branch to perform
45                                   ; the desired # of
46                                   ; repetitions
47   ;
48   ; In-line code to clear the high bits of up to the maximum #
49   ; of bytes.
50   ;
51           rept    MAXIMUM_ARRAY_LENGTH-1
52                                   ;maximum # of bytes to clear
53                                   ; less 1
54           and     [bx],al         ;clear the high bit of this
55                                   ; byte
56           inc     bx              ;point to the next byte
57           endm
58   SingleRepetitionStart:          ;a single repetition of the
59                                   ; loop code, so we can
```

```
60                                 ; calculate the length of
61                                 ; a single repetition
62           and      [bx],dl      ;clear the high bit of this
63                                 ; byte
64           inc      bx           ;point to the next byte
65    InLineBitClearEnd:
66           ret
67    ;
68    Skip:
69           call     ZTimerOn
70           mov      bx,offset ByteArray
71                                 ;array in which to clear
72                                 ; high bits
73           mov      cx,ARRAY_LENGTH ;# of bytes to clear
74                                 ; (always less than
75                                 ; MAXIMUM_ARRAY_LENGTH)
76           call     ClearHighBits ;clear the high bits of the
77                                 ; bytes
78           call     ZTimerOff
```

any instruction or sequence of instructions without branching, just as **rep** does for string instructions. It's true that branched-to in-line code doesn't really eliminate the prefetch queue cycle eater as **rep** does, because each instruction byte in branched-to in-line code must still be fetched. On the other hand, it's also true that branched-to in-line code eliminates the constant prefetch queue flushing of **loop**, and that's all to the good.

In short, branched-to in-line code allows repetitive processing based on nonstring instructions to approach its performance limits on the 8088 by eliminating branching, thereby doing away with not only the time required to branch but also the nasty prefetch queue effects of branching. When you need flat-out speed for repetitive tasks, branched-to in-line code is often a good bet.

That's not to say that branched-to in-line code is perfect. The hitch is that you must allow for the maximum number of repetitions when setting up branched-to in-line code. If you're performing checksums on data blocks no larger than 64 bytes, the maximum size is no problem, but if you're working with large arrays, the maximum size can easily be either unknown or so large that the resulting in-line code would simply be too large to use. For example, the in-line code in Listing 13-23 is 600 bytes long, and would swell to 60,000 bytes long if the maximum number of repetitions were 20,000 rather than 200. In-line code can also become too large to be practical after just a few repetitions if the code to be repeated is lengthy. Finally, lengthy branched-to in-line code isn't well-suited for tasks such as scanning arrays, because the in-line code can easily be too long to allow the 1-byte displacements of conditional jumps to branch out of the in-line code when a match is found.

Clearly, branched-to in-line code is not the ideal solution for all situations. Branched-to in-line code is great if both the maximum number of repetitions and the code to be repeated are small, or if performance is so important that you're willing to expend a great many bytes to speed up your code. For applications that don't fit within those parameters, however, a still more flexible in-line solution is needed.

Which brings us to partial in-line code.

Partial In-Line Code

Partial in-line code is a hybrid of normal looping and pure in-line code. Partial in-line code performs a few repetitions back-to-back without branching, as in-line code does, and then loops. As such, partial in-line code offers much of the performance improvement of in-line code and much of the compactness of normal loops. Although partial in-line code isn't as fast as pure or branched-to in-line code, it's still fast, and because it's relatively compact, it overcomes most of the size-related objections to in-line code.

Let's go back to our familiar example of zeroing the high bit of each byte in an array to see partial in-line code in action. In Listing 13-19 we saw this example implemented with a loop; in Listing 13-20 we saw it implemented with pure in-line code; and in Listing 13-23 we saw it implemented with branched-to in-line code. Listing 13-24 shows yet another version, this time using partial in-line code.

The key to Listing 13-24 is that is performs four in-line bit clears, then loops. This means that Listing 13-24 loops just once for every 4 bits cleared. Although Listing 13-24 still branches 25 times, that's 75 times fewer than the loop-only version, Listing 13-19, certainly a vast improvement. And while the **ClearHighBits** subroutine is 13 bytes larger in Listing 13-24 than in Listing 13-19, it's nearly 300 bytes smaller than in the pure in-line version, Listing 13-20. If Listing 13-24 can run anywhere near as fast as Listing 13-20, it'll be a winner.

```
1    ;
2    ; *** Listing 13-24 ***
3    ;
4    ; Zeros the high-bit of each byte in a 100-byte array,
5    ; using partial in-line code.
6    ;
7            jmp     Skip
8    ;
9    ARRAY_LENGTH    equ     100
10   ByteArray       label   byte
11           db      ARRAY_LENGTH dup (80h)
12   ;
13   ; Clears the high bit of each byte in an array.
```

```
14      ;
15      ; Input:
16      ;         BX = pointer to the start of the array to clear
17      ;         CX = number of bytes to clear (must be a multiple
18      ;              of 4)
19      ;
20      ; Output: none
21      ;
22      ; Registers altered: AL, BX, CX
23      ;
24      ClearHighBits:
25              mov     al,not 80h              ;pattern to clear
26                                              ; high bits with
27              shr     cx,1                    ;# of passes through
28              shr     cx,1                    ; partial in-line
29                                              ; loop, which does
30                                              ; 4 bytes at a pop
31      ClearHighBitsLoop:
32              rept    4                       ;we'll put 4 bit-
33                                              ; clears back to
34                                              ; back, then loop
35              and     [bx],al                 ;clear the high bit
36                                              ; of this byte
37              inc     bx                      ;point to the next
38                                              ; byte
39              endm
40              loop    ClearHighBitsLoop
41              ret
42      ;
43      Skip:
44              call    ZTimerOn
45              mov     bx,offset ByteArray
46                                      ;array in which to clear
47                                      ; high bits
48              mov     cx,ARRAY_LENGTH ;# of bytes to clear
49                                      ; (always a multiple of 4)
50              call    ClearHighBits   ;clear the high bits of the
51                                      ; bytes
52              call    ZTimerOff
```

Listing 13-24 is indeed a winner, running in 688 μsec. That's certainly slower than pure in-line code—Listing 13-20 is about 24 percent faster—but it's a whole lot faster than pure looping. Listing 13-24 outperforms Listing 13-19 by close to 50 percent—*at a cost of just 13 bytes.* That's a terrific return for the extra bytes expended, proportionally much better than the 83 percent improvement Listing 13-20 brings at a cost of 295 bytes. To put it another way, in this example the performance improvement of partial in-line code over pure looping is about 49 percent, at a cost of 13 bytes, whereas the improvement of pure in-line code over partial in-line code is only 24 percent, at a cost of 282 bytes.

If you need absolute maximum speed, in-line code is the ticket, but partial in-line code offers similar performance improvements in a far more generally usable form. If size is your driving concern, then **loop** is the way to go.

As always, no one approach is perfect in all situations. The three approaches to handling repetitive code that we've discussed—in-line code, partial in-line code, and looping—give you a solid set of tools to use for handling repetitive tasks, but it's up to you to evaluate the tradeoffs between performance, size, and program complexity and select the proper techniques for your particular applications. There are no easy answers in top-notch assembler programming, but at least now you have a set of tools with which to craft good solutions.

There are many, many ways to use in-line code. We've seen some already, we'll see more over the remainder of this chapter, and you'll surely discover others yourself. Whenever you must loop in time-critical code, take a moment to see whether you can't use in-line code in one of its many forms instead.

The rewards can be rich indeed.

Partial In-Line Code: Limitations and Workarounds

The partial in-line code implementation in Listing 13-24 is somewhat but not much more flexible than the pure in-line code implementation in Listing 13-20. The partial in-line code in Listing 13-24 is capable of handling only repetition counts that happen to be multiples of four, since four repetitions are performed each time through the loop. That's fine for repetitive tasks that always involve repetition counts that happen to be multiples of four; unfortunately, such tasks are the exception rather than the rule. In order to be generally useful, partial in-line code must be able to support *any* number of repetitions.

As it turns out, that's not a problem. The flexibility of branched-to in-line code can easily be coupled with the compact size of partial in-line code. As an example, let's modify the branched-to in-line code of Listing 13-23 to use partial in-line code.

The basic principle when branching into partial in-line code is similar to that for standard branched-to in-line code. The key is still to branch to the location in the in-line code from which the desired number of repetitions will occur. The difference with branched-to partial in-line code is that the branching-to process needs to handle only any odd repetitions that can't be handled by a full loop, as shown in Figure 13.12. In other words, if partial in-line code performs n repetitions per loop and we want to perform m repetitions, the branching-to process needs to handle only m modulo n repetitions.

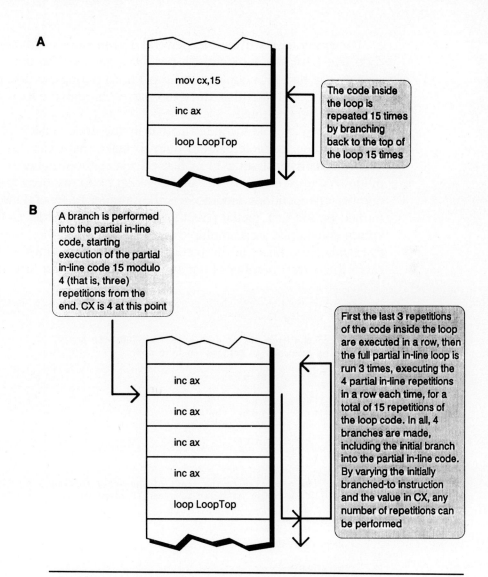

A

mov cx,15

inc ax

loop LoopTop

> The code inside the loop is repeated 15 times by branching back to the top of the loop 15 times

B

> A branch is performed into the partial in-line code, starting execution of the partial in-line code 15 modulo 4 (that is, three) repetitions from the end. CX is 4 at this point

inc ax

inc ax

inc ax

inc ax

loop LoopTop

> First the last 3 repetitions of the code inside the loop are executed in a row, then the full partial in-line loop is run 3 times, executing the 4 partial in-line repetitions in a row each time, for a total of 15 repetitions of the loop code. In all, 4 branches are made, including the initial branch into the partial in-line code. By varying the initially branched-to instruction and the value in CX, any number of repetitions can be performed

FIGURE 13.12   Branched-to partial in-line code can handle any number of repetitions. The trick with branched-to partial in-line code is that any odd portion of the desired repetition count—any portion that is not an even multiple of the number of repetitions per partial in-line loop—is handled by initially branching to perform that odd number of repetitions. All succeeding repetitions are handled by full passes through the partial in-line loop. **(A)** A loop that repeats 15 times. **(B)** A branched-to partial in-line version of that loop.

For example, if we want to perform 15 repetitions with partial in-line code that performs 4 repetitions per loop, we need to branch so as to perform the first 15 modulo 4 = 3 repetitions during the first, partial pass through the loop. After that, three full passes through the loop will handle the other 12 repetitions.

Listing 13-25, a branched-to partial in-line code version of our familiar bit-clearing example, should help to make this clear. The version of **ClearHighBits** in Listing 13-25 first calculates the number of repetitions modulo 4. Since each pass through the loop performs four repetitions, the number of repetitions modulo 4 is the number of repetitions to be performed on the first, partial pass through the loop in order to handle repetition counts that aren't multiples of 4. Listing 13-25 then uses this value to calculate the offset in the partial in-line code to branch to in order to cause the correct number of repetitions to occur on that first pass.

```
 1     ;
 2     ; *** Listing 13-25 ***
 3     ;
 4     ; Zeros the high-bit of each byte in a 100-byte array,
 5     ; using branched-to partial in-line code.
 6     ;
 7             jmp     Skip
 8     ;
 9     ARRAY_LENGTH    equ     100
10     ByteArray       label   byte
11             db      ARRAY_LENGTH dup (80h)
12     ;
13     ; Clears the high bit of each byte in an array.
14     ;
15     ; Input:
16     ;       BX = pointer to the start of the array to clear
17     ;       CX = number of bytes to clear (0 means 0)
18     ;
19     ; Output: none
20     ;
21     ; Registers altered: AX, BX, CX, DX
22     ;
23     ClearHighBits:
24     ;
25     ; Calculate the offset in the partial in-line code to which
26     ; to jump in order to perform CX modulo 4 repetitions (the
27     ; remaining repetitions will be handled by full passes
28     ; through the loop).
29     ;
30             mov     ax,cx
31             and     ax,3            ;# of repetitions modulo 4
32             mov     dx,ax
33             shl     ax,1
34             add     ax,dx           ;(# of reps modulo 4) * 3
35                                     ; is the # of bytes from the
36                                     ; the end of the partial
37                                     ; in-line code to branch to
```

```
38                                   ; in order to handle the
39                                   ; # of repetitions that
40                                   ; can't be handled in a full
41                                   ; loop
42              mov     dx,offset InLineBitClearEnd
43              sub     dx,ax         ;point back just enough
44                                   ; instruction bytes from
45                                   ; the end of the in-line
46                                   ; code to perform the
47                                   ; desired # of repetitions
48              shr     cx,1          ;divide by 4, since we'll do
49              shr     cx,1          ; 4 repetitions per loop
50              inc     cx            ;account for the first,
51                                   ; partial pass through the
52                                   ; loop
53              mov     al,not 80h    ;pattern to clear high bits
54                                   ; with
55              jmp     dx            ;finally, branch to perform
56                                   ; the desired # of
57                                   ; repetitions
58      ;
59      ; Partial in-line code to clear the high bits of 4 bytes per
60      ; pass through the loop.
61      ;
62      ClearHighBitsLoop:
63              rept    4
64              and     [bx],al       ;clear the high bit of this
65                                   ; byte
66              inc     bx            ;point to the next byte
67              endm
68      InLineBitClearEnd:
69              loop    ClearHighBitsLoop
70              ret
71      ;
72      Skip:
73              call    ZTimerOn
74              mov     bx,offset ByteArray
75                                   ;array in which to clear
76                                   ; high bits
77              mov     cx,ARRAY_LENGTH ;# of bytes to clear
78                                   ; (always less than
79                                   ; MAXIMUM_ARRAY_LENGTH)
80              call    ClearHighBits ;clear the high bits of the
81                                   ; bytes
82              call    ZTimerOff
```

Incidentally, multiplication by 3 in Listing 13-25 is performed not with **mul** but with a much faster shift-and-add sequence. As we mentioned earlier, the same could have been done in Listing 13-23, but **mul** was used there in order to handle the general case and avoid obscuring the mechanics of the branching-to process. In the next chapter we'll see a jump table–based approach that does away with the calculation of the target offset in the in-line code entirely, in favor of simply looking up the target address.

Next, Listing 13-25 divides the repetition count by 4, because four repetitions are performed each time through the loop. That value must then be incremented to account for the first pass through the loop—and that's it! All we need do is branch to the correct location in the partial in-line code and let it rip. And rip it does, running in just 713 μsec. Yes, that is indeed considerably slower than the 584-μsec time of the branched-to in-line code of Listing 13-23, but it's much faster than the 1023 μsec of Listing 13-19. Then, too, Listing 13-25 is only 32 bytes larger than Listing 13-19; in contrast, Listing 13-23 is more than 600 bytes larger.

Listing 13-25, the branched-to partial in-line code, has an additional advantage over Listing 13-23, the branched-to in-line code, and that's the ability to handle an array of *any* size up to 64 K—1. With in-line code, the largest number of repetitions that can be handled is determined by the number of times the code is physically repeated. Partial in-line code suffers from no such restriction, since it loops periodically. In fact, branched-to partial in-line code implementations can handle any case normal loops can handle, tend to be only a little larger, and are much faster for all but very small repetition counts.

Listing 13-25 itself isn't *quite* equivalent to a **loop**-based loop. Given an initial count of 0, **loop** performs 64 K repetitions, while Listing 13-25 performs 0 repetitions in the same case. That's not necessarily a disadvantage; **loop**-based loops are often preceded with **jcxz** in order to cause counts of 0 to produce 0 repetitions. However, Listing 13-25 can easily be modified to treat an initial count of 0 as 64 K; I chose to perform 0 repetitions given a 0 count in Listing 13-25 only because it made for code that was easier to explain and understand. Listing 13-26 shows the **ClearHighBits** subroutine of Listing 13-25 modified to perform 64 K repetitions given an initial count of 0.

```
1    ;
2    ; *** Listing 13-26 ***
3    ;
4    ; Replacement code for ClearHighBits in Listing 13-25.
5    ; This version performs 64K rather than 0 repetitions
6    ; when CX is 0.
7    ;-------------------------------------------------------------
8    ; Clears the high bit of each byte in an array.
9    ;
10   ; Input:
11   ;       BX = pointer to the start of the array to clear
12   ;       CX = number of bytes to clear (0 means 64K)
13   ;
14   ; Output: none
15   ;
16   ; Registers altered: AX, BX, CX, DX
17   ;
18   ClearHighBits:
```

```
19      ;
20      ; Calculate the offset in the partial in-line code to which
21      ; to jump in order to perform CX modulo 4 repetitions (the
22      ; remaining repetitions will be handled by full passes
23      ; through the loop).
24      ;
25              dec     cx              ;# of reps - 1, since 1 to 4
26                                      ; (rather than 0 to 3) repetitions
27                                      ; are performed on the first,
28                                      ; possibly partial pass through
29                                      ; the loop
30
31              mov     ax,cx
32              and     ax,3            ;# of repetitions modulo 4
33              inc     ax              ;(# of reps modulo 4)+1 in order to
34                                      ; perform 1 to 4 repetitions on the
35                                      ; first, possibly partial pass
36                                      ; through the loop
37              mov     dx,ax
38              shl     ax,1
39              add     ax,dx           ;(((# of reps - 1) modulo 4)+1)*3
40                                      ; is the # of bytes from the
41                                      ; the end of the partial
42                                      ; in-line code to branch to
43                                      ; in order to handle the
44                                      ; # of repetitions that
45                                      ; must be handled in the
46                                      ; first, possibly partial
47                                      ; loop
48              mov     dx,offset InLineBitClearEnd
49              sub     dx,ax           ;point back just enough
50                                      ; instruction bytes from
51                                      ; the end of the in-line
52                                      ; code to perform the
53                                      ; desired # of repetitions
54              shr     cx,1            ;divide by 4, since we'll do
55              shr     cx,1            ; 4 repetitions per loop
56              inc     cx              ;account for the first,
57                                      ; possibly partial pass
58                                      ; through the loop
59              mov     al,not 80h      ;pattern with which to clear
60                                      ; high bits
61
62              jmp     dx              ;finally, branch to perform
63                                      ; the desired # of repetitions
64      ;
65      ; Partial in-line code to clear the high bits of 4 bytes per
66      ; pass through the loop.
67      ;
68      ClearHighBitsLoop:
69              rept    4
70              and     [bx],al         ;clear the high bit of this
71                                      ; byte
72              inc     bx              ;point to the next byte
73              endm
74      InLineBitClearEnd:
75              loop    ClearHighBitsLoop
76              ret
```

It's worth noting that the **inc ax** in Listing 13-26 could be eliminated if the line

```
mov   dx,offset InLineBitClearEnd
```

were changed to

```
mov   dx,offset InLineBitClearEnd-3
```

This change has no effect on overall functionality, because the net effect of **inc ax** in Listing 13-26 is merely to subtract 3 from the offset of the end of the partial in-line code. I omitted this optimization in the interests of making Listing 13-26 comprehensible, but as a general practice arithmetic should be performed at assembly time rather than at run time whenever possible.

By the way, there's nothing special about using 4 repetitions in partial in-line code. Eight, or even 16, repetitions could serve as well, and, in fact, speed increases as the number of partial in-line repetitions increases. However, size increases proportionately as well, offsetting part of the advantage of using partial in-line code. Partial in-line code using four repetitions strikes a nice balance between size and speed, eliminating 75 percent of the branches without adding too many instruction bytes.

Partial In-Line Code and Strings: A Good Match

One case in which the poor repetition granularity of non-branched-to partial in-line code (that is, the inability of such partial in-line loops to deal unaided with repetition counts that aren't exact multiples of the number of repetitions per partial in-line loop) causes no trouble at all is in handling 0-terminated strings. As there is no preset repetition count for processing such strings, it doesn't matter in the least that the lengths of the strings won't always be multiples of the number of repetitions in a single partial in-line loop. When handling 0-terminated strings, it doesn't matter if the terminating condition occurs at the start of partial in-line code, at the end, or somewhere between, because a conditional jump will branch out equally well from anywhere in partial in-line code. As a result, there's no need to branch into partial in-line code when handling 0-terminated strings.

As usual, an example is the best explanation. Back in Listing 11-25, we used **lodsw** and **scasw** inside a loop to find the first difference between two 0-terminated strings. We used word- rather than byte-sized string instructions to speed processing; interestingly, much of the improvement came not from accessing memory a word at a time but from cutting the number of loops in half, as 2 bytes were processed per loop. We're going to use partial in-line code to speed up Listing 11-25 further by eliminating still more branches.

Listing 13-27 is our partial in-line version of Listing 11-25. I've chosen a repetition granularity of eight repetitions per loop, both for speed and to show you that granularities other than four can be used. There's no need to add code to branch into the partial in-line code, because there's no repetition count for a 0-terminated string. Note that I've separated the eighth repetition of the partial in-line code from the first seven, so that the eighth repetition can jump directly back to the top of the loop if it doesn't find the terminating 0. If I lumped all eight repetitions together in a **rept** block, an unconditional jump would have to follow the partial in-line code in order to branch back to the top of the loop. While that would work, it would result in a conditional jump/unconditional jump pair—and well we know to steer clear of those when we're striving for top performance.

```
1    ;
2    ; *** Listing 13-27 ***
3    ;
4    ; Determines whether two zero-terminated strings differ, and
5    ; if so where, using LODS/SCAS and partial in-line code.
6    ;
7            jmp     Skip
8    ;
9    TestString1     label   byte
10           db      'This is a test string that is '
11           db      'z'
12           db      'terminated with a zero byte...',0
13   TestString2     label   byte
14           db      'This is a test string that is '
15           db      'a'
16           db      'terminated with a zero byte...',0
17   ;
18   ; Compares two zero-terminated strings.
19   ;
20   ; Input:
21   ;       DS:SI = first zero-terminated string
22   ;       ES:DI = second zero-terminated string
23   ;
24   ; Output:
25   ;       DS:SI = pointer to first differing location in
26   ;               first string, or 0 if the byte wasn't found
27   ;       ES:DI = pointer to first differing location in
28   ;               second string, or 0 if the byte wasn't found
29   ;
30   ; Registers altered: AX, SI, DI
31   ;
32   ; Direction flag cleared
33   ;
34   ; Note: Does not handle strings that are longer than 64K
35   ;       bytes or cross segment boundaries.
```

```
36    ;
37    CompareStrings:
38            cld
39    CompareStringsLoop:
40    ;
41    ; First 7 repetitions of partial in-line code.
42    ;
43            rept    7
44            lodsw           ;get the next 2 bytes
45            and     al,al   ;is the first byte the terminating
46                            ; zero?
47            jz      CompareStringsFinalByte
48                            ;yes, so there's only one byte left
49                            ; to check
50            scasw           ;compare this word
51            jnz     CompareStringsDifferent ;the strings differ
52            and     ah,ah   ;is the second byte the terminating
53                            ; zero?
54            jz      CompareStringsSame
55                            ;yes, we've got a match
56            endm
57    ;
58    ; Final repetition of partial in-line code.
59    ;
60            lodsw           ;get the next 2 bytes
61            and     al,al   ;is the first byte the terminating
62                            ; zero?
63            jz      CompareStringsFinalByte
64                            ;yes, so there's only one byte left
65                            ; to check
66            scasw           ;compare this word
67            jnz     CompareStringsDifferent ;the strings differ
68            and     ah,ah   ;is the second byte the terminating
69                            ; zero?
70            jnz     CompareStringsLoop ;no, continue comparing
71                            ;the strings are the same
72    CompareStringsSame:
73            sub     si,si   ;return 0 pointers indicating that
74            mov     di,si   ; the strings are identical
75            ret
76    CompareStringsFinalByte:
77            scasb           ;does the terminating zero match in
78                            ; the 2 strings?
79            jz      CompareStringsSame ;yes, the strings match
80            dec     si      ;point back to the differing byte
81            dec     di      ; in each string
82            ret
83    CompareStringsDifferent:
84                            ;the strings are different, so we
85                            ; have to figure which byte in the
86                            ; word just compared was the first
87                            ; difference
88            dec     si
89            dec     si      ;point back to the first byte of the
90            dec     di      ; differing word in each string
91            dec     di
92            lodsb
93            scasb           ;compare that first byte again
94            jz      CompareStringsDone
```

```
95                                  ;if the first bytes are the same,
96                                  ; then it must have been the second
97                                  ; bytes that differed. That's where
98                                  ; we're pointing, so we're done
99              dec     si          ;the first bytes differed, so point
100             dec     di          ; back to them
101     CompareStringsDone:
102             ret
103     ;
104     Skip:
105             call    ZTimerOn
106             mov     si,offset TestString1 ;point to one string
107             mov     di,seg TestString2
108             mov     es,di
109             mov     di,offset TestString2 ;point to other string
110             call    CompareStrings  ;and compare the strings
111             call    ZTimerOff
```

Listing 13-27 runs in 278 μsec, 10 percent faster than Listing 11-25. Considering how heavily optimized Listing 11-25 already was, what with the use of word-sized string instructions, that's a healthy improvement. What's more, Listing 13-27 isn't markedly more complicated than Listing 11-25; actually, the only difference is that the contents of the loop are repeated eight times rather than once.

As you can see, partial in-line code is ideal for handling 0-terminated strings. Once again, partial in-line code is the poor man's **rep**; in fact, in string and similar applications, you might think of partial in-line code as a substitute for the sorely missed **rep** prefix for the flexible but slow **lods/stos** and **lods/scas** instruction pairs.

Labels and In-Line Code

That just about does it for our discussion of in-line code. However, there's one more in-line code item we need to discuss, and that's the use of labels.

Suppose that for some reason you need to use a label somewhere inside in-line code. For example, consider the following:

```
        rept  4
        lodsb
        cmp  al,'a'
        jb   NotUppercase
        cmp  al,'z'
        ja   NotUppercase
        and  al,not 20h
NotUppercase:
        stosb
        endm
```

In this example, the label **NotUppercase** is inside in-line code used to convert four characters in a row to upper case. Although the code seems simple enough, it nonetheless has one serious problem:

It won't assemble.

Why is that? The problem is that the line defining the label is inside a **rept** block, so it's literally assembled multiple times. As it would at any time, MASM complains when asked to define two labels with the same name.

The solution should be straightforward: declare the label local to the **rept** block with the **local** directive. For example, the following code should do the trick:

```
              rept  4
              local      NotUppercase
              lodsb
              cmp  al,'a'
              jb    NotUppercase
              cmp  al,'z'
              ja    NotUppercase
              and  al,not 20h
NotUppercase:
              stosb
              endm
```

It should, but it doesn't, at least not with MASM 5.0. Although the **local** directive does indeed solve our problem when assembled with TASM, it just doesn't work correctly when assembled with MASM 5.0. There's no use asking why—the bugs and quirks of MASM are just a fact of life in assembler programming.

So, what's the solution to our local label problem when using MASM? One possibility is counting bytes and jumping relative to the program counter, as in

```
rept  4
lodsb
cmp  al,'a'
jb    $+8
cmp  al,'z'
ja    $+4
and  al,not 20h
stosb
endm
```

It's not elegant, but it does work. Another possibility is defining a macro that contains the code in the **rept** block, as **local** *does* work in macros. For example, the following assembles properly under MASM 5.0:

```
MAKE_UPPER      macro
        local       NotUppercase
        lodsb
        cmp     al,'a'
        jb      NotUppercase
        cmp     al,'z'
        ja      NotUppercase
        and     al,not 20h
NotUppercase:
        stosb
        endm
            :
        rept    4
        MAKE_UPPER
        endm
```

13.8 ◆ A Note on Self-Modifying Code

Just so you won't think I've forgotten about it, let's briefly discuss self-modifying code. For those of you who are unfamiliar with this demon of modern programming, self-modifying code is a once popular coding technique whereby a program modifies its own code—changes its own instruction bytes—on the fly in order to alter its operation without the need for tests and branches. (Remember how back in Chapter 3 we learned that code is just one kind of data? Self-modifying code is a logical extension of that concept.) Nowadays, self-modifying code is severely frowned upon, on the grounds that it makes for hard-to-follow, hard-to-debug programs.

"Frowned upon, eh?" you think. "Sounds like fertile ground for a little Zen programming, doesn't it?" Yes, it does. Nonetheless, I *don't* recommend that you use self-modifying code, at least not self-modifying code in the classic sense. Not because it's frowned upon, of course, but rather because I haven't encountered any cases where in-line code, look-up tables, jump vectors, jumping through a register, or some other 8088 technique didn't work just about as well as self-modifying code.

Granted, there may be a small advantage to, say, directly modifying the displacement in a **jmp** instruction rather than jumping to the address stored in a word-sized memory variable, but in-line code really *is* hard to debug and follow—and hard to write, as well (consider the complexities of simply calculating a jump displacement). I haven't seen cases where in-line code brings the sort of significant performance improvement that would justify its drawbacks. That's not to say such cases don't exist; I'm sure they do. I just haven't encountered them.

Self-modifying code has an additional strike against it in the form of the prefetch queue. If you modify an instruction byte after it's been fetched by the bus interface unit (BIU), it's the original, unmodified byte that's executed, since that's the byte that the 8088 read. That's particularly troublesome because the various members of the 8086 family have prefetch queues of different lengths, so self-modifying code that works on the PC might not work at all on an AT or a Model 80. A branch always empties the prefetch queue and forces it to reload, but even that might not be true with future 8086-family processors.

To sum up, my experience is that in the context of the 8086 family, self-modifying code offers at best small performance improvements, coupled with significant risk and other drawbacks. That's not the case with some other processors, especially those with less rich instruction sets and no prefetch queue. However, *The Zen of Assembly Language* is concerned only with the 8086 family, and in that context my final word on self-modifying code of the sort we've been discussing is:

Why bother?

On the other hand, I've been discussing only classic self-modifying code, in which individual instructions are altered. For instance, the operand to **cmp al,*immed8*** might be modified to change an inclusion range; in such a case, why not just use **cmp al,*reg*** and load the new range bound into the appropriate register? It's simpler, easier to follow, and actually slightly faster.

There's another sort of self-modifying code that operates on a grander scale. Consider a program that uses code overlays. Code is swapped in from disk to memory and then executed; obviously the instruction bytes in the overlay region are changed, so that's self-modifying code. Or consider a program that builds custom code for a special, complex purpose in a buffer and then executes the generated code; that's self-modifying code as well. Some programs are built out of loosely coupled, relocatable blocks of code residing in a heap under a memory manager, with the blocks moved around memory and to and from disk as they're needed; that's certainly self-modifying code, in the sense that the instructions stored at particular memory locations change constantly. Finally, loadable drivers, such as graphics drivers for many windowing environments, are self-modifying code of a sort, as they are loaded from the disk into memory and executed by the driver-based program.

My point is that you shouldn't think of code as immovable and unchangeable. I've found that it's not worth the trouble and risk to modify individual instructions, but in large or complex programs it can be most worthwhile to treat blocks of code as if they were data. The topic is a broad one, and this is not the place to explore it, but always keep in mind that even if self-modifying code in its classic sense isn't a great idea on the 8088, the notion that code is just another sort of data is a powerful and perfectly valid one.

Conclusion

Who would have thought that not-branching could offer such variety, to say nothing of such substantial performance improvements? You'll find that not-branching is an excellent exercise for developing your assembler skills, requiring as it does a complete understanding of what your code needs to do, a thorough knowledge of the 8088 instruction set, the ability to approach programming problems in nonintuitive ways, knowledge about when the effort involved in not-branching is justified by the return, and balancing the relative importance of saving bytes and cycles in a given application.

In other words, not-branching is a perfect Zen exercise. Practice it often and well!

Chapter 14

If You Must Branch . . .

14.1	Don't Go Far
14.2	Replacing call and ret with jmp
14.3	Use int Only When You Must
14.4	Forward References Can Waste Time and Space
14.5	Saving Space with Branches
14.6	Double-Duty Tests
14.7	The Looping Instructions
14.8	Only jcxz Can Test *and* Branch in a Single Bound
14.9	Jump and Call Tables
14.10	Forward References Rear Their Collective Ugly Head Once More

Not-branching is a terrific performance tool, but realistically you *are* going to branch—and frequently at that, for the branching instructions are both compact and most useful for making decisions. Do your best to avoid branches in your time-critical code, and when you must branch, do so intelligently. By *intelligently* I mean, among other things, avoiding far branches whenever possible, getting multiple tests out of a single instruction, using the special looping instructions, and using jump tables. We'll look at these and various other cycle- and/or byte-saving branching techniques over the course of this chapter.

This chapter differs from the last few chapters in that it offers no spectacularly better approaches, no massive savings of cycles. Instead, it's a collection of things to steer clear of and tips that save a few cycles and/or bytes. Taken together, the topics in this chapter should give you some new perspectives on writing branching code, along with a few more items for your programming toolkit.

Remember, though, that relatively fast as some of the techniques in this chapter may be, it's still faster not to branch at all!

14.1 ◆ Don't Go Far

Far branches are branches that load both CS and IP, in contrast to near branches, which load only IP. Whatever you do, don't use far branches—jumps, calls, and returns—any more than you absolutely must. Far calls and returns, in particular, tend to bulk up code and slow performance greatly, as the bloated size and sluggish performance of C programs written in the large code model readily attest.

Surprisingly, far jumps—*direct* far jumps, at least—aren't all that bad. A direct far jump—a far jump to a label, such as **jmp far ptr Target**—is big, at 5 bytes, but its execution unit (EU) execution time is exactly the same as that of a near jump to a label—15 cycles. Of course, it can take extra cycles to fetch all 5 bytes, and, as with all branches, the prefetch queue is emptied; still and all, a direct jump isn't much worse than its near counterpart.

The same cannot be said for an indirect far jump—that is, a far jump to the segment:offset address contained in a memory variable, as in **jmp dword ptr [Vector]**. While such an instruction is no larger than its near counterpart—both are 1 byte long plus the usual 1 to 3 bytes of *mod-reg-rm* addressing—it *is* much slower than an indirect near jump, and that's saying a lot. Where an indirect near jump takes at least 27 cycles to execute, an indirect far jump takes at least 37 cycles; that's one reason why jump and call tables that branch to near routines are *much* preferred to those that branch to far routines. (We'll discuss jump and call tables at the end of this chapter.)

Far calls and returns are worse yet. Near returns must pop IP from the stack. Far returns must pop CS as well, and those two additional memory accesses cost at least 8 cycles. In all, far returns execute in 32 cycles, 12 cycles slower than near returns. In itself that's not so bad, especially when you consider that far returns are only 1 byte long, just like near returns.

Now, however, consider that far returns must be paired with far calls. So what, you ask? Simply this: no matter how you slice it, far calls are bad news. The basic problem is that far calls perform a slew of memory accesses. All far calls must push 4 bytes (the CS:IP of the return address) onto the stack: that alone takes 16 cycles. Direct far calls are 5 bytes long, which is likely to cause the prefetch queue to eat more than a few cycles; indirect far calls must read the 4 bytes that point to the destination from memory, at a cost of 16 more cycles. The total bill: direct far calls take 36 cycles and 5 bytes, and indirect far calls take at least 58 cycles.

Fifty-eight cycles—and where there's a far call, there's a far return yet to come. Together, an indirect far call and the corresponding return take at least 90 cycles—as long as or longer than an 8-bit divide! Even a direct far call and the corresponding return together take at least 68 cycles, and very possibly more when you add in the prefetch queue effects of fetching a 5-byte instruction and emptying the prefetch queue twice.

Let's see just how bad far calls are. In the previous chapter, we compared the performance of a subroutine in Listing 13-16 with that of a macro in Listing 13-17. The subroutine in Listing 13-16—**IsPrintable**—is called with a near **call** and returns with a near **ret**. Given that quite a bit besides the **call** and **ret** occurs each time the subroutine is called—including several branches and two memory accesses—how much slower do you suppose overall performance would be if **IsPrintable** were entered and exited with far branches?

Quite a bit, as it turns out. Listing 13-16 ran in 3.48 msec. Listing 14-1, which is identical to Listing 13-16 except that **IsPrintable** is a far procedure, takes 4.32 msec to finish. In other words, the simple substitution of a near **call/ret** for a far **call/ret** results in a 24 percent performance increase.

```
1   ;
2   ; *** Listing 14-1 ***
3   ;
4   ; Copies a zero-terminated string to another string,
5   ; filtering out non-printable characters by means of a
6   ; subroutine that performs the test. The subroutine is
```

```
 7        ; called with a far call and returns with a far return.
 8        ;
 9                  jmp       Skip
10        ;
11        SourceString    label     byte
12                  db        'This is a sample string, consisting of '
13        X=1
14                  rept      31
15                  db        X
16        X=X+1
17                  endm
18                  db        7fh
19                  db        'both printable and non-printable '
20                  db        'characters', 0
21        DestinationString        label     byte
22                  db        200 dup (?)
23        ;
24        ; Determines whether a character is printable (in the range
25        ; 20h through 7Eh).
26        ;
27        ; Input:
28        ;         AL = character to check
29        ;
30        ; Output:
31        ;         Zero flag set to 1 if character is printable,
32        ;                  set to 0 otherwise
33        ;
34        ; Registers altered: none
35        ;
36        IsPrintable     proc      far
37                  cmp       al,20h
38                  jb        IsPrintableDone ;not printable
39                  cmp       al,7eh
40                  ja        IsPrintableDone ;not printable
41                  cmp       al,al     ;set the Zero flag to 1, since the
42                                      ; character is printable
43        IsPrintableDone:
44                  ret
45        IsPrintable     endp
46        ;
47        ; Copies a zero-terminated string to another string,
48        ; filtering out non-printable characters.
49        ;
50        ; Input:
51        ;         DS:SI = source string
52        ;         ES:DI = destination string
53        ;
54        ; Output: none
55        ;
56        ; Registers altered: AL, SI, DI
57        ;
58        ; Direction flag cleared
59        ;
60        ; Note: Does not handle strings that are longer than 64K
61        ;       bytes or cross segment boundaries.
62        ;
63        CopyPrintable:
64                  cld
65        CopyPrintableLoop:
```

```
66              lodsb                   ;get the next byte to copy
67              call    IsPrintable     ;is it printable?
68              jnz     NotPrintable    ;nope, don't copy it
69              stosb                   ;put the byte in the
70                                      ; destination string
71              jmp     CopyPrintableLoop ;the character was
72                                      ; printable, so it couldn't
73                                      ; possibly have been 0. No
74                                      ; need to check whether it
75                                      ; terminated the string
76  NotPrintable:
77              and     al,al           ;was that the
78                                      ; terminating zero?
79              jnz     CopyPrintableLoop ;no, do next byte
80              stosb                   ;copy the terminating zero
81              ret                     ;done
82  ;
83  Skip:
84              call    ZTimerOn
85              mov     di,seg DestinationString
86              mov     es,di
87              mov     di,offset DestinationString
88                      ;ES:DI points to the destination
89              mov     si,offset SourceString
90                      ;DS:SI points to the source
91              call    CopyPrintable   ;copy the printable
92                                      ; characters
93              call    ZTimerOff
```

I don't think I really have to interpret those results for you, but just in case . . .

Don't branch. If you must branch, don't branch far. If you must branch far, don't use far calls and returns unless you absolutely, positively can't help it. (Don't even consider software interrupts; as we'll see later, interrupts make far calls look fast.) Unfortunately, it's easy to fall into using far calls and returns, since that's the obvious way to implement large applications on the PC. High level languages make it particularly easy to fall into the far call trap, because the source code for a large code model program (that is, a program using far calls by default) is no different than that for a small code model program.

Even in assembler, far calls seem fairly harmless at first glance. The Zen timer reveals the truth, however—far calls cost dearly in the performance department. Far calls, whether direct to a label or indirect through a call table (as we'll see later), cost dearly in code size, too.

If you catch my drift: don't use far calls unless you have no choice!

How to Avoid Far Branches

Ideally, all the code in a given program should fit in one 64-Kb segment, eliminating the need for far branching altogether. Even in bigger programs, however, it's often possible to keep most of the branches near.

For example, few programs with more than 64 Kb of code (large code model programs) are written in pure assembler. Usually the bulk of a program is written in C, Pascal, or the like; assembler is used only when speed is of the essence. In such programs all the assembler code often fits in a single 64-Kb segment, and the complete control assembler gives you over segment naming makes it easy to place multiple assembler modules in the same code segment. Once that's done, all branches within the assembler code can be near, even though branches between the high level language code and the assembler code must be far, as shown in Figure 14.1.

Many compilers allow you to specify the segment names used for individual modules, if you so desire. If your compiler supports code segment naming and also supports near procedures in the large code model (as, for example, Turbo C does), you could actually make near calls not only within your assembler code, but also *into* that code from the high level language. The key is giving selected high level language modules and your assembler code identical code segment names, so they'll share a single code segment, then using the **near** keyword to declare the assembler subroutines as near externals in the high level language code.

In fact, you can readily benefit from localized near branching even if you're not using assembler at all. You can use the **near** keyword to declare routines that are referenced only within one high level language module to be near routines, allowing the compiler to generate near rather than far calls to those routines. As noted above, you can even place several modules in the same code segment and use near calls for functions referenced only within those modules that share the same segment.

In short, in the code that really matters you can often enjoy the performance advantage of small code model programming—that is, near branches—even when your program has more than 64 Kb of code and so must use the large code model overall.

Whether you're programming in assembler or a high level language, one great benefit of using near rather than far subroutines is the reduction in the size of jump and call tables that near subroutines make possible. While the address of a near subroutine can be specified as a 1-word table entry, a full doubleword is required to specify the segment and offset of a far subroutine. It doesn't take a genius to figure out that we can cut the size of a jump or call table in half if we can convert the subroutines it branches to from far to near, as shown in Figure 14.2. When we add the space savings of near-branching jump and call tables to the performance advantages of indirect near branches that we explored earlier, we can readily see that it's worth going to a good deal of trouble to use the near-branching variety of jump and call tables whenever possible. We'll return to the topic of jump and call tables at the end of this chapter.

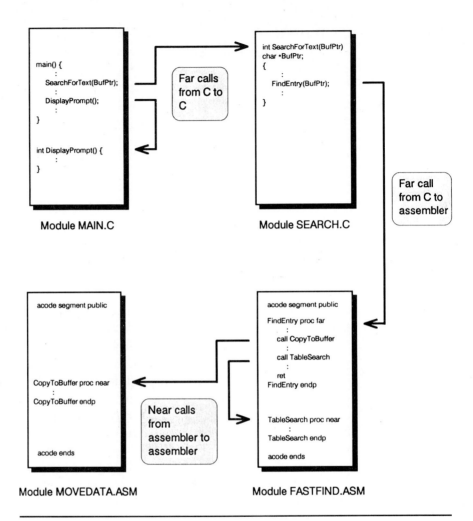

FIGURE 14.1   In large-model programs written primarily in C or Pascal, all the assembler code can be placed in a single segment, allowing near branches to be used within the assembler code even though far branches must be used whenever C or Pascal code is involved.

Odds and Ends on Branching Far

When programming in the large code model, you'll often encounter the case where one assembler subroutine calls another assembler subroutine that resides in the same code segment. Naturally, you'd like to use a near

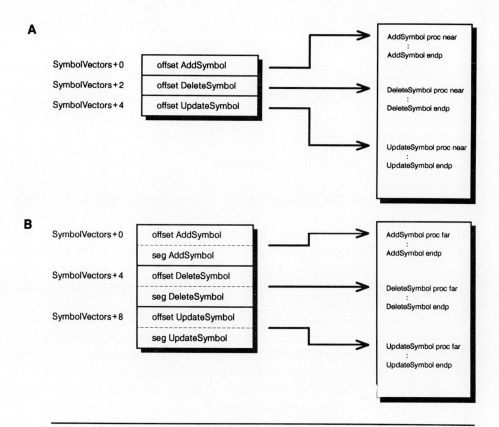

FIGURE 14.2 A jump table that contains the addresses of near subroutines is just half the size of a jump table that contains the
addresses of far subroutines. **(A)** The jump table **SymbolVectors** requires just 2 bytes per entry when used for
near branching. **(B) SymbolVectors** requires 4 bytes per
entry when used for far branching.

rather than far call; unfortunately, if the called subroutine is also called
from outside the module, it may well have to be a far subroutine—that is,
it may return with a far return. That means that a near call can't be used,
because the far return would attempt to pop CS:IP and the near call would
push only IP.

All is not lost, however. You can *fake* a far call, and save a byte in the
process. If you think about it, the only functional difference between a far
call to a near label and a near call is that the far call pushes CS before it

pushes IP, and we can accomplish that by pushing CS before making a near call. That is,

```
push cs
call near ptr FarSubroutine
```

is equivalent to

```
call far ptr FarSubroutine
```

when **FarSubroutine** is in the same segment as the calling code. Since a direct near call is 2 bytes shorter than a direct far call and **push cs** is only 1 byte long, we actually come out 1 byte ahead by pushing CS and making a near call. According to the official cycle counts, the push/near call approach is 1 cycle slower; however, the alternative approach requires that 1 more instruction byte be fetched, so the scales could easily tip the other way.

One more item on far calls, and then we'll get on to other topics. Often it's necessary to perform a far branch to an address specified by an entry in a look-up table. That's generally no problem—we point to the table entry, perform an indirect far branch, and away we go.

Sometimes, however—in certain types of reentrant interrupt handlers and dispatchers, for example—it's necessary to perform an indirect far branch without altering the registers in any way, and without modifying memory. How can we perform such a branch without building a double-word pointer in memory, to say nothing of leaving the registers unchanged?

The answer is that we *can* build a doubleword pointer in memory—on the stack. We can perform a far branch to anywhere in memory simply by putting CS and IP onto the stack (in that order, with CS at the higher address), then performing a far return. To wit:

```
;
; Branches to the entry in VectorTable that's indicated
; by the index in BX. All registers are preserved.
;
; VectorTable is in CS, so DS doesn't need to be set to
; any particular segment.
;
FarBranchByIndex    proc far
        sub    sp,4        ;make room for the target address
        push   bp          ;preserve all registers we'll change
```

```
        mov    bp,sp      ;point 1 word above the stack space
                          ; we've reserved for the target address
        push   bx
        push   ax
        shl    bx,1       ;convert index to doubleword look-up
        shl    bx,1
        mov    ax,cs:[VectorTable+bx]    ;get target offset
        mov    [bp+2],ax ;put target offset onto stack
        mov    ax,cs:[VectorTable+bx+2] ;get target segment
        mov    [bp+4],ax ;put target segment onto stack
        pop    ax         ;restore all registers we've changed
        pop    bx
        pop    bp
        ret
FarBranchByIndex    endp
```

To carry this line of thought to its logical extreme, we could even preserve the states of the flags by executing a **pushf** before allocating the stack space, and then performing an **iret** rather than a far **ret** to branch to the target.

The sort of branching shown above is an example of how flexible the 8088's instruction set can be, especially if you're willing to use instructions in unusual ways, like hand-constructing far return addresses on the stack. This example certainly isn't ideal for most tasks—but it's nice to know that it's available if you need the particular service it delivers. In truth, the only limit on the strange jobs the 8088 can be coaxed into doing is your creativity. Speed may sometimes be a problem with the 8088, but flexibility shouldn't be.

14.2 ◆ Replacing call and ret with jmp

Enough of far branches, already. Let's continue with some interesting ways to replace **call** and **ret** with **jmp**.

Suppose that we've got a subroutine that's called from only one place in an entire program. That might be the case with a subroutine called through a call table from a central dispatch point, for example. Well, then, there's really no reason to call and return; instead, we can simply jump to the subroutine, and then jump back to the instruction after the call point, saving some cycles in the process.

For example, consider the code in Listing 14-2, which is yet another modification of the printable character filtering program of Listing 13-16. The modification in Listing 14-2 is that the call to **IsPrintable** has been replaced with a jump to the subroutine, and the return from **IsPrintable** has been replaced with a second jump, this time to the instruction after the jump that invoked the subroutine.

```
1    ;
2    ; *** Listing 14-2 ***
3    ;
4    ; Copies a zero-terminated string to another string,
5    ; filtering out non-printable characters by means of a
6    ; subroutine that performs the test. The subroutine is
7    ; invoked with a JMP and returns with another JMP.
8    ;
9            jmp     Skip
10   ;
11   SourceString    label     byte
12           db      'This is a sample string, consisting of '
13   X=1
14           rept    31
15           db      X
16   X=X+1
17           endm
18           db      7fh
19           db      'both printable and non-printable '
20           db      'characters', 0
21   DestinationString       label     byte
22           db      200 dup (?)
23   ;
24   ; Determines whether a character is printable (in the range
25   ; 20h through 7Eh).
26   ;
27   ; Input:
28   ;       AL = character to check
29   ;
30   ; Output:
31   ;       Zero flag set to 1 if character is printable,
32   ;               set to 0 otherwise
33   ;
34   ; Registers altered: none
35   ;
36   IsPrintable:
37           cmp     al,20h
38           jb      IsPrintableDone ;not printable
39           cmp     al,7eh
40           ja      IsPrintableDone ;not printable
41           cmp     al,al   ;set the Zero flag to 1, since the
42                           ; character is printable
43   IsPrintableDone:
44           jmp     short IsPrintableReturn
45                           ;this hardwires IsPrintable to
46                           ; return to just one place
47   ;
48   ; Copies a zero-terminated string to another string,
49   ; filtering out non-printable characters.
50   ;
```

```
51    ; Input:
52    ;         DS:SI = source string
53    ;         ES:DI = destination string
54    ;
55    ; Output: none
56    ;
57    ; Registers altered: AL, SI, DI
58    ;
59    ; Direction flag cleared
60    ;
61    ; Note: Does not handle strings that are longer than 64K
62    ;       bytes or cross segment boundaries.
63    ;
64    CopyPrintable:
65            cld
66    CopyPrintableLoop:
67            lodsb                       ;get the next byte to copy
68            jmp     IsPrintable         ;is it printable?
69    IsPrintableReturn:
70            jnz     NotPrintable        ;nope, don't copy it
71            stosb                       ;put the byte in the
72                                        ; destination string
73            jmp     CopyPrintableLoop   ;the character was
74                                        ; printable, so it couldn't
75                                        ; possibly have been 0. No
76                                        ; need to check whether it
77                                        ; terminated the string
78    NotPrintable:
79            and     al,al               ;was that the
80                                        ; terminating zero?
81            jnz     CopyPrintableLoop   ;no, do next byte
82            stosb                       ;copy the terminating zero
83            ret                         ;done
84    ;
85    Skip:
86            call    ZTimerOn
87            mov     di,seg DestinationString
88            mov     es,di
89            mov     di,offset DestinationString
90                        ;ES:DI points to the destination
91            mov     si,offset SourceString
92                        ;DS:SI points to the source
93            call    CopyPrintable   ;copy the printable
94                                    ; characters
95            call    ZTimerOff
```

That simple change cuts overall execution time to 3.09 msec, an improvement of more than 12 percent. Granted, part of the improvement is due to the use of short jumps, each of which reduces prefetching by 1 byte over normal jumps; when

```
db 128 dup(?)
```

is placed between **IsPrintable** and the rest of the code, forcing the use of jumps with normal 2-byte displacements, overall execution time rises to

3.33 msec, less than 5 percent faster than the original version. All that means, however, is that the **jmp-jmp** technique as a replacement for **call-ret** is most desirable when short jumps can be used. That's particularly true because two normal jumps total 6 bytes in length, 2 bytes longer than a **call-ret** pair.

In truth, Listing 14-2 doesn't demonstrate a particularly good application for replacing **call-ret** with **jmp-jmp**. As Listing 14-2 shows, **IsPrintable** can be called from only one place in the program, the **CopyPrintable** subroutine, and we usually want more flexibility than that in invoking our subroutines. (Otherwise we might just as well make the subroutines macros and move them right into the calling code.) Subroutines called through call tables, which often are invoked from just one place, are better candidates for the **jmp-jmp** technique.

Flexibility *ad Infinitum*

If more flexibility is needed than the last example provides, are we fated always to use **call-ret** rather than **jmp-jmp**? Well, the theme of this chapter seems to be the infinite flexibility of the 8088's instruction set, so it should come as no surprise to you that the answer is: not at all. Usually, you *will* want to use **call-ret**, because it's by far the simplest solution and often the fastest as well, but there *are* alternatives, and they can be quite handy in a pinch.

Consider this. Suppose that you've got a set of subroutines that are called via a call table. Next, suppose that it's desirable that any of the subroutines be able to end at any point and return to the central dispatching point—*without cleaning up the stack.* That is, it must be possible to return from anywhere in any subroutine called through the call table, discarding whatever variables, return addresses, and so on happen to be on the stack at the time.

Well, that's no great trick; we can simply jump back to the dispatch point, where the original (precall) stack pointer can be retrieved from a memory variable and loaded into SP. I know it's a strange thought, but it's perfectly legal to clear the stack simply by reloading SP. Now, however, suppose that the call table can be started from any of several locations. That means that a simple direct jump no longer serves to return us to the calling code, as the calling code could be in any of several places. We can't use **call** and **ret** either, as the return address could well be buried under data pushed on the stack at any given time.

The solution is simple: place the return address in a register before jumping at the central dispatch point, preserve the register throughout each

subroutine, and return by branching to the offset in the register. The code
would look something like this:

```
        mov   [OriginalSP],sp          ;save the stack state
DispatchLoopTop:
                :                       ;point BX to desired entry
                :                       ; in VectorTable
        mov   di,offset DispatchReturn  ;put the return address in DI,
                                        ; pointing to the instruction
                                        ; after the jump
        jmp   [VectorTable+bx]          ;jump to desired subroutine
DispatchReturn:                         ;subroutines return here
        mov   sp,[OriginalSP]           ;restore the stack state
        jmp   DispatchLoopTop
                :
Subroutine1:                            ;one of the subroutines
                :                       ; called through VectorTable
                :                       ;DI is preserved throughout
                :                       ; Subroutine1
        jmp   di                        ;return to the calling code
```

Make no mistake: this approach has its flaws. For one thing, it ties up a
16-bit register for the duration of each subroutine, and registers are scarce
enough as it is. (The return address could instead be stored in a memory
variable, but that reduces performance and causes reentrancy problems.)
For another, it wastes bytes, because the **jmp di** instruction used to return
to the dispatcher is 1 byte longer than **ret**, and the **mov-jmp** pair used
by the dispatcher is 3 bytes longer than **call**. Yet another shortcoming
is the greater complexity of the code, which brings with it an increased
probability of bugs.

Nonetheless, the above approach offers the flexibility we need—and
then some. Think for a moment, and you'll realize that we can, if we wish,
return anywhere at all with the above approach. For example, the following
saves a branch by returning right to **DispatchLoopTop**:

```
        mov   [OriginalSP],sp          ;save the stack state
DispatchLoopTop:
        mov   sp,[OriginalSP]          ;restore the stack state
                :                      ;point BX to desired entry
                :                      ; in VectorTable
```

```
        mov   di,offset DispatchLoopTop ;put the return address in DI,
                                        ; pointing to the top of the loop
        jmp   [VectorTable+bx]          ;jump to desired subroutine
              :
Subroutine1:                            ;one of the subroutines
              :                         ; called through VectorTable
              :                         ;DI is preserved throughout
              :                         ; Subroutine1
        jmp   di                        ;return to the calling code
```

(You don't have to jump through a register to return to an instruction other than the one after the calling instruction; just push the desired return address onto the stack and jump to a subroutine. For example, the following:

```
DispatchLoopTop:
              :                         ;point BX to desired entry
              :                         ; in VectorTable
        mov ax,offset DispatchLoopTop   ;push the return address
        push ax                         ; on the stack
        jmp   [VectorTable+bx]          ;jump to desired subroutine
              :
Subroutine1:                            ;one of the subroutines
              :                         ; called through VectorTable
        ret                             ;return to the calling code
```

pushes **DispatchLoopTop** before jumping, so each subroutine returns to **DispatchLoopTop** rather than to the instruction after the **jmp**.)

Surprisingly, flexibility is not the only virtue of the return-through-register approach—under the right circumstances, performance can benefit as well, since a branch through a register is only 2 bytes long and executes in just 11 cycles. Listing 14-3 shows Listing 14-2 modified to store the return address in BP. Although this code is a tad longer than Listing 14-2, because BP must be loaded, Listing 14-3 executes in 3.03 msec—slightly *faster* than Listing 14-2. The key is that BP is loaded only once, outside the loop, in **CopyPrintable**, so the extra overhead of loading BP is spread over the many repetitions of the loop. Meanwhile, the 4-cycle performance advantage of **jmp bp** over **jmp short IsPrintableReturn** is gained every time through the loop.

What's more, the version of **IsPrintable** in Listing 14-3 can be called from anywhere, so long as the calling code sets BP to the return address.

```
 1   ;
 2   ; *** Listing 14-3 ***
 3   ;
 4   ; Copies a zero-terminated string to another string,
 5   ; filtering out non-printable characters by means of a
 6   ; subroutine that performs the test. The subroutine is
 7   ; invoked with a JMP and returns with a JMP through a
 8   ; register.
 9   ;
10           jmp       Skip
11   ;
12   SourceString    label    byte
13           db        'This is a sample string, consisting of '
14   X=1
15           rept      31
16           db        X
17   X=X+1
18           endm
19           db        7fh
20           db        'both printable and non-printable '
21           db        'characters', 0
22   DestinationString     label    byte
23           db        200 dup (?)
24   ;
25   ; Determines whether a character is printable (in the range
26   ; 20h through 7Eh).
27   ;
28   ; Input:
29   ;       AL = character to check
30   ;       BP = return address
31   ;
32   ; Output:
33   ;       Zero flag set to 1 if character is printable,
34   ;               set to 0 otherwise
35   ;
36   ; Registers altered: none
37   ;
38   IsPrintable:
39           cmp       al,20h
40           jb        IsPrintableDone ;not printable
41           cmp       al,7eh
42           ja        IsPrintableDone ;not printable
43           cmp       al,al    ;set the Zero flag to 1, since the
44                              ; character is printable
45   IsPrintableDone:
46           jmp       bp       ;return to the address in BP
47   ;
48   ; Copies a zero-terminated string to another string,
49   ; filtering out non-printable characters.
50   ;
51   ; Input:
52   ;       DS:SI = source string
53   ;       ES:DI = destination string
54   ;
55   ; Output: none
56   ;
57   ; Registers altered: AL, SI, DI, BP
58   ;
59   ; Direction flag cleared
```

```
60    ;
61    ; Note: Does not handle strings that are longer than 64K
62    ;       bytes or cross segment boundaries.
63    ;
64    CopyPrintable:
65            cld
66            mov     bp,offset IsPrintableReturn
67                                    ;set the return address for
68                                    ; IsPrintable. Note that
69                                    ; this is done outside the
70                                    ; loop for speed
71    CopyPrintableLoop:
72            lodsb                   ;get the next byte to copy
73            jmp     IsPrintable     ;is it printable?
74    IsPrintableReturn:
75            jnz     NotPrintable    ;nope, don't copy it
76            stosb                   ;put the byte in the
77                                    ; destination string
78            jmp     CopyPrintableLoop ;the character was
79                                    ; printable, so it couldn't
80                                    ; possibly have been 0. No
81                                    ; need to check whether it
82                                    ; terminated the string
83    NotPrintable:
84            and     al,al           ;was that the
85                                    ; terminating zero?
86            jnz     CopyPrintableLoop ;no, do next byte
87            stosb                   ;copy the terminating zero
88            ret                     ;done
89    ;
90    Skip:
91            call    ZTimerOn
92            mov     di,seg DestinationString
93            mov     es,di
94            mov     di,offset DestinationString
95                        ;ES:DI points to the destination
96            mov     si,offset SourceString
97                        ;DS:SI points to the source
98            call    CopyPrintable   ;copy the printable
99                                    ; characters
100           call    ZTimerOff
```

By contrast, **IsPrintable** is hard wired to return only to **CopyPrintable** in Listing 14-2.

Once again, the point is not that you should generally replace **call-ret** with one of the many flavors of **jmp-jmp**, but rather that you should understand the unusual flexibility that **jmp-jmp** offers. It's a bonus that **jmp-jmp** can sometimes improve performance; the main point is that the flexibility of this approach lets you perform an odd lot of slightly improbable but sometimes most useful tasks.

Tinkering with the Stack in a Subroutine

Let's look at an example of a slightly improbable task that jumping through a register makes easy. Suppose that we want to be able to call a subroutine that allocates a specified number of bytes on the stack, then returns. That doesn't seem at first glance to be possible, because the allocated bytes would bury the return address beneath them, preventing the subroutine from returning until it deallocated the bytes.

Ah, but now we know about jumping through a register, so the solution's obvious. Here's the desired subroutine:

```
;
; Allocates space on the stack.
;
; Input:
;    CX = # of bytes to allocate
;
; Output: none
;
; Registers altered: AX, SP
;
AllocateStackSpace proc near
      pop   ax        ;retrieve the return address
      sub   sp,cx     ;allocate the space on the stack
      jmp   ax        ;return to the calling code
AllocateStackSpace endp
```

If we can tinker with the stack in a subroutine with such impunity, it would seem that with the 8088's instruction set we could do just about anything one could imagine—and indeed we can. Given the in-depth understanding of the 8088 that we've acquired, there's really nothing we can't do, given enough execution time. It's just a matter of putting the pieces of the puzzle—the 8088's instructions—together, and that's what the Zen of assembly language is all about.

As another example, consider the following. Once upon a time, Jeff Duntemann needed to obtain the IP of a particular instruction. Normally, that's no problem: the value of any label can be loaded into a general-purpose register as an immediate value. That wouldn't do in Jeff's situation, however, because his code was in-line assembler code in a Pascal program. The code was nothing more than a series of hex bytes that could be compiled directly into the program at any location at all; because the code could be placed at any location, the current IP couldn't be represented by any label or immediate value. Given that IP can't be read directly, what was Jeff to do?

The solution was remarkably simple, given a solid understanding of the 8088's instruction set and a flexible mind. The **call** instruction pushes the

IP of the next instruction, so Jeff just called the very next instruction and popped the IP of that instruction from the stack as follows:

```
call $+3        ;pushes IP and branches to the next instruction
pop  ax         ;gets the IP of this instruction
```

It's not exactly what **call** was intended for, but it solved Jeff's problem—and results are what matter most in assembler programming.

14.3 ◆ Use int Only When You Must

Before we get on with more ways to branch efficiently, let's discuss **int** for a moment. Among branching instructions, **int** is an oddball in that it performs a far branch to the address stored at the corresponding interrupt vector in the 1-Kb table of interrupt vectors starting at 0000:0000. Not only does **int** push a return CS:IP address, as would a far call, but it pushes the flags register as well.

The **int** instruction operates as it does because it's really more of a hardware instruction than a software instruction. When interrupts are enabled (via the interrupt flag) and a hardware interrupt occurs, the 8088 automatically executes an **int** instruction at the end of the current instruction. Because the currently executing code can be interrupted at any time, the exact state of the registers and flags *must* be preserved; hence the pushing of the flags register. The **iret** instruction provides a neat method for restoring the flags and branching back to continue the interrupted code.

From the perspective of servicing hardware that can require attention at any time, the 8088's interrupt mechanism is ideal. Interrupts are location- and code-independent; no matter what code you're executing, where that code resides, or what the register settings are, a hardware interrupt will cause a branch to the correct interrupt handler and allow you to restore the state of the 8088 when you're done.

From a software perspective, the interrupt mechanism is considerably less ideal. Because an **int** instruction must be executed to perform a software interrupt, there's no possibility of asynchronous execution of a software interrupt and hence no real need to save the state of the flags. What's more, **int** is astonishingly slow, making almost any sort of branch—yes, even a far call—preferable.

How slow is **int**? *Slow.* By itself **int** takes 71 cycles and empties the prefetch queue, and **iret** takes an additional 44 cycles and empties the prefetch queue again. At 115 cycles and two queue flushes a pop, you won't be using **int** too often in your time-critical code!

Why would you ever want to use **int**? The obvious answer is that you *must* use **int** to invoke DOS and BIOS functions. These services are provided via **int** because it's a handy way to provide entry points into routines that may move around in memory. No matter where the BIOS keyboard interface resides (and it may well move from one version of the BIOS to another, to say nothing of memory-resident programs that intercept keystrokes), it can always be accessed with **int 16h**. Basically, **int** is a useful way to access code that's external to the program that's running and consequently can't be branched to directly.

IBM left a number of interrupt vectors free for application program use, and that, along with the knowledge that **int** is a compact 2 bytes in length, might start you thinking that you could use **int** rather than **call** to branch to routines *within* a program. After all, in a large code model program **int** is 3 bytes shorter than a direct call.

It's a nice idea—but not, as a general rule, a *good* one. For one thing, you might well find that your chosen interrupt vectors conflict with those used by a memory-resident program. There aren't very many available vectors, and interrupt conflicts can easily crash a computer. Also, **int** is just too slow to be of much use; you'd have to have a powerful need to save space and an equally powerful insensitivity to performance to even consider using **int**. Also, because there aren't many interrupt vectors, you'll probably find yourself using a register to pass function numbers. Having to load a register pretty much wipes out the space savings **int** offers, and because the interrupt handler will have to perform another branch internally in order to vector to the code for the desired function, performance will be even worse.

In short, reserve **int** for accessing DOS and BIOS services and for applications where there simply is no substitute—applications in which location independence is paramount.

Beware of Letting DOS Do the Work

Interrupts are so slow that it often pays to go to considerable trouble to move them out of loops. Consider character-by-character processing of a text file, as, for example, when converting the contents of a text file to upper case. In such an application it's easiest to avoid the complications of buffering text by letting DOS feed you one character at a time, as shown in Figure 14.3.

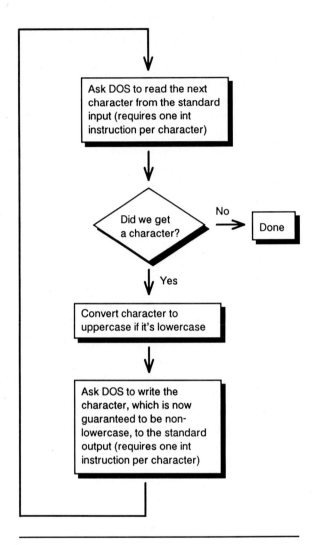

FIGURE 14.3   It's easiest—but not fastest—to communicate with DOS one character at a time, letting DOS handle the details of buffering data.

Listing 14-4 illustrates the approach of letting DOS do the work on a character-by-character basis. Listing 14-4 reads characters from the standard input, converts them to upper case, and prints the results to the standard output, interacting with DOS a character at a time at both the input and output stages. Listing 14-4 takes 2.009 seconds to convert the contents of

```
 1   ;
 2   ; *** Listing 14-4 ***
 3   ;
 4   ; Copies the standard input to the standard output,
 5   ; converting all characters to uppercase. Does so
 6   ; one character at a time.
 7   ;
 8           jmp     Skip
 9   ; Storage for the character we're processing.
10   Character       db      ?
11   ErrorMsg        db      'An error occurred', 0dh, 0ah
12   ERROR_MSG_LENGTH equ    $-ErrorMsg
13   ;
14   Skip:
15           call    ZTimerOn
16   CopyLoop:
17           mov     ah,3fh  ;DOS read fn
18           sub     bx,bx   ;handle 0 is the standard input
19           mov     cx,1    ;we want to get 1 character
20           mov     dx,offset Character ;the character goes here
21           int     21h     ;get the character
22           jc      Error   ;check for an error
23           and     ax,ax   ;did we read any characters?
24           jz      Done    ;no, we've hit the end of the file
25           mov     al,[Character]  ;get the character and
26           cmp     al,'a'          ; convert it to uppercase
27           jb      WriteCharacter  ; if it's lowercase
28           cmp     al,'z'
29           ja      WriteCharacter
30           and     al,not 20h      ;it's uppercase-convert to
31           mov     [Character],al  ; uppercase and save
32   WriteCharacter:
33           mov     ah,40h  ;DOS write fn
34           mov     bx,1    ;handle 1 is the standard output
35           mov     cx,1    ;we want to write 1 character
36           mov     dx,offset Character ;the character to write
37           int     21h     ;write the character
38           jnc     CopyLoop ;if no error, do the next character
39   Error:
40           mov     ah,40h  ;DOS write fn
41           mov     bx,2    ;handle 2 is standard error
42           mov     cx,ERROR_MSG_LENGTH ;# of chars to display
43           mov     dx,offset ErrorMsg ;error msg to display
44           int     21h     ;notify of error
45   Done:
46           call    ZTimerOff
```

the file TEST.TXT (shown in Figure 14.4) to upper case and send the result to the standard output.

(There's a slight complication in timing Listing 14-4. Listing 14-4 must be assembled and linked with LZTIME.BAT, because it takes more than 54 msec to run; however, Listing 14-4 expects to receive characters from the standard input when it executes. When run with the standard input *not* redirected, as occurs when LZTIME.BAT completes assembly and linking, Listing 14-4 waits indefinitely for input from the keyboard. Consequently,

This is the first line of the test file.
This is the second line of the test file.
This is the third line of the test file.
This is the fourth line of the test file.
This is the fifth line of the test file.
This is the sixth line of the test file.
This is the seventh line of the test file.
This is the eighth line of the test file.
This is the last line of the test file.

FIGURE 14.4   The contents of the file TEST.TXT, which is used as redirected input to Listings 14-4 and 14-5.

after the link is complete—when the program is waiting for keyboard
input—you must press Ctrl-Break to stop the program and type

   LZTEST <TEST.TXT

at the DOS prompt to time the code in Listing 14-4. The same is true for
Listing 14-5.)

```
1    ;
2    ; *** Listing 14-5 ***
3    ;
4    ; Copies the standard input to the standard output,
5    ; converting all characters to uppercase. Does so in
6    ; blocks of 256 characters.
7    ;
8            jmp     Skip
9    ; Storage for the characters we're processing.
10   CHARACTER_BLOCK_SIZE      equ     256
11   CharacterBlock  db        CHARACTER_BLOCK_SIZE dup (?)
12   ErrorMsg        db        'An error occurred', 0dh, 0ah
13   ERROR_MSG_LENGTH equ      $-ErrorMsg
14   ;
15   Skip:
16           call    ZTimerOn
17   CopyLoop:
18           mov     ah,3fh  ;DOS read fn
19           sub     bx,bx   ;handle 0 is the standard input
20           mov     cx,CHARACTER_BLOCK_SIZE
21                           ;we want to get a block
22           mov     dx,offset CharacterBlock
23                           ;the characters go here
24           int     21h     ;get the characters
25           jc      Error   ;check for an error
```

```
26              mov      cx,ax      ;get the count where it does us the
27                                  ; most good
28              jcxz     Done       ;if we didn't read anything, we've
29                                  ; hit the end of the file
30              mov      dx,cx      ;remember how many characters we read
31              mov      bx,offset CharacterBlock
32                                  ;point to the first character to
33                                  ; convert
34   ConvertLoop:
35              mov      al,[bx]           ;get the next character and
36              cmp      al,'a'            ; convert it to uppercase
37              jb       ConvertLoopBottom ; if it's lowercase
38              cmp      al,'z'
39              ja       ConvertLoopBottom
40              and      al,not 20h        ;it's uppercase-convert to
41              mov      [bx],al           ; uppercase and save
42   ConvertLoopBottom:
43              inc      bx                ;point to the next character
44              loop     ConvertLoop
45              mov      cx,dx      ;get back the character count in
46                                 ; this block, to serve as a count of
47                                 ; bytes for DOS to write
48              mov      ah,40h     ;DOS write fn
49              mov      bx,1       ;handle 1 is the standard output
50              mov      dx,offset CharacterBlock
51                                 ;point to the characters to write
52              push     cx         ;remember # of characters read
53              int      21h        ;write the character
54              pop      ax         ;get back the # of characters in
55                                  ; this block
56              jc       Error      ;check for an error
57              cmp      ax,CHARACTER_BLOCK_SIZE
58                                  ;was it a partial block?
59              jz       CopyLoop   ;no, so we're not done yet
60              jmp      short Done ;it was a partial block, so that
61                                  ; was the end of the file
62   Error:
63              mov      ah,40h     ;DOS write fn
64              mov      bx,2       ;handle 2 is standard error
65              mov      cx,ERROR_MSG_LENGTH ;# of chars to display
66              mov      dx,offset ErrorMsg ;error msg to display
67              int      21h        ;notify of error
68   Done:
69              call     ZTimerOff
```

The problem with the approach of Listing 14-4 is that all the overhead of calling a DOS function—including an **int** and an **iret**—occurs twice for each character, once during input and once during output. We can easily avoid all that simply by reading a sizeable block of text with a single DOS call, processing it one character at a time *in place* (thereby avoiding the overhead of interrupts and DOS calls), and printing it out as a block with a single DOS call, as shown in Figure 14.5. This process can be repeated a block at a time until the source file runs out of characters.

Listing 14-5, which implements the block-handling approach, runs in

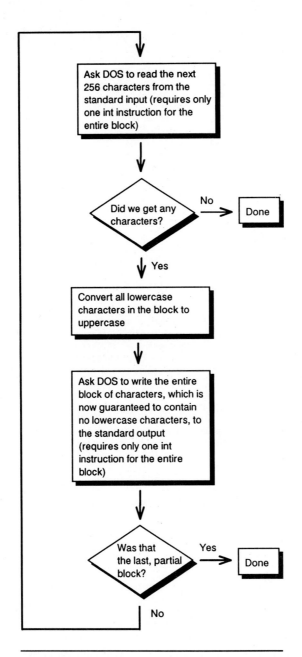

FIGURE 14.5   It's fastest to transfer characters to and from DOS in sizable blocks, avoiding the overhead of invoking DOS functions by performing data buffering within your own code.

818 ms—about 145 percent faster that Listing 14-4. Forget about disk access time and screen input and output time, to say nothing of the time required to loop and convert characters to upper case—*Listing 14-4 spends well over half its time just performing the overhead associated with asking DOS to handle characters one at a time.*

I rest my case.

14.4 ◆ Forward References Can Waste Time and Space

Many 8088 instructions offer special compressed forms. For example, **jmp**, which is normally 3 bytes long, can use the 2-byte **jmp short** form when the target is within the range of a 1-byte displacement, as we found in Chapter 12. The word-sized forms of the arithmetic instructions—**cmp**, **add**, and **and**, and the like—have similarly shortened forms when used with immediate operands that can fit within a signed byte; such operands are stored in a byte rather than a word and are automatically sign extended before being used.

As yet another example, any instruction that uses a *mod-reg-rm* byte and has a displacement field—**Index** in **mov al,[bx+Index]**, for example—is a byte shorter if the displacement fits within a signed byte. In fact, if **Index** is 0 in **mov al,[bx+Index]**, the displacement field can be done away with entirely, saving 2 bytes. (The potential waste of 2 bytes also applies when SI or DI is used with a displacement, but not when BP is used; the organization of the *mod-reg-rm* byte requires that BP-based addressing have at least a 1-byte displacement, so only 1 byte at most can be wasted.)

Obviously, we'd like the assembler to use the shortest possible forms of compressible instructions such as those mentioned above, and the assembler does just that *when it knows enough to do so*—which is not always the case.

Consider this. If the assembler comes to a **jmp** instruction, a great deal depends on whether the jump goes backward or forward. If it's a backward jump, the target label is already defined, and the assembler knows exactly how far away the jump destination is. If a backward destination is within the range of a 1-byte displacement, a short jump is generated; otherwise, a normal jump with a 2-byte displacement is generated. Either way, you can rest assured that the assembler has assembled the shortest possible jump.

Not so with a forward jump. In this case, the target label hasn't been reached yet, so the assembler hasn't the faintest idea how far away it is. Either type of jump *might* be appropriate, but the assembler won't know until the target label is reached in the course of assembly. The assembler can't wait until then to decide how big to make the jump, though. The jump size *must* be set before assembly can continue past the jump instruction; otherwise, the assembler wouldn't know where to place the next instruction.

Faced with such a dilemma, the assembler takes the only possible way out: it reserves space for the larger possibility, a normal jump. Later, when the target label becomes defined, the jump is assembled as a short jump if possible, but the damage has already been done; since 3 bytes were originally reserved for the jump, 3 bytes must be used, and a **nop** is stuffed in after the short jump. That is, a jump to the very next instruction, as in

```
        jmp   NearLabel
NearLabel:
```

assembles to the following:

```
        jmp   short NearLabel
        nop
NearLabel:
```

From a speed perspective, that's fine, but why waste a byte on a **nop**? The correct code is:

```
        jmp   short NearLabel
NearLabel:
```

Now consider the case of forward references to structure elements. The following **mov**:

```
        mov   ax,[bx+FirstEntry]
          :
EntryList struc
FirstEntry      dw   ?
SecondEntry     dw   ?
ThirdEntry      dw   ?
EntryList struc
```

assembles with a 2-byte displacement field. On the other hand, this **mov**:

```
EntryList struc
FirstEntry      dw   ?
```

```
SecondEntry      dw   ?
ThirdEntry       dw   ?
EntryList struc
        :
   mov  ax,[bx+FirstEntry]
```

assembles with no displacement field at all. Again, the assembler has no way of knowing on a forward reference how much space will be required for the displacement field and must assume the worst. Unlike the previous **jmp** example, however, performance as well as code size suffers in this case, because the additional displacement bytes must be fetched and a more complex effective address calculation must be made.

The same is true of forward-referenced immediate operands to the arithmetic instructions, and, indeed, of forward-referenced operands to any instruction that has a compressed form. You can improve the quality of your code considerably by avoiding forward references to data of all sorts (this will also speed up assembly a bit) and by explicitly using **jmp short** whenever it will reach on forward jumps.

The Right Assembler Can Help

Avoiding inefficient forward references can be a frustrating task, involving many assembly errors from short jumps that you thought *might* reach their destinations but which turned out not to. What's more, MASM doesn't tell you when it encounters inefficient forward references, so there's no easy way to identify opportunities to save bytes and/or cycles by using short jumps and by moving data and equates so as to avoid forward references.

In short, there's no good way to avoid inefficient code with *MASM*—but it's a different story with TASM and OPTASM. TASM can detect inefficient code as it assembles, issuing warnings to that effect if you so desire. You do then need to reedit your source code to correct the inefficient code, but once that's done you can relax in the knowledge that the assembler is generating the best possible machine language code from your source code.

OPTASM goes TASM one better. OPTASM can actually assemble the most efficient possible code automatically, with no intervention required on your part. Be warned, however, that I've heard that OPTASM is mostly, but not 100 percent, MASM compatible. On the other hand, Borland claims TASM is 100 percent MASM compatible, and I've found no reason to dispute that claim.

I wouldn't be surprised if MASM added similar features in a future version, because it's so obviously useful and because it's easy to do (at least to the extent of issuing inefficient code warnings). In any case, if you're interested in generating the tightest, fastest code possible, it's generally worth your while to use an assembler that can handle inefficient code in one way or another. Unlike almost everything else we've encountered in this book, saving bytes and/or cycles by eliminating inefficient code requires virtually no effort, given an assembler that helps you do the job.

If you aren't using an assembler that can help you generate efficient forward branches, use backward branches whenever possible. One reason is that MASM can select the smallest possible displacement for unconditional backward jumps. Another reason is that macros can be used to generate efficient code for backward *conditional* jumps, as we'll see later in this chapter.

14.5 ◆ Saving Space with Branches

When you're interested in saving space while losing as little performance as possible, you should use jumps in order to share as much code as possible between similar routines. For example, suppose you've got a routine, **SampleSub**, that performs the equivalent of a switch statement with three separate cases, depending on the value in BX. Suppose that each of the cases can succeed or fail, and that **TestSub** returns AX equal to 0 for success and 1 for failure. Suppose further that on failure the byte-sized memory variable **ErrorCode** must be set to indicate which case failed.

One possible implementation is

```
SampleSub proc near
       and    bx,bx
       jz     Case0
       dec    bx
       jz     Case1
; Default    case.
              :                ;code to handle the default case
       jz     SampleSubSuccess ;if success, set AX properly
       mov    [ErrorCode],DEFAULT_CASE_ERROR
       mov    ax,1
       ret
Case0:
              :                ;code to handle the case of BX=1
       jz     SampleSubSuccess ;if success, set AX properly
```

```
        mov     [ErrorCode],CASE0_ERROR
        mov     ax,1
        ret
Case1:
        :                       ;code to handle the case of BX=2
        jz      SampleSubSuccess ;if success, set AX properly
        mov     [ErrorCode],CASE1_ERROR
        mov     ax,1
        ret
SampleSubSuccess:
        sub     ax,ax           ;return success status
        ret
SampleSub endp
```

In this implementation, all cases jump to the common code at **Success** when they succeed, so that the code to return a success status appears just once but serves all three cases.

Although it's not quite so obvious, we can shrink the code a good bit by doing the same for the failure case, as follows:

```
SampleSub proc near
        and     bx,bx
        jz      Case0
        dec     bx
        jz      Case1
; Default case.
        :                       ;code to handle the default case
        jz      SampleSubSuccess ;if success, set AX properly
        mov     al,DEFAULT_CASE_ERROR
        jmp     short SampleSubFailure   ;set error code & status
Case0:
        :                       ;code to handle the case of BX=1
        jz      SampleSubSuccess ;if success, set AX properly
        mov     al,CASE0_ERROR
        jmp     short SampleSubFailure   ;set error code & status
Case1:
        :                       ;code to handle the case of BX=2
        jz      SampleSubSuccess ;if success, set AX properly
        mov     al,CASE1_ERROR
SampleSubFailure:
        mov     [ErrorCode],al
```

```
        mov    ax,1
        ret
SampleSubSuccess:
        sub    ax,ax            ;return success status
        ret
SampleSub endp
```

Although this latter version doesn't look much different from the original, it's a full 10 bytes shorter and functionally equivalent. (If there were more cases, we'd save proportionally more bytes, too.) This substantial reduction in size results from two factors: the instruction pair **mov ax,1/ret** appears once rather than three times, saving 8 bytes, and three **mov al,*immed*** instructions along with one accumulator-specific direct-addressed memory access replace three *mod-reg-rm* direct-addressed memory accesses, saving 6 bytes. Those 14 bytes saved more than offset the 4 bytes added by two **jmp short** instructions.

There are two points to be made here. First, we can save many bytes by jumping to common exit code from various places in a subroutine, provided that the common exit code performs a reasonably lengthy task that would otherwise have to be performed at the end of a number of code sequences. (If the common exit code is just a **ret**, we're better off executing a 1-byte **ret** in several places in the subroutine than we are executing a 2-byte **jmp short** just to get to the **ret**, as we saw in the last chapter.)

Second, we can save bytes by altering our code a bit to allow common exit code to do more than it normally would. This is illustrated in the above example, in that each of the cases loads an error code into AL rather than storing it to memory, so that a single accumulator-specific direct-addressed **mov** can store the error code to memory. Off the top, it would seem that the error-code setting belongs in the separate cases, since each case stores a different error value, but with a little ingenuity, a single memory-accessing instruction can do the trick.

The idea of sharing common exit code can be extended across several functions. Suppose that we've got two subroutines that end by popping DI, SI, and BP, then returning. Suppose also that in case of success these subroutines return AX set to 0, and that in case of failure they return AX set to a nonzero error code.

There's absolutely no reason why the two subroutines shouldn't share a considerable amount of exit code, along the following lines:

```
Subroutine1        proc near
        push  bp
```

```
            mov   bp,sp
            push  si
            push  di
                  :         ;body of subroutine, putting an error code in AX and
                  :         ; branching to Exit on failure, or falling through in
                  ;         ; case of success
Success:
            sub   ax,ax
Exit:
            pop   di
            pop   si
            pop   bp
            ret
Subroutine1         endp
Subroutine2         proc near
            push  bp
            mov   bp,sp
            push  si
            push  di
                  :         ;body of subroutine, putting an error code in AX and
                  :         ; branching to Exit on failure, or falling through in
                  ;         ; case of success
            jmp   Success
Subroutine2         endp
```

Here we've saved 3 or 4 bytes by replacing 6 bytes of exit code that would normally appear at the end of **Subroutine2** with a 2- or 3-byte jump. What's more, we could do the same for any number of subroutines that can use the same exit code; at worst, a 3-byte jump would be required to reach **Success** or **Exit**. Naturally, larger savings would result from sharing lengthier exit code.

The key here is realizing that in assembler there's no need for a clean separation between subroutines. If multiple subroutines end with the same instructions, they might as well share those instructions. Of course, performance will suffer a little from the extra branch all but one of the subroutines will have to make in order to reach the common code. Once again, we've acquired a new tool that has both costs and benefits; this time it's a tool that saves bytes while expending cycles. Deciding when that's a good tradeoff is your business, to be judged on a case by case basis. Sometimes this new tool is desirable, sometimes not—but either way, making that sort of decision properly is a key to good assembler code.

Multiple Entry Points

We can save bytes at the other end of a subroutine by providing multiple entry points. In one use, multiple entry points are an extension of the common exit code concept we just discussed, with the idea being to share as much code as possible, via branches into the middle as well as the start of subroutines. If two subroutines share the whole last half of their code in common, then one can branch into the other at that point. If some tasks require only the last one third of the code in a subroutine, then a call can be made directly to the appropriate point in the subroutine; in this case, one subroutine would be a proper subset of the other and wouldn't exist as separate code at all.

Assembler facilitates that sort of code sharing, because if we really want to, we can always set up the registers, flags and stack to match the requirements of a subroutine's code at any entry point. In other words, if we want to branch into the middle of a subroutine, the complete control of the PC that is possible only in assembler allows us to set up the state of the PC as needed to enter that code. (Recall our tinkering with the stack earlier in this chapter.) Whether it's worth going to the trouble of doing so is another question entirely, but never forget that assembler lets you put the PC into any state you choose at any time.

There's another meaning to multiple entry points, and that's the technique of using several front-end entry points to a subroutine in order to set up commonly used parameters. I can explain this best by way of an example.

Imagine that we've got a subroutine, **SpeakerControl**, that's called with one parameter, passed in AX. A call to **SpeakerControl** with AX set to 0 turns off the PC's speaker; a call with AX set to 1 turns on the speaker.

Now imagine that **SpeakerControl** is called from dozens—perhaps hundreds—of places in a program. Every time **SpeakerControl** is called, a 2- or 3-byte instruction must be used to set AX to the desired state. If there are 100 calls to **SpeakerControl**, approximately 250 bytes are used simply selecting the mode of operation of **SpeakerControl**.

Instead, why not simply provide two front-end entry points to **SpeakerControl**, one to turn the speaker on (**SpeakerOn**) and one to turn the speaker off (**SpeakerOff**)? The code would be as simple as this:

```
; Turns the speaker on.
SpeakerOn proc near
      mov    ax,1
      jmp    short SpeakerControl
```

```
SpeakerOn endp
; Turns the speaker off.
SpeakerOff        proc near
       sub   ax,ax
SpeakerOff        endp
;
; Turns the speaker on or off.
;
; Input:
;       AX = 1 to turn the speaker on
;          = 0 to turn the speaker off
;
; Output:
;       none
;
SpeakerControl    proc near
               :
```

Given these front-end functions, we could, for example, use **SpeakerOff** instead of calling **SpeakerControl** with AX equal to 0. At the cost of the 7 bytes taken by the two front-end functions, we would save 250 bytes worth of parameter-setting code, for a net saving of 243 bytes.

The principle of using front-end functions that set common parameter values applies to high level language code as well. In fact, it may apply even better to high level language code, since it takes 3 to 4 bytes to push a constant parameter onto the stack. The downside of using this technique in a high level language is much the same as the downside of using it in assembler—it involves extra branching, so it's slower. (In high level language code, performance will also be slowed by the time required to push any additional parameters that must be passed through the front-end functions.)

Trading off cycles for bytes—so what else is new?

A Brief Zen Exercise in Branching (and Not-Branching)

Just for fun, we're going to take a moment to look at several ways in which branching and not-branching can be used to improve a simple bit of code. I'm not going to dwell on the mechanisms or merits of the various approaches; by this point you should have the knowledge and tools to do that yourself.

The task at hand is simple: increment a 32-bit value in DX:AX. The obvious solution is

```
add   ax,1
adc   dx,0
```

which comes in at 6 bytes and 8 execution unit (EU) cycles.

If we're willing to sacrifice performance, we can save 2 bytes by branching:

```
      inc   ax
      jnz   IncDone
      inc   dx
IncDone:
```

However, this approach usually takes 18 cycles and empties the prefetch queue, since the case where AX turns over to 0 (and so no branch occurs) is only one out of 64 K possible cases. We can adjust for that at the cost of an additional byte with

```
      inc   dx
      inc   ax
      jz    IncDone
      dec   dx
IncDone:
```

which preincrements DX, then usually falls through the conditional jump and decrements DX back to its original state. This approach is 5 bytes long but usually takes 10 cycles to execute.

Along the lines of our discussion of 32-bit negation in the last chapter, we can also use conditional branching to improve performance, as follows:

```
      inc   ax
      jz    IncDX
IncDone:
         :

IncDX:
      inc   dx
      jmp   IncDone
```

This approach requires the same 6 bytes as the original approach but takes only 3 bytes and 6 cycles along the usual execution path.

Finally, if the branch-out technique of the last case isn't feasible, we could preload two registers with the values 1 and 0, to speed and shorten the addition:

```
mov  bx,1
sub  cx,cx
      :
add  ax,bx
adc  dx,cx
```

This would reduce the actual addition code to 4 bytes and 6 cycles, although it would require 9 bytes overall. Such an approach would make little sense unless BX and CX were preloaded outside a loop and the 32-bit addition occurred repeatedly inside the loop—but then it doesn't make sense expending the energy for *any* of these optimizations unless either the code is inside a time-critical loop or bytes are in extremely short supply.

Remember, you must pick and choose your spots when you optimize at a detailed instruction-by-instruction level. When you optimize for speed, identify the portions of your programs that significantly affect overall performance and/or make an appreciable difference in response time, and focus your detailed optimization efforts on fine-tuning that code, especially inside loops.

Optimizing for space rather than speed is less focused—you should save bytes wherever you can—but most assembler optimization on the PC is, in fact, for speed, as there's a great deal of memory available relative to the few bytes that can be saved over the course of a few assembler instructions. However, in certain applications, such as BIOS code and ROMable process-control code, size optimization is sometimes critical. In such applications, you'd want to use subroutines as much as possible (and, yes, perhaps even interrupts), and design those subroutines to share as much code as possible. You'd probably also want to use mini-interpreters, which we'll discuss in Volume II of *Zen of Assembly Language.*

At any rate, knowing when and where optimization is worth the effort is as important as knowing how to optimize. Without the when and where, the how is useless; you'll spend all your time tweaking code without seeing the big picture, and you'll never accomplish anything of substance.

14.6 ◆ Double-Duty Tests

There are a number of ways to get multiple uses out of a single instruction that sets the flags. Sometimes a multiple use is available because multiple flags are set, and sometimes a multiple use is available because the instruction that sets the flags performs other tasks as well. Let's look at some examples.

Suppose that we have eight 1-bit flags stored in a single byte-sized memory variable, **StateFlags**, as shown in Figure 14.6. In order to check whether a high- or medium-priority event is pending, as indicated by bits 7 and 6 of **StateFlags**, we'd normally use something like

```
mov   al,[StateFlags]
test  al,80h                              ;high-priority event pending?
jnz   HandleHighPriorityEvent             ;yes
test  al,40h                              ;medium-priority event pending?
jnz   HandleMediumPriorityEvent ;yes
```

or perhaps, if we were clever, the slightly faster sequence

```
mov   al,[StateFlags]
shl   al,1                                ;high-priority event pending?
jc    HandleHighPriorityEvent             ;yes
shl   al,1                                ;medium-priority event pending?
jc    HandleMediumPriorityEvent ;yes
```

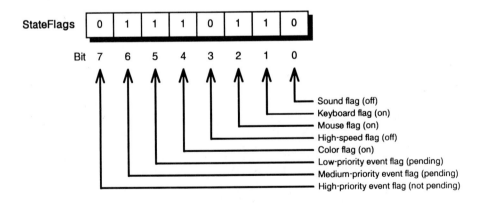

FIGURE 14.6   The byte-sized variable **StateFlags** contains eight separate 1-bit flags. The interpretation of the current state of each flag is shown in parentheses.

If we think for a moment, however, we'll realize that shifting a value to the left has a most desirable property. The **shl** instruction not only sets the carry flag (CF) to reflect carry out of the most significant bit of the result, but also sets the sign flag (SF) to reflect the value stored *into* the most significant bit of the result.

Do you see it now? After a register is shifted 1 bit to the left, CF and SF are set to reflect the states of the *two* most significant bits originally stored in that register. That means that we can replace the above code with

```
mov    al,[StateFlags]
shl    al,1                       ;high- or medium-priority event pending?
jc     HandleHighPriorityEvent    ;high-priority event pending
js     HandleMediumPriorityEvent  ;medium-priority event pending
```

which is one full instruction shorter.

Stretching this idea still further, we could relocate three of our flags to bits 7, 6, and 5 of **EventFlags**, with bits 4 to 0 always set to 0, as shown in Figure 14.7. Then, if the first two tests failed, a zero-nonzero test would serve to determine whether the flag in bit 5 is set, and we could get *three* tests out of a single operation:

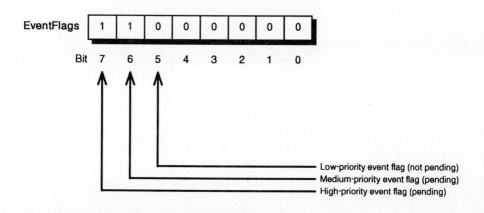

FIGURE 14.7   The byte-sized variable **EventFlags** contains three separate 1-bit flags in bits 7 to 5, with bits 4 to 0 always set to 0. The interpretation of the current state of each flag is shown in parentheses.

```
        mov    al,[EventFlags]
        shl    al,1                                  ;high-, medium-, or low-
                                                     ; priority event pending?
        jc     HandleHighPriorityEvent    ;high-priority event pending
        js     HandleMediumPriorityEvent  ;medium-priority event pending
        jnz    HandleLowPriorityEvent     ;low-priority event pending
```

Using Loop Counters as Indexes

There's another way to get double-duty from tests, in this case by combining the counting function of a loop counter with the indexing function of an index used inside the loop.

Consider the following, which is a standard way to generate a checksum byte for an array:

```
        mov    cx,TEST_ARRAY_LENGTH
        sub    bx,bx
        sub    al,al
ChecksumLoop:
        add    al,[TestArray+bx]
        inc    bx
        loop   ChecksumLoop
```

(Yes, I know that this could be speeded up and shrunk by loading BX with the offset of **TestArray** outside the loop, but bear with me while we look at a specific optimization.)

Now consider the following:

```
        mov    bx,TEST_ARRAY_LENGTH
        sub    al,al
ChecksumLoop:
        add    al,[TestArray+bx-1]
        dec    bx
        jnz    ChecksumLoop
```

This second version generates the same checksum as the earlier code, but is one instruction and 2 bytes shorter, and slightly faster, as well. Rather than maintaining separate loop counter and array index values, the second version uses BX for both purposes. The key to being able to do this is the realization that it's equally valid to start processing at either end of the array. Whenever that's the case, look to process at the high end and count toward 0 if you can, because it's easier to test for 0 than for any other value.

By the way, while it's easiest to check for counting down to 0, it's reasonably easy to check for counting *past* 0 as well, so long as the initial count is 32 K or less: just test SF. For instance, the following is yet another version of the checksum code, this time ending the loop when BX counts down past 0 to 0FFFFh:

```
        mov   bx,TEST_ARRAY_LENGTH-1
        sub   al,al
ChecksumLoop:
        add   al,[TestArray+bx]
        dec   bx
        jns   ChecksumLoop
```

Note that BX now starts off with the index of the last element of the array rather than the length of the array, so no adjustment by 1 is needed when each element of the array is addressed. So long as TEST_ARRAY_LENGTH is 32 K or less, this version isn't generally better or worse than the last version; both versions are the same length and execute at the same speed. However, SF is set when either 0 *or* any value greater than 32 K is decremented, so if TEST_ARRAY_LENGTH exceeds 32 K the checksum loop in the last example will end prematurely—and incorrectly.

14.7 ♦ The Looping Instructions

And so we come to the 8088's special looping instructions: **jcxz**, **loop**, **loopz**, and **loopnz**. You undoubtedly know how **jcxz** and **loop** work by now—we've certainly used them often enough over the last few chapters. As a quick refresher, **jcxz** branches if and only if CX is 0, and **loop** decrements CX and branches *unless* the new value in CX is zero. None of the looping instructions—not even **loop**, which decrements CX—affects the 8088's flags in any way; we saw that put to good use in a loop that performed multi-word addition in Chapter 9.

(In fact, the only branching instructions of the 8088 that affect the flags register are the interrupt-related instructions. The **int** instruction sets the interrupt flag to 0, disabling maskable interrupts right away, as does **into** when the overflow flag is 1; **iret** sets the entire flags register to the 16-bit value popped from the stack.)

Given that we're already familiar with **jcxz** and **loop**, we'll take a look at the useful and often overlooked **loopz** and **loopnz**, and then we'll touch on a few items of interest involving **jcxz** and **loop**. Always bear in mind, however, that while the special looping instructions are more efficient than the other branching instructions, they're still branching instructions, and that means that they're still slow. When performance matters, not-branching is the way to go.

loopz and loopnz

The **loopz** and **loopnz** instructions (also known as **loope** and **loopne**, respectively) are essentially **loop** with a little something extra added. The **loopz** instruction (which we can remember as *loop while 0,* as we did with **repz**) decrements CX and then branches unless either CX is 0 *or* ZF is 0. Likewise, **loopnz** (*loop while not 0*) decrements CX and branches unless either CX is 0 *or* ZF is one. Depending on whether they branch or not, these instructions are anywhere from 0 to 2 cycles slower than **loop**, but all three instructions are the same size, 2 bytes.

The instructions **loopz** and **loopnz** afford an extremely compact way to repeat a loop up to a maximum number of repetitions while waiting for an event that affects ZF to occur. If, when the loop ends, ZF isn't in the sought after state, then the event hasn't occurred within the maximum number of repetitions.

For example, suppose that we want to search an array for the first entry that matches a particular character. Normally, we would do that with **repnz scasb**, but in this particular case we need to perform a case-insensitive search. Listing 14-6 shows a standard solution to this problem, which tests for a match and branches out of the loop when a match is found or falls through the bottom of the loop if no match exists. Listing 14-6 runs in 1134 μsec for the test case.

```
1    ;
2    ; *** Listing 14-6 ***
3    ;
4    ; Searches for the first appearance of a character, in any
5    ; case, in a byte-sized array by using JZ and LOOP.
6    ;
7            jmp     Skip
8    ;
9    ByteArray       label   byte
10           db      'Array Containing Both Upper and Lowercase'
11           db      ' Characters And Blanks'
12   ARRAY_LENGTH    equ     ($-ByteArray)
13   ;
14   ; Finds the first occurrence of the specified character, in
15   ; any case, in the specified byte-sized array.
16   ;
17   ; Input:
18   ;       AL = character for which to perform a
```

```
19    ;            case-insensitive search
20    ;      CX = array length (0 means 64K long)
21    ;      DS:SI = array to search
22    ;
23    ; Output:
24    ;      SI = pointer to first case-insensitive match, or 0
25    ;            if no match is found
26    ;
27    ; Registers altered: AX, CX, SI
28    ;
29    ; Direction flag cleared
30    ;
31    ; Note: Does not handle arrays that are longer than 64K
32    ;       bytes or cross segment boundaries.
33    ;
34    ; Note: Do not pass an array that starts at offset 0 (SI=0),
35    ;       since a match on the first byte and failure to find
36    ;       the byte would be indistinguishable.
37    ;
38    CaseInsensitiveSearch:
39          cld
40          cmp     al,'a'
41          jb      CaseInsensitiveSearchBegin
42          cmp     al,'z'
43          ja      CaseInsensitiveSearchBegin
44          and     al,not 20h      ;make sure the search byte
45                                  ; is uppercase
46    CaseInsensitiveSearchBegin:
47          mov     ah,al           ;put the search byte in AH
48                                  ; so we can use AL to hold
49                                  ; the bytes we're checking
50    CaseInsensitiveSearchLoop:
51          lodsb                   ;get the next byte from the
52                                  ; array being searched
53          cmp     al,'a'
54          jb      CaseInsensitiveSearchIsUpper
55          cmp     al,'z'
56          ja      CaseInsensitiveSearchIsUpper
57          and     al,not 20h      ;make sure the array byte is
58                                  ; uppercase
59    CaseInsensitiveSearchIsUpper:
60          cmp     al,ah           ;do we have a
61                                  ; case-insensitive match?
62          jz      CaseInsensitiveSearchMatchFound ;yes
63          loop    CaseInsensitiveSearchLoop
64                                  ;check the next byte, if any
65          sub     si,si           ;no match found
66          ret
67    CaseInsensitiveSearchMatchFound:
68          dec     si              ;point back to the matching
69                                  ; array byte
70          ret
71    ;
72    Skip:
73          call    ZTimerOn
74          mov     al,'K'          ;character to search for
75          mov     si,offset ByteArray ;array to search
76          mov     cx,ARRAY_LENGTH ;# of bytes to search
77                                  ; through
```

```
78              call    CaseInsensitiveSearch
79                                      ;perform a case-insensitive
80                                      ; search for 'K'
81              call    ZTimerOff
```

You can probably see where we're heading. The **jz/loop** pair at the bottom of the loop in Listing 14-6 is an obvious candidate for conversion to **loopnz**, and Listing 14-7 takes advantage of just that conversion. Essentially, the test for a match is moved out of the loop in Listing 14-7, with **loopnz** replacing **loop** in order to allow the loop to end either on a match or at the end of the array. The result: Listing 14-7 runs in 1036 μsec, more than 9 percent faster than Listing 14-7. Not a *massive* improvement, but not a bad payoff for replacing one instruction and moving another.

```
1    ;
2    ; *** Listing 14-7 ***
3    ;
4    ; Searches for the first appearance of a character, in any
5    ; case, in a byte-sized array by using LOOPNZ.
6    ;
7              jmp     Skip
8    ;
9    ByteArray       label   byte
10             db      'Array Containing Both Upper and Lowercase'
11             db      ' Characters And Blanks'
12   ARRAY_LENGTH    equ     ($-ByteArray)
13   ;
14   ; Finds the first occurrence of the specified character, in
15   ; any case, in the specified byte-sized array.
16   ;
17   ; Input:
18   ;      AL = character for which to perform a
19   ;              case-insensitive search
20   ;      CX = array length (0 means 64K long)
21   ;      DS:SI = array to search
22   ;
23   ; Output:
24   ;      SI = pointer to first case-insensitive match, or 0
25   ;              if no match is found
26   ;
27   ; Registers altered: AX, CX, SI
28   ;
29   ; Direction flag cleared
30   ;
31   ; Note: Does not handle arrays that are longer than 64K
32   ;       bytes or cross segment boundaries.
33   ;
34   ; Note: Do not pass an array that starts at offset 0 (SI=0),
35   ;       since a match on the first byte and failure to find
36   ;       the byte would be indistinguishable.
37   ;
38   CaseInsensitiveSearch:
39             cld
40             cmp     al,'a'
41             jb      CaseInsensitiveSearchBegin
```

```
42                cmp     al,'z'
43                ja      CaseInsensitiveSearchBegin
44                and     al,not 20h      ;make sure the search byte
45                                        ; is uppercase
46    CaseInsensitiveSearchBegin:
47                mov     ah,al           ;put the search byte in AH
48                                        ; so we can use AL to hold
49                                        ; the bytes we're checking
50    CaseInsensitiveSearchLoop:
51                lodsb                   ;get the next byte from the
52                                        ; array being searched
53                cmp     al,'a'
54                jb      CaseInsensitiveSearchIsUpper
55                cmp     al,'z'
56                ja      CaseInsensitiveSearchIsUpper
57                and     al,not 20h      ;make sure the array byte is
58                                        ; uppercase
59    CaseInsensitiveSearchIsUpper:
60                cmp     al,ah           ;do we have a
61                                        ; case-insensitive match?
62                loopnz  CaseInsensitiveSearchLoop
63                                        ;fall through if we have a
64                                        ; match, or if we've run out
65                                        ; of bytes. Otherwise, check
66                                        ; the next byte
67                jz      CaseInsensitiveSearchMatchFound
68                                        ;we did find a match
69                sub     si,si           ;no match found
70                ret
71    CaseInsensitiveSearchMatchFound:
72                dec     si              ;point back to the matching
73                                        ; array byte
74                ret
75    ;
76    Skip:
77                call    ZTimerOn
78                mov     al,'K'          ;character to search for
79                mov     si,offset ByteArray ;array to search
80                mov     cx,ARRAY_LENGTH ;# of bytes to search
81                                        ; through
82                call    CaseInsensitiveSearch
83                                        ;perform a case-insensitive
84                                        ; search for 'K'
85                call    ZTimerOff
```

(Food for thought: Listings 14-6 and 14-7 could be speeded up by storing upper case and lower case versions of the search byte in separate registers and simply comparing each byte of the array to *both* versions. The extra comparison would be a good deal faster than the code used in Listings 14-6 and 14-7 to convert each byte of the array to upper case.)

How You Loop Matters More than You Might Think

In the previous chapter, I lambasted **loop** as a slow looping instruction. Well, it *is* slow—but if you must perform repetitive tasks by branching—that is, if you must loop—**loop** is a good deal faster than other branching in-structions. To drive that point home, I'm going to measure the performance of the case-insensitive search program of Listing 14-6 with the looping code implemented as follows: with **loop**, with **dec reg16/jnz**, with **dec reg8/jnz**, with **dec mem8/jnz**, and with **dec mem16/jnz**. (Remember that **dec reg16** is faster than **dec reg8**, and that byte-sized memory ac-cesses are faster than word-sized accesses.)

Listing 14-6 already shows the **loop**-based implementation. Listings 14-8 through 14-11 show the other implementations. The results are shown in Table 14.1. Although the incremental performance differences between the various implementations are fairly modest, **loop** is clearly the winner and is the shortest of the bunch as well.

Whenever you must branch in order to loop, use the **loop** instruction if you possibly can. The performance of the **loop** instruction is superior only in the realm of branching instructions, for notbranching is *much* faster than looping with any of the branching instructions, but when space is at a premium, **loop** is hard to beat.

```
 1   ;
 2   ; *** Listing 14-8 ***
 3   ;
 4   ; Searches for the first appearance of a character, in any
 5   ; case, in a byte-sized array by using JZ, DEC REG16, and
 6   ; JNZ.
 7   ;
 8           jmp     Skip
 9   ;
10   ByteArray       label   byte
11           db      'Array Containing Both Upper and Lowercase'
12           db      ' Characters And Blanks'
13   ARRAY_LENGTH    equ     ($-ByteArray)
14   ;
15   ; Finds the first occurrence of the specified character, in
16   ; any case, in the specified byte-sized array.
17   ;
18   ; Input:
19   ;       AL = character for which to perform a
20   ;               case-insensitive search
21   ;       CX = array length (0 means 64K long)
22   ;       DS:SI = array to search
23   ;
24   ; Output:
25   ;       SI = pointer to first case-insensitive match, or 0
26   ;               if no match is found
27   ;
28   ; Registers altered: AX, CX, SI
29   ;
30   ; Direction flag cleared
31   ;
32   ; Note: Does not handle arrays that are longer than 64K
```

```
33  ;       bytes or cross segment boundaries.
34  ;
35  ; Note: Do not pass an array that starts at offset 0 (SI=0),
36  ;       since a match on the first byte and failure to find
37  ;       the byte would be indistinguishable.
38  ;
39  CaseInsensitiveSearch:
40          cld
41          cmp     al,'a'
42          jb      CaseInsensitiveSearchBegin
43          cmp     al,'z'
44          ja      CaseInsensitiveSearchBegin
45          and     al,not 20h      ;make sure the search byte
46                                  ; is uppercase
47  CaseInsensitiveSearchBegin:
48          mov     ah,al           ;put the search byte in AH
49                                  ; so we can use AL to hold
50                                  ; the bytes we're checking
51  CaseInsensitiveSearchLoop:
52          lodsb                   ;get the next byte from the
53                                  ; array being searched
54          cmp     al,'a'
55          jb      CaseInsensitiveSearchIsUpper
56          cmp     al,'z'
57          ja      CaseInsensitiveSearchIsUpper
58          and     al,not 20h      ;make sure the array byte is
59                                  ; uppercase
60  CaseInsensitiveSearchIsUpper:
61          cmp     al,ah           ;do we have a
62                                  ; case-insensitive match?
63          jz      CaseInsensitiveSearchMatchFound ;yes
64          dec     cx              ;count down bytes remaining
65                                  ; in array being searched
66          jnz     CaseInsensitiveSearchLoop
67                                  ;check the next byte, if any
68          sub     si,si           ;no match found
69          ret
70  CaseInsensitiveSearchMatchFound:
71          dec     si              ;point back to the matching
72                                  ; array byte
73          ret
74  ;
75  Skip:
76          call    ZTimerOn
77          mov     al,'K'          ;character to search for
78          mov     si,offset ByteArray ;array to search
79          mov     cx,ARRAY_LENGTH ;# of bytes to search
80                                  ; through
81          call    CaseInsensitiveSearch
82                                  ;perform a case-insensitive
83                                  ; search for 'K'
84          call    ZTimerOff


1   ;
2   ; *** Listing 14-9 ***
3   ;
4   ; Searches for the first appearance of a character, in any
5   ; case, in a byte-sized array by using JZ, DEC REG8, and
```

```
6    ; JNZ.
7    ;
8            jmp     Skip
9    ;
10   ByteArray       label   byte
11           db      'Array Containing Both Upper and Lowercase'
12           db      ' Characters And Blanks'
13   ARRAY_LENGTH    equ     ($-ByteArray)
14   ;
15   ; Finds the first occurrence of the specified character, in
16   ; any case, in the specified byte-sized array.
17   ;
18   ; Input:
19   ;       AL = character for which to perform a
20   ;                    case-insensitive search
21   ;       CL = array length (0 means 256 long)
22   ;       DS:SI = array to search
23   ;
24   ; Output:
25   ;       SI = pointer to first case-insensitive match, or 0
26   ;                    if no match is found
27   ;
28   ; Registers altered: AX, CL, SI
29   ;
30   ; Direction flag cleared
31   ;
32   ; Note: Does not handle arrays that are longer than 256
33   ;       bytes or cross segment boundaries.
34   ;
35   ; Note: Do not pass an array that starts at offset 0 (SI=0),
36   ;       since a match on the first byte and failure to find
37   ;       the byte would be indistinguishable.
38   ;
39   CaseInsensitiveSearch:
40           cld
41           cmp     al,'a'
42           jb      CaseInsensitiveSearchBegin
43           cmp     al,'z'
44           ja      CaseInsensitiveSearchBegin
45           and     al,not 20h      ;make sure the search byte
46                                   ; is uppercase
47   CaseInsensitiveSearchBegin:
48           mov     ah,al           ;put the search byte in AH
49                                   ; so we can use AL to hold
50                                   ; the bytes we're checking
51   CaseInsensitiveSearchLoop:
52           lodsb                   ;get the next byte from the
53                                   ; array being searched
54           cmp     al,'a'
55           jb      CaseInsensitiveSearchIsUpper
56           cmp     al,'z'
57           ja      CaseInsensitiveSearchIsUpper
58           and     al,not 20h      ;make sure the array byte is
59                                   ; uppercase
60   CaseInsensitiveSearchIsUpper:
61           cmp     al,ah           ;do we have a
62                                   ; case-insensitive match?
63           jz      CaseInsensitiveSearchMatchFound ;yes
64           dec     cl              ;count down bytes remaining
```

```
65                                  ; in array being searched
66          jnz     CaseInsensitiveSearchLoop
67                                  ;check the next byte, if any
68          sub     si,si           ;no match found
69          ret
70  CaseInsensitiveSearchMatchFound:
71          dec     si              ;point back to the matching
72                                  ; array byte
73          ret
74  ;
75  Skip:
76          call    ZTimerOn
77          mov     al,'K'          ;character to search for
78          mov     si,offset ByteArray ;array to search
79          mov     cx,ARRAY_LENGTH ;# of bytes to search
80                                  ; through
81          call    CaseInsensitiveSearch
82                                  ;perform a case-insensitive
83                                  ; search for 'K'
84          call    ZTimerOff
```

```
1   ;
2   ; *** Listing 14-10 ***
3   ;
4   ; Searches for the first appearance of a character, in any
5   ; case, in a byte-sized array by using JZ, DEC MEM8, and
6   ; JNZ.
7   ;
8           jmp     Skip
9   ;
10  ByteArray       label   byte
11          db      'Array Containing Both Upper and Lowercase'
12          db      ' Characters And Blanks'
13  ARRAY_LENGTH    equ     ($-ByteArray)
14  BCount  db      ?       ;used to count down the # of bytes
15                          ; remaining in the array being
16                          ; searched (counter is byte-sized)
17  ;
18  ; Finds the first occurrence of the specified character, in
19  ; any case, in the specified byte-sized array.
20  ;
21  ; Input:
22  ;       AL = character for which to perform a
23  ;               case-insensitive search
24  ;       CL = array length (0 means 256 long)
25  ;       DS:SI = array to search
26  ;
27  ; Output:
28  ;       SI = pointer to first case-insensitive match, or 0
29  ;               if no match is found
30  ;
31  ; Registers altered: AX, SI
32  ;
33  ; Direction flag cleared
34  ;
35  ; Note: Does not handle arrays that are longer than 256
36  ;       bytes or cross segment boundaries.
37  ;
```

```
38      ; Note: Do not pass an array that starts at offset 0 (SI=0),
39      ;        since a match on the first byte and failure to find
40      ;        the byte would be indistinguishable.
41      ;
42      CaseInsensitiveSearch:
43              cld
44              mov     [BCount],cl     ;set the count variable
45              cmp     al,'a'
46              jb      CaseInsensitiveSearchBegin
47              cmp     al,'z'
48              ja      CaseInsensitiveSearchBegin
49              and     al,not 20h      ;make sure the search byte
50                                      ; is uppercase
51      CaseInsensitiveSearchBegin:
52              mov     ah,al           ;put the search byte in AH
53                                      ; so we can use AL to hold
54                                      ; the bytes we're checking
55      CaseInsensitiveSearchLoop:
56              lodsb                   ;get the next byte from the
57                                      ; array being searched
58              cmp     al,'a'
59              jb      CaseInsensitiveSearchIsUpper
60              cmp     al,'z'
61              ja      CaseInsensitiveSearchIsUpper
62              and     al,not 20h      ;make sure the array byte is
63                                      ; uppercase
64      CaseInsensitiveSearchIsUpper:
65              cmp     al,ah           ;do we have a
66                                      ; case-insensitive match?
67              jz      CaseInsensitiveSearchMatchFound ;yes
68              dec     [BCount]        ;count down bytes remaining
69                                      ; in array being searched
70                                      ; (counter is byte-sized)
71              jnz     CaseInsensitiveSearchLoop
72                                      ;check the next byte, if any
73              sub     si,si           ;no match found
74              ret
75      CaseInsensitiveSearchMatchFound:
76              dec     si              ;point back to the matching
77                                      ; array byte
78              ret
79      ;
80      Skip:
81              call    ZTimerOn
82              mov     al,'K'          ;character to search for
83              mov     si,offset ByteArray ;array to search
84              mov     cx,ARRAY_LENGTH ;# of bytes to search
85                                      ; through
86              call    CaseInsensitiveSearch
87                                      ;perform a case-insensitive
88                                      ; search for 'K'
89              call    ZTimerOff


1       ;
2       ; *** Listing 14-11 ***
3       ;
4       ; Searches for the first appearance of a character, in any
5       ; case, in a byte-sized array by using JZ, DEC MEM16, and
```

```
 6   ; JNZ.
 7   ;
 8           jmp        Skip
 9   ;
10   ByteArray       label      byte
11           db         'Array Containing Both Upper and Lowercase'
12           db         ' Characters And Blanks'
13   ARRAY_LENGTH    equ        ($-ByteArray)
14   WCount  dw         ?         ;used to count down the # of bytes
15                                ; remaining in the array being
16                                ; searched (counter is word-sized)
17   ;
18   ; Finds the first occurrence of the specified character, in
19   ; any case, in the specified byte-sized array.
20   ;
21   ; Input:
22   ;       AL = character for which to perform a
23   ;                 case-insensitive search
24   ;       CX = array length (0 means 64K long)
25   ;       DS:SI = array to search
26   ;
27   ; Output:
28   ;       SI = pointer to first case-insensitive match, or 0
29   ;                 if no match is found
30   ;
31   ; Registers altered: AX, SI
32   ;
33   ; Direction flag cleared
34   ;
35   ; Note: Does not handle arrays that are longer than 64K
36   ;       bytes or cross segment boundaries.
37   ;
38   ; Note: Do not pass an array that starts at offset 0 (SI=0),
39   ;       since a match on the first byte and failure to find
40   ;       the byte would be indistinguishable.
41   ;
42   CaseInsensitiveSearch:
43           cld
44           mov        [WCount],cx     ;set the count variable
45           cmp        al,'a'
46           jb         CaseInsensitiveSearchBegin
47           cmp        al,'z'
48           ja         CaseInsensitiveSearchBegin
49           and        al,not 20h      ;make sure the search byte
50                                      ; is uppercase
51   CaseInsensitiveSearchBegin:
52           mov        ah,al           ;put the search byte in AH
53                                      ; so we can use AL to hold
54                                      ; the bytes we're checking
55   CaseInsensitiveSearchLoop:
56           lodsb                      ;get the next byte from the
57                                      ; array being searched
58           cmp        al,'a'
59           jb         CaseInsensitiveSearchIsUpper
60           cmp        al,'z'
61           ja         CaseInsensitiveSearchIsUpper
62           and        al,not 20h      ;make sure the array byte is
63                                      ; uppercase
64   CaseInsensitiveSearchIsUpper:
```

```
65              cmp     al,ah           ;do we have a
66                                      ; case-insensitive match?
67              jz      CaseInsensitiveSearchMatchFound ;yes
68              dec     [WCount]        ;count down bytes remaining
69                                      ; in array being searched
70                                      ; (counter is word-sized)
71              jnz     CaseInsensitiveSearchLoop
72                                      ;check the next byte, if any
73              sub     si,si           ;no match found
74              ret
75      CaseInsensitiveSearchMatchFound:
76              dec     si              ;point back to the matching
77                                      ; array byte
78              ret
79      ;
80      Skip:
81              call    ZTimerOn
82              mov     al,'K'          ;character to search for
83              mov     si,offset ByteArray ;array to search
84              mov     cx,ARRAY_LENGTH ;# of bytes to search
85                                      ; through
86              call    CaseInsensitiveSearch
87                                      ;perform a case-insensitive
88                                      ; search for 'K'
89              call    ZTimerOff
```

14.8 ◆ Only jcxz Can Test *and* Branch in a Single Bound

The **jcxz** instruction is the only 8088 instruction that can both test a register and branch according to the outcome. Most of the applications for this unusual property of **jcxz** are well known, most notably avoiding division by 0 and guarding against 0 counts in loops. You may, however, find other, less obvious, applications if you stretch your mind a little.

For example, suppose that we have an animation program that needs to

TABLE 14.1   The relative performance of various looping approaches.

Looping code	Listing	Time
loop CaseInsensitiveSearchLoop	14–6	1134 μsec
dec cx/jnz CaseInsensitiveSearchLoop	14–8	1199 μsec
dec cl/jnz CaseInsensitiveSearchLoop	14–9	1252 μsec
dec [BCount]/jnz CaseInsensitiveSearchLoop	14–10	1540 μsec
dec [WCount]/jnz CaseInsensitiveSearchLoop	14–11	1652 μsec

be speed synchronized. This program has a delay loop built into each pass through the main loop; however, the proper delay will vary from processor to processor and from one display adapter to another, so the delay will need to be adjusted as the program runs.

Let's say that ideally the program should perform exactly 600 passes through the main loop every 10 seconds. In order to monitor its compliance with that standard, the program counts down a word-sized counter every time it completes the main loop. In a perfect world, the counter would reach 0 precisely as the 10-second mark is reached.

That's not very likely to happen, of course. The program can easily detect whether it's running too fast; if the counter reaches 0 before the 10-second mark is reached, the delay needs to be increased. The quicker the counter reaches 0, the greater the necessary increase in the delay.

If the program does reach the 10-second mark without the counter reaching 0, then it's running too slowly, and the delay needs to be decreased. The higher the remaining count, the greater the amount by which the delay needs to be decreased, so we need to know not only that the counter hasn't reached 0 but also the exact count remaining. At the same time, we need to reset the counter to its initial value in preparation for the next 10-second timing period.

We could do that easily enough with

```
mov   ax,[SyncCount]     ;get remaining count
mov   [SyncCount],INITIAL_COUNT
                         ;set count back to initial value
and   ax,ax              ;is the count 0?
jz    MainLoop           ;yes, so we're dead on and no
                         ; adjustment is needed
; The count isn't zero, so the program is running too slowly.
; Decrease the delay proportionately to the value in AX.
```

With **jcxz** and a little creativity, however, we can tighten the code considerably:

```
mov   cx,INITIAL_COUNT
xchg  [SyncCount],cx     ;get remaining count and set count
                         ; back to initial value
jcxz  MainLoop           ;if the count is 0, we're dead on
                         ; and no adjustment is needed
; The count isn't zero, so the program is running too slowly.
; Decrease the delay proportionately to the value in CX.
```

With these changes, we've managed to trim a 13-byte sequence by 4 bytes—30 percent—even though the original sequence used the accumulator-specific direct-addressed form of **mov**. There's nothing more profound here than familiarity with the 8088's instruction set and a willingness to mix and match instructions inventively—which, when you get right down to it, is where some of the best 8088 code comes from.

Try it yourself and see!

14.9 ◆ Jump and Call Tables

Given that you've got an index that's associated with the execution of certain code, jump and call tables allow you to branch very quickly to the corresponding code. A jump or call table is nothing more than an array of code addresses organized to correspond to some index value; the index can then be used to look up the matching address in the table, so that a branch can be made to that address.

The only difference between call tables and jump tables is the type of branch made. Both types of tables consist of nothing but addresses, and the distinction lies solely in whether the code using the table chooses to call or jump to the addresses looked up. Jump tables are used in switch-type situations, where one of several paths through a routine is chosen; call tables are used for applications such as function dispatchers, where one of several subroutines is executed. For simplicity, I'll refer to both sorts of tables as jump tables from now on.

The operation of a sample jump table is shown in Figure 14.8. An index into the table is used to look up one of the entries in the table, and an indirect branch is performed to the address contained in that entry.

The size of a jump table entry can be either 2 or 4 bytes, depending on whether near or far branches are used by the code that branches through the jump table. As we discussed earlier, the 2-byte jump table entries used with near branches are vastly preferable to the 4-byte jump table entries used with far branches, for two reasons: 2-byte-per-entry jump tables are half the size of equivalent 4-byte-per-table jump tables, and near indirect branches are much faster than far indirect branches, especially when **call** and **ret** are used.

So, what's so great about jump tables? Simply put, they're usually the fastest way to turn an index into execution of the corresponding code. In the sorts of applications jump tables are best suited to, we basically already know which routine we want to branch to, thanks to the index—it's just a

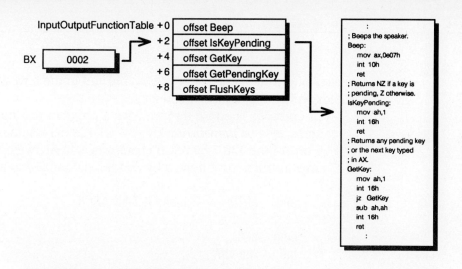

FIGURE 14.8 The operation of a sample jump table. Here the function **JumpToInputOutputFunction** in the code

```
InputOutputFunctionTable label        word
        dw    Beep
        dw    IsKeyPending
        dw    GetKey
        dw    GetPendingKey
        dw    FlushKeys
    ;
    ; On entry, BX contains the entry number of the
    ; desired function in InputOutputFunctionTable.
    ;
JumpToInputOutputFunction:
        shl   bx,1      ;function # times 2
        jmp   word ptr [InputOutputFunctionTable+bx]
```

is executed, with BX set to 1 when **JumpToInputOutputFunction** is called. A BX setting of 1 indicates that the second function in the jump table (function number 1, **IsKeyPending**) should be executed; if BX were 0, function number 0, **Beep**, would be executed, and if BX were 2, function number 2, **GetKey**, would be executed.

Since each entry in **InputOutputFunctionTable** is 2 bytes long, the function number in BX must be multiplied by 2 before it can serve as a pointer into **InputOutputFunctionTable**. Once it has been multiplied by 2, the function number in BX is used to point to the entry for the desired function in **InputOutputFunctionTable**, and an indirect jump to the offset stored in that entry is performed.

matter of getting there as fast as possible and in the fewest bytes, and jump tables are winners on both counts.

For example, suppose that we have a program that monitors the serial port and needs to branch quickly to 1 of 128 subroutines, depending on which one of the 128 7-bit ASCII characters is in AL. We could do that with 127 **cmp** instructions followed by conditional jumps, something like this:

```
        and    al,7fh        ;make it 7-bit ASCII
               :
        cmp    al,8
        jae    Above7
        cmp    al,4
        jae    Above3
        cmp    al,2
        jae    Above1
        and    al,al
        jnz    ls1
; The character is ASCII 0.
               :
; The character is ASCII 1.
ls1:
```

However, this approach would take a *lot* of code to handle all 128 characters—somewhere between 4 and 7 bytes for each character after the first, or between 508 and 889 bytes in all. It would be slow as well, as seven comparisons and conditional jumps would be required to identify each character. Worse yet, some of the conditional jumps would have to be implemented as reversed-polarity conditional jumps around unconditional jumps, because conditional jumps have a range of only +127 to −128 bytes—and we know how slow jumps around jumps can be.

The failing of the above approach is that it uses code to translate a value in AL into a routine's offset to be loaded into IP. Because the mapping of values to offsets covers every value from 0 through 127 and is well defined, it can be handled far more efficiently in the form of data than in the form of endless test-and-branch code. How? By constructing a table of offsets—a jump table—with the position of each routine's offset in the table corresponding to the value used to select that routine:

```
Jump7BitASCIITable     label     word
        dw     ls0, ls1, ls2, ls3, ls4, ls5, ls6, ls7
        dw     ls8, ls9, ls10, ls11, ls12, ls13, ls14, ls15
               :
```

```
mov   bl,al
and   bx,7fh      ;make it 7-bit ASCII and make it a word
shl   bx,1        ;*2 for lookup in a table of word-sized offsets
jmp   [Jump7BitASCIITable+bx]   ;jump to handler for value
```

The jump table approach is not only faster (by a long shot—only four instructions and one branch are involved), it's also *much* more compact. Only 267 bytes are needed, less than half as many as are required by the compare-and-branch approach.

It's not much of a contest, is it?

This may remind you of our experience with look-up tables in Chapter 7, and well it might, for a jump table is just another sort of look-up table. When a task is such that it can be solved by looking up a result rather than calculating it, the look-up approach almost invariably wins. It matters not a whit whether the desired result is a bit pattern, a multiplication product, or a code address.

Partial Jump Tables

Jump tables work well even with less neatly organized index-to-offset mappings. Suppose, for example, that the ASCII character handler of the last example needs to branch to unique handlers only for the 32 control characters and that the other 96 characters can be handled by a single routine. That would greatly reduce the number of comparisons required by the compare-and-branch approach, improving performance and shrinking the code to less than 150 bytes. On the other hand, our jump table implementation wouldn't shrink at all, because one jump table entry would still be needed for each 7-bit ASCII character, although the entries for all the non-control character entries would be the same, as follows:

```
Jump7BitASCIITable      label     word
      dw    Is0, Is1, Is2, Is3, Is4, Is5, Is6, Is7
      dw    Is8, Is9, Is10, Is11, Is12, Is13, Is14, Is15
      dw    Is16, Is17, Is18, Is19, Is20, Is21, Is22, Is23
      dw    Is24, Is25, Is26, Is27, Is28, Is29, Is30, Is31
      dw    96 dup (IsNormalChar)
      :
      mov   bl,al
      and   bx,7fh      ;make it 7-bit ASCII and make it a word
      shl   bx,1        ;*2 for lookup in a table of word-sized offsets
      jmp   [Jump7BitASCIITable+bx]   ;jump to handler for value
```

While the duplicate entries work perfectly well, all branching to the same place, they do waste bytes.

What of jump tables in this case?

Well, the pure jump table code would indeed be somewhat larger than the compare-and-branch code, but it would still be much faster. One of the wonders of jump tables is that they never require more than one branch, and no compare-and-branch approach that performs anything more complex than a yes-no decision can make that claim.

Matters are not so clear cut as they might seem, however. We've learned that there are always other options, and this is no exception. Just as we achieved good results with a hybrid of in-line code and looping in the last chapter, we can come up with a better solution here by mixing the two approaches. We can compare-and-branch to handle the 96 normal characters, then use a reduced jump table to handle the 32 control characters, as follows:

```
JumpControlCharTable    label     word
        dw      ls0, ls1, ls2, ls3, ls4, ls5, ls6, ls7
        dw      ls8, ls9, ls10, ls11, ls12, ls13, ls14, ls15
        dw      ls16, ls17, ls18, ls19, ls20, ls21, ls22, ls23
        dw      ls24, ls25, ls26, ls27, ls28, ls29, ls30, ls31
        :
        cmp     al,20h      ;is it a control character?
        jnb     IsNormalChar   ;no-handle as a normal character
        mov     bl,al       ;handle control characters through look-up table
        and     bx,7fh      ;make it 7-bit ASCII and make it a word
        shl     bx,1        ;*2 for lookup in a table of word-sized offsets
        jmp     [JumpControlCharTable+bx]   ;jump to handler for value
```

This partial jump table approach requires the execution of a maximum of only six instructions and one branch and is just 79 bytes long—still vastly superior to the compare-and-branch approach, and, on balance, superior to the pure jump table approach as well.

Granted, pure jump table code would be slightly faster, being two instructions shorter, but that's just our familiar tradeoff of speed for size. In this case that's an easy tradeoff to make, because the speed differential is negligible and the size differential is great. The greater the number of tests required before performing the branch through the jump table in a partial jump table approach, the greater the performance loss and the less the space saving relative to a pure jump table approach. As usual, the decision is yours to make on a case-by-case basis.

Generating Jump Table Indexes

There are many ways to generate indexes into jump tables. Sometimes indexes are passed in as parameters by calling routines, as in a function dispatcher. Sometimes they are read from ports or from memory. Indexes also may be looked up in *other* tables. For example, a keyboard handler might use **repnz scasw** to find the index for the current 16-bit key code in a key-mapping table, then use that index to jump to the appropriate key-handling routine via a jump table, as shown in Listing 14-12, which runs in 504 μsec for the sample keystrokes. (Listing 14-12 is a modification of the key-handling jump table code we saw in Listing 11-17.)

```
1    ;
2    ; *** Listing 14-12 ***
3    ;
4    ; Demonstrates scanning a table with REPNZ SCASW in
5    ; order to generate an index to be used with a jump table.
6    ;
7            jmp     Skip
8    ;
9    ; Branches to the routine corresponding to the key code in
10   ; AX. Simply returns if no match is found.
11   ;
12   ; Input:
13   ;       AX = 16-bit key code, as returned by the BIOS
14   ;
15   ; Output: none
16   ;
17   ; Registers altered: CX, DI, ES
18   ;
19   ; Direction flag cleared
20   ;
21   ; Table of 16-bit key codes this routine handles.
22   ;
23   KeyLookUpTable  label   word
24           dw      1e41h, 3042h, 2e43h, 2044h      ;A-D
25           dw      1245h, 2146h, 2247h, 2347h      ;E-H
26           dw      1749h, 244ah, 254bh, 264ch      ;I-L
27           dw      324dh, 314eh, 184fh, 1950h      ;M-P
28           dw      1051h, 1352h, 1f53h, 1454h      ;Q-T
29           dw      1655h, 2f56h, 1157h, 2d58h      ;U-X
30           dw      1559h, 2c5ah                    ;Y-Z
31   KEY_LOOK_UP_TABLE_LENGTH_IN_WORDS equ (($-KeyLookUpTable)/2)
32   ;
33   ; Table of addresses to which to jump when the corresponding
34   ; key codes in KeyLookUpTable are found. All the entries
35   ; point to the same routine, since this is for illustrative
36   ; purposes only, but they could easily be changed to point
37   ; to any label in the code segment.
38   ;
39   KeyJumpTable    label   word
40           dw      HandleA_Z, HandleA_Z, HandleA_Z, HandleA_Z
41           dw      HandleA_Z, HandleA_Z, HandleA_Z, HandleA_Z
42           dw      HandleA_Z, HandleA_Z, HandleA_Z, HandleA_Z
```

```
43              dw      HandleA_Z, HandleA_Z, HandleA_Z, HandleA_Z
44              dw      HandleA_Z, HandleA_Z, HandleA_Z, HandleA_Z
45              dw      HandleA_Z, HandleA_Z, HandleA_Z, HandleA_Z
46              dw      HandleA_Z, HandleA_Z
47      ;
48      VectorOnKey     proc    near
49              mov     di,cs
50              mov     es,di
51              mov     di,offset KeyLookUpTable
52                              ;point ES:DI to the table of keys
53                              ; we handle, which is in the same
54                              ; code segment as this routine
55              mov     cx,KEY_LOOK_UP_TABLE_LENGTH_IN_WORDS
56                              ;# of words to scan
57              cld
58              repnz   scasw   ;look up the key
59              jnz     VectorOnKeyDone ;it's not in the table, so
60                                      ; we're done
61              jmp     cs:[KeyJumpTable+di-2-offset KeyLookUpTable]
62                              ;jump to the routine for this key
63                              ; Note that:
64                              ;   DI-2-offset KeyLookUpTable
65                              ; is the offset in KeyLookUpTable of
66                              ; the key we found, with the -2
67                              ; needed to compensate for the
68                              ; 2-byte (1-word) overrun of SCASW
69      HandleA_Z:
70      VectorOnKeyDone:
71              ret
72      VectorOnKey     endp
73      ;
74      Skip:
75              call    ZTimerOn
76              mov     ax,1e41h
77              call    VectorOnKey     ;look up 'A'
78              mov     ax,1749h
79              call    VectorOnKey     ;look up 'I'
80              mov     ax,1f53h
81              call    VectorOnKey     ;look up 'S'
82              mov     ax,2c5ah
83              call    VectorOnKey     ;look up 'Z'
84              mov     ax,0
85              call    VectorOnKey     ;finally, look up a key
86                                      ; code that's not in the
87                                      ; table
88              call    ZTimerOff
```

Why not simply put the address of each key handler right next to the corresponding 16-bit key code in a single look-up table, so no calculation is needed in order to perform the second look-up? For one thing, the second look-up takes hardly any time at all in Listing 14-12, since the calculation of the jump table address is performed as a *mod-reg-rm* calculation by

```
jmp cs:[KeyJumpTable+di-2-offset KeyLookUpTable]
```

Even if the second look-up were slow, however, the two-table approach would still be preferable. You see, contiguous data arrays are required in order to use **repnz scasw**, and, as we learned a few chapters back, it's worth structuring your code so that repeated string instructions can be used whenever possible.

Does it really make that much difference to structure the table so that **rep scasw** can be used? It surely does. Listing 14-13, which uses a single look-up table containing both key codes and handler addresses, takes 969 μsec to run, nearly twice as long as Listing 14-12.

Design your code to use repeated string instructions!

```
1   ;
2   ; *** Listing 14-13 ***
3   ;
4   ; Demonstrates that it's much slower to scan a table
5   ; in a loop than to use REP SCASW; look-up tables should
6   ; be designed so that repeated string instructions can be
7   ; used.
8   ;
9           jmp     Skip
10  ;
11  ; Branches to the routine corresponding to the key code in
12  ; AX. Simply returns if no match is found.
13  ;
14  ; Input:
15  ;       AX = 16-bit key code, as returned by the BIOS
16  ;
17  ; Output: none
18  ;
19  ; Registers altered: CX, DI, ES
20  ;
21  ; Direction flag cleared
22  ;
23  ; Table of 16-bit key codes this routine handles, each
24  ; paired with the address to jump to if that key code is
25  ; found.
26  ;
27  KeyLookUpTable   label    word
28          dw      1e41h, HandleA_Z, 3042h, HandleA_Z      ;A-B
29          dw      2e43h, HandleA_Z, 2044h, HandleA_Z      ;C-D
30          dw      1245h, HandleA_Z, 2146h, HandleA_Z      ;E-F
31          dw      2247h, HandleA_Z, 2347h, HandleA_Z      ;G-H
32          dw      1749h, HandleA_Z, 244ah, HandleA_Z      ;I-J
33          dw      254bh, HandleA_Z, 264ch, HandleA_Z      ;K-L
34          dw      324dh, HandleA_Z, 314eh, HandleA_Z      ;M-N
35          dw      184fh, HandleA_Z, 1950h, HandleA_Z      ;O-P
36          dw      1051h, HandleA_Z, 1352h, HandleA_Z      ;Q-R
37          dw      1f53h, HandleA_Z, 1454h, HandleA_Z      ;S-T
38          dw      1655h, HandleA_Z, 2f56h, HandleA_Z      ;U-V
39          dw      1157h, HandleA_Z, 2d58h, HandleA_Z      ;W-X
40          dw      1559h, HandleA_Z, 2c5ah, HandleA_Z      ;Y-Z
41  KEY_LOOK_UP_TABLE_LEN_IN_ENTRIES equ (($-KeyLookUpTable)/4)
42  ;
43  VectorOnKey      proc     near
```

```
44              mov     di,cs
45              mov     es,di
46              mov     di,offset KeyLookUpTable
47                              ;point ES:DI to the table of keys
48                              ; we handle, which is in the same
49                              ; code segment as this routine
50              mov     cx,KEY_LOOK_UP_TABLE_LEN_IN_ENTRIES
51                              ;# of entries to scan
52              cld
53      VectorOnKeyLoop:
54              scasw
55              jz      VectorOnKeyJump ;we've found the key code
56              inc     di              ;point to the next entry
57              inc     di
58              loop    VectorOnKeyLoop
59              ret                     ;the key code is not in the
60                                      ; table, so we're done
61      VectorOnKeyJump:
62              jmp     word ptr cs:[di]
63                              ;jump to the routine for this key
64      HandleA_Z:
65              ret
66      VectorOnKey     endp
67      ;
68      Skip:
69              call    ZTimerOn
70              mov     ax,1e41h
71              call    VectorOnKey     ;look up 'A'
72              mov     ax,1749h
73              call    VectorOnKey     ;look up 'I'
74              mov     ax,1f53h
75              call    VectorOnKey     ;look up 'S'
76              mov     ax,2c5ah
77              call    VectorOnKey     ;look up 'Z'
78              mov     ax,0
79              call    VectorOnKey     ;finally, look up a key
80                                      ; code that's not in the
81                                      ; table
82              call    ZTimerOff
```

At any rate, jump tables operate in the same basic way no matter how indexes are generated; an index is used to look up an address to branch to. The rule as to when you should use a jump table is equally simple: whenever you find yourself branching to one of several addresses based on one of a set of consecutive values, you should almost certainly use a jump table. If the values aren't consecutive but are bunched, you might want to use the partial jump table approach, filtering out the oddball cases and branching on those that are tightly grouped. Finally, if speed is paramount, the pure jump table approach is the way to go, even if that means making a large table containing many unused or duplicate entries.

Jump Tables, Macros, and Branched to In-Line Code

In the last chapter, we simply calculated the destination offset whenever we needed to branch into in-line code. That approach is fine when the offset calculations involve nothing more than a few shifts and adds, but it can reduce performance considerably if a **mul** instruction must be used. Then, too, the calculated offset approach works only if every repeated code block in the target in-line code is exactly the same size. That won't be the case if, for example, some repeated code blocks use short branches while others use normal branches, as shown in Figure 14.9.

In such a case, a jump table is the preferred solution. Selecting an offset and branching to it through a jump table takes only a few instructions, and is certainly faster than multiplying. Jump tables can also handle repeated in-line code blocks of varying sizes, because jump tables store offsets that can point anywhere and can be arranged in any order, rather than being limited to calculations based on a fixed block size.

Let's look at the use of a jump table to handle a case where in-line code blocks do vary in size. Suppose that we're writing a subroutine that will search the first n bytes of a 0-terminated string up to 80 bytes long for a given character. We want to use pure in-line code for speed, but that's more easily said than done. The in-line code performs conditional jumps when checking for both matches and terminating zeros; unfortunately, the entire in-line code sequence is so long that the 1-byte displacement of a conditional jump can't reach the termination labels from the in-line code blocks that are smack in the middle of the in-line code. We could solve this problem by using conditional jumps around unconditional jumps in all cases, but that seems like an awful waste, given that many of the blocks *could* use conditional jumps.

What we really want to do is use conditional jumps in some in-line code blocks—whenever a 1-byte displacement will reach—and jumps around jumps in other blocks. Unfortunately, that would mean that some blocks were larger than others, and *that* would mean that there was no easy way to calculate the start offset of the desired block.

The answer (surprise!) is to use a jump table, as shown in Listing 14-14. The jump table simply stores the start offset of each in-line code block, regardless of how large that block may be. Although the jump table takes up 162 bytes, there's no speed penalty for using it, since the process of looking up a table entry and branching accordingly requires only a few instructions. Indeed, it's often faster to use a jump table in this way than it

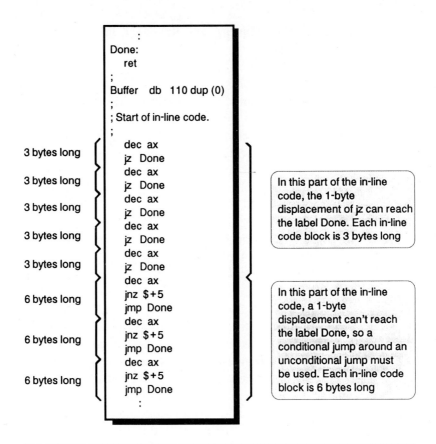

FIGURE 14.9   An example of in-line code in which the in-line code
blocks vary in size. Each in-line code block decrements
AX and branches to **Done** if AX becomes 0. However,
the 1-byte displacement of **jz** can reach **Done** only from
the first five in-line code blocks; the longer **jnz/jmp**
sequence must be used in the rest of the in-line code
blocks, making those blocks 3 bytes longer than the first
five blocks.

is to calculate the target offset even when the repeated in-line code blocks
are all the same size.

How does Listing 14-14 generate in-line code blocks of varying sizes?
The macro **CHECK_CHAR**, which is used to generate each in-line code
block, actually calculates the distance from the end of each conditional
jump to the target label and then uses the **if** directive to assemble a single

```
 1   ;
 2   ; *** Listing 14-14 ***
 3   ;
 4   ; Demonstrates the use of a jump table to branch into
 5   ; in-line code consisting of repeated code blocks of
 6   ; varying lengths. The approach of using a jump table to
 7   ; branch into in-line code is speedy enough that
 8   ; it's often preferable even when all the repeated code
 9   ; blocks are the same size, although the jump table does
10   ; take extra space.
11   ;
12   ; Searches up to N bytes of a zero-terminated string for
13   ; a character.
14   ;
15           jmp     Skip
16   TestString      label   byte
17           db      'This is a string containing the letter '
18           db      'z but not containing capital q', 0
19   ;
20   ; Searches a zero-terminated string for a character.
21   ; Searches until a match is found, the terminating zero
22   ; is found, or the specified number of characters have been
23   ; checked.
24   ;
25   ; Input:
26   ;       AL = character to search for
27   ;       BX = maximum # of characters to search. Must be
28   ;                    less than or equal to 80
29   ;       DS:SI = string to search
30   ;
31   ; Output:
32   ;       SI = pointer to character, or 0 if character not
33   ;                    found
34   ;
35   ; Registers altered: AX, BX, SI
36   ;
37   ; Direction flag cleared
38   ;
39   ; Note: Don't pass a string starting at offset 0, since a
40   ;        match there couldn't be distinguished from a failure
41   ;        to match.
42   ;
43   MAX_SEARCH_LENGTH equ   80      ;longest supported search
44                                   ; length
45   ;
46   ; Macro to create SearchTable entries.
47   ;
48   MAKE_CHECK_CHAR_LABEL   macro   NUMBER
49           dw      CheckChar&NUMBER&
50           endm
51   ;
52   ; Macro to create in-line code to search 1 character.
53   ; Gives the code block a unique label according to NUMBER.
54   ; Each conditional branch uses the shortest possible jump
55   ; sequence to reach NoMatch and MatchFound.
56   ;
57   CHECK_CHAR      macro   NUMBER
58           local   CheckMatch, Continue
59   CheckChar&NUMBER&:
```

```
60              lodsb           ;get the character
61              and     al,al   ;done if terminating zero
62      ;
63      ; Assemble a single conditional jump if it'll reach, or
64      ; a conditional jump around an unconditional jump if the
65      ; 1-byte displacement of a conditional jump won't reach.
66      ;
67      if ($+2-NoMatch) le 128
68              jz      NoMatch
69      else
70              jnz     CheckMatch
71              jmp     NoMatch
72      endif
73      CheckMatch:
74              cmp     ah,al   ;done if matches search character
75      ;
76      ; Again, assemble shortest possible jump sequence.
77      ;
78      if ($+2-MatchFound) le 128
79              jz      MatchFound
80      else
81              jnz     Continue
82              jmp     MatchFound
83      endif
84      Continue:
85              endm
86      ;
87      ; Table of in-line code entry points for maximum search
88      ; lengths of 0 through 80.
89      ;
90      SearchTable     label   word
91              dw      NoMatch         ;we never match on a
92                                      ; maximum length of 0
93      BLOCK_NUMBER=MAX_SEARCH_LENGTH-1
94              rept    MAX_SEARCH_LENGTH
95              MAKE_CHECK_CHAR_LABEL   %BLOCK_NUMBER
96      BLOCK_NUMBER=BLOCK_NUMBER-1
97              endm
98      ;
99      SearchNBytes    proc    near
100             mov     ah,al           ;we'll need AL for LODSB
101             cmp     bx,MAX_SEARCH_LENGTH
102             ja      NoMatch         ;if the maximum length's
103                                     ; too long for the in-line
104                                     ; code, return a no-match
105                                     ; status
106             shl     bx,1            ;*2 to look up in word-sized
107                                     ; table
108             jmp     [SearchTable+bx] ;branch into the in-line
109                                      ; code to do the search
110     ;
111     ; No match was found.
112     ;
113     NoMatch:
114             sub     si,si           ;return no-match status
115             ret
116     ;
117     ; A match was found.
118     ;
```

```
119   MatchFound:
120           dec     si              ;point back to matching
121                                   ; location
122           ret
123   ;
124   ; This is the in-line code that actually does the search.
125   ; Each repetition is uniquely labelled, with the labels
126   ; running from CheckChar0 through CheckChar79.
127   ;
128   BLOCK_NUMBER=0
129   ;
130   ; These in-line blocks use 1-byte displacements whenever
131   ; possible to branch backward; otherwise 2-byte
132   ; displacements are used to branch backward, with
133   ; conditional jumps around unconditional jumps.
134   ;
135           rept    MAX_SEARCH_LENGTH
136           CHECK_CHAR      %BLOCK_NUMBER
137   BLOCK_NUMBER=BLOCK_NUMBER+1
138           endm
139   ;
140   ; If we make it here, we haven't found the character.
141   ;
142           sub     si,si   ;return no-match status
143           ret
144   SearchNBytes    endp
145   ;
146   Skip:
147           call    ZTimerOn
148           mov     al,'Q'
149           mov     bx,20                   ;search up to the
150           mov     si,offset TestString    ; first 20 bytes of
151           call    SearchNBytes            ; TestString for 'Q'
152           mov     al,'z'
153           mov     bx,80                   ;search up to the
154           mov     si,offset TestString    ; first 80 bytes of
155           call    SearchNBytes            ; TestString for 'z'
156           mov     al,'a'
157           mov     bx,10                   ;search up to the
158           mov     si,offset TestString    ; first 10 bytes of
159           call    SearchNBytes            ; TestString for 'a'
160           call    ZTimerOff
```

conditional jump if a 1-byte displacement will reach the target label or a conditional jump around an unconditional jump if necessary. In some cases a conditional jump does reach the target, and in others it doesn't; as a result, the in-line code blocks vary in size.

Listing 14-14 illustrates the use of a clever technique that's most useful for generating jump tables that point to in-line code: macro text substitution. In order to generate a unique label for each repeated code block, the assembler variable **BLOCK_NUMBER** is initially set to 0 and then incremented each time a new code block is created. (Note that **BLOCK_NUMBER** is a variable used during assembly, not a variable used by the assembler program. Such variables are used to control assembly, and the program being assembled has no knowledge of them at run time.)

The value of **BLOCK_NUMBER** is passed to **CHECK_CHAR**, the macro that creates each instance of the repeated code, as follows:

```
CHECK_CHAR   %BLOCK_NUMBER
```

The macro sees this passed parameter as the parameter **NUMBER**. Thanks to the percent sign, the assembler actually makes the value of **BLOCK_NUMBER** into a text string when it passes it to **CHECK_CHAR**; that text string is then substituted wherever the parameter **NUMBER** appears in the macro.

What's really interesting is what comes of butting **&NUMBER&** up against the text "CheckChar" in the macro **CHECK_CHAR**, as follows:

```
CheckChar&NUMBER&:
```

(The ampersands (&) around **NUMBER** ensure that the assembler knows that parameter substitution should take place; otherwise, when **NUMBER** is butted up against other text, as it is above, the assembler has no way of knowing whether to treat **NUMBER** as a parameter or as part of a longer text string.) A text representation of the value of **NUMBER** is substituted into the above line, so if **NUMBER** is 2, the line becomes

```
CheckChar2:
```

If **NUMBER** is 10, the line becomes

```
CheckChar10:
```

Do you see what we've done? We've created a unique label for each repeated code block, since **BLOCK_NUMBER** is incremented after each code block is created. Better yet, the labels are organized in a predictable manner, with the first code block labelled with **CheckChar0**, the second labelled with **CheckChar1**, and so on.

It should be pretty clear that this is an ideal setup for a jump table. There are a couple of tricks here, however. First, if we want to check at most one character, we must branch to not the first but the *last* repeated in-line code block, and that code block is labelled with **CheckChar79**. That means that our jump table should look something like this:

```
CheckCharJumpTable   label     word
     dw    NoMatch
     dw    CheckChar79, CheckChar78, CheckChar77, CheckChar76
     dw    CheckChar75, CheckChar74, CheckChar73, CheckChar72
             :
     dw    CheckChar3, CheckChar2, CheckChar1, CheckChar0
```

with the maximum number of characters to check used as the index into the table. That way, a maximum check count of 1 will branch to the last repeated in-line code block, a maximum count of 2 will branch to the next to last block, and so on.

That brings us to the second trick: why do all the typing involved in creating the above table when we've already seen that labels created with macros can do the work for us? The following is a *much* easier way to create the jump table:

```
MAKE_CHECK_CHAR_LABEL    macro    NUMBER
     dw    CheckChar&NUMBER&
     endm
             :
SearchTable    label    word
     dw    NoMatch
BLOCK NUMBER=MAX_SEARCH_LENGTH-1
     rept   MAX_SEARCH_LENGTH
     MAKE_CHECK_CHAR_LABEL    %BLOCK_NUMBER
BLOCK_NUMBER=BLOCK_NUMBER-1
     endm
```

Listing 14-14 puts all of the above together, creating and using unique labels in both the in-line code and the jump table. Figure 14.10 illustrates Listing 14-14 in action. Study both the listing and the figure carefully, for macros, repeat blocks, jump tables, and in-line code working together are potent indeed.

Now for the kicker: all that fancy coding actually doesn't even pay off in this particular case. Listing 14-14 runs in 1013 μsec. Listing 14-15, which uses a standard loop approach, runs in 988 μsec! Not only is Listing 14-15 faster, but it's also hundreds of bytes shorter and much simpler than Listing 14-14—and, unlike Listing 14-14, Listing 14-15 can handle strings of any length. Frankly, there's no reason to recommend Listing 14-14 over Listing 14-15, and good reason not to.

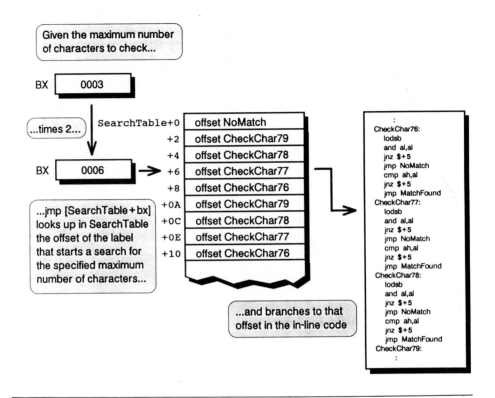

FIGURE 14.10   Listing 14-14 in action. Here a maximum search length of 3 is passed to **SearchNBytes**. That value is multiplied by 2 in order to look up the corresponding entry in the word-sized table **SearchTable**. A branch is then performed to the offset stored in the entry looked up; in this case, the entry contains the offset of **CheckChar77**.

```
1    ;
2    ; *** Listing 14-15 ***
3    ;
4    ; For comparison with the in-line-code-branched-to-via-a-
5    ; jump-table approach of Listing 14-14, this is a loop-based
6    ; string-search routine that searches at most the specified
7    ; number of bytes of a zero-terminated string for the
8    ; specified character.
9    ;
10            jmp     Skip
11   TestString      label   byte
12           db      'This is a string containing the letter '
```

```
13              db          'z but not containing capital q', 0
14      ;
15      ; Searches a zero-terminated string for a character.
16      ; Searches until a match is found, the terminating zero
17      ; is found, or the specified number of characters have been
18      ; checked.
19      ;
20      ; Input:
21      ;       AL = character to search for
22      ;       BX = maximum # of characters to search
23      ;       DS:SI = string to search
24      ;
25      ; Output:
26      ;       SI = pointer to character, or 0 if character not
27      ;            found
28      ;
29      ; Registers altered: AX, CX, SI
30      ;
31      ; Direction flag cleared
32      ;
33      ; Note: Don't pass a string starting at offset 0, since a
34      ;       match there couldn't be distinguished from a failure
35      ;       to match.
36      ;
37      SearchNBytes     proc     near
38              mov      ah,al              ;we'll need AL for LODSB
39              mov      cx,bx              ;for LOOP
40      SearchNBytesLoop:
41              lodsb
42              and      al,al
43              jz       NoMatch            ;terminating 0, so no match
44              cmp      ah,al
45              jz       MatchFound         ;match, so we're done
46              loop     SearchNBytesLoop
47      ;
48      ; No match was found.
49      ;
50      NoMatch:
51              sub      si,si   ;return no-match status
52              ret
53      ;
54      ; A match was found.
55      ;
56      MatchFound:
57              dec      si                 ;point back to matching
58                                          ; location
59              ret
60      SearchNBytes     endp
61      ;
62      Skip:
63              call     ZTimerOn
64              mov      al,'Q'
65              mov      bx,20              ;search up to the
66              mov      si,offset TestString ; first 20 bytes of
67              call     SearchNBytes         ; TestString for 'Q'
68              mov      al,'z'
69              mov      bx,80              ;search up to the
70              mov      si,offset TestString ; first 80 bytes of
71              call     SearchNBytes         ; TestString for 'z'
```

```
72        mov     al,'a'
73        mov     bx,10                    ;search up to the
74        mov     si,offset TestString     ; first 10 bytes of
75        call    SearchNBytes             ; TestString for 'a'
76        call    ZTimerOff
```

Why have I spent all this time developing *slower* code? Forget the specific example: the idea was to show you how jump tables can be used to branch into in-line code, even when the in-line code consists of code blocks of varying lengths. The particular example I chose doesn't benefit from these techniques because it was selected for illustrative rather than practical purposes. Although there are good applications for jump tables that branch into in-line code—plenty of them!—they tend to be lengthy and complex, and I decided to choose an example that was short enough so that the decidedly nonobvious techniques used could be readily understood.

Why does this particular example not benefit much from the use of branched-to in-line code? The answer is that too few of the branches in Listing 14-14 are able to use 1-byte conditional jumps. As a result, many of the branches—especially those between the middle and end of the in-line code, which tend to be executed most often—must use jumps around jumps. Consequently, *two* branches, in the form of jumps around jumps, are often performed for each byte checked in Listing 14-14. In contrast, only one branch—a **loop**—is performed for each byte checked in Listing 14-15.

In truth, the best way to speed up this code would be partial in-line code, which would allow *all* the branches to use 1-byte displacements. A double-scan approach, using a repeated string instruction to search for the terminating 0 and then another string instruction to search for the desired character, might also serve well.

Just to demonstrate the flexibility of macros, jump tables, and branched-to in-line code, however, Listing 14-16 is a modification of Listing 14-14 that branches out with 1-byte displacements at *both* ends of the in-line code, using conditional jumps around unconditional jumps only in the middle of the in-line code, where 1-byte displacements can't reach past either end. As predicted, Listing 14-16 is, at 908 μsec, a good bit faster than Listings 14-14 and 14-15. (Bear in mind that the relative performances of these listings could change considerably given different search parameters. *There is no such thing as absolute performance.* Know the conditions under which your code will run!)

Listing 14-16 isn't *lightning* fast, but it is fast enough to remind us that branched-to in-line code is a most attractive option—and now jump tables let us use branched-to in-line code in more situations than ever.

```
 1    ;
 2    ; *** Listing 14-16 ***
 3    ;
 4    ; Demonstrates the use of a jump table to branch into
 5    ; in-line code consisting of repeated code blocks of
 6    ; varying lengths. Branches out of the in-line code with
 7    ; 1-byte displacements at both ends of the in-line code,
 8    ; for improved speed.
 9    ;
10    ; Searches up to N bytes of a zero- terminated string for
11    ; a character.
12    ;
13            jmp     Skip
14    TestString      label   byte
15            db      'This is a string containing the letter '
16            db      'z but not containing capital q', 0
17    ;
18    ; Searches a zero-terminated string for a character.
19    ; Searches until a match is found, the terminating zero
20    ; is found, or the specified number of characters has been
21    ; checked.
22    ;
23    ; Input:
24    ;       AL = character to search for
25    ;       BX = maximum # of characters to search. Must be
26    ;               less than or equal to MAX_SEARCH_LENGTH
27    ;       DS:SI = string to search
28    ;
29    ; Output:
30    ;       SI = pointer to character, or 0 if character not
31    ;               found
32    ;
33    ; Registers altered: AX, BX, SI
34    ;
35    ; Direction flag cleared
36    ;
37    ; Note: Don't pass a string starting at offset 0, since a
38    ;       match there couldn't be distinguished from a failure
39    ;       to match.
40    ;
41    MAX_SEARCH_LENGTH equ   80      ;longest supported search
42                                    ; length
43    ;
44    ; Macro to create SearchTable entries.
45    ;
46    MAKE_CHECK_CHAR_LABEL   macro   NUMBER
47            dw      CheckChar&NUMBER&
48            endm
49    ;
50    ; Macro to create in-line code to search 1 character.
51    ; Gives the code block a unique label according to NUMBER.
52    ; Each conditional branch uses the shortest possible jump
53    ; sequence to reach NoMatch and MatchFound.
54    ;
55    CHECK_CHAR      macro   NUMBER
56            local   CheckMatch, Continue
57    CheckChar&NUMBER&:
58            lodsb                   ;get the character
59            and     al,al   ;done if terminating zero
```

```
60    ;
61    ; Assemble a single conditional jump if it'll reach, or
62    ; a conditional jump around an unconditional jump if the
63    ; 1-byte displacement of a conditional jump won't reach.
64    ;
65    if ($+2-NoMatch) le 128
66            jz      NoMatch
67    else
68            jnz     CheckMatch
69            jmp     NoMatch
70    endif
71    CheckMatch:
72            cmp     ah,al   ;done if matches search character
73    ;
74    ; Again, assemble shortest possible jump sequence.
75    ;
76    if ($+2-MatchFound) le 128
77            jz      MatchFound
78    else
79            jnz     Continue
80            jmp     MatchFound
81    endif
82    Continue:
83            endm
84    ;
85    ; Macro to create in-line code to search 1 character.
86    ; Gives the code block a unique label according to NUMBER.
87    ; All branches use a 1-byte displacement to branch to
88    ; NoMatch2 and MatchFound2.
89    ;
90    CHECK_CHAR2     macro   NUMBER
91    CheckChar&NUMBER&:
92            lodsb           ;get the character
93            and     al,al   ;done if terminating zero
94            jz      NoMatch2
95            cmp     ah,al   ;done if matches search character
96            jz      MatchFound2
97            endm
98    ;
99    ; Table of in-line code entry points for maximum search
100   ; lengths of 0 through 80.
101   ;
102   SearchTable    label   word
103           dw      NoMatch         ;we never match on a
104                                   ; maximum length of 0
105   BLOCK_NUMBER=MAX_SEARCH_LENGTH-1
106           rept    MAX_SEARCH_LENGTH
107           MAKE_CHECK_CHAR_LABEL    %BLOCK_NUMBER
108   BLOCK_NUMBER=BLOCK_NUMBER-1
109           endm
110   ;
111   SearchNBytes   proc    near
112           mov     ah,al           ;we'll need AL for LODSB
113           cmp     bx,MAX_SEARCH_LENGTH
114           ja      NoMatch         ;if the maximum length's
115                                   ; too long for the in-line
116                                   ; code, return a no-match
117                                   ; status
118           shl     bx,1            ;*2 to look up in word-sized
```

```
119                                   ; table
120            jmp      [SearchTable+bx] ;branch into the in-line
121                                   ; code to do the search
122     ;
123     ; No match was found.
124     ;
125     NoMatch:
126            sub      si,si           ;return no-match status
127            ret
128     ;
129     ; A match was found.
130     ;
131     MatchFound:
132            dec      si              ;point back to matching
133                                     ; location
134            ret
135     ;
136     ; This is the in-line code that actually does the search.
137     ; Each repetition is uniquely labelled, with labels
138     ; CheckChar0 through CheckChar79.
139     ;
140     BLOCK_NUMBER=0
141     ;
142     ; These in-line code blocks use 1-byte displacements
143     ; whenever possible to branch backward; otherwise 2-byte
144     ; displacements are used to branch backwards, with
145     ; conditional jumps around unconditional jumps.
146     ;
147            rept     MAX_SEARCH_LENGTH-14
148            CHECK_CHAR       %BLOCK_NUMBER
149     BLOCK_NUMBER=BLOCK_NUMBER+1
150            endm
151     ;
152     ; These in-line code blocks use 1-byte displacements to
153     ; branch forward.
154     ;
155            rept     14
156            CHECK_CHAR2      %BLOCK_NUMBER
157     BLOCK_NUMBER=BLOCK_NUMBER+1
158            endm
159     ;
160     ; If we make it here, we haven't found the character.
161     ;
162     NoMatch2:
163            sub      si,si    ;return no-match status
164            ret
165     ;
166     ; A match was found.
167     ;
168     MatchFound2:
169            dec      si              ;point back to matching
170                                     ; location
171            ret
172     SearchNBytes     endp
173     ;
174     Skip:
175            call     ZTimerOn
176            mov      al,'Q'
177            mov      bx,20                   ;search up to the
```

```
178        mov     si,offset TestString    ; first 20 bytes of
179        call    SearchNBytes            ; TestString for 'Q'
180        mov     al,'z'
181        mov     bx,80                   ;search up to the
182        mov     si,offset TestString    ; first 80 bytes of
183        call    SearchNBytes            ; TestString for 'z'
184        mov     al,'a'
185        mov     bx,10                   ;search up to the
186        mov     si,offset TestString    ; first 10 bytes of
187        call    SearchNBytes            ; TestString for 'a'
188        call    ZTimerOff
```

14.10 ◆ Forward References Rear Their Collective Ugly Head Once More

You may have noticed that **CHECK_CHAR2**, the macro in Listing 14-16 that assembles in-line code blocks that use conditional jumps forward to **NoMatch2** and **MatchFound2**, is a bit different from **CHECK_CHAR**, which assembles blocks that use backward jumps. **CHECK_CHAR** uses the **if** directive to determine whether a conditional jump can be used, assembling a jump around a jump if a conditional jump won't reach. **CHECK_CHAR2**, on the other hand, always assembles a conditional jump.

The reason is this: when the assembler performs arithmetic for use in **if** directives, all the values in the expression must already be known when the **if** is encountered. In particular, the offset of a forward-referenced label can't be used in **if** arithmetic. Why? When performing **if** arithmetic with a forward-referenced label, the assembler doesn't know whether the **if** is true until the forward-referenced label has been assembled. That creates a nasty paradox, because the assembler can't assemble the label, which follows the **if**, until the **if** has been evaluated and the code associated with the **if** has or hasn't been assembled. The assembler resolves this chicken-and-egg problem by reporting an error.

The upshot is that although a line like

```
if ($-BackwardReferencedLabel)
```

is fine, a line like

```
if (ForwardReferencedLabel-$)
```

is not. Alas, that means that there's no way to have a macro do automatic jump sizing for branches to forward-referenced labels—hence the lack of conditional assembly in **CHECK_CHAR2**—although there's no problem with backward-referenced labels, as evidenced by **CHECK_CHAR**. In fact, I arrived at the optimal number of repetitions of **CHECK_CHAR2** in Listing 14-16 by rough calculation followed by trial and error, and that's what you'll have to do when trying to get maximum performance out of forward branches in in-line code.

Actually, there is an alternative to trial and error: assemblers that detect and/or correct suboptimal branches can help optimize forward in-line branches. If you're using MASM, however, backward branches, which macros (or even the assembler, for unconditional branches) can easily optimize, should be used whenever possible.

A final note: macros can easily obscure the true nature of your code, since you don't see the actual code that's assembled when you scan a listing containing macros. That problem becomes all the more acute when the **if** directive is used to produce conditionally assembled code. Whenever you're not sure exactly what code you're assembling, generate an assembler listing file that shows macro expansions or take a look at the actual code with a debugger.

Still and All . . . Don't Jump!

All the wonderful branching tricks we've encountered in this chapter notwithstanding, you're still better off from a performance perspective when you don't branch. Granted, branching can often be beneficial from a code size perspective, but performance is more often an issue than size. Also, the improvements in performance that can be achieved by not-branching are relatively far greater than the improvements in size that can be achieved by judicious branching.

Think back again to Listing 11-27, in which we sped up a case-insensitive string comparison considerably simply by looking up the upper case version of each character in a table instead of using a mere five instructions—and at most one branch—to convert each character to upper case. *Only rarely can code-only calculations, especially calculations that involve branching, beat table look-ups.* What's more, we could speed up the code a good deal more by using pure or partial in-line code rather than looping every two characters. If we wanted to, we could effectively eliminate nearly every single branch in the string-comparison code—and the code would be much faster for it.

No matter how tight your code is, if it branches it *can* be made faster. Whether it *is* made faster is purely a matter of your ability to bring techniques such as table look-ups and in-line code to bear, your willingness to trade the extra bytes those techniques require for the cycles they save, and the degree to which the performance of the code matters.

Never waste your time optimizing noncritical code for speed. There's too much time-critical code in the world that *needs* improving to squander effort on initialization code, code outside loops, and the like.

This Concludes Our Tour of the 8088's Instruction Set

And with that, we've come to the end of our long journey through the 8088's strange but powerful instruction set. We haven't covered all the variations of all the instructions—not by a long shot—but we have done the principal ones, and we've gotten a good look at what the 8088 has to offer. As a sort of continuing education on the instruction set, you would do well to scan through Appendix A or another instruction set summary periodically. I've been doing that for 7 years now, and I still find useful new tidbits in the instruction set from time to time.

We've also come across a great many tricks, tips, and optimizations in our travels—but Lord knows we haven't seen them all! Thanks to the virtually infinite combinations and permutations of which the 8088's instruction set is capable, as well as the inherent and unpredictable variation of the execution time of any given instruction, PC code optimization is now and forever an imperfect art. Nonetheless, we've learned a great deal, and with that knowledge and the Zen timer in hand, we're well along the path to becoming expert code artists.

Chapter 15

◆◆

Other Processors

15.1   Why Optimize for the 8088?

15.2   Which Processors Matter?

15.3   Things Mother Never Told You, Part II

15.4   New Instructions and Features

15.5   Optimization Rules: The More Things Change . . .

15.6   popf and the 80286

15.7   Coprocessors and Peripherals

Now that we've spent 14 chapters learning how to write good assembler code for the 8088, it's time to acknowledge that there are other widely used processors in the 8088's family: the 8086, the 80286, and the 80386, to name only a few. None of the other processors is as popular as the 8088 yet, but some—most notably the 80386—are growing in popularity, and it's likely that any code you write for general distribution will end up running on those processors as well as on the 8088.

Omigod! Does that mean that you need to learn as much about those processors as you've learned about the 8088? Not at all. We'll see why shortly, but for now, take my word for it: the 8088 is the processor for which you should optimize.

Nonetheless, in this chapter we'll take a quick look at optimizations for other processors, primarily the 80286 and the 80386. Why? Well, many of the optimizations for those processors are similar to those for the 8088, and it's useful to know which of the rules we've learned are generally applicable to the whole family (all the major ones, as it turns out). Also, one particular optimization for other 8086-family processors—data alignment—is so easy to implement, costs so little, and has such a large payback that you might want to apply it routinely to your code even though it has no effect on 8088 performance.

Finally, I'd like to get you started in the right direction if you *are* primarily interested in optimization for the 80286 and its successors. After all, the 8088 is going to go out of style *someday* (although that's certainly not happening any time soon), and OS/2 and its ilk are creeping up on us. You have the Zen timer, and you've learned much about how to evaluate and improve code performance; with a bit of a head start here, you should be able to develop your own expertise in 80286/80386 coding if you so desire.

15.1 ◆ Why Optimize for the 8088?

The great lurking unanswered question is: given that the 80286 and the 80386 (and the 80486 someday) are the future of PC-compatible computing, why optimize for the 8088? Why not use all the extra instructions and features of the newer processors to supercharge your code so it will run as fast as possible on the fastest computers?

There are several reasons. Each by itself is probably ample reason to optimize for the 8088; together, they make a compelling argument for 8088-specific optimization. Briefly put, the reasons are as follows:

♦ The 8088 is the lowest common denominator of the 8086 family for both compatibility and performance.

♦ The market for software that runs on the 8088 is enormous.

♦ The 8088 is the 8086-family processor for which optimization pays off most handsomely.

♦ The 8088 is the only 8086-family processor that comes in a single consistent system configuration—the IBM PC.

♦ The major 8088 optimizations work surprisingly well on the 80286 and 80386.

As we discuss these reasons below, bear in mind that when I say *8088,* I mean *8088 as used in the IBM PC,* because it's the widespread use of the PC that makes the 8088 the assembler programmer's chip of choice.

That said, let's tackle our original question again, this time in more detail: why optimize for the 8088?

For starters, the 8088 is the lowest common denominator of the 8086 family, unless you're writing applications for an operating system that doesn't even run on an 8088—OS/2, an 80286/80386-specific version of Unix, or the like. Code written for the 8088 will run on all of the other chips in the 8086 family, but code written for the 80286 or the 80386 won't run on the 8088 if any of the special features or instructions of those chips are used.

It stands to reason, then, that code written for the 8088 has the broadest market and is the most generally useful code around. That status should hold well into the 21st century, given that every 8086-family processor Intel has ever introduced has provided full backward compatibility with the 8088. If any further proof is needed, hardware and/or software packages that allow 8088 code to be run are available for a number of computers built around non-Intel processors, including the Apple Macintosh, the Commodore Amiga, and a variety of 68XXX-based workstations.

The 8088 is the lowest common denominator of the 8086 family in terms of performance as well as code compatibility. No 8086-family chip runs slower than the 8088, and it's a safe bet that none ever will. By definition, any code that runs adequately fast on an 8088 is bound to be more than adequate on any other 8086-family processor. Unless you're willing to forgo the 8088 market altogether, then, it certainly makes sense to optimize your code for the 8088.

The 8088 is also the processor for which optimization pays off best. The slow memory access, too small 8-bit bus, and widely varying instruction execution times of the 8088 mean that careful coding can produce stunning improvements in performance. Over the past few chapters we've seen that it's possible to double and even triple the performance of already tight 8088 assembler code. While the 80286 and 80386 certainly offer optimization possibilities, their superior overall performance results partly from eliminating some of the worst bottlenecks of the 8088, so it's harder to save cycles by the bushel. Then, too, the major optimizations for the 8088—keep instructions short, use the registers, use string instructions, and the like—also serve well on the 80286 and 80386, so optimization for the 8088 results in code that is reasonably well optimized across the board.

Finally, the 8088 is the only 8086-family processor that comes in one consistent system configuration, the IBM PC. There are 8088-based computers that run at higher clock speeds than the IBM PC, but, to the best of my knowledge, all 8088-based PC-compatible computers have 0–wait state memory. By contrast, the 80286 comes in two flavors, classic 1–wait state AT, and souped-up 0–wait state AT, and additional variations will surely appear as high-speed 80286s become available. The 80386 is available in a multitude of configurations: static-column RAM, cached memory, and interleaved memory, to name a few, with each of those available in several versions.

What all that means is that although you can rely on fast code on one PC being fast code on any PC, that's not the case with 80286 and 80386 computers. The performance of 80286–80386 computers can vary considerably, depending on how your code interacts with a particular computer's memory architecture. As a result, it's only on the PC that it pays to fine tune your assembler code down to the last few cycles.

So. I hope I've convinced you that the 8088 is the best place to focus your optimization efforts. In any case, let's tour the rest of the 8086 family.

15.2 ◆ Which Processors Matter?

While the 8086 family is a large one, only a few members of the family—which includes the 8088, 8086, 80188, 80186, 80286, 80386SX, and 80386—really matter.

The 80186 and 80188 never really caught on for use in PC compatibles and don't require further discussion.

The 8086, which is a good bit faster than the 8088, was used fairly widely for a while, but has largely been superseded by the 80286 as the chip of choice for better-than-8088 performance. (The 80386 is the chip of choice for flat-out performance, but it's the 80286 that's generally used in computers that are faster but not much more expensive than 8088-based

PCs.) Besides, the 8086 has exactly the same execution unit (EU) instruction execution times as the 8088, so much of what we've learned about the 8088 is directly applicable to the 8086. The only difference between the two processors is that the 8086 has a 16- rather than 8-bit bus, as we found back in Chapter 3. That means that the 8086 suffers less from the prefetch queue and 8-bit bus cycle eaters than does the 8088.

That's not to say that the 8086 isn't affected at all by those cycle eaters; it just suffers less than the 8088 does. Instruction fetching is certainly still a bottleneck on the 8086. For example, the 8086's EU can execute register-only instructions such as **shl** and **inc** twice as fast as the bus interface unit (BIU) can fetch them. Of course, that is a considerable improvement over the 8088, which can execute those instructions *four* times as fast as they can be fetched.

Oddly enough, the 8-bit bus cycle eater is also still a problem on the 8086, even though the 8086's bus is 16 bits wide. Although the 8086 is indeed capable of fetching words as rapidly as bytes, that's true only for words that start at even addresses. Words that start at odd addresses are fetched with two memory accesses, because the 8086 is capable of performing word-sized accesses only to even addresses. We'll discuss this phenomenon in detail when we get to the 80286.

In summary, the 8086 is much like the 8088, except that the prefetch queue cycle eater is less of a problem and that word-sized accesses should be made to even addresses. Both these differences mean that code running on an 8086 always runs either exactly as fast as or faster than it would run on an 8088, so the rule still is: optimize for the 8088, and the code will perform even better on an 8086.

That leaves us with the high-end chips: the 80826, the 80386SX, and the 80386. At this writing, it's unclear whether the 80386SX is going to achieve widespread popularity; it may turn out that the relatively small cost advantage the 80386SX enjoys over the 80386 isn't enough to offset its relatively large performance disadvantage. After all, the 80386SX suffers from the same debilitating problem that looms over the 8088—a too small bus. Internally, the 80386SX is a 32-bit processor, but externally, it's a 16-bit processor—and we know what *that* sort of mismatch can lead to!

Given the uncertainty of its acceptance, I'm not going to discuss the 80386SX in detail. If you do find yourself programming for it, follow the same general rules we've established for the 8088: use short instructions, use the registers as much as possible, and don't branch. In other words, avoid memory, because the 80386SX is by definition better at processing data internally than it is at accessing memory.

Which leaves us with just two processors, the 80286 and the 80386.

The 80286 and the 80386

There's no question but what the 80286 and 80386 are very popular processors. The 8088 is still more widely used than either of its more powerful descendants, but the gap is narrowing, and the more powerful processors can only gain in popularity as their prices come down and memory—which both can use in huge quantities—becomes cheaper. All in all, it's certainly worth our while to spend some time discussing 80286/80386 optimization.

We're only going to talk about real-mode operation of the 80286 and 80386, however. Real mode is the mode in which the processors basically function as 8088s (albeit with some new instructions), running good old MS-DOS. By contrast, protected mode offers a whole new memory management scheme, one that isn't supported by the 8088. Only code specifically written for protected mode can run in that mode; it's an alien and hostile environment for MS-DOS programs.

In particular, segments are different creatures in protected mode. They're selectors—indexes into a table of segment descriptors—rather than plain old registers, and can't be set arbitrarily. That means that segments can't be used for temporary storage or as part of a fast indivisible 32-bit load from memory, as in:

```
les   ax,dword ptr [LongVar]
mov   dx,es
```

which loads **LongVar** into DX:AX faster than:

```
mov   ax,word ptr [LongVar]
mov   dx,word ptr [LongVar+2]
```

Protected mode uses those altered segment registers to offer access to a great deal more memory than real mode: the 80286 supports 16 megabytes of memory, while the 80386 supports 4 gigabytes (4 K megabytes) of physical memory and 64 *terabytes* (64 K gigabytes!) of virtual memory. There's a price to pay for all that memory: protected-mode code tends to run a bit more slowly than equivalent real-mode code, because instructions that load segments run more slowly in protected mode than in real mode.

Also, in protected mode your programs generally run under an operating system (OS/2, Unix, or the like) that exerts much more control over the computer than does MS-DOS. Protected-mode operating systems can generally run multiple programs simultaneously, and the performance of any one program may depend far less on code quality than on how efficiently the program uses operating system services and how often and under what circumstances the operating system preempts the program. Protected mode programs are often nothing more than collections of operating system calls, and the performance of whatever code *isn't* operating system oriented may depend primarily on how large a timeslice the operating system gives that code to run in.

In short, protected-mode programming is a different kettle of fish altogether from what we've seen in *Zen of Assembly Language*. There's certainly a Zen to protected mode, but it's not the Zen we've been learning, and now is not the time to pursue it further.

15.3 ◆ Things Mother Never Told You, Part II

Under the programming interface, the 80286 and 80386 differ considerably from the 8088. Nonetheless, with one exception and one addition, the cycle eaters remain much the same on computers built around the 80286 and 80386. Next, we'll review each of the familiar cycle eaters as it applies to the 80286 and 80386, and we'll look at the new member of the gang, the data alignment cycle eater.

The one cycle eater that vanishes on the 80286 and 80386 is the 8-bit bus cycle eater. The 80286 is a 16-bit processor both internally and externally, and the 80386 is a 32-bit processor both internally and externally, so the EU/BIU size mismatch that plagues the 8088 is eliminated. Consequently, there's no longer any need to use byte-sized memory variables in preference to word-sized variables, at least so long as word-sized variables start at even addresses, as we'll see shortly. On the other hand, access to byte-sized variables still isn't any *slower* than access to word-sized variables, so you can use whichever size best suits a given task.

You might think that the elimination of the 8-bit bus cycle eater would mean that the prefetch queue cycle eater would also vanish, since on the 8088 the prefetch queue cycle eater is a side effect of the 8-bit bus. That would seem all the more likely given that both the 80286 and the 80386 have larger prefetch queues than the 8088 (6 bytes for the 80286, 16 bytes for the 80386) and can perform memory accesses, including instruction fetches, in far fewer cycles than the 8088.

However, the prefetch queue cycle eater *doesn't* vanish on either the 80286 or the 80386, for several reasons. For one thing, branching instructions still empty the prefetch queue, so instruction fetching still slows things down after most branches; when the prefetch queue is empty, it doesn't much matter how big it is. (Even apart from emptying the prefetch queue, branches aren't particularly fast on the 80286 or the 80386, at a minimum of 7-plus cycles apiece. Avoid branching whenever possible.)

After a branch it *does* matter how fast the queue can refill, and there we come to the second reason the prefetch queue cycle eater lives on: the 80286 and 80386 are so fast that sometimes the EU can execute instructions faster than they can be fetched, even though instruction fetching is *much* faster on the 80286 and 80836 than on the 8088.

(All other things being equal, too slow instruction fetching is more of a problem on the 80286 than on the 80386, since the 80386 fetches 4 instruction bytes at a time versus the 2 instruction bytes fetched per memory access by the 80286. However, the 80386 also typically runs at least twice as fast as the 80286, meaning that it can easily execute instructions faster than they can be fetched unless very high–speed memory is used.)

The most significant reason that the prefetch queue cycle eater not only survives but prospers on the 80286 and 80386, however, lies in the various memory architectures used in computers built around the 80286 and 80386. Owing to those memory architectures, the 8-bit bus cycle eater is replaced by a new form of the wait-state cycle eater: wait states on accesses to normal system memory.

System Wait States

The 80286 and 80386 were designed to lose relatively little performance to the prefetch queue cycle eater *when used with 0–wait state memory*—memory that can complete memory accesses so rapidly that no wait states are needed. However, true 0–wait state memory is almost never used with those processors. Why? Because memory that can keep up with an 80286 is fairly expensive, and memory that can keep up with an 80386 is *very* expensive. Instead, computer designers use alternative memory architectures that offer more performance for the dollar but less performance overall than 0–wait state memory. (It *is* possible to build 0–wait state systems for the 80286 and 80386; it's just so expensive that it's rarely done.)

The IBM AT and true compatibles use 1–wait state memory (some AT clones use 0–wait state memory, but such clones are less common than 1–wait state AT clones). Systems built around the 80386 use a wide variety of memory systems, including high-speed caches, interleaved memory, and static-column RAM, that insert anywhere from 0 to about 5 wait states (and many more if 8- or 16-bit memory expansion cards are used); the exact number of wait states inserted at any given time depends on the interaction between the code being executed and the memory system it's running on

The performance of most 80386 memory systems can vary greatly from one memory access to another, depending on factors such as what data happens to be in the cache and which interleaved bank or RAM column was accessed last.

The many memory systems in use make it impossible for us to optimize for 80286/80386 computers with the precision to which we've become accustomed on the 8088. Instead, we must write code that runs reasonably well under the varying conditions found in the 80286/80386 arena.

The wait states that occur on most accesses to system memory in 80286 and 80386 computers mean that nearly every access to system memory—memory in DOS's normal 640-Kb memory area—is slowed down. (Accesses in computers with high-speed caches may be wait state free if the desired data are already in the cache but will certainly encounter wait states if the data isn't cached; this phenomenon produces highly variable instruction execution times.) Although this is our first encounter with system memory wait states, we have run into a wait state cycle eater before: the display adapter cycle eater, which we discussed way back in Chapter 4. System memory generally has fewer wait states per access than display memory. However, system memory is also accessed far more often than display memory, so system memory wait states hurt plenty—and the place they hurt most is instruction fetching.

Consider this. The 80286 can store an immediate value to memory, as in **mov [WordVar],0**, in just 3 cycles. However, that instruction is 6 bytes long. The 80286 is capable of fetching 1 word every 2 cycles; however, the 1–wait state architecture of the AT stretches that to 3 cycles. Consequently, 9 cycles are needed to fetch the 6 instruction bytes. On top of that, 3 cycles are needed to write to memory, bringing the total memory access time to 12 cycles. On balance, memory access time—especially instruction prefetching—greatly exceeds execution time, to the extent that this particular instruction can take up to four times as long to run as it does to execute in the EU.

And that, my friend, is unmistakably the prefetch queue cycle eater. I might add that the prefetch queue cycle eater is in rare good form in the above example: a 4:1 ratio of instruction fetch time to execution time is in a class with the best (or worst!) we've found on the 8088.

Let's check out the prefetch queue cycle eater in action. Listing 15-1 times **mov [WordVar],0**. The Zen timer reports that on a 1–wait state 10-MHz AT clone (the computer used for all tests in this chapter), Listing 15-1 runs in 1.27 μsec per instruction. That's 12.7 cycles per instruction, just as we calculated above. (That extra 7/10 cycle comes from DRAM refresh, which we'll get to shortly.)

```
1    ;
2    ; *** Listing 15-1 ***
3    ;
4    ; Measures the performance of an immediate move to
5    ; memory, in order to demonstrate that the prefetch
6    ; queue cycle-eater is alive and well on the AT.
7    ;
8            jmp     Skip
9    ;
10           even                    ;always make sure word-sized memory
11                                   ; variables are word-aligned!
12   WordVar dw      0
13   ;
14   Skip:
15           call    ZTimerOn
16           rept    1000
17           mov     [WordVar],0
18           endm
19           call    ZTimerOff
```

What does this mean? It means that, practically speaking, the 80286 as used in the AT doesn't have a 16-bit bus. From a performance perspective, the 80286 in an AT has two thirds of a 16-bit bus (a 10.7-bit bus?), since every bus access on an AT takes 50 percent longer than it should. An 80286 running at 10 MHz *should* be able to access memory at a maximum rate of one word every 200 nsec; in a 10-MHz AT, however, that rate is reduced to one word every 300 nsec by the 1–wait state memory.

In short, a close relative of our old friend the 8-bit bus cycle eater—the system memory wait state cycle eater—haunts us still on all but 0–wait state 80286 and 80386 computers, and that means that the prefetch queue cycle eater is alive and well. (The system memory wait state cycle eater isn't really a new cycle eater, but rather a variant of the general wait state cycle eater, of which the display adapter cycle eater is another variant.) Although the 80286 in the AT can fetch instructions much faster than can the 8088 in the PC, it can execute those instructions faster still.

The picture is less clear in the 80386 world, because there are so many different memory architectures, but similar problems can occur in any computer built around an 80286 or 80386. The prefetch queue cycle eater is even a factor—albeit a lesser one—on 0–wait state machines, both because branching empties the queue and because some instructions can outrun even 0–wait state instruction fetching. (Listing 15-1 would take at least 8 cycles per instruction on a 0–wait state AT—5 cycles longer than the official execution time.)

To summarize:

♦ Memory-accessing instructions don't run at their official speeds on non-0–wait state 80286/80386 computers.

♦ The prefetch queue cycle eater reduces performance on 80286/80386 computers, particularly when non-0–wait state memory is used.

♦ Branches generally execute at less than their rated speeds on the 80286 and 80386, because the prefetch queue is emptied.

♦ The extent to which the prefetch queue and wait states affect performance varies from one 80286/80386 computer to another, making precise optimization impossible.

What's to be learned from all this? Several things:

♦ Keep your instructions short.

♦ Keep it in the registers; avoid memory, as memory generally can't keep up with the processor.

♦ Don't jump.

Of course, those are exactly the rules we've developed for the 8088. Isn't it convenient that the same general rules apply across the board?

Data Alignment

Thanks to its 16-bit bus, the 80286 can access word-sized memory variables just as fast as it can access byte-sized variables. There's a catch, however: that's true only for word-sized variables that start at even addresses. When the 80286 is asked to perform a word-sized access starting at an odd address, it actually performs two separate accesses, each of which fetches 1 byte, just as the 8088 does for all word-sized accesses.

Figure 15.1 illustrates this phenomenon. The conversion of word-sized accesses to odd addresses into double byte-sized accesses is transparent to memory-accessing instructions; all any instruction knows is that the requested word has been accessed, no matter whether 1 word-sized access or 2 byte-sized accesses were required.

The penalty for performing a word-sized access starting at an odd address is easy to calculate: two accesses take twice as long as one. In other words, the effective capacity of the 80286's external data bus is *halved* when a word-sized access to an odd address is performed.

That, in a nutshell, is the data alignment cycle eater, the one new cycle eater of the 80286 and 80386. (The data alignment cycle eater is a close relative of the 8088's 8-bit bus cycle eater, but as it behaves differently—occurring only at odd addresses—and is avoided with a different workaround, we'll consider it a new cycle eater.)

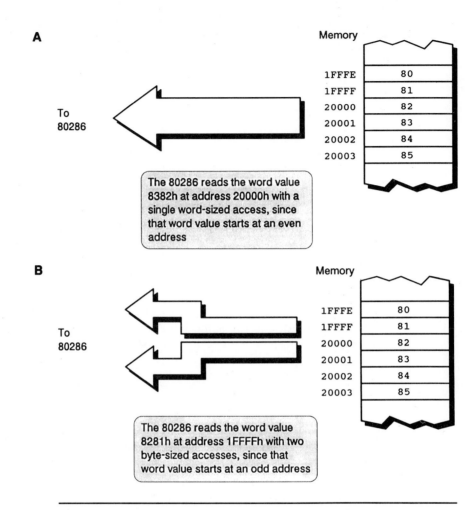

A

Memory

To 80286

1FFFE	80
1FFFF	81
20000	82
20001	83
20002	84
20003	85

The 80286 reads the word value 8382h at address 20000h with a single word-sized access, since that word value starts at an even address

B

Memory

To 80286

1FFFE	80
1FFFF	81
20000	82
20001	83
20002	84
20003	85

The 80286 reads the word value 8281h at address 1FFFFh with two byte-sized accesses, since that word value starts at an odd address

FIGURE 15.1   The data alignment cycle eater. **(A)** The 80286 needs just one word-sized memory access to read or write a word of memory that starts at an even address. **(B)** However, the 80286 must perform two byte-sized memory accesses— which together take twice as long as one word-sized access—when asked to read or write a word of memory that starts at an odd address. Apart from execution time, the whole process is transparent to instructions that access memory, which know only that a word of memory has been accessed in either case.

The way to deal with the data alignment cycle eater is straightforward: *don't perform word-sized accesses to odd addresses on the 80286 if you can help it.* The easiest way to avoid the data alignment cycle eater is to place the directive **even** before each of your word-sized variables. This forces the offset of the next byte assembled to be even by inserting a **nop** if the current offset is odd; consequently, you can ensure that any word-sized variable can be accessed efficiently by the 80286 simply by preceding it with **even**.

Listing 15-2, which accesses memory one word at a time with each word starting at an odd address, runs on a 10-MHz AT clone in 1.27 μsec per repetition of **movsw**, or 0.64 μsec per word-sized memory access. That's 6-plus cycles per word-sized access, which breaks down to two separate memory accesses—3 cycles to access the high byte of each word and 3 cycles to access the low byte of each word, the inevitable result of non-word-aligned word-sized memory accesses—plus a little extra for DRAM refresh.

```
1    ;
2    ; *** Listing 15-2 ***
3    ;
4    ; Measures the performance of accesses to word-sized
5    ; variables that start at odd addresses (are not
6    ; word-aligned).
7    ;
8    Skip:
9            push    ds
10           pop     es
11           mov     si,1     ;source and destination are the same
12           mov     di,si    ; and both are not word-aligned
13           mov     cx,1000  ;move 1000 words
14           cld
15           call    ZTimerOn
16           rep     movsw
17           call    ZTimerOff
```

On the other hand, Listing 15-3, which is exactly the same as Listing 15-2 save that the memory accesses are word aligned (start at even addresses), runs in 0.64 μsec per repetition of **movsw**, or 0.32 μsec per word-sized memory access. That's 3 cycles per word-sized access—exactly twice as fast as the non-word-aligned accesses of Listing 15-2, just as we predicted.

The data alignment cycle eater has intriguing implications for speeding up 80286/80386 code. The expenditure of a little care and a few bytes to make sure that word-sized variables and memory blocks are word aligned can literally double the performance of certain code running on the 80286; even if it doesn't double performance, word alignment usually helps and never hurts.

```
1    ;
2    ; *** Listing 15-3 ***
3    ;
4    ; Measures the performance of accesses to word-sized
5    ; variables that start at even addresses (are word-aligned).
6    ;
7    Skip:
8            push    ds
9            pop     es
10           sub     si,si   ;source and destination are the same
11           mov     di,si   ; and both are word-aligned
12           mov     cx,1000 ;move 1000 words
13           cld
14           call    ZTimerOn
15           rep     movsw
16           call    ZTimerOff
```

In fact, word alignment provides such an excellent return on investment on the 80286 that it's the one 80286-specific optimization that I recommend for assembler code in general. (Actually, word alignment pays off on the 80386 too, as we'll see shortly.) True, word alignment costs a few bytes and doesn't help the code that most needs help—code running on the 8088. Still, it's hard to resist a technique that boosts 80286 performance so dramatically without losing 8088 compatibility in any way or hurting 8088 performance in the least.

Code Alignment

Lack of word alignment can also interfere with instruction fetching on the 80286, although not to the extent that it interferes with access to word-sized memory variables. The 80286 prefetches instructions a word at a time; even if a given instruction doesn't begin at an even address, the 80286 simply fetches the first byte of that instruction at the same time that it fetches the last byte of the previous instruction, as shown in Figure 15.2, then separates the bytes internally. That means that in most cases instructions run just as fast whether they're word aligned or not.

There is, however, a non-word alignment penalty on *branches* to odd addresses. On a branch to an odd address, the 80286 is able to fetch only 1 useful byte with the first instruction fetch following the branch, as shown in Figure 15.3. In other words, lack of word alignment of the target instruction for any branch effectively cuts the instruction-fetching power of the 80286 in half for the first instruction fetch after that branch. Although that may not sound like much, you'd be surprised at what it can do to tight loops; in fact, a brief story is in order.

When I was developing the Zen timer, I used my trusty 10-MHz AT clone to verify the basic functionality of the timer by measuring the performance

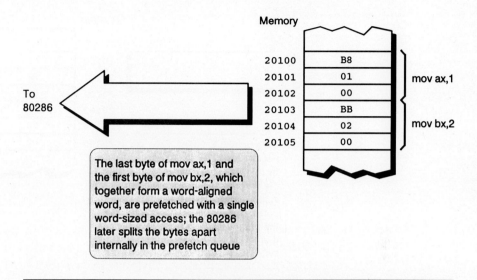

Memory

20100	B8
20101	01
20102	00
20103	BB
20104	02
20105	00

mov ax,1

mov bx,2

To 80286

The last byte of mov ax,1 and the first byte of mov bx,2, which together form a word-aligned word, are prefetched with a single word-sized access; the 80286 later splits the bytes apart internally in the prefetch queue

FIGURE 15.2   Normally, it doesn't matter whether instructions are word aligned or not, because the 80286 fetches instructions into the prefetch queue one word-aligned word at a time, then internally separates the bytes in the prefetch queue on an as-needed basis.

of simple instruction sequences. I was cruising along with no problems until I timed the following code:

```
        mov     cx,1000
        call    ZTimerOn
LoopTop:
        loop    LoopTop
        call    ZTimerOff
```

Now, the above code *should* run in about 12 cycles per loop at most. Instead, it took over 14 cycles per loop, an execution time that I could not explain in any way. After rolling it around in my head for a while, I took a look at the code under a debugger, and the answer leaped out at me. *The loop began at an odd address!* That meant that two instruction fetches were required each time through the loop; one to get the opcode byte of the **loop** instruction, which resided at the end of one word-aligned word, and another to get the displacement byte, which resided at the start of the next word-aligned word.

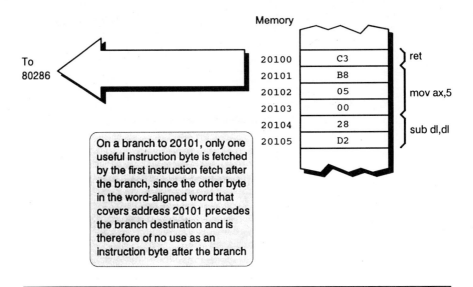

On a branch to 20101, only one useful instruction byte is fetched by the first instruction fetch after the branch, since the other byte in the word-aligned word that covers address 20101 precedes the branch destination and is therefore of no use as an instruction byte after the branch

FIGURE 15.3   On the 80286, only one useful instruction byte is obtained by the first instruction fetch after a branch to an odd address. The reason: a single word-sized, word-aligned instruction fetch that includes the byte at the branch target address would also fetch the byte *before* the branch target address. That preceding byte is useless, as it isn't part of the code that's about to be executed.

One simple change brought the execution time down to a reasonable 12.5 cycles per loop:

```
        mov     cx,1000
        call    ZTimerOn
        even
LoopTop:
        loop    LoopTop
        call    ZTimerOff
```

Although word aligning branch destinations can improve branching performance, it's a nuisance and can increase code size a good deal, so it's not worth doing in most code. Besides, **even** inserts a **nop** instruction if necessary, and the time required to execute a **nop** can sometimes cancel the performance advantage of having a word-aligned branch destination.

Consequently, it's best to word align only those branch destinations that can be reached solely by branching. I recommend that you go out of your way to word align only subroutine start offsets, as in

```
        even
FindChar  proc near
        :
```

In my experience, this simple practice is the one form of code alignment that consistently provides a reasonable return for bytes and effort expended, although sometimes it also pays to word align tight, time-critical loops.

Alignment and the 80386

So far we've discussed alignment only as it pertains to the 80286. What, you may well ask, of the 80386?

The 80386 benefits most from *doubleword* alignment. Every memory access that crosses a doubleword boundary forces the 80386 to perform two memory accesses, effectively doubling memory access time, just as happens with memory accesses that cross word boundaries on the 80286.

The rule for the 80386 is: word-sized memory accesses should be word aligned (it's impossible for word-aligned word-sized accesses to cross doubleword boundaries), and doubleword–sized memory accesses should be doubleword aligned. However, in real (as opposed to protected) mode, doubleword–sized memory accesses are rare, so the simple word alignment rule we've developed for the 80286 serves for the 80386 in real mode as well.

As for code alignment—the subroutine start word alignment rule of the 80286 serves reasonably well there, too, since it avoids the worst case, where just 1 byte is fetched on entry to a subroutine. While optimal performance would dictate doubleword alignment of subroutines, that takes 3 bytes, a high price to pay for an optimization that improves performance only on the 80386.

Alignment and the Stack

One side effect of the data alignment cycle eater of the 80286 and 80386 is that you should *never* allow the stack pointer to become odd. (You can make the stack pointer odd by adding an odd value to it or subtracting an odd value from it, or by loading it with an odd value.) An odd stack pointer on the 80286 or 80386 will significantly reduce the performance of **push**,

pop, **call**, and **ret**, as well as **int** and **iret**, which are executed to invoke DOS and BIOS functions, handle keystrokes and incoming serial characters, and manage the mouse. I know of a Forth programmer who vastly improved the performance of a complex application on the AT simply by forcing the Forth interpreter to maintain an even stack pointer at all times.

An interesting corollary to this rule is that you shouldn't **inc** SP twice to add 2, even though that's more efficient than using **add sp,2**. The stack pointer is odd between the first and second **inc**s, so any interrupt occurring between the two instructions will be serviced more slowly than it normally would. The same goes for decrementing twice; use **sub sp,2** instead.

Keep the stack pointer even at all times.

The DRAM Refresh Cycle Eater: Still an Act of God

The DRAM refresh cycle eater is the cycle eater that's least changed from its 8088 form on the 80286 and 80386. In the AT, DRAM refresh uses a little over 5 percent of all available memory accesses, slightly less than it uses in the PC, but in the same ballpark. While the DRAM refresh penalty varies somewhat on various AT clones and 80386 computers (in fact, a few computers are built around static RAM, which requires no refresh at all), the 5 percent figure is a good rule of thumb.

Basically, the effect of the DRAM refresh cycle eater is pretty much the same throughout the PC-compatible world: fairly small, so it doesn't greatly affect performance; unavoidable, so there's no point in worrying about it anyway; and a nuisance, because it results in fractional cycle counts when the Zen timer is used. Just as with the PC, a given code sequence on the AT can execute at varying speeds at different times, as a result of the interaction between the code and the DRAM refresh timing.

There's nothing much new with DRAM refresh on 80286/80386 computers, then. Be aware of it, but don't concern yourself overly—DRAM refresh is still an act of God, and there's not a blessed thing you can do about it.

The Display Adapter Cycle Eater

And finally we come to the last of the cycle eaters, the display adapter cycle eater. There are two ways of looking at this cycle eater on 80286/80386 computers: (1) it's much worse than it was on the PC or, (2) it's just about the same as it was on the PC.

Either way, the display adapter cycle eater is extremely bad news on 80286/80386 computers.

The two ways of looking at the display adapter cycle eater on

80286/80386 computers are actually the same. As you'll recall from Chapter 4, display adapters offer only a limited number of accesses to display memory during any given period of time. The 8088 is capable of making use of most, but not all, of those slots with **rep movsw**, so the number of memory accesses allowed by a display adapter such as an EGA is reasonably well matched to an 8088's memory access speed. Granted, access to an EGA slows down the 8088 considerably, but, as we're about to find out, considerably is a relative term. What an EGA does to PC performance is nothing compared to what it does to faster computers.

Under ideal conditions, an 80286 can access memory much, much faster than an 8088. A 10-MHz 80286 is capable of accessing a word of system memory every 0.20 μsec with **rep movsw**, dwarfing the 1 byte every 1.31 μsec that the 8088 in a PC can manage. However, access to display memory is anything but ideal for an 80286. For one thing, most display adapters are 8-bit devices. (While a few are 16-bit devices, they're the exception.) One consequence of that is that only 1 byte can be read or written per access to display memory; word-sized accesses to 8-bit devices are automatically split into two separate byte-sized accesses by the AT's bus. Another consequence is that accesses are simply slower; the AT's bus always inserts 3 wait states on accesses to 8-bit devices, because it must assume that such devices were designed for PCs and may not run reliably at AT speeds.

However, the 8-bit size of most display adapters is but one of the two factors that reduce the speed with which the 80286 can access display memory. Far more cycles are eaten by the inherent memory-access limitations of display adapters—that is, the limited number of display memory accesses that display adapters make available to the 80286. Look at it this way: if **rep movsw** on a PC can use more than half of all available accesses to display memory, then how much faster can code running on an 80286 or 80386 possibly run when accessing display memory?

That's right—less than twice as fast.

In other words, instructions that access display memory won't run a whole lot faster on ATs and faster computers than they do on PCs. That explains one of the two viewpoints expressed at the beginning of this section: the display adapter cycle eater is just about the same on high end computers as it is on the PC, in the sense that it allows instructions that access display memory to run at just about the same speed on all computers.

Of course, the picture is quite a bit different when you compare the performance of instructions that access display memory to the *maximum* performance of those instructions. Instructions that access display memory receive many more wait states when running on an 80286 than they do on an 8088. Why? While the 80286 is capable of accessing memory much more often than the 8088, we've seen that the frequency of access to display memory is determined not by processor speed but by the display adapter. As a result, both processors are actually allowed just about the same maximum number of accesses to display memory in any given time. By definition, then, the 80286 must spend many more cycles waiting than does the 8088.

And that explains the second viewpoint expressed above regarding the display adapter cycle eater vis-a-vis the 80286 and 80386. The display adapter cycle eater, as measured in cycles lost to wait states, is indeed much worse on AT-class computers than it is on the PC, and it's worse still on more powerful computers.

How bad is the display adapter cycle eater on an AT? Back in Chapter 3, we measured the performance of **rep movsw** accessing system memory in a PC and display memory on an EGA installed in a PC. Access to EGA memory proved to be more than twice as slow as access to system memory. Listing 3-1, which accessed EGA memory, ran in 26.06 msec; Listing 3-2, which accessed system memory, ran in 11.24 msec.

When the same two listings are run on an EGA-equipped 10-MHz AT clone, the results are startling. Listing 3-2 accesses system memory in just 1.31 msec, more than eight times faster than on the PC. Listing 3-1 accesses EGA memory in 16.12 msec—considerably less than twice as fast as on the PC, and well over 10 times as slow as Listing 13-1. *The display adapter cycle eater can slow an AT—or even an 80386 computer—to near-PC speeds when display memory is accessed.*

I know that's hard to believe, but the display adapter cycle eater gives out just so many display memory accesses in a given time, and no more, no matter how fast the processor is. In fact, the faster the processor, the more the display adapter cycle eater hurts the performance of instructions that access display memory. Not only is the display adapter cycle eater still present in 80286/80386 computers, it's worse than ever.

What can we do about this new, more virulent form of the display adapter cycle eater? The workaround is the same as it was on the PC:

Access display memory as little as you possibly can.

15.4 ◆ New Instructions and Features

The 80286 and 80386 offer a number of new instructions. The 80286 has a relatively small number of instructions that the 8088 lacks; the 80386 has those instructions and quite a few more, plus new addressing modes and data sizes. We'll discuss the 80286 and the 80386 separately in this regard.

The 80286

The 80286 has a number of instructions designed for protected-mode operations. As I've said, we're not going to discuss protected mode in *Zen of Assembly Language;* in any case, protected-mode instructions generally are used only by operating systems. (I should mention that the 80286's protected mode brings with it the ability to address 16 Mb of memory, a considerable improvement over the 8088's 1 Mb. In real mode, however, programs are still limited to 1 Mb of addressable memory on the 80286. In either mode, individual segments are still limited to 64 Kb.)

There are also a few 80286-specific real-mode instructions, and they can be quite useful. The **bound** instruction checks array bounds. The instructions **enter** and **leave** support compact and speedy stack frame construction and removal, ideal for interfacing to high level languages such as C and Pascal. The new string instructions **ins** and **outs** support efficient data transfer between memory and I/O ports. Finally, **pusha** and **popa** push and pop all eight general-purpose registers.

A couple of old instructions gain new features on the 80286. For one, the 80286 version of **push** is capable of pushing a constant on the stack. For another, the 80286 allows all shifts and rotates to be performed for not just 1 bit or the number of bits specified by CL but for any constant number of bits.

These new instructions are fairly powerful, if not earthshaking. Nonetheless, it would be foolish to use them unless you're intentionally writing a program that will run only on the 80286 and 80386. That's because none of the 80286-specific instructions does anything that can't be done reasonably well with some combination of 8088 instructions—and if you do use even one of the 80286-specific instructions, you've thrown 8088 compatibility out the window. In other words, you'll be sacrificing the ability to run on most of the computers in the PC-compatible market in return for a relatively minor improvement in performance and program size.

If you're programming in protected mode or if you've already decided that you don't want your programs to run on 8088-based computers, sure, go ahead and use the 80286-specific instructions. Otherwise, give them a wide berth.

The 80386

The 80386 is somewhat more complex than the 80286 as regards new features. Once again, we won't discuss protected mode, which on the 80386 comes with the ability to address up to 4 gigabytes per segment and 64 terabytes in all. In real mode (and in virtual-86 mode, which allows the 80386 to multitask MS-DOS applications and is identical to real mode so far as MS-DOS programs are concerned), programs running on the 80386 are still limited to 1 Mb of addressable memory and 64 Kb per segment.

The 80386 has many new instructions, as well as new registers, addressing modes, and data sizes that have trickled down from protected mode. Let's take a quick look at these new real-mode features.

Even in real mode, it's possible to access many of the 80386's new and extended registers. Most are simply 32-bit extensions of the 16-bit registers of the 8088. For example, EAX is a 32-bit register that contains AX as its lower 16 bits, EBX is a 32-bit register that contains BX as its lower 16 bits, and so on. There are also two new segment registers, FS and GS.

The 80386 also comes with a slew of new real-mode instructions beyond those supported by the 8088 and 80286. These instructions can scan data bit by bit, set the carry flag (CF) to the value of a specified bit, sign extend or zero extend data as it's moved, set a register or memory variable to 1 or 0 on the basis of any of the conditions that can be tested with conditional jumps, and more. What's more, both old and new instructions support 32-bit operations on the 80386. For example, it's relatively simple to copy data in chunks of 4 bytes on an 80386, even in real mode, by using the **movsd** (*move string double*) instruction, or to negate a 32-bit value with **neg eax**. (That's a whole lot less complicated than our fancy 32-bit negation code of past chapters, eh?)

Finally, it's possible in real mode to use the 80386's new addressing modes, in which *any* 32-bit general-purpose register can be used to address memory. What's more, multiplication of memory-addressing registers by 2, 4, or 8 for look-ups in word, doubleword, or quadword tables can be built right into the memory-addressing mode. In protected mode, these new addressing modes allow you to address a full 4 gigabytes per segment, but in real mode you're still limited to 64 Kb, even with 32-bit registers and the new addressing modes.

Having shown you these wonders, I'm going to snatch them away. All these features are available only on the 80386; code using them won't even run on the 80286, let alone the 8088. If you're going to go to the trouble of using 80386-specific features, thereby eliminating any chance of running on PCs and ATs, you might as well go all the way and write 80386 protected-mode code. That way, you'll be able to take full advantage of the new addressing modes and larger segments, rather than working with the subset of 80386 features that's available in real mode.

And 80386 protected mode programming, my friend, is quite a different journey from the one we've been taking. Although the 80386 in protected mode bears some resemblance to the 8088, the resemblance isn't all that strong. The protected-mode 80386 is a wonderful processor to program, and a good topic—a *terrific* topic—for some book to cover in detail, but this is not that book.

To sum up: stick to the 8088's instruction set, registers, and addressing modes, unless you're willing to sacrifice completely the ability to run on the bulk of PC-compatible computers. The 80286-specific instructions don't have a big enough payback to compensate for the inability to run on 8088-based computers, and 80386-specific instructions limit your market so sharply that you might as well go to protected mode and get the full benefits of the 80386.

15.5 ◆ Optimization Rules: The More Things Change . . .

Let's see what we've learned about 80286/80386 optimization. Mostly what we've learned is that our familiar PC cycle eaters still apply, although in somewhat different forms, and that the major optimization rules for the PC hold true on ATs and 80386-based computers. You won't go wrong on high-end MS-DOS computers if you keep your instructions short, use the registers heavily and avoid memory, don't branch, and avoid accessing display memory like the plague.

Although we haven't touched on them, repeated string instructions are still desirable on the 80286 and 80386, as they provide a great deal of functionality per instruction byte and eliminate both the prefetch queue cycle eater and branching. However, string instructions are not quite so spectacularly superior on the 80286 and 80386 as they are on the 8088, because nonstring memory-accessing instructions have been speeded up considerably on the newer processors.

There's one cycle eater with new implications on the 80286 and 80386, and that's the data alignment cycle eater. From the data alignment cycle eater we get a new rule: word align your word-sized variables, and start your subroutines at even addresses. This rule doesn't hurt 8088 performance or compatibility, improves 80286 and 80386 performance considerably, is easy to implement, and costs relatively few bytes, so it's worth applying even though it doesn't improve the performance of 8088 code.

Basically, what we've found is that the broad optimization rules for the 8088, plus the word-alignment rule, cover the 80286 and 80386 quite nicely. What *that* means is that if you optimize for the 8088 and word align word-sized memory accesses, you'll get solid performance on all

PC-compatible computers. What's more, it means that if you're writing code specifically for the 80286 or 80386, you already have a good feel for optimizing that code.

In short, what you've already learned in *Zen of Assembly Language* will serve you well throughout the PC family.

Detailed Optimization

Although the major 8088 optimization rules hold true on computers built around the 80286 and 80386, many of the instruction-specific optimizations we've learned no longer hold, for the execution times of most instructions are quite different on the 80286 and 80386 than on the 8088. We have already seen one such example of the sometimes vast difference between 8088 and 80286/80386 instruction execution times: **mov [WordVar],0**, which has an EU execution time of 20 cycles on the 8088, has an EU execution time of just 3 cycles on the 80286 and 2 cycles on the 80386.

In fact, the performance of virtually all memory-accessing instructions has been improved enormously on the 80286 and 80386. The key to this improvement is the near elimination of effective address (EA) calculation time. Where an 8088 takes from 5 to 12 cycles to calculate an EA, an 80286 or 80386 usually takes no time whatsoever to perform the calculation. If a base+index+displacement addressing mode, such as **mov ax,[WordArray+bx+si]**, is used on an 80286 or 80386, 1 cycle is taken to perform the EA calculation, but that's both the worst case and the only case in which there's any EA overhead at all.

The elimination of EA calculation time means that the EU execution time of memory-addressing instructions is much closer to the EU execution time of register-only instructions. For instance, on the 8088 **add [WordVar],100h** is a 31-cycle instruction and **add dx,100h** is a 4-cycle instruction—a ratio of nearly 8:1. By contrast, on the 80286 **add [WordVar],100h** is a 7-cycle instruction and **add dx,100h** is a 3-cycle instruction—a ratio of just 2.3:1.

It would seem, then, that it's less necessary to use the registers on the 80286 than it was on the 8088, but that's simply not the case, for reasons we've already seen. The key is this: the 80286 can execute memory-addressing instructions so fast that there's no spare instruction prefetching time during those instructions, so the prefetch queue runs dry, especially on the AT, with its 1–wait state memory. On the AT, the 6-byte instruction **add [WordVar],100h** is effectively at least a 15-cycle instruction, because 3 cycles are needed to fetch each of the three instruction words and 6 more cycles are needed to read **WordVar** and write the result back to memory.

Granted, the register-only instruction **add dx,100h** also slows down—to 6 cycles—because of instruction prefetching, leaving a ratio of 2.5:1. Now, however, let's look at the performance of the same code on an 8088. The register-only code would run in 16 cycles (4 instruction bytes at 4 cycles per byte), while the memory-accessing code would run in 40 cycles (6 instruction bytes at 4 cycles per byte, plus two word-sized memory accesses at 8 cycles per word). That's a ratio of 2.5:1, *exactly the same as on the 80286*.

This is all theoretical. We put our trust not in theory but in actual performance, so let's run this code through the Zen timer. On a PC, Listing 15-4, which performs register-only addition, runs in 3.62 msec, while Listing 15-5, which performs addition to a memory variable, runs in 10.05 msec. On a 10-MHz AT clone, Listing 15-4 runs in 0.64 msec, while Listing 15-5 runs in 1.80 msec. Obviously, the AT is much faster, but the ratio of Listing 15-5 to Listing 15-4 is virtually identical on both computers, at 2.78 for the PC and 2.81 for the AT. If anything, the register-only form of **add** has a slightly *greater* advantage on the AT than it does on the PC in this case.

Theory confirmed.

```
1   ;
2   ; *** Listing 15-4 ***
3   ;
4   ; Measures the performance of adding an immediate value
5   ; to a register, for comparison with Listing 15-5, which
6   ; adds an immediate value to a memory variable.
7   ;
8           call    ZTimerOn
9           rept    1000
10          add     dx,100h
11          endm
12          call    ZTimerOff
```

What's going on? Simply this: instruction fetching is controlling overall execution time on *both* processors. Both the 8088 in a PC and the 80286 in an AT can execute the bytes of the instructions in Listings 15-4 and 15-5 faster than they can be fetched. Because the instructions are exactly the same lengths on both processors, it stands to reason that the ratio of the overall execution times of the instructions should be the same on both processors as well. Instruction length controls execution time, and the instruction lengths are the same—therefore the ratios of the execution times are the same. The 80286 can both fetch and execute instruction bytes faster than the 8088 can, so code executes much faster on the 80286; nonetheless, because the 80286 can also execute those instruction bytes much faster than it can fetch them, overall performance is still determined largely by the size of the instructions.

```
1   ;
2   ; *** Listing 15-5 ***
3   ;
4   ; Measures the performance of adding an immediate value
5   ; to a memory variable, for comparison with Listing 15-4,
6   ; which adds an immediate value to a register.
7   ;
8           jmp     Skip
9   ;
10          even                    ;always make sure word-sized memory
11                                  ; variables are word-aligned!
12  WordVar dw      0
13  ;
14  Skip:
15          call    ZTimerOn
16          rept    1000
17          add     [WordVar],100h
18          endm
19          call    ZTimerOff
```

Is this always the case? No. When the prefetch queue is full, memory-accessing instructions on the 80286 and 80386 are much faster relative to register-only instructions than they are on the 8088. Given the system wait states prevalent on 80286 and 80386 computers, however, the prefetch queue is likely to be empty quite a bit, especially when code consisting of instructions with short EU execution times is executed. Of course, that's just the sort of code we're likely to write when we're optimizing, so the performance of high-speed code is more likely to be controlled by instruction size than by EU execution time on most 80286 and 80386 computers, just as it is on the PC.

All of which is just a way of saying that faster memory access and EA calculation notwithstanding, it's just as desirable to keep instructions short and memory accesses to a minimum on the 80286 as it is on the 8088. And we know full well that the way to do that is to use the registers as heavily as possible, use string instructions, use short forms of instructions, and the like.

The more things change, the more they remain the same. . .

Don't sweat the details.   We've just seen how a major difference between the 80286 and 8088—the virtual elimination of effective address calculation time—leaves the major optimization rules pretty much unchanged. Although there are many details about 80286 and 80386 code performance that differ greatly from the 8088 (for example, the 80386's barrel shifter allows you to shift or rotate a value *any* number of bits in just 3 cycles, and **mul** and **div** are much, much faster on the newer processors), those details aren't worth worrying about unless you're abandoning the 8088 entirely.

Even then, the many variations in memory architecture and performance between various 80286 and 80386 computers make it impractical to focus too closely on detailed 80286/80386 optimizations.

In short, there's little point in even considering 80286/80386 optimizations when you're writing code that will also run on the 8088. If the 8088 isn't one of the target processors for a particular piece of code, you can use Intel's publications, which list cycle times for both real and protected mode, and the Zen timer to optimize for the 80286 or the 80386. (You will probably have to modify the Zen timer before you can run it under a protected-mode operating system; it was designed for use under MS-DOS in real mode and has been tested only in that mode. Some operating systems provide built-in high-precision timing services that could be used in place of the Zen timer.)

Always bear in mind, however, that your optimization control is not so fine on 80286/80386 computers as it is on the PC, unless you can be sure that your code will run only on a particular processor (either the 80286 or the 80386, but not both) with a single, well-understood memory architecture. As 80286 and 80386 machines of various designs proliferate, that condition becomes increasingly difficult to fulfill.

On balance, my final word on 80286/80386 real-mode optimization in this: *with the sole exception of word aligning your word-sized variables and subroutines, optimize only for the 8088.* You'll get the best possible performance on the slowest computer—the PC—and excellent performance across the entire spectrum of PC-compatible computers.

When you get right down to it, isn't that everything you could ask for from a real-mode program?

15.6 ◆ popf and the 80286

We've one final 80286-related item to discuss: the hardware malfunction of **popf** under certain circumstances on the 80286.

The problem is this: sometimes **popf** permits interrupts to occur when interrupts are initially off and the setting popped into the interrupt flag (IF) from the stack keeps interrupts off. In other words, an interrupt can happen even though IF is never set to 1. (For further details, see "Chips in Transition," *PC Tech Journal,* April 1986.)

Now, I don't want to blow this particular bug out of proportion. It causes problems only in code that cannot tolerate interrupts under any circumstances, and that's a rare sort of code, especially in user programs.

Still, some code does need to have interrupts absolutely disabled, with no chance of an interrupt sneaking through. For example, a critical portion of a disk BIOS might need to retrieve data from the disk controller the instant it becomes available; even a few hundred microseconds of delay could result in a sector's worth of data misread. In this case, one interrupt during a **popf** could result in a trashed hard disk if that interrupt occurs while the disk BIOS is reading a sector of the File Allocation Table.

There is a workaround for the **popf** bug. Although the workaround is easy to use, it's considerably slower than **popf** and costs a few bytes as well, so you won't want to use it in code that can tolerate interrupts. On the other hand, in code that truly cannot be interrupted, you should view those extra cycles and bytes as cheap insurance against mysterious and erratic program crashes.

One obvious reason to discuss the **popf** workaround is that it's useful. Another reason is that the workaround is an excellent example of the Zen of assembly language, in that there's a well-defined goal to be achieved but no obvious way to do so. The goal is to reproduce the functionality of the **popf** instruction without using **popf**, and the place to start is by asking exactly what **popf** does.

All **popf** does is pop the word on top of the stack into the flags register, as shown in Figure 15.4. How can we do that without **popf**? Of course, the 80286's designers intended us to use **popf** for this purpose and didn't intentionally provide any alternative approach, so we'll have to devise an alternative approach of our own. To do that, we'll have to search for instructions that contain some of the same functionality as **popf**, in the hope that one of those instructions can be used in some way to replace **popf**.

Well, there's only one instruction other than **popf** that loads the flags register directly from the stack, and that's **iret**, which loads the flags register from the stack as it branches, as shown in Figure 15.5. The **iret** instruction has no known bugs like the one that plagues **popf**, so it's certainly a candidate to replace **popf** in noninterruptible applications. Unfortunately, **iret** loads the flags register with the *third* word down on the stack, not the word on top of the stack, as is the case with **popf**; the far return address that **iret** pops into CS:IP lies between the top of the stack and the word popped into the flags register.

Obviously, the segment:offset that **iret** expects to find on the stack above the pushed flags isn't present when the stack is set up for **popf**, so we'll have to adjust the stack a bit before we can substitute **iret** for **popf**. What we'll have to do is push the segment:offset of the instruction after our workaround code onto the stack right above the pushed flags. The **iret**

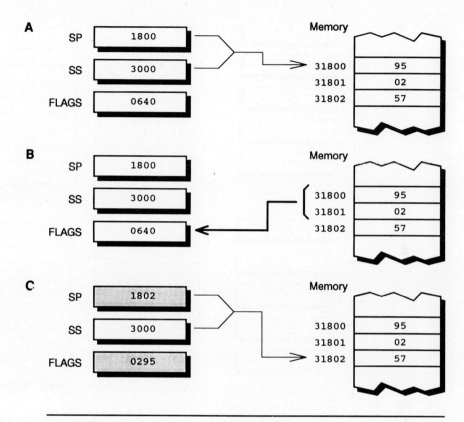

FIGURE 15.4   An example of the operation of **popf**. **(A)** The state of the PC before **popf** is executed. **(B)** The state of the PC as **popf** executes. **(C)** The state of the PC after **popf** is finished.

instruction will then branch to that address and pop the flags, ending up at the instruction after the workaround code with the flags popped. That's just the result that would have occurred had we executed **popf**—with the bonus that no interrupts can accidentally occur when IF is 0 both before and after the pop.

How can we push the segment:offset of the next instruction? Well, think back to our discussion in the last chapter of finding the offset of the next instruction by performing a near call to that instruction. We can do something similar here, but in this case we need a far call, since **iret** requires both a segment and an offset. We'll also branch backward so that

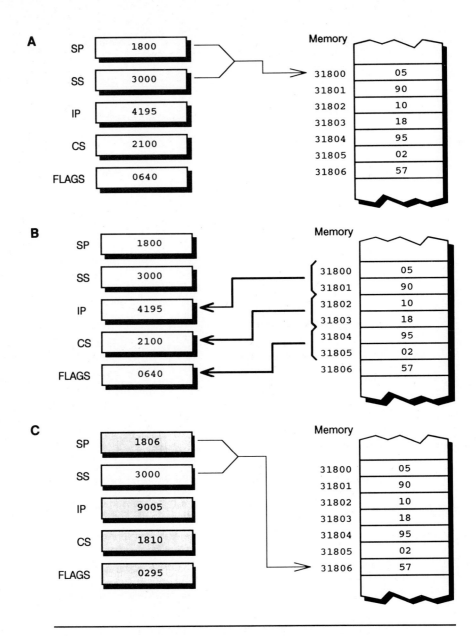

FIGURE 15.5 An example of the operation of **iret**. **(A)** The state of the PC before **iret** is executed. **(B)** The state of the PC as **iret** executes. **(C)** The state of the PC after **iret** is finished.

the address pushed on the stack will point to the instruction we want to continue with. The code works out like this:

```
        jmp short popfskip
popfiret:
        iret            ;branches to the instruction after the
                        ; call, popping the word below the address
                        ; pushed by CALL into the FLAGS register
popfskip:
        call far ptr popfiret
                        ;pushes the segment:offset of the next
                        ; instruction on the stack just above
                        ; the flags word, setting things up so
                        ; that IRET will branch to the next
                        ; instruction and pop the flags
; When execution reaches the instruction following this comment,
; the word that was on top of the stack when JMP SHORT POPFSKIP
; was reached has been popped into the FLAGS register, just as
; if a POPF instruction had been executed.
```

The operation of this code is illustrated in Figure 15.6.

The **popf** workaround can best be implemented as a macro; we can also emulate a far call by pushing CS and performing a near call, thereby shrinking the workaround code by 1 byte:

```
EMULATE_POPF    macro
        local       popfskip, popfiret
        jmp    short popfskip
popfiret:
        iret
popfskip:
        push   cs
        call   popfiret
        endm
```

By the way, the flags can be popped much more quickly if you're willing to alter a register in the process. For example, the following macro emulates **popf** with just one branch but wipes out AX:

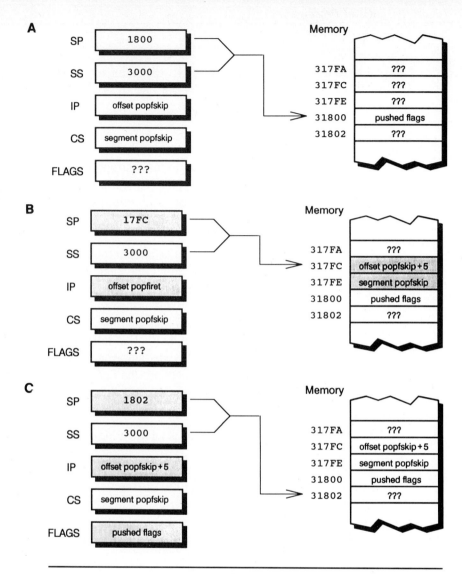

FIGURE 15.6   An example of the operation of the workaround code for the **popf** bug. The workaround code is

```
        jmp short popfskip
popfiret:
        iret
popfskip:
        call far ptr popfiret
```

(A) The state of the PC after **jmp short popfskip**. **(B)** The state of the PC after **call far ptr popfiret**. **(C)** The state of the PC after **iret**.

```
EMULATE_POPF_TRASH_AX      macro
      push cs
      mov  ax,offset $+5
      push ax
      iret
      endm
```

It's not a perfect substitute for **popf**, since **popf** doesn't alter any registers, but it's faster and shorter than **EMULATE_POPF** when you can spare the register. If you're using 286-specific instructions, you can use

```
.286
   :

EMULATE_POPF     macro
      push  cs
      push  offset $+4
      iret
      endm
```

which is shorter still, alters no registers, and branches just once. (Of course, this version of **EMULATE_POPF** won't work on an 8088.)

The standard version of **EMULATE_POPF** is 6 bytes longer than **popf** and much slower, as you'd expect given that it involves three branches. Anyone in his or her right mind would prefer **popf** to a larger, slower, three-branch macro, given a choice. In noninterruptible code, however, there's no choice; the safer—if slower—approach is the best. (Having people associate your programs with crashed computers is *not* a desirable situation, no matter how unfair the circumstances under which it occurs.)

Anyway, the overall inferiority of **EMULATE_POPF** is almost never an issue, because **EMULATE_POPF** is unlikely to be used either often or in situations where performance matters. The **popf** instruction is neither a frequently used instruction nor one that's used often in time-critical code; as we found in Chapter 8, **lahf/sahf** is superior to **pushf/popf** for most applications. Besides, all this matters only when the flags need to be popped in noninterruptible code, a situation that rarely arises.

And now you know the nature of and the workaround for the **popf** bug. Whether you ever need the workaround or not, it's a neatly packaged example of the tremendous flexibility of the 8088's instruction set and of the value of the Zen of assembly language.

15.7 ◆ Coprocessors and Peripherals

Up to this point we've concentrated on the various processors in the 8088 family. There are also a number of coprocessors in use in the PC world, and they can affect the performance of some programs every bit as much as processors can. Unfortunately, while processors are standard equipment (I should hope every computer comes with one!) not a single coprocessor is standard. Every PC-compatible computer can execute the 8088 instruction **mov al,1**, but the same cannot be said of the 8087 numeric coprocessor instruction **fld [MemVar]**, to say nothing of instructions for the coprocessors on a variety of graphics, sound, and other adapters available for the PC. Then, too, there are many PC peripherals that offer considerable functionality without being true coprocessors—VGAs and serial adapters, to name just two—but none of those is standard either.

Coprocessors and peripherals are just about as complex as processors and require similarly detailed explanations of programming techniques. However, because of the lack of standards, you'll want to learn about a given coprocessor or peripheral only if it affects your work. By contrast, you had no choice but to learn about the 8088, as it affects everything you do on a PC.

If you're interested in programming a particular coprocessor or peripheral, you can always find a book, an article, or at least a data sheet that addresses that interest. You may not find reference material of the quality or in the quantity you'd like, especially for the more esoteric coprocessors, but there is surely enough information available to get you started; otherwise no one else would be able to program that coprocessor or peripheral either. (Remember, as an advanced assembler programmer you're now among the programming elite. There just aren't very many people who understand as much about microcomputer programming as you do. That may be a strange thought, but roll it around in your head for a while. I suspect you'll get to like it.)

Once you've gotten started with a given coprocessor or adapter, you can put the Zen approach to work in a new context. Gain a thorough understanding of the resources and capabilities the new environment has to offer, and learn to think in terms of matching those capabilities to your applications.

A Brief Note on the 8087

The 8087, 80287 and 80387 are the most common and important PC coprocessors. These numeric coprocessors improve the performance of floating-point arithmetic far beyond the speeds possible with an 8088 alone, performing floating-point operations such as addition, subtraction, multiplication, division, absolute value, comparison, and square root. The 80287 is similar to the 8087, but with protected-mode support; the 80387 adds some new functions, including sine and cosine. (For the remainder of this section I'll use the term *8087* to cover all 8087-family numeric coprocessors.)

While the 8087 is widely used and is used frequently in high level language programs, it is rarely programmed directly in assembler. This is true partly because floating-point arithmetic is relatively slow, even with an 8087, so the cycle savings achievable via assembler are relatively small as a percentage of overall execution time. Also, 8087 instructions are so specialized that they generally offer less rich optimization opportunities than do 8088 instructions.

Given the specialized nature of 8087 assembler programming, and given that 8087 programming is largely a separate topic from 8088 programming (although the processors do have their common points, such as addressing modes), I'm not going to tackle the 8087 in this book. I will offer one general tip, however:

Keep your arithmetic variables in the 8087's data registers as much as you possibly can. (There are eight 80-bit data registers, organized as an internal stack.) "Keep it in the registers" is a rule we've become familiar with on the 8088, and it will stand us in equally good stead on the 8087.

Why? Well, the 8087 works with an internal 10-byte format, rather than the 2-, 4-, and 8-byte integer and floating-point formats we're familiar with. Whenever an 8087 instruction loads data from or stores data to a memory variable that's in a 2-, 4-, or 8-byte format, the 8087 must convert the data format accordingly, and it takes the 8087 dozens of cycles to perform those conversions. Even apart from the conversion time, it takes quite a few cycles just to copy 2 to 10 bytes to or from memory.

For example, it takes the 8087 between 51 and 97 cycles (including effective address calculation time and the 4–cycle per word 8-bit bus penalty) just to push a floating-point value from memory onto the 8087's data register stack. By contrast, it takes just 17 to 22 cycles to push a value from an internal register onto the data register stack. Ideally, the value you need will have been left on top of the 8087 register stack as the result of the last operation, in which case no load time at all is required.

Intensive use of the 8087's data registers is one area in which assembler code can substantially outperform high level language code. High level languages tend to use the 8087 for only one operation—or, at most, one high level language statement—at a time, loading the data registers from scratch for each operation. Most high level languages load the operands for each operation into the 8087's data registers, perform the operation, and store the result back to memory, then start the whole process over again for the next operation, even if the two operations are related.

What you can do in assembler, of course, is use the 8087's data registers much as you've learned to use the 8088's general-purpose registers: load often-used values into the data registers, keep results around if you'll need them later, and keep intermediate results in the data registers rather than storing them to memory. Also, remember that you often have the option of either popping or not popping source operands from the top of the stack and that data registers other than ST(0) can often serve as destination operands.

In short, the 8087 has both a generous set of data registers and considerable flexibility in how those registers can be used. Take full advantage of those resources when you write 8087 code.

Before we go, one final item about the 8087. The 8087 is a true coprocessor, fully capable of executing instructions in parallel with the 8088. In other words, the 8088 can continue fetching and executing instructions while the 8087 is processing one of its lengthy instructions. Although that makes for excellent performance, problems can arise if a second 8087 instruction is fetched and started before the first has finished. To avoid such problems, MASM automatically inserts a **wait** instruction before each 8087 instruction. That **wait** simply tells the 8088 to wait until the 8087 has finished its current instruction before continuing. In short, MASM neatly and invisibly avoids one sort of potential 8087 synchronization problem.

There's a second sort of potential 8087 synchronization problem, however, and this one you must guard against, for it isn't taken care of by MASM: instructions accessing memory out of sequence. The 8088 is fully capable of executing new instructions while a lengthy 8087 instruction that precedes those 8088 instructions executes. One of those later 8088 instructions can, for example, easily read a memory location before the 8087 instruction writes to it. In other words, given an 8087 instruction that accesses a memory variable, it's possible for an 8088 instruction that follows that 8087 instruction to access the memory variable *before* the 8087 instruction does.

Clearly, serious problems can arise if instructions access memory out of sequence. To avoid such problems, you should explicitly place a **wait** instruction between any 8087 instruction that accesses a memory variable and any following 8088 instructions that could possibly access that same variable.

That doesn't by any stretch of the imagination mean that you should put **wait** after all of your 8087 instructions. On the contrary, the rule is that you should use **wait** only when there's the potential for out-of-sequence 8087 and 8088 memory accesses, and then only immediately before the instructions during which the conflict might arise. The rest of the time, you can boost performance by omitting **wait** and letting the 8088 and 8087 coprocess.

Conclusion

Despite all the other processors, coprocessors, and peripherals in the PC family, the 8088 is still the best place to focus your optimization efforts. If your code runs well on an 8088, it will run well on every 8086-family processor well into the 21st century, and even on a number of computers built around other processors. Good performance and the largest possible market—what more could you want?

That's enough of being practical. No one programs extensively in assembler just because it's useful; a certain fondness for the kinds of puzzles assembler programming presents is also required. For that sort of programmer, there's nothing better than the weird but wonderful 8088. Admit it—strange as 8088 assembler programming is . . .

. . . isn't it *fun?*

Chapter 16

Onward to the Flexible Mind

16.1 A Taste of What You've Learned

16.2 Zenning

16.3 Knowledge and Beyond

And so we come to the end of our journey through knowledge. More precisely, we've come to the end of that part of *Zen of Assembly Language* that's dedicated to knowledge, for no matter how long you or I continue to program the 8088, there will always be more to learn about this surprising processor.

If the Zen of assembly language were merely a matter of instructions and cycle times, I would spend a few pages marvelling at the wonders we've seen, then congratulate you on arriving at a mastery of assembly language and bid you farewell. I won't do that, though, for in truth we've merely arrived at a resting place from whence our journey will continue anew in Volume II of *Zen of Assembly Language.* There are marvels aplenty to come, so we'll just catch our breath, take a brief look back to see how far we've come—and then it's on to the flexible mind.

The flexible mind notwithstanding, congratulations are clearly in order *right now,* for you've mastered a great deal. In fact, you've absorbed just about as much knowledge about assembler as any mortal could in so short a time. You've undoubtedly learned much more than you realize just yet; only with experience will everything you've seen in this volume sink in fully.

As important as the amount you've learned is the nature of your knowledge. We haven't just thrown together a collection of unrelated facts in this volume; we've divined the fundamental nature and basic optimization rules of the PC. We've explored the architectures of the PC and the 8088, and we've seen how those underlying factors greatly influence the performance of all assembler code (and, by extension, the performance of all code that runs on the PC). We've learned which members of the instruction set are best suited to various tasks; we've come across unexpected talents in many instructions; and we've learned to view instructions in light of what they *can* do, not what they were designed to do. Best of all, we've learned to use the Zen timer to check our assumptions and to help us continue to learn and to hone our skills.

What all this amounts to is a truly excellent understanding of instruction performance on the PC. That's important—critically important—but it's not the whole picture. The knowledge we've acquired is merely the foundation for the flexible mind, which enables us to transform task specifications into superior assembler code. In turn, application implementations—whole programs—are built upon the flexible mind. So, while we've built a strong foundation, we've a ways yet to go in completing our mastery of the Zen of assembly language.

The flexible mind and implementation are what Volume II of *Zen of Assembly Language* is all about. Volume II develops the concept of the flexible mind from the bottom up, starting at the level of implementing the most efficient code for a small, well-defined task, continuing on through algorithm implementation, and extending to designing custom assembler-based mini-languages tailored to various applications. We'll learn how to search and sort data quickly, how to squeeze every cycle out of a line-drawing routine, how to let data replace code (with tremendous program-size benefits), and how to do animation. The emphasis every step of the way will be on outperforming standard techniques by using our new knowledge in innovative ways to create the best possible 8088 code for each task.

Finally, we'll put everything we've learned together by designing and implementing an animation application. The PC isn't renowned as a game machine (to put it mildly!), but by the time we're through, I promise you won't be able to tell the difference between the graphics on your PC and those in an arcade. The key, of course, is the flexible mind, the ability to bring together the needs of the application and the capabilities of the PC, often with spectacular results.

So, while we've gone a mighty long way toward mastering the Zen of assembly language, we haven't arrived yet. That's all to the good, though. Until now, interesting as our explorations have been, we've basically been doing grunt work—learning cycle times and the like. What's coming up next is the *really* fun stuff—taking what we've learned and using that knowledge to create the wondrous tasks and applications that are possible only with the very best assembler code.

In short, in Volume II we'll experience the full spectrum of the Zen of assembly language, from the details that we now know so well to the magnificent applications that make it all worthwhile.

16.1 ◆ A Taste of What You've Learned

Before we leave Volume I, I'd like to give you a taste of both what's to come and what you already know. Why do you need to see what you already know? The answer is that you've surely learned much more than you realize right now. The example we'll look at involves strong elements of the flexible mind, and what we'll find is that there's no neat dividing line between knowledge and the flexible mind—and that we have already ventured much farther across the fuzzy boundary between the two than you'd ever imagine.

We'll also see that the flexible mind involves knowledge and intuition—but no deep dark mysteries. Knowledge you have in profusion, and, as you'll see, your intuition is growing by leaps and bounds. (Try to stay one step ahead of me as we optimize the following routine. I suspect you'll be surprised at how easy it is.) I'm presenting this last example precisely because I'd like you to see how well you already understand the flexible mind.

On to our final example . . .

16.2 ◆ Zenning

In the third edition of Jeff Duntemann's excellent book *Complete Turbo Pascal* (published by Scott, Foresman and Company), there's a small assembler subroutine that's designed to be called from a Turbo Pascal program in order to fill the screen or a system-memory screen buffer with a specified character-attribute pair in text mode. This subroutine involves only 21 instructions and works perfectly well; nonetheless, with what we know we can compact the subroutine tremendously and speed it up a bit as well. To coin a verb, we can "Zen" this already tight assembler code to an astonishing degree. In the process, I hope you'll get a feel for how advanced your assembler skills have become.

The code is as follows (the code is Jeff's, with many letters converted to lower case in order to match the style of *Zen of Assembly Language,* but the comments are mine):

```
OnStack    struc        ;data that's stored on the stack after PUSH BP
OldBP      dw   ?       ;caller's BP
RetAddr    dw   ?       ;return address
Filler     dw   ?       ;character to fill the buffer with
Attrib     dw   ?       ;attribute to fill the buffer with
BufSize    dw   ?       ;number of character/attribute pairs to fill
BufOfs     dw   ?       ;buffer offset
BufSeg     dw   ?       ;buffer segment
EndMrk     db   ?       ;marker for the end of the stack frame
OnStack    ends
;
ClearS     proc near
    push   bp                          ;save caller's BP
    mov    bp,sp                       ;point to stack frame
    cmp    word ptr [bp].BufSeg,0      ;skip the fill if a null
    jne    Start                       ; pointer is passed
```

```
        cmp    word ptr [bp].BufOfs,0
        je     Bye
Start:  cld                                 ;make STOSW count up
        mov    ax,[bp].Attrib               ;load AX with attribute parameter
        and    ax,0ff00h                    ;prepare for merging with fill char
        mov    bx,[bp].Filler               ;load BX with fill char
        and    bx,0ffh                      ;prepare for merging with attribute
        or     ax,bx                        ;combine attribute and fill char
        mov    bx,[bp].BufOfs               ;load DI with target buffer offset
        mov    di,bx
        mov    bx,[bp].BufSeg               ;load ES with target buffer segment
        mov    es,bx
        mov    cx,[bp].BufSize              ;load CX with buffer size
        rep    stosw                        ;fill the buffer
Bye:    mov    sp,bp                        ;restore original stack pointer
        pop    bp                           ; and caller's BP
        ret    EndMrk-RetAddr-2             ;return, clearing the parms from the stack
ClearS  endp
```

The first thing you'll notice about this code is that **ClearS** uses a **rep stosw** instruction. That means that we're not going to improve performance by any great amount, no matter how clever we are. Although we can eliminate some cycles, the bulk of the work in **ClearS** is done by that one repeated string instruction, and there's no way to improve on that.

Does that mean that the code is as good as it can be? Hardly. While the speed of **ClearS** is very good, there's another side to the optimization equation: size. The whole of **ClearS** is 52 bytes long as it stands—but, as we'll see, that size is hardly graven in stone.

Where do we begin with **ClearS**? For starters, there's an instruction in there that serves no earthly purpose—**mov sp,bp**. SP is guaranteed to be equal to BP at that point anyway, so why reload it with the same value? Removing that instruction saves us 2 bytes.

Well, that was certainly easy enough! We're not going to find any more totally nonfunctional instructions in **ClearS**, however, so let's get on to some serious optimizing. We'll look first for cases where we know of better instructions for particular tasks than those that were chosen. For example, there's no need to load any register, whether segment or general-purpose, through BX; we can eliminate two instructions by simply loading ES and DI directly:

```
ClearS      proc near
    push  bp                          ;save caller's BP
    mov   bp,sp                       ;point to stack frame
    cmp   word ptr [bp].BufSeg,0      ;skip the fill if a null
    jne   Start                       ; pointer is passed
    cmp   word ptr [bp].BufOfs,0
    je    Bye
Start: cld                            ;make STOSW count up
    mov   ax,[bp].Attrib              ;load AX with attribute parameter
    and   ax,0ff00h                   ;prepare for merging with fill char
    mov   bx,[bp].Filler              ;load BX with fill char
    and   bx,0ffh                     ;prepare for merging with attribute
    or    ax,bx                       ;combine attribute and fill char
    mov   di,[bp].BufOfs              ;load DI with target buffer offset
    mov   es,[bp].BufSeg              ;load ES with target buffer segment
    mov   cx,[bp].BufSize             ;load CX with buffer size
    rep   stosw                       ;fill the buffer
Bye:
    pop   bp                          ;restore caller's BP
    ret   EndMrk-RetAddr-2            ;return, clearing the parms from the stack
ClearS      endp
```

(The **OnStack** structure definition doesn't change in any of our examples, so I'm not going clutter up this chapter by reproducing it for each new version of **ClearS**.)

Okay, loading ES and DI directly saves another 4 bytes. We've squeezed a total of 6 bytes—about 11%—out of **ClearS**. What next?

Well, **les** would serve better than two **mov** instructions for loading ES and DI:

```
ClearS      proc near
    push  bp                          ;save caller's BP
    mov   bp,sp                       ;point to stack frame
    cmp   word ptr [bp].BufSeg,0      ;skip the fill if a null
    jne   Start                       ; pointer is passed
    cmp   word ptr [bp].BufOfs,0
    je    Bye
Start: cld                            ;make STOSW count up
    mov   ax,[bp].Attrib              ;load AX with attribute parameter
    and   ax,0ff00h                   ;prepare for merging with fill char
```

```
        mov   bx,[bp].Filler              ;load BX with fill char
        and   bx,0ffh                     ;prepare for merging with attribute
        or    ax,bx                       ;combine attribute and fill char
        les   di,dword ptr [bp].BufOfs    ;load ES:DI with target buffer segment:offset
        mov   cx,[bp].BufSize             ;load CX with buffer size
        rep   stosw                       ;fill the buffer
Bye:
        pop   bp                          ;restore caller's BP
        ret   EndMrk-RetAddr-2            ;return, clearing the parms from the stack
ClearS  endp
```

That's good for another 3 bytes. We're down to 43 bytes, and counting. We can save 3 more bytes by clearing the low and high bytes of AX and BX, respectively, by using **sub *reg8,reg8*** rather than **and**ing 16-bit values:

```
ClearS  proc near
        push  bp                          ;save caller's BP
        mov   bp,sp                       ;point to stack frame
        cmp   word ptr [bp].BufSeg,0      ;skip the fill if a null
        jne   Start                       ; pointer is passed
        cmp   word ptr [bp].BufOfs,0
        je    Bye
Start:  cld                               ;make STOSW count up
        mov   ax,[bp].Attrib              ;load AX with attribute parameter
        sub   al,al                       ;prepare for merging with fill char
        mov   bx,[bp].Filler              ;load BX with fill char
        sub   bh,bh                       ;prepare for merging with attribute
        or    ax,bx                       ;combine attribute and fill char
        les   di,dword ptr [bp].BufOfs    ;load ES:DI with target buffer segment:offset
        mov   cx,[bp].BufSize             ;load CX with buffer size
        rep   stosw                       ;fill the buffer
Bye:
        pop   bp                          ;restore caller's BP
        ret   EndMrk-RetAddr-2            ;return, clearing the parms from the stack
ClearS  endp
```

Now we're down to 40 bytes—more than 20 percent smaller than the original code. That's pretty much it for simple instruction-substitution optimizations. Now let's look for instruction-rearrangement optimizations.

It seems strange to load a word value into AX and then throw away AL.

Likewise, it seems strange to load a word value into BX and then throw away BH. Nevertheless, those steps are necessary because the two modified word values are **or**ed into a single character-attribute word value that is then used to fill the target buffer.

Let's step back and see what this code really *does*, though. All it does in the end is load 1 byte addressed relative to BP into AH and another byte addressed relative to BP into AL. Heck, we can just do that directly! Presto! We've saved another 6 bytes, and turned two word-sized memory accesses into byte-sized memory accesses as well:

```
ClearS      proc near
    push  bp                          ;save caller's BP
    mov   bp,sp                       ;point to stack frame
    cmp   word ptr [bp].BufSeg,0      ;skip the fill if a null
    jne   Start                       ; pointer is passed
    cmp   word ptr [bp].BufOfs,0
    je    Bye
Start: cld                            ;make STOSW count up
    mov   ah,byte ptr [bp].Attrib[1]  ;load AH with attribute
    mov   al,byte ptr [bp].Filler     ;load AL with fill char
    les   di,dword ptr [bp].BufOfs    ;load ES:DI with target buffer segment:offset
    mov   cx,[bp].BufSize             ;load CX with buffer size
    rep   stosw                       ;fill the buffer
Bye:
    pop   bp                          ;restore caller's BP
    ret   EndMrk-RetAddr-2            ;return, clearing the parms from the stack
ClearS      endp
```

(We could get rid of yet another instruction by having the calling code pack both the attribute and the fill value into the same word, but that's not part of the specification for this particular routine.)

Another nifty instruction-rearrangement trick saves 6 more bytes. **ClearS** checks to see whether the far pointer is null (0) at the start of the routine, then loads and uses that same far pointer later on. Let's get that pointer into memory and keep it there; that way we can check to see whether it's null with a single comparison and can use it later without having to reload it from memory:

```
ClearS      proc near
    push  bp                          ;save caller's BP
    mov   bp,sp                       ;point to stack frame
```

```
        les    di,dword ptr [bp].BufOfs    ;load ES:DI with target buffer segment:offset
        mov    ax,es                       ;put segment where we can test it
        or     ax,di                       ;is it a null pointer?
        je     Bye                         ;yes, so we're done
Start:  cld                                ;make STOSW count up
        mov    ah,byte ptr [bp].Attrib[1]  ;load AH with attribute
        mov    al,byte ptr [bp].Filler     ;load AL with fill char
        mov    cx,[bp].BufSize             ;load CX with buffer size
        rep    stosw                       ;fill the buffer
Bye:
        pop    bp                          ;restore caller's BP
        ret    EndMrk-RetAddr-2            ;return, clearing the parms from the stack
ClearS  endp
```

Well. Now we're down to 28 bytes, having reduced the size of this subroutine by nearly 50 percent. Only 13 instructions remain. Realistically, how much smaller can we make this code?

About one third smaller yet, as it turns out—but in order to do that, we must stretch our minds and use the 8088's instructions in unusual ways. Let me ask you this: what do most of the instructions in the current version of **ClearS** do?

Answer: they either load parameters from the stack frame or set up the registers so that the parameters can be accessed. Mind you, there's nothing wrong with the stack frame–oriented instructions used in **ClearS**; those instructions access the stack frame in a highly efficient way, exactly as the designers of the 8088 intended and just as the code generated by a high level language would. That means that we aren't going to be able to improve the code if we don't bend the rules a bit.

Let's think: the parameters are sitting on the stack, and most of our instruction bytes are being used to read bytes off the stack with BP-based addressing. We need a more efficient way to address the stack . . . *the stack* . . . THE STACK!

Ye gods! That's easy—we can use the *stack pointer* to address the stack. While it's true that the stack pointer can't be used for *mod-reg-rm* addressing, as BP can, it *can* be used to pop data off the stack—and **pop** is a 1-byte instruction. Instructions don't get any shorter than that.

There is one detail to be taken care of before we can put our plan into action: the return address—the address of the calling code—is on top of the stack, so the parameters we want can't be reached with **pop**. That's easily solved, however—we'll just pop the return address into an unused register, then branch through that register when we're done, as we learned to do in Chapter 14. As we pop the parameters, we'll also be removing them from the stack, thereby neatly avoiding the need to discard them when it's time to return.

With that problem dealt with, here's the Zenned version of **ClearS**:

```
ClearS      proc near
      pop   dx          ;get the return address
      pop   ax          ;put fill char into AL
      pop   bx          ;get the attribute
      mov   ah,bh        ;put attribute into AH
      pop   cx          ;get the buffer size
      pop   di          ;get the offset of the buffer origin
      pop   es          ;get the segment of the buffer origin
      mov   bx,es        ;put the segment where we can test it
      or    bx,di        ;null pointer?
      je    Bye          ;yes, so we're done
      cld                ;make STOSW count up
      rep   stosw        ;do the string store
Bye:
      jmp   dx           ;return to the calling code
ClearS      endp
```

At long last, we're down to the bare metal. This version of **ClearS** is 19 bytes long. That's just 37 percent of the length of the original version, *without any change whatsoever in the functionality* **ClearS** *makes available to the calling code.* The code is bound to run a bit faster too, given that there are far fewer instruction bytes and fewer memory accesses.

All in all, the Zenned version of **ClearS** is a vast improvement over the original. Probably not the best possible implementation—*never say never!*—but an awfully good one.

16.3 ◆ Knowledge and Beyond

There is a point to all this Zenning above and beyond showing off some neat tricks we've learned (and a trick or two we'll learn more about in Volume II). The real point is to illustrate the breadth of knowledge you now possess and the tremendous power that knowledge has when guided by the flexible mind.

Consider the optimizations we made above to **ClearS**. Our initial optimizations resulted purely from knowing particular facts about the 8088, and nothing more. We knew, for example, that segment registers do not have to be loaded from memory by way of general-purpose registers but can instead be loaded directly, so we made that change.

As optimizations became harder to come by, however, we shifted from applying pure knowledge to coming up with creative solutions that involved understanding and reworking the code as a whole. We started out by compacting individual instructions and bits of code, but in the end we came up with a solution that applied our knowledge of the PC to implementing the functionality of the entire subroutine as efficiently as possible.

And that, simply put, is the flexible mind.

Think back. Did you have any trouble following the optimizations to **ClearS**? I very much doubt it; in fact, I would guess that you were ahead of me much of the way. So, you see, you already have a good feel for the flexible mind.

There will be much more of the flexible mind in Volume II of *Zen of Assembly Language,* but it won't be an abrupt change from what we've been doing; rather, it will be a gradual raising of our focus from learning the nuts and bolts of the PC to building applications with those nuts and bolts. We've trekked through knowledge and beyond; now it's time to seek out ways to bring the magic of the Zen of assembly language to the real world of applications.

I hope you'll join me for the journey.

Appendix A

◆◆◆

8086/8088 Instruction Set Reference

Adapted from "Assembly Language from Square One," by Jeff Duntemann (Scott, Foresman and Company, 1989), by permission of the author.

What follows is a summary of the 8088's instruction set. Valid instruction forms, execution times, sizes, and examples are given for each instruction. A short summary of each instruction is provided as well. This is not a complete reference on the 8088's instruction set; rather, it is a quick reference summary that is particularly useful for calculating execution unit (EU) execution time and code size. This reference is also handy in that it lists all forms of each instruction, including the special, shorter forms that many instructions have.

References that provide more comprehensive information about the 8088's instruction set are listed below.

Notes on the Instruction Set Reference

Instruction Operands
When an instruction takes two operands, the destination operand is the one on the *left,* and the source operand is the operand on the *right.* In general, when a result is produced by an instruction, the result is stored in the destination operand. For example, in the instruction **add bx,si,** the BX register (the destination operand) is added to the SI register (the source operand), and the sum is then placed back in the BX register, overwriting whatever was in BX before the addition.

Flag Results
Each instruction contains a flag summary that looks like this (the asterisks will vary from instruction to instruction):

```
O D I T S Z A P C        OF:  Overflow flag   TF:  Trap flag   AF:  Aux carry
F F F F F F F F F         DF:  Direction flag  SF:  Sign flag   PF:  Parity flag
*       * * * *           IF:   Interrupt flag  ZF:  Zero flag   CF:  Carry flag
```

The nine flags are all represented here. An asterisk indicates that the instruction on that page affects that flag. If a flag is affected at all (that is, if it has an asterisk beneath it) it will generally be affected according to these rules:

OF: Set if the result is too large to fit in the destination operand.

DF: Set by the **std** instruction; cleared by **cld.**

IF: Set by the **sti** and **int** instructions; cleared by **cli.**

TF: For debuggers; not used in normal programming and may be ignored.

SF: Set when the sign of the result is negative.

ZF: Set if the result of an operation is zero. If the result is nonzero, ZF is cleared.

AF: *Auxiliary carry* used for 4-bit BCD math. Set when an operation causes a carry out of a 4-bit BCD quantity.

PF: Set if the number of 1 bits in the low byte of the result is even; cleared if the number of 1 bits in the low byte of the result is odd. Used in data communications applications but little else.

CF: Set if the result of an add or shift operation "carries out" a bit beyond the destination operand; otherwise cleared. May be manually set by **stc** and manually cleared by **clc** when CF must be in a known state before an operation begins.

In addition, all flags may be either set or cleared by **popf** and **iret,** and CF, PF, AF, ZF, and SF may be either set or cleared by **sahf.**

Some instructions force certain flags to become undefined. When this is the case for a given instruction, it will be so stated under *Notes. Undefined* means *don't count on its being in any particular state.*

Accounting for the Time Consumed by Memory Accesses

Each byte-sized access to memory takes 4 cycles. That time is normally built into execution times; however, many instructions may work with either byte- or word-sized memory operands. In such cases, *each* additional byte-sized access to memory incurred by the use of word-sized operands adds 4 cycles to the instruction's official execution time. For example, **add ax,[si]** takes 4 cycles longer to execute than **add al,[si].**

Some instructions access memory more than once. In such cases, 4 cycles are required for *each* extra access. So, for example, **add [si],ax,** takes not 4 but 8 cycles longer than **add [si],al,** because the word-sized memory operand pointed to by SI must be both read from and written to. The 8- and 16-bit forms of various instructions are shown separately in this appendix, with the cycle times adjusted appropriately in the case of 16-bit instructions, so you need not add any additional execution time for word-sized memory operands.

These Are Only Execution Unit Execution Times

The execution times given below describe how many cycles each instruction takes to execute *once it has reached the EU.* This does not account for the time required to *reach* the EU—that is, the time required to fetch the instruction byte. Instruction fetch time for a given instruction can vary from no time at all to more than 4 cycles per byte, depending on how quickly the EU executes the preceding instructions, how often those instructions access memory, and how effectively the bus interface unit (BIU) can prefetch that instruction's bytes into the prefetch queue.

Overall execution time is a complex topic, to which Chapters 3, 4, and 5 are largely dedicated. Refer to those chapters for a detailed discussion. For the purposes of this appendix, simply understand that the execution times given here are EU execution times only, and so are only part of the overall execution picture.

Effective Address Calculations

As described in Chapter 7, instructions that use *mod-reg-rm* memory operands require extra cycles, known as effective address calculation time, in order to calculate the address of the memory location being addressed. Effective address calculation time varies with the *mod-reg-rm* memory-addressing mode selected but does not depend on the instruction selected. In this appendix, effective address calculation time will be denoted as +EA; this will mean that the instruction takes the specified number of cycles *plus* the number of cycles required for effective address calculation by the selected addressing mode, as follows:

Memory-addressing mode	*Additional cycles required for EA calculation*
Base	
[bp]	5 cycles
[bx]	5 cycles
Index	
[si]	5 cycles
[di]	5 cycles
Direct	
[MemVar]	6 cycles

Memory-addressing mode	Additional cycles required for EA calculation
Base+index	
[bp+di]	7 cycles
[bx+si]	7 cycles
Base+index	
[bx+di]	8 cycles
[bp+si]	8 cycles
Base+displacement	
[bx+*disp*]	9 cycles
[bp+*disp*]	9 cycles
Index+displacement	
[si+*disp*]	9 cycles
[di+*disp*]	9 cycles
Base+index+displacement	
[bp+di+*disp*]	11 cycles
[bx+si+*disp*]	11 cycles
Base+index+displacement	
[bx+di+*disp*]	12 cycles
[bp+si+*disp*]	12 cycles

For example, **mov bl,[si]** takes 13 cycles: 8 cycles for the execution of the basic instruction and 5 cycles for effective address calculation.

Two additional cycles are required if a segment override prefix, as in **mov al,es:[di],** is used.

If you want to know whether a given form of any instruction uses *mod-reg-rm* memory addressing, the rule is: if +EA appears in the cycles field for that instruction form, *mod-reg-rm* memory addressing is used; if +EA does not appear, *mod-reg-rm* memory addressing is not used. There is no way to tell whether or not *mod-reg-rm* register addressing is used; the references listed below provide that information if you need it.

Note that segment override prefixes can be used on all *mod-reg-rm* memory accesses. Note also that all *mod-reg-rm* memory accesses default to accessing the segment pointed to by DS, except when BP is used to point to memory, in which case *mod-reg-rm* memory accesses default to accessing the segment pointed to by SS. Segment defaults used by non-*mod-reg-rm* instructions are noted on a case-by-case basis in this appendix, as are the cases in which segment override prefixes can and cannot be used.

Instruction Forms Shown

This appendix shows the various forms of each instruction. This does *not* mean that all forms accepted by the assembler are shown. Rather, forms that assemble to different opcodes, with different size or performance characteristics, are shown.

For example, **xlat, xlat [*mem8*],** and **xlatb** are all forms of **xlat** that the assembler accepts. However, since all three forms assemble to exactly the same instruction byte, I will only show one of the forms, **xlat.** On the other hand, **or [WordVar],1000h** and **or [ByteVar],10h,** which appear to be two instances of the same instruction, actually assemble to two different instruction opcodes, with different sizes and performance characteristics, so I will show those forms of **or** separately, as **or [*mem16*],*immed16*** and **or [*mem8*],*immed8*,** respectively.

Note that some word-sized immediate operands to some instructions can be stored as bytes and sign extended to a word at execution time. This can be done with immediate operands in the range of −128 to +127 (0FF80h to 07Fh). This is a distinct instruction form and is shown separately. To continue the example above, **or [WordVar],10h** would be another form of **or,** denoted as **or [*mem16*],*sext-immed*.**

Finally, I haven't shown general forms of instructions that are always replaced by special shorter forms. For example, there's a *mod-reg-rm* form of **mov *reg16,immed16*** that's 4 bytes long. There's also a special form of the same instruction that's only 3 bytes long. The special form is superior, so MASM always assembles that form; there's no good reason to want the other form. The only way to get the long form is to hand assemble the desired instruction and then use **db** to create the instruction. Since it's almost certain that you'll never want to use long forms of instructions that have special short forms, to avoid confusion I've omitted the long forms. The references listed below can be used to look up the long forms if you so desire.

Cycle Times

There is no definitive source for the execution times of 8088 instructions that I am aware of. Intel's documentation has a number of mistakes, and so do all other sources I know of. I have done my best to provide correct cycle times in this appendix. I have cross-referenced the cycle times from three sources: Intel's *iAPX 86,88 User's Manual* (Santa Clara, CA, 1981, available directly from Intel or in technical bookstores), the *Microsoft Macro Assembler 5.0 Reference* that comes with MASM 5.0, and *The 8088 Book* (by Rector and Alexy, Osborne/McGraw-Hill, Berkeley, CA, 1980). I have corrected all documented cycle times that I know to be wrong, and I have checked dubious times to the extent possible with the Zen timer.

Nonetheless, there is no certainty that all times listed here are correct; I have no magic insight into the innards of the 8088, and the Zen timer has its limitations in determining EU execution times. In any case, rarely is any reference totally free of errors. That's merely one more reason to follow the practice recommended throughout *Zen of Assembly Language:* time your code. Even if all the cycle times in this chapter are correct, cycle times are only one part of overall execution time (instruction fetching, wait states, and the like also influence overall execution time)—so you *must* time your code if you want to know how fast it really is.

By the way, 8086/80186/80286/80386/8087/80287/80387 cycles times are not given in this appendix. The *Microsoft Macro Assembler 5.0 Reference* is an excellent cycle time reference for those processors.

Instruction Sizes

Instruction sizes in bytes are given in this appendix. However, the size of a given form of a given instruction that uses *mod-reg-rm* memory addressing may vary, depending on whether 0, 1, or 2 displacement bytes are present. In such cases, instruction sizes are given as a maximum/minimum range; for example, **adc [*mem16*],*immed16*** may be anywhere from 4 to 6 bytes in size, depending on the displacement used. Both the *Microsoft Macro Assembler 5.0 Reference* and *The 8086 Book* are good references on exact instruction formats and sizes.

AAA   ASCII Adjust after Addition

Flags Affected

O D I T S Z A P C		
F F F F F F F F F		
* * * * * *		

OF: Overflow flag   TF: Trap flag   AF: Aux carry
DF: Direction flag   SF: Sign flag   PF: Parity flag
IF: Interrupt flag   ZF: Zero flag   CF: Carry flag

Instruction Forms

	Cycles	Bytes	
aaa	4	1	aaa

Notes

Given the binary result of the addition of two decimal digits (that is, two values bits 3 to 0 of which are in the range 0 to 9; the values of bits 7 to 4 are ignored, facilitating addition of ASCII digits but allowing addition of unpacked BCD values as well) in AL, with the flags still set from the addition, **aaa** corrects that binary result to one decimal digit (unpacked BCD) in AL and increments AH if the result of the previous addition was greater than 9.

OF, SF, ZF, and PF are left undefined by **aaa.** AF and CF are set to 1 if the result of the previous addition was greater than 9.

reg8 = AL AH BL BH CL CH DL DH	*reg16* = AX BX CX DX BP SP SI DI
[*mem8*] = 8-bit memory data	[*mem16*] = 16-bit memory data
immed8 = 8-bit immediate data	*immed16* = 16-bit immediate data
sext-immed = 8-bit sign-extendable value	*segreg* = CS DS SS ES
disp8 = 8-bit branch displacement	[*mem32*] = 32-bit memory data
disp16 = 16-bit branch displacement	[*mem*] = memory data of any size
segment:offset = 32-bit segment:offset address	

AAD   ASCII Adjust before Division

Flags Affected

O D I T S Z A P C			
F F F F F F F F F	OF: Overflow flag	TF: Trap flag	AF: Aux carry
* * * * * *	DF: Direction flag	SF: Sign flag	PF: Parity flag
	IF: Interrupt flag	ZF: Zero flag	CF: Carry flag

Instruction Forms

	Cycles	*Bytes*	
aad	60	2	aad

Notes

The aad instruction converts a two-digit unpacked BCD number stored in AX (with the most significant digit in AH) into a binary number in AX by multiplying AH by 10 and adding it to AL, then zeroing AH. The name derives from the use of this instruction to convert a two-digit unpacked BCD value to a binary value in preparation for using that number as a dividend.

OF, AF, and CF are left undefined by **aad.** AH is always set to 0; SF is set on the basis of bit 7 of AL.

reg8 = AL AH BL BH CL CH DL DH
[*mem8*] = 8-bit memory data
immed8 = 8-bit immediate data
sext-immed = 8-bit sign-extendable value
disp8 = 8-bit branch displacement
disp16 = 16-bit branch displacement
segment:offset = 32-bit segment:offset address

reg16 = AX BX CX DX BP SP SI DI
[*mem16*] = 16-bit memory data
immed16 = 16-bit immediate data
segreg = CS DS SS ES
[*mem32*] = 32-bit memory data
[*mem*] = memory data of any size

AAM   ASCII Adjust after Multiplication

Flags Affected

O D I T S Z A P C			
F F F F F F F F F	OF: Overflow flag	TF: Trap flag	AF: Aux carry
* * * * * *	DF: Direction flag	SF: Sign flag	PF: Parity flag
	IF: Interrupt flag	ZF: Zero flag	CF: Carry flag

Instruction Forms

	Cycles	*Bytes*	
aam	83	2	aam

Notes

The **aam** instruction converts a binary value in the range 0 to 99 stored in AL into a two-digit unpacked BCD number in AX, with the most significant digit in AH, by dividing AL by 10 and storing the quotient in AH and the remainder in AL. The name derives from the use of this instruction to convert the binary result of the multiplication of two unpacked BCD values (two values in the range 0 to 9) to an unpacked BCD result.

OF, AF, and CF are left undefined by **aam.** PF and ZF are set according to the contents of AL, not AX. SF is also set according to the contents of AL; practically speaking, however, SF is always set to 0, since the sign bit of AL is always 0 after **aam.**

reg8 = AL AH BL BH CL CH DL DH	*reg16* = AX BX CX DX BP SP SI DI
[*mem8*] = 8-bit memory data	[*mem16*] = 16-bit memory data
immed8 = 8-bit immediate data	*immed16* = 16-bit immediate data
sext-immed = 8-bit sign-extendable value	*segreg* = CS DS SS ES
disp8 = 8-bit branch displacement	[*mem32*] = 32-bit memory data
disp16 = 16-bit branch displacement	[*mem*] = memory data of any size
segment:offset = 32-bit segment:offset address	

AAS   ASCII Adjust after Subtraction

Flags Affected

O D I T S Z A P C			
F F F F F F F F F	OF: Overflow flag	TF: Trap flag	AF: Aux carry
* * * * * *	DF: Direction flag	SF: Sign flag	PF: Parity flag
	IF: Interrupt flag	ZF: Zero flag	CF: Carry flag

Instruction Forms

	Cycles	*Bytes*	
aas	4	1	aas

Notes

Given the binary result of the subtraction of two decimal digits (that is, two values bits 3 to 0 of which are in the range 0 to 9; the values of bits 7 to 4 are ignored, facilitating subtraction of ASCII digits but allowing addition of unpacked BCD values as well) in AL, with the flags still set from the subtraction, **aas** corrects that binary result to a decimal digit (unpacked BCD) in AL. Note that if the result of the subtraction was less than 0 (borrow occurred), AH is decremented by **aas,** and AF and CF are set to 1.

OF, SF, ZF, and PF are left undefined by **aas.**

reg8 = AL AH BL BH CL CH DL DH
[*mem8*] = 8-bit memory data
immed8 = 8-bit immediate data
sext-immed = 8-bit sign-extendable value
disp8 = 8-bit branch displacement
disp16 = 16-bit branch displacement
segment:offset = 32-bit segment:offset address

reg16 = AX BX CX DX BP SP SI DI
[*mem16*] = 16-bit memory data
immed16 = 16-bit immediate data
segreg = CS DS SS ES
[*mem32*] = 32-bit memory data
[*mem*] = memory data of any size

ADC   Arithmetic Add with Carry

Flags Affected

O D I T S Z A P C		
F F F F F F F F F	OF: Overflow flag	TF: Trap flag	AF: Aux carry
* * * * * *	DF: Direction flag	SF: Sign flag	PF: Parity flag
	IF: Interrupt flag	ZF: Zero flag	CF: Carry flag

Instruction Forms

	Cycles	*Bytes*	
adc *reg8,reg8*	3	2	adc al,bl
adc [*mem8*],*reg8*	16+EA	2 to 4	adc [bx],ch
adc *reg8,*[*mem8*]	9+EA	2 to 4	adc dl,[bx+si]
adc *reg16,reg16*	3	2	adc bx,di
adc [*mem16*],*reg16*	24+EA	2 to 4	adc [WordVar+2],cx
adc *reg16,*[*mem16*]	13+EA	2 to 4	adc si,[di]
adc *reg8,immed8*	4	3	adc ah,1
adc [*mem8*],*immed8*	17+EA	3 to 5	adc [ByteVar],10h
adc *reg16,sext-immed*	4	3	adc bx,7fh
adc *reg16,immed16*	4	4	adc dx,1000h
adc [*mem16*], *sext-immed*	25+EA	3 to 5	adc [WordVar],0ffffh
adc [*mem16*], *immed16*	25+EA	4 to 6	adc [WordVar],000ffh
adc al,*immed8*	4	2	adc al,40h
adc ax,*immed16*	4	3	adc ax,8000h

Notes

The **adc** instruction adds the source operand and CF to the destination operand; after the operation, the result replaces the destination operand. The add is an arithmetic add, and the carry allows multiple-precision additions across several registers or memory locations. (To add without taking CF into account, use the **add** instruction.) All affected flags are set according to the operation. Most importantly, if the result does not fit into the destination operand CF is set to 1.

reg8 = AL AH BL BH CL CH DL DH	*reg16* = AX BX CX DX BP SP SI DI
[*mem8*] = 8-bit memory data	[*mem16*] = 16-bit memory data
immed8 = 8-bit immediate data	*immed16* = 16-bit immediate data
sext-immed = 8-bit sign-extendable value	*segreg* = CS DS SS ES
disp8 = 8-bit branch displacement	[*mem32*] = 32-bit memory data
disp16 = 16-bit branch displacement	[*mem*] = memory data of any size
segment:offset = 32-bit segment:offset address	

ADD   Arithmetic Add (Ignore Carry)

Flags Affected

O D I T S Z A P C	OF: Overflow flag	TF: Trap flag	AF: Aux carry
F F F F F F F F F	DF: Direction flag	SF: Sign flag	PF: Parity flag
* * * * * *	IF: Interrupt flag	ZF: Zero flag	CF: Carry flag

Instruction Forms

	Cycles	*Bytes*	
add *reg8,reg8*	3	2	add ah,al
add [*mem8*],*reg8*	16+EA	2 to 4	add [bx+1],dh
add *reg8,*[*mem8*]	9+EA	2 to 4	add ch,[bx]
add *reg16,reg16*	3	2	add dx,ax
add [*mem16*],*reg16*	24+EA	2 to 4	add [bp+5],ax
add *reg16,*[*mem16*]	13+EA	2 to 4	add ax,[Base+di]
add *reg8,immed8*	4	3	add dl,16
add [*mem8*],*immed8*	17+EA	3 to 5	add byte ptr [si+6], 0c3h
add *reg16,sext-immed*	4	3	add si,0ff80h
add *reg16,immed16*	4	4	add si,8000h
add [*mem16*], *sext-immed*	25+EA	3 to 5	add [WordVar],3
add [*mem16*], *immed16*	25+EA	4 to 6	add [WordVar],300h
add al,*immed8*	4	2	add al,1
add ax,*immed16*	4	3	add ax,2

Notes

The **add** instruction adds the source operand to the destination operand; after the operation the result replaces the destination operand. The add is an arithmetic add, and does *not* take CF into account. (To add using CF, use the **adc**—add with carry—instruction.) All affected flags are set according to the operation. Most importantly, if the result does not fit into the destination operand, CF is set to 1.

reg8 = AL AH BL BH CL CH DL DH	*reg16* = AX BX CX DX BP SP SI DI
[*mem8*] = 8-bit memory data	[*mem16*] = 16-bit memory data
immed8 = 8-bit immediate data	*immed16* = 16-bit immediate data
sext-immed = 8-bit sign-extendable value	*segreg* = CS DS SS ES
disp8 = 8-bit branch displacement	[*mem32*] = 32-bit memory data
disp16 = 16-bit branch displacement	[*mem*] = memory data of any size
segment:offset = 32-bit segment:offset address	

AND   Logical And

Flags Affected

O D I T S Z A P C	OF: Overflow flag	TF: Trap flag	AF: Aux carry
F F F F F F F F F	DF: Direction flag	SF: Sign flag	PF: Parity flag
* * * * * *	IF: Interrupt flag	ZF: Zero flag	CF: Carry flag

Instruction Forms

	Cycles	*Bytes*	
and *reg8,reg8*	3	2	and dl,dl
and [*mem8*],*reg8*	16+EA	2 to 4	and [si−1],dl
and *reg8*,[*mem8*]	9+EA	2 to 4	and ah,[si+bx]
and *reg16,reg16*	3	2	and si,bp
and [*mem16*],*reg16*	24+EA	2 to 4	and [WordVar],dx
and *reg16*,[*mem16*]	13+EA	2 to 4	and si,[WordVar−2]
and *reg8,immed8*	4	3	and ah,07fh
and [*mem8*],*immed8*	17+EA	3 to 5	and byte ptr [di],5
and *reg16,sext-immed*	4	3	and dx,1
and *reg16,immed16*	4	4	and cx,0aaaah
add [*mem16*], *sext-immed*	25+EA	3 to 5	and word ptr [bx], 10h
add [*mem16*], *immed16*	25+EA	4 to 6	and word ptr [di], 05555h
and al,*immed8*	4	2	and al,0f0h
and ax,*immed16*	4	3	and ax,0ff00h

Notes

The **and** instruction performs the logical operation "and" on its two operands. Once the operation is complete, the result replaces the destination operand. This operation is performed on a bit-by-bit basis, such that bit 0 of the source is **and**ed with bit 0 of the destination, bit 1 of the source is **and**ed with bit 1 of the destination, and so on. The **and** operation yields a 1 if *both* of the operands are 1 and a 0 if *either* operand is 0. Note that **and** makes AF undefined. CF and OF are cleared to 0, and the other affected flags are set according to the operation's results.

reg8 = AL AH BL BH CL CH DL DH	*reg16* = AX BX CX DX BP SP SI DI
[*mem8*] = 8-bit memory data	[*mem16*] = 16-bit memory data
immed8 = 8-bit immediate data	*immed16* = 16-bit immediate data
sext-immed = 8-bit sign-extendable value	*segreg* = CS DS SS ES
disp8 = 8-bit branch displacement	[*mem32*] = 32-bit memory data
disp16 = 16-bit branch displacement	[*mem*] = memory data of any size
segment:offset = 32-bit segment:offset address	

CALL   Call Subroutine

Flags Affected

O D I T S Z A P C		
F F F F F F F F F	OF: Overflow flag	TF: Trap flag	AF: Aux carry
<none>	DF: Direction flag	SF: Sign flag	PF: Parity flag
	IF: Interrupt flag	ZF: Zero flag	CF: Carry flag

Instruction Forms

	Cycles	*Bytes*	
call *disp16*	23	3	call near ptr NearTarget
call *reg16*	20	2	call bx
call [*mem16*]	29+EA	2 to 4	call word ptr [Vecs+si]
call *segment:offset*	36	5	call far ptr FarTarget
call [*mem32*]	53+EA	2 to 4	call dword ptr [FarVec]

Notes

The **call** instruction branches to the destination specified by the single operand; that is, **call** sets IP (and CS, for far jumps) so that the next instruction executed is at the specified location. If the call is a far call, **call** then pushes CS onto the stack; then, whether the call is far or near, **call** pushes the offset of the start of the next instruction onto the stack. The pushed address can later be used by **ret** to return from the called subroutine to the instruction after **call.**

In addition to branching directly to either near or far labels, **call** can branch anywhere in the segment pointed to by CS by setting IP equal to an offset stored in any general-purpose register. It can also branch to an address (either near or far) stored in memory and accessed through any *mod-reg-rm*–addressing mode; this is ideal for calling addresses stored in jump tables.

reg8 = AL AH BL BH CL CH DL DH	*reg16* = AX BX CX DX BP SP SI DI
[*mem8*] = 8-bit memory data	[*mem16*] = 16-bit memory data
immed8 = 8-bit immediate data	*immed16* = 16-bit immediate data
sext-immed = 8-bit sign-extendable value	*segreg* = CS DS SS ES
disp8 = 8-bit branch displacement	[*mem32*] = 32-bit memory data
disp16 = 16-bit branch displacement	[*mem*] = memory data of any size
segment:offset = 32-bit segment:offset address	

CBW   Convert Signed Byte in AL to Signed Word in AX

Flags Affected

O D I T S Z A P C
F F F F F F F F F
<none>

OF: Overflow flag   TF: Trap flag   AF: Aux carry

DF: Direction flag   SF: Sign flag   PF: Parity flag

IF: Interrupt flag   ZF: Zero flag   CF: Carry flag

Instruction Forms

	Cycles	*Bytes*	
cbw	2	1	cbw

Notes

The **cbw** instruction sign extends a signed byte in AL to a signed word in AX. In other words, bit 7 of AL is copied to all bits of AH.

reg8 = AL AH BL BH CL CH DL DH
[*mem8*] = 8-bit memory data
immed8 = 8-bit immediate data
sext-immed = 8-bit sign-extendable value
disp8 = 8-bit branch displacement
disp16 = 16-bit branch displacement
segment:offset = 32-bit segment:offset address

reg16 = AX BX CX DX BP SP SI DI
[*mem16*] = 16-bit memory data
immed16 = 16-bit immediate data
segreg = CS DS SS ES
[*mem32*] = 32-bit memory data
[*mem*] = memory data of any size

CLC   Clear Carry Flag

Flags Affected

O D I T S Z A P C	OF: Overflow flag	TF: Trap flag	AF: Aux carry
F F F F F F F F F	DF: Direction flag	SF: Sign flag	PF: Parity flag
*	IF: Interrupt flag	ZF: Zero flag	CF: Carry flag

Instruction Forms

	Cycles	Bytes	
clc	2	1	clc

Notes

The **clc** instruction clears CF to 0. Use **clc** in situations where CF *must* be in a known cleared state before work begins, as when you are rotating a series of words or bytes using **rcl** or **rcr,** or before performing multi-word addition in a loop with **adc.** It can also be useful for returning a status in CF from a subroutine, or for presetting CF before a conditional jump that tests CF, such as **jc.**

reg8 = AL AH BL BH CL CH DL DH	*reg16* = AX BX CX DX BP SP SI DI
[*mem8*] = 8-bit memory data	[*mem16*] = 16-bit memory data
immed8 = 8-bit immediate data	*immed16* = 16-bit immediate data
sext-immed = 8-bit sign-extendable value	*segreg* = CS DS SS ES
disp8 = 8-bit branch displacement	[*mem32*] = 32-bit memory data
disp16 = 16-bit branch displacement	[*mem*] = memory data of any size
segment:offset = 32-bit segment:offset address	

CLD   Clear Direction Flag

Flags Affected

O D I T S Z A P C		
F F F F F F F F F		
*		

OF: Overflow flag   TF: Trap flag   AF: Aux carry
DF: Direction flag   SF: Sign flag   PF: Parity flag
IF: Interrupt flag   ZF: Zero flag   CF: Carry flag

Instruction Forms

	Cycles	Bytes	
cld	2	1	cld

Notes

The **cld** instruction clears DF to 0. This affects the pointer-register adjustments performed after each memory access by the string instructions **lods, stos, scas, movs,** and **cmps.** When DF=0, pointer registers (SI and/or DI) are incremented by 1 or 2; when DF=1, pointer registers are decremented by 1 or 2. DF is set to 1 by **std.**

reg8 = AL AH BL BH CL CH DL DH
[*mem8*] = 8-bit memory data
immed8 = 8-bit immediate data
sext-immed = 8-bit sign-extendable value
disp8 = 8-bit branch displacement
disp16 = 16-bit branch displacement
segment:offset = 32-bit segment:offset address

reg16 = AX BX CX DX BP SP SI DI
[*mem16*] = 16-bit memory data
immed16 = 16-bit immediate data
segreg = CS DS SS ES
[*mem32*] = 32-bit memory data
[*mem*] = memory data of any size

CLI   Clear Interrupt Flag

Flags Affected

O D I T S Z A P C		
F F F F F F F F F	OF: Overflow flag	TF: Trap flag	AF: Aux carry
*	DF: Direction flag	SF: Sign flag	PF: Parity flag
	IF: Interrupt flag	ZF: Zero flag	CF: Carry flag

Instruction Forms

	Cycles	**Bytes**	
cli	2	1	cli

Notes

This instruction clears IF to 0, disabling maskable hardware interrupts (IRQ0 through IRQ7) until IF is set to 1. (Software interrupts via **int** are not affected by the state of IF.) The **sti** instruction sets IF to 1, enabling maskable hardware interrupts.

reg8 = AL AH BL BH CL CH DL DH
[*mem8*] = 8-bit memory data
immed8 = 8-bit immediate data
sext-immed = 8-bit sign-extendable value
disp8 = 8-bit branch displacement
disp16 = 16-bit branch displacement
segment:offset = 32-bit segment:offset address

reg16 = AX BX CX DX BP SP SI DI
[*mem16*] = 16-bit memory data
immed16 = 16-bit immediate data
segreg = CS DS SS ES
[*mem32*] = 32-bit memory data
[*mem*] = memory data of any size

CMC   Complement Carry Flag

Flags Affected

O D I T S Z A P C	OF: Overflow flag TF: Trap flag AF: Aux carry	
F F F F F F F F F	DF: Direction flag SF: Sign flag PF: Parity flag	
*	IF: Interrupt flag ZF: Zero flag CF: Carry flag	

Instruction Forms

	Cycles	Bytes	
cmc	2	1	cmc

Notes

The **cmc** instruction flips the state of CF. If CF is 0, **cmc** sets it to 1; if CF is 1, **cmc** sets it to 0.

reg8 = AL AH BL BH CL CH DL DH
[*mem8*] = 8-bit memory data
immed8 = 8-bit immediate data
sext-immed = 8-bit sign-extendable value
disp8 = 8-bit branch displacement
disp16 = 16-bit branch displacement
segment:offset = 32-bit segment:offset address

reg16 = AX BX CX DX BP SP SI DI
[*mem16*] = 16-bit memory data
immed16 = 16-bit immediate data
segreg = CS DS SS ES
[*mem32*] = 32-bit memory data
[*mem*] = memory data of any size

CMP   Compare by Subtracting without Saving Result

Flags Affected

O	D	I	T	S	Z	A	P	C
F	F	F	F	F	F	F	F	F
*				*	*	*	*	*

OF: Overflow flag   TF: Trap flag   AF: Aux carry
DF: Direction flag   SF: Sign flag   PF: Parity flag
IF: Interrupt flag   ZF: Zero flag   CF: Carry flag

Instruction Forms

	Cycles	Bytes	
cmp *reg8,reg8*	3	2	cmp ah,al
cmp [*mem8*],*reg8*	9+EA	2 to 4	cmp [si],cl
cmp *reg8*,[*mem8*]	9+EA	2 to 4	cmp ah,[bx]
cmp *reg16,reg16*	3	2	cmp dx,ax
cmp [*mem16*],*reg16*	13+EA	2 to 4	cmp [bx+di+ RecPtr],bx
cmp *reg16*,[*mem16*]	13+EA	2 to 4	cmp bp,[bx+1]
cmp *reg8,immed8*	4	3	cmp ah,9
cmp [*mem8*],*immed8*	10+EA	3 to 5	cmp [ByteVar],39h
cmp *reg16,sext-immed*	4	3	cmp dx,8
cmp *reg16,immed16*	4	4	cmp sp,999h
cmp [*mem16*], *sext-immed*	14+EA	3 to 5	cmp [WordVar],12
cmp [*mem16*], *immed16*	14+EA	4 to 6	cmp [WordVar],92h
cmp al,*immed8*	4	2	cmp al,22
cmp ax,*immed16*	4	3	cmp ax,722

Notes

The **cmp** operation compares two operands and sets the flags to indicate the results of the comparison. *Neither operand is affected.* The operation itself is identical to subtraction of the source from the destination without borrow (the operation of the **sub** instruction) except that the result is only used to set the flags and does not replace the destination. Typically, **cmp** is followed by one of the conditional jump instructions; for example, **jz** to jump if the operands were equal, **jnz** if they were unequal, and so on.

reg8 = AL AH BL BH CL CH DL DH	*reg16* = AX BX CX DX BP SP SI DI
[*mem8*] = 8-bit memory data	[*mem16*] = 16-bit memory data
immed8 = 8-bit immediate data	*immed16* = 16-bit immediate data
sext-immed = 8-bit sign-extendable value	*segreg* = CS DS SS ES
disp8 = 8-bit branch displacement	[*mem32*] = 32-bit memory data
disp16 = 16-bit branch displacement	[*mem*] = memory data of any size
segment:offset = 32-bit segment:offset address	

CMPS   Compare String

Flags Affected

```
O D I  T S Z A P C      OF:  Overflow flag   TF:  Trap flag    AF:  Aux carry
F F F F F F F F F        DF:  Direction flag  SF:  Sign flag    PF:  Parity flag
*       * * * * *        IF:  Interrupt flag  ZF:  Zero flag    CF:  Carry flag
```

Instruction Forms

	Cycles	*Bytes*	
cmpsb	22	1	cmpsb
repz cmpsb	9+(22*CX)	2	repz cmpsb
repnz cmpsb	9+(22*CX)	2	repnz cmpsb
cmpsw	30	1	cmpsw
repz cmpsw	9+(30*CX)	2	repz cmpsw
repnz cmpsw	9+(30*CX)	2	repnz cmpsw

Notes

The **cmps** instruction compares either the byte (**cmpsb**) or word (**cmpsw**) pointed to by DS:SI to the byte or word pointed to by ES:DI, adjusting both SI and DI after the operation, as described below. The use of DS as the destination segment can be overridden, but ES must be the segment of the source and cannot be overridden. SI must always be the destination offset, and DI must always be the source offset. The comparison is performed via a trial subtraction of the location pointed to by ES:DI from the location pointed to by DS:SI; just as with **cmp,** this trial subtraction alters only the flags, not any memory locations.

By placing an instruction repeat count in CX and preceding **cmpsb** or **cmpsw** with the **repz** or **repnz** prefix, it is possible to execute a single **cmps** up to 65,535 (0FFFFh) times, just as if that many **cmps** instructions had been executed, but without the need for any additional instruction fetching. Repeated **cmps** instructions end either when CX counts down to 0 or when the state of ZF specified by **repz/repnz** ceases to be true. ZF should be tested to determine whether a match-nonmatch was found after **repz cmps** or **repnz cmps** ends.

Note that if CX is 0 when repeated **cmps** is started, 0 repetitions of **cmps**—not 65,536 repetitions—are performed. After each **cmps,** SI and DI are adjusted (as described in the next paragraph) by either 1 (for **cmpsb**) or 2 (for **cmpsw**), and, if the **repz** or **repnz** prefix is being used, CX is decremented by 1. Note that the accumulator is not affected by **cmps.**

Adjusting SI and DI means incrementing them if DF is cleared (0) or decrementing them if it is set (1).

reg8 = AL AH BL BH CL CH DL DH	*reg16* = AX BX CX DX BP SP SI DI
[*mem8*] = 8-bit memory data	[*mem16*] = 16-bit memory data
immed8 = 8-bit immediate data	*immed16* = 16-bit immediate data
sext-immed = 8-bit sign-extendable value	*segreg* = CS DS SS ES
disp8 = 8-bit branch displacement	[*mem32*] = 32-bit memory data
disp16 = 16-bit branch displacement	[*mem*] = memory data of any size
segment:offset = 32-bit segment:offset address	

CWD   Convert Signed Word in AX to Signed Doubleword in DX:AX

Flags Affected

O D I T S Z A P C   OF: Overflow flag   TF: Trap flag   AF: Aux carry
F F F F F F F F F   DF: Direction flag   SF: Sign flag   PF: Parity flag
     <none>   IF: Interrupt flag   ZF: Zero flag   CF: Carry flag

Instruction Forms

	Cycles	*Bytes*	
cwd	5	1	cwd

Notes

The **cwd** instruction sign extends a signed word in AX to a signed doubleword in DX:AX. In other words, bit 15 of AX is copied to all bits of DX.

reg8 = AL AH BL BH CL CH DL DH
[*mem8*] = 8-bit memory data
immed8 = 8-bit immediate data
sext-immed = 8-bit sign-extendable value
disp8 = 8-bit branch displacement
disp16 = 16-bit branch displacement
segment:offset = 32-bit segment:offset address

reg16 = AX BX CX DX BP SP SI DI
[*mem16*] = 16-bit memory data
immed16 = 16-bit immediate data
segreg = CS DS SS ES
[*mem32*] = 32-bit memory data
[*mem*] = memory data of any size

DAA   Decimal Adjust after Addition

Flags Affected

```
O D I  T S Z A P C      OF: Overflow flag    TF: Trap flag      AF: Aux carry
F F F  F F F F F F       DF: Direction flag   SF: Sign flag      PF: Parity flag
*      * * * *           IF:  Interrupt flag  ZF: Zero flag      CF: Carry flag
```

Instruction Forms

	Cycles	*Bytes*	
daa	4	1	daa

Notes

Given the binary result of the addition of two packed BCD values in AL, with the flags still set from the addition, **daa** corrects that binary result to two packed BCD digits in AL.

OF is left in an undefined state by **daa.**

reg8 = AL AH BL BH CL CH DL DH
[*mem8*] = 8-bit memory data
immed8 = 8-bit immediate data
sext-immed = 8-bit sign-extendable value
disp8 = 8-bit branch displacement
disp16 = 16-bit branch displacement
segment:offset = 32-bit segment:offset address

reg16 = AX BX CX DX BP SP SI DI
[*mem16*] = 16-bit memory data
immed16 = 16-bit immediate data
segreg = CS DS SS ES
[*mem32*] = 32-bit memory data
[*mem*] = memory data of any size

DAS   Decimal Adjust after Subtraction

Flags Affected

O D I T S Z A P C		
F F F F F F F F F	OF: Overflow flag	TF: Trap flag	AF: Aux carry
* * * * * *	DF: Direction flag	SF: Sign flag	PF: Parity flag
	IF: Interrupt flag	ZF: Zero flag	CF: Carry flag

Instruction Forms

	Cycles	*Bytes*	
das	4	1	das

Notes

Given the binary result of the subtraction of two packed BCD values in AL, with the flags still set from the subtraction, **das** corrects that binary result to two packed BCD digits in AL.

OF is left in an undefined state by **das.**

reg8 = AL AH BL BH CL CH DL DH	*reg16* = AX BX CX DX BP SP SI DI
[*mem8*] = 8-bit memory data	[*mem16*] = 16-bit memory data
immed8 = 8-bit immediate data	*immed16* = 16-bit immediate data
sext-immed = 8-bit sign-extendable value	*segreg* = CS DS SS ES
disp8 = 8-bit branch displacement	[*mem32*] = 32-bit memory data
disp16 = 16-bit branch displacement	[*mem*] = memory data of any size
segment:offset = 32-bit segment:offset address	

DEC   Decrement Operand

Flags Affected

O D I	T S Z A P C		
F F F	F F F F F F		
*	* * * *		

OF: Overflow flag   TF: Trap flag   AF: Aux carry
DF: Direction flag   SF: Sign flag   PF: Parity flag
IF: Interrupt flag   ZF: Zero flag   CF: Carry flag

Instruction Forms

	Cycles	*Bytes*	
dec *reg8*	3	2	dec ah
dec [*mem8*]	15+EA	2 to 4	dec byte ptr [bx]
dec *reg16*	2	1	dec si
dec [*mem16*]	23+EA	2 to 4	dec [WordVar]

Notes

The **dec** instruction decrements (subtracts 1 from) the operand. Decrementing an operand with **dec** is similar to subtracting 1 from the operand with **sub;** however, **dec** is more compact, since no immediate operand is required, and, unlike **sub,** CF is not affected by **dec.** Note the special, shorter 16-bit-register form of **dec.**

reg8 = AL AH BL BH CL CH DL DH
[*mem8*] = 8-bit memory data
immed8 = 8-bit immediate data
sext-immed = 8-bit sign-extendable value
disp8 = 8-bit branch displacement
disp16 = 16-bit branch displacement
segment:offset = 32-bit segment:offset address

reg16 = AX BX CX DX BP SP SI DI
[*mem16*] = 16-bit memory data
immed16 = 16-bit immediate data
segreg = CS DS SS ES
[*mem32*] = 32-bit memory data
[*mem*] = memory data of any size

DIV   Unsigned Divide

Flags Affected

O D I T S Z A P C	
F F F F F F F F F	
* * * * *	

OF: Overflow flag   TF: Trap flag   AF: Aux carry
DF: Direction flag   SF: Sign flag   PF: Parity flag
IF: Interrupt flag   ZF: Zero flag   CF: Carry flag

Instruction Forms

	Cycles	Bytes	
div *reg8*	80 to 90	2	div bh
div [*mem8*]	86+EA to 96+EA	2 to 4	div byte ptr [si+3]
div *reg16*	144 to 162	2	div cx
div [*mem16*]	154+EA to 172+EA	2 to 4	div [WordVar]

Notes

The **div** instruction performs a 16×8 unsigned division of AX by a byte operand, storing the quotient in AL and the remainder in AH, or a 32×16 unsigned division of DX:AX by a word operand, storing the quotient in AX and the remainder in DX. Note that in order to use a byte value in AL as a dividend, you must zero-extend it to a word in AX (**sub ah,ah** can be used for this purpose). Similarly, in order to divide a word value in AX by another word value, you must zero-extend it to a doubleword in DX:AX, generally with **sub dx,dx.** Also note that for 16×8 division, the quotient must be no larger than 8 bits, and for 32×16 division, the quotient must be no larger than 16 bits. If the quotient is too large or if the divisor is 0, a divide-by-0 interrupt, **int 0,** is executed.

OF, SF, ZF, AF, PF, and CF are left in undefined states by **div.**

reg8 = AL AH BL BH CL CH DL DH	*reg16* = AX BX CX DX BP SP SI DI
[*mem8*] = 8-bit memory data	[*mem16*] = 16-bit memory data
immed8 = 8-bit immediate data	*immed16* = 16-bit immediate data
sext-immed = 8-bit sign-extendable value	*segreg* = CS DS SS ES
disp8 = 8-bit branch displacement	[*mem32*] = 32-bit memory data
disp16 = 16-bit branch displacement	[*mem*] = memory data of any size
segment:offset = 32-bit segment:offset address	

HLT   Halt

Flags Affected

O D I T S Z A P C			
F F F F F F F F F	OF: Overflow flag	TF: Trap flag	AF: Aux carry
<none>	DF: Direction flag	SF: Sign flag	PF: Parity flag
	IF: Interrupt flag	ZF: Zero flag	CF: Carry flag

Instruction Forms

	Cycles	*Bytes*	
hlt	2	1	hlt

Notes

The **hlt** instruction stops the 8088 until a hardware interrupt, a nonmaskable interrupt, or a processor reset occurs. This instruction is almost never used in normal PC programs.

reg8 = AL AH BL BH CL CH DL DH
[*mem8*] = 8-bit memory data
immed8 = 8-bit immediate data
sext-immed = 8-bit sign-extendable value
disp8 = 8-bit branch displacement
disp16 = 16-bit branch displacement
segment:offset = 32-bit segment:offset address

reg16 = AX BX CX DX BP SP SI DI
[*mem16*] = 16-bit memory data
immed16 = 16-bit immediate data
segreg = CS DS SS ES
[*mem32*] = 32-bit memory data
[*mem*] = memory data of any size

IDIV   Signed Divide

Flags Affected

```
O D I T S Z A P C      OF: Overflow flag    TF: Trap flag    AF: Aux carry
F F F F F F F F F       DF: Direction flag   SF: Sign flag    PF: Parity flag
*       * * * * *       IF:  Interrupt flag  ZF: Zero flag    CF: Carry flag
```

Instruction Forms

	Cycles	*Bytes*	
idiv *reg8*	101 to 112	2	idiv cl
idiv [*mem8*]	107+EA to 118+EA	2 to 4	idiv [ByteVar]
idiv *reg16*	165 to 184	2	idiv bx
idiv [*mem16*]	175+EA to 194+EA	2 to 4	idiv word ptr [bx+si]

Notes

The **idiv** instruction performs a 16×8 signed division of AX by a byte operand, storing the quotient in AL and the remainder in AH, or a 32×16 signed division of DX:AX by a word operand, storing the quotient in AX and the remainder in DX. Note that in order to use a byte value in AL as a dividend, you must sign-extend it to a word in AX (**cbw** can be used for this purpose). Similarly, in order to divide a word value in AX by another word value, you must sign extend it to a doubleword in DX:AX, generally with **cwd.** Also note that for 16×8 division, the quotient must be no larger than 8 bits (including the sign bit), and for 32×16 division, the quotient must be no larger than 16 bits (including the sign bit). If the quotient is too large, or if the divisor is 0, a divide-by-0 interrupt, **int 0,** is executed.

OF, SF, ZF, AF, PF, and CF are left in undefined states by **idiv.**

reg8 = AL AH BL BH CL CH DL DH
[*mem8*] = 8-bit memory data
immed8 = 8-bit immediate data
sext-immed = 8-bit sign-extendable value
disp8 = 8-bit branch displacement
disp16 = 16-bit branch displacement
segment:offset = 32-bit segment:offset address

reg16 = AX BX CX DX BP SP SI DI
[*mem16*] = 16-bit memory data
immed16 = 16-bit immediate data
segreg = CS DS SS ES
[*mem32*] = 32-bit memory data
[*mem*] = memory data of any size

IMUL   Signed Multiply

Flags Affected

```
ODI TSZAPC
FFF FFFFFF
 *      * * * *
```

OF: Overflow flag   TF: Trap flag   AF: Aux carry
DF: Direction flag   SF: Sign flag   PF: Parity flag
IF: Interrupt flag   ZF: Zero flag   CF: Carry flag

Instruction Forms

	Cycles	*Bytes*	
imul *reg8*	80 to 98	2	imul ch
imul [*mem8*]	86+EA to 104+EA	2 to 4	imul byte ptr [bx]
imul *reg16*	128 to 154	2	imul bp
imul [*mem16*]	138+EA to 164+EA	2 to 4	imul [WordVar+si]

Notes

The instruction **imul** performs an 8 × 8 signed multiplication of AL by a byte operand, storing the result in AX, or a 16 × 16 signed multiplication of AX by a word operand, storing the result in DX:AX. Note that AH is changed by 8 × 8 multiplication, even though it is not an operand; the same is true of DX for 16 × 16 multiplication.

CF and OF are set to 1 if and only if the upper half of the result (AH for 8 × 8 multiplies, DX for 16 × 16 multiplies) is not a sign extension of the lower half and set to 0 otherwise. SF, ZF, AF, and PF are left in undefined states.

reg8 = AL AH BL BH CL CH DL DH
[*mem8*] = 8-bit memory data
immed8 = 8-bit immediate data
sext-immed = 8-bit sign-extendable value
disp8 = 8-bit branch displacement
disp16 = 16-bit branch displacement
segment:offset = 32-bit segment:offset address

reg16 = AX BX CX DX BP SP SI DI
[*mem16*] = 16-bit memory data
immed16 = 16-bit immediate data
segreg = CS DS SS ES
[*mem32*] = 32-bit memory data
[*mem*] = memory data of any size

IN   Input Byte from I/O Port

Flags Affected

O D I T S Z A P C		
F F F F F F F F F		
<none>		

OF: Overflow flag   TF: Trap flag   AF: Aux carry
DF: Direction flag   SF: Sign flag   PF: Parity flag
IF: Interrupt flag   ZF: Zero flag   CF: Carry flag

Instruction Forms

	Cycles	Bytes	
in al,dx	8	1	in al,dx
in al,*immed8*	10	2	in al,1
in ax,dx	12	1	in ax,dx
in ax,*immed8*	14	2	in ax,92h

Notes

The **in** instruction reads data from the specified I/O port into the accumulator. Note that data *must* go to the accumulator and that only DX or a constant may be used to address the I/O port. Note also that only I/O ports in the range 0 to 255 may be addressed with a constant; DX must be used to address I/O ports in the range 256 to 65,535.

reg8 = AL AH BL BH CL CH DL DH
[*mem8*] = 8-bit memory data
immed8 = 8-bit immediate data
sext-immed = 8-bit sign-extendable value
disp8 = 8-bit branch displacement
disp16 = 16-bit branch displacement
segment:offset = 32-bit segment:offset address

reg16 = AX BX CX DX BP SP SI DI
[*mem16*] = 16-bit memory data
immed16 = 16-bit immediate data
segreg = CS DS SS ES
[*mem32*] = 32-bit memory data
[*mem*] = memory data of any size

INC   Increment Operand

Flags Affected

O D I	T S Z A P C
F F F	F F F F F F
*	* ‡ * *

OF: Overflow flag   TF: Trap flag   AF: Aux carry
DF: Direction flag   SF: Sign flag   PF: Parity flag
IF: Interrupt flag   ZF: Zero flag   CF: Carry flag

Instruction Forms

	Cycles	*Bytes*	
inc *reg8*	3	2	inc ah
inc [*mem8*]	15+EA	2 to 4	inc byte ptr [bx]
inc *reg16*	2	1	inc si
inc [*mem16*]	23+EA	2 to 4	inc [WordVar]

Notes

The **inc** instruction increments (adds 1 to) the operand. Incrementing an operand with **inc** is similar to adding 1 to the operand with **add;** however, **inc** is more compact, since no immediate operand is required, and unlike **add,** CF is not affected by **inc.** Note the special, shorter 16-bit-register form of **inc.**

reg8 = AL AH BL BH CL CH DL DH
[*mem8*] = 8-bit memory data
immed8 = 8-bit immediate data
sext-immed = 8-bit sign-extendable value
disp8 = 8-bit branch displacement
disp16 = 16-bit branch displacement
segment:offset = 32-bit segment:offset address

reg16 = AX BX CX DX BP SP SI DI
[*mem16*] = 16-bit memory data
immed16 = 16-bit immediate data
segreg = CS DS SS ES
[*mem32*] = 32-bit memory data
[*mem*] = memory data of any size

INT   Software Interrupt

Flags Affected

O	D	I	T	S	Z	A	P	C			
F	F	F	F	F	F	F	F	F			
			*	*							

OF: Overflow flag   TF: Trap flag   AF: Aux carry
DF: Direction flag   SF: Sign flag   PF: Parity flag
IF: Interrupt flag   ZF: Zero flag   CF: Carry flag

Instruction Forms

	Cycles	*Bytes*	
int *immed8*	71	2	int 10h
int 3	72	1	int 3

Notes

The **int** instruction generates a software interrupt to one of 256 segment:offset vectors stored in the first 1024 bytes of memory. The operand specifies which vector, in the range 0 to 255, is to be used; **int *n*** branches to the address specified by the segment:offset pointer stored at address 0000:*n**4. When an interrupt is performed, the flags register is pushed on the stack, followed by the current CS and then the IP of the instruction after the **int,** so that a later **iret** can restore the pre-interrupt flags register and return to the instruction following the **int** instruction. IF is cleared by **int,** preventing hardware interrupts from being recognized until IF is set again. TF is also cleared.

There's also a special 1-byte form of **int** specifically for executing interrupt 3. Debuggers use interrupt 3 to set breakpoints in code by replacing an instruction byte to be stopped at with the single-byte opcode for **int 3.** Normal programs use the 2-byte form of **int,** which takes an 8-bit immediate operand.

reg8 = AL AH BL BH CL CH DL DH
[*mem8*] = 8-bit memory data
immed8 = 8-bit immediate data
sext-immed = 8-bit sign-extendable value
disp8 = 8-bit branch displacement
disp16 =.16-bit branch displacement
segment:offset = 32-bit segment:offset address

reg16 = AX BX CX DX BP SP SI DI
[*mem16*] = 16-bit memory data
immed16 = 16-bit immediate data
segreg = CS DS SS ES
[*mem32*] = 32-bit memory data
[*mem*] = memory data of any size

INTO   Execute int 4 if Overflow Flag Set

Flags Affected

O D I T S Z A P C	OF: Overflow flag	TF: Trap flag	AF: Aux carry
F F F F F F F F F	DF: Direction flag	SF: Sign flag	PF: Parity flag
* *	IF: Interrupt flag	ZF: Zero flag	CF: Carry flag

Instruction Forms

	Cycles	Bytes	
into	73 (OF=1)/4 (OF=0)	1	into

Notes

The **into** instruction executes an **int 4** if OF is set (equal to 1); otherwise, it does nothing. This is a compact (1 byte) way to check for overflow after arithmetic operations and to branch to a common handler if overflow does occur. IF is cleared by **into.** TF is also cleared.

reg8 = AL AH BL BH CL CH DL DH	*reg16* = AX BX CX DX BP SP SI DI
[*mem8*] = 8-bit memory data	[*mem16*] = 16-bit memory data
immed8 = 8-bit immediate data	*immed16* = 16-bit immediate data
sext-immed = 8-bit sign-extendable value	*segreg* = CS DS SS ES
disp8 = 8-bit branch displacement	[*mem32*] = 32-bit memory data
disp16 = 16-bit branch displacement	[*mem*] = memory data of any size
segment:offset = 32-bit segment:offset address	

IRET   Return from Interrupt

Flags Affected

```
O D I  T S Z A P C        OF: Overflow flag   TF: Trap flag   AF: Aux carry
F F F F F F F F F          DF: Direction flag  SF: Sign flag   PF: Parity flag
* * * * * * * * *          IF:  Interrupt flag  ZF: Zero flag   CF: Carry flag
```

Instruction Forms

	Cycles	*Bytes*	
iret	44	1	iret

Notes

The **iret** instruction is the proper way to exit from an interrupt service routine; that is, from code branched to with **int** or started by hardware that generates hardware interrupts, such as serial ports, the timer chip, the computer keyboard, and the like. The **iret** instruction pops the return address from the top of the stack into CS:IP (IP must be on top of the stack, followed by CS) and then pops the next word from the stack into the flags register. (This is the state in which both hardware and software interrupts leave the stack.) *All flags are affected.*

For interrupts triggered by hardware, additional steps, such as issuing an *end of interrupt* (EOI) command, are generally required in order to prepare the hardware for another interrupt before **iret** is executed; the exact steps depend on the hardware involved. Consult your PC and peripheral hardware documentation.

reg8 = AL AH BL BH CL CH DL DH
[*mem8*] = 8-bit memory data
immed8 = 8-bit immediate data
sext-immed = 8-bit sign-extendable value
disp8 = 8-bit branch displacement
disp16 = 16-bit branch displacement
segment:offset = 32-bit segment:offset address

reg16 = AX BX CX DX BP SP SI DI
[*mem16*] = 16-bit memory data
immed16 = 16-bit immediate data
segreg = CS DS SS ES
[*mem32*] = 32-bit memory data
[*mem*] = memory data of any size

J? Jump on Condition

Flags Affected

O D I T S Z A P C		
F F F F F F F F F	OF: Overflow flag	TF: Trap flag	AF: Aux carry
<none>	DF: Direction flag	SF: Sign flag	PF: Parity flag
	IF: Interrupt flag	ZF: Zero flag	CF: Carry flag

Instruction Forms

	Descriptions	*Jump Conditions*	
ja *disp8*	Jump above	CF=0 and ZF=0	ja OutOfRange
jae *disp8*	Jump above or equal	CF=0	jae XLabel
jb *disp8*	Jump below	CF=1	jb TooLow
jbe *disp8*	Jump below or equal	CF=1 or ZF=1	jbe Exit
jc *disp8*	Jump CF set	CF=1	jc NextTest
je *disp8*	Jump equal	ZF=1	je Same
jg *disp8*	Jump greater	ZF=0 and SF=OF	jg Greater
jge *disp8*	Jump greater than or equal	SF=OF	jge GtThanEq
jl *disp8*	Jump less than	SF<>OF	jl IsLessThan
jle *disp8*	Jump less than or equal	ZF=1 or SF<>OF	jle LessThanEq
jna *disp8*	Jump not above	CF=1 or ZF=1	jna NotAbove
jnae *disp8*	Jump not above or equal	CF=1	jnae Skip1
jnb *disp8*	Jump not below	CF=0	jnb OffTop
jnbe *disp8*	Jump not below or equal	CF=0 and ZF=0	jnbe TooHigh
jnc *disp8*	Jump CF not set	CF=0	jnc TryAgain
jne *disp8*	Jump not equal	ZF=0	jne Mismatch
jng *disp8*	Jump not greater	ZF=1 or SF<>OF	jng Loop-Bottom
jnge *disp8*	Jump not greater than or equal	SF<>OF	jnge Point2
jnl *disp8*	Jump not less than	SF=OF	jnl NotLess
jnle *disp8*	Jump not less than or equal	ZF=0 and SF=OF	jnle ShortLab

	Descriptions	**Jump Conditions**	
jno *disp8*	Jump OF not set	OF=0	jno NoOver-flow
jnp *disp8*	Jump PF not set	PF=0	jnp EndText
jns *disp8*	Jump SF not set	SF=0	jns NoSign
jnz *disp8*	Jump not zero	ZF=0	jnz Different
jo *disp8*	Jump OF set	OF=1	jo Overflow
jp *disp8*	Jump PF set	PF=1	jp ParCheck1
jpe *disp8*	Jump parity even	PF=1	jpe ParityEven
jpo *disp8*	Jump parity odd	PF=0	jpo OddParity
js *disp8*	Jump SF set	SF=1	js Negative
jz *disp8*	Jump zero	ZF=1	jz Match

All conditional jumps take 16 cycles if the condition is true and the branch is taken or 4 cycles if the condition is false and the branch is not taken. All conditional jump instructions are 2 bytes long.

Notes

Each conditional jump instruction makes a short jump (a maximum of 127 bytes forward or 128 bytes back from the start of the instruction after the conditional jump) if the specified condition is true, or falls through if the condition is not true. The conditions all involve flags; the flag conditions tested by each conditional jump are given to the right of the mnemonic and its description, above.

The mnemonics incorporating *above* and *below* are for use after unsigned comparisons, whereas the mnemonics incorporating *less* and *greater* are for use after signed comparisons. *Equal* and *zero* may be used after either signed or unsigned comparisons.

Note that two or three different mnemonics often test the same condition; for example, **jc, jb,** and **jnae** all assemble to the same instruction, which branches only when CF is set to 1. The multiple mnemonics provide different logical ways to think of the instruction; for example, **jc** could be used to test a status returned in the CF by a subroutine, while **jb** or **jnae** might be used after an unsigned comparison. Any of the three mnemonics would work, but it's easier to use one that's logically related to the task at hand.

reg8 = AL AH BL BH CL CH DL DH
[*mem8*] = 8-bit memory data
immed8 = 8-bit immediate data
sext-immed = 8-bit sign-extendable value
disp8 = 8-bit branch displacement
disp16 = 16-bit branch displacement
segment:offset = 32-bit segment:offset address

reg16 = AX BX CX DX BP SP SI DI
[*mem16*] = 16-bit memory data
immed16 = 16-bit immediate data
segreg = CS DS SS ES
[*mem32*] = 32-bit memory data
[*mem*] = memory data of any size

JCXZ   Jump if CX = 0

Flags Affected

O D I T S Z A P C		
F F F F F F F F F	OF: Overflow flag	TF: Trap flag	AF: Aux carry
<none>	DF: Direction flag	SF: Sign flag	PF: Parity flag
	IF: Interrupt flag	ZF: Zero flag	CF: Carry flag

Instruction Forms

	Cycles	*Bytes*	
jcxz *disp8*	18 (CX=0)/6 (CX<>0)	2	jcxz SkipTest

Notes

Many instructions use CX as a counter. The **jcxz** instruction, which branches only if CX=0, allows you to test for the case where CX is 0, as for example to avoid executing a loop 65,536 times when the loop is entered with CX=0. The branch can only be a short branch (that is, no more than 127 bytes forward or 128 bytes back from the start of the instruction following **jcxz**) and will be taken only if CX=0 at the time the instruction is executed. If CX is any other value than 0, execution falls through to the next instruction.

reg8 = AL AH BL BH CL CH DL DH	*reg16* = AX BX CX DX BP SP SI DI
[*mem8*] = 8-bit memory data	[*mem16*] = 16-bit memory data
immed8 = 8-bit immediate data	*immed16* = 16-bit immediate data
sext-immed = 8-bit sign-extendable value	*segreg* = CS DS SS ES
disp8 = 8-bit branch displacement	[*mem32*] = 32-bit memory data
disp16 = 16-bit branch displacement	[*mem*] = memory data of any size
segment:offset = 32-bit segment:offset address	

JMP Jump

Flags Affected

O D I T S Z A P C	OF:	Overflow flag	TF:	Trap flag	AF:	Aux carry
F F F F F F F F F	DF:	Direction flag	SF:	Sign flag	PF:	Parity flag
<none>	IF:	Interrupt flag	ZF:	Zero flag	CF:	Carry flag

Instruction Forms

	Cycles	*Bytes*	
jmp *disp8*	15	2	jmp short SkipAdd
jmp *disp16*	15	3	jmp NearLabel
jmp *reg16*	11	2	jmp dx
jmp [*mem16*]	22+EA	2 to 4	jmp word ptr [Vecs+bx]
jmp *segment:offset*	15	5	jmp FarLabel
jmp [*mem32*]	32+EA	2 to 4	jmp dword ptr [FarVec]

Notes

The **jmp** instruction branches to the destination specified by the single operand; that is, **jmp** sets IP (and CS, for far jumps) so that the next instruction executed is at the specified location. In addition to branching to either near or far labels, **jmp** can branch anywhere in the segment pointed to by CS by setting IP equal to an offset stored in any general-purpose register. It can also branch to an address (either near or far) stored in memory and accessed through any *mod-reg-rm*-addressing mode; this is ideal for branching to addresses stored in jump tables.

Note that short jumps can reach only labels within +127 or −128 bytes of the start of the instruction after the jump, but are 1 byte shorter than normal 16-bit-displacement jumps, which can reach anywhere in the current code segment.

reg8 = AL AH BL BH CL CH DL DH	*reg16* = AX BX CX DX BP SP SI DI
[*mem8*] = 8-bit memory data	[*mem16*] = 16-bit memory data
immed8 = 8-bit immediate data	*immed16* = 16-bit immediate data
sext-immed = 8-bit sign-extendable value	*segreg* = CS DS SS ES
disp8 = 8-bit branch displacement	[*mem32*] = 32-bit memory data
disp16 = 16-bit branch displacement	[*mem*] = memory data of any size
segment:offset = 32-bit segment:offset address	

LAHF   Load AH from 8080 Flags

Flags Affected

O D I T S Z A P C		
F F F F F F F F F	OF: Overflow flag	TF: Trap flag	AF: Aux carry
<none>	DF: Direction flag	SF: Sign flag	PF: Parity flag
	IF: Interrupt flag	ZF: Zero flag	CF: Carry flag

Instruction Forms

	Cycles	*Bytes*	
lahf	4	1	lahf

Notes

This instruction copies the lower byte of the flags register to AH. This action, which can be reversed with **sahf,** is intended to allow the 8088 to emulate the **push psw** instruction of the 8080; however, it can also be used to save five of the 8088's flags—SF, ZF, AF, PF, and CF—quickly and without involving the stack. Note that OF is *not* copied to AH.

reg8 = AL AH BL BH CL CH DL DH
[*mem8*] = 8-bit memory data
immed8 = 8-bit immediate data
sext-immed = 8-bit sign-extendable value
disp8 = 8-bit branch displacement
disp16 = 16-bit branch displacement
segment:offset = 32-bit segment:offset address

reg16 = AX BX CX DX BP SP SI DI
[*mem16*] = 16-bit memory data
immed16 = 16-bit immediate data
segreg = CS DS SS ES
[*mem32*] = 32-bit memory data
[*mem*] = memory data of any size

LDS   Load DS Pointer

Flags Affected
```
O D I  T S Z A P C
F F F F F F F F F
    <none>
```
OF: Overflow flag   TF: Trap flag   AF: Aux carry
DF: Direction flag   SF: Sign flag   PF: Parity flag
IF: Interrupt flag   ZF: Zero flag   CF: Carry flag

Instruction Forms

	Cycles	*Bytes*	
lds [*mem32*]	24+EA	2 to 4	lds bx,[DwordVar]

Notes
The **lds** instruction loads DS and a general-purpose register from a memory doubleword. This is useful for loading a segment:offset pointer to any location in the 8088's address space in a single instruction. Note that segment:offset pointers loaded with **les** must be stored with the offset value at memory address *n* and the segment value at memory address *n*+2.

reg8 = AL AH BL BH CL CH DL DH
[*mem8*] = 8-bit memory data
immed8 = 8-bit immediate data
sext-immed = 8-bit sign-extendable value
disp8 = 8-bit branch displacement
disp16 = 16-bit branch displacement
segment:offset = 32-bit segment:offset address

reg16 = AX BX CX DX BP SP SI DI
[*mem16*] = 16-bit memory data
immed16 = 16-bit immediate data
segreg = CS DS SS ES
[*mem32*] = 32-bit memory data
[*mem*] = memory data of any size

LEA   Load Effective Address

Flags Affected

O D I T S Z A P C			
F F F F F F F F F	OF: Overflow flag	TF: Trap flag	AF: Aux carry
<none>	DF: Direction flag	SF: Sign flag	PF: Parity flag
	IF: Interrupt flag	ZF: Zero flag	CF: Carry flag

Instruction Forms

	Cycles	*Bytes*	
lea *reg16,*[*mem*]	2+EA	2 to 4	lea bx,[bp+si+100h]

Notes

The **lea** instruction calculates the offset of the source operand within its segment, then loads that offset into the destination operand. The destination operand must be a 16-bit register and *cannot* be memory. The source operand must be a memory operand but may be of any size. In other words, the value stored in the destination operand is the offset of the first byte of the source operand in memory. The source operand is not actually read.

reg8 = AL AH BL BH CL CH DL DH
[*mem8*] = 8-bit memory data
immed8 = 8-bit immediate data
sext-immed = 8-bit sign-extendable value
disp8 = 8-bit branch displacement
disp16 = 16-bit branch displacement
segment:offset = 32-bit segment:offset address

reg16 = AX BX CX DX BP SP SI DI
[*mem16*] = 16-bit memory data
immed16 = 16-bit immediate data
segreg = CS DS SS ES
[*mem32*] = 32-bit memory data
[*mem*] = memory data of any size

LES   Load ES Pointer

Flags Affected

O D I T S Z A P C		
F F F F F F F F F	OF: Overflow flag	TF: Trap flag	AF: Aux carry
<none>	DF: Direction flag	SF: Sign flag	PF: Parity flag
	IF: Interrupt flag	ZF: Zero flag	CF: Carry flag

Instruction Forms

	Cycles	*Bytes*	
les [*mem32*]	24+EA	2 to 4	les di,dword ptr [bx]

Notes

This instruction loads both ES and a general-purpose register from a memory doubleword. This is useful for loading a segment:offset pointer to any location in the 8088's address space in a single instruction. Note that segment:offset pointers loaded with **les** must be stored with the offset value at memory address *n* and the segment value at memory address *n*+2.

reg8 = AL AH BL BH CL CH DL DH
[*mem8*] = 8-bit memory data
immed8 = 8-bit immediate data
sext-immed = 8-bit sign-extendable value
disp8 = 8-bit branch displacement
disp16 = 16-bit branch displacement
segment:offset = 32-bit segment:offset address

reg16 = AX BX CX DX BP SP SI DI
[*mem16*] = 16-bit memory data
immed16 = 16-bit immediate data
segreg = CS DS SS ES
[*mem32*] = 32-bit memory data
[*mem*] = memory data of any size

LODS   Load String

Flags Affected

```
O D I  T S Z A P C        OF: Overflow flag   TF: Trap flag    AF: Aux carry
F F F F F F F F F         DF: Direction flag  SF: Sign flag    PF: Parity flag
       <none>             IF:  Interrupt flag ZF: Zero flag    CF: Carry flag
```

Instruction Forms

	Cycles	*Bytes*	
lodsb	12	1	lodsb
rep lodsb	9+(13*CX)	2	rep lodsb
lodsw	16	1	lodsw
rep lodsw	9+(17*CX)	2	rep lodsw

Notes

The **lods** instruction loads either AL (**lodsb**) or AX (**lodsw**) from the location pointed to by DS:SI, adjusting SI after the operation, as described below. DS may be overridden as the source segment, but SI must always be the source offset.

By placing an instruction repeat count in CX and preceding **lodsb** or **lodsw** with the **rep** prefix, it is possible to execute a single **lods** up to 65,535 (0FFFFh) times; however, this is not particularly useful, since the value loaded into AL or AX by each repeated **lods** will wipe out the value loaded by the previous repetition. After each **lods**, SI is adjusted (as described in the next paragraph) by either 1 (for **lodsb**) or 2 (for **lodsw**), and, if the **rep** prefix is being used, CX is decremented by 1.

Adjusting SI means incrementing SI if DF is cleared (0) or decrementing SI if DF is set (1).

reg8 = AL AH BL BH CL CH DL DH	*reg16* = AX BX CX DX BP SP SI DI
[*mem8*] = 8-bit memory data	[*mem16*] = 16-bit memory data
immed8 = 8-bit immediate data	*immed16* = 16-bit immediate data
sext-immed = 8-bit sign-extendable value	*segreg* = CS DS SS ES
disp8 = 8-bit branch displacement	[*mem32*] = 32-bit memory data
disp16 = 16-bit branch displacement	[*mem*] = memory data of any size
segment:offset = 32-bit segment:offset address	

LOOP   Loop while CX Not Equal to 0

Flags Affected

O D I T S Z A P C	OF: Overflow flag	TF: Trap flag	AF: Aux carry
F F F F F F F F F	DF: Direction flag	SF: Sign flag	PF: Parity flag
\<none\>	IF: Interrupt flag	ZF: Zero flag	CF: Carry flag

Instruction Forms

	Cycles	*Bytes*	
loop *disp8*	17 (CX \<\>0)/5 (CX=0)	2	loop WaitLoop

Notes

The **loop** instruction is similar to the two-instruction sequence **dec cx/jnz disp8.** When the **loop** instruction is executed, it first decrements CX, then it tests to see if CX equals 0. If CX is *not* 0 after being decremented, **loop** branches *disp8* bytes relative to the start of the instruction following **loop;** if CX is 0, execution falls through to the instruction after **loop.**

The difference between **loop** and the above two-instruction sequence is that **loop** does not alter any flags, even when CX is decremented to 0. Be aware that if CX is initially 0, **loop** will decrement it to 65,535 (0FFFFh) and then perform the loop another 65,535 times.

reg8 = AL AH BL BH CL CH DL DH	*reg16* = AX BX CX DX BP SP SI DI
[*mem8*] = 8-bit memory data	[*mem16*] = 16-bit memory data
immed8 = 8-bit immediate data	*immed16* = 16-bit immediate data
sext-immed = 8-bit sign-extendable value	*segreg* = CS DS SS ES
disp8 = 8-bit branch displacement	[*mem32*] = 32-bit memory data
disp16 = 16-bit branch displacement	[*mem*] = memory data of any size
segment:offset = 32-bit segment:offset address	

LOOPNZ   Loop while CX Not Equal to 0 and Zero Flag Equal to 0
LOOPNE   Loop while CX Not Equal to 0 and Last Result Was Not Equal

Flags Affected

O D I T S Z A P C		
F F F F F F F F F	OF: Overflow flag	TF: Trap flag	AF: Aux carry
<none>	DF: Direction flag	SF: Sign flag	PF: Parity flag
	IF: Interrupt flag	ZF: Zero flag	CF: Carry flag

Instruction Forms

	Cycles	*Bytes*	
loopnz *disp8*	19 (CX<>0 and ZF=0)/ 5 (CX=0 or ZF=1)	2	loopnz PollLp

Notes

The instruction **loopnz** (also known as **loopne**) is identical to **loop,** except that **loopnz** branches to the specified displacement only if CX isn't equal to 0 after CX is decremented *and* ZF is cleared to 0. This is useful for handling a maximum number of repetitions of a loop that normally terminates on a ZF setting of 1.

reg8 = AL AH BL BH CL CH DL DH
[*mem8*] = 8-bit memory data
immed8 = 8-bit immediate data
sext-immed = 8-bit sign-extendable value
disp8 = 8-bit branch displacement
disp16 = 16-bit branch displacement
segment:offset = 32-bit segment:offset address

reg16 = AX BX CX DX BP SP SI DI
[*mem16*] = 16-bit memory data
immed16 = 16-bit immediate data
segreg = CS DS SS ES
[*mem32*] = 32-bit memory data
[*mem*] = memory data of any size

LOOPZ   Loop while CX Not Equal to 0 and Zero Flag Equal to 1
LOOPE   Loop while CX Not Equal to 0 and Last Result Was Equal

Flags Affected

O D I T S Z A P C	OF: Overflow flag	TF: Trap flag	AF: Aux carry
F F F F F F F F F	DF: Direction flag	SF: Sign flag	PF: Parity flag
<none>	IF: Interrupt flag	ZF: Zero flag	CF: Carry flag

Instruction Forms

	Cycles	*Bytes*	
loopz *disp8*	18 (CX<>0 and ZF=1)/	2	loopz
	6 (CX=0 or ZF=0)		MaxWtLp

Notes

The instruction **loopz** (also known as **loope**) is identical to **loop,** except that it branches to the specified displacement only if CX isn't equal to 0 after CX is decremented *and* ZF is set to 1. This is useful for handling a maximum number of repetitions of a loop that normally terminates on a ZF setting of 0.

reg8 = AL AH BL BH CL CH DL DH
[*mem8*] = 8-bit memory data
immed8 = 8-bit immediate data
sext-immed = 8-bit sign-extendable value
disp8 = 8-bit branch displacement
disp16 = 16-bit branch displacement
segment:offset = 32-bit segment:offset address

reg16 = AX BX CX DX BP SP SI DI
[*mem16*] = 16-bit memory data
immed16 = 16-bit immediate data
segreg = CS DS SS ES
[*mem32*] = 32-bit memory data
[*mem*] = memory data of any size

MOV   Move (Copy) Right Operand into Left Operand

Flags Affected

O D I T S Z A P C	OF: Overflow flag	TF: Trap flag	AF: Aux carry
F F F F F F F F F	DF: Direction flag	SF: Sign flag	PF: Parity flag
<none>	IF: Interrupt flag	ZF: Zero flag	CF: Carry flag

Instruction Forms

	Cycles	*Bytes*	
mov *reg8,reg8*	2	2	mov ch,al
mov [*mem8*],*reg8*	9+EA	2 to 4	mov [bx+10h],dh
mov *reg8,*[*mem8*]	8+EA	2 to 4	mov bl,[si]
mov *reg16,reg16*	2	2	mov ax,dx
mov [*mem16*],*reg16*	13+EA	2 to 4	mov [WordVar],cx
mov *reg16,*[*mem16*]	12+EA	2 to 4	mov bx,[Table+bx]
mov *reg8,immed8*	4	2	mov dl,1
mov [*mem8*],*immed8*	10+EA	3 to 5	mov [ByteVar],1
mov *reg16,immed16*	4	3	mov ax,88h
mov [*mem16*], *immed16*	14+EA	4 to 6	mov [WordVar],1000h
mov al,[*mem8*] (direct)	10	3	mov al,[Flag]
mov [*mem8*],al (direct)	10	3	mov [ByteVar],al
mov ax,[*mem16*] (direct)	14	3	mov ax,[WordVar]
mov [*mem16*],ax (direct)	14	3	mov [Count],ax
mov *segreg,reg16*	2	2	mov es,ax
mov *segreg,*[*mem16*]	12+EA	2 to 4	mov ds,[DataPtrs+bx]
mov *reg16,segreg*	2	2	mov dx,ds
mov [*mem16*],*segreg*	13+EA	2 to 4	mov [StackSeg],ss

Notes

The **mov** instruction copies the contents of the source operand to the destination operand. The source operand is not affected, and no flags are affected. Note that, unlike other instructions that accept immediate operands, 16-bit immediate operands to **mov** are never stored as a single byte that is sign extended at execution time. Note also that the special, shorter accumulator-specific form of **mov** applies only to direct-addressed operands and that there is a special, 1-byte-shorter form of **mov** to load a register (but not a memory operand) with an immediate value.

reg8 = AL AH BL BH CL CH DL DH
[*mem8*] = 8-bit memory data
immed8 = 8-bit immediate data
sext-immed = 8-bit sign-extendable value
disp8 = 8-bit branch displacement
disp16 = 16-bit branch displacement
segment:offset = 32-bit segment:offset address

reg16 = AX BX CX DX BP SP SI DI
[*mem16*] = 16-bit memory data
immed16 = 16-bit immediate data
segreg = CS DS SS ES
[*mem32*] = 32-bit memory data
[*mem*] = memory data of any size

MOVS   Move String

Flags Affected

O D I T S Z A P C			
F F F F F F F F F	OF: Overflow flag	TF: Trap flag	AF: Aux carry
<none>	DF: Direction flag	SF: Sign flag	PF: Parity flag
	IF: Interrupt flag	ZF: Zero flag	CF: Carry flag

Instruction Forms

	Cycles	*Bytes*	
movsb	18	1	movsb
rep movsb	9+(17*CX)	2	rep movsb
movsw	26	1	movsw
rep movsw	9+(25*CX)	2	rep movsw

Notes

This instruction copies either the byte (**movsb**) or word (**movsw**) pointed to by DS:SI to the location pointed to by ES:DI, adjusting both SI and DI after the operation, as described below. The use of DS as the source segment can be overridden, but ES must be the segment of the destination and cannot be overridden. SI must always be the source offset, and DI must always be the destination offset.

By placing an instruction repeat count in CX and preceding **movsb** or **movsw** with the **rep** prefix, it is possible to execute a single **movs** up to 65,535 (0FFFFh) times, just as if that many **movs** instructions had been executed, but without the need for any additional instruction fetching. Note that if CX is 0 when **rep movs** is started, 0 repetitions of **movs**—not 65,536 repetitions—are performed. After each **movs**, SI and DI are adjusted (as described in the next paragraph) by either 1 (for **movsb**) or 2 (for **movsw**), and, if the **rep** prefix is being used, CX is decremented by 1.

Adjusting SI and DI means incrementing them if DF is cleared (0) or decrementing them if it is set (1).

Note that the accumulator is not affected by **movs.**

reg8 = AL AH BL BH CL CH DL DH	*reg16* = AX BX CX DX BP SP SI DI
[*mem8*] = 8-bit memory data	[*mem16*] = 16-bit memory data
immed8 = 8-bit immediate data	*immed16* = 16-bit immediate data
sext-immed = 8-bit sign-extendable value	*segreg* = CS DS SS ES
disp8 = 8-bit branch displacement	[*mem32*] = 32-bit memory data
disp16 = 16-bit branch displacement	[*mem*] = memory data of any size
segment:offset = 32-bit segment:offset address	

MUL   Unsigned Multiply

Flags Affected

O D I T S Z A P C	OF: Overflow flag	TF: Trap flag	AF: Aux carry
F F F F F F F F F	DF: Direction flag	SF: Sign flag	PF: Parity flag
* * * * * *	IF: Interrupt flag	ZF: Zero flag	CF: Carry flag

Instruction Forms

	Cycles	*Bytes*	
mul *reg8*	70 to 77	2	mul ah
mul [*mem8*]	76+EA to 83+EA	2 to 4	mul byte ptr [bx+si]
mul *reg16*	118 to 133	2	mul cx
mul [*mem16*]	128+EA to 143+EA	2 to 4	mul [WordVar]

Notes

The **mul** instruction performs an 8×8 unsigned multiplication of AL by a byte operand, storing the result in AX, or a 16×16 unsigned multiplication of AX by a word operand, storing the result in DX:AX. Note that AH is changed by 8×8 multiplication even though it is not an operand; the same is true of DX for 16×16 multiplication.

CF and OF are set to 1 if and only if the upper half of the result (AH for 8×8 multiplies, DX for 16×16 multiplies) is nonzero, and set to 0 otherwise. SF, ZF, AF, and PF are left in undefined states.

reg8 = AL AH BL BH CL CH DL DH	*reg16* = AX BX CX DX BP SP SI DI
[*mem8*] = 8-bit memory data	[*mem16*] = 16-bit memory data
immed8 = 8-bit immediate data	*immed16* = 16-bit immediate data
sext-immed = 8-bit sign-extendable value	*segreg* = CS DS SS ES
disp8 = 8-bit branch displacement	[*mem32*] = 32-bit memory data
disp16 = 16-bit branch displacement	[*mem*] = memory data of any size
segment:offset = 32-bit segment:offset address	

NEG   Negate [Two's Complement; i.e., Multiply by −1]

Flags Affected

O D I	T S Z A P C			
F F F	F F F F F F	OF: Overflow flag	TF: Trap flag	AF: Aux carry
*	* * * *	DF: Direction flag	SF: Sign flag	PF: Parity flag
		IF: Interrupt flag	ZF: Zero flag	CF: Carry flag

Instruction Forms

	Cycles	*Bytes*	
neg *reg8*	3	2	neg cl
neg [*mem8*]	16+EA	2 to 4	neg [ByteVar]
neg *reg16*	3	2	neg si
neg [*mem16*]	24+EA	2 to 4	neg word ptr [bx+si+1]

Notes

The **neg** instruction performs the assembly language equivalent of multiplying a value by −1. Keep in mind that negation is not the same as simply inverting each bit in the operand; another instruction, **not,** does that. The process of negation is also known as generating the *two's complement* of a value; the two's complement of a value added to that value yields 0.

If the operand is 0, CF is cleared and ZF is set; otherwise CF is set and ZF is cleared. This property can be useful in multi-word negation. If the operand contains the maximum negative value (80h = −128 for byte operands, 8000h = −32,768 for word operands), there is no corresponding positive value that will fit in the operand, so the operand does not change; this case can be detected because it is the only case in which OF is set by **neg.**

reg8 = AL AH BL BH CL CH DL DH	*reg16* = AX BX CX DX BP SP SI DI
[*mem8*] = 8-bit memory data	[*mem16*] = 16-bit memory data
immed8 = 8-bit immediate data	*immed16* = 16-bit immediate data
sext-immed = 8-bit sign-extendable value	*segreg* = CS DS SS ES
disp8 = 8-bit branch displacement	[*mem32*] = 32-bit memory data
disp16 = 16-bit branch displacement	[*mem*] = memory data of any size
segment:offset = 32-bit segment:offset address	

NOP   No Operation

Flags Affected

```
O D I  T S Z A P C
F F F F F F F F F
   <none>
```

OF: Overflow flag   TF: Trap flag   AF: Aux carry
DF: Direction flag   SF: Sign flag   PF: Parity flag
IF: Interrupt flag   ZF: Zero flag   CF: Carry flag

Instruction Forms

	Cycles	*Bytes*	
nop	3	1	nop

Notes

This, the easiest to understand of all 8086-family machine instructions, does nothing; its job is simply to take up space or time. The opcode for **nop** is actually the opcode for **xchg ax,ax,** which changes no registers and alters no flags but takes up 1 byte and requires 3 cycles to execute. It is used for patching out machine instructions during debugging, leaving space for future procedure or interrupt calls, and padding timing loops. The **nop** instruction is also inserted by MASM to fill reserved space that turns out not to be needed, such as the third byte of a forward **jmp** that turns out to be a **jmp short.**

reg8 = AL AH BL BH CL CH DL DH
[*mem8*] = 8-bit memory data
immed8 = 8-bit immediate data
sext-immed = 8-bit sign-extendable value
disp8 = 8-bit branch displacement
disp16 = 16-bit branch displacement
segment:offset = 32-bit segment:offset address

reg16 = AX BX CX DX BP SP SI DI
[*mem16*] = 16-bit memory data
immed16 = 16-bit immediate data
segreg = CS DS SS ES
[*mem32*] = 32-bit memory data
[*mem*] = memory data of any size

NOT   Logical Not (One's Complement)

Flags Affected

O D I T S Z A P C		
F F F F F F F F F	OF: Overflow flag	TF: Trap flag	AF: Aux carry
<none>	DF: Direction flag	SF: Sign flag	PF: Parity flag
	IF: Interrupt flag	ZF: Zero flag	CF: Carry flag

Instruction Forms

	Cycles	Bytes	
not *reg8*	3	2	not al
not [*mem8*]	16+EA	2 to 4	not byte ptr [bx]
not *reg16*	3	2	not dx
not [*mem16*]	24+EA	2 to 4	not [WordVar]

Notes

The **not** instruction inverts each bit within the operand. In other words, every bit that was 1 becomes 0, and every bit that was 0 becomes 1, just as if the operand had been **xor**ed with 0FFh (for byte operands) or 0FFFFh (for word operands). The **not** instruction performs the logical **not,** or one's complement, operation. See the **neg** instruction for the negation, or two's complement, operation.

Note that no flag is altered.

reg8 = AL AH BL BH CL CH DL DH
[*mem8*] = 8-bit memory data
immed8 = 8-bit immediate data
sext-immed = 8-bit sign-extendable value
disp8 = 8-bit branch displacement
disp16 = 16-bit branch displacement
segment:offset = 32-bit segment:offset address

reg16 = AX BX CX DX BP SP SI DI
[*mem16*] = 16-bit memory data
immed16 = 16-bit immediate data
segreg = CS DS SS ES
[*mem32*] = 32-bit memory data
[*mem*] = memory data of any size

OR Logical or

Flags Affected

O D I T S Z A P C	OF: Overflow flag	TF: Trap flag	AF: Aux carry
F F F F F F F F F	DF: Direction flag	SF: Sign flag	PF: Parity flag
* * * * * *	IF: Interrupt flag	ZF: Zero flag	CF: Carry flag

Instruction Forms

	Cycles	*Bytes*	
or *reg8,reg8*	3	2	or al,dl
or [*mem8*],*reg8*	16+EA	2 to 4	or [ByteVar],ch
or *reg8*,[*mem8*]	9+EA	2 to 4	or bh,[si]
or *reg16,reg16*	3	2	or bp,ax
or [*mem16*],*reg16*	24+EA	2 to 4	or [bp+si],cx
or *reg16*,[*mem16*]	13+EA	2 to 4	or ax,[bx]
or *reg8,immed8*	4	3	or cl,03h
or [*mem8*],*immed8*	17+EA	3 to 5	or [ByteVar+1],29h
or *reg16,sext-immed*	4	3	or ax,01fh
or *reg16,immed16*	4	4	or ax,01ffh
or [*mem16*],*sext-immed*	25+EA	3 to 5	or [WordVar],7fh
or [*mem16*],*immed16*	25+EA	4 to 6	or [WordVar],7fffh
or al,*immed8*	4	2	or al,0c0h
or ax,*immed16*	4	3	or ax,01ffh

Notes

The **or** instruction performs the **or** logical operation between its two operands. Once the operation is complete, the result replaces the destination operand. The **or** is performed on a bit-by-bit basis, such that bit 0 of the source is **or**ed with bit 0 of the destination, bit 1 of the source is **or**ed with bit 1 of the destination, and so on. The **or** operation yields a 1 if *either one* of the operands is 1, and a 0 only if both operands are 0. Note that **or** makes AF undefined. CF and OF are cleared to 0, and the other affected flags are set according to the operation's results.

reg8 = AL AH BL BH CL CH DL DH	*reg16* = AX BX CX DX BP SP SI DI
[*mem8*] = 8-bit memory data	[*mem16*] = 16-bit memory data
immed8 = 8-bit immediate data	*immed16* = 16-bit immediate data
sext-immed = 8-bit sign-extendable value	*segreg* = CS DS SS ES
disp8 = 8-bit branch displacement	[*mem32*] = 32-bit memory data
disp16 = 16-bit branch displacement	[*mem*] = memory data of any size
segment:offset = 32-bit segment:offset address	

OUT   Output Byte to I/O Port

Flags Affected

```
ODI T S Z A P C
F F F F F F F F F
    <none>
```

OF: Overflow flag	TF: Trap flag	AF: Aux carry
DF: Direction flag	SF: Sign flag	PF: Parity flag
IF: Interrupt flag	ZF: Zero flag	CF: Carry flag

Instruction Forms

	Cycles	*Bytes*	
out dx, al	8	1	out dx,al
out *immed8*,al	10	2	out 21h,al
out dx,ax	12	1	out dx,ax
out *immed8*,ax	14	2	out 10,ax

Notes

The **out** instruction writes the data in the accumulator to the specified I/O port. Note that data *must* come from the accumulator and that only DX or a constant may be used to address the I/O port. Note also that only I/O ports in the range of 0 to 255 may be addressed with a constant; DX must be used to address I/O ports in the range of 256 to 65,535.

reg8 = AL AH BL BH CL CH DL DH	*reg16* = AX BX CX DX BP SP SI DI
[*mem8*] = 8-bit memory data	[*mem16*] = 16-bit memory data
immed8 = 8-bit immediate data	*immed16* = 16-bit immediate data
sext-immed = 8-bit sign-extendable value	*segreg* = CS DS SS ES
disp8 = 8-bit branch displacement	[*mem32*] = 32-bit memory data
disp16 = 16-bit branch displacement	[*mem*] = memory data of any size
segment:offset = 32-bit segment:offset address	

Pop from Top of Stack

Flags Affected

```
ODI TS ZAP C        OF: Overflow flag   TF: Trap flag    AF: Aux carry
F F F F F F F F F    DF: Direction flag  SF: Sign flag    PF: Parity flag
     <none>          IF:  Interrupt flag ZF: Zero flag    CF: Carry flag
```

Instruction Forms

	Cycles	*Bytes*	
pop *reg16*	12	1	pop cx
pop [*mem16*]	25+EA	2 to 4	pop word ptr [si+1]
pop *segreg* (not CS)	12	1	pop es

Notes

The **pop** instruction pops the word on top of the stack into the specified operand. SP is incremented by 2 *after* the word comes off the stack. Remember that a word can be popped directly to memory, without passing through a register.

It is impossible to pop a byte-sized item from the stack; it's words or nothing. There is a separate instruction, **popf,** for popping the flags register.

Note that CS cannot be loaded with **pop;** in order to load CS from the stack, it must be loaded simultaneously with IP, usually via **retf.**

The top of the stack is always located at SS:SP; the segment cannot be overridden, and **pop** always uses SP to address the source operand. However, when a memory location is popped into, *mod-reg-rm* addressing is used to point to the destination operand, and the default segment of DS for that operand can be overridden.

reg8 = AL AH BL BH CL CH DL DH	*reg16* = AX BX CX DX BP SP SI DI
[*mem8*] = 8-bit memory data	[*mem16*] = 16-bit memory data
immed8 = 8-bit immediate data	*immed16* = 16-bit immediate data
sext-immed = 8-bit sign-extendable value	*segreg* = CS DS SS ES
disp8 = 8-bit branch displacement	[*mem32*] = 32-bit memory data
disp16 = 16-bit branch displacement	[*mem*] = memory data of any size
segment:offset = 32-bit segment:offset address	

POPF   Pop Top of Stack into Flags Reg

Flags Affected

O D I T S Z A P C	OF: Overflow flag	TF: Trap flag	AF: Aux carry
F F F F F F F F F	DF: Direction flag	SF: Sign flag	PF: Parity flag
* * * * * * * * *	IF: Interrupt flag	ZF: Zero flag	CF: Carry flag

Instruction Forms

	Cycles	**Bytes**	
popf	12	1	popf

Notes

The **popf** instruction pops the word on top of the stack into the flags register. SP is incremented by 2 *after* the word comes off the stack.

There is a separate instruction, **pop,** for popping into register and memory operands.

The top of the stack is always located at SS:SP; the segment cannot be overridden, and **popf** always uses SP to address memory.

reg8 = AL AH BL BH CL CH DL DH	reg16 = AX BX CX DX BP SP SI DI
[mem8] = 8-bit memory data	[mem16] = 16-bit memory data
immed8 = 8-bit immediate data	immed16 = 16-bit immediate data
sext-immed = 8-bit sign-extendable value	segreg = CS DS SS ES
disp8 = 8-bit branch displacement	[mem32] = 32-bit memory data
disp16 = 16-bit branch displacement	[mem] = memory data of any size
segment:offset = 32-bit segment:offset address	

PUSH   Push onto Top of Stack

Flags Affected

O D I T S Z A P C	OF: Overflow flag TF: Trap flag AF: Aux carry
F F F F F F F F F	DF: Direction flag SF: Sign flag PF: Parity flag
<none>	IF: Interrupt flag ZF: Zero flag CF: Carry flag

Instruction Forms

	Cycles	*Bytes*	
push *reg16*	15	1	push ax
push [*mem16*]	24+EA	2 to 4	push word ptr [bx]
push *segreg*	14	1	push ds

Notes

This instruction pushes the specified operand onto the top of the stack. sp is decremented by 2 *before* the word goes onto the stack. Remember that memory operands can be pushed directly onto the stack without passing through a register.

It is impossible to push a byte-sized item onto the stack; it's words or nothing. There is a separate instruction, **pushf,** for pushing the flags register.

The top of the stack is always located at SS:SP; the segment cannot be overridden, and **push** always uses SP to address the destination operand. However, when a memory location is pushed from, *mod-reg-rm* addressing is used to point to the source operand, and the default segment of DS for that operand can be overridden.

reg8 = AL AH BL BH CL CH DL DH	*reg16* = AX BX CX DX BP SP SI DI
[*mem8*] = 8-bit memory data	[*mem16*] = 16-bit memory data
immed8 = 8-bit immediate data	*immed16* = 16-bit immediate data
sext-immed = 8-bit sign-extendable value	*segreg* = CS DS SS ES
disp8 = 8-bit branch displacement	[*mem32*] = 32-bit memory data
disp16 = 16-bit branch displacement	[*mem*] = memory data of any size
segment:offset = 32-bit segment:offset address	

PUSHF   Push Flags Register onto Top of Stack

Flags Affected

O D I T S Z A P C			
F F F F F F F F F	OF: Overflow flag	TF: Trap flag	AF: Aux carry
\<none>	DF: Direction flag	SF: Sign flag	PF: Parity flag
	IF: Interrupt flag	ZF: Zero flag	CF: Carry flag

Instruction Forms

	Cycles	Bytes	
pushf	14	1	pushf

Notes

The **pushf** instruction pushes the current contents of the flags register onto the top of the stack. SP is decremented *before* the word goes onto the stack.

There is a separate instruction, **push,** for pushing other register data and memory data.

The flags register is not affected when you *push* the flags, but only when you pop them back with **popf.**

The top of the stack is always located at SS:SP; the segment cannot be overridden, and **pushf** always uses SP to address memory.

reg8 = AL AH BL BH CL CH DL DH
[*mem8*] = 8-bit memory data
immed8 = 8-bit immediate data
sext-immed = 8-bit sign-extendable value
disp8 = 8-bit branch displacement
disp16 = 16-bit branch displacement
segment:offset = 32-bit segment:offset address

reg16 = AX BX CX DX BP SP SI DI
[*mem16*] = 16-bit memory data
immed16 = 16-bit immediate data
segreg = CS DS SS ES
[*mem32*] = 32-bit memory data
[*mem*] = memory data of any size

RCL   Rotate through Carry Left

Flags Affected

O D I T S Z A P C	OF: Overflow flag	TF: Trap flag	AF: Aux carry
F F F F F F F F F	DF: Direction flag	SF: Sign flag	PF: Parity flag
* *	IF: Interrupt flag	ZF: Zero flag	CF: Carry flag

Instruction Forms

	Cycles	Bytes	
rcl *reg8*,1	2	2	rcl dl,1
rcl [*mem8*],1	15+EA	2 to 4	rcl byte ptr [bx+di],1
rcl *reg16*,1	2	2	rcl dx,1
rcl [*mem16*],1	23+EA	2 to 4	rcl word ptr [di],1
rcl *reg8*,cl	8+(4*CL)	2	rcl ah,cl
rcl [*mem8*],cl	20+EA+(4*CL)	2 to 4	rcl [ByteVar],cl
rcl *reg16*,cl	8+(4*CL)	2	rcl ax,cl
rcl [*mem16*],cl	28+EA+(4*CL)	2 to 4	rcl word ptr [bx+Index],cl

Notes

The instruction **rcl** rotates the bits within the destination operand to the left, where left is toward the most significant bit, bit 15 for word operands, bit 7 for byte operands. A rotate is a shift (see **shl** and **shr**) that wraps around; with **rcl**, the leftmost bit (bit 15 for word operands, bit 7 for byte operands) of the operand is rotated into CF, CF is rotated into the rightmost bit of the operand (bit 0), and all intermediate bits are rotated one bit to the left.

The number of bit positions rotated may be specified either as the literal 1 or by the value in CL (not CX!). It is generally faster to perform sequential rotate-by-1 instructions for rotations of up to about 4 bits, and faster to use rotate-by-CL instructions for longer rotations. Note that while CL may contain any value up to 255, it is meaningless to rotate by any value larger than 17, *even though the rotations are actually performed—wasting cycles—on the 8088.*

OF is modified predictably *only* by the rotate-by-1 forms of **rcl;** after rotate-by-CL forms, OF becomes undefined.

reg8 = AL AH BL BH CL CH DL DH	*reg16* = AX BX CX DX BP SP SI DI
[*mem8*] = 8-bit memory data	[*mem16*] = 16-bit memory data
immed8 = 8-bit immediate data	*immed16* = 16-bit immediate data
sext-immed = 8-bit sign-extendable value	*segreg* = CS DS SS ES
disp8 = 8-bit branch displacement	[*mem32*] = 32-bit memory data
disp16 = 16-bit branch displacement	[*mem*] = memory data of any size
segment:offset = 32-bit segment:offset address	

RCR   Rotate through Carry Right

Flags Affected

ODI TSZAPC	OF: Overflow flag	TF: Trap flag	AF: Aux carry
FFFFFFFFF	DF: Direction flag	SF: Sign flag	PF: Parity flag
* *	IF: Interrupt flag	ZF: Zero flag	CF: Carry flag

Instruction Forms

	Cycles	*Bytes*	
rcr *reg8*,1	2	2	rcr cl,1
rcr [*mem8*],1	15+EA	2 to 4	rcr byte ptr [di],1
rcr *reg16*,1	2	2	rcr bx,1
rcr [*mem16*],1	23+EA	2 to 4	rcr word ptr [bx+di],1
rcr *reg8*,cl	8+(4*CL)	2	rcr dh,cl
rcr [*mem8*],cl	20+EA+(4*CL)	2 to 4	rcr [ByteVar+ 100h],cl
rcr *reg16*,cl	8+(4*CL)	2	rcr bx,cl
rcr [*mem16*],cl	28+EA+(4*CL)	2 to 4	rcr [WordVar],cl

Notes

The **rcr** instruction rotates the bits within the destination operand to the right, where right is toward the least significant bit, bit 0. A rotate is a shift (see **shl** and **shr**) that wraps around; with **rcr,** the rightmost bit (bit 0) of the operand is rotated into CF, CF is rotated into the leftmost bit of the operand (bit 15 for word operands, bit 7 for byte operands), and all intermediate bits are rotated one bit to the right.

The number of bit positions rotated may be specified either as the literal 1 or by the value in CL (not CX!). It is generally faster to perform sequential rotate-by-1 instructions for rotations of up to about 4 bits, and faster to use rotate-by-CL instructions for longer rotations. Note that while CL may contain any value up to 255, it is meaningless to rotate by any value larger than 17, *even though the rotations are actually performed—wasting cycles—on the 8088.*

OF is modified predictably *only* by the rotate-by-1 forms of **rcr;** after rotate-by-CL forms, OF becomes undefined.

reg8 = AL AH BL BH CL CH DL DH	*reg16* = AX BX CX DX BP SP SI DI
[*mem8*] = 8-bit memory data	[*mem16*] = 16-bit memory data
immed8 = 8-bit immediate data	*immed16* = 16-bit immediate data
sext-immed = 8-bit sign-extendable value	*segreg* = CS DS SS ES
disp8 = 8-bit branch displacement	[*mem32*] = 32-bit memory data
disp16 = 16-bit branch displacement	[*mem*] = memory data of any size
segment:offset = 32-bit segment:offset address	

RET   Return from Subroutine Call

Flags Affected

O D I T S Z A P C	OF: Overflow flag	TF: Trap flag	AF: Aux carry
F F F F F F F F F	DF: Direction flag	SF: Sign flag	PF: Parity flag
<none>	IF: Interrupt flag	ZF: Zero flag	CF: Carry flag

Instruction Forms

	Cycles	*Bytes*	
retn	20	1	ret (in near proc)
retf	34	1	retf
retn *immed16*	24	3	retn 10
retf *immed16*	33	3	ret 512 (in far proc)

Notes

There are two kinds of returns, near and far; near pops IP from the stack (returning to an address within the current code segment) and far pops both CS and IP from the stack (usually returning to an address in some other code segment). Ordinarily the **ret** form is used, with the assembler resolving it to a near or far return opcode to match the current **proc** directive's use of the **near** or **far** specifier. Alternatively, **retf** or **retn** may be used to select explicitly the type of return; however, be aware that the **retf** and **retn** forms are *not* available in MASM prior to version 5.0.

The **ret** instruction may take an operand indicating how many bytes of stack space are to be released (the amount to be added to the stack pointer) as the return is executed. This is used to discard parameters that were pushed onto the stack for the procedure's use immediately prior to the procedure call.

No two references agree on the execution times of **ret** *immed16* and **retf** *immed16.* The times shown above are from *Microsoft Macro Assembler 5.0 Reference,* which are closest to the times measured with the Zen timer. The Zen timer actually measured longer execution times still, most likely as a result of the prefetch queue and DRAM refresh cycle eaters.

reg8 = AL AH BL BH CL CH DL DH	*reg16* = AX BX CX DX BP SP SI DI
[*mem8*] = 8-bit memory data	[*mem16*] = 16-bit memory data
immed8 = 8-bit immediate data	*immed16* = 16-bit immediate data
sext-immed = 8-bit sign-extendable value	*segreg* = CS DS SS ES
disp8 = 8-bit branch displacement	[*mem32*] = 32-bit memory data
disp16 = 16-bit branch displacement	[*mem*] = memory data of any size
segment:offset = 32-bit segment:offset address	

ROL   Rotate Left

Flags Affected

O D I T S Z A P C			
F F F F F F F F F	OF: Overflow flag	TF: Trap flag	AF: Aux carry
* *	DF: Direction flag	SF: Sign flag	PF: Parity flag
	IF: Interrupt flag	ZF: Zero flag	CF: Carry flag

Instruction Forms

	Cycles	*Bytes*	
rol *reg8*,1	2	2	rol cl,1
rol [*mem8*],1	15+EA	2 to 4	rol byte ptr [di],1
rol *reg16*,1	2	2	rol ax,1
rol [*mem16*],1	23+EA	2 to 4	rol word ptr [Base+bx],1
rol *reg8*,cl	8+(4*CL)	2	rol dl,cl
rol [*mem8*],cl	20+EA+(4*CL)	2 to 4	rol byte ptr [bx],cl
rol *reg16*,cl	8+(4*CL)	2	rol di,cl
rol [*mem16*],cl	28+EA+(4*CL)	2 to 4	rol [WordVar],cl

Notes

The **rol** instruction rotates the bits within the destination operand to the left, where left is toward the most significant bit, bit 15 for word operands and bit 7 for byte operands. A rotate is a shift (see **shl** and **shr**) that wraps around; with **rol,** the leftmost bit of the operand (bit 15 for word operands, bit 7 for byte operands) is rotated into the rightmost bit, and all intermediate bits are rotated one bit to the left.

The number of bit positions rotated may be specified either as the literal 1 or by the value in CL (not CX!). It is generally faster to perform sequential rotate-by-1 instructions for rotations of up to about 4 bits and faster to use rotate-by-CL instructions for longer rotations. Note that while CL may contain any value up to 255, it is meaningless to rotate by any value larger than 17, *even though the rotations are actually performed—wasting cycles—on the 8088.*

The leftmost bit is copied into CF on each rotate operation. OF is modified predictably *only* by the rotate-by-1 forms of **rol;** after rotate-by-CL forms, OF becomes undefined.

reg8 = AL AH BL BH CL CH DL DH	*reg16* = AX BX CX DX BP SP SI DI
[*mem8*] = 8-bit memory data	[*mem16*] = 16-bit memory data
immed8 = 8-bit immediate data	*immed16* = 16-bit immediate data
sext-immed = 8-bit sign-extendable value	*segreg* = CS DS SS ES
disp8 = 8-bit branch displacement	[*mem32*] = 32-bit memory data
disp16 = 16-bit branch displacement	[*mem*] = memory data of any size
segment:offset = 32-bit segment:offset address	

ROR   Rotate Right

Flags Affected

O	D	I	T	S	Z	A	P	C
F	F	F	F	F	F	F	F	F
*								*

OF: Overflow flag   TF: Trap flag   AF: Aux carry
DF: Direction flag   SF: Sign flag   PF: Parity flag
IF: Interrupt flag   ZF: Zero flag   CF: Carry flag

Instruction Forms

	Cycles	Bytes	
ror *reg8*,1	2	2	ror dl,1
ror [*mem8*],1	15+EA	2 to 4	ror [ByteVar],1
ror *reg16*,1	2	2	ror bx,1
ror [*mem16*],1	23+EA	2 to 4	ror word ptr [bx+si],1
ror *reg8*,cl	8+(4*CL)	2	ror ah,cl
ror [*mem8*],cl	20+EA+(4*CL)	2 to 4	ror byte ptr [si+100h],cl
ror *reg16*,cl	8+(4*CL)	2	ror si,cl
ror [*mem16*],cl	28+EA+(4*CL)	2 to 4	ror [WordVar +1],cl

Notes

The **ror** instruction rotates the bits within the destination operand to the right, where right is toward the least significant bit, bit 0. A rotate is a shift (see **shl** and **shr**) that wraps around; with **ror,** the rightmost bit (bit 0) of the operand is rotated into the leftmost bit (bit 15 for word operands, bit 7 for byte operands), and all intermediate bits are rotated one bit to the right.

The number of bit positions rotated may be specified either as the literal 1 or by the value in CL (not CX!). It is generally faster to perform sequential rotate-by-1 instructions for rotations of up to about 4 bits, and faster to use rotate-by-CL instructions for longer rotations. Note that while CL may contain any value up to 255, it is meaningless to rotate by any value larger than 17, *even though the rotations are actually performed—wasting cycles—on the 8088.*

Bit 0 of the operand is not only copied to the leftmost bit, but is also copied into CF by each rotation. OF is modified predictably *only* by the rotate-by-1 forms of **ror;** after rotate-by-CL forms, OF becomes undefined.

reg8 = AL AH BL BH CL CH DL DH
[*mem8*] = 8-bit memory data
immed8 = 8-bit immediate data
sext-immed = 8-bit sign-extendable value
disp8 = 8-bit branch displacement
disp16 = 16-bit branch displacement
segment:offset = 32-bit segment:offset address

reg16 = AX BX CX DX BP SP SI DI
[*mem16*] = 16-bit memory data
immed16 = 16-bit immediate data
segreg = CS DS SS ES
[*mem32*] = 32-bit memory data
[*mem*] = memory data of any size

SAHF   Store AH to 8080 Flags

Flags Affected

O D I T S Z A P C			
F F F F F F F F F	OF: Overflow flag	TF: Trap flag	AF: Aux carry
* * * * *	DF: Direction flag	SF: Sign flag	PF: Parity flag
	IF: Interrupt flag	ZF: Zero flag	CF: Carry flag

Instruction Forms

	Cycles	Bytes	
sahf	4	1	sahf

Notes

The **sahf** instruction copies AH to the lower byte of the flags register. This reverses the action of **lahf** and is intended to allow the 8088 to emulate the **pop psw** instruction of the 8080; however, it can also be used to restore five of the 8088's flags—SF, ZF, AF, PF, and CF—quickly and without involving the stack. Note that OF is *not* affected.

reg8 = AL AH BL BH CL CH DL DH	*reg16* = AX BX CX DX BP SP SI DI
[*mem8*] = 8-bit memory data	[*mem16*] = 16-bit memory data
immed8 = 8-bit immediate data	*immed16* = 16-bit immediate data
sext-immed = 8-bit sign-extendable value	*segreg* = CS DS SS ES
disp8 = 8-bit branch displacement	[*mem32*] = 32-bit memory data
disp16 = 16-bit branch displacement	[*mem*] = memory data of any size
segment:offset = 32-bit segment:offset address	

SAR   Shift Arithmetic Right

Flags Affected

O D I T S Z A P C			
F F F F F F F F F	OF: Overflow flag	TF: Trap flag	AF: Aux carry
* * * * * *	DF: Direction flag	SF: Sign flag	PF: Parity flag
	IF: Interrupt flag	ZF: Zero flag	CF: Carry flag

Instruction Forms

	Cycles	Bytes	
sar *reg8*,1	2	2	sar bh,1
sar [*mem8*],1	15+EA	2 to 4	sar [ByteVar],1
sar *reg16*,1	2	2	sar dx,1
sar [*mem16*],1	23+EA	2 to 4	sar word ptr [bx+1],1
sar *reg8*,cl	8+(4*CL)	2	sar ch,cl
sar [*mem8*],cl	20+EA+(4*CL)	2 to 4	sar byte ptr [bx],cl
sar *reg16*,cl	8+(4*CL)	2	sar ax,cl
sar [*mem16*],cl	28+EA+(4*CL)	2 to 4	sar [WordVar],cl

Notes

The **sar** instruction shifts all bits within the destination operand to the right, where right is toward the least significant bit, bit 0. The number of bit positions shifted may be specified either as the literal 1 or by the value in CL (not CX!). It is generally faster to perform sequential shift-by-1 instructions for shifts of up to about 4 bits, and faster to use shift-by-CL instructions for longer shifts. Note that while CL may contain any value up to 255, it is meaningless to shift by any value larger than 17, *even though the shifts are actually performed—wasting cycles—on the 8088.*

The rightmost bit of the operand is shifted into CF by each shift; *the leftmost bit is left unchanged.* This preservation of the most significant bit, which is the difference between **sar** and **shr,** maintains the sign of the operand. AF becomes undefined after this instruction. OF is modified predictably *only* by the shift-by-one form of **sar;** after shift-by-CL forms, OF becomes undefined.

reg8 = AL AH BL BH CL CH DL DH	*reg16* = AX BX CX DX BP SP SI DI
[*mem8*] = 8-bit memory data	[*mem16*] = 16-bit memory data
immed8 = 8-bit immediate data	*immed16* = 16-bit immediate data
sext-immed = 8-bit sign-extendable value	*segreg* = CS DS SS ES
disp8 = 8-bit branch displacement	[*mem32*] = 32-bit memory data
disp16 = 16-bit branch displacement	[*mem*] = memory data of any size
segment:offset = 32-bit segment:offset address	

SBB   Arithmetic Subtract with Borrow

Flags Affected

O D I T S Z A P C		
F F F F F F F F F	OF: Overflow flag	TF: Trap flag AF: Aux carry
* * * * *	DF: Direction flag	SF: Sign flag PF: Parity flag
	IF: Interrupt flag	ZF: Zero flag CF: Carry flag

Instruction Forms

	Cycles	Bytes	
sbb *reg8,reg8*	3	2	sbb ah,dh
sbb [*mem8*],*reg8*	16+EA	2 to 4	sbb [ByteVar],al
sbb *reg8,*[*mem8*]	9+EA	2 to 4	sbb al,[si+bp+18h]
sbb *reg16,reg16*	3	2	sbb bx,cx
sbb [*mem16*],*reg16*	24+EA	2 to 4	sbb [WordVar+2],ax
sbb *reg16,*[*mem16*]	13+EA	2 to 4	sbb dx,[si]
sbb *reg8,immed8*	4	3	sbb cl,0
sbb [*mem8*],*immed8*	17+EA	3 to 5	sbb [ByteVar],20h
sbb *reg16,sext-immed*	4	3	sbb dx,40h
sbb *reg16,immed16*	4	4	sbb dx,8000h
sbb [*mem16*],*sext-immed*	25+EA	3 to 5	sbb word ptr [bx],1
sbb [*mem16*],*immed16*	25+EA	4 to 6	sbb word ptr [bx],1000h
sbb al,*immed8*	4	2	sbb al,10
sbb ax,*immed8*	4	3	sbb ax,−1

Notes

The **sbb** instruction performs a subtraction with borrow, where the source is subtracted from the destination, and then CF is subtracted from the result. The result replaces the destination. If the result is negative, CF is set, indicating a borrow. To subtract without taking CF into account (i.e., without borrowing) use the **sub** instruction.

reg8 = AL AH BL BH CL CH DL DH	*reg16* = AX BX CX DX BP SP SI DI
[*mem8*] = 8-bit memory data	[*mem16*] = 16-bit memory data
immed8 = 8-bit immediate data	*immed16* = 16-bit immediate data
sext-immed = 8-bit sign-extendable value	*segreg* = CS DS SS ES
disp8 = 8-bit branch displacement	[*mem32*] = 32-bit memory data
disp16 = 16-bit branch displacement	[*mem*] = memory data of any size
segment:offset = 32-bit segment:offset address	

SCAS   Scan String

Flags Affected

```
O D I  T S Z A P C       OF:  Overflow flag   TF:  Trap flag    AF:  Aux carry
F F F  F F F F F F F      DF:  Direction flag  SF:  Sign flag    PF:  Parity flag
*        * * * * *        IF:  Interrupt flag  ZF:  Zero flag    CF:  Carry flag
```

Instruction Forms

	Cycles	Bytes	
scasb	15	1	scasb
repz scasb	9+(15*CX)	2	repz scasb
repnz scasb	9+(15*CX)	2	repnz scasb
scasw	19	1	scasw
repz scasw	9+(19*CX)	2	repz scasw
repnz scasw	9+(19*CX)	2	repnz scasw

Notes

The **scas** instruction compares either AL (**scasb**) or AX (**scasw**) to the location pointed to by ES:DI, adjusting DI after the operation, as described below. ES must be the segment of the source and cannot be overridden. Similarly, DI must always be the source offset. The comparison is performed via a trial subtraction of the location pointed to by ES:DI from AL or AX; just as with **cmp,** this trial subtraction alters only the flags, not AL/AX or the location pointed to by ES:DI.

By placing an instruction repeat count in CX and preceding **scasb** or **scasw** with the **repz** or **repnz** prefix, it is possible to execute a single **scas** up to 65,535 (0FFFFh) times, just as if that many **scas** instructions had been executed, but without the need for any additional instruction fetching. Repeated **scas** instructions end either when CX counts down to 0 or when the state of ZF specified by **repz/repnz** ceases to be true. ZF should be used to determine whether a match-nonmatch was found after **repz scas** or **repnz scas** ends.

Note that if CX is 0 when **repz scas** or **repnz scas** is started, 0 repetitions of **scas**—not 65,536 repetitions—are performed. After each **scas,** DI is adjusted (as described in the next paragraph) by either 1 (for **scasb**) or 2 (for **scasw**), and, if the **repz** or **repnz** prefix is being used, CX is decremented by 1.

Adjusting DI means incrementing DI if DF is cleared (0) or decrementing DI if DF is set (1).

reg8 = AL AH BL BH CL CH DL DH
[*mem8*] = 8-bit memory data
immed8 = 8-bit immediate data
sext-immed = 8-bit sign-extendable value
disp8 = 8-bit branch displacement
disp16 = 16-bit branch displacement
segment:offset = 32-bit segment:offset address

reg16 = AX BX CX DX BP SP SI DI
[*mem16*] = 16-bit memory data
immed16 = 16-bit immediate data
segreg = CS DS SS ES
[*mem32*] = 32-bit memory data
[*mem*] = memory data of any size

SHL   Shift Logical Left
SAL   Shift Arithmetic Left

Flags Affected

O D I T S Z A P C	OF:	Overflow flag	TF:	Trap flag	AF:	Aux carry
F F F F F F F F F	DF:	Direction flag	SF:	Sign flag	PF:	Parity flag
* * * * * *	IF:	Interrupt flag	ZF:	Zero flag	CF:	Carry flag

Instruction Forms

	Cycles	*Bytes*	
shl *reg8*,1	2	2	shl dl,1
shl [*mem8*],1	15+EA	2 to 4	shl byte ptr [bx+si],1
shl *reg16*,1	2	2	shl cx,1
shl [*mem16*],1	23+EA	2 to 4	shl word ptr [di],1
shl *reg8*,cl	8+(4*CL)	2	shl al,cl
shl [*mem8*],cl	20+EA+(4*CL)	2 to 4	shl [ByteVar],cl
shl *reg16*,cl	8+(4*CL)	2	shl bp,cl
shl [*mem16*],cl	28+EA+(4*CL)	2 to 4	shl [WordVar+1],cl

Notes

The **shl** instruction (also known as **sal;** the two mnemonics refer to the same instruction) shifts the bits within the destination operand to the left, where left is toward the most significant bit, bit 15 for word operands and bit 7 for byte operands. The number of bit positions shifted may be specified either as the literal 1 or by the value in CL (not CX!). It is generally faster to perform sequential shift-by-1 instructions for shifts of up to about 4 bits, and faster to use shift-by-CL instructions for longer shifts. Note that while CL may contain any value up to 255, it is meaningless to shift by any value larger than 17, *even though the shifts are actually performed—wasting cycles—on the 8088.*

The leftmost bit of the operand is shifted into CF; the rightmost bit is cleared to 0. AF becomes undefined after this instruction. OF is modified predictably *only* by the shift-by-1 forms of **shl;** after shift-by-CL forms, OF becomes undefined.

reg8 = AL AH BL BH CL CH DL DH	*reg16* = AX BX CX DX BP SP SI DI
[*mem8*] = 8-bit memory data	[*mem16*] = 16-bit memory data
immed8 = 8-bit immediate data	*immed16* = 16-bit immediate data
sext-immed = 8-bit sign-extendable value	*segreg* = CS DS SS ES
disp8 = 8-bit branch displacement	[*mem32*] = 32-bit memory data
disp16 = 16-bit branch displacement	[*mem*] = memory data of any size
segment:offset = 32-bit segment:offset address	

SHR   Shift Logical Right

Flags Affected

O	D	I	T	S	Z	A	P	C			
F	F	F	F	F	F	F	F	F	OF: Overflow flag	TF: Trap flag	AF: Aux carry
*				*	*	*	*	*	DF: Direction flag	SF: Sign flag	PF: Parity flag
									IF: Interrupt flag	ZF: Zero flag	CF: Carry flag

Instruction Forms

	Cycles	*Bytes*	
shr *reg8*,1	2	2	shr al,1
shr [*mem8*],1	15+EA	2 to 4	shr [ByteVar],1
shr *reg16*,1	2	2	shr bx,1
shr [*mem16*],1	23+EA	2 to 4	shr word ptr [si],1
shr *reg8*,cl	8+(4*CL)	2	shr dl,cl
shr [*mem8*],cl	20+EA+(4*CL)	2 to 4	shr [ByteVar+bx],cl
shr *reg16*,cl	8+(4*CL)	2	shr si,cl
shr [*mem16*],cl	28+EA+(4*CL)	2 to 4	shr [WordVar+si],cl

Notes

The **shr** instruction shifts the bits within the destination operand to the right, where right is toward the least significant bit, bit 0. The number of bit positions shifted may be specified either as the literal 1 or by the value in CL (not CX!). It is generally faster to perform sequential shift-by-1 instructions for shifts of up to about 4 bits and faster to use shift-by-CL instructions for longer shifts. Note that while CL may contain any value up to 255, it is meaningless to shift by any value larger than 17, *even though the shifts are actually performed—wasting cycles—on the 8088.*

The rightmost bit of the operand is shifted into CF; the leftmost bit is cleared to 0. AF becomes undefined after this instruction. OF is modified predictably *only* by the shift-by-1 forms of **shr;** after shift-by-CL forms, OF becomes undefined.

reg8 = AL AH BL BH CL CH DL DH	*reg16* = AX BX CX DX BP SP SI DI
[*mem8*] = 8-bit memory data	[*mem16*] = 16-bit memory data
immed8 = 8-bit immediate data	*immed16* = 16-bit immediate data
sext-immed = 8-bit sign-extendable value	*segreg* = CS DS SS ES
disp8 = 8-bit branch displacement	[*mem32*] = 32-bit memory data
disp16 = 16-bit branch displacement	[*mem*] = memory data of any size
segment:offset = 32-bit segment:offset address	

STC   Set Carry Flag

Flags Affected

 O D I T S Z A P C
F F F F F F F F F
                *

OF: Overflow flag   TF: Trap flag   AF: Aux carry
DF: Direction flag   SF: Sign flag   PF: Parity flag
IF: Interrupt flag   ZF: Zero flag   CF: Carry flag

Instruction Forms

	Cycles	*Bytes*	
stc	2	1	stc

Notes

This instruction sets CF to 1. It can be useful for returning a status in CF from a subroutine or for presetting CF before **adc, sbb,** or a conditional jump that tests CF, such as **jc.**

reg8 = AL AH BL BH CL CH DL DH
[*mem8*] = 8-bit memory data
immed8 = 8-bit immediate data
sext-immed = 8-bit sign-extendable value
disp8 = 8-bit branch displacement
disp16 = 16-bit branch displacement
segment:offset = 32-bit segment:offset address

reg16 = AX BX CX DX BP SP SI DI
[*mem16*] = 16-bit memory data
immed16 = 16-bit immediate data
segreg = CS DS SS ES
[*mem32*] = 32-bit memory data
[*mem*] = memory data of any size

STD   Set Direction Flag

Flags Affected

```
O D I T S Z A P C        OF: Overflow flag   TF: Trap flag    AF: Aux carry
F F F F F F F F F         DF: Direction flag  SF: Sign flag    PF: Parity flag
        *                IF:  Interrupt flag  ZF: Zero flag    CF: Carry flag
```

Instruction Forms

	Cycles	*Bytes*	
std	2	1	std

Notes

The **std** instruction sets DF to the set (1) state. This affects the pointer register adjustments performed after each memory access by the string instructions **lods, stos, scas, movs,** and **cmps.** When DF=0, pointer registers (SI and/or DI) are incremented by 1 or 2; when DF=1, pointer registers are decremented by 1 or 2. DF is set to 0 by **cld.**

reg8 = AL AH BL BH CL CH DL DH
[*mem8*] = 8-bit memory data
immed8 = 8-bit immediate data
sext-immed = 8-bit sign-extendable value
disp8 = 8-bit branch displacement
disp16 = 16-bit branch displacement
segment:offset = 32-bit segment:offset address

reg16 = AX BX CX DX BP SP SI DI
[*mem16*] = 16-bit memory data
immed16 = 16-bit immediate data
segreg = CS DS SS ES
[*mem32*] = 32-bit memory data
[*mem*] = memory data of any size

STI   Set Interrupt Flag

Flags Affected

```
O D I  T S Z A P C
F F F  F F F F F F
     *
```

OF: Overflow flag   TF: Trap flag   AF: Aux carry
DF: Direction flag SF: Sign flag   PF: Parity flag
IF: Interrupt flag ZF: Zero flag   CF: Carry flag

Instruction Forms

	Cycles	*Bytes*	
sti	2	1	sti

Notes

The **sti** instruction sets IF to the set (1) state, allowing maskable hardware interrupts (IRQ0 through IRQ7) to occur. (Software interrupts via **int** are not affected by the state of IF.) Both **cli** and **int** clear IF to 0, disabling maskable hardware interrupts.

reg8 = AL AH BL BH CL CH DL DH
[*mem8*] = 8-bit memory data
immed8 = 8-bit immediate data
sext-immed = 8-bit sign-extendable value
disp8 = 8-bit branch displacement
disp16 = 16-bit branch displacement
segment:offset = 32-bit segment:offset address

reg16 = AX BX CX DX BP SP SI DI
[*mem16*] = 16-bit memory data
immed16 = 16-bit immediate data
segreg = CS DS SS ES
[*mem32*] = 32-bit memory data
[*mem*] = memory data of any size

STOS   Store String

Flags Affected

O D I T S Z A P C		
F F F F F F F F F	OF: Overflow flag	TF: Trap flag	AF: Aux carry
<none>	DF: Direction flag	SF: Sign flag	PF: Parity flag
	IF: Interrupt flag	ZF: Zero flag	CF: Carry flag

Instruction Forms

	Cycles	*Bytes*	
stosb	11	1	stosb
rep stosb	9+(10*CX)	2	rep stosb
stosw	15	1	stosw
rep stosw	9+(14*CX)	2	rep stosw

Notes

The **stos** instruction stores either AL (**stosb**) or AX (**stosw**) to the location pointed to by ES:DI, adjusting DI after the operation, as described below. ES must be the segment of the destination and cannot be overridden. Similarly, DI must always be the destination offset.

By placing an instruction repeat count in CX and preceding **stosb** or **stosw** with the **rep** prefix, it is possible to execute a single **stos** up to 65,535 (0FFFFh) times, just as if that many **stos** instructions had been executed, but without the need for any additional instruction fetching. Note that if CX is 0 when **rep stos** is started, 0 repetitions of **stos**—not 65,536 repetitions—are performed. After each **stos,** DI is adjusted (as described in the next paragraph) by either 1 (for **stosb**) or 2 (for **stosw**), and, if the **rep** prefix is being used, CX is decremented by 1.

"Adjusting" DI means incrementing DI if DF is cleared (0) or decrementing DI if DF is set (1).

reg8 = AL AH BL BH CL CH DL DH	*reg16* = AX BX CX DX BP SP SI DI
[*mem8*] = 8-bit memory data	[*mem16*] = 16-bit memory data
immed8 = 8-bit immediate data	*immed16* = 16-bit immediate data
sext-immed = 8-bit sign-extendable value	*segreg* = CS DS SS ES
disp8 = 8-bit branch displacement	[*mem32*] = 32-bit memory data
disp16 = 16-bit branch displacement	[*mem*] = memory data of any size
segment:offset = 32-bit segment:offset address	

SUB   Arithmetic Subtraction (No Borrow)

Flags Affected

O D I T S Z A P C	OF: Overflow flag	TF: Trap flag	AF: Aux carry
F F F F F F F F F	DF: Direction flag	SF: Sign flag	PF: Parity flag
* * * * * *	IF: Interrupt flag	ZF: Zero flag	CF: Carry flag

Instruction Forms

	Cycles	Bytes	
sub *reg8,reg8*	3	2	sub al,dl
sub [*mem8*],*reg8*	16+EA	2 to 4	sub [ByteVar],ah
sub *reg8,*[*mem8*]	9+EA	2 to 4	sub dl,[si+1]
sub *reg16,reg16*	3	2	sub ax,dx
sub [*mem16*], *reg16*	24+EA	2 to 4	sub [WordVar],ax
sub *reg16,*[*mem16*]	13+EA	2 to 4	sub cx,[di+bp]
sub *reg8,immed8*	4	3	sub dl,10h
sub [*mem8*], *immed8*	17+EA	3 to 5	sub [ByteVar],01h
sub *reg16, sext-immed*	4	3	sub dx,−1
sub *reg16,immed16*	4	4	sub dx,80h
sub [*mem16*], *sext-immed*	25+EA	3 to 5	sub word ptr [bp], 10h
sub [*mem16*], *immed16*	25+EA	4 to 6	sub word ptr [bp], 100h
sub al,*immed8*	4	2	sub al,20h
sub ax,*immed16*	4	3	sub ax,100h

Notes

The **sub** instruction performs a subtraction without borrow, where the source is subtracted from the destination; the result replaces the destination. If the result is negative, CF is set, indicating a borrow. Multiple-precision subtraction can be performed by following **sub** with **sbb**—subtract with borrow—which takes CF into account as a borrow.

reg8 = AL AH BL BH CL CH DL DH	*reg16* = AX BX CX DX BP SP SI DI
[*mem8*] = 8-bit memory data	[*mem16*] = 16-bit memory data
immed8 = 8-bit immediate data	*immed16* = 16-bit immediate data
sext-immed = 8-bit sign-extendable value	*segreg* = CS DS SS ES
disp8 = 8-bit branch displacement	[*mem32*] = 32-bit memory data
disp16 = 16-bit branch displacement	[*mem*] = memory data of any size
segment:offset = 32-bit segment:offset address	

TEST   Compare by Anding without Saving Result

Flags Affected

O D I	T S Z A P C			
F F F	F F F F F F	OF: Overflow flag	TF: Trap flag	AF: Aux carry
*	* * * * *	DF: Direction flag	SF: Sign flag	PF: Parity flag
		IF: Interrupt flag	ZF: Zero flag	CF: Carry flag

Instruction Forms

	Cycles	*Bytes*	
test *reg8,reg8*	3	2	test dl,bl
test [*mem8*],*reg8*	9+EA	2 to 4	test [si],al
test *reg8,*[*mem8*]	9+EA	2 to 4	test dh,[bx]
test *reg16,reg16*	3	2	test si,cx
test [*mem16*],*reg16*	13+EA	2 to 4	test [WordVar],dx
test *reg16,*[*mem16*]	13+EA	2 to 4	test ax,[bx−2]
test *reg8,immed8*	5	3	test bh,040h
test [*mem8*],*immed8*	11+EA	3 to 5	test byte ptr [di],44h
test *reg16,immed16*	5	4	test bx,08080h
test [*mem16*], *immed16*	15+EA	4 to 6	test word ptr [bp], 0101h
test al,*immed8*	4	2	test al,0f7h
test ax,*immed16*	4	3	test ax,09001h

Notes

This instruction performs the logical operation **and** on its two operands, but does not store the result. The **and** operation is performed on a bit-by-bit basis, such that bit 0 of the source is **and**ed with bit 0 of the destination, bit 1 of the source is **and**ed with bit 1 of the destination, and so on. The **and** operation yields a 1 if *both* of the operands are 1, and a 0 if *either* operand is 0. Note that **test** makes AF undefined. CF and OF are cleared to 0, and the other affected flags are set according to the operation's results. Note also that the ordering of the operands doesn't matter; **test al,[bx]** and **test [bx],al** function identically.

Unlike **and, test** cannot store sign-extendable 16-bit values as bytes and sign extend them to words at execution time.

reg8 = AL AH BL BH CL CH DL DH	*reg16* = AX BX CX DX BP SP SI DI
[*mem8*] = 8-bit memory data	[*mem16*] = 16-bit memory data
immed8 = 8-bit immediate data	*immed16* = 16-bit immediate data
sext-immed = 8-bit sign-extendable value	*segreg* = CS DS SS ES
disp8 = 8-bit branch displacement	[*mem32*] = 32-bit memory data
disp16 = 16-bit branch displacement	[*mem*] = memory data of any size
segment:offset = 32-bit segment:offset address	

WAIT   Wait for Interrupt or Test Signal

Flags Affected

```
O D I  T S Z A P C       OF: Overflow flag   TF: Trap flag   AF: Aux carry
F F F F F F F F F         DF: Direction flag  SF: Sign flag   PF: Parity flag
     <none>              IF:  Interrupt flag  ZF: Zero flag   CF: Carry flag
```

Instruction Forms

	Cycles	*Bytes*	
wait	3	1	wait

Notes

This instruction stops the 8088 until either a hardware interrupt occurs or the signal on the 8088's TEST pin becomes true. It is often used for synchronization with coprocessors, notably the 8087, to make sure that the coprocessor has finished its current instruction before starting another coprocessor instruction or to make sure that memory variables aren't accessed out of sequence by different processors. Note that when a hardware interrupt occurs during **wait,** the **iret** that ends that interrupt returns to the **wait** instruction, not the following instruction. Also note that 3 is the minimum number of cycles that **wait** can take, in the case where the signal on the TEST pin is already true; the actual number of cycles can be much higher, depending on the coprocessor.

This instruction is also known as **fwait.**

reg8 = AL AH BL BH CL CH DL DH
[*mem8*] = 8-bit memory data
immed8 = 8-bit immediate data
sext-immed = 8-bit sign-extendable value
disp8 = 8-bit branch displacement
disp16 = 16-bit branch displacement
segment:offset = 32-bit segment:offset address

reg16 = AX BX CX DX BP SP SI DI
[*mem16*] = 16-bit memory data
immed16 = 16-bit immediate data
segreg = CS DS SS ES
[*mem32*] = 32-bit memory data
[*mem*] = memory data of any size

XCHG   Exchange Operands

Flags Affected

```
O D I T S Z A P C        OF: Overflow flag   TF: Trap flag    AF: Aux carry
F F F F F F F F F         DF: Direction flag  SF: Sign flag    PF: Parity flag
      <none>             IF: Interrupt flag  ZF: Zero flag    CF: Carry flag
```

Instruction Forms

	Cycles	Bytes	
xchg *reg8,reg8*	4	2	xchg al,ah
xchg [*mem8*],*reg8*	17+EA	2 to 4	xchg [ByteVar],dl
xchg *reg8,*[*mem8*]	17+EA	2 to 4	xchg dh,[ByteVar]
xchg *reg16,reg16*	4	2	xchg dx,bx
xchg [*mem16*],*reg16*	25+EA	2 to 4	xchg [bx],cx
xchg *reg16,*[*mem16*]	25+EA	2 to 4	xchg ax,[bx]
xchg ax,*reg16*	3	1	xchg ax,bx

Notes

The **xchg** instruction exchanges the contents of its two operands. Note that the ordering of the operands doesn't matter; **xchg al,ah** and **xchg ah,al** function identically.

reg8 = AL AH BL BH CL CH DL DH
[*mem8*] = 8-bit memory data
immed8 = 8-bit immediate data
sext-immed = 8-bit sign-extendable value
disp8 = 8-bit branch displacement
disp16 = 16-bit branch displacement
segment:offset = 32-bit segment:offset address

reg16 = AX BX CX DX BP SP SI DI
[*mem16*] = 16-bit memory data
immed16 = 16-bit immediate data
segreg = CS DS SS ES
[*mem32*] = 32-bit memory data
[*mem*] = memory data of any size

XLAT   Translate from Table

Flags Affected

O D I T S Z A P C	OF: Overflow flag	TF: Trap flag	AF: Aux carry
F F F F F F F F F	DF: Direction flag	SF: Sign flag	PF: Parity flag
<none>	IF: Interrupt flag	ZF: Zero flag	CF: Carry flag

Instruction Forms

	Cycles	*Bytes*	
xlat	11	1	xlat

Notes

This instruction loads into AL the byte of memory addressed by the sum of BX and AL. It defaults to accessing the segment pointed to by DS, but this can be overridden with a segment override prefix.

Also known as **xlatb**.

reg8 = AL AH BL BH CL CH DL DH
[*mem8*] = 8-bit memory data
immed8 = 8-bit immediate data
sext-immed = 8-bit sign-extendable value
disp8 = 8-bit branch displacement
disp16 = 16-bit branch displacement
segment:offset = 32-bit segment:offset address

reg16 = AX BX CX DX BP SP SI DI
[*mem16*] = 16-bit memory data
immed16 = 16-bit immediate data
segreg = CS DS SS ES
[*mem32*] = 32-bit memory data
[*mem*] = memory data of any size

XOR   Exclusive or

Flags Affected

O D I T S Z A P C			
F F F F F F F F F	OF: Overflow flag	TF: Trap flag	AF: Aux carry
* * * * *	DF: Direction flag	SF: Sign flag	PF: Parity flag
	IF: Interrupt flag	ZF: Zero flag	CF: Carry flag

Instruction Forms

	Cycles	Bytes	
xor reg8,reg8	3	2	xor dh,dl
xor [mem8],reg8	16+EA	2 to 4	xor [ByteVar],bh
xor reg8,[mem8]	9+EA	2 to 4	xor al,[si]
xor reg16,reg16	3	2	xor ax,ax
xor [mem16],reg16	24+EA	2 to 4	xor [WordVar+1],bp
xor reg16,[mem16]	13+EA	2 to 4	xor si,[di]
xor reg8,immed8	4	3	xor ad,1
xor [mem8],immed8	17+EA	3 to 5	xor [ByteVar],11h
xor reg16,sext-immed	4	3	xor bx,−1
xor reg16,immed16	4	4	xor bx,2222h
xor [mem16], sext-immed	25+EA	3 to 5	xor word ptr [bx], 17h
xor [mem16], immed16	25+EA	4 to 6	xor word ptr [bx], 100h
xor al,immed8	4	2	xor al,33h
xor ax,immed16	4	3	xor ax,0cccch

Notes

The **xor** instruction performs an exclusive-**or** logical operation between its two operands. Once the operation is complete, the result replaces the destination operand. This instruction is performed on a bit-by-bit basis, such that bit 0 of the source is **xor**ed with bit 0 of the destination, bit 1 of the source is **xor**ed with bit 1 of the destination, and so on. The **xor** operation yields a 1 if the operands are different and a 0 if the operands are the same. Note that **xor** makes AF undefined. CF and OF are cleared to 0, and the other affected flags are set according to the operation's results.

reg8 = AL AH BL BH CL CH DL DH	reg16 = AX BX CX DX BP SP SI DI
[mem8] = 8-bit memory data	[mem16] = 16-bit memory data
immed8 = 8-bit immediate data	immed16 = 16-bit immediate data
sext-immed = 8-bit sign-extendable value	segreg = CS DS SS ES
disp8 = 8-bit branch displacement	[mem32] = 32-bit memory data
disp16 = 16-bit branch displacement	[mem] = memory data of any size
segment:offset = 32-bit segment:offset address	

Appendix B

The Extended ASCII Code and Symbol Set

Dec	Hex	Binary	Symbol		Dec	Hex	Binary	Symbol
0	00	00000000			32	20	00100000	
1	01	00000001	☺		33	21	00100001	!
2	02	00000010	●		34	22	00100010	"
3	03	00000011	♥		35	23	00100011	#
4	04	00000100	♦		36	24	00100100	$
5	05	00000101	♣		37	25	00100101	%
6	06	00000110	♠		38	26	00100110	&
7	07	00000111	•		39	27	00100111	'
8	08	00001000	◘		40	28	00101000	(
9	09	00001001	○		41	29	00101001	)
10	0A	00001010	◙		42	2A	00101010	*
11	0B	00001011	♂		43	2B	00101011	+
12	0C	00001100	♀		44	2C	00101100	,
13	0D	00001101	♪		45	2D	00101101	–
14	0E	00001110	♫		46	2E	00101110	.
15	0F	00001111	☼		47	2F	00101111	/
16	10	00010000	►		48	30	00110000	0
17	11	00010001	◄		49	31	00110001	1
18	12	00010010	↕		50	32	00110010	2
19	13	00010011	‼		51	33	00110011	3
20	14	00010100	¶		52	34	00110100	4
21	15	00010101	§		53	35	00110101	5
22	16	00010110	▬		54	36	00110110	6
23	17	00010111	↨		55	37	00110111	7
24	18	00011000	↑		56	38	00111000	8
25	19	00011001	↓		57	39	00111001	9
26	1A	00011010	→		58	3A	00111010	:
27	1B	00011011	←		59	3B	00111011	;
28	1C	00011100	∟		60	3C	00111100	<
29	1D	00011101	↔		61	3D	00111101	=
30	1E	00011110	▲		62	3E	00111110	>
31	1F	00011111	▼		63	3F	00111111	?

Dec	Hex	Binary	Symbol		Dec	Hex	Binary	Symbol
64	40	01000000	@		106	6A	01101010	j
65	41	01000001	A		107	6B	01101011	k
66	42	01000010	B		108	6C	01101100	l
67	43	01000011	C		109	6D	01101101	m
68	44	01000100	D		110	6E	01101110	n
69	45	01000101	E		111	6F	01101111	o
70	46	01000110	F		112	70	01110000	p
71	47	01000111	G		113	71	01110001	q
72	48	01001000	H		114	72	01110010	r
73	49	01001001	I		115	73	01110011	s
74	4A	01001010	J		116	74	01110100	t
75	4B	01001011	K		117	75	01110101	u
76	4C	01001100	L		118	76	01110110	v
77	4D	01001101	M		119	77	01110111	w
78	4E	01001110	N		120	78	01111000	x
79	4F	01001111	O		121	79	01111001	y
80	50	01010000	P		122	7A	01111010	z
81	51	01010001	Q		123	7B	01111011	{
82	52	01010010	R		124	7C	01111100		
83	53	01010011	S		125	7D	01111101	}
84	54	01010100	T		126	7E	01111110	~
85	55	01010101	U		127	7F	01111111	▓
86	56	01010110	V		128	80	10000000	Ç
87	57	01010111	W		129	81	10000001	ü
88	58	01011000	X		130	82	10000010	é
89	59	01011001	Y		131	83	10000011	â
90	5A	01011010	Z		132	84	10000100	ä
91	5B	01011011	[		133	85	10000101	à
92	5C	01011100	\		134	86	10000110	å
93	5D	01011101	]		135	87	10000111	ç
94	5E	01011110	^		136	88	10001000	ê
95	5F	01011111			137	89	10001001	ë
96	60	01100000	`		138	8A	10001010	è
97	61	01100001	a		139	8B	10001011	ï
98	62	01100010	b		140	8C	10001100	î
99	63	01100011	c		141	8D	10001101	ì
100	64	01100100	d		142	8E	10001110	Ä
101	65	01100101	e		143	8F	10001111	Å
102	66	01100110	f		144	90	10010000	É
103	67	01100111	g		145	91	10010001	æ
104	68	01101000	h		146	92	10010010	Æ
105	69	01101001	i		147	93	10010011	ô

Dec	Hex	Binary	Symbol	Dec	Hex	Binary	Symbol
148	94	10010100	ö	190	BE	10111110	⅃
149	95	10010101	ò	191	BF	10111111	┐
150	96	10010110	û	192	C0	11000000	└
151	97	10010111	ù	193	C1	11000001	┴
152	98	10011000	ÿ	194	C2	11000010	┬
153	99	10011001	Ö	195	C3	11000011	├
154	9A	10011010	Ü	196	C4	11000100	─
155	9B	10011011	¢	197	C5	11000101	┼
156	9C	10011100	£	198	C6	11000110	╟
157	9D	10011101	¥	199	C7	11000111	╠
158	9E	10011110	₧	200	C8	11001000	╚
159	9F	10011111	ƒ	201	C9	11001001	╔
160	A0	10100000	á	202	CA	11001010	╩
161	A1	10100001	í	203	CB	11001011	╦
162	A2	10100010	ó	204	CC	11001100	╠
163	A3	10100011	ú	205	CD	11001101	═
164	A4	10100100	ñ	206	CE	11001110	╬
165	A5	10100101	Ñ	207	CF	11001111	╧
166	A6	10100110	ª	208	D0	11010000	╨
167	A7	10100111	º	209	D1	11010001	╤
168	A8	10101000	¿	210	D2	11010010	╥
169	A9	10101001	⌐	211	D3	11010011	╙
170	AA	10101010	¬	212	D4	11010100	╘
171	AB	10101011	½	213	D5	11010101	╒
172	AC	10101100	¼	214	D6	11010110	╓
173	AD	10101101	¡	215	D7	11010111	╫
174	AE	10101110	«	216	D8	11011000	╪
175	AF	10101111	»	217	D9	11011001	┘
176	B0	10110000	░	218	DA	11011010	┌
177	B1	10110001	▒	219	DB	11011011	█
178	B2	10110010	▓	220	DC	11011100	▄
179	B3	10110011	│	221	DD	11011101	▌
180	B4	10110100	┤	222	DE	11011110	▐
181	B5	10110101	╡	223	DF	11011111	▀
182	B6	10110110	╢	224	E0	11100000	α
183	B7	10110111	╖	225	E1	11100001	β
184	B8	10111000	╕	226	E2	11100010	Γ
185	B9	10111001	╣	227	E3	11100011	π
186	BA	10111010	║	228	E4	11100100	Σ
187	BB	10111011	╗	229	E5	11100101	σ
188	BC	10111100	╝	230	E6	11100110	µ
189	BD	10111101	╜	231	E7	11100111	τ

Dec	Hex	Binary	Symbol	Dec	Hex	Binary	Symbol
232	E8	11101000	Φ	244	F4	11110100	∫
233	E9	11101001	θ	245	F5	11110101	∫
234	EA	11101010	Ω	246	F6	11110110	÷
235	EB	11101011	δ	247	F7	11110111	≈
236	EC	11101100	∞	248	F8	11111000	°
237	ED	11101101	φ	249	F9	11111001	•
238	EE	11101110	ε	250	FA	11111010	·
239	EF	11101111	∩	251	FB	11111011	√
240	F0	11110000	≡	252	FC	11111100	η
241	F1	11110001	±	253	FD	11111101	²
242	F2	11110010	≥	254	FE	11111110	•
243	F3	11110011	≤	255	FF	11111111	

Index

=, assembler directive, 260
68000, 269
68XXX, 697
80-column color text mode, 284
8-bit adapters, 263
8-bit bus cycle eater, 75–81, 83, 93, 110, 113, 128, 129, 699, 701, 704, 705
  interaction with DRAM refresh cycle eater, 115
  location, 78, 83
  penalty for word-sized accesses, 79, 80, 84, 110, 321, 376, 662
  penalty for word-sized accesses doubles when memory is destination, 321
  prefetch queue cycle eater as manifestation of, 83, 84
  what to do about, 80–83
  with multiple word-sized accesses, 79
8-bit data bus, 69, 71, 76, 78, 263, 525, 697
  address lines of, 117, 121
80186, 71, 698
80188, 71, 698
80286, 71, 142, 156, 160, 169, 184, 211, 263, 266, 306, 390, 537, 696–707, 709–722, 727
  bug in **popf**, 145, 721–723, 725–727
  handles pushing SP differently than 8088, 141
  imbalance between processing speed and memory speed, 72
80287, 728, 729
80386, 30, 63, 71, 108, 142, 156, 160, 169, 185, 211, 266, 269, 306, 390, 696–705, 707, 708, 711–718, 720, 721
  imbalance between processing speed and memory speed, 72
80386SX, 63, 71, 698, 699
80387, 728, 729
80486, 696
8080, 69, 71, 134, 155, 266–272, 285, 289, 290, 294, 295
8080 legacy, 266, 269
8080-specific instructions, 270
8085, 71, 266, 267
8086, 69, 71, 72, 76, 78–80, 263, 266, 390, 525, 616, 696–699, 731
8087, 291, 728–731
  can coprocess with the 8088, 730, 731
  ensuring synchronization with 8088, 730, 731

keep variables in data registers as much as possible, 729, 730
8088, 5, 6, 8, 11, 13, 14, 25, 26, 63, 65, 69–73, 75, 76, 78–80, 117, 118, 123, 169, 266–272, 274, 281, 289–291, 295, 297, 304–306, 309, 312, 316, 326, 332, 344, 346, 390, 396, 508, 509, 514, 517, 519, 524, 535, 560, 592, 616, 694, 696–701, 703–705, 708, 712–721, 727–731, 733
  16-bit processor that often performs like an 8-bit processor, 76
  16-bit processor with an 8-bit data bus, 133, 134
  architecture, 266, 267, 295
  bug in disabling of interrupts while loading segment registers, 144
  can address no more than four 64-Kb blocks at any one time, 134
  capable of addressing 1 Mb of memory, 133, 134, 152, 154–156, 160
  clock speed in PC is slow, 134
  compared to 8086, 69, 71, 72, 78, 80, 84
  data lines of, 117, 121
  derivation from 8086, 69, 72, 134
  display memory access, restricted, 102, 103
  effect on performance, 62
  externally an 8-bit processor, 67, 76, 78
  fairly low-performance processor that's hard to program, 134
  handles pushing SP differently than 80286, 141
  hodgepodge of a processor, 134
  influenced by 8080, 134
  instruction execution and memory access relatively slow, 134, 158, 346
  instruction set. *See* instruction set
  internal parallelism (internal coprocessing), 65–68, 85, 92, 119, 122, 124, 125
  internally a 16-bit processor, 67, 75–78, 83
  memory architecture, 152, 154–156, 167
  minimum memory access time, 82, 130
  mismatched internal and external bus sizes, 69, 71, 72, 76, 78, 80, 701
  programming interface, 63, 133
  register space is limited, 134
  resources, 133, 135
  rests on PC's hardware, 64, 65, 73
  sets tone for PC, 133

8088 (*continued*)
  speed of accessing the second byte of a word-sized
      operand, 82, 219, 384
  two processors in one, 65, 66
8237 DMA controller chip
  documentation, 52
  DRAM refresh, 95
8253 timer chip, 8, 14, 23, 24, 25, 28, 37
  accuracy, 30
  configuration in the PC, 24
  counting rate, 30
  counting resolution, 30
  documentation, 52
  in PS/2 computers, 36, 37
  interrupts, 25, 27
  latching a timer count, 28, 36
  mode 2, divide-by-*N* mode, 23, 25, 26
  mode 3, square wave mode, 25, 26
  modes, 25
  programmability, 23–26, 36
  stopping a timer, 25, 28, 36
8259 interrupt controller chip, 25
  configuration in the PC, 26
  documentation, 52
  edge triggering, 25, 26
  timer interrupt, 27
  aaa instruction, 139, 147, 333, 335, 339–342
  aad instruction, 139, 333, 335–337
  aam instruction, 139, 333, 335–337
  aas instruction, 139, 147, 333, 335, 339, 341, 342
accumulator, 138, 139, 267, 270, 275–277, 290, 298,
      302, 351, 359, 412, 436, 444
  and **in** and **out**, 138, 261
  multiplication and division, 138
  sign extension, 139, 312
  string instructions, 139

A

accumulator-specific, 278, 284
  AX-specific form of **xchg**. *See* **xchg**
  direct-addressing form of **mov**, 219, 231, 271–280,
      282, 298, 299, 302, 343, 344, 648, 670
  immediate-addressing form of **test**, 286
  immediate-addressing instructions, 231, 271, 281–
      283, 285, 342, 344
  instructions, 139, 270, 284, 285

adc instruction, 281–283, 309, 320, 343, 560, 563
add instruction, 147, 222, 281–283, 294, 305, 306,
      309, 320, 334, 342, 343, 643, 712
addressing modes. *See* memory addressing modes
AF (auxiliary carry flag), 144, 145, 147, 329, 330, 334,
      340–342, 354
AH register, 137, 138, 289–291, 294, 307, 312, 315,
      335, 341, 362, 440, 449
  not an accumulator, 138, 275, 276
AL register, 137, 138, 159, 261, 298, 301, 307, 312, 315,
      322, 334, 335, 337, 339, 341, 342, 343, 347, 351,
      352, 354, 355, 359, 405, 407, 440, 449
  8-bit accumulator, 138, 275–277
algorithms, 59, 131, 482, 734
and instruction, 146, 148, 229, 281–285, 301, 302, 320,
      335, 343, 561, 563, 643
animation, 109, 404, 489–492, 496–499, 504, 505, 594,
      596, 598, 668, 734
  block-move animation, 497–499, 504, 505, 596
  xor animation, 489–492, 496–499, 504, 505, 594
ANSI.SYS device driver, poor performance of, 61
Apple II, 135, 136, 497
Apple Macintosh, 697
application programs, 60, 63
arg directive, 244
arithmetic logic unit (ALU), 65, 66
arrays, comparing, 359, 371, 457, 458, 462, 482, 483,
      485
arrays, copying, 351, 404, 406, 407
arrays, searching, 354, 400, 430, 432, 433, 439, 454,
      471–473, 479, 482, 572, 601, 656
arrays, setting, 375, 376, 590, 602, 608
ASCII, 246, 335, 336, 338, 340, 672, 673
ASCII adjust, 333–335, 340, 341
ASCII arithmetic, 139, 147, 333, 339, 340
assembler code
  advantages of mixing with high level languages, 241
  and stack frames, 240–242
  no complete solution to writing, 114
  versus compiled code, 10, 174, 240
assembler programmer
  can think more flexibly than high level language,
      174, 400, 533
  knows exactly what code must do, 164, 166, 167
  knows more about what code must do than high
      level language, 174, 542
assembler programming, 560, 589
  high performance must be intuitive art, 131, 505,
      560, 589, 604, 649, 694

no hard and fast rules, 316, 560
science of, 113
assemblers, 645, 646, 693
and precalculation, 249, 251, 258, 260
manuals, importance of reading, 192
relationship to machine language, 7, 8
assembly language, 4–9, 13, 166, 589, 623, 624, 650, 731, 733
bad code, 10
complete control over segments, 163, 623, 624
difficulty of learning, 7, 8
excellent data-definition capabilities, 258, 260
framework, 11
good at handling multiple segments and larger than 64 KB blocks, 155, 163, 164, 167, 173, 179–181, 191
good code, 10
hardware, 8
high-performance programming, 64, 73, 110, 505, 510, 530, 531, 560, 589, 593, 597, 601–604, 611, 649
lack of transformation loss, 7
low-level control, 8
need for forethought and planning, 10
objectives of good programming, 9
objectives of high-performance programming, 9
optimization, 10
performance, 10
porting 8080 code, 267, 269, 270, 272
potential of, 5
produces best code, 10, 241
programmers, 8, 58
programmers and responsibility for code quality, 8
superior information and adaptability, 10
traditional programming model, 59, 60
versus high level languages, 10, 163, 164, 167, 173, 174, 191, 240, 246, 258, 400, 488, 533, 542, 560, 729, 730
when to use, 10
assume directive, 168, 196, 393
and segment override prefixes, 196, 197
assume nothing, 13, 250, 344
assuming and related problems, 13
automatic (dynamic) variables, 233, 240
AUX device driver for reporting timer results, 29
auxiliary carry flag. *See* AF
AX register, 137, 138, 261, 267, 275, 298, 307, 312, 314, 315, 335, 337, 339, 343, 347, 351, 352, 354, 355, 359, 405, 407, 449, 680

16-bit accumulator, 138
accessible as AH and AL, 138

B

barrel shifter of the 80386, 720
base addressing, 207, 209, 211, 213, 214, 218, 219, 221
base addressing component, 200, 202, 207
base+displacement, 214, 220, 255
base+index addressing, 213, 214, 255
base+index+displacement addressing, 200, 202, 207, 214, 718
based relative addressing, 206
BASIC, 166
BC register pair of 8080, 267
BCD arithmetic, 139, 147, 334, 335
beneath the programming interface, importance of understanding, 75, 701
best code, rarely such a beast, 174, 257
BH register, 137, 139
not used as memory-addressing register, 139
BIOS, 8, 25, 28, 35, 59–61, 75, 133, 152, 194, 363, 637, 653, 712, 722
adapter-select bits, 284
as an assembly language program, 61
documentation, 52
equipment flag, 284
inadequacy of some services, 61
interrupt 17h, printer control, 29
time of day count. *See* time of day count
bit doubling, 250–254, 256, 257, 332
BL register, 137, 139
not used as memory-addressing register, 139
blocks of data, comparing, 359, 457, 458
blocks of data, copying, 351, 413, 414, 416–420, 424
blocks of data, setting, 365–367, 384, 389
Borland, 645
bound instruction, 715
BP register, 137, 140, 159, 193, 239, 245, 643
base addressing component, 207
no addressing mode that uses only BP, 207, 643
normally addresses the stack segment, 140, 143, 192
specializes as stack frame-addressing register, 140, 208, 239, 240, 245
used as memory-addressing register, 140, 200, 208, 223, 233, 239, 245, 246, 309
branched-to in-line code, 598, 599, 601, 602, 604, 607, 608, 679, 688

branched-to partial in-line code, 605, 606, 608
branches, 150, 192, 297, 346, 366, 471, 508, 509, 512,
        517, 519, 521–525, 527–531, 533, 534, 537–540,
        542, 543, 545, 555–557, 560–562, 564, 565, 569,
        571, 572, 574, 577, 579, 581, 582, 586, 587,
        589–594, 596, 599, 601, 602, 604–608, 610, 611,
        615, 619–621, 627, 631, 632, 636, 637, 649–653,
        657, 658, 661, 662, 668, 670, 672, 674, 678, 679,
        686, 688, 693, 701, 702, 705, 708, 710, 711, 717,
        723
    absolute, 510, 511
    desirability of eliminating, 251, 368, 440, 444, 479,
        499, 508, 509, 514, 530, 531, 555, 560, 574,
        577, 579, 582, 586, 592–594, 596, 601, 602, 611,
        619–621, 658, 699, 702, 705, 717
    empty the prefetch queue, 66, 67, 86, 294, 518, 519,
        522–525, 527, 528, 530, 531, 539, 556, 582, 589,
        590, 601, 616, 619, 620, 636, 637, 652, 701, 702,
        704, 705
    first prefetch after is included in execution time,
        523–525, 527, 530
    not-branching. *See* not-branching
    relative, 510–515, 565
bus, 62, 63, 65, 68, 70, 71
    bug in splitting 16-bit accesses to 8-bit adapters in
        certain computers, 263
    effect on performance, 62, 64, 72, 77–80, 83, 84
    maximum data transfer rate, 67, 70, 73, 77, 78, 84
    sizes in 8086 family, 69
    splits 16-bit accesses to 8-bit adapters with some
        processors, 263
    transparency to programs, 62
bus interface unit (BIU), 65–72, 78, 158, 520, 524–529,
        616, 699, 701
    bottleneck, 70–72, 78
    can coprocess with EU, 66–68, 85, 92, 119, 122, 124,
        519, 520
    converts 16-bit memory accesses into 8-bit accesses,
        69, 78, 263
    features contained within, 67
    inability to fetch instruction bytes as fast as EU can
        execute them, 75, 77, 84, 85, 130, 699
    interleaves instruction fetches with memory operand
        accesses, 125
    minimum transfer time for bytes from the prefetch
        queue to the EU, 130
    path for all memory and I/O accesses, including
        instruction fetches, 69
    performs all memory and I/O accesses, 66, 67
    potentially greatest cycle eater of all, 69
    prefetches, 66, 67, 85, 519–521, 523, 616, 699
    provides instruction bytes for EU, 66, 67
    provides only 8-bit access to bus, 67, 78
BX register, 137, 139, 159, 267, 643
    accessible as BH and BL, 139
    base addressing component, 207
    normally addresses the data segment, 140
    used as memory-addressing register, 139, 200, 208,
        223, 246, 309, 316
Byte magazine, 52
byte-sized accesses, desirability of, 80, 81, 110
byte-sized versus word-sized operations, 80–83
byte-to-word conversion, 312, 313
bytes versus cycles, 9, 160, 249, 255, 257, 471, 537,
        554, 581, 588–590, 592, 596, 602–604, 610, 617,
        637, 649, 651, 674, 694, 711

C

C, 6, 58, 166, 233, 240, 433, 488, 542, 589, 619, 623,
        624, 715
    switch, 303, 646, 670
cache memory, 698, 702, 703
call instruction, 141–144, 517, 568, 582, 584, 620, 627,
        630, 631, 633, 635–637, 670, 712, 726
call tables. *See* jump tables
calls, subroutine, 508, 517, 526, 581, 582, 584, 586,
        588, 589, 592, 627, 628, 670
    direct, 620, 622, 626, 637
    far. *See* far calls
    indirect, 187, 620, 622, 623, 626, 670, 671
    moving called code into loop, 582, 584, 586
    near. *See* near calls
    replacing with macros, 582, 584, 630
carry flag. *See* CF
carrying results along in a flag, 310–312
cbw instruction, 139, 140, 312, 313, 315
CF (carry flag), 144–147, 309, 310, 322, 323, 327–330,
        332, 341, 354, 488, 547, 560, 562, 563, 564, 655,
        716
    can sometimes be used to avoid branching,
        561–564
CGA. *See* Color/Graphics Adapter
CH register, 137, 139
    not used as counting register, 139

"Chips in Transition," 721
CL register, 137, 139, 324–327, 329, 331
   used as counting register, 139
clc instruction, 146
cld instruction, 149, 362, 363, 420
clearing the screen, 58
cli instruction, 149
cmc instruction, 146
cmp instruction, 277, 278, 281–283, 301–304, 321,
   343, 354, 356, 359, 436, 444, 540, 643
cmps instruction, 140, 359–361, 368, 371, 372, 377,
   381, 391, 393, 457, 462, 466, 471, 482, 483, 485,
   499
   repeated. *See* **repz cmps** and **repnz cmps**
cmpsb. *See* **cmps**
cmpsw. *See* **cmps**
COBOL, 166, 589
code
   as data that 8088 interprets as instructions, 65,
      68–70, 73, 615, 617
   desirability of keeping short. *See* shorter is better
   equivalence with data, 65
   seemingly similar sequences can perform quite
      differently, 289
code maintenance, 9
code segment. *See* CS register
Codeview
   run from a remote terminal, 29
cold boot and system clock, 26, 27
Color/Graphics Adapter (CGA), 14, 106, 262
   and display adapter cycle eater, 105
Commodore Amiga, 697
common exit code. *See* sharing code
compilers, 6, 240–242, 362, 400, 533, 542, 623
   as data transformation programs, 65, 533
   information available to, 10, 542
Complete Turbo Pascal, 735
conditional jumps. *See* jumps, conditional
constants, handling efficiently, 297, 298
context, 58, 85, 91, 92, 116, 129, 130, 174, 517, 542,
   554, 563
coprocessors, 728, 731
CP/M, 266
CS register, 137, 142, 158, 159, 169, 192, 193, 396,
   509–512, 514, 619, 620, 625, 626, 636, 722,
   725
   can't be used for temporary storage, 170
   default access to, 142, 159

must be loaded, together with IP, in a single
   instruction, 142, 170
CS: segment override prefix, 193
cursor, 58
cwd instruction, 139, 312–314, 338
CX register, 137, 139, 267, 363, 364, 371, 373–375,
   377, 378, 382, 452
   accessible as CH and CL, 139
   used as counting register, 139, 316
cycle counting, 14
cycle eaters, 62–64, 70, 75–77, 110, 111, 504, 510, 517,
   530, 597, 701, 717
   8-bit bus. *See* 8-bit bus cycle eater
   assembler programming can't be reduced to a
      science because of, 113
   can't be eliminated, 111
   cause performance to vary with context and time,
      116, 119, 126, 130, 517, 697
   display adapter. *See* display adapter cycle eater
   don't change the effects of code, but do change
      performance, 129
   dynamic RAM (DRAM) refresh. *See* dynamic RAM
      refresh cycle eater
   foundation of Zen of assembler, 131
   importance, 62, 63, 65
   interaction between, 111, 114–116, 122
   interaction with instruction execution, 117, 123, 128
   live outside execution unit, 75
   locations in PCs, 77
   must understand to be able to interpret Zen timer
      results, 110
   no compiler can deal with as well as good
      assembler programmer, 116
   no need to understand all interactions between, 115
   part of knowledge aspect of Zen of assembly
      language, 131
   prefetch queue. *See* prefetch queue cycle eater
   underlie programming interface, 131, 701
   wait state. *See* wait state cycle eater
cycles versus bytes. *See* bytes versus cycles

D

daa instruction, 139, 147, 333, 334, 341, 344
das instruction, 139, 147, 333, 334, 341
data, equivalence with code, 65, 615, 617

data alignment, 696, 699, 705–711
  code, 708–711, 717, 721
  doubleword, 390, 711
  word, 390, 525, 705–707, 709–711, 717, 721
data alignment cycle eater, 699, 701, 705–707, 711, 717
  dealing with, 707, 708, 710, 711, 717, 721
data bus. *See* bus
data segment. *See* DS register
Date command, 25, 35
db directive, 168
DE register pair of 8080, 267
debugger, 28
  using to see actual code generated, 197, 208, 244, 284, 693, 709
dec instruction, 5, 80, 81, 147, 303, 304–309, 318, 342, 590, 597, 662
  16-bit register-only form, 305–308, 342, 662
  doesn't affect CF, 309
decimal adjust, 333, 334
development environment, 9
device drivers, 59–61
  extending DOS's capabilities, 61
  poor performance of, 61
DF (direction flag), 144, 145, 149, 291, 294, 347, 348, 351–355, 359, 360, 362, 363, 379, 416–425, 427, 445
  must be in a known state before using string instructions, 362
DH register, 137
DI register, 137, 140, 149, 159, 351–356, 358–360, 380, 643
  index addressing component, 207
  specializes as memory-addressing register for string instructions, 140, 192, 193, 351, 354, 359
  used as memory-addressing register, 140, 200, 208, 223, 246, 309, 391, 396
direct addressing, 207, 208, 213, 218, 219, 270, 272, 274–277, 280, 298, 302, 343, 648
  accumulator-specific. *See* accumulator-specific direct-addressing
  always uses a 16-bit displacement, 208, 271
direct indexed addressing, 206
direct memory access. *See* DMA
direction flag. *See* DF
directives, 168
disk, 60, 64, 133
disk-backup software, 61

displacements, branch/call/jump, 510, 512–515, 517, 522, 531, 564, 565, 601, 615, 616, 629, 643, 646, 679–680, 683, 688
  forward references, 643–645
displacements, memory addressing, 187, 200, 202, 205, 208, 213, 255, 271, 643–645
  and addressing mode naming, 207
  can always reach anywhere in a segment, 224
  forward references, 643–645
  impact on size and performance, 205, 206, 209, 214, 218, 264, 643
  must be numbers or symbols equated to numbers in order to sign extend, 206
  negative, 224
  sign extension, 205, 206, 231, 643
  use 1-byte displacements whenever possible, 214, 243, 263, 601, 628
display adapter, 8, 29, 60, 64, 133, 136, 669, 713, 714
  8088 may get as little as 10 percent of display memory accesses, 102, 103
  allows same access speed regardless of speed of computer, 104, 108, 713, 714
  may stretch out access time based on pixel clock, 102, 104
  must guarantee video circuitry all needed accesses, 102
  not very fast compared to system memory, 105
  provides memory accesses only at certain intervals, 102, 104, 713, 714
  serves two masters, 101
  slows up CPU, 101–105
  usually 8-bit devices, 713
  video circuitry may take up to 90 percent of display memory accesses, 102, 103
"Display Adapter Bottleneck," 110
display adapter cycle eater, 62, 76, 77, 101, 110, 113, 114, 122, 129, 499, 597, 703, 704, 712–714
  can more than double the execution time of 8088 code, 107, 110
  effect on performance, 105–110
  effect on performance varies with display mode, 105
  effect on performance varies with type of adapter, 105
  effects tend to even out over time, 129
  impact is proportional to time spent accessing display memory, 107
  impact varies with intensity of access to display memory, 108–110

impact varies with time, 114, 128
in text mode, 106
interaction with prefetch queue cycle eater, 115
makes exclusive-or animation less-than-ideal, 109, 499
matters most in high-resolution EGA and VGA graphics modes, 106
much worse on ATs and 80386 machines, 108
rarely a factor in text mode, 105
what to do about, 108, 109
worst with EGA and VGA, 105, 106
display memory, 107, 152, 401, 489, 491, 496–498, 594, 597, 713, 714
access as little as possible, 108–110, 594, 714, 717
access speed in the EGA's high-resolution graphics mode, 107
and word-sized string instructions, 390, 391, 392
avoid read/modify/write accesses to, 109
compared to system memory, 107
don't put code in, 105, 115
perform multiple accesses to very rapidly, 109
performance of, 63
set all pixels in a byte at once for speed, 109
display memory wait states, 85, 100–104, 106, 107, 109
div instruction, 335–339, 720
divide-by-0 interrupt, 339
division, 138, 140, 312, 329–331, 335, 336, 338–340, 620, 668
effect on EU/BIU coprocessing, 68
rounding with **sar**, 331
DL register, 137
DMA, 8, 24, 95
Doctor Dobb's Journal magazine, 344
documentation, 8
don't assume intended instruction uses are always best, 304, 315, 333
don't jump, 508, 530, 531, 693, 705
DOS, 25, 59–61, 75, 133, 169, 363, 637, 638, 641, 642, 700, 712, 717, 721
as an assembly-language program, 61
calls part of programming interface, 131
file system, 59
function 4, auxiliary output, 29
function 5, printer output, 29
function 9, print string, 28
functions 2Ah to 2Dh, time and date, 25, 35
inadequacy of some services, 61

interrupts, use to obtain blocks, not single characters, 582, 637, 638, 641–643
dot operator, 245
double duty from a single instruction, 656
doubleword alignment. *See* data alignment
doublewords, loading, 184, 185, 189, 700
DS register, 137, 142, 143, 158, 159, 173, 192, 193, 347, 351, 358, 359, 396, 400
can be used for temporary storage when free, 171
default access to, 142, 143, 159, 208, 239, 246, 247, 347, 351, 359, 381, 391, 395
loading with **lds**, 176, 177
DS: segment override prefix, 193
dual 8/16-bit registers, 137
Duntemann, Jeff, 135, 635, 735
duplicating code, 568–572, 574, 579, 588
dw directive, 168
DX register, 137, 139, 267, 312, 314, 315, 337, 338
accessible as DH and DL, 139
least specialized general-purpose register, 139
used as I/O-addressing register, 261
dynamic RAM (DRAM), 94
dynamic RAM (DRAM) refresh, 24, 25, 75, 76, 83, 85, 94, 95, 113, 114, 251, 294, 368, 531, 703, 707, 712
act of God, 94, 99
can scarcely be addressed at all, 111
can't make less frequent, 99, 712
code can't directly control, 94
doesn't necessarily stop 8088, 97
holds up PC via READY line, 117
in PC, 95, 96
lowest level, 93, 94
dynamic RAM (DRAM) refresh cycle eater, 62, 76, 77, 79, 87, 110, 122, 275, 316, 517, 530, 712
affects high-performance assembler code most, 98
affects performance of every program, 93
affects slower instructions least, 99
can cause fractional Zen timer counts, 99
can't structure code to avoid, 99
effect on performance, 95–98, 110, 123
effect on Zen timer accuracy, 30
effects tend to even out over time, 129
external to 8088, 94
impact varies with time, 114, 126, 128
interaction with 8-bit bus cycle eater, 115
what to do about, 98–99

E

EA calculations. *See* effective address calculations
EAX, 716
EBCDIC, 248
EBX, 716
effective address (EA) calculations, 210–214, 219–221,
    531, 645, 676, 718, 720
  only *mod-reg-rm* memory operands require, 212,
    217
EGA. *See* Enhanced Graphics Adapter
ends directive, 168
Enhanced Graphics Adapter (EGA), 62, 262, 263, 492,
    499, 713, 714
  and display adapter cycle eater, 105, 713
  and word-sized string instructions, 390–392
enter instruction, 715
ES register, 137, 142, 143, 158, 159, 173, 192, 193, 351,
    354, 358, 359, 396, 400, 401
  and loading doublewords, 184
  can be used for temporary storage, 171–173
  default access to, 143, 159, 351, 354, 359, 381, 391,
    393, 396
  loading with **les**, 176, 177, 737
ES: segment override prefix, 193
even directive, 707, 710
event timeline, 118
execution
  as two parallel chains of execution, 122, 124
  as three interleaved streams of events, 119, 122,
    123, 125, 126
execution unit (EU), 65–70, 72, 75, 77, 78, 117, 520,
    522, 524, 525, 527, 528, 530, 699, 701
  ability to execute instruction bytes faster than BIU
    can fetch them, 75, 77, 84, 85, 130, 702–704
  can coprocess with BIU, 66–68, 85, 92, 119, 122,
    124, 519, 520
  can process during DRAM refresh unless bus access
    needed, 97
  can process while wait states are inserted unless
    bus access needed, 101
  does not perform direct memory and I/O accesses,
    65–67
  don't double-count execution time overlapped with
    instruction fetching, 92, 124
  execution times, 85, 210, 251, 279, 325, 364, 619,
    652, 699, 718, 720
  features contained within, 65

fully 16-bit, 67
gets instruction bytes from BIU, 66, 67, 519–521,
    523
minimum transfer time for bytes from the prefetch
    queue to the EU, 130
transfers to from prefetch queue, 118
usually stopped by wait states, 101
extra segment. *See* ES register

F

far calls, 187, 517, 619–621, 623–626, 636, 670, 723,
    725, 726
  emulating, 625, 725
far data, 397, 398, 400, 413
far jumps, 514, 517, 619–621, 623–626, 670
  ending subroutines with, 567, 568
far pointers, organization in memory, 187
far returns, 568, 619–621, 623–627, 722
filling the screen. *See* screen filling
flags, 65, 66, 145, 289–291, 293, 294, 298, 307, 310,
    359, 372, 375, 378, 380, 432, 448, 449, 482, 488,
    560, 627, 636, 653, 654, 657, 722, 723
  double duty, 656
  multiple tests, 619, 653–655
  used by interrupt handler, 318
flags register, 137, 144, 145, 267, 289, 310, 322, 636,
    657, 722
flexible mind, 9–12, 109, 131, 471, 504, 506, 508, 635,
    733–735, 741, 742
  developing skill, 10
for statement, 58
Forth, 712
forward references, 244, 643–645, 646, 692, 693
front-end entry points. *See* multiple entry points
further reading, 52, 53

G

Geary, Michael, 129
general-purpose registers, 136–138, 170, 270, 316, 343,
    349
  and *mod-reg-rm* byte, 204, 205
  loading segment registers via, 174
  use as operands, 138
global variables, 193

graphics support by DOS and BIOS, 61
group directive, 199

H

hardware, 8, 59, 60, 62, 133
   documentation, 52
   foundation for 8088, 63, 65
   independence, 59
   transparency to programs, 62
Heinlein, Robert, 380
Hercules Graphics Card (HGC), and display adapter
   cycle eater, 105
hexadecimal, 8, 156–158
high level languages, 6, 9, 10, 58, 163, 164, 167, 173,
   179, 191, 193, 240, 241, 244, 258, 400, 488, 535,
   542, 560, 622, 623, 651, 729, 730
   advantages of mixing with assembler, 241
   and segment sharing, 192, 199, 623
   interfacing assembler to, 241, 242, 623
   limitations, 10
   low-level control, 8
   transformation inefficiencies, 6, 10
HL register pair of 8080, 267
horizontal retrace, 106
Hoyt, Michael, 249–251

I

IBM, 72, 154, 269, 637
   AT, 30, 53, 63, 101, 108, 616, 698, 702–704, 707,
   708, 712–714, 717–719
   Model 30, 30, 53
   Models 50 and 60, 53
   Model 80, 53, 616
   PC, 5, 8, 9, 53, 58, 72, 101, 113, 114, 152–155, 489,
   616, 694, 697, 698, 704, 712–714, 717, 719–721,
   733, 734
   PC *jr*, all memory was display memory, 105
   PS/2 computers, 30, 37
   technical reference manuals, 53
   XT, 30, 53
idiv instruction, 338
IF (interrupt flag), 143–145, 148, 149, 291, 294, 636,
   721, 723
if directive, 680, 692, 693

if . . . then . . . else, 560
Illowsky, Dan, 332, 497, 545
immediate addressing, 208, 224, 226–232, 281, 284,
   298, 302, 343
   forward references, 645
   no sign extension for **mov**, 231, 232, 299
   sign extension, 231, 282–284, 643
   sign extension of operands to logical instructions,
   284
implementation. *See* program implementation
implied addressing, 206
imul instruction, 146, 337
in instruction, 138, 140, 261, 262
in-line assembler (in high level language), 241, 242
in-line code, 5, 155, 160, 440, 471, 504, 535, 572, 589,
   592–596, 598, 599, 601–605, 607, 608, 613–615,
   679–680, 683, 685, 688, 692, 693
   branched-to. *See* branched-to in-line code
   handling blocks of varying size, 679–680, 683, 688
   labels in. *See* labels in in-line code
   partial. *See* partial in-line code
   pure. *See* pure in-line code
inc instruction, 145, 147, 182, 226, 302, 304–310,
   340, 342, 349, 356, 366, 547, 556, 563, 699,
   712
   16-bit register-only form, 231, 305–307, 342
   and byte order in memory, 190
   doesn't affect CF, 309
incrementing 32-bit values, 652
index addressing, 209, 212–214, 218, 221
index addressing component, 200, 202, 207
index registers, 137
index+displacement addressing, 207, 214
indirect addressing, 208
indirect branching, 208
indivisible doubleword reads, 185, 186, 700
input/output (I/O)
   not performed directly by EU, 65, 66
   performed directly by BIU, 66
input/output (I/O) addressing, 140, 261, 262
input/output (I/O) instructions, 261, 262
input/output (I/O) ports, 62, 261
input/output to the real world
   needed by all useful programs, 61
ins instruction, 715
instruction execution time, 13, 279
   assumes instruction already prefetched, 68, 85
   inaccuracy due to prefetch queue cycle eater, 84, 85

instruction execution time (*continued*)
    individual instruction times less useful than overall performance, 129
    minimum of 4 cycles times the number of all memory accesses, 90, 92, 175, 471
    must be measured for working code sequences, not individual instructions, 91
    no exact interval during which one and only one instruction executes, 92, 122–124
    no such beast as true, 86, 90, 91, 116, 126
    only meaningful in context, 91, 92, 129, 130, 517
    shown in an event timeline, 126
    varies depending on preceding code, 85, 86, 90
    working definition of, 92, 123, 126, 523
instruction fetch time, 13, 251, 517, 524
    benefits of using short instructions. *See* shorter is better
    controls execution time when prefetch queue is empty, 68, 300, 719, 720
    counts as part of execution time when not overlapped with execution, 68
    determines maximum execution speed, 84, 369, 719, 720
    don't double-count when overlapped with EU execution time, 92
    varies depending on context, 85, 524
instruction fetching, 14, 53, 84, 346, 519–525, 528, 529, 538, 557, 589, 601, 702, 703, 708–710, 718
    can proceed during shifts and rotates by CL, 325, 538
    effect on performance, 85, 88–90, 209, 210, 213, 214, 251, 369, 444, 471, 479, 701, 719, 720
    maximum rate, 84
    often subject to wait states in AT, 101
    rarely subject to wait states in PC, 101
    subject to cycle eaters, 69, 70, 75, 77
instruction mix, effect on performance, 68, 85, 88–90, 542
instruction pointer. *See* IP register
instruction prefetch queue. *See* prefetch queue
instruction prefetching, 75, 262, 519–521, 523, 703
    determines execution time of sequence of register-only instructions, 88
    most important coprocessing BIU performs, 68
instruction set, 8, 59, 75, 76, 134, 150, 169, 263, 266, 269, 270, 274, 285, 295, 297, 344, 346, 535, 563, 616, 617, 627, 630, 635, 670, 694, 717, 727, 733
    view as capable of being used, not as intended to be used, 304, 315, 333, 449, 733, 740

instructions, 297, 305
    desirability of keeping short. *See* shorter is better
    instruction selection often matters, 289
    part of programming interface, 131
int 0, 339
int 1, 149
int 4, 148
int instruction, 141–145, 149, 636, 637, 641, 657, 712
    flags affected by, 657
Intel, 13, 23, 25, 34, 156, 187, 190, 267, 295, 363, 519, 524, 721
    Microsystem Components Handbook, 52
interleaved memory, 698, 702, 703
interleaving of memory accesses and instruction execution, 119
interrupt flag. *See* IF
interrupt handlers, 193, 318, 363, 626, 637
interrupt vectors, 187, 636, 637
interrupts, 148, 319, 401, 508, 517, 581, 622, 636, 641, 653, 657, 712, 721–723
    can use the stack at any time, 237, 238
    disabling, 143, 144, 149, 319, 401
    divide-by-0, 339
    don't change the effects of code, but do change performance, 129
    flush the prefetch queue and change execution patterns, 129
    loading vectors is only memory access that doesn't involve a segment, 159
    should be disabled for as short a time as possible, 149, 401
into instruction, 148
INTR pin, 148
IP register (instruction pointer), 66, 67, 137, 142, 144, 226, 227, 509–511, 513–515, 517, 519, 531, 582, 619, 620, 625, 626, 635, 636, 722
    complications arising from prefetching handled internally by 8088, 144
iret instruction, 141–145, 362, 401, 627, 636, 641, 712, 722–724, 726
    all flags are affected by, 657
IRQ0, 24–26

J

ja instruction, 146
jae instruction, 146
jb instruction, 146

jbe instruction, 146
jc instruction, 146
jcxz instruction, 139, 374, 432, 448, 449, 462, 543, 544, 608, 657, 668, 669
  doesn't affect any flags, 657
je instruction, 147
jg instruction, 147, 148
jge instruction, 148
jl instruction, 148
jle instruction, 148
jmp instruction, 142, 144, 509–511, 513, 514, 517–519, 524–529, 531, 568–570, 572, 582, 598, 615, 627, 630–633, 643, 645, 680
jmp short, 509, 512, 522, 525, 569, 570, 572, 628, 630, 643–645, 648, 679, 726
jna instruction, 146
jnae instruction, 146
jnb instruction, 146
jnbe instruction, 146
jnc instruction, 146, 552
jne instruction, 147
jng instruction, 147, 483
jnge instruction, 148
jnl instruction, 148
jnle instruction, 148
jno instruction, 148
jnp instruction, 147
jns instruction, 148, 563
jnz instruction, 5, 147, 309, 318, 567, 590, 597, 662, 680
jo instruction, 148
jp instruction, 147
jpe instruction, 147
jpo instruction, 147
js instruction, 148
jump tables, 193, 194, 257, 450, 452, 607, 619, 620, 623, 625, 630, 670–676, 678, 679, 683–686, 688
  letting assembler do the work of creating, 685
  partial jump tables. *See* partial jump tables
  pure jump tables. *See* pure jump tables
jumps, 508–514, 563, 565, 581, 615, 616, 627–629, 632, 635, 644, 646, 670
  around jumps, 457, 563, 567, 611, 672, 679, 683, 688
  backward references, 643, 646
  conditional, 510, 512, 539–541, 545, 560, 562–565, 567, 569, 577, 586, 601, 610, 611, 646, 652, 672, 679–680, 683, 688, 692
  direct, 619, 630
  far. *See* far jumps

  forward references, 643–646
  indirect, 619, 623, 626, 670, 671
  near. *See* near jumps
  short. *See* **jmp short**
  replacing calls, 628
  to other subroutines in place of **ret**, 567, 568, 630, 633
  unconditional, 563, 565, 567–569, 572, 611, 679, 688, 693
jz instruction, 147, 540, 565, 567, 660, 680

K

keyboard, 8, 35, 59, 60, 64, 129, 401, 675, 676, 712
  interrupt, 136, 149
  macro software, 61
knowledge, 8, 9, 11, 58, 59, 131, 471, 504, 508, 733, 734, 741, 742

L

labels in in-line code, 613, 614, 684
lahf instruction, 139, 145, 267, 289–291, 294, 309, 312, 727
latches, EGA/VGA, 391, 392
layered system software, 59, 60, 63, 64
lds instruction, 143, 176, 177, 182
lea instruction, 198, 214, 221–223
leave instruction, 715
les instruction, 143, 170, 176–179, 182, 184, 737
  and byte order in memory, 189
  and loading doublewords, 184–186, 189, 700, 736
  and performance, 179
libraries, subroutine and macro, 589
link, 32
listing file, using to see actual code generated, 197, 244, 284, 588, 693
local directive, 244, 614
  bug when used in **rept** blocks, 614
local variables, 239, 240, 242–244
lods instruction, 82, 139, 140, 182, 288, 347–351, 357, 359, 361, 377, 381, 391, 404–407, 412, 413, 420, 421, 435, 436, 439, 440, 442–444, 458, 464, 466, 534, 610, 613
  doesn't affect any flags, 375
  repeated. *See* **rep lods**

lods instruction (*continued*)
    synergy with other instructions, 404–407, 412, 413, 464, 613
lodsb. *See* **lods**
lodsw. *See* **lods**
look-up tables, 14, 153, 154, 160, 249–252, 254, 256–258, 260, 297, 303, 332, 333, 404, 450, 452, 456, 457, 468, 471, 538, 539, 607, 615, 626, 673, 676–678, 686, 693
loop instruction, 139, 179, 192, 309, 310, 318, 366, 368, 375, 378, 483, 533, 534, 537, 538, 572, 574, 589–592, 594, 597, 598, 601, 604, 608, 657, 658, 660–662, 688, 709
    doesn't affect any flags, 310, 657
loope instruction, 658
loopne instruction, 658
loopnz instruction, 139, 657, 658, 660
    doesn't affect any flags, 657
loops, 508, 534, 535, 537, 538, 542, 565, 567, 569, 572, 574, 577, 579, 581, 582, 586–599, 602–606, 608, 611, 613, 632, 637, 653, 656–658, 660–662, 668, 669, 685, 693, 709, 711
loopz instruction, 139, 657, 658
    doesn't affect any flags, 657
lss instruction, doesn't exist, 190
LZTEST.ASM long-period Zen timer test bed program, 49
LZTEST.EXE long-period Zen timer executable program, 50
LZTIME.BAT long-period Zen timer batch file, 50, 51, 164, 639
LZTIMER.ASM long-period Zen timer source code, 37, 50

M

machine language, 6, 8, 10, 645
    ultimate form of all source code, 63–65, 73
macros, 582, 584, 586, 588, 589, 615, 620, 630, 646, 679–680, 683, 684, 685, 688, 692, 693, 725, 727
    text substitution, 683, 684, 685
MAD magazine, 168
many ways to approach any task in assembler, 231, 254, 257, 292, 404, 448, 458, 470, 545, 554
maskable interrupts. *See* interrupts
MASM (Microsoft Macro Assembler), 32, 50, 52, 168, 170, 190, 192, 196, 197, 198, 242, 253, 284, 372, 373, 393–396, 614, 645, 646, 693, 730

memory, 8, 9, 60, 64, 133, 152, 219
    8-bit as a cycle eater in AT, 62, 713
    accessed directly by BIU, 66
    avoid accessing whenever possible for performance, 92, 153, 182, 210, 218, 263, 316, 440, 471, 699, 705, 720
    constant access by programs, 62
    effect on performance, 62, 279
    initializing, 258, 259, 301
    initializing when defined (at assembly time), desirability of, 260
    is slow, 210, 346, 697
    not accessed directly by EU, 65
    part of the PC's hardware, 61
    should not be destination operand, 319–321
    tradeoff for performance, 160
    use to improve performance, 9, 154, 160
    versus processing horsepower, 9
memory accessing instructions, effect on instruction prefetching, 68, 90
    are slow, 152, 158, 211, 246, 704
    never faster than register-only instructions, 217
    often slower than 4 cycles per memory access, 90
    suffer less from the prefetch queue than register-only instructions, 217
memory addresses, calculate outside loops, 214, 220–222
memory addressing, 6, 59, 149, 150, 154, 157, 198, 263
    can only address memory pointed to by at least one segment register, 160, 161
    difficulty of dealing with blocks larger than 64 Kb, 161, 162, 167
    difficulty of handling blocks that cross a segment boundary, 162, 167
    part of programming interface, 131
    use of square brackets to denote, 154, 246
memory addressing modes, 152, 153, 159, 198–200, 202, 211, 212, 232, 715–717, 729
    16 completely distinct memory-addressing modes, 205, 206, 271, 349
    24 distinct ways to generate a memory offset, 204
    immediate addressing. *See* immediate addressing
    mod-reg-rm addressing. *See* *mod-reg-rm* addressing
    naming *mod-reg-rm* addressing modes, 206, 207, 209
    specifying *mod-reg-rm* addressing modes, 245
    stack addressing. *See* stack addressing
memory architecture in 80286- and 80386-based computers, 698, 702–704, 721

memory resident programs, 254, 637

MEMR line, 117, 121, 123, 124

MEMW line, 117, 121, 123, 124

microcode, 211

Microsoft Linker, 29, 32, 50

Miller, Dave, 129

mini-interpreters, 260, 653, 734

mod-reg-rm addressing, 199, 200, 203, 205, 208, 213, 218, 221, 223–226, 231–233, 239, 245, 246, 255, 272, 274–279, 281–286, 288, 306, 307, 342, 343, 344, 648, 676, 740

  allow only word-sized registers to be used to address memory, 248

  and code size, 209, 210, 217, 218, 234, 237

  and performance, 209–214, 216–218, 235, 237

  avoid whenever possible for performance, 210, 263

  can be forced to access any segment, 208

  can select a memory offset or register as an operand in any of 16 ways, 205, 271, 349

  can specify 256 possible source/destination combinations, 203, 204

  defaults to accessing DS except when BP is used, 208, 239

  direct addressing as anomaly, 207

  doesn't work with all instructions, 209

  has two performance components, 211

  naming modes, 206, 207, 209

  no addressing mode that uses only BP, 207, 208, 245

  no inherent support for constant operands, 205

  slow, but less slow than you might think relative to registers, 216

  some instructions can only use *mod-reg-rm* addressing, 210

  specifying, 245, 246

  suffer less from the prefetch queue than register-only instructions, 217

  use displacement-free modes whenever you can, 214

  used by many register-only instructions, 210

  varies in performance due to EA calculation time, 211–213

  very flexible, 203, 205, 209, 224

  workhorse memory addressing mode of the 8088, 210, 224

mod-reg-rm bytes, 199, 201–204, 207, 208, 213, 224, 226, 227, 245, 270, 271, 343, 393, 511, 643

  time required to calculate addresses from (EA calculation time), 209, 210, 219, 220

with one-operand instructions, 200, 204

Mode command, 29

Monochrome Display Adapter (MDA), and display adapter cycle eater, 105

"More optimizing for Speed," 251

mouse, 35, 49, 129, 401, 712

mov instruction, 34, 143, 145, 170, 182, 221, 226, 232, 272–277, 282, 285, 298, 299, 300, 311, 315, 342–344, 347, 349–351, 366, 367, 413, 468, 631, 644, 648, 670

  accumulator-specific direct-addressing form. *See* accumulator-specific

  and byte order in memory, 187, 188, 190

  and segment copying, 174

  byte versus word, 79, 81, 84

  doesn't affect any flags, 311

  doesn't sign extend immediate operands, 231

  no non-*mod-reg-rm* memory immediate form, 344

  non-*mod-reg-rm* register immediate form, 231, 232, 343, 344

movs instruction, 140, 173, 351, 353, 359, 377, 380, 381, 391, 393, 405, 413, 414, 420, 428, 497, 499, 581

  doesn't affect any flags, 375

  repeated. *See* **rep movs**

movsb. *See* **movs**

movsd, 716

movsw. *See* **movs**

MS_DOS. *See* DOS

mul instruction, 146, 205, 336, 337, 598, 607, 679, 720

  doesn't suffer from DRAM refresh, 97

  effect on prefetch queue, 87, 89, 90

multi-bit shifts and rotates, 324, 325, 538, 715

multi-byte values, storage organization in memory, 186–190, 379

multi-word shifts and rotates, 328

multi-word values, addition and subtraction of, 309, 310

multiple entry points, 650

  front-end entry points, 650, 651

multiple tests from a single instruction, 619, 653–655

multiplication, 138, 140, 146, 329, 335, 336, 607, 673

  effect on EU/BIU coprocessing, 68

N

Navas, John, 244

near calls, 192, 517, 619, 620, 623–626, 670, 723, 725

near jumps, 514, 517, 619, 620, 623–625, 670
  ending subroutines with, 567, 568
near keyword in C, 623
near returns, 568, 619, 620, 623–625
NEC, 267
neg instruction, 147, 321–324, 546–549, 716
negating 32-bit values, 322, 323, 544–552, 554, 555, 652, 716
negation, 322, 323, 544–552, 554, 555
NMI pin, 149
non-mod-reg-rm addressing, 199, 208, 214, 218, 224, 225, 231, 343
  generally faster than *mod-reg-rm* addressing, 210, 224, 225
  generally less flexible than *mod-reg-rm* addressing, 210, 224
  requires no EA calculation time, 224
nonmaskable interrupts, 136, 149
nop instruction, 569, 644, 707, 710
not instruction, 321–323, 546, 547, 552
  doesn't affect any flags, 322
not-branching, 533, 535, 537, 617, 619, 651, 658, 662

O

OF (overflow flag), 144–148, 291, 294, 329–331, 354
official execution times, 252, 257, 514, 524, 530, 539
  can't simply add up times for individual instructions, 91
  inaccuracy of, 84–86, 91, 106, 111, 324, 325
offset operator, 198, 199
  and segment groups, 199
offsets, 155–159, 198, 510, 511, 513, 514, 564, 607, 631, 671, 679, 686, 723
  24 distinct ways to generate, 204
  calculating, 159, 198, 199, 200, 208–210, 245–248, 607
  just 16-bit numbers, 222, 223
  loading, 198, 221, 736
  loading for a variable in a segment group, 199
  offsets greater than 16 bits wrap around to 0, 162, 223–225, 382, 383, 385, 420
  use in addressing memory, 198
  very flexible portion of memory addressing, 198, 203
Omnilab electronic test instrument, 117
"On Graphics," 244

operating system, 8, 60
OPTASM, 645
optimization, 4, 59, 81, 292, 542, 550, 554, 579, 581, 693, 694, 696–700, 708, 711, 717, 718, 721, 729, 733, 736, 741, 742
  8088 is best place to focus efforts, 696–699, 715–717, 731
  8088 optimizations serve well on other processors, 698, 699, 717, 720, 721
  concentrate on loops and time-critical code, 153, 166, 182, 186, 214, 218, 219, 227, 240, 241, 264, 538, 554, 572, 574, 579, 581, 582, 588, 589, 617, 619, 632, 637, 653, 656, 660, 694, 711
  detailed 80286/80386 optimization, 718–721
  don't become fixated on a particular trick, 288, 315
  don't use nifty tricks for their own sake, 279
  for space (size), 653, 662, 693, 736
  optimize for the common case, 449, 539–545, 551, 552, 559, 560
  understand conditions under which it will run, 541, 542, 554, 688
  worst-case, 541, 542
"Optimizing for Speed," 249
or instruction, 146, 148, 229, 281–284, 301, 302, 320, 343, 412
OS/2, 696, 697, 700
out instruction, 138, 140, 261, 262
  desirability of byte-sized, 263
  hazards of word-sized, 262, 263
outs instruction, 715
overflow, 148
overflow flag. *See* OF

P

packed BCD, 334
paired-byte initialization, 300, 301
paired jumps. *See* jumps around jumps
parameter passing, 233, 239–241, 244, 576, 650, 651, 675, 740, 741
  macro parameters, 684
parity, 147
parity errors, 136
parity flag. *See* PF
partial in-line code, 537, 602–606, 608, 610, 611, 613, 688, 693
partial jump tables, 673, 674, 678

Pascal, 6, 242, 589, 623, 624, 635, 715
Paterson, Tim, 344
PC data bus. *See* bus
PC Tech Journal magazine, 110, 721
peripherals, 728, 731
performance, 9, 542, 588, 592, 593, 601–604, 611, 617, 623, 632, 633, 645, 662, 668, 693, 697, 698, 700, 710, 717, 733, 736
 can only be improved by reducing code's limiting factor, 91
 can only know by measuring, 91–93, 109, 113, 116, 128, 131, 164, 275, 293, 294, 316, 351, 517, 555
 can vary by up to 8.33 percent from DRAM refresh, 99
 controlled by instruction fetch time, EU execution time, or both, 90
 how to measure, 14
 importance of measuring, 13, 14
 may vary for same code sequence over time because of cycle eaters, 113, 114, 119, 122, 127, 697
 must be measured for working code sequences, not individual instructions, 91
 pointlessness of trying to understand exactly, 113, 114, 116, 117, 121, 126, 128, 130, 294, 530
 traditional assembler programming model, 60
 true nature of, 131
 true performance, 8, 13, 14
perspective, 5, 315
PF (parity flag), 144, 147, 329, 330, 354
plus operator, 246
pop instruction, 141, 143, 170, 211, 234–240, 289, 306, 317, 343, 712, 740
 and segment copying, 173, 174
 non-*mod-reg-rm* register form, 234, 237
psw on 8088, 290
popa instruction, 715
popf instruction, 145, 291, 294, 309, 312, 362, 721–723, 725–727
 80286 bug and workaround for, 721–727
portability, 60
precalculation, desirability of, 249, 253, 258, 260, 539, 610
prefetch queue, 14, 66, 68, 71, 106, 300, 326, 368, 518–525, 527, 528, 530, 531, 538, 539, 542, 556, 582, 589, 590, 601, 616, 619, 620, 636, 637, 652, 701, 702, 709, 718, 720
 allowed to fill by **mul**, 89, 90

and performance of *mod-reg-rm* instructions, 216
 can add as much as 4 cycles per byte to instruction execution time, 91
 drained by register-only instruction, 88, 90
 drained by short instructions, 93
 effect on Zen timer accuracy, 30, 53, 86
 emptied by branches, 66, 67
 located in BIU, 67
 size, 67, 69, 616, 701
 state varies with code mix, 85
 transfers from to EU, 118
prefetch queue cycle eater, 62, 69, 72, 76, 77, 79, 83, 93, 110, 113, 122, 126, 205, 217, 227, 250–252, 258, 275, 281, 305, 313, 316, 325, 326, 455, 499, 517, 523, 525, 527–531, 538, 552, 601, 699, 701–705, 717
 as manifestation of 8-bit bus cycle eater, 83
 effect on performance, 84, 85, 110, 123, 214
 effect on register-only code, 88
 interaction with display adapter cycle eater, 115
 looms over the performance of all 8088 code, 93
 minimum transfer time for bytes from the prefetch queue to the EU, 130
 observed, 130
 undocumented and unpredictable, 84
 variation during different executions of same code sequence, 85, 93
 what to do about, 92, 93
prefetching. *See* instruction prefetching
prefix bytes, 363, 401
 avoid multiple, 149, 401
preloading values, 555–557, 559, 560, 569, 572
printer, 250
printer ports, 8
program
 commenting, 9
 conception, 5
 design, 6, 9, 59
 execution, true nature, 65
 implementation, 5, 6, 131, 504, 508, 733
 specification and Zen of assembly language, 9
Programmer's Journal magazine, 244, 249, 251
"Programming Insight: High-Performance Software Analysis on the IBM PC," 52
programming interface, 59–65, 68–70, 73
 beneath, 75, 110, 701
 component parts, 133

programming interface (*continued*)
   part of knowledge aspect of Zen of assembly
      language, 131
   rests on cycle eaters, 131
protected mode, 142, 169, 170, 184, 700, 701, 711,
   715–717
PS2 equate for assembling PS/2 version of long-
   period timer, 36, 37
public option to the **segment** directive, 192
pure in-line code, 598, 599, 602, 603, 679, 693
pure jump tables, 674, 678
push instruction, 141, 143, 211, 234–237, 239, 240,
   289, 306, 317, 343, 582, 626, 711, 715
   and segment copying, 173, 174
   non-*mod-reg-rm* register form, 234, 237
psw on 8088, 290
pusha instruction, 715
pushf instruction, 145, 291, 294, 309, 312, 627, 727
PZTEST.ASM precision Zen timer test bed program, 31,
   32, 34
PZTEST.EXE precision Zen timer executable program,
   32
PZTIME.BAT precision Zen timer batch file, 32, 34
PZTIMER.ASM precision Zen timer source code, 15,
   32, 34

Q

QS0 line, 117, 118
QS1 line, 117, 118

R

RAM disk, 154
rcl instruction, 139, 328
rcr instruction, 328, 560
READY line, 117
real mode, 169, 170, 700, 711, 715, 716, 721
ReferenceZTimerOff, 29
ReferenceZTimerOn, 29
register hidden agenda, 135, 136
register set, 135–137, 149, 267–269
register-only instructions, 217, 258, 263, 468, 534
   effect on instruction prefetching, 68, 217, 346
   many use *mod-reg-rm* addressing, 210, 217
registers, 59, 65, 66, 75, 319, 412, 466, 557, 559, 631,
   632, 716, 717

desirability of using as much as possible, 83, 93,
   110, 135, 153, 210, 217, 218, 227, 229, 230, 232,
   234, 235, 237, 245, 246, 263, 305, 316, 321, 698,
   699, 705, 717, 720
initializing multiple registers to same value, 299,
   300
initializing two bytes with a single **mov**, 300, 301
irregularity of, 135
part of programming interface, 131
register selection often matters, 289
should be destination operand whenever possible,
   319–321
use to store frequently used constants, 298, 356,
   563, 594, 616, 653
use to store variables, 83, 305, 616, 656
rep cmps, 372
rep movs, 79, 173, 363, 373, 405, 413, 416–420, 497,
   596, 597, 707, 713, 714
rep prefix, 139, 351, 361, 363–365, 372, 373, 375, 378,
   380, 401, 404, 405, 497, 499, 537, 598, 601, 613
   don't use with segment override prefixes, 401
rep lods, 373
rep scas, 372
rep stos, 58, 298, 365–368, 370, 373, 376, 736
repe prefix, 371
repeated string instructions, 109, 139, 319, 346, 354,
   356, 363–365, 368, 375, 377, 381, 386, 390, 405,
   412, 413, 471, 538, 688, 717, 736
   always alter CX, 373, 374
   don't use with segment override prefixes, 401
   execution time, 364
   handling 0-byte and 64 K-byte blocks, 377, 380,
      382, 384, 385, 389, 432
   handling blocks larger than 64 K, 505, 506
   much less flexible than normal instructions, 368
   no branching, 366–368, 538, 717
   no instruction fetching, 364, 366–368, 370, 538, 717
   operation when CX equals zero, 377, 378, 380, 382,
      384, 432, 448, 449, 462
   try to use whenever possible, 368, 677
   use ZF, not CX, to evaluate comparison results, 371,
      374, 375
   word-sized operations, advantages of, 376, 384, 389,
      420, 449, 450, 581
   word-sized operations, hazards of, 390–392, 420,
      421
repne prefix, 371
repnz cmps, 371–375, 378, 448, 449, 482, 485
repnz prefix, 368, 371, 372, 433, 482

repnz scas, 323, 354, 356, 357, 371–375, 378, 380, 430, 432–435, 439, 442–445, 448–450, 452, 454, 456, 457, 464, 471, 474, 479, 482, 658, 675, 677

rept assembler directive, 52, 260, 592, 598, 611, 614, 685

repz cmps, 371–375, 378, 380, 448, 449, 458, 464, 471, 472, 474, 479, 482, 485

repz prefix, 368, 371, 372, 433, 482, 658

repz scas, 354, 356, 371–375, 378, 432–434, 442–445, 448–450, 454, 482

ret instruction, 141–144, 517, 567–569, 572, 582, 584, 620, 627, 630, 631, 633, 648, 670, 712

return addresses, organization in memory, 187

returns, subroutine, 508, 581, 582, 584, 586, 588, 589, 627, 628, 631–633, 635

   far. *See* far returns

   near. *See* near returns

   to anywhere, 631, 632

rol instruction, 327

ROMable code, 653

ror instruction, 139, 327

rotate instruction affects fewer flags than you might think, 329

rotates, multi-bit. *See* multi-bit shifts and rotates

S

sahf instruction, 139, 145, 267, 289, 290, 291, 294, 309, 312, 362, 727

shl instruction, 329, 563, 564, 655, 699

sar instruction, 257, 330–333

sbb instruction, 147, 281–283, 309, 320, 323, 341, 343, 548, 550–552

scas instruction, 139, 140, 171, 354–356, 359, 368, 371, 372, 377, 381, 391, 393, 404, 430, 432, 433, 440, 450, 454, 457, 458, 462, 464, 466, 482, 581, 610, 613

repeated. *See* **repz scas** and **repnz scas**

scasb. *See* **scas**

scasw. *See* **scas**

screen filling, 735–741

seg operator, 190, 191, 198, 358

segment directive, 168, 192

segment:offset addressing, 156–159, 162, 167, 198, 200, 202, 514

   4096 pairs point to each address, 159

   don't count on wrapping back to 0, 160

   not particularly fast, 158

   offset portion very flexible, 198

   sums greater than 20 bits normally wrap around to 0, 160, 162

segment:offset pointers

   loading, 176, 198, 736

   organization in memory, 187, 722, 723

   passing in stack frames, 176

   usually loaded with **les**, 176, 737

segment override prefixes, 142, 143, 171, 179, 192–196, 211, 246, 347, 351, 359, 361, 363, 381, 391, 394–398, 401

   and the **assume** directive, 196, 197

   don't use with **rep**, 401

segment registers, 66, 67, 141, 142, 155, 158, 168, 343, 380, 383, 397, 506, 716

   and protected mode, 142, 169, 170, 700

   avoid loading whenever possible, 177, 182

   avoiding loading by sharing segments across modules, 192, 623, 624

   bug in disabling of interrupts while loading, 144

   can be loaded directly from any addressable memory location, 175, 176, 736, 742

   can each only point to a 64-Kb chunk, 160–162, 167, 380, 381

   common, 192

   copying, 173, 174

   copying and storing, 142, 169

   directives, 168

   disabling of interrupts while loading, 143, 149

   grouping, 192, 199

   loading with a segment that can vary during program execution, 175

   manipulating, 169, 170

   must be loaded when a high level language passes a far pointer, 177

   organize so that override prefixes aren't needed inside loops, 194–196, 397

   setting, 173–175, 198, 358

   speed of manipulation, 169, 170

   use for temporary storage, 142, 170–173, 700

segment selectors, 169, 170, 700

segmented memory architecture, 6, 133, 155, 167, 269, 505

segments, 155–159, 167, 168, 198, 380–383, 396, 400, 401, 420, 700, 723

   default memory-addressing segments, 142, 143, 159, 192, 208, 239, 391, 393, 397, 401

   joining or separating via the **segment** directive, 191, 192

segments (*continued*)
  sharing among multiple modules, 191, 192, 623, 624
  sharing between high level language and assembler, 199
  shifted when used to address memory, 156–158
  working with multiple segments, 193, 194
  working with multiple segments in multi-module programs, 191, 623, 624
self-modifying code, 65, 615–617
self-reliance, 7
serial communications support by DOS and BIOS, 61
serial ports/adapters, 8, 28, 29, 129, 401, 672, 712, 728
SF (sign flag), 144, 148, 291, 292, 329, 330, 354, 561, 655, 657
sharing code, 646–650
Sheppard, Byron, 52
shifting and rotating memory, 326
shifts and rotates by 1 bit, relative undesirability of, 324–327
shifts and rotates by CL bits, 324–327, 538
  relative desirability of, 324–327
shifts and rotates by CL bits don't affect CL, 326, 373
shifts, multi-bit. *See* multi-bit shifts and rotates
shl instruction, 139, 329
short jumps. *See* **jmp short**
shorter is better (smaller/faster), 83, 92, 93, 110, 281, 299, 305, 333, 589, 698, 699, 705, 717, 720
shr instruction, 68, 116, 325, 329–331, 538
  effect on prefetch queue, 86–89
  suffers from DRAM refresh, 97, 98
SI register, 137, 140, 149, 159, 347, 349, 350, 353, 358–361, 380, 643
  index addressing component, 207
  specializes as memory-addressing register for string instructions, 140, 193, 316, 350, 351, 359
  used as memory-addressing register, 140, 200, 208, 223, 246, 309, 347, 391
sign flag. *See* SF
size versus speed. *See* bytes versus cycles
smaller is better. *See* shorter is better
smaller is slower, 589
source code control, 9
SP register (stack pointer), 135, 137, 144, 159, 170, 232, 233, 237–239, 291, 306, 630, 711, 740
  always addresses the stack segment, 141
  is a general-purpose register when not being used to maintain a stack, 136, 141

never push directly, 141
not usually available as a general-purpose register, 136, 141, 172
points to top of stack, 136, 141, 232, 233, 237
should always be even, 306, 711, 712
used as memory-addressing register, 232, 233, 239
speaker, 24, 25, 60, 64, 650
special forms of common instructions, 224, 226, 230, 232
  assembler automatically selects whenever possible, 226, 232, 274, 287, 306, 342
  look the same as more general forms, 273
  two legitimate machine language forms of, 274, 306, 342, 344
special compressed forms of instructions, 643
  assembler automatically uses only when it knows enough to do so, 643
  forward references to, 643–645
speed of development, 9
speed versus size. *See* bytes versus cycles
SS register, 137, 142–144, 158, 159, 190, 192, 193, 396
  default access to, 143, 159, 208, 239
  don't use for temporary storage, 170
  together with SP must point to a valid stack, 143, 190
SS: segment override prefix, 193
stack, 136, 232–234, 237–240, 291, 294, 517, 568, 582, 626, 627, 630, 632, 633, 635, 650, 651, 657, 711, 721, 722, 725, 740, 741
  allocating space on in a subroutine, 635
  clearing by reloading SP, 630
  don't access popped stack data, 237, 238
  not inactive even when not accessed directly because of interrupts, 136, 143
stack addressing, 224, 232, 237, 244
stack addressing registers, 137
stack frames, 141, 175, 179, 193, 208, 233, 239–245, 286, 544, 715, 740
  all *mod-reg-rm* addressing modes can often be used to point to, 244
  negative displacements, 242, 243
  try to use 1-byte displacements, 243, 244
stack-oriented instructions, 224
stack pointer. *See* SP register
stack segment. *See* SS register
standard input, 638, 639
  redirected, 639, 640
standard output, 638, 639

static-column RAM, 698, 702, 703
static RAM (SRAM), 94, 712
static variables, 193
statuses, carrying along. *See* carrying results along in a flag
statuses, saving, 291
status flags, 144–147
stc instruction, 146
std instruction, 149, 362, 363, 420
sti instruction, 149
stos instruction, 139, 140, 288, 351, 352, 359, 365, 377, 381, 391, 393, 404–407, 412, 413, 613
    doesn't affect any flags, 375
    repeated. *See* **rep stos**
stosb. *See* **stos**
stosw. *See* **stos**
string instructions, 79, 109, 139, 140, 143, 149, 158, 159, 182, 192, 209, 211, 218, 219, 221, 224–226, 264, 288, 297, 319, 344, 346, 347, 351, 357–359, 362–364, 367, 381–383, 393, 395–397, 400, 401, 404, 407, 413, 416, 417, 424, 466, 479, 482, 488, 497, 504, 506, 534, 538, 601, 613, 698, 720
    advance their pointer registers, 350, 359, 377, 391, 407, 444
    byte- and word-sized operations, hazards of mixing, 420, 422–425, 427
    data size, 361, 375, 377, 393, 394
    definition of advancing pointer registers, 359, 361, 362
    operands to, 393–396
    pointing back to last element processed, 377–379, 444
    repeated. *See* repeated string instructions
strings, comparing, 359, 404, 457, 462, 464, 610, 611, 613
strings, copying, 351, 405, 576, 582, 610, 611, 613
strings, searching, 354, 404, 433–436, 439, 442–445, 454, 457, 464, 471–473, 479, 482, 565, 610, 611, 613, 679, 685
    case-insensitive, 457, 466, 658, 661, 662, 693
    double-search approach, 433–435, 445, 462, 688
    substrings. *See* substrings, searching for
    word-sized operations, advantages of, 440, 449, 450, 610, 611
struc directive, 179, 242
    negative displacements, 242, 243
structure elements, forward references to, 644, 645
sub instruction, 147, 281–283, 298, 300, 305, 306, 309, 311, 313, 314, 319–321, 323, 341, 343, 448, 449

subroutines, 508
    returning status from, 147, 487, 488
substrings, searching for, 457, 471–473, 479
Symdeb
    run from a remote terminal, 29
    screen flipping, 28
system clock, 25
system memory performance relative to display memory, 63, 703
system memory wait state cycle eater, 702–704, 720
system software, 59, 60, 63, 64

T

TASM (Turbo Assembler), 32, 168, 244, 372, 614, 645
test instruction, 285, 321, 343
TESTCODE Zen timer file containing code to be timed, 29–31, 50
TF (trap flag), 144, 145, 149
think functionally, 533, 535
Time command, 25, 35
time of day count, 25, 36, 37, 185
timer channel 0 of the 8253, 24–28, 36, 37
    interrupts, 25, 26
timer channel 1 of the 8253, 24, 25
    DRAM refresh, 25, 95
timer channel 2 of the 8253, 24–26
    interrupts, 25, 26
    system clock, 25, 26
timer interrupt, 26, 35, 129, 136, 149, 186
    BIOS code to handle, 35, 51
timer. *See* 8253 timer chip
TIMER-INT BIOS routine, 25
timing diagrams, 118
tlink, 32
traditional assembler programming model, 59, 60
    compatibility benefits, 59, 60
    inadequacy of hardware representation, 61
    knowing well, 59, 61
    knowing when to break the rules, 61
    performance shortcomings, 60, 61
    portability benefits, 59, 60
    replacing with own code, 61
trap flag. *See* TF
"Tricks of the Trade," 344
Turbo C, 241, 623
Turbo Pascal, 735
two's complement arithmetic, 322, 323, 546

U

unconditional jumps. *See* jumps, unconditional
Unix, 697, 700
unpacked BCD, 334, 335, 339, 340
upper case, converting to, 351, 405–407, 466, 468, 470, 471, 576, 577, 579, 614, 637, 638, 661, 693
user interaction, 9

V

V20, 267
vertical retrace, 106
VGA. *See* Video Graphics Array
Video Graphics Array (VGA), and display adapter cycle eater, 105, 262, 728
  and word-sized string instructions, 390–392
video registers, indexed, setting, 262, 263
VisiCalc, 269

W

wait instruction, 730, 731
wait state cycle eater, 83, 702–704
wait states, 14, 62, 75–77, 100, 106, 698, 703–705, 713, 718
  affect everything, even other cycle eaters, 100
  allow slower devices to complete bus accesses, 100
  are of no particular duration, 100
  as they relate to display memory, 100, 101
  can occur only during a memory or I/O read or write, 100
  code can't directly control, 94
  compared to DRAM refresh, 100
  controlled by device being accessed, 100
  do not occur on a regularly scheduled basis, 100
  don't stop the 8088 completely, 101
  external to 8088, 94
  lowest level, 94, 100
  only display adapter wait states seriously affect PC performance, 101
  system memory. *See* system memory wait state cycle eater
  transparent to code, 100
  usually do stop the 8088, 101
warm boot and system clock, 26, 27

white space, 488
word alignment. *See* data alignment
word-to-doubleword conversion, 312–314
word-sized memory access
  advantage over two byte-sized accesses by two instructions, 81, 83
  penalty for using, 79, 80, 84
  split into two byte-sized accesses, 67, 78, 79
WordStar, 269

X

xchg instruction, 139, 172, 226, 267, 285, 287, 288, 316–319, 342
  AX-specific form of, 285–288, 306, 318, 342
  used to get and set a memory variable, 318
xlat instruction, 139, 158, 193, 209, 211, 224, 246–249, 256, 257, 264, 312, 333, 468, 471
xor instruction, 146, 148, 281–284, 298, 311, 320–322, 343, 489–492, 496–499, 504, 505, 533–537, 594

Z

Z80, 266, 267, 509
Zen (coined verb form; also Zenned, Zenning), 735, 741
Zen of assembly language, 3–11, 13, 14, 53, 73, 113, 114, 117, 164, 167, 182, 237, 289, 315, 332, 396, 489, 504, 508, 509, 533–535, 537, 545, 559, 589, 615, 617, 635, 651, 701, 722, 727, 728, 733–735, 742
  inquisitive, skeptical mind, 81
  learning, 10
  mastering, 10
Zen timer, 14, 15, 22, 23, 26, 30, 53, 87, 93, 113, 115, 164, 251, 275–279, 281, 291, 293, 294, 456, 492, 514, 517, 518, 557, 622, 694, 696, 703, 708, 719, 721, 733
  accuracy, 29, 30, 34, 53, 86
  accurate only for the particular code sequence you've timed, 116, 129
  avoiding interrupts while long-period Zen timer runs, 49
  alternative output methods, 28, 29
  assembling the long-period timer for PS/2 computers, 36, 37

calling interface, 15, 23, 27–29, 34, 48
choosing the long-period timing mode, 36, 37
compatibility with PC-compatible computers, 30
DS set equal to CS to allow data in TESTCODE, 30–32
effect of DRAM refresh on accuracy, 30, 34
effect of preceding code on accuracy, 86
effect of prefetch queue on accuracy, 30, 34, 53, 86
effect on calling code, 29
erratic operation when undocumented timer stop is used, 37
excluding execution time of start-up code, 32
far calls to, 29
fractional counts can result from DRAM refresh, 99, 128, 712
fractional counts can result from display adapter cycle eater, 99, 128
ideally used to measure the performance of an entire subroutine, 86
imperfections, 53
inability to measure across midnight, 35
inaccuracy introduced into system clock, 23, 26, 27, 35, 36
interrupts, 23, 25, 26, 28, 35
least variable over longer periods, 129
long-period inaccuracy in PS/2 computers, 36
long-period timer, 26, 34–37, 48–51, 164, 186, 492
maximum timing intervals, 34, 35
minimum timing interval, 86
overflow detection, 26–28

overhead adjustment, 27, 28
precision timer, 35, 37, 48, 50, 51, 492
rebooting at the end of timing sessions, 26, 27, 35–37
rebooting immediately in case of erratic results, 37
repeating tests multiple times, 37
rounding results, 34
sample use of long-period timer, 48, 49
sample use of precision timer, 30
sequence of calls to subroutines, 28
short code sequences may vary greatly from one measurement to next, 129
use with assembly language, 29
use with high level languages, 29
using, 30–32, 34, 48–52
variation of results on computers other than PCs, 30
variations can result from DRAM refresh, 99
zero, handling efficiently, 229, 230, 277–279, 297–299, 301, 302, 303, 311, 657, 738
zero flag. *See* ZF
ZF (zero flag), 144–148, 277, 301, 307, 329, 330, 354, 371, 372, 375, 432, 433, 448, 449,482, 488, 586, 658
Zilog, 266
ZTimerOff, 15, 23, 26–28, 30–32, 34
ZTimerOn, 15, 23, 26–28, 30–32, 34, 49
interrupts are turned off and must remain off for precision timer, 23
ZTimerReport, 15, 28–31, 34